STUDIES OF THE HARRIMAN INSTITUTE

Columbia University

The W. Averell Harriman Institute for Advanced Study of the Soviet Union, Columbia University, sponsors the *Studies of the Harriman Institute* in the belief that their publication contributes to scholarly research and public understanding. In this way the Institute, while not necessarily endorsing their conclusions, is pleased to make available the results of some of the research conducted under its auspices.

THE MAKING OF THREE RUSSIAN REVOLUTIONARIES

THE MAKING OF THREE RUSSIAN REVOLUTIONARIES

Voices from the Menshevik past

LEOPOLD H. HAIMSON

W. Averell Harriman Institute
for Advanced Study of the Soviet Union,
Columbia University

in collaboration with
Ziva Galili y Garcia and Richard Wortman

Introduction by Leopold H. Haimson,
Notes by Ziva Galili y Garcia

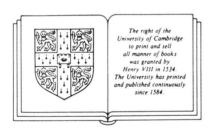

The right of the
University of Cambridge
to print and sell
all manner of books
was granted by
Henry VIII in 1534.
The University has printed
and published continuously
since 1584.

CAMBRIDGE UNIVERSITY PRESS

Cambridge
New York   New Rochelle   Melbourne   Sydney

EDITIONS DE LA MAISON DES SCIENCES DE
L'HOMME

Paris

Published by the Press Syndicate of the University of Cambridge
The Pitt Building, Trumpington Street, Cambridge CB2 1RP
32 East 57th Street, New York, NY 10022, USA
10 Stamford Road, Oakleigh, Melbourne 3166, Australia
and   88—　　976
Editions de la Maison des Sciences de l'Homme
54 Boulevard Raspail, 75720 Paris, Cedex 06, France

First published 1987

Printed in the United States of America

Library of Congress Cataloging-in-Publication Data
Haimson, Leopold H.
The making of three Russian revolutionaries.
1. Dan, Lidiia.   2. Nicolaevsky, Boris I., 1887–1966.
3. Denike, George.   4. Revolutionists – Soviet Union –
Biography.   5. Rossiiskaia sotsial-demokraticheskaia
rabochaia partiia.   I. Galili y Garcia, Ziva.
II. Wortman, Richard.   III. Title.
DK253.H34   1987   947.08′092′2   87-6651

British Cataloguing in Publication Data
Haimson, Leopold H.
The making of three Russian revolutionaries:
voices from the Menshevik past.
1. Rossiskaia sotsial-demokratiches-kaia
rabochaia partiia (men'sheviki)
I. Title   II. Galili y Garcia, Ziva
III. Wortman, Richard
324.247′075   JN6598.R8/

ISBN 0 521 26325 5
ISBN 2 7351 0199 1 (France only)

CONTENTS

ILLUSTRATIONS

PREFACE

The three life histories from which the reminiscences in this volume have been drawn were originally recorded on tape in the course of an interviewing program conducted between 1960 and 1965, as part of an interuniversity project on the history of the Menshevik movement. All the interviews were transcribed as faithfully as possible, but our informants were given and usually availed themselves of the opportunity to edit their remarks, and especially to correct the inevitable errors in the transcripts.

For reasons more fully explained in the Introduction, I concluded soon after beginning my interviews with three survivors of the Menshevik movement that the interest their reminiscences presented warranted a systematic effort to trace the trajectory of their lives, and in particular the shaping of their ideas, attitudes, and values. If the end product of this effort proves of enduring interest and value, thanks are owed first and foremost to these three informants – Lydia Dan, Boris Nicolaevsky, and George Denike – for the time and energy that they invested, notwithstanding advanced age and failing health, in this long and arduous interviewing program.

Long after the conclusion of the interviews – which by the time of the deaths of these informants comprised thousands of pages of transcripts – several readers expressed the view that the light shed by these life histories on Menshevik political culture and the radical intelligentsia of which it was a part warranted dissemination of edited versions among a broader circle of readers. Most encouraging in this regard was Professor Richard Wortman, who offered me his collaboration in selecting and eventually editing those portions of the transcripts that most deserved broader circulation. With his help, and eventually that of Professor Ziva Galili y Garcia, I embarked on the difficult task of selecting portions of the interviews for translation into English. These translations, which often proved extremely demanding, were undertaken by Mr. Martin Lopes Morillas and eventually by Ms. Lynn Solotaroff, to whom I wish to express our gratitude for the efforts they invested in what sometimes seemed an almost impossible task.

The final selection and editing of the excerpts to be published, which Richard Wortman, Ziva Galili, and I undertook after the completion of these translations, was itself no easy job. We had jointly concluded that in the reminiscences of Lydia Dan and Boris Nicolaevsky preference should be accorded in this process of selection to the reminiscences that these two informants had left us of their childhood and youth, and of their early political careers. We drew this conclusion partly because of the much greater vividness with which these earlier stages of their life experience had remained imprinted upon their memories, but also because of the light that they jointly shed – especially given these two informants' very different social origins and backgrounds – on the processes of socialization that had been at work in the shaping of Menshevik political culture, and in the evolution of the radical intelligentsia as a whole. (Our considerations on this issue are elaborated in the Introduction.)

But even after this decision was reached, we were confronted with the problem of reconciling our objective of making these reminiscenses accessible and hopefully interesting to a broader readership with that of rendering as faithfully as possible the actual transcripts. One of our working rules, in this connection, was to eliminate most of the inevitable repetitions in these long series of interviews. Another was to eliminate major digressions from the narrative flow (usually biographical details concerning secondary figures in Russian Social Democracy and other currents of the revolutionary movement). We also condensed the introductory remarks with which I had usually opened our interview sessions in an effort to provide a framework and chronological points of reference for the chapters in their lives which my informants would seek to recount; and we eliminated many of the follow-up questions with which the sessions had been punctuated to elicit fuller responses, and to provide pauses for memory to do its work.

The final preparation of the manuscript consequently involved occasional "splicing" of the interviews to bridge gaps left by the editing process. But we took considerable care not to allow these efforts to achieve greater readability to distort the record that the interviews provided of my informants' processes of recall.

This description of the preparation of the volume will hopefully suggest that for all those who were involved in it, it came to constitute a labor of love as much as a work of scholarship. I have already mentioned the debt we owe to the memory of our three informants (two of whom, Lydia Dan and George Denike, died shortly after the completion of my interviews with them), as well as to the translators of these interviews, Martin Lopes Morillas and Lynn Solotaroff. But I particularly wish to acknowledge indebtedness to Richard Wortman and Ziva Galili for their help in the final shaping of this volume. Ziva Galili played an especially important part in the final editing, and contributed elaborate endnotes that will make the historical record provided here more valuable to interested readers. I wish to thank Madame Marianne Dumont – as remarkable a person as the informants in which she took such a deep personal interest – for her assistance in the preparation of the introductory section during my stays in Paris. I also owe a special debt to Ruth Mathewson for her help in turning the draft of the introduction into serviceable English prose, to Lola Peters who took charge of the final editing, as well as to Jan Sammer who patiently recorded the various versions on the word processor. Last but not least, I wish to acknowledge our debt to the Ford and Atran Foundations, which funded the work of the Menshevik project during the years when these interviews were conducted, and to the American Council of Learned Societies, which provided the grant that enabled us to present them in this edited version.

EDITORS' NOTE

All editorial additions to the text of the interviews have been placed in brackets. These include the translation into English of certain Russian terms; the Russian origin of certain words rendered into English in the text; surnames otherwise identified in the text only by proper name and patronymic; and the interjection of a word or a phrase to clarify an incomplete sentence or a misleading statement. Introductory or connecting passages are also in brackets.

In transliterating Russian names we generally adhered to the more precise Library of Congress system, but deliberately allowed for certain exceptions, especially in the text. Thus, Lydia Dan's first name, and Boris Nicolaevsky's last name, have been anglicized both for aesthetic reasons and to conform to their preferences. In the notes, however, these are treated as Russian names and transliterated as Lidia Dan and Boris Nikolaevskii. Only in one case did we use the more familiar anglicized version throughout; namely, in the case of Trotsky.

All the abbreviations in the text are those actually used during the interviews, most notably, *SRs* for Socialist Revolutionaries and *SDs* for Social Democrats. In the notes, the abbreviation *CC* is often used for Central Committee, *NSs* for the Party of People's Socialists, *PSR* for the Party of Socialist Revolutionaries, and *RSDRP* for the Russian Social Democratic Labor Party.

Unless otherwise indicated, all pre-1918 dates follow the Julian or "Old Style" calendar, twelve days behind the Gregorian or "Western" calendar in the nineteenth century and thirteen days behind in the twentieth.

INTRODUCTION:
MENSHEVISM AND THE
EVOLUTION OF THE
RUSSIAN INTELLIGENTSIA

I

The voices of the Menshevik past heard in this volume were originally recorded on tape in the course of a project on the history of Menshevism that I directed from 1960 to 1965 at the joint invitation of a group of Menshevik survivors and a number of specialists in Russian and Soviet studies teaching at various American universities.

The impulse for this effort had originated in 1959 with these survivors of the Menshevik Party themselves – more precisely, with nine members of its last coherent *kollektiv*, which was still functioning in New York after four decades in the emigration. Six of them – Gregory Aronson, David Dallin, Lydia Dan, Boris Dvinov, Boris Nicolaevsky, and Solomon Schwarz – were survivors of the RSDRP Delegation Abroad *(Zagranichnaia Delegatsiia RSDRP)*, established by Julius Martov and his political associates following their expulsion from Soviet Russia by a decree of the Supreme Soviet in 1922. This group had continued to function uninterruptedly as a political entity, with representation in the Labor Socialist International – first in Berlin, until Hitler's rise to power, and later in Paris, until the German occupation of France in the spring of 1940. The other three members of the group – Leo Lande, Boris Sapir, and Simon Wolin – were survivors of the Mensheviks' Union of Youth *(Soyuz molodezhev)*, which had maintained a shadow underground existence in Soviet Russia and contacts with the Menshevik Delegation Abroad until the mid-1920s. Most of these survivors were still active as contributors to *Sotsialisticheskii Vestnik* (The Socialist Herald), the journal launched by the Delegation Abroad immediately after its inception, which had continued publication even after the Delegation's dissolution in 1940. This journal was still appearing in New York as our project got under way, having stubbornly continued breathing – issuing its political message and responses to events – over four tumultuous and tormented decades, marked by the rise to power of Hitler and Stalin, their respective terrors, and the holocaust of World War II, and punctuated in the lives of most of its contributors by successive transplantations to Germany, to France, and eventually to the United States.

These nine aging but indomitable men and women (Lydia Dan, the matriarch of the group, was then in her late seventies, and even the three survivors of the Menshevik Union of Youth, well into their sixties) had decided to embark, as the last major act of their collective existence, on the writing of a history of their party. Indeed, some two years before the project was actually launched, they had collectively drawn up an outline for such a history, assigning among themselves each of the chapters to be completed. They had even appealed, on their own initiative, for foundation support, turning to sympathetic members of the American academic community only after their original request had been turned down.

I was blissfully unaware of all this when I was approached by these Menshevik survivors to direct their undertaking. They only told me, ingenuously, that they had reached the conclusion that a history of Menshevism needed to be written and were now turning to us for help to turn the idea into reality. Yet this background may well suggest some of the problems and opportunities that we confronted in preparing our research design, as well as the psychological atmosphere in which the project was eventually launched.

In the first place, notwithstanding their advanced age, fading health (several contributors died before the end of the project), and the trials and tribulations to which they had been subjected, these survivors could hardly be described as flotsam of a long-lost past – let alone as "rejects of history," to use the cruel and inaccurate term once used by Trotsky (before he, by his own definition, became one). In fact, of all the constituent groups of the remarkably resilient post-1917 emigration of the Russian intelligentsia, they had proven probably the hardiest – at least in their ability to continue functioning as a collective political entity.

Some of this extraordinary vitality was clearly rooted in political ideas and attitudes. For it was at least in part the Marxist ideology that the members of this group espoused, and the political values they associated with it – their idealization of the working class, but also their deterministic faith in the ultimate effects of industrialization and modernization – that had inspired for so many years their confidence in the ultimate future of Soviet Russia even as they opposed its current rulers. This ideology had confirmed them in their diagnoses of Russia's contemporary situation and in their prescriptions for its future. But perhaps even more important, the concepts, political language, and values they drew from it had enabled them to relate more comfortably than any other contemporary group of the Russian emigration to certain of the intellectual and political milieus of the Western countries in which they had settled, as well as to the international socialist movement as a whole. A few of them had managed to assimilate the distinctive cultural characteristics of their new environments. But even those who did not had responded to them with sufficient interest and zest to draw from them intellectual and emotional sustenance.

Indeed, the most salient characteristic of these members of the Menshevik emigration was their cosmopolitanism: a cosmopolitanism not merely of political ideals and values, but also of culture, of language, of style. To visit them in their apartments was to be constantly reminded – by the books and newspapers piled up on their tables but also on the floor, by the range of topics raised and the various languages in which they were discussed – that most of them were down-to-the-bone members of a truly European, if not universal, culture, perhaps already on its way to extinction, but of which they remained as vital exemplars.

Another, less obvious feature of their collective psychology also helped account for their remarkable intellectual vitality, and for their indomitable confidence, through the vagaries of their émigré existence, that they had their own word to say and the collective ability to say it. This was an ingrown "family" spirit, a clannishness that partially contradicted their cosmopolitanism, and the openness that was supposed to distinguish it. This clannishness had its roots in the circles *(kruzhki)* and "circle spirit" *(kruzhkovshchina)* which had played so large a role in the lives of the members of the Russian intelligentsia during their formative years at the *gymnazium* and the university, and in a less accentuated form in later adult life. More than any other group of the intelligentsia, the Mensheviks maintained through these vehicles of its life and spirit patterns of social relations and organization that reminded an outside observer of the functioning of extended families, or of tribal clans or religious sects, rather than of a modern political party.

In the interviews devoted to her formative years during the 1890s as well as to the Iskra period of her revolutionary career, Lydia Dan repeatedly refers to the emotional closeness and intellectual comfort she had drawn from the sense of belonging to such an extended family or clan, even while acknowledging its negative aspects: the elitism, sectarianism, and intolerance it had fostered. She also observes that she and her comrades had irretrievably lost the sense of belonging to such an extended family when the Revolution of 1905 had suddenly lifted them from life in the underground to the open political arena, where they had to confront the other parties which had burgeoned on the political scene and the even more uncontrollable masses of the Russian people. Admittedly, this dramatic change in circumstances shook their belief in their ability to control events. Yet her remarks exaggerate somewhat the radicalness of the break that this change wrought in their basic psychological orientations and mutual relations.

Lydia Osipovna herself recalls that, when she and her husband, Theodore Dan, returned to Petersburg in the fall of 1905 they immediately repaired – along with her brothers Iu. O. Martov, S. O. Ezhov, and V. O. Levitsky (to use their respective party pseudonyms), and several of their party comrades and friends – to the Zederbaum family's spacious apartment, then still occupied by her parents, as if to resurrect within its walls the circle of brothers and sisters, friends and comrades, that had flourished around her brother Iulii Osipovich in the magic days of their youth. From this apartment, and imbued with the circle spirit that reigned there, its occupants headed during the October days of 1905 to their endless series of factional and editorial board meetings, and to the sessions of the Petersburg Soviet; and it was to this apartment they returned when the day, or rather the night, was out. There they eventually ruminated and argued about the causes of the crash of their great revolutionary expectations, and over the responsibility that they bore for it, individually and collectively. It was also there that, as late as 1906 and early 1907, they still sought collectively to define the party's political line and to manage the political behavior of the Menshevik faction, including its Georgian deputies, in the State Duma. And after the long years of exile or deportation that most of them experienced following the coup d'etat of June 1907, it was to a similar apartment that the Zederbaums and their clan instinctively homed in the Petrograd of 1917, seeking once more to recreate the intellectual unity and affective bonds of such a circle.

The rambling apartment that the Zederbaums occupied in 1917 constitutes for a historian of the period a source of immense, if ultimately unsatisfiable, curiosity. For despite the sharp ideological differences that now separated them, and the fact that they now headed opposing political factions in the Menshevik party and the councils of Soviet democracy, wrestling over its policies and the fate of the revolution, Martov and Dan managed somehow to coexist in it – with Lydia Osipovna, Martov's sister and Dan's wife, ministering to them both – along with several of their party comrades, including Boris Nicolaevsky, for whom a place had been found in the traditional servant quarters. From this apartment they headed for their now different and conflicting factional meetings, (Martov for those of the Menshevik Internationalists, Dan for those of the Revolutionary Defensists), as well as for the nightly sessions of the Petrograd Soviet where they untiringly and mercilessly assaulted each other's positions. They would return to the apartment in the early morning, often in the company of Tsereteli and other major party figures, to pursue the argument – unable to convince each other, yet unable to stop – over the tea and *zakuski* that Lydia Osipovna usually prepared for them.

All too little of these arguments was ever written down, or could be really reconstructed from the memories of Lydia Osipovna and Nicolaevsky when I pressed them to recall their substance in the course of our interviews. Yet enough of the atmosphere was revived to confirm the impression that, notwithstanding the acuteness of the conflicts and the dramatic and ultimately tragic circumstances in which they had taken place, the spirit of the clan did somehow survive within the walls of this Petrograd apartment. That spirit accounted, almost as much as the ultimate turn of the events over which the conflicts had ranged, for the swift and private – perhaps even subliminal – character of the process of reconciliation between the leaders of the two party factions after the Bolsheviks took power.

Indeed, when one explores the psychological and social texture of the Mensheviks' collective experience, it is difficult to escape the impression that throughout its history, this party's leadership maintained the character of a series of clans, which coalesced and gravitated together, although they periodically, and in some cases irrevocably, split. This was true particularly of the clan represented by the Zederbaums and their immediate associates, perhaps the most vital intellectual and spiritual center of the party. But it was also evident in the overlapping clans of the Georgian Social Democrats and in the different, less stable, psychological constellations represented by the circles which gravitated around P. B. Axelrod and A. N. Potresov and his literary associates on the Menshevik right. A few individuals, such as Iraklii Tsereteli, and, in their own fashion, George Denike and Boris Nicolaevsky, served as somewhat precarious bridges connecting these often warring circles.

To be admitted to one of these clans demanded far more than the broad consensus on a political program and on the strategy and tactics to achieve it characteristic of a modern political party. What it required was nothing less than the assimilation of certain patterns of collective behavior – of a shared language, a shared ritual of discussion and of decision making, a shared system of references and evaluation regarding all major aspects of public, and often private, life – that could be absorbed only through the accumulation of shared experience.

Anecdotes – sometimes verging on caricature – abounded about the stylized patterns of behavior in which the psychological features I have described were often articulated, especially in the emigration. I shall cite but two, recounted to me with fond amusement by one participant observer. The first, duly entered in the protocols of one of the sessions in the mid-1920s of the Delegation Abroad, concerned a half-serious resolution offered by one of its small minority of *praktiki* and publicists of the Menshevik right, at the conclusion of a particularly long and irritating monologue by a representative of its Internationalist majority. The resolution proposed that the word "dialectic" be banned in the Delegation's deliberations for a period of no less than three years. The other example was the response of Iu. O. Martov, the dominant figure in the Delegation until his death in late 1923, when a young faithful attendant of the sessions of the Menshevik club in Berlin requested admission to the Menshevik Party. "One does not join the party in the emigration!" was Martov's reply. As if, indeed, one could become a member of the Menshevik Party, especially by this time, by an act of personal choice rather than by history's dictate, or, more precisely, by the weight of accumulated experience.

These distinctive characteristics of the inner circles of the Menshevik Party – the resilient intellectual categories that their world view provided for filtering experience and drawing ready-made responses to events, as well as the equally resilient circle spirit and clannish social relationships that so strongly sustained it – did not always serve the Mensheviks well when they were thrust to the center of a particularly agitated and swiftly changing political scene. They fostered dogmatic, sometimes sectarian, attitudes, which frequently caused them to misperceive the movement of events, as well as a hermetic language and a distinctive style of public behavior which caused many of them (particularly those in the Internationalist wing of the party, who had spent the longest and most uninterrupted periods in the emigration) to repel even those they sought to convert. Consider the impression recorded by Denike that Martov and his small band of Menshevik Internationalists made on most of the delegates to the Unification Congress of the Menshevik Party in August 1917. On this decisive occasion, Martov and his followers (most of whom had just returned to Russia after their long years in the emigration) repelled many representatives of the provincial organizations of the party, who had had no previous encounters with them, not only by the substance of their arguments, but also by the strange and foreign language in which these were voiced, and by the even stranger apparel and manners displayed by those who voiced them – their ridiculous large hats, and periodic hysterical outcries. Under these circumstances, it was all too easy for many provincial delegates, including Denike himself, to dismiss the pleas of Martov and his comrades as coming from Paris *kafeiniki*, entirely oblivious of Russian realities.

Even more fundamentally, it may be argued that at certain crucial points the coherence and resilience of their world view fatally hindered many leading Mensheviks from shaping – and in certain cases, even seeking to shape – political realities. It was not merely that this world view, and the dogmatism that often marked it, frequently blinded them to those realities; or even that when they did recognize the untoward movement of events, it provided them all too easily with ready-made rationalizations for political setbacks and the often illusory promise that these setbacks would be redressed by the laws of history. It was also that in certain crucial situations, it crippled their very capacity to act or to react politically – their world view, and the ethical code and intellectual preconceptions that underlay it, being more precious to them than the pursuit or preservation of political power. This, it seems to me, was at least partially the case in 1917 with Martov – in his contemporary diagnoses, probably the most lucid of the Menshevik leaders – if not with most of his Revolutionary Defensist opponents in the party, who so appalled Denike by their failure to grapple with political realities when he visited them in the "madhouse atmosphere" of the capital.

In Martov, caught as he was in the probably insoluble contradictions of 1917, these psychological features – including the stubborn attachment to principles that they induced – had a sublime, indeed tragic, quality. In the case of figures of lesser political importance whom I came to know and love in the course of our project, some of the same traits, while no less touching, frequently assumed an incongruous, tragicomic character.

As I write these words, I think particularly of Solomon Schwarz, a Menshevik *praktik* and publicist of considerable experience and stature, who during the years between 1905 and 1917 had invested all his energies in the effort to build a mass Europeanized labor movement on Russian soil. When I once asked Schwarz to describe the St. Petersburg labor scene on the eve of World War I, and in particular the contemporary evolution of the St. Petersburg Union of Metal Workers (whose journal he had edited up to the Bolsheviks' seizure of control of the union in the summer and fall of 1913), his mind focused, to the exclusion of any other topic, on the social-insurance campaign which he had led during this period, and sought to infuse with the Mensheviks' hallowed principles of working-class initiative and independent activity. Similarly, when I asked Schwarz to reconstruct, this time from the vantage point of October 1917 (when he was vice-minister of labor), the days immediately preceding the Bolshevik seizure of power, his mind again stubbornly focused on the social-insurance legislation he had been drafting on the night the Bolsheviks took power, still faithfully seeking to incorporate in its provisions the principles of workers' self-help and self-administration. And when in the spring of 1918 Schwarz addressed the workers at the Putilov plants – at the request of leaders of the Menshevik right seeking to organize a movement of workers' representatives *(dvizhenie upolnomochennykh)* to challenge the Bolsheviks' domination of the Soviets – he delivered to his eager but increasingly bewildered workers' audience a passionate speech culminating in the, for him, sacred phrase: "Forward to Capitalism!" (I need hardly add that Schwarz's conception of "capitalist development," as of most other earthly things, consistently retained a highly abstract quality.)

To be sure, Schwarz's stubbornness and political innocence appeared idiosyncratic even to many of his comrades. But in a less pristine form, some of the ingredients that made for these qualities were in fact characteristic of the political culture in which he had been formed and remained absorbed. These attributes of Menshevik political culture also may account, at least in part, for the shape that Bolshevism – which originally grew out of the same political soil as Menshevism and yet became in so many ways its psychological as well as political opposite – increasingly assumed.

I have more in view by this observation than the will to power that Lenin ostensibly incarnated, or the political opportunism of which the Mensheviks so frequently and bitterly accused him. More to the point for the comparison of Menshevism and Bolshevism as political cultures I am seeking to draw was the conception of a revolutionary party which Lenin had already outlined on the eve of the Bolshevik–Menshevik split, and to which, with changed emphases, he periodically returned.

I have in mind the image originally drawn in *What Is To Be Done* of the party as an army of professional revolutionaries headed by an ideological center setting the "party line" to be followed through all changing political conjunctures. This organizational center of the party, in turn, was to dictate the allocation of men and resources required for the fulfillment of its strategic and tactical plans – wherever they might be needed, regardless of local or particular interests and loyalties. This army was to be as centralized and disciplined as the earlier circles had been fragmented and unstable. And the relations within its ranks were to be as impersonal and subordinated to the execution of the revolutionary tasks defined from the center as earlier relations had been embedded in the spirit of "circle" and "family" relations.

There was a grandeur to this organizational vision, a quality of revolutionary asceticism and dedication, but also a clarity, a surface rationality – characteristic of Lenin's political diagnoses and especially of the strategy and tactics that he deduced from them – which had proven enormously appealing to many of the future Mensheviks during the Iskra period when the vision had originally been articulated, and even in 1905, as long as the revolution appeared close at hand. It bears recalling that many future Mensheviks, especially those who eventually assumed organizational responsibilities as *praktiki* of the Menshevik Party (including such eventual collaborators of our project as George Denike and Solomon Schwarz) had in fact been Bolsheviks in 1905. Indeed, it is fair to state that Menshevism did not really begin to take shape as a distinct political movement, and especially as a political culture, until after the collapse of the great revolutionary expectations of 1905, and the searing criticism and self-criticism that this revolutionary maximalism generated within the Menshevik camp.

From this point onward, a variety of factors contributed to the crystallization of Menshevik political culture and to the process of its demarcation from Bolshevism. First came the criticism of Lenin and his followers for stubbornly holding onto their revolutionary expectations and continuing to translate them in their strategy and tactics until the Stolypin coup d'etat of June 1907. Along with this went the increasingly loud denunciations of the ruthless political infighting that marked Lenin's pursuit of these maximalist goals – goals which seemed to the Mensheviks increasingly detached from political realities. And during the period of relative political stability that followed the Stolypin coup d'etat, there came a growing sense of revulsion inspired by the activities of the collapsing revolutionary underground.

Most important of all, reinforcing the revulsion now induced by the putrefying remains of life in the underground, was the growing attraction exercised by the various possibilities of life "in the open" which this era, for all its severe political restrictions, afforded, at least for those members of the Menshevik movement who remained in Russia. For Menshevik *praktiki*, there were apparent opportunities to build a mass Europeanized labor movement, as well as to educate a new generation of working-class intelligentsia (perceived all too readily in the Mensheviks' own image) to lead it. For Menshevik publicists, there was the possibility of articulating their views, albeit sometimes in thinly disguised Aesopian language, in existing legal journals and newspapers, and eventually in the open labor press. For the party as a whole, there were the opportunities for political agitation arising from the presence of the Menshevik deputies in the State Duma and the legal immunities covering their activities, outside as well as inside the Taurus Palace. And as Denike's account reminds us, there was also for some the irresistible attraction exercised by the rich and many-faceted cultural life of the period; and more generally, for youths who earlier had been absorbed into the revolutionary underground, the increasingly compelling urge to train for and eventually assume professional careers and the cares of a more normal day-to-day existence.

When we interviewed those Menshevik survivors who had initially been drawn to Bolshevism about the sources of their differences and ultimate break with Lenin and his followers, issues of individual and group morality almost invariably figured large. But they also conveyed the impression – precisely when discussing the immediate aftermath of 1905, which was in some ways more decisive in the process of their self-definition than the years of their youth – that it was during this period that Bolshevism, and the life in the underground and code of the professional revolutionary with which it was identified in their minds, began to appear to them not only immoral but abnormal: abnormal in its pathologies, but more fundamentally in its subordination of all other considerations – all other loyalties, interests, and concerns – to the pursuit of revolutionary goals. This psychological break was necessarily sharper and more dramatic among those Mensheviks who remained in Russia during these years than among those who elected or were compelled to spend most of them in the emigration, giving rise to differences in psychological orientations and political attitudes not fully recognized until 1917. Yet even in the more shuttered circles of the Menshevik emigration, this break – and specifically the repudiation of the ethos of the professional revolutionary – proved extremely important in the crystallization of the more stable patterns of collective life and of the intellectual and moral values that came to distinguish Menshevik political culture.

The Bolsheviks too underwent a significant psychological evolution during this period – indeed, a crisis of identity in some ways even more painful and more dramatic, as Lenin and those who remained faithful to him, as well as the new followers he managed to recruit, also sought to adapt to the new conditions in Russian political life by using existing "legal" possibilities to mobilize a new mass revolutionary movement. They were impelled in the process to part ways with those in their own ranks who criticized them, at least initially in the name of "true" Bolshevism, for the adoption of these new tactics.

Both Bolshevism and Menshevism subsequently underwent enormous changes and divisions, especially in the course of the revolution of 1917, as they became mass parties and each in turn had to shoulder the responsibilities of power. Yet both movements, or more precisely their inner circles, brought quite distinctive political orientations to these unprecedented problems and opportunities.

Given the rapid turnover in the Bolshevik leadership during these years, as well as Lenin's psychological ascendancy (for which there was no full counterpart in the Menshevik party, as the reception that Martov received at the August Unification Congress amply suggests), one hesitates to speak, at least as of 1917, of a coherent Bolshevik political culture. But precisely because of Lenin's personal ascendancy, and the grip that the image of the revolutionary underground continued to exercise on the Bolsheviks' inner circles, most of them undoubtedly brought to the crucible of 1917 an already distinctive political style. It was characterized by an identification of the revolutionary struggle with the pursuit of political power, and a consequent readiness for tactical flexibility, a steady focus on mass political mobilization and organization, and a self-conscious emphasis on tough-mindedness, self-discipline, and economy of effort. And however blurred, these traits reflected Lenin's 1903 picture of his army of professional revolutionaries, and the imprint left on many of his followers by a life in the underground punctuated by periods of deportation and administrative exile.

With respect to the inner circles of the Menshevik party in 1917, one can speak more confidently of a political culture, some features of which I have already suggested and to which I shall return. As I have noted, this political culture did not always serve the Mensheviks well during their periods at the center of the political stage. But one can state far more unambiguously that through at least two decades of their last, post-1921 emigration, it sustained them as a collective entity with a remarkable life force. By the time our project was launched, those survivors of this movement who worked at our side still radiated some of this force. Yet their very decision to embark on this project implied at least at some level a recognition that their days as a political movement were over, or at least coming to an end.

*   *   *

This recognition, and the conclusion these survivors had drawn from it that the time had come to review their party's experience not as an eternal present but a history, stemmed in part from a realization of the corrosion of the flesh induced by illness and old age, as well as of the depletions that their ranks had suffered, most recently with the death of Theodore Dan – for so many years the dominant figure among the Menshevik Internationalists, who since the Bolshevik seizure of power had constituted the most prominent and coherent group in the party. But also contributing to this recognition were certain major psychological blows that the members of the Menshevik emigration, and especially their inner circle of Internationalists, had suffered well before Dan's death in the mid-1950s. Two of these should be singled out for the massiveness and irreversibility of the damage they inflicted on the hitherto so resilient world view that had kept the Menshevik emigration infused with its remarkable collective spirit.

The first was the shattering effect of the changes in Soviet Russia during the 1930s. It was not that the Mensheviks in the emigration failed to keep abreast of these developments. In fact, in their journal and other publications, a number of them offered unusually well-informed accounts of many of the events, and indeed of the broader political, social, and economic processes of the Stalin era. Their records appear more reliable in many respects than those of most contemporary Western observers. One need only cite such examples as Nicolaevsky's "Letter of an Old Bolshevik," recording in the pages of *Sotsialisticheskii Vestnik* Bukharin's views – on the very eve of his arrest and trial – of contemporary Soviet developments and of Stalin's role in them. And in a different, more scholarly, vein, there were the various monographs on Soviet affairs, most of them published after their transplantation to the United States, by David Dallin, Boris Nicolaevsky, and Solomon Schwarz (to mention only those members of the Menshevik emigration who were intimately associated with our project).

Yet notwithstanding the impressive range of information recorded in these writings, the Menshevik emigration proved collectively unable to draw from it an interpretation sufficiently compelling to keep even the members of their inner Internationalist circle together. At issue were not merely differences over what was actually happening but, more fundamentally, an inability to make sense of it. Indeed, what proved so shattering about these events, and about such processes as collectivization and the Great Purges, as the holocaust they had wrought began to be perceived, was not merely the horror and revulsion they inspired, but also that they seemed to defy any rational explanation, at least in the terms to which the Mensheviks were accustomed.

Until that time, although admittedly with growing difficulty, the members of the Menshevik emigration, and especially their Internationalist circle, had felt collectively able to comprehend and interpret the major developments they had witnessed since 1917: War Communism and NEP; the Great Depression and the rise of Fascism; and, at the very outset, the victory of Stalin over his political opponents and the inception of the Five Year Plans. By the late 1930s, however, this was no longer the case. Even the Internationalists found themselves unable to formulate a persuasive interpretation of developments in Stalin's Russia on the basis of the definitions of the laws of history from which they had derived their notions of cause and effect; on the basis of the images of historical precedent, especially of past revolutionary events, in which these notions had been embodied, or modified; or even on the basis of the larger constructs that their world view had provided for ordering their experience. Capitalism, socialism, not to speak of Thermidorian reaction – indeed revolution and counterrevolution (necessarily of the right in their historical cosmology, just as the concept of reaction in contemporary European experience had been necessarily associated with capitalism) – no longer seemed adequate for making sense of the processes of collectivization, forced-draft industrialization, let alone the Great Purges, and their political and social consequences, at least to the extent that the shape of the new Soviet society and state could be discerned by the end of the decade. Neither these constructs, nor the peculiar blend of economic determinism and sense of revolutionary dynamics (largely drawn from the example of the French Revolution) that most Menshevik publicists had applied to Soviet developments, could really explain the primacy of politics over economics that these developments appeared to demonstrate, the extraordinary importance of the role of personality (in this instance, indeed, a personality which had inspired them with so little respect), and the extraordinary element of arbitrariness that this personality appeared to have introduced into Russian politics.

To be sure, certain Menshevik publicists of the period sought to invent new constructs, or to refurbish old ones, in their efforts to unravel the puzzle that these developments presented. But these constructs – such as the concept of state capitalism, or even the embryonic conception of totalitarianism for which some were already groping – sowed even greater intellectual confusion in their own ranks, for their own ideology was even more resistant to their elaboration than the contemporary Soviet experience they were meant to elucidate.

By the eve of World War II, the developments of the Stalin era – far more than any other events of the 1930s – had precipitated a major intellectual, moral, and political crisis in the Menshevik emigration that proved irresolvable. Even within the small and hitherto extraordinarily coherent circle of Internationalists, which had dominated the Delegation Abroad since its inception, a group of erstwhile followers of Theodore Dan – including Boris Nicolaevsky and David Dallin – now challenged with increasing vigor and directness the dogmas that Dan indomitably still sought to apply to the interpretation of Soviet experience. The issues involved could no longer be buried or plastered over; nor could the Delegation Abroad be revived as a political entity after its survivors moved to the United States. The confrontation between ideology and reality was too cruel, the intellectual and moral passions it unleashed too great, to make even a surface restoration of unity possible.

In this context, Dan's *Origins of Bolshevism (Proiskhozhdenie bol'shevizma)*, published soon after his arrival in the United States, constituted not only an ideological testament but also a political swan song. For the basic themes drawn in the concluding section of this remarkable book – its interpretation of the evolution of Bolshevism as an almost inevitable product of the implantation of Marxism on Russian soil and of its grafting onto the Russian revolutionary tradition, and especially the hopeful view that Dan still insisted on drawing from social and economic changes in the Soviet Union – were not recognized, even by Dan's erstwhile followers, as elaborations of his own earlier views, let alone as a legitimate expression of the world view they had once shared.

In any event, by the time the book appeared, this world view – and the shared experience and mutual loyalties that had sustained it – had suffered a second and more immediate psychological blow. This one was induced by the Mensheviks' confrontation with the new wave of the Soviet emigration – or, more precisely, with those representatives of it who reached American soil in the early postwar period. From the outset, a few Menshevik survivors – including, predictably, Dan – greeted these first representatives of the postwar Soviet emigration (who had come to the United States from the parts of German-occupied Europe liberated by the Western armies) with considerable suspicion. They saw hovering over some of them the shadow of possible collaboration with the Nazis, but more generally they discerned in their wholesale hostility to the Soviet regime a rejection of socialist ideals and values as they themselves understood and cherished them. But many members of the Menshevik community, including Boris Nicolaevsky and several other survivors of the Delegation Abroad, were far more receptive to the new immigrants, seeing in them a bridge to the Russia from which they had been so cruelly separated, and indeed potential political allies, perhaps even recruits for their own movement, capable of infusing it with a renewed political vitality.

Most Menshevik survivors, however, emerged deeply disappointed from the encounter. At issue were not only the differences in political assessments, or the deeper differences in political ideals and values that all too rapidly emerged from this confrontation, but also the gulf that it exposed between the ethos and the very life style of these two generations of the Russian emigration, shaped as they had been by such radically different historical experiences. Most of the Menshevik survivors detected in the new Soviet emigration a pragmatism, a materialism, and what seemed to them a lack of critical judgment, if not of intellectual and moral responsibility, which they found incomprehensible and ultimately unacceptable. Most of the newcomers who established contact with the Menshevik émigrés for any period of time (a much smaller number than they had expected, it turned out) soon came to view them as a sect of aging men and women, clinging to an outlived and obviously discredited set of political dogmas and values bearing no meaningful relationship to contemporary realities. With few exceptions, the members of the two generations involved in this encounter emerged from it as strangers, and each group quickly went its own way, the new Soviet émigrés usually taking the initiative.

This experience probably left deeper personal scars on the survivors of the Menshevik emigration than had the disputes of the 1930s about Soviet

Russia and its future. It shook far more profoundly their own personal sense of relevance. By the same token, it undoubtedly contributed to the mood that made possible the inception of our project and the eventual fruitfulness of its efforts. Not only did it contribute to these survivors' realization that their days as a political movement were over – probably a psychological prerequisite for their conclusion that the time had come for them to record its history – but it also helped to defuse past factional differences, making it possible to persuade all of them (some, however, reluctantly at first) to join in our collective effort.

II

I have drawn in detail this historical background not only because of the light it sheds on these Menshevik survivors' psychology and mood, but also because it dictated some of our project's objectives. We managed to persuade the foundation officers we approached that our Menshevik associates should not be confined to the role of "sources" for Western scholars who would be associated with the project, but should also be encouraged to reach for their original goal of recording their own history. We also argued, however, that in this effort to reconstruct the history of their party, each of them should be encouraged to pay particular attention to those aspects of this experience in which they had been most directly involved.

In pursuit of these objectives, we outlined a number of strategies. We would make available to our Menshevik collaborators all of the relevant primary sources that we could assemble: copies of articles they had written, speeches they had delivered, and resolutions they had helped formulate, along with fuller records of the newspapers and periodicals to which they had contributed and of the party conferences and congresses in which they had participated. In this fashion, and with the help of our own questions, we hoped to encourage an interplay between the sources in which their experiences had originally been recorded and our informants' recollection of them – the written sources refreshing our informants' recall, and memory in turn filling in the gaps and illuminating the sometimes deliberate obscurities in the written record.

To this end, an informal library of primary sources, including the materials that Boris Nicolaevsky and Anna Bourguina had assembled over the years, was established in the basement apartment, facing the Columbia Law School, which had been turned into the project's offices. In the course of the project many of our Menshevik associates spent long evenings there reading, rereading, and often discussing among themselves the documentary and memoir materials we had asked them to interpret. This basement apartment (which also served as the meeting place for our seminars and many of our interview sessions) thus came to provide a setting for our Menshevik associates to relive, individually and collectively, the events in the history of their movement and in their own lives that we were seeking to recapture.

A variety of flexible formats was adopted for recording this interplay between memory and the written word, ranging from memoirs of those aspects of Menshevik history in which their authors had been most directly involved (which we distributed in mimeographed form) to more scholarly individual and collective studies, eventually published as monographs. Drafts of many of these works were discussed at the weekly seminars of the project. We expected that additional insights and reconsiderations would result from the confrontation at these seminars of the range of viewpoints represented among our Menshevik associates, since this group included survivors of factions which at various critical points in the party's history had advocated bitterly conflicting political views and radically different courses of action. We also hoped that the presence at these sessions, side by side with the survivors of these factions, of the Western historians associated with the project might increase the light and decrease the heat of these confrontations. We counted on the sheer atmospheric effect of their physical presence, but also on the questions that these Western scholars might put from their own very different angles of vision as to why certain steps had been taken and certain actions performed, or left unperformed, by the party's various factions.

Seeking to probe below the level of rationalization and stereotype for deeper sources of political motivation, we also asked some of the Western historians in our midst to pose the same kinds of questions in individual and more informal interviews with our Menshevik associates and other survivors within our reach. Our Western collaborators were asked to concentrate on those aspects of the history of Menshevism in which their informants had been most deeply involved, thereby aiding the process of historical reconstruction pursued in our program of written memoirs. But more important, it seemed to us that these interviews would provide a last chance to trace the genesis and subsequent evolution of Menshevik political culture: the processes of socialization – immediate family relationships, and the various concentric and intertwining associations in the *gymnazium*, at the university, and in the broader circles of intelligentsia life – through which our informants had been recruited into this political culture; as well as the norms, the values, the *byt* – the patterns of collective daily life – that had distinguished the internal functioning of this culture and its relationship to others.

My two collaborators in these interviews, Walter Sablinsky and Alan Wildman, and I were specialists on the history of the period, if not on all of the specific events that were recounted to us. Indeed, both my collaborators were conducting these interviews partly to gather additional information for the monographs that each was then preparing (Wildman, on the Russian Social Democratic intelligentsia and the workers' movement in the 1890s and during the Iskra period; Sablinsky, on Father Gapon's Assembly of Factory Workers and the interaction between its members and the Social Democrats in the inception of labor unrest in Petersburg in 1905). I had already published a monograph on the origins of Bolshevism and Menshevism.

All three of us used whatever knowledge we had already accumulated or managed to absorb in our ongoing studies to provide at the outset of each session a framework for our informants' recollections. We tried to set the events and experiences they were to recount in the context of their own lives, of the milieus of the Russian intelligentsia in which they had moved, and of the political and social life of the country as a whole. We also sought through follow-up questions to probe for greater detail and depth in their responses, and to elicit information about experiences and events they had barely mentioned, or left entirely untouched.

The results of these additional probes, it now seems to me, were somewhat mixed. Usually, we did manage to elicit considerable supplementary factual information, as well as additional impressions and evaluations; but these usually concerned topics which our informants had from the outset been eager to discuss. About events originally left blank or blurred, our further probes – despite our informants' otherwise superb capacity for recall – most often elicited elliptic or at best vague or stilted responses, wanting not only in concreteness but also in spontaneity and vitality.

*   *   *

I shall return to certain of the specific problems I encountered in this regard in my discussion of the reminiscences included in this volume. But I would now like to summarize some of the more general impressions we drew about memory and capacity for recall in the course of our interviews with these survivors of the Russian revolutionary movement.

Some of these impressions and observations are perhaps banal, likely to be familiar to anyone who has conversed with persons of advanced age. It is almost always the case, for example, that the aged remember most vividly and by and large most faithfully their experience of childhood and youth, and that their ability to recall becomes more fragmentary, more blurred, more stilted, as they move forward toward the more recent past. This was certainly our experience with most of the Menshevik survivors we interviewed. For even when we were unable to elicit from them more than fragmentary accounts of various episodes in their adult lives, their reminiscences of childhood and youth were almost invariably fresh, concrete, filled with distinctive detail, usually recounted with vitality and zest. It was as if the usury of time had not in the least eroded these traces of their earliest past, and the adult mind had not imposed on them, at least in any obvious way, its screen and principles of selection.

Indeed, the easiest course would have been to devote exclusive attention in our interview program to accounts of childhood and youth. Instead, under the compulsion of the other goals of our project, we sought to follow our informants through their subsequent political journeys; and with the three figures to whom this volume is devoted, to do so consecutively. That this proved so much more difficult a task was not merely due to the peculiar usury of time to which I have referred: that the human memory among the aged appears to become enfeebled as it moves toward the present. This was undoubtedly the case, but there were, I think, other reasons for the difficulties we experienced in drawing from most of our informants, especially in any consecutive fashion, equally vivid accounts of their adult lives.

To explore the sources of these difficulties, we must bear in mind that the period after 1905, which saw the crystallization of Menshevik political culture, was nonetheless marked by abrupt and dramatic changes in Russia's political life, in the attendant fortunes of the Menshevik Party, and in the individual lives of most of our informants. For some of them, such as George Denike, the years of reaction after the Stolypin coup d'etat in 1907 opened the way for a return to life in the open. For others, however, such as Lydia and Theodore Dan, the years of reaction meant the resumption of a new period of political exile in Western Europe, interrupted only in 1913, when the political amnesty declared on the tercentenary of the Romanov dynasty enabled them to return to Russia. For still others, such as Boris Nicolaevsky, the years between the Stolypin coup d'etat and the summer of 1914 brought periods of administrative exile. Nicolaevsky spent two years in the North (1908–10), followed by the resumption of a political career in Baku as a journalist and Menshevik Party activist, and eventually in Petersburg as an aid to the Mensheviks' Duma fraction. Another break was induced by World War I, which for most of the Menshevik Internationalists who opposed it involved a renewed experience of arrest, deportation, and administrative exile, interrupted by the outbreak of the Revolution, which brought most of them back from Siberia or Western Europe, this time to the very center of the political scene. There followed months of febrile political activity, interrupted equally abruptly by the Bolshevik seizure of power; and after the conclusion of the Civil War and the launching of NEP, a new period of political exile in the emigration, marked by the successive uprootings that I already discussed.

As we tried to reconstruct the extraordinarily disjointed phases of experience and dramatically shifting scenes that distinguished these individual life journeys as well as the political history of the Menshevik Party as a whole, it seemed that our informants' ability to recall them was in part a function of the upturns and downturns in their political fortunes. Thus our interview experience – particularly with the psychologically strongest, most vital, most intact of our informants – appeared at least partially to confirm the common sense rule that, especially many years after the event, the mind recalls most easily and vividly moments of victory rather than moments of defeat, times of hope rather than times of despair.

By itself, however, this axiom did not provide an altogether adequate explanation of our results. Precisely because of the coherence of their political culture, our informants' ability to recall various events seemed even more sharply affected by the degree to which they had been able to filter and order them, *even while experiencing them*, through the extraordinarily resilient worldview upon which their individual and collective identity so largely depended.

One of the greatest disappointments of our interviewing experience, for example, was our inability to draw from our informants detailed and vivid accounts of their experience of the Revolution of 1917. (Denike's interviews were a major exception, for reasons to which I shall return.) In most cases, notwithstanding our best efforts, we were unable to elicit from them recollections of any depth of factual detail or any freshness or spontaneity of tone, even concerning events in which they had been centrally involved; or indeed to draw even a rudimentary reconstruction of their own lives and daily activities during the Revolution. Some informants were able to recall activities that fitted into an habitual pattern (such as Schwarz's account of the social-insurance legislation that he was still drafting on the night of the Bolshevik seizure of power, and some of Lydia Dan's descriptions of the all-night sessions at the Dan's Petrograd apartment). But as soon as they left these few orderly reference points, their recollections usually became extraordinarily foggy or chaotic – the fragments detached from any larger frame or sequence, as if time itself had exploded, or become suspended, during these months.

I often reflected, during the life of our project and subsequently, upon the sources of this failure of memory – a failure that presented so sharp a contrast to the vividness with which most of our informants recalled their experiences of 1905. The contrast, I believe, cannot be ascribed solely to the greater vividness of memories of youth (although, notwithstanding the prominent roles that some of them played in 1905, most of our informants were still very young), or even to the much more searing and irrevocable defeat that the outcome of the revolution of 1917 brought to their political and personal lives. More to the point is the fact that for most of them the course that the revolution of 1917 had taken had been not merely a defeat, but one that did not fit into any established frame of reference, and the experience of which, therefore, could not be integrated and recorded in memory.

The impression that most of our informants rendered of this experience, sometimes quite unconsciously, was that almost from the outset they had found themselves valiantly trying to master a chaos that had gradually overwhelmed them. Nothing about the experience had proven familiar, or run according to expectations (notwithstanding their frequent attempts to attach to it familiar labels): the identities of friends and foes, the sources of major threats, the behavior of various collective actors, including the industrial workers they had tried so hard to lead, and whose interests they had sought to represent. Even the outcome, the final outcome as it turned out, had failed to make sense, to lend itself, even in hindsight, to a historical rationale (at least in terms of *their* understanding of the laws of history).

Indeed, in their own terms, how was the Bolshevik seizure of power in October to be perceived, or even classified? It was not a revolution – Russia had already experienced a revolution, in February, and the conditions were obviously unripe for another, socialist, revolution. Neither could it be viewed – in any of the terms to which the Mensheviks were accustomed – as a counterrevolution. For a genuine counterrevolution could only come from the right, from the forces of reaction, and whatever their sins the Bolsheviks (and especially the working-class following which they had undeniably drawn in their wake) could not be so classified. And so the Mensheviks, and most of their erstwhile allies on the left, insisted on calling October an "overturn" *(perevorot);* the Bolsheviks having succeeded in seizing the reins of power by taking advantage of the wholesale disintegration that the country and the Revolution had experienced under the unbearable strains imposed by the war. Indeed, most of them viewed the October Revolution, at least at the time, as a lunatic act which could only precipitate an inevitable civil war, and lead ultimately to an equally inevitable, and genuine, counterrevolution of the right.

From this perspective the whole process of unraveling that had led to this senseless outcome *could only then be perceived,* and later only dimly recalled, as a maelstrom that had eventually overwhelmed the Mensheviks' best efforts to control it. And of the activities that our informants had pursued until they had been overwhelmed by this sea of chaos, only fragments could be remembered; while the settings in which they had taken place assumed in recall the stilted, two-dimensional quality of standing portraits, or the foggy quality of dreams. It was as if the labels originally applied to them had never really quite fitted, had not been persuasive even at the time – all of them masking, and yet simultaneously suggesting, as in a veritable living nightmare, a frightful reality yawning below.

To all this, our informants' recollection of the revolutionary experience of 1905 presented an enormous contrast. That experience, too, had ended in defeat, but a defeat perceived as merely the postponement of an inevitable outcome. That defeat, moreover, had come at the hands of a familiar enemy, and in a form which, at least after the fact, could be rationalized, if not easily accepted – that of a Thermidorean reaction, precipitated perhaps by the Revolution's own excesses. This fitted well within the terms of the historical lessons which our informants felt they should have drawn from the revolutionary experiences of the past: from the Revolution of 1848 and the Paris Commune, and especially from the great French Revolution of 1789, which most of them had studied in the days of their youth, when they had first sought to define the historical roles that they would play in the course of their revolutionary careers.

This is not to suggest that 1905 had not also shattered certain assumptions and precipitated certain important political reassessments. In fact, it was only in the wake of this experience that several of our informants had repudiated Bolshevism, and committed themselves to the Menshevik cause. But they had been able to make these changes in orientation without great intellectual difficulty or psychological strain, not only because this first defeat had come when they were young, but also because it had not inflicted on them a trauma even barely comparable to the one they eventually suffered in 1917. Hence our informants could still vividly recall, so many years after the event, in almost every detail and with considerable zest, their own "revolutionary excesses" during the first revolutionary experience.

III

The three informants whose reminiscences are presented here were by no means altogether exempt from these constrictions of memory. I persisted, nonetheless, for several years in my efforts to record their respective life histories because I was convinced that each of them brought to this process of reconstruction certain extraordinary qualities of intellect and temperament, and equally distinctive personal and political backgrounds.

I will begin with their human qualities, which stood out from the very outset. All three informants had been deeply involved in the events they now sought to describe – even after so many years they became fully absorbed in recounting them – but their accounts also assumed a quality of detachment and indeed a genuine philosophical perspective, punctuated by notes of irony. In each of them, this detachment derived in part from profoundly ingrained personal traits. All three, but especially Lydia Dan, positively hated any manifestation of sentimentality, self-deception, or emotional excess, especially when speaking as historical observers. But these common psychological traits were reinforced by certain distinctive characteristics drawn from the roles each had assumed in the course of their political journeys.

Lydia Dan's detachment stemmed in part from the woman's perspective she contributed to the description of a political world which had been largely dominated by men, but also from the fact that after her second emigration to Western Europe (following the Stolypin coup d'etat in June 1907) she had stood increasingly at the periphery of the political conflicts that periodically tore apart the ranks of Russian Social Democracy. Largely because of this psychological distance, her memory of those developments lacks sharpness and depth of detail. But there is an extraordinary freshness and immediacy in her recollections of earlier years: of her childhood and early teens, and of her initiation and early career as a professional revolutionary in the late 1890s and during the Iskra period. Concerning the events she had witnessed, the milieus in which she had moved, and the historical figures she had met and worked with during those formative years – both in her own life, and in the development of Russian Social Democracy – Lydia Dan's memory was not only miraculously intact but also remarkably undistorted by subsequent political divisions and conflicts.

In George Denike and Boris Nicolaevsky, this capacity for detachment was enhanced by the ability of each of these informants to act as his own historian. Indeed, both of them brought to our interviews a depth of historical knowledge, sophistication, and intellectual self-discipline drawn from their earlier efforts at such historical reconstruction. Denike had begun an academic career as a professional historian, first at the University of Kazan and later at the University of Moscow. Nicolaevsky had devoted much of his adult life, especially in the emigration, to acting as the informal historian and archivist of the Menshevik party and other revolutionary groups. In fact, during his years in the emigration he had recorded the reminiscences of some of the major participants in pre-revolutionary political life in much the same way as I now tried to record his own life.[1]

But even more important than these qualities in accounting for the richness and texture of these three life histories (and contributing, I believe, to the value of the volume that we were eventually able to derive from them) was their complementariness: the differences in the angles of vision that these three informants brought to bear not only on the history of Menshevism, but also on the broader milieus in which the ideas and attitudes of the Russian intelligentsia had been shaped. This complementariness of vision, reflected particularly in their reminiscences of childhood and youth, was due in large measure to the range of their respective social backgrounds. Indeed, by virtue of their family origins, each provided a prototype of one of the major social and psychological elements in the cultural melting pot from which the intelligentsia had emerged in Russia's otherwise highly particularistic and compartmentalized society.

George Denike was, on his father's side, a descendant of a family of the provincial service nobility – at least until the Great Reforms of the 1860s, the most important source of what eventually became the Russian intelligentsia. As has often been noted, the sons and daughters of this service nobility, from which the state had traditionally staffed its officer corps and the upper ranks of its bureaucracy, brought to their life concerns and occupations, even when they refused to serve the state, an ethos of service but also a sense of their destiny to lead. From the Decembrist uprising of 1825 onward, but especially by the late nineteenth century, this sense of destiny was usually translated into the collective image of themselves as, at least potentially, an alternative political leadership to that constituted by the autocracy and its official servants.

In the representations of the origins and role of the Russian intelligentsia that became rooted in radical circles by the end of the nineteenth century, this sense of service and of the destiny to lead was perceived as having been transferred from the state power to the benighted masses of the People. The historical mission of the intelligentsia was equally automatically identified as that of leading the People, or at least certain of its constituent groups, to liberation from the state and the social structure of privilege and inequity with which it was seen as inextricably intertwined. Long after the conclusion in the early 1880s of the classical era of Russian Populism, this heroic version of the genesis of the intelligentsia continued to provide for the youths who eventually joined its various radical circles their earliest inspiration in articulating their disaffection from the existing order: their images of right and wrong and of heroic behavior in seeking to right the wrongs. The legacy of Russian Populism also provided some of the "sacred

---

[1] The extraordinary range of information that Nicolaevsky had compiled in collecting these reminiscences, combined with his own extraordinary powers of recall, hampered our efforts to reconstruct systematically his own political journey. His mind often wandered off, by an almost endless process of association, over the details of the life histories of the various political figures he mentioned in the course of our interviews – while I listened, usually spellbound, unwilling and unable to interrupt.

texts" on which these youngsters drew – in the highly self-conscious process of formulating their world views – the conceptions of the natural and historical laws that would guide them in their efforts to create a new world of freedom and cooperation. Indeed the heritage of Russian Populism, along with the exemplars of the libertarian tradition in nineteenth-century Russian literature, figure very large in Lydia Dan's and Boris Nicolaevsky's early recollections of the works they read and the figures they discussed as they first sought to define their political and social attitudes and the life paths they would seek to follow.

But notwithstanding the grip that these heroic images of the intelligentsia's revolutionary tradition continued to exercise even as late as the turn of the century, there had also emerged, especially among certain elements of the liberal nobility, an alternative definition of its character and role. This was the view that the intelligentsia constituted the intellectual and moral elite of *obshchestvo* – of educated, indeed privileged, "census" society. By the late 1870s, this alternative representation of the intelligentsia had already come into wide public usage not only among spokesmen for various currents of liberal and eventually radical opinion, but even in the pronouncements of certain state officials. Its very emergence rested on the premise that a civil society was developing in Russian life, transcending the particularistic and antagonistic interests of its traditional estates *(sosloviia)*, and that this emerging civil society represented at least potentially a "public interest" which could legitimately be opposed to the superordinate authority of the state. Thus among those who came to identify themselves as members of the liberal intelligentsia, the notion of service as well as of the destiny to lead, originally rooted in the ethos of the Russian service nobility, was transferred from the state to an existing or potentially existing civil society. In contrast to their fathers, who had sought to act as "statesmen" *(gosudarstvennye deiateli)* serving a transcendent "state interest," the scions of the service nobility who became members of this new liberal intelligentsia came to view themselves as "public figures" *(obshchestvennye deiateli)* working on behalf of an even more legitimate and transcendent "public weal" *(obshchestvennoe delo)*.

At the end of the seventies and the beginning of the eighties, when the image emerged of a developing civil society with its own set of common values and principles of order which could be counterposed to the overarching structure of the state, this *obshchestvo* was still largely perceived by most educated opinion and by officialdom to be separated from the masses of the People by a profound cultural gulf, if not by basic differences of interests. But the attempts, however halfhearted and ultimately unsuccessful, to establish political coalitions between the liberal and radical circles of the intelligentsia in order to gain political freedom already reflected the emergence, even among radicals, of the sense of a convergence of interests between certain elements of privileged society and the benighted masses of the People.

Although much of the energy invested in the efforts to build such coalitions was temporarily dissipated during the decade of reaction that followed the assassination of Alexander II in 1881, the continued dissemination of the term intelligentsia to designate both the radical and liberal wings of the intellectual elite clearly suggested that hopes for such a convergence had not entirely been abandoned. Indeed, even during this seemingly thankless decade, the vision of a common role for the various constituent groups of the intelligentsia continued to be articulated, however modestly, in the doctrine of "small deeds" *(malye dela)*, in which all "People-loving" elements of the intelligentsia should engage to achieve gradual but tangible improvements in the cultural and material conditions of the People.

By the late 1890s, and especially during the years immediately preceding the Revolution of 1905, when George Denike imbibed the ideas and attitudes that eventually drew him to the revolutionary movement, the political situation had dramatically changed. A massive opposition movement emerged with dramatic speed among the various liberal and radical circles of educated society, its development resting on the much more ambitious and seemingly substantial image of an "All-Nation Struggle" directed at the overthrow of absolutism and the conquest of political freedom. All radical as well as liberal political factions and parties now subscribed to this objective, at least as a first stage "minimum program" for which they would seek to mobilize the masses whose interests they claimed to represent.

To be sure, for the radical factions represented in this coalition, the suspension of their final, divisive, revolutionary objectives, which this consensus implied, was perceived as temporary. The shaping of the nation to be born would ultimately be decided by the struggles that would resume after the overthrow of autocracy, and by the same token by the dictates of the laws of history to which these political groupings so confidently subscribed. But notwithstanding this qualification, the emerging consensus on the immediate political objectives to be achieved in the "All-Nation Struggle against Absolutism" and its translation into the strategy and tactics of various radical as well as liberal circles of the intelligentsia, reflected an amalgamation of the conceptions of "Society" and "People," which had kept radicals and liberals apart through most of the Populist era.

Indeed, the implicit rationale for the leadership role the intelligentsia sought to assume in the "All-Nation Struggle" was that they would play the role of "midwives" in the birth of this new political nation. They would assist in bringing political maturity, independent initiative *(samodeiatel 'nost)*, and collective organization to the various groups they claimed to represent, even while mobilizing them to win the political freedoms that would eventually enable them to exercise their own independent consciousness and will. This image of the dynamics of the "All-Nation Struggle" and the special role it assigned to the members of the intelligentsia, obviously still reflected beneath the veneer of the various ideological formulations advanced to justify it, the sense of their own special qualities of leadership and service – transcending all individual, group, and factional interests – which the scions of the service nobility who had originally defined themselves as members of the intelligentsia had introduced into the collective representation of this group.

In the wake of 1905, this conception of an "All-Nation Struggle" based on a consensus among liberals and radicals on the immediate objective of attaining political freedom underwent considerable strain, as the various factions in the coalition blamed one another for their political setbacks. The radicals (including the Mensheviks) bitterly criticized the liberals for political timidity and opportunism; the liberals in turn condemned the radicals for their dogmatism and revolutionary excesses. Yet this conception proved to have a hardy life in the subsequent evolution of the intelligentsia, and in fact played a considerable role in the crystallization of Menshevik political culture.

Menshevism distanced itself from Bolshevism during these years over two related sets of political issues. The first concerned the legitimacy of coalitions with liberal parties and parliamentary groups in the political setting created by the establishment of Russia's new national representative institutions. The issue originally arose during the elections to the Second Duma, as a result of the Mensheviks' willingness to consider electoral agreements with the Kadets when these were deemed necessary to forestall the election of "Black Hundred" reactionary candidates. But it resurfaced even after the Stolypin coup d'etat over the formation of tactical alliances in the Duma between Social Democratic deputies and those of the Kadet and Progressist factions – most dramatically so on the eve of the war, when an opposition majority, resting on such a liberal–radical coalition, appeared within reach.

A second doctrinal conflict between Mensheviks and Bolsheviks after 1905 concerned the use of existing "legal possibilities" for building an open labor party and labor movement. By the eve of the War, when the Bolsheviks had been converted to the exploitation of such "legal possibilities," the debate came to focus over a narrower issue: were the "open" organizations of labor to serve as instruments of the revolutionary underground in the pursuit of the revolutionary perspectives traced by Lenin and his followers (a "general political strike" leading to an "armed uprising" culminating in the establishment of a "firm democratic regime"), or should they be left to pursue the more modest aims for which they had been ostensibly organized, and serve as recruiting grounds for the labor intelligentsia that would eventually assume the leadership of a Europeanized labor party and labor movement on Russian soil?

The two issues were closely interrelated both doctrinally and politically. They were doctrinally related because both ultimately raised the question whether, in the immediate future, Russia would continue to undergo a "bourgeois" phase of political and social development, which would necessarily be contained, even in the eventuality of a revolution, within the framework of institutions essentially comparable to those already functioning in Western Europe. They were related politically because if this *was* the only realistic perspective, coalition tactics with "bourgeois" parties and factions were fully justified, partly to achieve such an institutional frame-work in the longer term, but also in the shorter term to protect and extend the open labor organizations' existing legal immunities against arbitrary acts of repression. By the eve of World War I, these issues were becoming all the more pressing in view of increasingly desperate efforts by some mod-erate and liberal parliamentary groups to mobilize an opposition majority to use the Duma's budgetary powers to resist the government's infractions of existing legal safeguards, and to mobilize public opinion in the face of the increasingly urgent rumors of an impending coup d'etat.

As George Denike's reminiscences of his stays in Kazan on the eve of the war suggest, members of the radical and ex-radical intelligentsia living in provincial cities during these years, including Mensheviks and non-fac-tional Social Democrats, perceived these issues very differently from those active in the capital and in the emigration. The severe political constraints to which members of the intelligentsia were subjected in provincial Russia, the abuses by provincial bureaucrats, the weakness of local party organi-zations, and the absence of politically mobilized and militant mass follow-ings all fostered a less partisan and ideologically "loaded" political climate. Various elements of the liberal and radical intelligentsia naturally gravi-tated together, not only in the performance of "small deeds" to bring mar-ginal improvements in cultural, social, and economic conditions, but also to pursue all possibilities for political action through participation in elec-tions to local and national bodies and publicistic activity in "progressive" newspapers and journals.

But the underlying issue – whether those who identified themselves as socialists should view themselves, in however qualified a fashion, as mem-bers of, or indeed spokesmen for, an emerging nation – surfaced even among Menshevik activists in the capital and in the emigration after the outbreak of World War I. The threat of Russia's military defeat at the hands of the Central Powers suddenly loomed very large following the mil-itary setbacks of the late spring and summer of 1915, and so did the need for full-scale mobilization of the war effort if such an outcome was to be avoided. Under the circumstances, the question of whether the constituent groups of Russian Social Democracy had any political stake in this mobi-lization – and if so under what conditions and on what terms – assumed great urgency. The Menshevik deputies in the State Duma had been one of the few parliamentary groups of the various belligerent countries to vote against war credits when the Duma had been briefly convened to consider the issue, well after the outbreak of the war. (All Bolshevik deputies had been arrested by this time and sent into administrative exile). Even so, just as had been the case among other European Socialist parties, deep fissures had opened in Russia's Social Democratic circles (as indeed in the radical intelligentsia as a whole) between Internationalist and Defensist groups of various hues.

Among the Defensist groups represented within the RSDRP, positions ranged from the outright militant support of the war effort advocated by

Plekhanov and the small circle of collaborators associated with him in the publication of the journal *Edinstvo (Unity)*, to the slightly more modulated position articulated by Potresov and those Menshevik publicists who joined with him in the publication of the miscellany *Samozashchita (Self-Defense)*, to the even more qualified, more varied, and fluid positions assumed by those Menshevik *praktiki* of the open labor movement who became associated with the labor groups of the war industrial committees that sprang up by late 1915 and early 1916. Even so, what was basically involved in all these early manifestations of Defensism and Revolutionary Defensism was an effort, or more precisely, an irresistible impulse on the part of various Social Democratic circles to identify themselves – in the face of the threat of Russia's defeat and its implications for her future development – with a conception of national interest, and at least potentially of state interest, however much the interests of this nation-state were to be distinguished from those of the regime currently in power.

The overthrow of the autocracy in February–March 1917, and the wholesale collapse of much of the institutional structure on which it had rested, greatly eased the articulation and legitimation of an outright Defensist stand. Support of the war effort, it could now be argued, was identified with the defense, indeed the salvation, of both the country and the revolution. The Revolutionary Defensist wing of the Menshevik party came to insist that all the "vital forces of the nation" – workers and peasants, but also the "progressive" bourgeoisie, and the "democratic" nonsocialist intelligentsia – should be mobilized for this purpose. This formula provided the ideological justification for the eventual abandonment of the experiment in dual power and the formation of a coalition government.

In the capital itself, this process of definition and self-definition would consume months of agonizing debate, marked by qualifications, reservations, and ideological and political obscurities. But in most provincial cities, as Denike's reminiscences remind us, this process occurred much more swiftly, if not automatically – as if no other outcome could be conceived, no other conclusion drawn, in the face of existing realities. For most of the radical as well as liberal members of the provincial intelligentsia, the world – the real world in these provincial towns and the surrounding countryside – now clearly consisted of deeply divided social groups: small numbers of workers, artisans, shopkeepers, garrisons of increasingly disgruntled soldiers, as well as islands of educated society, surrounded by large masses of peasants. And the only group conceivably capable of bridging these differences amid the chaos left by the collapse of the old regime was the intelligentsia.

Of course, this sense of the inevitability of coalition and of their own leadership of it, which Denike now shared with so many other radical and erstwhile radical members of the provincial intelligentsia, reflected not only an appreciation of current political and social realities, but also a sense of their destiny to lead. Indeed, it appeared as if, with the collapse of the autocracy, those scions of the service nobility who had contributed so much to the formation of the intelligentsia, and to its sense of political mission, had reached, for however brief a moment, the ultimate formulation of that sense of mission in the vision that they and other members of the intelligentsia now articulated so sharply of leading and serving the new nation-state that they sought to erect on the ruins of the old order.

*   *   *

Boris Nicolaevsky, a descendant of seven generations of village priests in Central and East European Russia, provides a striking example of the role played by another group of Russian society, the *popovichi* (the offspring of members of the orthodox clergy and graduates of its religious academies and seminaries) in the development of the intelligentsia. The appearance on the cultural scene of such *raznochintsy* – members of the intelligentsia drawn from other ranks and estates than the nobility – greatly reinforced, in the intellectual and political climate generated by the emancipation of the serfs in 1861, the sense of duty and debt to the People which constituted so important an element in Russian Populism, and more generally in the ethos of "People loving" liberal and radical circles of the intelligentsia. The immediacy and sense of urgency with which this group infused the ethos of service to the People are well expressed in Nicolaevsky's recollection that he had drawn from his childhood experience the irresistible conviction that "something had to be done" to introduce "more justice" into the life of the peasants of his native village.

The emergence of the *raznochintsy* as a major constituent group of the intelligentsia also added legitimacy to its claim to national leadership: the intelligentsia could now claim to be not only for the People, but also of the People, and thus all the more entitled to voice its aspirations and needs. By 1905 this collective representation of the intelligentsia was reinforced by the addition to its ranks of significant numbers of *"intelligenty"* and *polu-* (semi-) *intelligenty* drawn from various tributary estates and lower socio-economic groups of urban and rural Russia: members of the lower professions, technicians, artisans, and skilled workers; village teachers, medical assistants *(feldshery)*, and veterinarians; and, in even larger numbers, students of the secondary and special technical schools which had sprung up to provide training in various trades and menial professions.

The recruits it drew from these lower legal estates and socioeconomic groups obviously added considerable substance to the intelligentsia's claim to constitute a non-caste, non-*soslovie*, non-class group, transcending the sharp differences of interests and values separating other groups in national life – including the hitherto seemingly insurmountable barriers between "census society" and the masses of the People. As the experience of 1905 would demonstrate, especially during the heady and exhilarating months leading up to the issuance of the October Manifesto, it also greatly reinforced the ability of the intelligentsia to rouse various groups in both rural and urban Russia in its efforts to mobilize an "All-Nation Struggle against Absolutism," not only by virtue of the heterogenous social origins of its members, but also because of the opportunities for contacts with various strata of the population that their professional occupations afforded them. But the experience of 1905 would also demonstrate – precisely as this process of political and social mobilization progressed – the fragility of the intelligentsia's claim to bridge the differences of interests and values of the social groups it sought to lead in this "All-Nation Struggle."

Actually, the fragility of this "All-Nation" coalition was apparent from the very outset in the political constructs used to describe it. According to the various radical and liberal circles of the intelligentsia, the "All-Nation Struggle" was to be waged in the name of "democracy" and "democratic" objectives. But what relationship did "democracy" bear to privileged "census" society, and "democratic" objectives to the institutional framework to be created for the political nation that would emerge after the overthrow of autocracy? Inevitably, differences over these issues surfaced in the course of the 1905 Revolution, splitting the ranks of the liberal and radical intelligentsia, including those of the Social Democrats. They would just as inevitably recur during the Revolution of 1917 between the Menshevik Internationalists, who opposed a coalition government with the "bourgeoisie" (first in the name of "dual power," and eventually in the name of an "all-democratic" government from which "bourgeois" parties were to be excluded), and the Revolutionary Defensist wing of the Menshevik Party, which continued up to October to support a coalition of all the "vital forces of the nation," including the "progressive elements of the bourgeoisie." But even before 1905 the problem had already arisen in a variety of forms in the intelligentsia's programmatic debates about the "minimum" objectives to be pursued in the "All-Nation Struggle," and the relationship of these "minimum" programs to its radical factions' ultimate socialist goals.

Nicolaevsky's reminiscences – and the contrasts that they present to George Denike's – suggest that lurking beneath these ideological and political conflicts, especially in rural Russia, were persistent social differences between the liberal and "democratic" elements of the intelligentsia, the full significance of which would be revealed in the course of the Revolution. Nicolaevsky recalls that such social differences were reflected, even after the turn of the century, in the process of recruitment into the student circles he joined during his *gymnazium* years. For what distinguished these circles was that their members were "democratic" by virtue of their social origins as well as of their political and social attitudes – excluding from their midst almost automatically the offsprings of noble families. This process of natural selection clearly indicated – and the experience of 1905 would amply confirm – the persistent social as well as psychological dimensions of the conflicts between the *raznochintsy* and the established liberal elements of the intelligentsia (largely of noble origin) originally acted out in the sixties and seventies, when provincial *raznochintsy*, most of them recruited from priestly families and ecclesiastical seminaries, had appeared as a dissonant presence on the Russian intellectual scene.

Nicolaevsky's reminiscences also strikingly illustrate how the recruitment of these *popovichi* greatly reinforced two major characteristics of the intelligentsia's collective consciousness and self-consciousness. The first was an intense preoccupation with ethical issues and moral values, and the effort to apply them systematically to individual conduct as well as to political and social programs. The *popovichi* conferred on this preoccupation a quasireligious quality. But just as important – indeed inextricably linked with this sense of moral urgency – was an intellectual need to find substitutes for the "cosmology" – the conception of the universe, and of the principles and laws governing it – that the traditions of Russian orthodoxy had provided. The accretion of the *popovichi* to the ranks of the intelligentsia thus greatly strengthened, or at least made more self-conscious and refined, a connection between these intellectual and moral preoccupations already profoundly embedded in traditional Russian culture. It reinforced, especially but not exclusively among the Populists, the idealization of the double meaning of the word *pravda* – as both truth and justice – and even more widely, the dual meaning assigned to the terms *soznanie* and *soznatel 'nost'*, consciousness and conscience. These two concepts were fused in the intelligentsia's vision of its destiny to lead, and in its sense that this mission should involve – both among the masses of the people and within its own ranks – a task of "enlightenment" *(prosveshchenie)* whose intellectual and moral dimensions were inextricably linked. Indeed, for the generation of "Realists" among whom these *popovichi* emerged as such a major force, it became a categorical imperative that their ethical views and the programs into which they were translated be rooted in a "realistic" understanding of "scientific" laws. Their ideals, their visions of the future – however seemingly at odds with current political and social realities – were to be grounded in the even more basic, transcendent "realities" defined by the laws of nature and of history.

The intellectual and moral imperatives articulated by the "Realists" of the 1860s, and the body of writings in which they were spelled out, had become by the 1890s an integral part of the heritage of both the Populist and Marxist camps of the intelligentsia. From the outset, however, the Populists and neo-Populists introduced into this common heritage a subjectivist cast: they assigned a considerable degree of autonomy in the delineation of political ideals and programs to human conscience and consciousness, and by the same token discerned a considerable degree of "indeterminacy" in the dynamics of historical development. Conversely, the Russian Marxists infused this common intellectual heritage, especially during the 1890s, with an opposite emphasis on the determining role of "objective" factors, insisting that the strategy and tactics of the Russian revolutionary movement strictly conform to the "objective" laws of historical development.

It is remarkable the degree to which the Russian Marxists, and especially those who were recruited into their ranks from relatively humble "democratic" provincial milieus, were influenced during their early years by the writings of the Realists of the sixties, and continued thereafter to share some of their more basic intellectual and especially moral attitudes, even while translating them into quite different political and social programs. Nicolaevsky emphasizes in his reminiscences the profound impression that the writings of the Realists, and especially those of Pisarev, made upon him during his years in the *gymnazium*, when he ransacked the holdings of the local public library to read as many of them as he could find. Even more striking are the echoes of the sixties in his descriptions of the intellectual and moral impulses that drew him to the revolutionary movement, and eventually to Social Democracy.

"Justice was what mattered to us, above everything else." Nicolaevsky summarizes in this phrase the basic preoccupation of the members of the "democratic" circles that he joined during his *gymnazium* years. But from his earliest years he combined this preoccupation with an immense intellectual curiosity and a need to elaborate for himself a new "scientific" cosmogony. Even in childhood he had been profoundly interested in the natural and physical sciences – astronomy, geology, botany. These interests antedated even his interest in history. And like the Realists of the sixties, Nicolaevsky was driven by the conviction that moral and political ideals must be rooted in "objective" realities. Hence "the primitive realism" of the generation of 1860s greatly appealed to him, and the writings of Pisarev, even those on literature and art, impressed him by the "soundness" of their "rationalist approach."

It was precisely this fusion of intellectual and moral imperatives, so characteristic of the world view of the Realists of the 1860s, that eventually attracted Nicolaevsky to Marxism. Marxism – specifically the labor theory of value – signified for him the infusion of "humanism into the social sciences." He identified almost immediately this conception of socialism with Western models, and especially with the example of German Social Democracy. It was "intellectually serious," and had proven remarkably successful in developing into a mass movement to reconstruct human society. Indeed, the various educational activities that German Social Democracy conducted for this purpose were the epitome of the essential role of "cultivation and enlightenment" that the Russian revolutionary movement should perform.

In large measure, it was this very emphasis on the educational role to be played by Russian Social Democracy in the building of a mass movement on a European, and specifically German, model which also eventually drew Nicolaevsky to Menshevism. But the original definition of that role, with its underlying intellectual and moral imperatives, can justifiably be traced to the contribution made by the Realists of the 1860s, and specifically by the *popovichi* in their midst.

* * *

Just as sharply, the reminiscences of Lydia Dan remind us of the critical contribution to the intelligentsia's "mentalité" and sense of identity made by elements from the various non-Russian, non-Orthodox, national and religious minorities of the Empire. The magnetic attraction that the Russian intelligentsia exercised by the late nineteenth century for the intellectual elites of these minority groups greatly reinforced the substance of its claim to transcend the conflicting particular interests and values of other social groups, and thereby to assume the mantle of political leadership and service that had been borne by the nobility of the Empire, in part also precisely by virtue of its multinational and multireligious origins. Indeed, even by comparison with the intelligentsias of other societies of Eastern and Central Europe, the Russian intelligentsia displayed a remarkable willingness and ability to assimilate recruits from various national minorities, and especially members of their more highly educated and socially mobile strata. By the turn of the century, these recruits had in turn contributed greatly to the shaping of the psychological orientations of other members of the intelligentsia.

Lydia Dan's recollections provide us, in this respect, with dramatic illustrations of the contributions made to the ideas and attitudes that crystallized by the end of the century in Russian Social Democracy by recruits drawn from the more assimilated elements of the Jewish cultural elite. First and foremost, I have in mind the emphasis on reason as the only legitimate mode of cognition, and more specifically the stress on the building of an explicit, all-embracing, and intellectually consistent world view to guide one's apprehension of all aspects of reality, as well as to provide a set of guiding criteria – a code – for all forms of political, social, and indeed moral action.

The demand for such a world view as a guide to knowledge and to action had become by the turn of the century a general characteristic of the intelligentsia, but the emphases on rationality and intellectualization were particularly important in shaping the conception of consciousness and self-consciousness that circles of the Social Democratic intelligentsia espoused, and of which they claimed to be the incarnation on Russian soil. Recruits from the Jewish cultural elite contributed even more notably to the accentuation of the demand for objectivity and realism, and to the distrust of all "subjective" or romantic impulses, which by the end of the 1890s had become such central points of reference for "orthodox" Social Democrats in their conflicts with the neo-Populists and with the emerging liberal currents of the intelligentsia. Specifically, the Jewish members of "orthodox" Social Democratic circles substantially reinforced two complementary aspects of these emphases on rationality and objectivity. The first was a profound instinctive distrust, in the formulation of political and social programs, of any positive stress upon the distinctive "autochthonous" features in Russia's political, social, and cultural development. This rejection extended not only to the heritage of autocracy and semi-serfdom, but also to the distinctive institutions, mores, and values of the Russian peasantry. The reverse side of this rejection of any positive emphases on Russian *samobytnost'* was a profound Occidentalism, indeed an idealization of Western patterns of development as models to be emulated in the shaping of Russia's immediate future.

To be sure, both emphases had already surfaced in the doctrinal tenets articulated in the late 1880s and early 1890s by the founders of Russian Marxism in their debates with the Russian Populists. They had been reflected in their insistence on the universal historical laws governing Russia's development, and therefore on the axiom that a "bourgeois" revolution (which would enable Russia to rejoin the historical path already traversed by Western nations) was necessarily to precede by a significant historical interval the eventual advent of socialism.

These deterministic themes, with their resolutely "Westerner" and "anti-Slavophile" emphases, were sounded even more triumphantly during the 1890s by the young men and women who joined the ranks of Social Democracy on Russian soil. And just as these themes proved so important in the shaping of Russian Marxism in its conflicts with Russian Populism during the 1880s and 1890s, so they came to play a crucial role after 1905 in the demarcation of the Menshevik movement from Bolshevism. In this process, too, members of the Jewish intellectual elite exercised a major influence. The publicists among them – including Lydia Dan's brother, Iu. O. Martov, her husband Fedor Dan, and many others – were instrumental in hammering out the conception of "bourgeois revolution" to which the Mensheviks returned after 1905 (even if they did ultimately split after the outbreak of the war and especially in 1917 over its precise interpretation). These publicists and the many Jewish *praktiki* in the Menshevik movement played an even more central role in the efforts to erect the scaffolding of a mass Europeanized labor movement on Russian soil, exploiting for this purpose all possibilities for work "in the open."

The tactical and organizational style that increasingly distinguished these efforts reflected in part a deterministic faith that historical processes once launched assumed their own dynamics, and the belief that such dynamics were ultimately more important in the development of mass movements than the plans, the strategies, the tactics, and the organizational designs of any underground revolutionary party. But equally important was the emphasis laid on education and enlightenment *(prosveshchenie)* as the primary task to be pursued by the Menshevik party in bringing to life a truly working-class intelligentsia, at least until the downfall of the Czarist regime, promised by the laws of history, actually occurred.

IV

We can find still another complementary dimension in these reminiscences, particularly in the angles of vision they respectively bring to bear on the development of Menshevism. More sharply than one might infer from their dates of birth (Lydia Dan was born in 1878, Boris Nicolaevsky and George Denike in 1887), these three informants provide representative examples of the contributions made to the development of Menshevism, and indeed of Social-Democracy as a whole, by successive "political" generations.

The patterns that distinguished the development of Menshevism and Bolshevism can hardly be traced exclusively from the perspective of the unfolding, however tortuous, of long-term processes of change. One must also consider the impact of delimited historical conjunctures, and indeed of specific historical events. If we conceive of the development of the Menshevik movement in terms of a series of historical, if not geological, layers, each contributed by successive political generations, Lydia Dan stands out as an example of the contribution made by those members of the Social Democratic intelligentsia of the 1890s who opted for Menshevism rather than for Bolshevism, when the split between the two factions at the Second Party Congress of 1903 impelled them, however reluctantly in many cases, to choose. Boris Nicolaevsky provides an example of the role played, particularly during the prewar period, by those who joined the movement during and immediately after the Revolution of 1905; while George Denike illustrates even more clearly the eventual contribution made in this convoluted process of self-definition by members of the Social Democratic intelligentsia who, after years of wandering, finally opted for Menshevism only when confronted by the Revolution of 1917 itself.

From this perspective the dominant theme that emerges in Lydia Dan's reminiscences of her youth – and which consistently recurs in her comments about herself, her siblings, and other members of her circle (frequently in parody, but more often than she realized in notes that she unconsciously struck) – is the veritable cult of rationality that distinguished the younger generation of the Social Democratic intelligentsia in the first half of the 1890s. Lydia Dan pithily sums up the major source of their attraction to Marxism with the phrase that it signified for them "the path of reason." In seeking to account for the attraction of this "path" for the younger generation of the 1890s, and especially for the conceptions of "consciousness" and "self-consciousness" that its members articulated and acted out, it is important to remember that these conceptions were honed in the intellectual and psychological climate created by the famine of 1891, in opposition to the ideas and attitudes that had distinguished the two major currents of intelligentsia opinion during the previous decade: Legal Populism and "small deed" liberalism.

Stories circulated during the famine and the cholera epidemic that followed of peasants' attacks on the doctors and *feldshery* who sought to inoculate them; the peasants allegedly thought they were being poisoned. These tales epitomized for the younger generation of the Marxist intelligentsia not only the collapse of Populist ideology and its idealized image of the Russian peasantry, but also the bankruptcy of the modes of conduct by which, during most of the 1880s, the adepts of both Legal Populism and small-deed liberalism had sought to express their "People-loving" sentiments. In this context, Lydia Dan recalls, it became "almost improper" for a student not to become a Marxist, and by the same token the atmosphere created by the famine generated among the new young adepts of the Marxist faith what can only be termed a mood of intellectual "triumphalism."

In this mood the recruits to Marxism among Lydia Osipovna's generation flocked to the debates organized by the Free Economic Society and cheered on Struve, Tugan Baranovsky, and other luminaries of Legal Marxism as they "routed" their Legal Populist opponents with their demonstrations of the inevitability of capitalist development in Russia and the fraudulence of all notions of a distinctive "autochthonous" Russian path. In the same spirit, they infused their demands for "objectivity" with a contempt for all "romantic flights" and sentimental gestures, whether terroristic acts or equally futile and meaningless involvements in "charitable" organizations such as the committees to combat the famine. In this spirit, as well, they identified their conception of objectivity and their demand for a "firm and well grounded world view" with an almost mechanistically deterministic representation of the inevitable unfolding of the universal laws of history through which Russia' development would necessarily rejoin the path already travelled by Western nations.

It is easy to read into Lydia Dan's observations about herself and her siblings during this period solely a reflection of attitudes shaped in the milieus of St. Petersburg's assimilated Jewish high culture in which they had been raised: their "superior attitude" toward, but also ignorance of, the peasantry and of the countryside ("The peasantry was and remained little known to Martov"); their profoundly urban outlook and values which had contributed to the shaping of these attitudes ("We were city people through and through"); their "bookishness" ("We knew little about life: we had a ready-made outlook drawn from books"); and above all, their intellectual elitism. From the perspective of old age, Lydia Osipovna consciously parodied this elitism, as she "graded" the individuals and groups she had encountered during these years ("Social Democracy was first rate; the student movement was second rate"), but she also often acted it out quite unconsciously, and sometimes quite unjustly ("Potresov was not brilliant, but well educated [!]").

Yet, while these attitudes undoubtedly stemmed in part from predispositions drawn from Lydia Dan's family milieu, they also found fertile soil in a more general and pervasive mood characteristic during this period of the Social Democratic intelligentsia as a whole. This mood was perhaps most clearly expressed in the sense of discovery, awe, indeed veritable worship evoked by the contemporary writings of G. V. Plekhanov – in particular, his *Monistic View of History*, which was published legally and therefore widely circulated and read. In these writings the young who rallied to Social Democracy found grounds for their uncompromising identification with the West, and for their equally uncompromising rejection of all forms of Russian *samobytnost'*. (The debates between Marxists and Populists represented, according to Plekhanov, the last and ultimate chapter of the century-old struggle between Westerners and Slavophiles in Russian thought.) But Plekhanov's readers also found in this work an even more lyrical apotheosis of the role of the city, as against the countryside, in Russia's development. The city was the vehicle for all forms of progress and enlightenment; the countryside, still fertile soil for *Aziatchina* – for all manifestations of arbitrariness and slavish submission, savagery and superstition in contemporary Russian life. Indeed, those who had occasion to read Plekhanov's essay "Russian Workers in the Revolutionary Movement," also published during this period, could draw from it an almost mystical sense of the variety of ways in which the city swiftly, almost magically, transformed the barbarous peasants who settled there to work in industry into civilized and ultimately revolutionary class-conscious proletarians. Above all, from *The Monistic View of History* Plekhanov's young readers were able to derive not only a sense of the inevitability of the journey through which Russia would rejoin the path of Western nations and ultimately move on to socialism, but also the conviction that they themselves, by virtue of their own superior consciousness, had been "elected" to act as agents of these inevitable historical laws.

The ideological changes involved in the transition from what Lydia Dan described as this "ready-made outlook" to that which distinguished the Iskra period were by no means so great as they were often perceived in retrospect by some spokesmen of the Menshevik movement. Indeed, much of the authenticity and value of Lydia Dan's account lies precisely in her unvarnished recognition of this fact. It was, after all, not Lenin but the diffident and gentle Pavel Borisovich Axelrod who had contributed most to shaping the conception of "proletarian hegemony" and justifying the leadership role that Social Democracy should assume in the birth of a new age, in view of the failure of the Russian liberal movement to fulfill its proper responsibility in the "bourgeois" revolution prescribed by history. The patronizing attitude that Iskra and its agents assumed, after the turn of the century, toward all of its actual and potential political rivals (and yet allies of necessity) – liberals, Legal Marxists, and neo-Populists alike – continued to be rooted, as Lydia Dan expressed it, in the firm conviction that "history was with us." By the same token, all that Lenin had done – or so it appeared right up to the Bolshevik–Menshevik split – was to translate this vision into an organizational blueprint. ("Everything in Lenin's *What Is To Be Done* seemed perfectly reasonable.")

But there was also, for Lydia Osipovna, a profound psychological continuity between her experience of the circles of the nineties and her life in Munich with the members of the Iskra editorial board, and eventually as one of Iskra's underground agents. For the professional revolutionary that she became (as for many others of Iskra's agents, workers and *intelligenty* alike), Iskra and its underground organization came to represent a new extended family. This family assigned to its members clearly defined identities as well as roles grounded in "definite," "firmly held," world views – another "sign" of their being "chosen," and thus of their superiority over others ("Kleinbort was shallow: he did not have a firmly grounded point of view"). Thus, compensating for the deprivations to which Lydia Dan and others like her were exposed in their underground existence was not only the conviction that they were "history's agents," but also the sense of being members of a large family, one which they had joined, and indeed had helped create, in an act of free and conscious will.

It is hardly surprising, therefore, that when, more than sixty years later, Lydia Osipovna reminisced about this period in her New York tenement apartment bordering on Harlem, it appeared to her as a golden and heroic era, its major actors – Plekhanov, her brother Martov, even Lenin – figuring in it surrounded by halos. Never again would she be so active and also feel as confident and comfortable about the role, the very identity, that she assumed. ("We were a political party, but in addition a group of people exceptionally closely linked, not only by a program, but also by an entire world view.")

Even in the wake of the Bolshevik–Menshevik split in 1903, Lydia Osipovna and almost all of the members of her circle who had been involved in Iskra still felt that the period of Iskra's founding had been "one of the most important and fruitful in the history of Social Democracy." There is little reason to gainsay those words. Indeed, the same sense of fruitfulness – and of importance and self-importance – pervades Potresov's account of this period in the retrospective essay that he contributed in 1909 to the Menshevik compendium on the Revolution of 1905 *(Obshchestvennoe dvizhenie v Rossii v nachale XXgo veka),* as well as the political and historical testament *(Proiskhozhdenie bol'shevizma)* that Lydia's own husband, Fedor Dan, recorded shortly before his death.

Another reason why those who had been involved in Iskra would remember this period as "golden" also emerges from Lydia Dan's account. Almost immediately thereafter, life became much more complicated and difficult to fathom. First came the Bolshevik–Menshevik split, which broke asunder their sense of unity as "one big family." There followed the even sharper jolt that the events of 1905 – at least from October onward – inflicted upon their sense of being the agents, indeed the "sources" of history. ("For the first time, we were confronted by large scale phenomena, in the face of which we felt proportionately a very small party. Before October 1905, we had felt ourselves to be the source of history; everything else was simply 'material.' Now this 'material' had grown up, become an independent quantity.")

Indeed, during the high point of the Revolution – in late 1905 – "elemental forces" appeared to sweep away the rationalism and rationality in which Lydia Dan and her circle had taken such pride and comfort. Their sense of rationality was overcome partly from the outside – as the workers' movement they sought to lead now appeared uncontrollable – but also from the inside. Some of the leading Mensheviks on the Petersburg scene, including Fedor Dan, now succumbed (or so they would feel in retrospect) to a revolutionary intoxication which caused them momentarily to forget the "objective," "rational," boundary line between a "bourgeois" and a "socialist" revolution, and to pursue political goals well beyond the limits dictated by the historical laws which, in earlier years, they had sought to observe and called on others to heed.

It was this experience, as much as the sense of political defeat that the Mensheviks would endure in the wake of 1905, and especially after the Stolypin coup d'etat of 1907, which induced the members of this first political generation to feel that they were now travelling in uncharted and turbulent waters and which caused them to define for themselves new strategies and tactics, and indeed a new, or at least a refurbished, political identity.

*   *   *

In fact, this process of redefinition had begun almost at the outset of the Revolution of 1905, well before the great expectations that it raised had been frustrated. For already during this period the Mensheviks' tactical and organizational prescriptions of creating a new institutional framework de facto *(v iavnom poriadke)* – exploiting for this purpose all legal opportunities, however slender, that opened before them – while as yet consciously directed and justified in terms of immediate revolutionary perspectives, came to focus increasingly on the organization of a mass labor movement. In this sense, the events of 1905 – from the elections to the Shidlovsky Commission through the experience of the October general strike and the inception of the Petersburg Soviet which it precipitated – already provided the Mensheviks with an accumulated capital of political experience on which they were able to draw after the revolutionary tide began to recede.

Ironically, the leaders of the Menshevik movement who had come out of Iskra's ranks were helped in drawing the lessons of this experience by individuals and groups in Social Democracy whom in the heyday of the Iskra period they had identified as their ideological and political opponents in their struggle for "proletarian hegemony" in the bourgeois revolution.

A major role was played in this regard by another current contributed to the development of Russian Social Democracy by Russian Jewry – this one drawn mainly from the less assimilated elements of the "Pale," the urban concentrations of Jewish workers, *polu-intelligenty*, and *intelligenty* of White Russia, Russian Poland, Lithuania, and the Western Ukraine. During the 1890s these elements had coalesced around the Bund and turned it into one of the few genuine working-class organizations in Russian Social Democracy. The Jewish members of the Iskra directorate, Martov included, had been among the fiercest opponents of the Bund's claims for autonomy as a representative organization of Jewish workers within the RSDRP. They had voted against these claims at the Second Party Congress before they had themselves emerged, as this congress unfolded, as members of an outvoted minority. But the experience of 1905 greatly attenuated these divisions, and from the Stockholm party congress of 1906 onward the Bund in fact became one of the most reliable allies in the coalition that the Mensheviks sought to forge against Bolshevism.

Recruits for the Mensheviks' cause also came from the so-called "Economists," whom the Iskra directorate has singled out as their chief ideological opponents in their struggle for "hegemony" in the RSDRP. What the erstwhile "Economists," most notably Martynov, accentuated in Menshevik praxis was the conception of "tactics process" (as opposed to "tactics plan") that they had originally articulated in their struggle against Iskra. This was the view that the tactics, indeed the organizational practices, of Social Democracy should emerge in the very "process" of the experience of the workers' movement rather than be imposed a priori by any organizational center, let alone one directed exclusively by a would-be "conscious" elite of the intelligentsia.

In the reshuffling of allegiances that this political regrouping involved, history – in part, at least – was coming full circle, since the conception of "tactics process" had in fact constituted a more faithful translation than Iskra's political program of the theory of stages (from "economic" to "political" struggle) which in the mid-1890s had provided the doctrinal grounds for the shift of the activities of Social Democratic circles in Russia from "propaganda" to "agitation." The pamphlet in which this theory had originally been spelled out *(Ob agitatsii)* had also contained a prefiguration of the political maximalism that Martynov and Dan displayed in 1905 in "transcending" the boundaries of a "bourgeois" revolution. In the aftermath of the defeat of 1905, however, the Mensheviks' application of the notion of "tactics process" necessarily took the quite different form of using the new possibilities for work "in the open" to build a mass labor party and labor movement.

In these efforts to define and establish a new political presence "in the open" for Russian Social Democracy – and especially to exploit the opportunities afforded for this purpose by the establishment of Russia's new national legislature – the political representatives of yet another national minority, the Georgian Social Democrats, played a major role. By 1905 the Social Democrats had established a dominant political presence in Georgia; from 1905 onward, as well, the Georgian Mensheviks had reduced the influence of Bolshevism in Georgia to that of a rather insignificant political minority. In the process they carved out for themselves a distinct political identity which henceforth coexisted, at times uncomfortably, with other currents of the Menshevik movement.

Because of their highly pragmatic political orientation, as well as their dominant presence on the Georgian political scene (obviously the two phenomena were not unrelated), the Georgian Social Democrats did not hesitate to exploit the political processes opened by the creation of Russia's new legislative institutions. They participated from the outset in the elections to the First State Duma and eventually sent their representatives to it, even before the Mensheviks in the rest of the Empire had repudiated decisively the idea of boycotting participation in Russia's new representative assembly. This early participation, and their majority support among their own constituents, enabled the Georgian Social Democrats to become the dominant group in the Social Democratic parliamentary group which eventually coalesced in the First Duma. But even after the Menshevik, and eventually the Bolshevik, organizations in the rest of the Empire had overcome their initial resistance to participation in the Duma, the Georgian deputies continued to play an exceptionally prominent role in it. They substantially contributed to shaping the tactics of the Duma faction of the RSDRP, and indeed of the radical opposition as a whole – making effective use of the protected political arena that the Duma afforded not only to represent the interests of their own constituents, but also to assert, even under existing political conditions, the presence of Social Democracy, as a quasi-parliamentary party.

After 1905 the Georgian Social Democrats were joined in this effort to use all existing legal possibilities by a new political generation of Social Democratic activists from other parts of the Empire, many of whom shifted their allegiance from Bolshevism to Menshevism precisely because of an imperative need – following the collapse of their great revolutionary expectations – to find new, more effective ways to build a mass labor party and labor movement. Indeed, some of these young erstwhile Bolshevik militants now became so absorbed in the effort to build an "open" labor movement as to veer toward "liquidationism" in the vehemence of their repudiation of all "underground" work.

This was not the case, however, with Boris Nicolaevsky, who still considered the preservation of Social Democracy as a revolutionary political entity to be a prerequisite for the development and eventual hegemony of a genuine workers' party on Russian soil. In this as in other respects, Nicolaevsky was and remained a highly distinctive figure in this "second" political generation of the Menshevik movement.

In practical politics he managed to display a nonfactional spirit, indeed an affective as well as intellectual openness, uncharacteristic of most Mensheviks at the time. He remained until the eve of the war a *primirenets*, seeking to restore peace among the various warring factions of the party. And even after these efforts at reconciliation had failed, and the divisions between Mensheviks and Bolsheviks became irreconcilable, he continued to maintain bonds of personal friendship and esteem with a number of major figures in the Bolshevik party: with Enukidze, whom he first met during his stay in Baku in 1911; with Riazanov, who continued to publish his writings even after his deportation from Soviet Russia in the early 1920s; with Rykov, with whom he shared an apartment after the October Revolution; and with Bukharin, whose political testament (delivered during Bukharin's brief stay in Paris in early 1936) he paraphrased in his *Letter of an Old Bolshevik*. These ties were not severed until most of these figures were liquidated during the Stalin purges of the late 1930s. (We should note as well that one of Nicolaevsky's younger brothers was himself a Bolshevik, who eventually became a Red Army officer, and died in the Civil War.)

But Nicolaevsky's essentially nonfactional spirit and range of personal sympathies also extended, especially during the prewar period, to others on the radical left: He considered most members of the PSR he encountered, including those engaged in terrorist activities, as "fine fellows," even though he considered their acts, at least after 1905, impractical and in fact a diversion from the central task of building a mass labor movement. Neither did Nicolaevsky share – indeed he deplored – the distrust entertained by many of his fellow Mensheviks toward the Russian peasants in whose midst he had lived during his childhood years – although he had no doubt, precisely on the basis of his dealings with them, that the peasants, while constituting a potentially valuable revolutionary force, were far too "unenlightened" to provide likely recruits for the socialist cause. ("The city rather than the country was the arena in which the struggle for progress and socialism would ultimately be won.") Indeed, Nicolaevsky's identification of the city as the arena of Russia's cultural as well as political progress was so firm during these prewar years that he was prepared to engage without hesitation in coalition politics with representatives of the liberal parties and factions of urban Russia. In this approach to practical politics, and especially in the absence of any sense of personal hostility toward the liberal groups of the Russian intelligentsia, Nicolaevsky differed not only from Lenin and his Bolshevik followers – with whom he had parted ways after 1905, over this very issue among others – but also from many of the members of the Menshevik movement with whom he became associated.

It is not surprising, therefore, that Nicolaevsky displayed a special political affinity with the Georgian Social Democrats. He felt profoundly attracted to Tsereteli from the very moment of his emergence as a major political figure (with his speech on behalf of the Social Democratic faction at the opening of the Second State Duma). He subsequently established a lifelong friendship with him, which was strained but remained unbroken even in 1917. As secretary to the Menshevik faction in the Fourth State Duma, after his return to Petersburg from administrative exile following the 1913 political amnesty, Nicolaevsky was close to deputies Chkeidze and Skobelev. And during his years in the emigration, in the 1920s and 1930s, he maintained cordial relations with other figures in Georgian Social Democracy, including Zhordania and many who served in his government during Georgia's brief existence as an independent republic. For it was among the Georgians more than among any other group in the RSDRP that Nicolaevsky found a political approach, indeed political reflexes, akin to his own, in the efforts to translate into practical terms his vision of building a mass labor party capable of eventually achieving power in a democratic Russia.

Yet – and this is what made him so singular a figure, even in his own political generation of the Menshevik movement – Nicolaevsky consistently combined this essentially pragmatic approach to politics with a strict attachment to Marxist orthodoxy, reminiscent in its quasi-religious quality of the *popovichi* of the 1860s. At no point in his political career did he display the least degree of sympathy for any of the revisionist or "liquidationist" currents in Russian Social Democracy or in the international socialist movement as a whole. From the days of his youth, Marxism represented for him a revealed truth, and Marx's writings the sacred texts embodying this truth. (The labor theory of value, as we have noted, constituted for him the veritable incarnation of "humanism in the social sciences.") Notwithstanding his less than adequate knowledge of German (or for that matter any foreign language), Nicolaevsky became a formidable master of these sacred texts (he was one of the few scholars able to decipher Marx's script). And his political biography of Marx, written during his years in the emigration, combined genuine scholarship with a veritable paean to Marx's contribution to the march of human progress.

For Nicolaevsky (even more than for most other Russian Social Democrats), German Social Democracy represented up to the outbreak of World War I the exemplar of the kind of party that he hoped would eventually emerge on Russian soil: a truly mass party, which appeared to have managed – through its trade unions, its cooperatives, and last but not least its various cultural organizations – to enlighten, educate, and politically mobilize the working-class base on which it rested. He also saw it as a party which succeeded in carrying its weight in parliamentary politics and yet also managed to resist the sirens of "reformism" and "opportunism," thus steering an effective and yet truly orthodox socialist course in its dealings with "bourgeois" parties and "bourgeois society."

It was precisely for these reasons that the response to the outbreak of World War I by the majority of the German Social Democratic deputies in the Reichstag, most of the cadres of German Social Democracy, and indeed by the vast majority of the German working class, inflicted so profound a psychological shock on Nicolaevsky. Their initial support for the war appeared to him a repudiation not only of the international solidarity of the working class, but also of the "humanist" values that he profoundly identified with Marxism. Nicolaevsky never deviated from this profound, indeed instinctive, response to the war. And it was his conviction that the war must at all costs be stopped on all fronts which caused him in 1917 to tie his fate to Martov and the Menshevik Internationalists in their desperate efforts to end the butchery and destruction; and to part ways temporarily with the Revolutionary Defensists, including Tsereteli, with whom he otherwise shared so many personal as well as political affinities.

*   *   *

If among our three informants Boris Nicolaevsky provides an example – even if a highly idiosyncratic one – of the second political generation of the Menshevik movement, George Denike affords a more representative illustration of the third, which on the basis of quite different psychological impulses if not political values, rallied to Menshevism only in 1917. Most of the members of the Social Democratic intelligentsia – including ex-Bolsheviks as well as nonfactional Social Democrats – who joined the Menshevik party at this crucial point in its history did so largely because it provided them with a political mantle which enabled them to assume unambiguously the role of political actors in the defense of the country and the Revolution.

To be sure, some members of the Menshevik and indeed of the Bolshevik factions had already assumed Defensist stands even before the outbreak of the Revolution – feeling instinctively, as if by a reflex, and then seeking to translate these feelings into plausible doctrinal terms, that they could not remain indifferent to the prospect of a military defeat at the hands of the Central Powers which would condemn Russia (as they saw it) to semicolonial status, perhaps to territorial dismemberment. In seeking to avoid this outcome of what they perceived to be an imperialist contest between the Czarist regime and the Central Powers, some of them had even sought to draw a distinction between Russia's bourgeois democratic allies, in particular France and Great Britain, and the authoritarian, militaristic imperial regimes of the Hapsburgs and the Hohenzollerns. But notwithstanding their intellectual ingenuity, such rationalizations were bound to retain a tortured quality as long as the defense of Russia's national interest appeared linked to the survival of the Romanov dynasty and the Czarist regime.

By the same token, the coming of the Revolution brought psychological liberation for those in the Social Democratic intelligentsia, and indeed in the "democratic" intelligentsia as a whole, who following 1905 had come to identify themselves – usually more than they knew – with a vision of Russia's national interest, as a result of their reabsorption into the processes of national life. The political mantle of Menshevism provided, especially for those elements of the radical intelligentsia who had identified themselves with the West, the opportunity to espouse openly this sense of Russia's national interest without explicitly repudiating their radical past. Thus in the process of reshuffling which the Revolution precipitated between the Bolshevik and the Menshevik factions of Social Democracy, those who now rallied to Menshevism did so in the name of Revolutionary Defensism. Those who eventually joined the Bolsheviks did so in the name of proletarian internationalism – to bring about the world revolution which would not only end the war but also raise the proletariat to power, in Russia and throughout the capitalist world.

In Petrograd, this last process of redefinition and realignment in the respective developments of Bolshevism and Menshevism assumed right up to October an extraordinarily convoluted and tormented character. The definition of appropriate lines to follow imposed on Menshevik leaders the painful task of seeking to reconcile hallowed principles, as well as ingrained perceptions of the past, with confusing and contradictory apprehensions of pressing current realities. Such confusion, by and large, marked the evolution of the line toward the issue of war and peace for which the leaders of the Revolutionary Defensists groped throughout the Revolution, and the increasingly disastrous efforts to translate into policy the ambiguities and contradictions which this line sought to reconcile, especially after the exhilarating effects of Tsereteli's rhetoric had been dissipated by the disastrous outcome of the June offensive. Even more notably, such confusion was characteristic of the attitudes that these leaders displayed toward the crucial issue of "power" – in the process of their conversion from the advocacy of "dual power" to a willingness to participate in a coalition government which would seek to unite all the "vital forces of the nation."

For most of the Mensheviks who found themselves during these critical months in the provinces or at the front – especially for those who like George Denike were recent recruits to the Menshevik movement (i.e., members of its third political generation) – the situation appeared far starker and much simpler. From the outset it appeared to them self-evident – now that the Czarist regime had been swept away, and the door opened for the establishment of a democratic state and society – that the country and the Revolution had to be defended. And it seemed to them equally evident – all the conditions surrounding them made this glaringly apparent – that the only political leadership potentially available for this purpose, let alone for the establishment under the immensely difficult conditions created by the war of a truly democratic order and institutions, was that provided by their own ranks, and by the "democratic" intelligentsia as a whole.

George Denike's reminiscences provide in this regard an extraordinarily valuable "corrective" to accounts left by Menshevik leaders whose contemporary experience was limited almost entirely to the obsessive and often "delusional" atmosphere of the capital. For Denike has given us a faithful record of the behavior and mood that members of the provincial organizations of the Menshevik Party – suddenly loaded with the responsibilities of trying to run the country, or at least most of urban Russia – actually displayed during these months. He draws a striking picture of the overwhelming practical responsibilities that were now thrust upon the ranks of this provincial democratic intelligentsia. He also conveys the sense they had from the very outset of the thinness of their own ranks in trying to control the chaos that threatened to overwhelm them – given the collapse of most existing administrative structures and the pressures of the unleashed grievances and aspirations of the *nizi*, the lower strata of the population which they, like the Bolsheviks, sought to mobilize in their support, but also had to govern.

From such a perspective, the whole issue of dual power versus coalition did not really arise. From the outset, Denike had assumed in his native provincial capital of Kazan (and thus combined in his own person) a multitude of functions: that of vice-chairman of the Committee of Public Safety, which in theory at least sought to represent the "vital forces" of "census society"; of vice-chairman of the local Soviet of Workers' and eventually Soldiers' Deputies, which equally theoretically sought to represent on a nonfactional basis the lower "democratic" strata of the local population (in particular, its workers and the soldiers of its military garrison); and the editorship of a newspaper which itself sought to combine the functions of providing an organ for this local "nonfactional" Soviet and for the local Menshevik party organization.

In this respect – and he was perfectly conscious of this – the responsibilities that Denike sought to combine were but the microcosm of a much broader phenomenon: that under existing local conditions there was not and could not be any dual power, or for that matter any coalition regime – the only political leadership with any hope of mobilizing mass support, or at least of maintaining a semblance of order, let alone of building democratic institutions, being the local democratic intelligentsia, Social Democrats and non–Social Democrats alike.

For the more partisan leaders of the Menshevik party in Petrograd, the perception of these truths involved a tortured and never completed process of discovery. For Denike and most members of this third political generation of the Menshevik movement – especially those in the provinces at the front – the recognition was instinctive and instantaneous, and so too was their collective self-definition as "democrats" animated by a sense of the "state interest" – would-be leaders, since no others were available, of a new democratic nation-state, born under the terrible strains generated by the war.

Denike and his fellow members of this third political generation ultimately failed in their efforts to carry the burdens that were now thrust upon them. But for these few months they acted out – at first with enormous energy, vitality, and indeed self-confidence and zest, and later with growing pessimism and a sense of impending doom – this last, ironic, and ultimately tragic chapter in the long and complicated evolution of the Menshevik movement, and of the democratic intelligentsia of which it was a part.

V

I hope that the three life histories traced in this volume will provide the reader with a better understanding of the psychological dynamics that distinguished the evolution of the Russian intelligentsia in this, the most crucial chapter in its history. In a broader historical perspective, they may also illuminate the formative processes involved in the shaping of the mentalities of its members, and especially of the representations they drew in the process of defining and redefining their political identities. Most significantly, I believe, these informants' unusually candid accounts of their early years should provide significant correctives to certain received ideas about the Russian intelligentsia, and the factors that made it what it originally was, and eventually became.

First and foremost, the evidence that these three life histories provide of the evolution of these informants' attitudes toward the world about them – toward the *nizi*, the lower strata, but also toward the *verkhi*, the milieus of more privileged "census society" – challenges traditional explanations of the mentality of the Russian intelligentsia as an example of psychological "alienation." In the records that these informants have left us of their formative years, and in particular in their descriptions of the impulses and pressures that contributed to their initial radical questioning of the existing political and social order, the reader will find no indication of any profound psychological conflicts with parental authority; no traces of an even momentary intellectual vacuum or confusion, let alone of a crisis of identity.

On the contrary, each appears propelled from the very outset by all the major influences in his or her environment on a single trajectory – leading undeviatingly onto the revolutionary path that they eventually followed. Indeed, we come away impressed with the sense of inevitability as well as of enormous self-confidence and self-assurance generated by the psychological climate in which these crucial life choices were made, at least up to the process of reevaluation that the outcome of the Revolution of 1905 induced. Until then, at least, everything in their experience seems to have contributed consistently, and by and large coherently, to the political direction that they elected to follow, and to the intellectual "triumphalism" which, in different forms and to different degrees, underlay their image of themselves as members of an intellectual, moral, and political elite, chosen by history to lead Russian society on the road to progress, enlightenment, and justice.[2]

---

[2] Admittedly these formative years unfolded in the lives of all three informants during a period which marked the *apogee* of the intelligentsia as a central political and social phenomenon in Russian national life.

Actually, notwithstanding the momentary collapse of their great revolutionary expectations in 1905 and their trials and tribulations in the years that followed, this fundamental confidence in the future and in themselves does not appear to have been sapped until the Revolution of 1917 thrust the leadership of the Menshevik Party once again – this time in positions of far greater responsibility – to the center of the political stage. I have discussed some of the ways in which the experience of the Revolution shook the world views that most members of the Menshevik party had elaborated by this time. But in the broader perspective of the historical development of the intelligentsia, as well as of the individual life experiences of our three informants, one should bring out another dimension in the trauma that 1917 inflicted on them.

As we have seen, the evolution of the Russian intelligentsia in the late nineteenth and early twentieth centuries, and the successive collective representations that it involved, can be viewed, at least in part, as a process of overcoming – of transcending rather than simply reflecting – a sense of alienation from national life. Indeed, the very dissemination of the term "intelligentsia" in public discourse in the 1870s and 1880s, and especially the application of this term to designate *both* the radical and liberal groups of the politicized strata of the intellectual elite, had reflected the inception of this process of transcendence. For the emergence of this representation of the intelligentsia had rested on the perception of a society distinct from, and potentially opposed to, the existing political order, and on an incipient sense of shared values – if not of a shared identity – between even the most radicalized members of the intellectual elite and this society in the making. From this historical perspective, the outbreak of the Revolution in 1917 – the sudden collapse of the Czarist regime and of the entire institutional structure on which it rested, and the exhilarating atmosphere generated by the revolutionary experience of the February days – marked a climactic, if ultimately deceptive moment in the process of reconciliation between most members of the intelligentsia and their political and social environment, and in the process of their assertion and fulfillment of a claim to the leadership of a new nation-state.

At this moment of truth as well as of ultimate fulfillment in the evolution of the intelligentsia's collective representations, those of its members who most fully partook and displayed these orientations, including the leading circles of the Menshevik party, were not followed by the masses, whose interests they claimed and sought to represent. There, òf course, lay the tragedy. For from its very inception, the intelligentsia had rested on this claim the legitimation of its urge to lead as well as to serve, and by the same token, the sense of manifest destiny in which, also from the very outset, this urge had been reflected and historically acted out.

1
LYDIA DAN

Plate 1. Lydia Osipovna Dan, Olekminsk, 1904

Plate 2. Lydia Osipovna Dan, circa 1960
(courtesy of Boris Sapir)

First interview

D: You are interested in the relations in our family. I think I can say forthrightly that our family always consisted of two clans – children and parents. Of course, we loved our parents. We respected our father greatly and thought highly of him. We had a much lower opinion (and undeservedly so) of our mother. I think the fact that we understood that Mother was not a particularly intellectual person greatly lessened her qualities in our eyes. This was unjust, but so it was. She was very loving and really did everything for her children. We could never say she behaved badly toward us. But she had totally different ideas of how women should live. About her sons she would think, "Now things are different; let them be like the rest." But daughters, they were supposed to repeat her past, which we didn't have the faintest desire to do. She soon gave in on this point as well. Occasionally there would be misunderstandings, but usually Father would straighten them out. If she was angry with us, she would announce that she had a migraine headache. When father came home from work, he would ask, "Where's Mother?" "She's lying down in her room." "What happened?" "I don't know." Father would then say, "Go say you are sorry."

Once an acquaintance came by when I wasn't home; he had visited us and we were on very good terms with him. He said, "Lidia Osipovna was at my place yesterday and left her gloves, so I brought them back." For Mother it was a dreadful shock that I would visit a young man who rented a room. This was not done, of course. We did it, and generally nothing was said. And we assumed that Mother understood and had decided not to interfere. But evidently she was not exactly aware, and when [the young man] came and said that I had left my gloves with him she was horrified. Later, Father arrived and said, "Go say you are sorry. Apologize, then it will be over with, and we can eat." He took me by the hand and we went to Mother's room. Mother cried, "But what will his landlady think of you?" It was really funny! Even Father laughed. I am describing this to show how in general we, people of different eras, got along fairly peaceably. With Father it was generally very easy, since he was a real intellectual and, I think, a rather good teacher: he knew how to approach his children. I have never seen parents or fathers who treated their children with as much respect as my father did. We all owed him a lot. Mother spoke good, correct Russian, without any accent, and was very musical, but could not read. And, needless to say, she could not write. But she learned about Russian literature from us. We liked to read aloud together.

Another real member of the family was the nurse. She had been Vladimir Osipovich's wet-nurse and later remained with us (her own child had died).[1] She addressed us all as *ty*,[2] and we always used *vy*[3] to her. She used to call my brother Vladimir Osipovich, *synok* ["little son"], and since children are mean we laughed at this. Sergei[4] would say, "Hey you, Vladimir Pelageevich (she was named Pelageia Zakhar'evna). Vladimir took this as a dreadful insult. Sergei was very good but he pestered and tormented all of us dreadfully. "Why am I Vladimir Pelageevich?" "Because you're Nurse's child; she calls you *synok.*" "And what does Father call you?" "Father also says, 'my son.' Therefore I am Sergei Tsederbaumovich." This manner of speaking and of deriving patronymics from last names was so common among us that in Martov's[5] letter to Anan'ev he writes "Dear Evgenii Anan' evich," although he was Arkad'evich.[6] Martov had been used to this since childhood, and in general I think it was a characteristic of our family that having formed our domestic group, we would even later, as adults, like to draw comrades and outsiders into it. I think that this was of some importance.

I remember best the earliest years of my relationship with my brother Sergei. He was a year younger than I, and therefore we were close. My sister [Nadezhda] was three years older, and Iulii five. For a while, therefore, there was a division between big children and small children. But gradually, when I was eight or even seven, we became one group. It is rather strange that Iulli Osipovich, even when he was relatively grown up and had changed a lot, kept his childhood interests and was an active member of our children's group. This was true even at the beginning of the 1890s. He felt a need to tell us about everything: what had happened in school, or what he had read. I don't think he did this with any special purpose. But as a child he had few friends because he was lame, and yet he needed some company, and he created it for himself in the home. He was not close to his older brother, Moris, who was very unwell and somewhat outside of the group. Moris had severe rheumatism and heart disease, and could not go to school regularly.

H: And who was Nadezhda particularly close to?[7]

D: First of all to Iulli, and later she was a member of our group. I think it was a characteristic of our family that all the children, regardless of age, became involved in common interests extremely early. I recall that when [my younger sister] Margarita was very small, she came in and said that she wanted to know what we were talking about. It was a nuisance for us to explain, and someone said, "We are talking about the class struggle, and you won't understand." She asked, "What's the class struggle?" Sergei gave her a fairly simple reply. She said, "I understand very well. It's the same for workers as for big people and children. Some people want to do things their way, and others won't let them. What do you mean, I won't understand?" That was a natural topic of conversation.

We knew little about life. We lived in a narrow intellectual Russian-Jewish environment, and were very contemptuous of our parents' friends. When I was still very young, at the end of the 1890s, all kinds of Russian intellectuals would visit my father. Later, these ties gradually weakened. He started to work in the New York Insurance Company, an American company, where he was the "secretary general," and gradually he became involved in a circle of people who were of no interest to us. I remember one of them: a very important man with a very fat wife. Father treated them respectfully, but we called them Mr. Lump and Madam Lump.

H: What kinds of games and reading did you have in the 1880s?

D: We liked the journal *Detskoe Chtenie* [Reading for Children] a lot. Then the journal *Vokrug Sveta* [Around the World] appeared, and we subscribed to it, and received it for many years. There we read all sorts of stories of adventure and travel. Father considered it useful, because it taught us geography. In the evenings, when he would ask what we were reading, we would reply saying "Something about Sumatra." He would then pull out a map and an atlas and show us, and tell us a great deal. But his talk was out of books, not from experience. Gradually came other kinds of reading. Iulii Osipovich was five years older than I, so that when I was nine he was 14 and already an adolescent. He could not use the public library (which was closed to *gimnazium* students in those days), but he read and listened and told us everything.

I think that most typical of our childhood was the social element, that is, each of us was a group member to such an extent that independent or separate life was impossible. Perhaps this played some part later – each of us felt a need to live in some group. Of course, we fought a great deal. Sergei was a very good boy, but, like boys of his age, he was mean. For example, we would receive *Vokrug Sveta*. I would say, "Today I will read it first." "No, I will." "Why?" "Because I'm your older brother." "What do you mean, you know I'm older than you." "Aren't I older than Volodia?" "You're older than Volodia, but I'm older than you." In this way he would reduce me to tears – I cried very readily. He would take the magazine and leave me holding the bag. But if anyone else treated me badly, he was ready to fight. Once, Father said to him, "If you treat Lidia badly, why do you fight with the boys when they do something to her?" He said, "Because she's my sister." It was entirely natural for him that he should order me about, but he wouldn't let anyone else. This was true until the end of his life.

H: When Iulii was a *gimmazium* student, do you remember his first accounts of social or revolutionary movements? I know that he was very interested in the history of the French Revolution even then.

D: All of us, I think, knew the history of the French Revolution very well and had very little interest in Russian history (and Iulii Osipovich was responsible for this). Old Russia, the tsars, and all that, wasn't interesting, but revolution, now, that was interesting. I think we had rather romantic and entirely unrealistic notions. If someone among us had said that there were fairly base motives and people abused their position during the Terror in France, we would have started a fight. We all imagined it very romantically. None of us, of course, was cruel. We were average, well-brought-up children. But we talked with delight of battles on the barricades. And when someone said that there would be shooting at the barricades, casualties would occur, it seemed natural. But it never entered my mind that anyone would die from the bullets. The entire revolution was viewed as a one-sided heroic process. If anyone had said to me that heroic processes have rather savage consequences, I would have answered, "I guess so," but it was never brought up.

H: How did Martov get interested in the French Revolution?

D: I think, first, that interest in the French Revolution was endemic to the Russian intelligentsia. Second, Father talked about Herzen, the martyrs of the Russian Revolution, et cetera,[8] and this made us curious about other countries. Our notions then were entirely un-Marxist, and our understanding of revolution was entirely romantic and unrealistic. In France there was oppression. Obviously, one had to fight. In Russia there had always been oppression, before the freeing of the serfs and even earlier. It was natural to fight and hate the autocracy. In short, the approach was purely idealistic. But when we read, and we read a great deal, this empty shell was filled out with some fairly good content.

H: You use the word "realistic." Could you explain what it means to be "romantic" and "realistic"?

D: I feel that realistic conceptions are the result of knowledge. When you learn about certain phenomena, you take a certain attitude toward them. But this is preceded by a romantic attitude, that is, heroic feelings, heroes, self-sacrifice, and these things are much less frequent in life than youth believes. I think that we all became realists very gradually. Iulii Osipovich writes in his memoirs, and this is a very interesting point, that while reading about political trials in Russia he became very intrigued by the Starodvorskii trial. Many years later, when he had emigrated, the accusation was made that Starodvorskii had petitioned for mercy and Martov was asked to be the judge in his trial.[9] You can imagine that this discovery left no place for romanticism. But that is where it began.

H: The first influence, in any case, was Father's?

D: Yes, and he succeeded in having good literature influence us. He found Herzen very appealing and also gave us a fairly romantic picture of him.

H: What did he tell you?

D: That this was a man of the gentry who could have lived a carefree life, but who could not accept the realities he saw and sacrificed all his well-being, so to speak. As Father said, times were different then; conditions were much worse, but Herzen risked everything because he believed in oppositional or revolutionary activity. Father, of course, did not want us to be revolutionaries. When it happened, he took it very badly, but he never said, as other fathers did, "At least think of me." He took the attitude that if the children had chosen this path, they should be allowed to follow it.

H: Do you recall when you yourself began to listen to this talk? How old were you?

D: Seven or eight, probably in 1886. I dimly remember talk in 1887 about the unsuccessful attempt on Alexander III, for which Lenin's brother was executed. We all knew very well that Alexander II had been assassinated in 1881. Nurse said that it was bad that Alexander II, the tsar-liberator, had been killed.[10] I didn't take part in the conversation, but only listened. But Iulii Osipovich, even then, tried to show that though Alexander was a liberator, still . . . In short, he already had his own opinions on this subject. He had read something. That was in 1887, when he was 14 or perhaps 13. He already had some notions about terrorists. He never posed the moral question of whether killing in general is permissible. He himself was probably incapable of killing a fly, but he thought that there was nothing better than the idea of assassinating a tsar or minister. I now recall with surprise that even Father never raised moral considerations.

H: But did he criticize the People's Will [*Narodnaia Volia*]?[11]

D: Not very sharply.

H: What did he say?

D: That these people were fighting not for themselves but for the people. This in itself was estimable. But more important was the fact that the People's Will included many noblemen, people who could live magnificently and who gave it all up. In other words, the moral aspect was of interest from the viewpoint of sacrifice. If it was necessary to kill, well . . .

H: What did your father say to you, directly or indirectly, regarding his feelings about injustices in Russia in the 1880s?

D: Of course, there had been serfdom in Russia. He could still remember it. Second, he had a European orientation. He was not a socialist (this didn't interest him), but he thought that there should be legal equality. Then, of course, there was the question of Jewish discrimination. This was important to him, and it became much more so after the first pogroms broke out in 1881.

H: How did he explain this to you?

D: He explained the pogroms by saying that the Russian people were not conscious of their own acts. It was the government that was at fault. I never heard him speak badly of the Russian peasantry.

You can see how important learning and education were. This rational and enlightened aspect was very evident in his life; he probably retained it from the 1860s.

H: I know that he considered himself a "man of the sixties." How did he explain this and what did it mean to him?

D: First of all, it meant faith in enlightenment. He wasn't a revolutionary and had little sympathy in general for revolution, but he felt that all evils could be rectified by enlightenment, particularly as regards the Jews. The first Jewish liberals, as we would now say, felt that Jewish Orthodoxy was much at fault (and it really was a dreadful milieu); both Father and Grandfather hated it. Only enlightenment could save Judaism. They even had the naive belief that the government could come to realize that the Jews were a very valuable part of the nation, provided that they were given opportunities for education, not confined to ghettos, and not deprived of residency rights, or Russian education. This was the origin of assimilationist tendencies. In this sense, my family was entirely assimilated.

H: Where and when was your father born?

D: I am not exactly sure, Zamoste I think; he was probably born at the end of the 1840s. He attended a *cheder*.[12] He didn't talk about it in detail; maybe he didn't like to, I don't know why. My grandfather was also born in Zamoste, in the province of Lublin, and left the village for Odessa very early. I think that he left his wife and children behind, and they grew up without him. They soon became independent and spread out, going to

Odessa and elsewhere. The mother died early, probably. Father never talked about his childhood, except for the *cheder*. But that was a long time ago. He had a diploma from the Higher School of Horticulture. He never made use of it, however, and understood nothing about it.

H: Where did he attend *gimnazium?*

D: He didn't. I don't even know how he came to learn his first foreign language. Later Grandfather, his father, got him a job in the Steam Navigation and Trade Company. In that capacity, he traveled about the East a great deal. He talked a lot about Beirut. I gather that he knew French, German, and English very well at that time.

H: What did he do for this organization?

D: He was "executive secretary" or something like that. Since this was a private company, he was involved with the Russian government somehow and, living in Constantinople, had more of a personal than a business relationship to the Russian embassy. When they gave receptions, he would be there for some reason. He was not an official, and, as a Jew, could not be, but he was an important person in the company and this evidently gave him a certain status. He was on familiar terms with Count Ignat'ev, who was then the ambassador in Constantinople. He lived there until the Russo-Turkish War of 1877, when all Russians had to leave. Then he went to Odessa. He apparently tried to do something with literature or journalism, but didn't succeed. He moved to Petersburg after the pogroms (where he remained until he died), and soon started to work for the New York Insurance Company. He was helped by his knowledge of languages, and, as he himself said, his tact. He knew how to talk to anyone; minister, count, or prince. He was a true *intelligent*. He knew European literature well.

H: Did Iulii remember the time spent in Constantinople?

D: Iulii described a few things about Constantinople which Mother claimed he could not remember. Probably, he was repeating stories he had heard rather than things he remembered. But his accounts were fairly long and colorful, all sorts of small daily affairs. He described the place where they lived, the apartment, the entry into the garden. Mother said that he could not remember all this, but he insisted that he did. We believed him, not Mother. If he said it, he knew.

H: Was it a positive impression?

D: Generally, yes.

H: Romanticized, of course?

D: Very romanticized. There was always a struggle within him. On the one hand, there was a tendency to romanticize life, but he always restrained himself because he felt that, first, as a revolutionary, and then as an *intelligent* or a revolutionary or a Marxist, it wasn't suitable. He always kept a very tight rein on himself. For example, I think that his personal history is quite revealing in this respect. When he went to Vilno [in 1893], he became acquainted with a girl, Polina Osipovna Gordon, also a Social Democrat, whom we all came to know subsequently and like very much. He even told us that she was his fiancée. He showed us a picture, and Nadezhda Osipovna and I were very disillusioned to see that she was hunchbacked. We said nothing. Later, after he had been arrested [on January 6, 1895], he asked Nadezhda Osipovna to write Polina a letter telling of his arrest. This began a correspondence, and after 1905 she even moved to Petersburg and worked there. She was a very good, intelligent person. When we learned that he would be sent to Siberia, we asked if Polina would be going with him. We wanted someone to be with him; he was a helpless person. He said, "Are you out of your mind? How could I do that?" Yet she herself had suggested that she go. The effect upon him was profound, and, strange as it may seem, negative. He wrote that he was thoroughly disillusioned in her – that she, an active revolutionary, was ready to abandon everything and go with him to Siberia, that he thought it was all a mistake, et cetera. Much later, when we again talked about it with him and I could speak as one adult to another, I asked him plainly if he didn't think that he simply didn't love her very much. He said he didn't think so. But in any case, I feel that it had a profound effect on his entire life. Here was a person whose psyche worked according to two principles. On the one hand, there was a very impulsive, idealistic, and romantic side; on the other hand, there was the effort to exercise rational control over this side, and he frequently forced himself to follow the path of reason.

H: Was this his first girl?

D: Yes. Many were surprised that he would choose her out of the entire Bund. She was by no means stupid and a very good person, but she was older than he and hunchbacked. Others were not encouraged by all this. For him, it was not of the slightest importance. I think, though, that this was simply because his feelings in fact were not very animated. I believe that the constant dichotomy in his relationships with women was very important. When approaching a person, he could regard him in a detached manner, as if wondering how it would work out. It didn't always work out well. But it is remarkable that, given this attitude, he could be very understanding to all of us in these situations. He didn't demand that we emulate him, although, given the influence that he had, he certainly had the opportunity. But he didn't have any desire or need to make people like himself.

I recall that when we were still fairly small and living together in the *dacha*, Mother would ask what we would be doing after breakfast or dinner. She wanted us to be occupied in some way, so that she could go lie down. We would look at Iulii and ask him what he was going to do. He would think, and we would say, "What you do, we'll do, we'll do the same!" and this would make him absolutely enraged. "Why must you do what I do? Leave me alone!" But then he would say that he was going to read, and we would say that we would too. And that was that. He could never get free of the group. Probably, he didn't want to. Strangely, he was happier playing croquet (we would play until late into the night) than, say, finding himself some suitable company. And when his friends came, he would involve them in our croquet games and our group. He felt better in these surroundings.

H: What did he remember about his childhood?

D: He talked a lot about the pogroms. He described (as he later wrote) how the servants convinced my mother to set out icons, and how nonetheless she thought it was dishonorable and the boys agreed. I think that she didn't do so largely for fear of his criticism. An instant aversion to any insincerity was very strong in him. Later it caused him much trouble in his life, particularly in party work.

H: You recall that he says in *Notes of a Social Democrat*[13] that this was the first time that he realized that he was Jewish.

D: We were very assimilated. We didn't go to church, but we didn't go to the synagoguge either. I think that, unconsciously, we felt that religion was generally for the common people. The servants went to church, but we didn't. For example, our nurse, Volodia's wet-nurse, whom we thought a lot of, went to church. She fasted at fast time, and Mother saw to this. We probably felt, though, that this was not for us. It was necessary for others, uncultured people.

H: You never went to the synagogue when you were small?

D: No.

H: Even on high holy days?

D: No, never. When we moved to Petersburg and were older, we went to Grandfather's *seders*,[14] but we never had them at home. It was interesting to go to Grandfather's; the boys were supposed to ask the four questions but were not forced to. In this regard the attitude toward religion was very liberal.

H: Of course, after 1881, the Jewish question became very acute in the *gimnazium*, et cetera.[15] When Iulii was a boy or even later, was it a psychological problem to be Jewish?

D: Of course, Iulii knew that it would be difficult for him to enter a *gimnazium;* that he had to study hard to win a medal, or otherwise he wouldn't be admitted to a university. But he was so contemptuous of the whole process that it created no problems for him.

H: He didn't feel himself in an inferior position?

D: No. For my own part, I first met Jews when I was small, when I visited my grandfather, but it had little impact. I was first in Jewish surroundings when Iulii Osipovich was arrested in 1896. I wasn't well; my lungs were bad and the doctor advised that I leave Petersburg because of the bad spring weather. Vladimir Osipovich was also in poor health; he also was tubercular. Then the wife of our comrade Liakhovskii from Vilno suggested that we come and live in their apartment. Vladimir and I went there. I had some introductions to members of the Bund at that time.[16] And for the first time I found myself in a Jewish environment. Vladimir Osipovich also mentions this in his memoirs. For us, this was something entirely new, and for me entirely unlike the Russian intelligentsia milieu. In addition to socialist culture, we were very much absorbed by Russian culture, Russian theater, Russian art. All this did not exist for these people, and it created certain barriers. But since we assumed that they were real revolutionaries and we were not, instead of being condescending I felt that they, and not I, were real people. This was a very important experience in my life; it revealed a greal deal to me. In the first place, I saw for the first time what it meant to be a poor Jew. We had never seen this at all in Petersburg. Our entire contact with Judaism consisted in going to Sadovaia Street to buy Jewish bread, because Father liked it. Grandfather was visited by Jewish intellectuals, but you couldn't imagine from them how poor Jews lived.

The following story shows the kind of man my father was. When I was around eleven or twelve, I believe, and Sergei was ten, I was anemic, and the doctor said I should go to the Caucasus, to take certain waters. Neither Father nor Mother could go, so they sent me and Sergei by ourselves. This was unheard of in my father's circle. Of course, they could have sent a governess, but that was too expensive. They bought us second-class tickets, told the conductor to look after us, and reserved us room in a pension in Kislovodsk by mail. The only thing they told us was that we should behave as at home and go to bed at 10 o'clock. This we did punctually, although we wanted to stay up. In Kislovodsk, we became acquainted with the artist Iaroshenko, simply because the entire resort knew who we were: those strange children, polite and well-dressed, behaving themselves well and living without adults. Some ladies started a conversation with us, and we behaved very politely. Iaroshenko was the brother of Madam Savinkova, and when we met him there were two nephews, Boris and Aleksandr Savinkov, staying with him.[17] I have known the family since then. Once Iaroshenko said that a fairly long trip was being arranged, and he was inviting us. Sergei and I exchanged glances and said yes, thank you, and then later we asked ourselves if this was all right. This was an unforeseen circumstance. We sent a telegram home. Father replied that we could go. He was very pleased that we followed the rules, even by ourselves. I think that we respected Father a great deal, because we never would have bothered to ask Mother.

H: Did your father consider himself a Russian?

D: He considered himself an assimilated Russian, of course. He could speak Yiddish, and once knew Hebrew, though I don't believe that he could read it, although possibly he could. In any case, he had educated himself on Russian literature. He could recite entire pages from Pushkin by memory. This was his natural literary idiom.

H: What writers did he particularly like?

D: Of the legal Russian writers, all the classics and, of course, Turgenev. Generally he felt that Turgenev was unsurpassed. But he felt equally comfortable in French and German literature. I don't recall that he had books in English, but perhaps they simply didn't interest me because I didn't know English. He had many books; the bookshelves filled an entire wall. And they didn't just lie there; he read them and loved to read aloud. He was constantly reading Victor Hugo aloud to us; he also read Balzac. My comprehension was poor, but I still listened, because it was interesting to me. Also, I didn't want to feel that I was one of the little ones. I wanted to sleep, but I sat up and listened instead.

H: This would be after dinner?

D: Yes. Beginning at 8:00, and at 10:00 we were invariably sent to bed.

H: Where would this be?

D: In Father's study. In addition to the living room there was also a study, with a large desk and books.

H: You would all sit on the sofa?

D: Yes, and he sat in his own chair. He could read well.

H: How many times a week would this be?

D: It would depend. Sometimes three times a week, sometimes once. If acquaintances came and they played *Preference*,[18] the children would be sent directly to their rooms, since they were not supposed to interfere with the conversation.

This all was before I finished the *gimnazium*. Father valued these evenings, and we valued the contact with Father, although we might have wished for something different. Sometimes, for example, Iulii would get certain pamphlets or he would begin to talk to Father about what he had heard regarding some trial. Opinions would be expressed; sometimes Father did not agree with him. He knew that things were bad even after the liberation of the serfs, but nonetheless the freeing of the serfs was a great legal and humanitarian act, and he defended his point of view. We would be condescending. How could he think that? We knew better.

H: I recall that when Iulii was finishing the *gimnazium*, he began to read about the trials involving the People's Will.

D: He first learned about the trials at home. Father knew some lawyers. For example, Passover, an important lawyer, was on very good terms with Father. He took only civil cases, but talked about what was being said among lawyers. And there were others who came and said that so-and-so's behavior at such-and-such a trial was remarkable, and so on. Of course, this impressed us very much. It was after this that Iulii sought out comments not only from lawyers but also from other sources. I remember, for example, that long before I met Vera Ivanovna Zasulich, we had heard stories about her at home.[19] Her defender was Petr Akimovich Aleksandrov, a renowned lawyer. He was on very good terms with my father and would come to dinner once every two months or so. After dinner everyone went into Father's study, where the older people would drink large cups of coffee; they didn't give us any but we would stand around and listen. And Petr Akimovich talked a great deal about Vera Zasulich. In 1905, when we returned from exile abroad [to Petersburg] and Vera Zasulich came, Father asked to be introduced. Vera Zasulich had an enormous moral influence on contemporary society, perhaps more than all the rest. For me it was Vera Nikolaevna Figner who had this influence.[20]

H: Let us return again to those evenings in your father's study, and what was read and discussed there.

D: The younger children were only tolerated, and then provided that we kept quiet. But the older ones, Iulii and Nadezhda, could take part in the conversation if no strangers from among Father's acquaintances were there. When they were, it was necessary to be quiet and behave properly. But we would listen very attentively and, a few days later, if Father spent an evening with us, we would ask him about what had been discussed. I think that what we drew from these accounts was a rather fragmentary acquaintance with the attitudes of Russian society, which were oppositional rather than revolutionary in those days.

H: This would be at the end of the 1880s?

D: Yes. At that time there was virtually no talk of revolution. There were echoes, like 1887,[21] but I remember them poorly and had little understanding at the time. There was no longer a revolutionary mood in Russia, but there was opposition. Lev Tolstoi was much talked about but was not a great authority in our family. Although Iulii Osipovich was interested in him, I don't recall that this affected the rest of us. Perhaps I personally (and others) had trouble with his Christian attitudes, because at that time I was unaware of his anticlericism. Yet Tolstoi was very important for us, as a great artist, and the fact that he belonged to Russian literature was of course immensely important.

H: What was said about public activity, and what needed to be done in Russian society?

D: The propagation of liberal ideas; we didn't go beyond that – equal justice, equality before the law, and struggle against the class system; serfdom had been abolished but the position of the peasant was very poor. I recall that, very early, we began to talk about Gleb Uspenskii. My father thought very highly of him, and therefore so did we. Simultaneously, though (and I think that this is interesting), I read Zlatovratskii and other *narodniki* [Populists], who described the dreadful, ignorant existence of the Russian peasantry.[22] This aroused in me, in addition to sympathy, a certain attitude, not exactly contemptuous, but superior. It seemed to me that such things would be impossible in Europe. I recall the following conversation: I was speaking with my father and the others about Ivan the Terrible. For me he was simply a dreadful tyrant; indeed, it was shameful that such a man could be on the throne in so large a country. Then Father said that if we were to look at Ivan the Terrible's contemporaries in Europe, they would scarcely seem better. I was astonished, because our admiration for Europe was very great; we knew only contemporary Europe, which was much more progressive.

H: Do you recall that Iulii Osipovich said anything about this?

D: I couldn't say. But he expressed his opinion about Philip II, who was apparently no better and tolerated as much cruelty. In this sense he was more inclined toward a historical approach. But his opinion of Ivan the Terrible was very negative, it never occurred to him to examine the more progressive historical features: that Ivan built the Russian state was completely alien to him.

H: What I have in mind is this: when you were small children, before the 1890s, when you were eleven or twelve, and Iulii was between fifteen and seventeen, how did you conceive of Western European reality? What positive and, particularly, negative aspects did you see?

D: We knew extremely little about the negative aspects. The positive side was some level of freedom and some democracy, which we valued greatly, and which, as compared to Russia, was vastly superior. At that time we had no idea of the relative value of democracy.

H: And what was your father's attitude?

D: My father considered himself a European and knew little about the European masses. How could he? For example, he would frequently compare the French and Russian peasantry. In the last analysis, he would say, there is as much drinking in France as in Russia. But in France, there is nothing as disgraceful as Russian peasant drunkenness, primarily because a Russian drinks because he is hungry, because he has nothing to eat. A French peasant drinks too, but eats differently. He had a great deal of admiration, even for externals. In Europe, my father would say, no one would be seen on the street in bare feet and a torn shirt. He had never seen such things in Paris or Berlin or elsewhere. (He wasn't aware, say, of the situation on the docks at Le Havre.) City life in Europe, of course, was very appealing. Then there was the matter of the relation of the police to the people. There you couldn't be picked up on the street and put in prison. Perhaps it happened, but he never saw it or heard about it. In Petersburg, on the other hand, even a respectable person, particularly if he was Jewish and without residency rights, could get into all sorts of trouble. Policemen were to be feared somewhat. This was not true in the case of the French *agent*, or the German *Schutzmann*. In those countries there was recourse to the law. This respect for the law was very prominent in my father, as it was in any Russian liberal, and he passed it on to us.

H: Did he talk at all about constitutional government?

D: He felt that it would probably come in the end. But it was hard for him to say or imagine just how. For a while there were high hopes for the heir, as was always the case. It was said that the new tsar was walking along the Nevskii Prospekt and did the unheard-of thing of entering a shop and buying gloves, and this democratic behavior was taken as an extremely favorable sign. And soon after that, upon receiving a delegation from the zemstva, the new tsar referred to "senseless dreams" and everything immediately collapsed.[23] I don't believe my father had a definite political outlook. He had a general attraction for culture which he attempted to pass on to us. The only thing that distinguished him from the average Russian liberal was his absence of patriotic sentiment. I think that this was fairly important, because patriotism caused the Russian liberals to take a benevolent view of negative phenomena.

H: What did he know and say about *narodnichestvo* [Populism] of the 1870s?

D: He knew only that [these were] gentry youth who left their elegant surroundings and went to the people. That was in effect all we learned. Nothing was said about the social aspects, namely, the push toward socialism on the part of the people. I heard nothing about that then, and wasn't interested.

H: Was the movement – "To the People" movement – talked about in general?[24]

D: Yes, the adults talked a great deal, and we talked among ourselves. Everyone was very impressed by the brave movement to the people, this abandonment of one's surroundings. We had little understanding of the difference. We imagined gentry families in which, for some reason, the younger generation rejected and scorned everything and departed. Their outlook was rather unclear to us. Part of the reason was Bazarov, although Iulii tried to explain to us that the model for Bazarov was Pisarev.[25] Possibly I read Pisarev then, but I remember nothing. At the same time, however, I had read Goncharov's *The Precipice*.[26] Mark Volokhov in that book is an entirely different person, much more of a nihilist. Bazarov and others considered the culture of enlightenment very important, while Volokhov didn't consider it important at all – he was its living negation. Of course, this left our impressions somewhat confused. Any protest movement, however, was good and valuable to us per se, even if we poorly understood its purpose.

H: Who were the heroes of this movement?

D: The heroes, of course, were the Russian revolutionaries and the People's Will. Secret printing shops, bomb factories, General Mezentsov on his trotting-horse and Kravchinskii stabbing him with a dagger – this would intoxicate anyone.[27]

H: Do you remember how you first heard of the People's Will?

K: I think that Iulii was again our source. He understood more than we did of what was being said in Father's circle and would tell us afterwards, with some distortion. Or perhaps our understanding was distorted. In any case, we were primarily attracted by the heroic and romantic aspects, and not at all by the social ones.

H: How early did you express a desire to have a "realistic" outlook?

D: To be frank, I don't recall a time when I didn't.

H: The need to be scientific, and so forth.

D: That came later. Clearly, it was necessary above all to protest and be a revolutionary. Exactly how would become apparent later. I should say that, as an adult, I felt that the fact that I had received a ready-made outlook, so to speak, was a fairly serious drawback in my development. Later in school, I encountered girls who described the painful process by which their attitudes were formed. Many from the provinces first had to reject religion and Russian Orthodoxy, become atheists, and then become involved in social protest. I didn't have to do this. Occasionally, I thought that if it was not achieved through suffering, it could be cast off at some point. In those times it happened fairly frequently that, say, a young man would have revolutionary inclinations as a student, then graduate from the university, obtain a position, and become a philistine. We knew specific cases of this, and I was greatly troubled that it might happen to me. The essential thing was that this "outlook was achieved without suffering," and in this sense I regard my childhood and family as a very positive factor in my life. For example, nationalistic Jewish attitudes became impossible for me; even in the days of Hitler I didn't regard myself as any more Jewish than before.

H: I know that when Iulii entered the university, he intended to go into the Faculty of Sciences. Was this of particular significance to him?

D: Yes, as a young Jew entering the University of Petersburg, Iulii had limited possibilities. There was no Faculty of Medicine at Petersburg. For that, it was necessary to enter the Military Academy, where Jews were not accepted. As for the Law Faculty, there wasn't a chance, and it was assumed that all law students were reactionary.

H: What about the Faculty of History?

D: No, because we were so contemptuous of the official Russian scholarship that it seemed pointless. The natural sciences, on the other hand, were independent of the regime and formed the basis of every world view.

H: I understand, but beyond that – scientific thinking, the laws of nature, et cetera? Was he influenced by this aspect in the thought of Chernyshevskii, Pisarev, and the nihilists?[28]

D: Yes, of course, particularly Pisarev's.

H: Did he talk about it?

D: Of course. Professor Lesgaft was an influential figure then and Iulii knew of him even before he entered the university.[29] And my sister Nadezhda Osipovna was also an ardent adherent of Lesgaft, and studied with him; he taught anatomy, but beyond that he felt that natural science and an understanding of the material aspects of existence is the basis of everything. However, Iulii Osipovich didn't get to the point of studying with him.

H: What novels was Iulii particularly fond of and what protagonists did he talk about?

D: French literature – Victor Hugo. George Sand was particularly important for all of us then. I now feel that we greatly overrated George Sand, but she was a great influence. A number of utopian and realistic notions came from her. First, there was the liberation of women. It is now difficult to realize how unenviable the position of women was under Russian law. This was a constant topic in daily life. For example, the entire process of divorce was exceptionally difficult, and the power of the husband was colossal. In effect, women could not leave their husbands. The husband could refuse to give the wife her passport, or if she left, he could use the police to make her return home. There were constant reports of such happenings in the newspapers and talk about them. The solution was simple: liberation of women, free love, et cetera.

H: Do you recall which of Victor Hugo's writings you particularly liked?

D: Of course, *1893* and *Les Miserables.* Hugo was an enormous influence. We read and reread him, and tried to find some inner meaning. I think I could describe the situation in general as follows: For a fairly long time in our family we attempted to build an outlook, despite all our materialistic inclinations, not from the facts of life but from literature. And therefore, when we met face to face with reality, the reaction was primarily one of amazement. We were cut off from day-to-day Russian realities. We were city people through and through, and naturally enough, since we lived in Petersburg. When Iulii Osipovich met students from the provinces, he discovered much that was entirely new and incomprehensible. He discovered much, but learned little. In particular, Russian peasant life always remained little known to him, and, perhaps, of little interest.

H: What Russian writers did you read in particular?

D: All the *narodniki:* Mikhailovskii,[30] Reshetnikov,[31] Uspenskii. Saltykov-Shchedrin[32] was our favorite. We knew him by heart. Needless to say, there were the classics – Pushkin, Lermontov, Tolstoi, Turgenev, Griboedov. These were all *livres de chevet* – they were indispensable to us. We became familiar with the Russian merchant class through Ostrovskii's plays, which are fairly one-sided. There was more to the Russian bourgeoisie than "kingdom of darkness," but for us the bourgeoisie was only what was described by Ostrovskii.[33] Unfortunately, there was no one then who could show us the good,.progressive, traits of the bourgeoisie.

H: I know that Iulii Osipovich read a great deal about the history of the French Revolution and even the French Utopians, at that time. Were these topics discussed in the *gimnazium*, the circle, or with his friends, Avgustovskii and Golovin?[34]

D: I think that utopian socialism – Saint-Simon and others – was the first thing they found significant. Then, much later, all that was replaced by Marxism. A factor here was George Sand, who was a vehicle for utopian socialist attitudes in those days and even earlier.

H: And what was of interest to them there? A vision of an ideal society?

D: Yes. These people were not religiously inclined, but since they felt a need for a higher good and a higher justice, they saw this in utopian socialism. I imagine that young people of the same degree of development but who were Christian believers probably had basically the same attitudes and found them in the Gospels, which were entirely outside of our interests. We were even somewhat contemptuous of religion, and later this was connected with our rejection of mysticism.

H: I know that one of the first illegal books that you read was Kravchinskii's.[35] Do you remember?

D: I remember that I read it very early, and it was of colossal importance for me. Now there is a new Soviet edition of Kravchinskii's works, and a very good one. I recently reread the book, and I reread it with the same pleasure that I had then. It is very well written and gives an impressive picture (though probably somewhat embellished) of revolutionary society of the times. The heroic elements, of course, were more effective then than now. Now I have some doubt that things were really like that, then I had none.

I remember that in *Andrei Kuzhukhov* [one of Kravchinskii's novels] a member of the People's Will talks of the necessity of regicide. And the woman who loves him gives all sorts of reasons against it; the main thing for her is that he not be involved. She says that the people love the tsar, and so forth. Finally, she says, "And what will happen to me if you are involved?" And this argument is convincing. We were upset – if he had chosen the course of the hero, why should it matter what happens to her?

H: Was the problem of one's debt to the people discussed?[36]

D: Of course, it was discussed, but it seems to me now that it was an alien topic. We did not feel ourselves indebted. The revolutionary democracy of the 1870s grew out of the soil of serfdom, and it did indeed owe something to the peasants. This wasn't a factor in our past, so we regarded it rather as history. We had other obligations: there was already some unclear talk about our obligations to the workers. For example, I remember a conversation between Iulii Osipovich and Nadezhda Osipovna when she was in the last year of *gimnazium*. She said that she wanted to be a teacher, go into the countryside, or something like that, because she felt that if a person could teach two hundred people to be literate it would be a great contribution to culture. I personally was amazed when Iulii Osipovich replied that this wasn't to the point; it would make much more sense to be involved with a dozen workers than to teach literacy to two hundred. I remember this conversation very well, because I still didn't know whether I would also be a teacher, but in any case it seemed to me that there were no objections, since nothing was more praiseworthy. And now, there was something higher.

Second interview

D: Today you want to begin with social and literary topics we discussed during our childhood and youth. I think that if I were to recall all the arguments that Iulii gave and that seemed very convincing to us (and that probably influenced us more than they deserved to), it would be mostly a repetition of the ideas of Pisarev, or of the "men of the sixties." They were aleady quite outdated by then, but we didn't know that there had been anything else said after that. And we took it as the final truth. But Iulii's tastes in literature were very good, and on many topics you could see a certain split in him. On the one hand, he sensed directly and emotionally that Pushkin wrote very well, but on the other hand he recalled Pisarev's comments on Pushkin and would align himself with the "correct position."[1] This was rather typical of him; I think it was typical of his entire mental outlook. On the one hand, there was a certain split in him, and, on the other, an unusual ability to concentrate on some idea if he thought it right. On the one hand, a monolith, and, on the other hand, there was a certain duality. When Blok wrote his poem, "The Twelve," in 1917, Iulii's first response was highly negative – he was very displeased, critical, abusive, etc. But my younger sister Evgeniia Osipovna, who liked Blok, modernism, and the rest, said to him, "Take it easy, you didn't read it right." And she read it to him. Then he said, "Yes, perhaps you are right. It's good." And after that he was fond of Blok's "The Twelve."

Many people thought this was a lack of character. This is not true. He was not without character because whatever he considered important, he would stick to under all circumstances and with a great deal of tenacity. But he was able to tell what was important and what not so important. And in what was not so important, he could make great concessions. I think this was typical of him.

H: Did Iulii regard himself as a sympathizer of Pisarev when he was in the upper forms of the *gimnazium?*

D: We all knew about Pisarev; he had been written about extensively. Needless to say, he was not a socialist, but the main thing for us was that he was a radical and had entirely overturned the old world view. At that time socialism was a remote goal and had more of an ethical character. There was a striving for absolute understanding and to absolute aspirations in all of us. I feel that the negative side of this was that we did not understand the importance of historicity at that time. Only later, because of Marxism and in particular the disputes with the *narodniki*, were we able to turn Marxism into a practical doctrine that showed what needed to be done. By then Pisarev did not seem so compelling.

H: Did Iulii read Chernyshevskii at that time?

D: Yes, of course, by no means all of him, but a lot. For example, I think that his novel *What is to be Done?*, a lackluster novel, was still very influential.[2] Now it is hard to see how one could get excited about it. But then it ruled our thought. And it seemed that if you read *What is to be Done?* as it should be read, you would know how to live. And this question, "How should one live?" had great importance for the youth of that time. Not for all, but at least for the progressive youth. This was a fairly compact group. So out of a *gimnazium* class of around 30, maybe three would be "progressive." This made the three feel themselves a tight-knit group, and it taught a lot, since it created a desire to unite these individual little groups somehow under a common world-view. Of course, there was no practical activity at that time.

I often remember a funny conversation which was, however, significant for me. Later, much later, when I was taking [university] courses, I talked with a classmate who condemned the members of the People's Will for murdering people. She said that to kill was bad. I didn't know her very well, so I had to be cautious, and I said, "Of course, killing is bad, but it ultimately depends on your point of view." And she said so sadly, "That's the whole problem, how to get that point of view." Poor thing, she thought that you could have a point of view handed to you. This longing for a point of view was very widespread, at least among the students. It distinguished us rather sharply from present-day Soviet youth, as I understand them. They have no such longing for a point of view – only a utilitarian attitude – this is what you need to know about this problem or that problem, but there is no point in trying to tie it into a unified outlook.

H: Did you children have your own library?

D: We had our own books, a rather random assortment. We had a complete collection of a biographical series, which yielded a great deal. They were little books that cost 25 kopecks apiece, and they gave a picture of one person and through him of an entire era. I think that there were around one hundred of these little books, and 25 kopecks was an amount we could afford.

H: You have told me that you read a biography of Pisarev. Did this series include also a biography of Chernyshevskii?

D: I don't think Chernyshevskii was included; he was still forbidden. There was a biography of Dobroliubov,[3] of course, and we could read between the lines. There was no biography of Herzen, for example. But for Granovskii, a respectable professor, there could be a biography.[4] And from it, through a fairly complex process, we could put together an impression of the 1840s. Beyond that, all branches of knowledge were there. Chemistry, for example: there was a very good biography of Mendeleev.[5] Of course, Mendeleev was a great scientist, but this meant very little to us. We knew for sure that he was not a revolutionary. This primitive utilitarian approach was characteristic of a great many youths.

H: What else in the way of progressive literature was there in this library?

D: Well, at that time the translation of Spielhagen's novel, *One in the Field is not a Soldier,* was considered progressive. Now this might seem strange. But this novel depicts the struggle of the lonely hero against the system, and so forth, and this was very important to us. Then there was Voinich's novel, *The Gadfly,* about the Italian carbonari, and we became engrossed in it. I am, of course, not speaking about popular literature. Then of course there was French literature, Hugo, Zola, and so forth. It might have been later than we read Zola and the Rougon Maquart novels. George Sand, of course, gave us a great deal. Sometimes we would ask Father questions. Perhaps about Saint-Simon. He was in no way an adherent of Saint-Simon or a socialist, but he was an educated person, and what he said was interesting.

H: Which of these figures particularly impressed you in those years when Iulii was completing his *gimnazium* studies?

D: The Russian revolutionaries, I think. It had nothing to do with whether we understood this, or whether we ourselves intended to become terrorists – that question wasn't asked. But revolutionary activity and the ability of lone individuals to take a heroic course against tsarism were very impressive. And of course, we wanted to learn all we could.

H: Can you recall conversations with your father on social or political topics?

D: I remember little. Probably I didn't think it was very important. In the first place, the feeling that, when "fathers and sons" had their differences, the children were always right arosè very early. As regards our father, we probably felt that he was somehow an exception. But he was still a father. Something else that was of importance, I think, was that he did not want to steer us toward Judaism. He himself was assimilated and probably didn't think it useful or honorable to foster any special "Jewish self-awareness." He loved his own father very much and was therefore restrained in what he said, although even Grandfather was an enlightened man with strong assimilationist tendencies. The only thing I remember very well, and this was extremely important in the childhood of all of us, was that Father gave us Bogrov's book *Notes of a Russian Jew,* which unexpectedly provoked a very negative attitude toward Jewish orthodoxy on our part.[6] That dark gloomy kingdom repelled us in every way. When Grandfather said to Iulii that Bogrov had been baptized and that it was an outrage, Iulii said, "That's not so important; if he didn't believe in the Jewish god he won't believe in the Russian Orthodox one either. Who cares?" Then Grandfather said, impassionedly, "The issue isn't whether he believes or not, but that he went from the camp of the oppressed to the camp of the oppressors." This wording made an enormous impression on us. I think that Grandfather's words were not chosen at random. He somehow perceived that we could be approached only on universalistic and civic terms, not on nationalist ones (and he evidently wanted to have some contact with his grandchildren). He was quite a smart man. But of course of an entirely different cast and mentality.

H: I would now like to take up the *gimnazium* experiences of Nadezhda, Sergei, and yourself, and the *gimnazia* you attended.

D: Nadezhda, Sergei, Volodia, and I went to state rather than private *gimnazia*. In the first place, it was cheaper, because we were a big family. I think that a *gimnazium* cost 60 rubles a year for boys and 100 for girls. Nadezhda and I both went to the Mariinskaia *gimnazium* in Petersburg, at Five Corners. The girls there came from petty-bourgeois backgrounds. I think there were very few children of intelligentsia parents, because even then there was a desire to send children to private *gimnazia*. We girls felt alien in the *gimnazium*, and the boys, Sergei and Vladimir, felt even more so.

H: What *gimnazia* were they in?

D: Both of them in public *gimnazium* No. 7, if I remember right. All those *gimnazia* were the same. I think that the boys felt the presence of antisemitism more. I couldn't complain because I never sensed it. Perhaps it was because the girls were less political in interest. In general, the *gimnazium* had no influence on either Nadezhda Osipovna or myself. We would leave as we had come; we were both beyond its influence. Both of us had a very good teacher of Russian, Balaev, who went on to open his own *gimnazium* after the revolution of 1905, and Nadezhda Osipovna taught there. They were on friendly terms for a long time. He was a liberal in his attitudes. He had been a *narodnik* in his youth, and then perhaps had suffered for it. He was a real teacher, but was scared of everything. In those days Belinskii was unheard-of in the *gimnazium*, but Balaev once said to Nadezhda Osipovna, "I would bring you a volume of Belinskii, if you like."[7] She replied, "No, thanks, we have it at home." He was terribly astonished, because nine out of ten girls would have known nothing about Belinskii. Then there was Russian history. We learned Russian history from Ilovaiskii's book.[8] Ilovaiskii was atrocious. Naturally, it was mostly about tsars, wars, and so forth. It left us completely dissatisfied. But we developed our minds apart from all this. Studying came easy to us and we were good students – we won medals. This was important for Jews, because it helped you get into higher institutions. I don't remember any troubles in this regard.

H: Were there any friends who shared your point of view?

D: None in the *gimnazium*. For this exchange of ideas we needed another environment. We had our parents' old acquaintances and family. There was Shekhter, an old friend of the family. He had two sons – one my age, the younger one the same age as Vladimir Osipovich.[9] Both later became Social Democrats, Shekhter was even an Internationalist.[10] I remember they also read, borrowed books from us and lent us others. But all this took place outside the *gimnazium*. In school it was better not to talk about such things. In general – and I feel that this is not just my own opinion – the more progressive youth had to be somewhat on guard in the *gimnazium*, and became accustomed to precautions. But Iulii managed to find comrades.

H: How did this situation change when Iulii Osipovich became a university student? Your relationship with him, and contacts with people?

D: His relationship to us did not change at all. This was strange: he was already an adult, but he still felt himself a member of this childhood organism. And some of his friends were drawn in . . . my sister even married one of his comrades.[11] His friends, like Nikolai Dmitrievich and Vasilii Dmitrievich Sokolov, were people with whom we were very close, because when they came to visit they found a sort of family.[12] They all regarded themselves as equal members of the group and we had to deal with this fact. When I was already taking courses (or perhaps it was in the last year of *gimnazium*), Mother was against our going out alone. To keep peace in the family, we pretended to obey. But this is what we did: say, Vasilii Dmitrievich (or, even better, Nikolai Dmitrievich, who was an attorney) would come and say to Mother that he was taking her daughters to go somewhere. They trusted him. It was fine. And once we were downstairs, we would say goodbye. We girls went wherever we wanted to. This was how we involved other people in this little game; they participated willingly, and they helped the emancipation of women.

H: So, in 1891, when Iulii Osipovich graduated and became a university student, he immediately started to bring home his new university friends?

D: Quite soon, I think. He was a sociable person and, I think, Father was an influence and even asked him to do so. Father thought that it was safer if he knew whom we were associating with. And since our parents always met young people warmly, they came quite willingly. Naturally, the conversations we had in our rooms were different from those in the dining-room over tea, but still . . .

H: Did Stavskii visit?[13]

D: Of course; Stavskii was a great influence on Sergei Osipovich. He was interested in children. Sergei was just a boy then, but Stavskii would ask him what he was reading, and he gave him suggestions. Maybe that was his way of helping youngsters to learn, or maybe he was simply interested.

H: Tell me what you remember about Stavskii, his character, and so forth.

D: That is difficult. He was an entirely new type. Our normal milieu was the Russian-Jewish intelligentsia. Stavskii was of an entirely different sort. First of all, there were his manners. They were unlike ours or those which

Mother thought of as necessary. My brothers obeyed her demands. But it was impossible to teach Iulii Osipovich how to use his handkerchief. His habit was that when he needed to blow his nose, he would take his handkerchief, twirl it in the air, and only then would he use it. This would make Mother absolutely hysterical. Of course, none of us would have ventured to do this. But he did. Stavskii was very shy. Then, for example, he didn't wear a formal student jacket; he wore a Russian blouse. This was regarded as rather strange. I remember that Iulii Osipovich longed to have such a blouse, and much later one of us made him one. Mother never would have permitted it. She preferred a starched collar with studs and a tie. Iulii would frequently forget about the tie, incidentally, but in any case his appearance was "proper." Stavskii's wasn't. Someone who had a more proper appearance was Gofman.[14] It seems that his father was of German extraction. He was very tidy and frequently wore a frock coat, and our parents had a high regard for him. In the dining-room, over tea, we would carry on the usual conversation about what was in the newspapers, and so forth. Later, when we went to our rooms, we would talk about politics or whatever. Neither Mother nor Father interfered.

I feel that both Stavskii and Gofman gave us a lot. They gave us some familiarity with Russia and Russian society outside of the Petersburg Russian-Jewish intellectual society in which we moved. And I know that there was a lot new to me in their stories. We always knew that we were activists; we were clearly aware and firmly convinced of this, and now we discovered that other people arrived at these views only through long agonizing sufferings and some strange incomprehensible process. Also, we grew up in a restricted environment, and knew neither real Russian "society" nor, needless to say, the Russian peasantry. And we weren't very interested. We felt that what we read about in Uspenskii was enough. We had no direct experience of them.

H: What did Stavskii talk about?

D: About that way of life. For me it was entirely unknown. He must have arrived in Petersburg with 10 rubles in his pocket. This meant that he had to begin to give lessons immediately to have some income. Then there was translation. But none of these people knew foreign languages – still, they translated and received a pittance for it. For example, three rubles for translation and galley-proofreading. But since they worked out of a dictionary and translated poorly, they would sometimes come to us for help. This was a totally different, more plebeian, milieu. It gave us an understanding of Russian realities which had not been there before. And it was through Iulii Osipovich's university friends, and later my classmates, that we gained it.

H: Can you recall conversations with Iulii Osipovich, before he was arrested, about the famine of 1891?[15]

D: I personally knew little about the famine. What I did know was stories about all the things that Tolstoi was doing, and so forth. But I doubt that Iulii Osipovich was interested in this. He had extremely little concern for the humanitarian or philanthropic aspects. He was not involved in any practical activity. But for myself and for the youth of that generation the famine was an extremely important landmark, an extremely important moment, because it demonstrated that the Russian system was completely bankrupt. It felt as though Russia was on the brink of something. The so-called Russian "society," naturally, was more interested in the purely humanitarian aspect, and did a great deal. But most people got off by giving money; enormous sums were collected. We were completely uninvolved in this and didn't conceive it as our duty. Some people perceived directly, and others picked it up, that the event was a sort of alarm signal that things couldn't go on like this. And when this then coincided with the Marxists' attitudes, it was quite portentous. For it turned out that the solution could not be found in the peasantry, which was stuck in a dead end because of its primitiveness and lack of culture, but in this new progressive force, the workers. This was the principal impact of the famine, I believe.

H: Before Iulii was arrested [in February 1892], did you know that he was involved in duplicating illegal literature?[16]

D: Of course, we knew, although he kept things from us. He was very clumsy, and couldn't handle the simplest practical matters himself. So he would turn to Nadezhda Osipovna or me for help. It was important to have good handwriting because there were no typewriters. I was no use for this purpose, since my handwriting is abominable. But Nadezhda Osipovna wrote very clearly, and he would sometimes make her write papers or letters. For example, there was Tsebrikova's letter.[17] We read it; he brought it to us and talked about it. I remember that it made a great impression.

H: Did he also read you the "declaration of the Russian liberals?"[18]

D: Of course. Nadezhda Osipovna had to copy it and she kept no secrets from me. So when they came for him, we were not at all surprised. He promptly instructed my sister and me (habits were rather patriarchal then) to write to so-and-so, say such-and-such, and so forth. He trusted us. This was a common feature of all of us. Each of us was involved, however slight our involvement might be. Iulii always tried to involve everyone in these doings. Much later, when it turned out that Vladimir Osipovich had different opinions from ours, we were greatly shocked. We had become so used to being together that it was a major psychological blow, in particular for Iulii Osipovich; Vladimir's involvement in the League for Freedom left him tremendously depressed.[19]

H: Was Sergei not involved?

D: Sergei began fairly early. There was only a one-year age difference between him and me. And he was a very healthy, strong boy, so that he even considered himself older than me and was protective of me. There was no question that Sergei was going to be involved. We always had doubts about Volodia, but not about Sergei.

H: What was his involvement?

D: It was sometimes necessary to deliver literature or a letter, and this was entrusted to Sergei. Sergei was going to *gimnazium* and could come home a half-hour late; no one would notice. He carried out these tasks pre-

cisely and conscientiously. He showed an aptitude for such technical functions very early, and carried them out very precisely.

H: Martov mentions in his memoirs that his first arrest made a very
great impression on him, both mentally and physically.

D: We more or less knew what he was involved in and more or less
understood that it might end abruptly, but still, when it happened, it made
a great impression. To be frank, both he and the rest of us were primarily
concerned that he not "get cold feet," crack under interrogation. After all,
it was pretty frightening. Then there was the notion that solitary confinement would be a frightening prospect. Each of us asked ourselves whether
he or she could handle such a situation. Any mention of prison would bring
to mind Shlissel'burg, which had no bearing on any situation.[20] Prosaic recollections of the place of preliminary detention were somehow forgotten
and of no interest. Talk about prison would conjure up psychological tor-
ment. The whole affair ended rather fortunately. But it was important, I
think, in terms of toughening one's character. Then, we thought that was
important.

H: What was the response of your parents?

D: Once he was in prison, we children were pushed aside and Father
and Grandfather took over. Grandfather had some connections, and he
started to use his pull. I don't know what he did because we weren't
involved, but Iulii was in jail a very short time, five weeks I think. It wasn't
so bad, and he was even able to remain in Petersburg. I think that, with
some effort, he could have returned to the university. But apparently certain conditions were required of him which he didn't care for, and he
remained outside the university. I guess that he had decided the university
was closed to him forever. I gather that Grandfather, and probably Father
to some extent, began to feel that he should be sent to America. This was
quite a common idea among Russian Jews. If, for some reason, things
didn't work out in Russia because of lack of residency rights or of opportunities to study, or because a young man had certain black marks, he
should be sent to America. For us it was that much simpler because my
father's brother had gone to America in 1882, ten years before. He had a
fine job; he was a doctor in Colorado and the organizer of the first sanato-
rium in Denver. He suggested that Iulii be sent to him. But Iulii said that
he wouldn't go, and it wasn't customary in our family to argue with the
children. If he didn't want to, he wouldn't go. "And what are you going to
do? Nothing?"

H: What did Iulii answer to such questions?

D: Nothing, he just shrugged his shoulders and said, "We'll see." I have
to say that in those times many other families and many of his friends had
to face the question of what precisely to live on. For him the problem didn't
exist. Father was not a rich man, but it never would have occurred to him
not to provide for his children. And, generally, we were on his neck for
quite a while. This problem didn't disturb us, and it didn't disturb Iulii.
When Iulii was living at home, it was no big deal, he had everything. When

he went to Vilno, he tried to earn something by giving lessons. Still, they sent him money. Not much, but they sent him some.

H: I have the impression that you became closer after his arrest.

D: You see, we had become more grown-up, naturally. And he could pretend, or perhaps even feel, that he was no longer talking to us as an older brother but as an equal. He tried hard to do that. He was uncomfortable being an older brother. It was as unlike Iulii to act the older brother as it was natural for Sergei to try to be the older brother and have his way. He began to accept us as equals very early and, of course, this strengthened our relationship. The situation changed gradually, and I don't even remember a moment at which it became different. But suddenly I noticed that he was no longer instructing us, but even asking our opinion.

H: I know that in the spring and summer of 1892, and particularly that autumn, he read a great deal and became a more serious follower of Marxism. Do you recall any discussions of this?

D: I can't say specifically. We spent that summer at the *dacha;* we went there every year.

H: Where was the *dacha?*

D: Near Petersburg, usually in Pavlovsk, or perhaps in Finland. In any case, he was free of obligations, didn't need to work, and could read. He could read remarkably fast. I know that members of the Bund mentioned later that they had never seen a man who read as fast and who remembered as much as he. He himself said that only one person had a better memory, that was Riazanov.[21] Iulii met him after the stint in Kresty prison. That summer Iulii read a great deal. I think it was then that he read *Das Kapital*, and maybe not just the first chapter, but others as well. We were more interested in Marx's historical works than in *Das Kapital*. We preferred to read about Marx than Marx himself. Marx was very difficult.

H: By this time, I know, Iulii was already friends with Potresov.[22]

D: He probably met him while he was still a *gimnazium* student. But Potresov was much older and Iulii was very shy. It was after his arrest, I think, that Golovin and Stavskii introduced him into that circle. But by his family and social position, Potresov was quite different. He was entirely apart from that milieu. You could feel perfectly at home with Stavskii or Gofman after two hours. But with Potresov it was not at all easy.

H: Why?

D: It's very hard to say. He came from an entirely different environment, well-to-do gentry circles, I think. I don't know his family background, but apparently his mother died when he was very young and he was raised by a governess. He was so impractical that when he was sent into exile he took the governess with him. Of course, everyone thought this was funny. In those times there were very few telephones, and it was natural that if you were free in the evening you would go visit Iulii Osipovich or someone else. If you found them home, fine; if not, it didn't matter. If they were home you would have tea and talk until one in the morning. With Potresov, however, it was different. Potresov could not be visited late or without sending a post card in advance, saying "I hope to find you home

. . ." This made the situation much more complicated. In short, he lived in a different world which was inaccessible to us. He was much closer to Struve than any of us, because they were older.[23] He was very close to Kalmykova, with whom we became very good friends many years later.[24] But while he was at home in that society, for us it was alien and inaccessible, and it might even have been boring. They were all extremely respectable people. And that left a great imprint on Potresov. In Munich, where life was almost communal, anyone might come and disturb you at any hour of the day or night – there was no time that was your own.[25] Not so with Potresov. Lenin tried to isolate himself also, but he wasn't half as successful as Potresov. Potresov required no effort to do so. I believe that this had a great effect on his entire political career. He was not a brilliant man, but he was thoroughly educated.

H: I know that when Martov was arrested, it was already felt, at least in this circle, that it was necessary to become involved in the workers' movement, and the question arose that year of how to do so. What do you recall? Were you involved?

D: No, that was something so inaccessible that even if we heard about it we probably wouldn't have had a concrete notion of what it was like. At that time, you see, it was possible, though not easy, to become involved in teaching Sunday schools, as a profession, if we had wanted to.[26] But we felt that this was do-gooding dilettantism [*kul'turnichestvo*], and insufficiently revolutionary. To be a schoolteacher beyond the *Nevskaia Zastava*[27] and teach a course in Russian history, you had to use an approved textbook. Of course, you could make additional comments, but it was risky. People were afraid and weren't always capable of doing it. So our attitude was somewhat condescending. I think that Nadezhda Osipovna had certain sympathies along these lines. She was naturally inclined to being a teacher, and later she was a good one. As a result, she was very prominent in the League of Youth when her son had already become a socialist.[28] But at that time, Iulii Osipovich and the rest of us regarded dilettantism with scorn. This attitude made it impossible for us to join the Sunday schools and reach the workers' milieu by this route. We had to wait until we were recruited into some circle and someone said, "Take this group and lead it." And then, it was very difficult for women to lead men's groups. For example, when I went to groups of women weavers I always dressed so that I looked like one of them and could go into any working family, where six or seven girls would get together. But I could not go to an apartment where there was a gathering of men. That was impossible. As a rule, therefore, women could lead only groups of women workers. We had to reconcile ourselves to this, although we were not happy with it. These were the conditions of Russian political life.

H: When Martov was arrested for the second time and went to Vilno, and before he returned in 1895,[29] how did you begin to discuss political freedom and how it might be used, and what did you say about the problem of working with the working class?

D: I have already said that the socialist aspects were in effect not very important in our outlook at that time, because we knew that they were a long way off. We dreamed that we would ultimately be able to assemble a workers' party. But I certainly don't recall that anyone thought at that time that we would create a powerful workers' party to seize power. That was absolutely excluded. The lack of political freedom was enormously important and became more and more prominent with each passing month and year. We thought we would help to create democratic freedoms. Maybe we even dreamed about a democratic republic.

At that time we did not say that our revolution was to be a bourgeois revolution.[30] We didn't even dream about revolution. I believe, though, that there was already an awareness that the working class had no ally as in Western Europe – a liberal bourgeoisie that would also take a revolutionary course. In addition, history (and in particular French history) had played a rather nasty trick on us. We were well aware of the history of the French revolution of 1848, and were extremely afraid of repeating it in Russia. We thought that we too would have a revolution, and, of course, the liberal bourgeoisie would be involved. It was better organized than the proletariat. The workers, who were more noble, naturally, would be drawn in. Workers' blood, naturally, would be shed, but why not? But then, what would come of it? To work only to provide grist for the mill of the bourgeoisie? We couldn't agree to that. So it was necessary somehow to insure the workers' party an independent function and meaning. I feel that this was the beginning of a certain repugnance to any coalition with liberal bourgeois elements. And it was here, I think (although I did not realize it at the time, of course), that disagreements with Marxists of Struve's type arose. They favored only limitations on the autocracy. They felt no less than we did that political freedom needed to be achieved, but the aim was somewhat different – for us what was important was freedom and the overthrow of the autocracy, but we didn't have the slightest concern for the state (this can be stated categorically). Struve understood better than the youth that a strong, powerful state was possible only with a well-developed capitalism. What was important for him wasn't important for us.

H: And did you know about the Russian constitutionalists?[31]

D: We didn't know and were little interested. These were probably prominent in the conceptions of Struve, but for us they simply didn't exist. In fact the constitutionalists were very weak then. We were already Marxist enough to know that some sort of base was necessary. We felt that even if we didn't in fact have such a base, we would in the future. And what kind of base did they have? None, and they would never have one. Such problems were solved very simply.

H: I know that when Potresov returned from Switzerland, he brought a copy of Plekhanov's work with him.[32] Did you read it and talk about it with Iulii that year?

D: No, I don't remember doing so at all.

H: Do you remember discussions, at any rate, regarding the classical problem of whether or not to help the countryside?

D: As I say, we were little acquainted with the Russian countryside. I think this was a major gap in our system of views at the time. For Russia the question of the countryside and the peasantry was a dominant one. Since we had become disillusioned with *narodnichestvo*, we simply discounted the problem.

H: What was said about helping the peasantry?

D: That it was one of the manifestations of dilettantism and "small deeds,"[33] because it was something impossible on any large scale under those conditions. We felt that the people interested in "petty activities" should go ahead and plug these holes, but that we understood too much for that. Now the proletariat, on the other hand, was something else. Disillusionment in the peasantry for the *narodniki* was the result of some activity or familiarity with the countryside. For us it was not disillusionment, but simply a ready-made attitude.

        *   *   *

H: When Iulii went to Vilno, did he consider himself to be a full-fledged Marxist?

D: Yes.

H: And you had started to take courses then?

D: I started in September 1893; I was still in the *gimnazium* when he left.

H: And Nadezhda?

D: She had been taking courses for two years; she went to Lesgaft's lectures and was generally involved in more of an oppositionist than a revolutionary movement. She knew more than she wanted to. She wanted to work as a teacher, so she started the courses in the Faculty of Philology.

H: Women's courses?

D: Yes, the Bestuzhev program.[34] But once you completed the program, you could become a teacher. It was very difficult for a Jew, but for some reason she gave this no thought. Her dilettantish tendencies were much more pronounced than mine or Iulii's. He was not at all interested in everyday matters.

H: Did Nadezhda have friends who shared her attitudes?

D: Of course. It was a very well-educated group of young people. She had a good friend, Ekaterina Genrikhovna Gurko, who became a friend of the entire family. She was a rather strange person. She was the daughter of a very important general, and she was a Marxist and an anarchist, both at the same time. Later she married some anarchist and went off to South America with him.

H: Did Nadezhda work in the Sunday schools?

D: I believe that she could not work there, because she was Jewish. Subsequently she was a *gimnazium* teacher, but that was after 1905. Ekaterina Gurko was a teacher beyond the Nevskaia Zastava, and she had contacts with workers somehow. In general, it was all not very serious. I remember that once in response to Nadezhda Osipovna's comments about becoming a teacher and spreading propaganda I said that it would be better to make a revolutionary out of one worker than to teach reading and writing to a hundred peasant children. Iulii said, "Well, I wouldn't say that." I was very hurt, because I counted on his support. I remember that very well. I thought about it, but didn't change my mind.

H: Where did you get the notion of the importance of the working class, that the workers were better? From Iulii?

D: From him, naturally, and from the entire mood. What had happened to the *narodniki*, after all? They had staked everything on the peasantry, and they had been rebuffed and nothing remained of them. We saw that they had made a mistake in their conception of the Russian peasantry, since the real advanced stratum was the proletariat . . . I recall now that we never used the word "industrialization" then, but actually we thought it was of enormous importance. It was characteristic that Struve ended his book with the words "We recognize our lack of sophistication and go to school to capitalism."[35] Our understanding of that phrase was somewhat different from Struve's but each of us could repeat it. In the first place, we placed tremendous importance on "culture" and to recognize one's own lack of culture was already a step forward. As for turning to "go to school to capitalism," for us capitalism was a very respectable aspect of the life of any country, so to speak, and more progressive. We looked to the West, we believed we could learn something there.

H: Did you consider yourself a full-fledged Marxist when you started taking courses?

D: Yes.

H: What had you read in the way of Marxist literature by that time? And what did Iulii read to you?

D: A number of Marx's pamphlets, naturally, the *Communist Manifesto.* Individual issues of *Neue Zeit.*[36] But we drew most of our wisdom from the history of the French revolution. I would say that we knew it rather well, but probably not in depth and we were carried away by the political aspects. But we knew 1848 well and drew many far-ranging conclusions, which were more harmful than useful, because they limited our horizons. We felt that, in backward Russia, we could make do with just a workers' movement, that it was possible to live apart from all the remaining classes of society. We left ourselves very much in isolation. This was to have a very negative result later.

H: Did you read Plekhanov's *Our Differences* at that time?[37]

D: Yes, that was available then. Iulii got such things for us. In general we knew the substance of the disagreements with the *narodniki* quite well.

H: Before you started [taking university courses], did you have friends who were radicals but not Marxists?

D: Yes, there were contacts. Not very many, but there were some. Even before I was in the student milieu I already knew, I can't say why, that the student movement was second-rate, so to speak. It was the social-democratic movement that was first-rate. When I started taking courses, I had the ready-made conviction that the students could be tolerated but it was impossible to identify with them. And we took advantage of the students.

We were not very clever tacticians and told them what we were doing. You can imagine that no student body would want to be only taken advantage of. This had its harmful aspect, of course, and I must say that our older comrades pushed us in this direction. They felt that those few students who could work in the social-democratic movement needed to operate clandestinely and not flaunt themselves before the police (and this was confirmed by the history of the revolutionary movement). In the student movement, and taking part in the students' debates, you would be spotted. Therefore they advised us not to expose ourselves, so to speak, in student society. On the other hand, it was natural to go and influence [the students] and it was stupid to say, "You are second-rate." But that was more or less what we said. This was always a major problem. Emotionally we gravitated toward the student movement, but intellectually we understood that it was not really the best thing for us to be doing. This ambivalence lasted a long time.

H: At that time, up to the summer of 1896 to be precise, did you have friends who regarded themselves as followers of the People's Will?

D: By then there were none from the People's Will, but there were girls who were *narodniki*, and some of them later became Socialist Revolutionaries.[38] The Petersburg women students tended not to be very activist. But from the provinces there were girls who were much more frequently *narodniki* than Marxists. And many of them joined the SR groups and became active SRs. I think this was a provincial phenomenon. I think that older *narodniki* who had ceased to be revolutionaries and were living in the provinces had some influence on the youth.

H: I am puzzled about the following. At that time there was already the problem of whether or not a revolution was needed to gain political freedom. And people who considered themselves at least the successors of the People's Will, who were quite scornful of the legal *narodniki* . . .

D: We all thought that revolution was absolutely necessary to gain political freedom. We did not believe in any constitutional concessions, and didn't particularly want them although we hardly knew what revolution meant. An acquaintance of mine now, a former Kadet,[39] says, "I can't understand why you had this dream of revolution. How can people dream of earthquakes?" We felt that revolution was a truly necessary process and one which was natural in every country, because there had been so many revolutions in France. Why then shouldn't there be revolution in Russia? At the same time, we wanted a freedom which would not just provide everything for the liberals but something for ourselves as well. This is why a moderate constitution did not suit us and we wanted a democratic republic and so forth. This was fairly widespread.

H: To return to when Iulii was arrested and in Kresty prison and was then exiled to Vilno, was it a great shock to you?

D: It was so much in the natural course of affairs that it was no shock, although it was a nuisance, a pity, and a hard thing to bear. We were all prepared for a life of complete self-sacrifice and suffering, so that when it happened we figured, being young, that it was normal.

H: But it seems to me that the situation had changed in two respects. First, he was leaving, and I imagine that he was the center of your life; second, you needed to become involved in life yourself and to take courses.

D: Well, he left after he had been in Kresty for five months, so we had gradually gotten used to it. We knew that when he left prison he would not be allowed to stay in Petersburg. Vilno was not bad, it could have been much worse. So there was no feeling of shock.

H: What conversations did you have with him before his departure? He knew that he was going away and leaving you and that you would now be in the wide world.

D: Well, there were all sorts of admonitions . . . he warned a lot about not being distracted by the lighter sides of student life. He urged us strongly to study hard. But Nadezhda Osipovna said to him, "I'm sure you'll agree that if we give a great deal of time to preparation for revolutionary activity, our course work will suffer."

H: What did he say?

D: That we had to arrange things, of course . . . education was very important. For our own self-development, he promised all sorts of assistance – advice and letters. He was very conscientious about doing all this, though he himself was highly impractical and a poor mentor. He could give general ideas.

H: What instructions did he give you about revolutionary activity?

D: First of all, to be a Marxist, of course. This idea was to accompany us to the end of our lives. It was best of all, naturally, to get into a workers' milieu somehow. In any case, we were to try to establish relationships with the social-democratic organization. This was still very unclear, how to go about it. He advised us to rely on Stavskii and Gofman, that they would help us in difficult moments with suggestions.

Third interview

H: I would like to begin with the autumn of 1894, when you began attending the Bestuzhev courses like your sister, and with your impressions of the groups and atmosphere among the students you knew.

D: You should keep in mind, first of all, that there were two currents in our life then that did not merge. First, there was student life. Here there was no special activity, and everything was fairly open and it was possible to talk freely. The other current was illegal activity, in which it was generally not easy to get involved. You had to wait until they asked you. It wasn't proper to say, "Hey, I want to do such-and-such," otherwise you could get an unflattering evaluation [*kharakteristika*] . . . a curious person . . . not serious. So you had to wait until they said, "Wouldn't you like to do such-and-such?" And this is a very important point. In school, for example, there were already some Marxists, and there were *narodniki*. None of them were engaged in any political activity, but they were under the sway of these ideas and they were their dominant interest. It was possible to be fairly open and, say, argue about the superiority of Marxism to *narodni-*

chestvo, etc. All life in Petersburg, or, more accurately, the life in this narrow sector, was intrigued with these ideas. Needless to say, the man in the
street was unaffected. Indeed, it was almost improper not to be interested
in Marxism in the student milieu. We were very poor Marxists, but this was
the only natural atmosphere to live in. There were hours-long discussions,
of course, and beyond that, there were meetings at the Free Economic
Society.[1]

The Free Economic Society was a very respected academic institution,
and it was probably then that it first became open to so broad a public. I
doubt that, before our time, any speaker had left the stage without
applause. The students also listened seriously, but were quite open about
expressing approval or disapproval. Of course, whistling would have been
too impolite, but there were ways of exchanging glances with each other so
that the speaker would have no doubt that his remarks were not being well-
received. And of course, this activity could greatly bother the speaker. I
doubt that Tugan-Baranovskii ever had as appreciative an audience at the
university.[2] At meetings of the Free Economic Society, there would be perhaps 200 in the audience, and of these only perhaps 30 would be distinguished people; the remaining 170 of us were students who understood little, but nonetheless we were convinced that we were the true audience. And
I think that Struve and Tugan-Baranovskii felt somewhat the same way.
They wanted some recognition from this group of listeners, and there was
nothing illegal and no risk in the situation. In a word, we felt completely
free there.

The situation was entirely different when it came to practical activity in
which it was necessary to be careful. Being labeled as a person who was
not serious was worse than a death sentence. That was our outlook then.
For example, Gorev in his memoirs complained bitterly even then that he
was never allowed into conspiratorial activity.[3] The reason he wasn't
allowed was that he was not regarded as serious, and his entire "lack of
seriousness" was that he spent some time running after some actress. That
was not all, however. Throughout his life he was a curious person and
could sometimes ask awkward questions. And he had one other trait: he
wanted recognition. Vanity was not considered good form, and ultimately
it would only get him arrested. But for him, underground work was like a
medal which was never given to him, and he took offense.

I think that, to some extent, each of us wanted some recognition. We were
asking for trouble and taking risks, but, of course, it was necessary to be
very careful, so that the older and more adult comrades took precautions
and didn't admit untested youth. For example, in the *gimnazium* Martov
had his friend Golovin, and so forth. I didn't have such friends, but all Martov's comrades would come to our house, even if it meant violating conspiratorial rules. I was very close with Gofman. In fact, I can now say that
I even intended to marry him. Fortunately, I didn't. Nadezhda Osipovna
was on the verge of marrying Treniukhin, and luckily she didn't. That was
how personal relationships were established.

H: When you became a university student, how did these relationships change?

D: It is very difficult to say, of course. They changed gradually. For example, I recall very well when I decided to marry Gofman. I came home early from class and waited for Father to come home from work to tell him. I sat with my younger sisters and sewed something for their dolls. When Father entered, I said, "Father, I intend to get married." He answered, "First stop playing with dolls." I was deeply hurt and thought I would stop there, but I went on. He said, "Well, that's up to you, but he . . . he's not Jewish! Are you sure that he will never reproach you for being Jewish? How naive you are! Just because that doesn't happen in our family . . . " But I remained a fiancee. He was arrested. I even went to visit him as his fiancee (in fact, you didn't have to be a fiancee to visit). Then he was exiled, and, fortunately, the whole thing ended. He was somewhat unbalanced, mentally.

H: I would like to discuss the two aspects of your student life in more detail. First, there was the open, public side, in which there were *narodniki* and Marxists, as you say. How do you think these tendencies were delineated, that is, where and on whom was the *narodnik* influence exercised, and which women responded to Marxism?

D: As I recall, the *narodniki* tended to be girls from the provinces; for some reason, many of them came from Siberia . . . The urban youth was more imbued with Marxist ideas. This was probably the result of literature from abroad which rarely reached the provinces. Petersburg students, even those not involved in illegal activity, were able to read works printed in, say, Geneva. Plekhanov was someone concrete for us. The girls from the provinces knew that Plekhanov had once made a speech on Kazan Square, and that was all they knew for sure, although a few could quote the speech.[4] But his Marxist streak was entirely unknown to them, and in this sense Beltov's book was the watershed, so to speak.[5] From that moment, it became clear what our differences were. I realized that we all had a very poor understanding of Marx. I knew before that the peasantry had not justified our hopes, and this was bad. But now there was a contrast – a new force, the workers' party. This was only dimly perceived, but it was the watershed.

So we had to go to the workers, but what we were to go with was unclear. For example, when I was asked to lead a group (this was after Iulii Osipovich's arrest, when I had become closer to active Social Democrats), I first learned, to my surprise, that a girl could attend only women's circles. The female proletariat was less educated and less intelligent, I felt, and therefore it was less interesting. It was easy to understand that cigarette-makers and weavers cannot readily be made into activists, whereas metal workers and typographers were ready-made revolutionaries. But, of course, we could not even dream of being involved in a metal workers' circle. This is now generally overlooked, but it was of great importance.

People who were regarded as Social Democrats, such as Nevzorova and Krupskaia, very good Social Democrats, felt that it was necessary to be

involved in educational work.[6] They taught in Sunday schools and had contact with male workers, because they met legally. They would go to lectures
and give some courses. I don't know what; sometimes it was simply reading
and writing. After the sessions, however, they could sometimes spend fifteen minutes and make some acquaintances. We were still so immature that
we avoided educational work. We naively thought that, by reading fifteen
pamphlets, we could become aware Social Democrats and do something.
What to do was rather unclear. In general, I think that our political level
was quite low. Naturally, in a student environment there were more active
interests and more active communication, and ultimately everything
turned into politics.

H: I would like to discuss the groups which existed in 1894 and 1895.
You have said that you had no contact with this new People's Will group,
but what did you find out about their ideology?[7]

D: I became acquainted with them and their ideas later, when they had
all been arrested. And since I regularly went to the place of preliminary
detention, I met people who were associated, for example, with Preis. And
later I was amazed to learn in school that a number of *narodnik* girls knew
about this group and were also concerned. They regarded themselves as
the successors of the People's Will. But of course they were not involved in
the most essential terrorist aspect of the activity. That was missing. The
Preis group somehow obtained a fairly well-equipped printing shop. But
they had no definite plans about what to print. Usually among the Social
Democrats in the provinces or elsewhere, a demand would arise for literature and in response an illegal print shop would be set up, with varying
degrees of risk and success. Here the situation was the reverse: the print
shop was available, but what was to be printed? Later, the Social Democratic organization learned about the printing shop, established contact
with these people, and gave them Hauptmann's *The Weavers* to print.[8]

H: In that year, 1894, did you have contact with Martov's friends?
Which ones?

D: Well, Gofman, Stavskii, and Treniukhin.[9]

H: Tell me about Treniukhin; I know virtually nothing about him.

D: Treniukhin was not a university student, but a student at the Institute of Means of Communication. This institute stood apart from other educational institutions. Treniukhin was very intelligent, and I think that, on a
theoretical level, he knew much more than all of us. But he was without
character and that was what made him leave. He disappeared altogether;
I never heard anything about him, in 1905 or any other time. But he read
a great deal and could answer any question put to him. As a result, his
impact upon my sister and me was doubtless fairly great. He knew German
fairly well, it seems; I gather that he read Marx and did so better and more
extensively than we. I think he gave us a lot in terms of general development. The most serious issue, of course, was the history of the Russian revolutionary movement, and he constantly engaged us about it, so that we
knew it fairly well. We read and learned willingly, and had mixed feelings,
as was often the case. On the one hand, there was an extraordinary respect

for the Russian revolutionaries, that is, for the revolutionary *narodniki.* With whatever justification, we distinguished between revolutionary *narodniki* and *narodniki* in general. There was nothing heroic in those *narodniki* whom we saw, say, at meetings of *Russkoe Bogatstvo* or the Free Economic Society.[10] Our notion was that it was indispensable for a revolutionary to be a hero; we assumed also that they had erred in their attitude toward the Russian people. Strangely, though, instead of saying that they had made a mistake, the impression was created that the "people" [i.e., the peasantry] had not lived up to expectations. But still, it was necessary to have some sort of hero, so we transferred our sympathies from the "people" to the proletariat. Of course, here as well we were wrong, not because the proletariat deceived us but because we knew little about them. For many this was to play a fatal role. In particular, I feel that it determined the entire subsequent course of events for a thoughtful person like Struve. He was carried away and decided that the active hero was the proletariat. Upon reflecting later, he saw that, whatever else it was, the proletariat was not heroic; it had little culture, was not self-aware . . . But it was still necessary to have heroes. It was at this point that he gravitated toward the liberal bourgeoisie, and this introduced a new opposition element which completely split and enervated the revolutionary movement, perhaps much more than the police persecutions.

H: Let us now deal with the illegal circles with which you were in contact that year.

D: Well, before Krupskaia's arrest I met her very frequently at the place of preliminary detention when she was visiting. Nevzorova was very well acquainted with her. They were on good terms with me, feeling that I was a sensible, no-nonsense person, and so forth. Beyond that, I didn't have other virtues on my side. I remember that Nevzorova once said to me, "Listen, we need someone to lead a circle of cigarette-makers at the Laferma Company." I was happy that they offered this to me. I started to visit the workers, but I couldn't establish a good exchange of views right away. I should tell you that the low cultural level of the Petersburg working woman was quite unexpected for me. Of course, they were almost all literate, that is, they could read, though badly. Their material circumstances were horrible. They came from the countryside. Learning to be a cigarette-maker was nothing, particularly at the factory. It was not even manual labor. Although in Vilno it was, and there it was necessary to have some skills. But at Laferma, everything was done by machine. The desire to learn something was very strong, but I soon became convinced that the way I spoke was too complex for them. I had to adapt to be understood, and that didn't happen immediately. Ultimately I got the hang of it, and, on the advice of Nevzorova and Gofman, who helped me, I concluded that it was pointless to make speeches to them. The best way was to meet once a week, on Saturday evenings (Saturday was a working day also), since they didn't have to get up early on Sunday. They read *Birzhovka* or *Kopeika* (that was somewhat later),[11] but they didn't know what was in the newspapers, particularly as regards Europe. Later one could expect questions, but at first, when I would speak, they would be shy. As a result, I had to find a topic myself. In general, I never found the workers unfavorable to the intelligentsia. Of course, there were individual cases, but I deny categorically that it was widespread. There might have been some distrust. For example, in discussions about Europe, I would say that the workers there could legally discuss wage increases, vote in parliamentary or Reichstag elections, etc. This was to encourage them to fight for these things – but, they would say, "What else do we need?" It seemed so unreal to them that it was hard for them to take it seriously. I decided that I could not reach them by talking about Western Europe; that I had to talk about Russian realities, and in particular, the economic aspects of their lives. They could teach me, not the other way around. Unwittingly, therefore, I came around to talking about police conditions. It was easier to interest them in politics. In the first place I (and the rest) were more *au courant* in this area. Second, they encountered examples of arbitrariness at every step, so that it was comprehensible to them. I think the impetus to politics had already begun.

H: What did this mean for them specifically, and what political topics were of significance to them?

D: First of all, there was the position of women. Don't forget that these girls all earned very little. Usually they were not living with their families, and their morals were rather low. Many of them engaged in prostitution on the side. Of course, none of them wanted to obtain the so-called yellow ticket, because prostitution was only to earn some extra money.[12] Every one of them hoped eventually to become an "honest" woman, marry, and have a family. In fact, however, they were entirely in the power of any policeman. This topic was a convenient *Anhaltspunkt* to start a discussion. In no other country, I would say, does the policeman have such power! Here there is no holding him in check! And indeed, this was the case. Then there was the attitude of the factory administration, which used these young girls unscrupulously. This was a very popular and easy topic.

H: More specifically?

D: Specifically, a foreman – or even just a worker – would push a girl into a corner and demand favors from her. And when this topic was discussed, the girls talked readily. I never heard any objections. They would say, "Indeed, how can such a situation be tolerated?" Then they would switch to the general problems of women with the police. The Russian woman, you see, was completely without rights. Even more so than the Russian man. This was again a convenient topic, namely the Russian citizen's lack of rights. This topic would interest them, since they were linked to the countryside. The following situation was very typical: the family remained in the country, in the province of Tver, for example, and the girl would come to the city to earn money. They were somewhat reluctant to talk about their domestic circumstances, and were not very interested, or at least I was not. I was not very interested in the situation of the Russian peasantry. But as regards the situation of city women, we tried to depict various rosy possibilities of what women could become, provided only that they were organized. No doubt these were pleasant fairy tales, but they listened eagerly.

Still, these girls lacked a specific "sense of organization" [*organizovannost'*], and when the cigarette-makers' strike at Laferma began, it immediately took on explosive proportions, despite our most energetic warnings, and, in 1896, they threw thousands and tens of thousands of cigarettes into the street. Afterwards I never heard, in Petersburg at any rate, of workers trying to destroy machinery during strikes. The women workers at Laferma did not destroy machinery (probably this would have been difficult for women), but the sight of huge boxes of cigarettes being thrown into the street – it was frightful. Somewhat later, at the Obukhov plant, a great deal was destroyed; this was during the "Obukhov defense."[13] This form of struggle was fairly primitive, but I believe this was the last case of it. Afterward there was a trial and the workers and their wives paid heavily. Therefore, even Kol'tsov's rather lackluster pamphlet, *The Machine*, was a great success and very important.[14] It showed that the enemy of the workers was not the machine but the entire structure of Russian life. This indicates the exceptionally low level which we encountered among the workers, though, of course, there were also workers like Babushkin[15] whose comprehension was much greater than that of all the girls put together, including those from the intelligentsia. And, once you were familiar with the situation, it was not easy to digest, because of the enormous illusions we had. In all these discussions there was the somewhat overworked notion of the progressive nature of capitalism, on the one hand, and, on the other, that capitalism was already the dominant phase of development in Russia. Of course, it was strange that the people should be so backward if the level of production was so high. This was fairly difficult to reconcile.

H: If we can return to 1894, when Martov was still in Vilno, do you know anything about his disagreements with his comrades at that time? Was the question of how to organize in Petersburg discussed?

D: Yes, I remember that idea. He wrote and talked about it. His letters, of course, were more circumspect. In any case, he had already gone through the phase (which matured only in Vilno, not in Petersburg) of changing over from propaganda to agitation.[16] I think that he himself was rather unaware of it, and we even less. There was an enormous difference between the Vilno proletariat, which was Jewish and in trades, and the Petersburg proletariat, which was truly industrial. Agitation was a better tactic for the western regions. First, there were exclusively Jewish enterprises. Second, these were not workers who had always been workers and who knew that they would always be workers. There was no need for lasting relationships with the exploiters. Many workers of both sexes intended, consciously or unconsciously, to get out of their situation.

For example, every stay-maker dreamed of marrying or of opening her own shop with two girls as employees. And, of course, she would treat them better than she was treated herself. But all the same, she would be a small proprietress, and for this it was important for them to have some knowledge and a better education. This included, among other things, a knowledge of Russian. None of these elements existed in the Petersburg proletariat, because a worker at Laferma knew that she could either get married or return to the countryside, but in either case she would be bound to her class or perhaps pushed out of her class, so to speak, but could not enter another social grouping. The same was true of the male workers, and the weavers. A weaver could remain only a weaver. Russian was her native language, and she might attend a Sunday school, and still she would remain a weaver. This was very important. For this reason, questions of agitation and propaganda were not as important in the well-developed capitalist economy of Petersburg as they were in the petty trade atmosphere of Vilno. We had a formula which originated, I believe, with Plekhanov: the difference between propaganda and agitation is that propaganda involves several ideas for a few people while agitation is one idea for many. This formula was much more applicable to Petersburg realities.

H: I would like to skip to the autumn of 1895, when Martov returned to Petersburg ... Did you know Chernyshev's group at that time, 1895?[17]

D: Yes, I knew Chernyshev; his was a group of engineers whom I met at parties. I knew that they led some workers' groups and I regarded them as lucky for being able to lead groups of male workers. What they talked about in those groups was probably the same as elsewhere. It was a milieu that was very undifferentiated ideologically.

H: Were you aware of what was going on when the Union for Struggle was created in 1895?[18]

D: Only a little. Martov would tell us bits and pieces. He was a very good pupil of the Vilno underground, which had a basic rule: "Don't speak with whom you can, but with whom you need to." And, needless to say, there wasn't the slightest necessity to talk to us. Still, there was a great temptation to do so, and he would break the rules and tell us things. He would come home late and Nadezhda Osipovna and I would deliberately stay up and wait for him to return. He would come to our room; our parents would have been asleep a long time, and we would talk. We would make tea for him, and it wasn't easy, because we could not wake the servants and we didn't know how to get the samovar going. Nonetheless, somehow we would manage to make tea and fix something for him, and he would give some first impressions. So he gradually introduced us not so much to what was going on but to the general atmosphere.

H: And when his activity with the Union began, particularly as regards the Putilov works,[19] did he mention it to you?

D: No, no, that he couldn't do; he was afraid and didn't want to. Don't forget that this was a very short period overall. By January 1896 he was already under arrest; January 9, I think ... I remember the day well; it was my parents' anniversary. They always had guests, and Mother was tremendously upset that all these relatives and guests were coming and Iulii wasn't around. He came very late, at 12:00, and the guests had already left. He was arrested that very night, so that he didn't even get a scolding because he hadn't been there in the evening . . .

H: And this was at the time of the arrest of those people with whom you subsequently became acquainted?

D: No, I had become friends with some of them earlier, like Gofman, for example, whom we knew earlier. And then I knew Dan because his mother was a good friend of my parents.[20] And young people would come to visit.

After Martov's arrest, when the makeup of the Union of Struggle changed . . . there were some factors at work that would now seem strange. For example, there was Radchenko, who was much older; he was over 30.[21] He was an engineer, God knows what sort, and he had an apartment. Radchenko probably never led a [workers'] group in his life, but he was important in the movement because at that time there was already some organization, and above all it was necessary to order a seal. This was a difficult matter because, as you can imagine, you could not go to a shop and order a seal for, say, the Russian League of Youth. An "illegal" could order one only through an acquaintance. In short, there was a seal, but where was it to be kept? It was very important that the seal appear on the circulars we distributed. It was important because the organization wanted to create a good reputation for itself, and because it was important for the workers to know that the material was in fact coming from the organization and not from God knows where. If, therefore, 200 copies were printed, it was necessary to put the seal on all of them. And the seal was kept by Stepan Ivanovich Radchenko himself. And when there were arrests, since he didn't attend workers' circles, he wasn't arrested for years. His entire power in the organization, and it was enormous, was because he had the seal, because he was the custodian of the traditions. His wife was Liubov Nikolaevna Radchenko, a very striking woman who was also a Social Democrat of long standing.

H: How did he obtain the seal?

D: I don't know how. It would have been a dreadful calamity if he had been arrested. He probably hid it in such a way that it wouldn't be taken, but if it had, the results would have been catastrophic. But, even if he had been arrested, Liubov Nikolaevna always knew where the seal was. And a new organization with a new makeup would eventually have arisen, and she would have offered them the seal. The power of the seal was not an illusion; it was a great power. I don't recall any such cases, but, for example, when there were already differences between the "politicals" and the "economists,"[22] she could have said, "No, I won't put the seal on that purely economist leaflet." Although it never happened, I can readily imagine that if someone had printed a leaflet on a purely political topic, others, say, people associated with *Rabochaia Mysl'*, would not have permitted the seal to be put on it.[23] As I recall, *Rabochaia Mysl'* had its own seal; there was a member of that group, Kok, a Finn, who had "his own seal," and this assured him an enormous role, though that wasn't the only reason, of course.[24]

H: I know that after Martov's arrest, as we have already mentioned, the Union and the scope of its activity expanded. Was it at this point that you became involved in the work?

D: Yes, precisely at this point. The entire atmosphere in Petersburg was beginning to become more specifically political, although I wouldn't quite say it was heating up. By now it was not enough to talk at school or to get together in student groups. We looked for some sort of practical activity. The whole atmosphere had become strongly politicized, and, naturally, the organization required a larger number of people who could be used either for purely technical work or in part for political activity.

It was at this time that typewriters first appeared. They were very expensive, and there were few who could use them. But, above all, to have a typewriter you needed permission from the City Governor. Now Vera Vasil'evna Kozhevnikova, who was then Dan's wife, had a typewriter, supposedly to earn money since she had a son from her first marriage . . . she was a widow and her husband had committed suicide.[25] So she submitted a petition to the City Governor, and she was allowed to have a typewriter. This represented enormous technical progress for our circles. Before the material had been written by hand, which I couldn't do, because my handwriting was so bad that I never imagined that I would be allowed to write leaflets. But now leaflets or articles could be done on a typewriter, and this was my first assignment. I already knew how to type, although slowly. Later, as mimeograph machines became available, methods became more and more sophisticated. Then it was possible not only to make a stencil but to set up a machine at the home of some acquaintance, and run things off and take them to a secret address from which they would be brought to Stepan Ivanovich Radchenko, who would put the seal on them. Now it seems funny to hear all this, of course, but that was what we regarded as political activity in those days. Later, when people saw that I could be careful and thorough, Nevzorova suggested that I lead a circle, and I started to go to circles.

H: Your first circle was a tobacco-workers' group?

D: Yes, cigarette-makers. And soon I had another circle of weavers, also in 1896. It was very difficult, because the weavers were even less educated. Even so, I managed somehow. It is difficult to say why I thought I was doing a decent job. In any event, people didn't run from the meetings, although someone would occasionally miss a session . . . So there was, I think, some contact.

H: You have told me that Krupskaia offered you this group of cigarette-workers . . .

D: She and Nevzorova. These two women had a great deal to do with pushing me forward, so to speak.

H: And they also offered you the weaver's group?

D: Yes. They were in the Central Group then, probably, and possibly in the Group of Propagandists.[26] I don't know, since I never asked. I was afraid of asking too many questions and being thought of as nonconspiratorial. It was a good school for me in this sense. I think that my ability to control and take care of myself comes from this.

H: Were you involved in the weavers' strike in the summer of 1896?

D: Yes. The situation of the workers at that time was really horrible. The working day was endless. One of the demands was for a shorter working day. And then it was considered a very great victory when the eleven-hour or eleven-and-a-half-hour working day was introduced.[27] Of course, there was also talk of the eight-hour day; it was known to exist. But it was so unreal as a demand that the workers did not particularly believe us when we would say that it existed somewhere. So we were supposed to meet on Saturday in a circle to talk about I don't know what. Instead of that, we came and brought leaflets. The leaflets would state certain demands which we had ascertained with the workers earlier. A leaflet might suggest what was necessary, how to prepare, in short, what to do. We did not write the leaflets ourselves. All the information would be given to Nevzorova, and the leaflet would be written and printed.

H: Who would write the leaflets?

D: It varied a good deal. Gofman would write leaflets, and he felt he did a good job. He wrote in a workmanlike, straightforward fashion, and this appealed to the workers.

H: I would like to know a little more about the process of formation of groups.

D: Well, you would become involved in a group. You would ask about the working conditions and the major complaints. At the same time, you had to watch yourself to see that you did more than just ask. Some of the [women] workers liked it that we treated them equally, and male workers, too – that we were interested in them and talked to them. But, on the other hand, it was very frequent that the workers would wonder why they were being asked, and thought it better that I talk instead. But say, for example, it would be mentioned in the Group of Propagandists that word had come that things were very tense, say, in the textile industry, and that the workers were talking about a strike. It was necessary to determine what they were specifically dissatisfied with at the particular moment . . .

H: Would these conversations begin spontaneously?

D: Of course, because there was constant inflation. More and more frequently there would be complaints and stories about such-and-such, in such-and-such a shop . . . there would be talk that they were fed up, that they needed something. We would gather material and information, which took not less than two weeks. On the other hand, we couldn't drag things out, because a spontaneous strike could have broken out. I don't know the situation at the Putilov works then; probably it was the same. The fear was that the situation would degenerate into chaos, unless the strike was organized. Organization was very important: first, because responsibility for disorders of this sort could be very heavy; second, if the workers were to suffer greatly it would probably cause a sharp aversion to any illegal activity.

H: Yes, I see, but I want to reconstruct the process step by step. If I follow what you have said, there would be rumors that there was talk of a strike among the workers, and you would first learn about it when it was discussed in the Group of Propagandists.

D: Yes, you see, we were all subordinate to the Group of Propagandists, so to speak. We would receive our instructions from them about what line to take, and . . .

H: Who were in the Group of Propagandists?

D: Well, there was Gofman. He was probably in the Committee also.[28] Then there was Nevzorova, Zinaida Pavlovna . . .

H: You first learned about it through Nevzorova?

D: Yes, most of my contact was with her. I would meet with Gofman unofficially, so to speak. Officially, however, I was directly in touch with Zinaida Pavlovna.

H: Now, what directives did you receive from her?

D: She would say something like this: There is a slowdown among the workers, that is, they are ceasing to work regularly. There is talk and muttering. In short, some sort of disturbance is building up. What is it about? What are they thinking? There was still a long way to go before formulating demands, so I would meet with Nastia or Masha, with the workers, and later describe what they had said . . . Other people would visit circles and also pick up information and impressions. All this was put together and we would try to draw conclusions from it.

H: Did your directives always instruct you to find out what was going on with the workers, and would you try to do so through the circles?

D: Yes. I would ask them, "They say there's a slowdown going on?" "Yes, well, in such-and-such a shop there is such-and-such going on," or "They hung around together at lunchtime and talked." "What about?" And it would turn out, say, that they were dissatisfied because management was requiring that a weaver who normally operated one loom be responsible for two or even three. In Europe a worker could handle even five or six, because everything was mechanized. But that was still not the case in Petersburg; everything was very primitive. So it was hard for a worker to handle two looms and she would explain that whether she paid attention or not, the threads would break, and she would have to tie them. And the output was reckoned partly in terms of the number of *arshins* produced (they reckoned in *arshins* [28 inches] in those days) . . .

H: Was there as yet no talk about shortening the working day?

D: No, that came later. The output was the main thing, and it must be said that we were quite ignorant in this respect. I had never seen a loom, and Gofman would frequently tell me, "You should read at least one pamphlet on how they work, because you can't go on like this," and indeed I knew nothing about it. Of course, if a thread broke you could tie a knot, but if there were five knots per *arshin* the piece would be rejected and on top of that you would be fined. That was why the workers couldn't agree to the demand that they handle three looms. They wanted the maximum to be two. This was much more important, because the output quotas would depend upon it.

Shortening of the working day came much later, and not in an individual sector of industry but in industry as a whole. An individual factory or company could not shorten the working day. There it had to be a universal demand. Raising the wage rates was another matter; workers could demand this because it was not standardized. So we would gather the information, and then we would go to the secret meeting-place and state that such-and-such was being said. Sometimes other comments would be made ... now it was necessary to write up a leaflet. We collected all the information. We would figure it out, sometimes correctly, sometimes not, because so much of it was secondhand, but in any case the pamphlet would be written. We always tried (although we were not always successful) to show the drafts of leaflets to workers to get their comments. This was difficult because we couldn't meet every evening. And if we waited a whole week, the entire situation might be different. Sometimes we could get together the next day with some bright worker, not the entire circle, and hear her opinion; then we would dash back to the secret meeting-place with the results. So a text would be produced, given a final editing, handed over to the technical department, and the leaflet would be ready.

The next time you went to your circle you would bring, say, 30 copies with you. I don't know of a case when the women workers refused to distribute them. Very frequently the leaflets would include, in addition to economic demands, the slogan "Down with autocracy." And I personally don't remember it happening to me that there was dissatisfaction at this inclusion of politics. But I frequently heard from others that it happened. Later, of course, it was entirely impossible for us to distribute the leaflets. The men could still do this, but we women could not. For example, a student (not wearing school uniform or a hat, naturally, but wearing a cap) would go to a tavern, and there you had to drink vodka, though you could also order a round of tea. You would be given a glass and two teapots, one with boiling water and the other with tea, and you could drink tea. The clientele was informal, and you could talk without being introduced. So you would begin to talk, usually using the familiar form *ty*, but sometimes using *vy* – "Where do you work?" Or sometimes you would begin talking about your circle. They knew which taverns people gathered in. Sometimes you could simply hand out leaflets, saying, "Take a look at this leaflet I got." "Yeah, let me have a look." Sometimes they would say, "No thanks, I don't need it;" it varied. Gofman, who was very good at doing these things, told me about it later. He became very adept at stuffing leaflets into the jacket pockets of the workers he would talk to in taverns. They either didn't notice or pretended not to notice.

In any case, you could bring 30 or 40 leaflets to the circle, and the women could give them to their fellow-workers at the factory without much risk. It was a fairly primitive method of dissemination. Later, at the end of the working day, the workers might hang around. In general, they were supposed to leave immediately, but sometimes management would not take measures to make them leave right away. Then an exchange of opinions would begin, or sometimes a delegate from a shop or section would be elected. Without any democratic rules, of course – someone would say, "There's that gal Nastia ... she's got a quick tongue. Let her speak for our shop." In this way a temporary, undefined sort of group would arise, and then it would submit demands to management. In general, the management was not very hostile to this. I now think (although I didn't think so at the time) that probably they felt that organized protest was more advantageous to them than trying to exchange words with the workers. After all, they might smash up the entire factory. I believe that this was the principal motive. And if the group did not receive a favorable answer, someone would come into the shop and say, "Let's knock off," and they would stop working. Although there was no voting or formal democratic procedure, the workers would usually go along.

H: All of them? Almost all?

D: Yes, almost all . . . I think it was less important for the women. The men were probably afraid that they would be beaten up if they didn't go along, while the women were not about to fight. But evidently this fear of public opinion already existed and was fairly strong.

H: How long did this particular strike [among the weavers] last?

D: More than a week, I think; perhaps ten days . . .

H: And what was the upshot?

D: First of all the penalty system was regularized. Then, if I remember correctly, they were not made to work with three looms, but only with two. I believe that this was quite acceptable in practice. I can't say whether there were improvements in the loom; I didn't know that aspect very well even then. But even this small victory greatly enhanced the authority and prestige of the organization. Now you could say, "I have some leaflets for you," and they knew what it was about. Probably the influence of those workers who were activists in the affair also increased. Still, there were arrests . . . of course, if they had arrested everyone, the whole thing would have been immediately suppressed, but they didn't. They might arrest a few of the noisier ones. Doubtless the successes were small; the demands were quite minimal. You could say that they left the factories' operation entirely unaffected. The management could make such concessions without any detriment to itself. And since these concessions came so late, it was pure profit for management.

H: So the Union flourished as a result of these successes in 1896?

D: Yes, because its prestige was enhanced. I think that the shortening of the working day came later, in 1897, but it was talked about even earlier, although this demand did not immediately take shape on the part of the workers, and then only after the strike. The fact is that this didn't even depend on the good will of management. It had to be done through the Factory Inspectorate,[29] so that it was a fairly complicated process. What was important, though, was that the issue could be placed on the agenda. And here there was success. I think that the role of the organization was quite considerable in this respect. It helped the workers to formulate their demands.

H: Were you involved in the big weavers' strike of 1897?

D: As for the weavers, I influenced them and, in turn, was influenced by them, so to speak. For me it was something new; we all learned. We did not arrive with ready-made opinions – we attempted to learn from the workers exactly what they wanted. And there was always some conflict of interest here. First, the workers were not very convinced that the demands could be achieved and regarded the effort as wasted time. They felt it was better to ask us questions. Sometimes they would just ask about geography, they were interested in that. We had to struggle somewhat to draw them out.

As I said, I was only involved with women workers and never went to men's circles. But I met a few men workers through Gofman. Then he was arrested, and since I knew some of his people I would meet with the better-educated workers at home. This was my contact with them. There we would speak, for example, about the history of the revolutionary movement. Since I was fairly well acquainted with it, I could take part and be useful. We would ask, for example, "Do you know who Kravchinskii was?" Somewhere they had read that Kravchinskii had killed Mezentsov. Since I read a lot and knew all that fairly well, I could describe it quite vividly. This was appreciated, but it was on another plane ... I knew little about the situation in the factories and workers' life. I must admit that I felt I had nothing to offer in this area.

For example, when Lenin was in jail he wrote a pamphlet about fines ... and many of us gathered material for it. I was a considerable authority in this respect. The women workers would tell me how much they earned – 11 or 18 rubles a month, I don't remember. A worker would count on it, and yet when payday came she would receive only 14 – she would be fined three rubles. Some worker at the Skorokhod factory[30] complained that they fined you mercilessly. You put a heel on crooked and they fine you almost a ruble for it. "But perhaps this is right," said Lenin, "Since we can't have footwear with crooked heels!" It was not just that you should have to pay for a slightly crooked heel – what was required was a much higher level, that the worker treat his labor with respect and have some professional aspirations so as to do good work. This did not come quickly to the Russian proletariat.

H: If we could return to the strikes of 1897, I would like to know the following: I imagine the workers had been saying for a long time that they worked too long, and so forth. What would be the first spark that would generate a strike? When did you yourself first learn that there was a possibility of a strike for shortening the working day?

D: Well, when you went to the women's circle and met with the workers, the constant topics were that they were at the end of their rope, that they were totally drained ... but it was a while before they realized that it was necessary to make demands on management. But, then, there were people who were always saying that the agreement of the management was not enough. Some sort of legislation, some act, some government regulation was necessary. And there were many conversations on this topic. There was no term like "planned economy" in those days. It seemed as though the management of Laferma or the Maxwell textile factory could declare a seven-hour or nine-hour working day tomorrow ... It was a fairly lengthy and complicated process to formulate the entire problem properly within the [framework of the] contemporary capitalist world and police state. And it was necessary to explain this, and yet at the same time, I remember very well their saying that the girls couldn't stand it any longer! Finally, members of the Union who were working regularly became more and more aware that the time was ripe. They began to collect demands, so to speak . . .

H: When did you first learn of it?

D: I don't remember, but in any case when we shared our information with the organization, it turned out that talk about it was becoming more and more frequent everywhere. Then it was proposed to prepare a leaflet . . . "Say, do you need a leaflet in your circle?" Not everyone would agree. Some would say, "No, it won't go over with us – the women aren't in favor," while others would say, "No, we need to try; perhaps they will respond." And ultimately, discussions of the matter would be held in the circles. People who had just told you that they were fed up and there was a slowdown were still afraid. They would say it was a good idea to go on strike, perhaps we would win, perhaps not . . . but then there would be no pay! This was a very serious problem. So the whole thing was a very gradual and somewhat painful process. But in the end, the activist minority gave a great impetus, and public opinion at the factory leaned toward a strike. I think that the strike lasted a fairly long time and it was very important that the workers receive some assistance on paydays during the strike. So funds were collected in Petersburg society to help the strikers. This was also of influence and enhanced [our prestige].

H: I would like to know if the Union for Struggle made the decision [on the strike].

D: It couldn't.

H: I understand, but would the leaflets mention a decision to strike?

D: Such leaflets would be written up and disseminated before the strike. But I don't remember that the leaflets ever specified a date for a strike to begin. In general, the situation heated up gradually. Finally, one day at some factory someone like a foreman (in those times only men, not women, could be foreman) would announce that there was a great deal of talk or that work was going badly . . . and eventually some worker would answer that they didn't want it any more, that they couldn't any longer, and so forth. Very frequently they would stop working at two o'clock and leave, not the factory but their work stations. And so it would begin. A meeting, a rather disorderly exchange of opinions, would be arranged . . . Some would say that a strike was needed, and here the older weavers would object, "Hey fellows, girls, stop this talk – you'll pay for it," and so forth. Then they would be rebuffed by others who claimed that they had endured enough already . . . In this way the entire situation would gradually become imbued with an atmosphere of combat. A decision would be made: "We're going on strike . . . " At this instant the most difficult thing for the people who were aware of the situation was to prevent it from turning into havoc and the smashing of machines. Many, many times I heard that this was a matter of great concern since, first, major repressions were feared, and, second, there was a feeling among the more aware proletariat that the fault did not lie in the machines. In the textile factories it was very easy to cut up the entire fabric – you simply took the stretched threads and cut them – but the damage could not be repaired. Even the workers themselves would not permit it. I would imagine that it was very difficult to carry out such sabotage in metal-working factories. There, there was something else: putting out the smelting furnaces. It was extremely expensive to start them up again.

H: Do you remember what happened immediately after this strike began?

D: Yes, if they had gone on strike, they would not go to work the next day. Or they would go and not be admitted to the factory. Then they would hang around the gates and an organized meeting would result. This would be dispersed, without the police, but rather mercilessly. Still, the workers would naturally go back to the office the next day to find out what was happening – "Well, you're striking – if you starve it's your problem!"

H: Was this strike a major event for society?

D: Yes. At that time it was very easy to collect money and to transmit it through the circles. I remember well that some assistance for the strikers came from abroad, from Belgium and Germany, I believe. It was in this way that talk of the solidarity of the proletariat went from being a base principle to something with flesh and blood, so to speak. It had colossal impact.

H: From what sectors of society did you receive money?

D: From the students. It was collected in the university. And then there was Kalmykova. I don't think that it was just her money that she gave. She might have collected it from teachers in the Sunday schools. They collected it in turn from the students. The sums were fairly large. I don't know how they were distributed; it was the workers' own affair.

H: Was this the first time that you received large amounts of money from society?

D: Relatively large amounts, yes. In addition, it was a symptom that the proletariat was entering the political arena. People from society felt themselves obligated to respond in some way. We could turn to a person like Tugan-Baranovskii and say that we were collecting for this purpose . . . that was very easy. But even less political people could be approached. Sometimes we said it was for a sick fellow-student. Earlier, that had always been the approach. Then gradually we could speak openly . . . "Yes, it's for striking workers." This evoked sympathy and it was considered almost improper not to give. Many of the givers were poor students – there were a great many of them. They would give 20 kopecks each. But in general the sums collected were quite respectable.

H: I know that at this time, between the summer of 1896 and the winter of 1897, when you were highly successful, not only did the organization expand, but its character and state of mind changed.

D: Yes, it became more political. New elements started to become prominent, and, as we said, the movement had advanced to a higher level. That was the formula used.

H: What did it mean?

D: It meant that, so to speak, the separate workers' movement, imbued with the desire to improve the position of the workers, was becoming more and more of a political factor. More in our awareness, perhaps, than in reality. But it seemed that any improvement had to deal with the obstacle of the police. So now it was necessary to move on and try to soften the political regime. There were debates as to whether this was possible by pressure on the government or on management, or whether it was possible at all, or whether a revolutionary, frontal attack was needed. The problem was not resolved, but I feel that it was great progress that this issue should appear on the agenda. It raised not only our self-assurance, but the workers' as well. Women workers were not very involved; their political level was low. Among men workers such as the typographers, however, there was already an awareness that they were a political factor. It is true, I can't recall a single strike by the typographers at that time; their situation was somewhat better than that of other workers. Perhaps such a strike would have become so immediately political that there was fear of doing it. When women workers struck in the city, society might be entirely unaware of it. While if *Novoe Vremia*[31] had not appeared, it would have been a European scandal.

Fourth interview

H: I would like to dwell on the years 1896 and 1897. How and when did you begin to feel that not all was well in the [Petersburg] Union of Struggle?

D: To be frank, it didn't happen all at once. First, I was very young and revolutionary organization had great prestige in my eyes. I, and everyone else too, felt that everything was going quite well. Our work was expanding. Earlier, we were printing a certain number of leaflets and now we could print even more. Such statistics were a great comfort to us; they made us very optimistic. I believe that the major disagreements were over the issue of assessing the economic struggle.

H: I know, but I would like to determine, if possible, how these disagreements developed as you observed them. First, were you aware at that time of the disagreements between the "oldsters" and the new leadership of the Union for Struggle in 1897?

D: I don't remember exactly, it was 60 years ago. But something filtered through. It had not yet taken on the proportions of an insuperable conflict. I think that the gradual sentiment [among the *intelligenty* in the organization] that "piecemeal tinkering" [*kustarnichestvo*] should be done away with was a factor.[1] People became aware, but very gradually, that the organization needed to be centralized and better organized. [At the same time], the Union for Struggle and other organizations included worker members. I believe that it is wrong to state, as is done now, that there was a bitter conflict between workers and *intelligenty*. I personally never saw any such thing on the part of either. But in general the workers gradually came to feel that, essentially, they could deal with the situation as well as members of the intelligentsia. There was that feeling. Of course, if they found some mature *intelligent*, they would eagerly try to learn from him. But if the *intelligent* was someone like myself, very young and inexperienced, well, for women workers such as weavers I think I was very good authority, but for a male metal worker I wasn't so great. It was not that they doubted my knowledge – I was still much more educated than they. But when I heard talk about workers' life and about the demands that grew out of that life, I would go blank and not understand. They were the masters in that realm.

H: I would like to establish step by step how the opposition to the Economist movement developed. As you saw it, who took control of the political tendencies and began to oppose the Economists in Petersburg in 1897 and 1898?

D: The situation was clearer by 1898. A longing and yearning for political action was very strong; there was an urge to organize, and a great many organizations formed. But because communication was very poor (everything was conspiratorial and people were afraid), there was sometimes duplication and lack of understanding. Why did the Group of Twenty[2] and the "Socialist"[3] group not join forces at the outset? Because of the conspiratorial conditions and so forth. But as soon as they began to associate with each other, they saw that they could work together. I think that such things led us to think that, given the backward conditions of Russia, we could organize only around party literature. Later this was one of Lenin's premises. Both Lenin and Martov felt equally that organization was possible only around a general Russian newspaper. As far as I remember, when we worked in the *Rabochee Znamia* group[4] and created an organ with a highly political line, we printed "Organ of Russian [*Russkaia*] Social Democracy" on the first issue. When, sometime later, we received the first issue of *Iskra*,[5] we were horrified to see that it called itself "*Rossiiskaia*."[6] Such was the lack of communication. This was a great catastrophe for us.

H: I would like to know more about the formation of *Rabochee Znamia*. Levitskii says that after 1898 this organization took over from another group with the same name, and he mentions the Russian Social-Democratic Party.

D: Rabochee Znamia arose at the same time, or perhaps a little earlier, in the western region (in Belostok, and so forth), and in Petersburg. In Petersburg there were considerable intellectual forces who could write and considered themselves well-informed politically. In the western regions there were Jewish workers, like Moisei Lur'e, who were miles ahead of us technically and who were infected by the general political climate.[7] But they were incapable of formulating their ideas. They had a printing shop and could print newspapers, but they didn't know what to print in them.

H: What specific details do you remember about how you and Sergei became involved in *Rabochee Znamia?*

D: It was in the air. We wanted political activity, and since we were sick of the Economism in the Union for Struggle, we tried to find like-minded people somewhere else.

H: And how did you find such people?

D: Well, Smirnov and Antropov – Sergei brought them around.[8] I don't know how he met them; perhaps it was through Ol'ga Zvezdochetova, who was in Petersburg then, or perhaps in some other way. They and Sergei were very good friends. I knew them less well. Sergei and I knew the Savinkovs from childhood. We met in the Caucasus. We also met Rutenberg through them.[9] Now it is very difficult to say. Such things somehow just happened. I knew Iordanskii and Lodyzhenskii earlier from student circles.[10]

H: I don't remember the details, but I know that you were involved in printing leaflets at that time. There were strikes at the Maxwell and Paul factories . . .[11]

D: Yes, the English textile mills.

H: Can you describe these strikes and your activities?

D: The sense of animation at that time affected even the most backward segment of the proletariat, the women. There were male textile workers, but I was only involved with the women weavers. Given the repressive conditions of the times, women could propagandize only among other women. I went to a circle regularly, once a week. The same girls would come regularly, almost every time – six or eight of them. I don't remember that there were more. The group was planned so that we would usually talk about the latest political events. Everything had to be discussed and explained to them in great detail. I should say that the lack of culture [*nekulturnost'*] of these girls was immense. For example, when we talked about the democratic system in Europe, they simply couldn't understand that the workers could need something more, once they already had that. They didn't even quite believe me when I told them that in France no one could come up to you on the street and arrest you.

H: I would like to establish how leaflets about the working day were printed.

D: A fellow named Tatarinov was involved. He was an *intelligent*, a legal person, and was involved with the Red Cross.[12] But [his help to us] was entirely apart from the Red Cross. He never would have risked that. There were problems with the mimeographing then. First, you had to write out the text by hand, in block letters. (If I remember rightly, it was in 1899 that Vera Vasil'evna Kozhevnikova obtained permission to buy a Remington machine.) Later this was given to Tatarinov, who gave us the copies. There was also a woman called Iuliia Toporkova, also a society woman.[13] Generally, it was people from society who furnished help such as mimeographing and other technical services. And it was very disinterestedly, because we only scorned them in return, as I have already said. But we couldn't have done without them. Of course, you might ask why we couldn't do it ourselves. It was because we felt (and perhaps with reason) that society people would arouse less suspicion and reduce the possibility of arrests. Iuliia Toporkova helped us continuously over a long time. These were people who later all turned out to be associated with the Union of Liberation and the liberals.[14] I understand now that they learned illegal techniques in our circle, though in fact they didn't belong to it. They simply generously let themselves be used for our purpose. Later they learned and began to make use of it for themselves.

From such facts, Axelrod came to the fairly generalized conclusion that it was precisely in this sense that the hegemony of the proletariat was to be understood;[15] not that the proletariat will command, but that it will guide the entire struggle. That was a noble and altruistic interpretation of hegemony, but one with which Lenin disagreed entirely.

H: I know that you first touched upon political topics in these leaflets. Do you recall what the results were?

D: At the moment I can't. But they often did not meet with sympathy on the part of the workers who were apprehensive about them. You could suffer for a leaflet which talked about wage increases; that, at least, was something to suffer for. But purely political and, in particular, anti-tsarist slogans always aroused some apprehension. This indicates that the workers were being radicalized quite slowly. Later the process was rapid, but this was the very beginning. And I remember the words, spoken not very openly, "Why is this [reference to politics] needed?" When we began to explain, the workers would reply, "Yes, all that's true, of course, we can't do without it, without freedom, but still . . . " In this respect there was a very great difference between the intelligentsia part of Social Democracy and the working mass. I even assume that if there had not been some push from the *intelligenty*, the general awareness would not have been so soon in coming. I think that the *narodniki* must have encountered the same difficulties among the peasantry.

*   *   *

H: I would like to turn back somewhat to put together a picture of the activities of your brother, Sergei Osipovich, from the autumn of 1896 when he entered the university, until he was arrested in December 1898.

D: Sergei spent only a short time in the student movement, which he didn't have much respect for. He wanted to be with workers from the beginning. Even earlier, when he was 15 or 16, and Nadezhda Osipovna was 19, he often said in our conversations that the hardest thing was to get into the working-class milieu. He would say, naively, "For your girls it's nothing. Marry a worker and you're with the workers." But neither Nadezhda nor I wanted to marry a worker. We couldn't tell him that, so we would ask, "And why don't you marry a worker yourself?" His answer was, "I know you – if I married a worker tomorrow you would make an *intelligent* out of her." He was no less educated than the rest of us. But for him practice overshadowed theory so much that he often seemed almost primitive. But he was not primitive at all.

H: What faculty was he in?

D: I don't remember. It might have been Natural Science or perhaps Jurisprudence. It played such a small part in his life that I don't remember at all.

H: And he was there only six months, until approximately January 1897 [when he was arrested for the first time]?

D: Yes, in general he had no contact with the students. Student life meant nothing to him. I must say that all his friends, Nogin,[16] Antropov, and the rest, were older than he. But he never lagged behind them in overall knowledge. Still, all this was of lesser importance; for him it was practice that was important. Such-and-such must be done today. He is remembered in the history of our party as a *praktik.*[17]

H: I would like to try to get a notion of your parents' attitude. They had already had trouble with Iulii Osipovich. You and Sergei were arrested around January 1897, and he was barred from reentering the university. What did he do?

D: He lived at home. Since he was a minor, he could live with his father. Probably he gave lessons and earned something. It was very little, but life at home was cheap – he never took money from our parents, he was always quite particular about that. The fact that we were living off our father in the apartment was unimportant; what was important was that we were not taking money. Naturally, Father wanted his children to graduate from a higher institution. This was very important among Jews, because it conferred residency rights.[18] This was important, in Father's opinion. Sergei was kicked out of the university, and poor Volodia didn't even get in. He was still in the *gimnazium* when he was arrested. What were things coming to? Father didn't think he had the right to persuade us by making us think of him. He understood that this was no argument, and never used it. He thought the following reasoning was proper: "Look, if you don't graduate from the university, you won't have residency rights. What if you want to live in a large city? And you know that it would be unpleasant for me if any of you were to be baptized." Sergei would reply, "And why would I be baptized?" "Well, just for residency rights. . . . " "You think that's a big deal? I'll make myself a false passport and live with that." Father didn't like that. First, he thought that to be a university graduate was a great honor. But to live on a false passport was already on the verge of ill-repute. And he would say, "Well, imagine if you were to fall in love with a Russian girl – then would you want to convert?" Sergei would say, "No." "And what will you do?" "Why should I get married in Church? I will have a civil marriage." In short, Sergei always had an answer for everything. Not a very convincing answer, perhaps, but one that satisfied him, and he never made any concessions. At this time he read a great deal and learned a lot. Primarily he was involved in various technical matters. He was very expert at that. He organized the printing of leaflets. He was very adept at disseminating them. He was considered simply remarkable in this respect. He could go to a tavern beyond the Nevskaia Zastava – you could drink tea there as well as vodka – and start talking to workers and was able to get chummy with them very rapidly. As a result he might hand out 50 leaflets in the tavern.

H: At this time, 1897, was his activity in workers' circles connected with the Union for Struggle?

D: Yes, of course, but he was not on the Committee of the Union because of his youth. But he was on the Board of Propagandists. . . .

H: Do you remember what worker circles Sergei frequented?

D: I think that there was one behind the Nevskaia Zastava and, if I remember correctly, at the Putilov works. He had connections with the metal workers, the most advanced workers. Though Sergei was very political, he was very much interested in the European trade union movement. And he told us a great deal. I think that he dreamt of becoming the secretary of a trade union. He didn't go beyond that. He thought that a trade-union secretary was a person who could answer all questions and be needed. He did not think of being number one; that didn't interest him at all. But to be absolutely indispensable – not to have power but to be needed so that it was impossible to get along without him – suited him very well.

H: Like Radchenko?

D: Yes, more or less like Radchenko, if you like. Except that Radchenko was very clandestine, while Sergei, because of his youth, needed contact with people more, to talk and so forth, which Radchenko wouldn't allow himself. Later, in 1905, when there were a number of party publishing houses, Sergei became passionately involved in all of them. He was very expert in this. He could start up a publishing house without a kopeck. He was a practical worker, beginning with the leaflets and going on to publishing concerns.

H: What was Nadezhda doing at this time?

D: Nadezhda was less involved in politics than we. First, she was a student and wanted to finish. Second, she felt more responsibility toward our parents. It seemed to her that someone in the end had to look after them. In this respect she had a very self-sacrificing nature. She felt that if none of the rest wanted to, then she should. Of course, she also watched out for us. We were three years apart in age, but that was a considerable difference at that time. Though she was two years younger than Iulii, she felt that she should watch out for and take care of him too. And he accepted this. When he was arrested, it was to her that he gave all his instructions at the last moment in the apartment – tell such-and-such to do so-and-so. He knew that she was very punctilious, pedantic, and so forth. I think that, of all of us, she had the greatest sense of responsibility. She was never involved in the circles, as far as I can remember. She tended more to open activity. Later, she was a good teacher. She was the favorite student of Professor Lesgaft. His were courses which didn't give you any rights so they were rather strange. Formally, they were about anatomy, but in practice they dealt with the moral philosophy of life. Lesgaft's courses were in effect a hangout where any person from the Social-Democratic organization could come and sit in on lectures. That wasn't important, but you could bring some political literature or get literature, all at Lesgaft's courses.

H: In December 1898 you were all arrested, yourself, Sergei, and other members of *Rabochee Znamia.* How long were you arrested for?

D: For a short time. After that I went to Orel province, and then to Yalta. In Orel province I was very much cut off from everything, but in Yalta I was living in a very political milieu. There were a fair number of people who were under surveillance in Yalta, and Gorkii, whom I got to know quite well, was living there. Later, Tugan-Baranovskii came there with his wife, whom I was very close to. There was a fairly broad group of Russian intelligentsia, in particular Marxist intelligentsia. This had to do with the Tokmakov family, a very rich family that had been living there a long time. They had two daughters. One married the Marxist Nikolai Vodovozov, the brother of Vasilii Vasil'evich Vodovosov, who was well known. He was one of the first Marxists, but he soon died of tuberculosis.[19] His widow, Mariia Ivanovna, the Tokmakov daughter, set up a publishing house in memory of her husband, and published various Marxist books. She lived close to Yalta. Her sister married Sergei Nikolaevich Bulgakov, who later became a priest. But at that time he was a Marxist, and groups of intelligentsia were always gathered around them.[20] They were not connected with Tolstoi personally, but all these groups were in contact. Life in Yalta was on a very high intellectual level. Though there was no movement, because it was a resort and not an industrial town, there was a constant coming and going of intelligentsia and life was very intense. We received all sorts of literature, "thick journals," and so forth. When Cherevanin came, we arranged a debate between him and Tugan-Baranovskii.[21] The topic was Marx, Marxism, and Bernsteinism and orthodox Marxism.[22] Such gatherings were possible because we could meet in Olenza, a few kilometers from Yalta, at the Tokmakovs' house. Then Martov came to visit me in Yalta, probably in the middle of 1900. He was very dissatisfied with my friendship with Tugan-Baranovskii.

H: Did he regard him as an enemy already?

D: Yes, in general he was fairly quick to do that. He also told us a great deal about his plans for *Iskra.* This was a constant topic – that it was necessary to set up a general Russian newspaper since this was the only, or at any rate the best, method of organizing a party. The first task was the creation of a party, a very centralized party with severe discipline of ideas and a very sharp aversion to Bernsteinism, which was already very much in vogue.

H: When you had these conversations with Iulii Osipovich, did he say that he intended to set up the newspaper in conjunction with the Emancipation of Labor group?[23]

D: For him it was clear that Emancipation of Labor was the ultimate authority. Now it is hard to imagine – it was really very dramatic – the colossal importance that Plekhanov had for Russian Social Democracy. At that time none of us had ever met him personally, so that many of his unpleasant traits were entirely unknown to us. But his erudition was enormous. We were very proud that our Russian Plekhanov ranked among the great minds of Europe. Plekhanov was almost a legendary figure. For example, take his speech on Kazan' Square. We had spoken on Kazan' Square ourselves, but in our imagination Plekhanov's appearance was entirely unique. Then there was his pamphlet, *Our Differences.* Finally, the Beltov book, which caused a complete change in outlook. I now often argue with Sapir, who thinks that the chief creator of Menshevism was Axelrod.[24] This is a serious error. Axelrod was an incomparable tactician, but Plekhanov was the real father of Russian Social Democracy.

H: I have the impression that they [Martov, Lenin] initially planned to publish a journal in Russia.

D: That was the dream, but it was clearly impossible. *Iuzhnii Rabochii* already existed at the time and had a very good reputation.[25] It was the prototype of a general Russian newspaper in the eyes of some, and it was natural to think that we too could also publish a newspaper in Russia. But it became clear very soon that no editorial board could be assured of continuity. Today you would get going, tomorrow either the editors would be arrested or the printing shop would be raided. Soon people began to think about publishing abroad, but in such a way that it would seem that the newspaper was being published in Russia.

*   *   *

H: Let us now turn to the time of your return to Petersburg in 1900. My first question is this: when you arrived in Petersburg from Yalta, what changes did you feel had taken place in the social climate over those two years, and what contacts did you have in literary circles, particularly the *Russkoe Bogatstvo* circle?

D: What struck me more than anything else about the people who gathered at *Russkoe Bogatstvo* was their new position. I had known them earlier, at the time of debates between Marxists and *narodniki.*[26] Then we were on the offensive; they, on the defensive. They were still imbued with the old attitudes, and drew all their strength from the respect we felt toward them as figures of a bygone era. Now these same people were starting to show some life; they felt that the time had not yet come for them to retire and that there was a place for them in contemporary Russia. This was connected with the political animation that began to be felt by 1900. For example, Annenskii was interesting not only because he had once done something, but also because he now had new questions regarding the current state of affairs.[27] It seemed to him that an age was dawning that would allow him and the others like him to have their way again. There was the lure of something new. Perhaps this explains why interest in the Legal Marxists had declined somewhat.[28] After Yalta, Tugan-Baranovskii and Bulgakov no longer seemed to be the friends they were during the debate with the *narodniki.* They had sort of lost their flavor. I think this was decisive in drawing me into democratic, and not just Marxist, intellectual circles.

There was also a purely personal element. My husband, Dr. Kantsel, though he also considered himself a socialist and a Social Democrat, was then intensely involved in the Literary Committee, and he had ties with these people.[29] So it was natural for me to frequent that milieu. But besides this quite extraneous matter, I now think – I was not so acutely aware of it then – the novelty of people who only yesterday seemed to have outlived their time, to have spent their life interests completely, was impressive, captivating. Not that I agreed with them, but they were interesting.

H: Was this spirit of the times, that you noticed in Annenskii and Mikhailovskii, also the result of the fact that they had the younger generation of students with them?

D: Probably.

H: Did you meet with the young generation – Peshekhonov,[30] Chernov,[31] and so forth?

D: I didn't know Chernov. Peshekhonov was respected but very drab. Miakotin was much more vivid.[32] He was very passionate and excitable, and was nicknamed "furious Vissarion." He would flare up, speak out loudly and ardently, and so forth. Of course, he was imbued with this contemporary spirit, and this was precisely what we younger people were so interested in at the meetings of *Russkoe Bogatstvo*. Here were people out of the past who were now acting as our contemporaries and opponents, and we had to argue with them. And there were things to argue about.

H: How do you explain this rebirth of *narodnichestvo?* When you saw these people, how did they seem?

D: I wouldn't swear to it, but I think it was like this: of course, the *narodniki*'s hopes in the peasantry had been wrong and this had left them bankrupt. But now a new era was beginning when it was not so much the struggle for socialism that was important for us as the political struggle. It seemed that the political struggle could and should become nation-wide. Which meant it was impossible to ignore the enormous mass of the peasantry, the principal part of the population. And perhaps the *narodniki*'s path to the peasantry was shorter than ours. If a nationwide movement really did arise, some part would fall to them; the *narodniki* too would contribute something. I wouldn't say that I formulated it in this way then. But it appeared that these apparently obsolete people could now become active participants in a process which perhaps we didn't name then, but which was conceived as a nation-wide political movement.

H: Did you feel that this neo-*narodnichestvo* would be any substantial competition for the Social-Democrats for the leadership of this nationwide movement?

D: I don't think we formulated it that way. We never used the word "hegemony" then. But I think that each of us felt that we would naturally be the vanguard. Without much justification, but that was the way we felt. And, like any commander, we were happy that the ranks were swelling. This was definitely the case. The students of the 1890s were very willing to offer all sorts of technical assistance to the Social-Democratic organization, and so forth. By 1900, there was something new. The student movement had not yet taken shape, but there appeared separate progressive [student] organizations and a great desire to form into a political movement. It is hard to say what the feelings of the students were toward the Populists and the Marxists, but I think they were split "fifty-fifty." They attached themselves to any political movement. I even believe that there was some preference for the *narodniki* among the students, because we Marxists spoke rather tactlessly.

H: In regard to the student movement?

D: Yes, to us it was second-class. . . .

H: What was the organization at St. Petersburg University that called itself the "Coalition"? Why was it called that?

D: Because it included *narodniki* and Marxists. There was already an unofficial, illegal, organization of student circles, with their *starosty.*[33] These were student leaders who did not pursue any formally political goals, but were involved with student conditions and student self-determination. Formally and in practice, the *starosty* were the go-betweens for the students and teaching staff. They were intended to deal with purely academic matters, but since the times were political, this organization rapidly grew into a political one. Since the *starosty* differed in their orientation, there was the so-called Coalition Committee. There were also unaffiliated people.

H: What was the *kassa* [treasury] of the radicals?

D: I think that it encompassed students who had more definite political attitudes and were inclined not to *narodnichestvo* but to the rebirth of the People's Will; in short, elements which were later to become Socialist Revolutionaries. This group was very clandestine, so that we did not know much about it; but the general impression was such.

So far as I know, there were leftist organizations in other institutions of higher education, like the Technological Institute, which was very radical, and even the Institute of Means of Communcation, where there were few radicals. The Institute of Forestry was very radical, perhaps because forestry was not a very good career, and there wasn't much one could do with forestry. For some reason, the writer Mikhailovskii was in touch with the Institute of Means of Communication more than the others. As I remember, it was said that this institute had a particularly strong contingent of Polish intelligentsia. Somehow, it was easy for Poles to go there. The Poles who became involved in Russian politics were very radical. But this was a rather separate group. In general, student life in 1900 struck me by its great animation – like a seething cauldron. Later, when there were student disturbances, it was not unexpected. We had already been prepared for this.

H: Were there Social Democrats in the radical *kassa?*

D: Formally, it was entirely possible, but I never heard of a Social Democrat who was involved. I imagine that they were.

H: I know that in general the Petersburg Union for Struggle took a negative view of participation in such organizations at that time.

D: The Union maintained that a person who became involved in a student organization and took part in the student movement was exposing himself a great deal and the police would know of him. If you admitted such a person to a workers' circle, you would destroy the entire circle. Psychologically, I think they underestimated the mood of the youth. There was a need to play some kind of role, and student circles attracted a great many.

But it certainly repelled party people. Gorev describes this situation in detail and very well in his memoirs.[34]

H: At this time did you also establish contacts with the *Rabochee Znamia?*

D: Yes, purely personal ones.

H: What changes did you notice in this organization as compared to 1897?

D: The *Rabochee Znamia* people had always been very politicized, so that there was no great difference. I think that the most serious feeling that I encountered was a striving for centralization and organization not just of local workers, as in any other city, but countrywide. I don't recall that there was much mention of the First Congress of the RSDRP prior to this time.[35] We even knew little about it and, truthfully, were not very interested – it was already in the remote past. As regards the feeling that it was necessary to organize a centralized party, I think that, subconsciously, many of us associated such a party with what the People's Will had been. Of course, we were more European in education and had the European type of social-ist party in mind, but since conditions were not exactly the same, we could not imagine a German-type party in illegal conditions. We read eagerly, asked our acquaintances, and tried to think up guidelines for how to act. But all of this was abstract, of course. In contrast, we understood, or thought we understood, the much more concrete notion of a strictly clan-destine party with very limited numbers. At this moment, centralization was a very important factor for us.

Moreover, it became apparent that we needed to organize not only our activity but also our brains, our ideology. Somehow organization had to lead to an intellectual discipline. We all believed firmly in the development of the workers' movement in Russia and in the victory of our ideas. But we could not ignore the fact that concretely people, even our people, were com-ing up with different solutions to these problems. This, of course, was harmful to the cause. Many of us felt that it might be quite harmful to orga-nize strikes over every trivial issue. It was not a very widespread notion, but there were such thoughts – that this fragmented our strength and that even though we were not preparing for the decisive moment, we still needed some sort of systematic planning, and not just within the limits of a circle or some single local group, but within a larger, unified entity. But for this it was first necessary to agree ideologically, so to speak.

The push toward unification involved everyone, I believe. Of course, if there had been any possibility for a trade union movement, it might have carried the day, but there was no such possibility. Hence, in the workers' milieu, unification was thought of only in terms of political organization, not trade union or economic. And the party was faced with the problem that the workers were demanding organization along these lines.

H: I would like to determine if the attitudes were in fact like this: now it was evident that all the potential for a national movement against abso-lutism was at hand. For the Social Democrats to mobilize and direct it, a central party was required. Did such a conception exist?

D: Yes, of course.

H: You said that ultimately the conception of such a centralized party was that of the People's Will. . . .

D: When we said that we have to direct the movement, this meant one thing in our meager experience: the Executive Committee of the People's Will. Naturally, we understood that this could not be repeated, but as a model of a center of practical activity, the idea was unquestionably in vogue. We didn't talk of an Executive Committee, but of a Central Committee. To direct the movement we also had to have some kind of common ideology. With our impoverished resources and the dreadful police conditions, propaganda and agitation were on a small, primitive [*kustar'*] scale. When talking to those workers whom you could talk to, we would speak of how they should demand ten kopecks more per box of cigarettes. But how could this be connected with the struggle with autocracy? It was rather hard. It was exactly these kopecks that interested the cigarette workers; the national struggle was far beyond their imaginations. So it was necessary to exert some influence on the workers along these lines too. The Economists of the time felt that it might even be harmful to discuss [the political question] because you might get the following answer [from the workers]: "This problem of the autocracy may be important for you intellectuals, but for us it isn't so basic; economic conditions must be improved first." I have put it rather crudely and primitively, but such attitudes unquestionably existed.

H: At that time did you foresee the possibility that there would be other revolutionary or oppositional parties?

D: We didn't give it much thought. The Socialist Revolutionaries were not far off in this sense, and no one even dreamed that the bourgeoisie might organize itself.

H: So, roughly, the picture was one of a centralized party which would direct a very broad and less well-organized movement.

D: There would be an organization over the movement, so to speak. This was considered natural and not alarming; we had to make the experiment in order to unify the leadership and the movement. This was not a pre-existing conviction; different people arrived at it gradually in their own time. It was not a starting point. And I think it is worth mentioning that at that time we did not believe an oppositionist party was possible, that is, one that could act within the bounds of autocracy, a constitutional party. No such example existed and we had no experience of such things.

H: As you have remarked, at this point there was a cooling-off of feeling toward the legal Marxists, Struve, Tugan-Baranovskii, and others. In Petersburg, how did you conceive of the part which these people might play (I am not thinking now of the views of the leadership of the party – Martov, Lenin, and so forth)?

D: We had all read Beltov's book by that time, and it really opened a gulf between us and the *narodniki.* As Gorev correctly says, people became Marxists in twenty-four hours.[36] But relations with the Legal Marxists were scarcely broken in twenty-four hours, as I understood it. It was a slow but palpable process.

H: So the feeling was, roughly, that they weren't "our people" or entirely our people. . . .

D: Not entirely our people – that's right.

H: What role could the Legal Marxists play then?

D: We didn't think about it much. Because we couldn't conceive of a single person who would have declared that anything other than revolutionary activity was possible. I believe that there was a subconscious notion that they themselves couldn't do anything, but that we could use them. In general, this idea of using people was enormously important . . .

H: For propaganda in society?

D: Yes, and for everything else. First there was propaganda in society and contacts. We were a small, isolated bunch of people faced with thousands of different demands. We had to meet them somehow. With our forces, what could we do? There were people who were older, more respected, of greater means. Something could be gotten from people in society in this respect. At that time there was already an awareness of the need to turn to illegal action, since propaganda and agitation had to be legal and therefore essentially not very effective. In this case, an all-Russian newspaper could become a powerful propaganda weapon. We all knew about Herzen's *Kolokol* to some degree and had an extremely high regard for it. An all-Russian newspaper that was not confined to purely local problems could play an enormous organizational role. This was the idea behind *Iuzhnyi Rabochii*, and the idea also figured in the creation of *Rabochee Znamia*. When *Iskra* first appeared, therefore, it was in keeping with this notion . . . it was not the ultimate answer, but I believe that this explains the truly stunning success that *Iskra* had. It gave a real answer to the question that was on everyone's lips. A newspaper which could be both a collective agitator and a collective organizer. The yearning for organization was very strong.

H: I would like to dwell somewhat on a topic which is of special interest to me. At that time there was already a Legal Marxist journal; *Nachalo* appeared in 1899, and so forth. It represented a literary trend.[37] How did you view your relationship to this? How did you explain it?

D: In this respect, probably, I personally belonged to an old-fashioned group. Gorkii appeared on the horizon at this time, and he was influential precisely because he stood in opposition to the Symbolists, and the rest. His influence was enormous, and we all terribly overrated his talent. Before him there were other writers, those who were called Decadents, Symbolists, and so on. I personally didn't understand them; they were alien to me. But I think that I was not typical in this respect. I was one of the "old believers," and this was entirely conscious and sincere; it was not forced on me.

H: If I remember correctly, you first met Gorkii in Yalta.

D: Yes, we got along well. For any writer, it is nice to have such an admirer, especially one who was young and Marxist. So it was very easy to become friends.

H: Did you talk politics with him?

D: Probably nothing but politics – what else could you talk to Gorkii about?

H: What were his political attitudes in 1900, as you remember them?

D: He favored the Social Democrats and the proletariat, of course. He took a negative view of the *narodnichestvo*, which I find rather hard to explain. He unquestionably had an antipathy toward the Russian *muzhik* as a conservative and retrograde, as a person incapable of submitting to public feeling, while any worker he thought of as a potential revolutionary. This was all very primitive but it was very common. After the *narodniki* had so overidealized the peasantry and had burned their fingers, you can understand why the Russian intelligentsia was so distrustful of the *muzhik*.

Fifth interview

H: In late 1900 you moved to Dvinsk with your husband and learned that the police were looking for you. How did you learn this?

D: Someone wrote from Petersburg – Savinkov or someone else. I talked it over with my husband, and he said it might be better to go abroad than to be in prison. He didn't have in mind that, once I went abroad, I wouldn't return. He wouldn't have relished that prospect at all. At that time, emigrating was not so formidable. Once I had decided to go abroad, I went to Vilno and met Sergei Osipovich there.

H: Did Sergei have a false passport?

D: Not a false one, just someone else's. I think that he went under the name of Shekhtman, but who Shekhtman was I don't know.

H: What did he live on?

D: As regards finances, we were fairly well off. My sister, Nadezhda Osipovna, or more accurately her husband, had received a large inheritance. And they were extremely magnanimous. I believe that Sergei lived entirely on these means. When I arrived in Berlin [after Sergei Osipovich had arranged for Lydia's illegal border crossing into Germany – ed.] the first thing I did was to telegraph Nadezhda Osipovna, and she sent me money.

H: Did Sergei tell you what he was doing?

D: I knew, I don't know how, that he was involved in transporting literature [from *Iskra*, in Germany, into Russia].

H: I would like to know specifically how this was done. He was linked with the editorial staff in Munich. Did he receive letters?

D: Yes, of course. He was the only one of us who had an aversion to emigration. Iulii Osipovich, Vladimir Osipovich, and I all emigrated; Sergei never wanted to. That was to have fateful consequences in his life. When we were all exiled (in 1920) he too could have left, but he refused. He ruined himself, his wife, and his children.

He was constantly in correspondence with Munich, sending and receiving letters in code. I think that he obtained purely technical guidance from the Berlin group. Such matters were not dealt with in Munich; we had the illusion, therefore, that we could be clandestine. *Iskra* would come out, be sent to Berlin, and from there onward. I never took part personally and know little about it, but I heard complaints that there was some playing of favorites. For example, things would be sent to Rostov but not to Ekaterinoslav. And I think that there was some basis for this. It was difficult or even impossible to write to Berlin to ask, say, for 300 copies of *Iskra*, but you could write to a clandestine address in Vilno. After he received these 300 copies, Sergei could use his own discretion. I am sure that he had reason to suppose that such-and-such people were good-for-nothings.

H: But, in principle, it was decided in Munich how many copies were to be sent and where?

D: Not entirely. I think that the Berlin group also had some say. And often people coming from Russia did not go directly to Munich but ended up in Berlin and had a secret address there, so that Berlin had its own notions about who was especially important. But there was no real competition between Berlin and Munich. I believe that the relationship was straightforward, not strained. In Vilno, on the other hand, Sergei or anyone else who transported literature liked to display their power.

H: But I would like to establish the following: say that a letter was received from Berlin asking that 50 issues be sent to Kazan and Odessa, etc. Did he already know where to send them?

D: But, you see, it was impossible to mail them. So he would have the literature on hand, and, say, no one came from Kazan, but someone from Rostov-on-Don showed up. It would be safer to hand out the literature today than to hold onto it. Often this was decisive. I assume, however, that there could also be "preferences."

H: I would like to try to retrace the process from Munich . . . *Iskra* was printed in Stuttgart?

D: First in Stuttgart, then in Munich.

H: In what form would issues be sent to Berlin?

D: In Munich there was Blumenfeld,[1] who had been involved in Social-Democratic printing shops, and who later worked as a typesetter for Dietz in Germany.[2] I don't know if he was a typesetter, but he knew all the technical aspects. He was a competent specialist in printing. When the paper was printed in Stuttgart, someone had to go there for final proofreading. This was inconvenient. Later Blumenfeld did it, and in fact, everything was done in Munich. Probably Blumenfeld did everything. This was considered more conspiratorial then. He would arrive, drop off material, and pick up some more. Attempts were made to keep others away from the shop. For example, an issue would come out. A hundred copies would be brought. The rest would be sent off immediately to Berlin. They would simply be mailed; there was no surveillance. In Berlin there were probably addresses and storage facilities. The Berlin group would be in correspondence with the "transporter," Ezhov or someone else. Occasionally someone living in Vilno could travel abroad. Illegally, of course. I think that Sergei himself traveled. There were others, I believe, whom he could send. Or the delivery would be arranged through smugglers. On the German side, the smugglers would deliver to some smuggler whom they knew in Russia and who was also connected with people from the organization. This was very sensitive work. A smuggler might be honest and not a traitor, but God only knew what might happen.

H: If I understand the steps correctly, someone from the group would deliver to a German smuggler, who would deliver to a Russian smuggler, who would ultimately give the material to Sergei. Is that right?

D: More or less. The smuggler would take two packages of literature and three packages of silk stockings, and it was up to him from there. On the other side, he would give the stockings to one person, and *Iskra* to another. Our man would then go to Vilno, where there was a storeroom. Apparently, there was once a storeroom location in Minsk as well. These matters were clandestine and not spoken about to those not involved.

H: I would like to determine the following. You have said that it was decided in Berlin where the material was to be sent, even if Ezhov had the right to change things. How was this arranged?

D: At the time, *Iskra* maintained a correspondence that was amazing under such circumstances. But I must tell you that no letters came to the Munich address, because there was an illusion that we could remain conspiratorial indefinitely. There were a number of addresses in Germany. Usually they belonged to German Social Democrats. They would transmit all these letters from Russia to Doctor Lehman, a Social-Democratic physician from Munich.

H: Was he also a Russian Social Democrat?

D: No, a German. For a Russian it would have been dangerous, but he was a respected German Social Democrat. There was no telephone at *Iskra*. There were few of them generally at that time, and every day someone went to Lehman to ask if there was any mail. And every day there was, sometimes a lot, sometimes a little. Sometimes Iulii Osipovich would go, although this wasn't particularly approved, because Lenin thought that there was no point. So Nadezhda Konstantinovna [Krupskaia] or I would go. We would pick up a bulky package which Lehman had received that day and bring it back to the office. There it would be sorted out. The mail was usually in code, either in a book or written in invisible ink. The procedure for writing in code in a book was fairly simple. Some Russian book would be taken and pencil-marks would be made on some letters, thus making up a word. This was very simple to decode. *Iskra*'s correspondence was transmitted this way, but not particularly clandestine matters. For these, invisible ink would be used, that is, milk or lemon juice. There were also other substances I don't know about. Letters were put under a hot iron, and the invisible ink would come out. This had the advantage that if the letter fell into the hands of the Okhrana and was read in this fashion, it could no longer be delivered. The code system was very simple. There would be a keyword, like "vile criminal," and messages were coded on this basis.

H: Perhaps you could describe a typical afternoon working session at *Iskra*, around the time you arrived in Munich, say in April of 1901.[3]

D: Martov and I would go to the editorial offices at around one o'clock every day. We would have lunch at twelve, which would take about an hour, and then go. By that time the mail would have arrived and we began to examine it immediately. Lenin was very unhappy about this, and rightly so, because he feared there would be disorder. What he wanted was to open the mail and look through everything himself, then give it to Nadezhda Konstantinovna, and have her pass it on from there. But there was too much impatience and too little subordination, for everyone was interested. At the same time the newspapers would arrive, and people were quick to take them too. Lenin was often also unhappy with this and would sometimes say to Martov, "Why do you snatch the Russian newspapers that way? You go to the Cafe Luipold in the evening and read French papers there, and I don't do that." But this was of no use since the hunger for newspapers was very great (for me it was somewhat less, since I had been in Russia so recently). In brief, there was constant talk about this.

Of course, opening the mail revealed rather little, because it was necessary to determine if there was clandestine writing in invisible ink. Very often there would be something even in legal letters, but to iron them for invisible writing was Nadezhda Konstantinovna's job, and no one else could do it. She would take an iron, pass it over the letter, and find that there was secret writing. Then it was my turn; she would give it to me, and say "decipher!" Iulii Osipovich could also decipher, but did it poorly, and didn't have enough patience. She would give it to me or to Dimka Smidovich,[4] and she would be off. Sometimes Blumenfeld was involved. He did not particularly like deciphering, but he was trusted with it. It was very inconvenient to work there, because Martov was constantly coming up and looking to see what was written. In short, this created, I would say, not a tense but a very animated atmosphere. There was no real irritation. It was very friendly.

After an hour or so, when what was in the mail had been more or less determined, and Lenin and Martov had read the papers, they would begin an exchange of opinions regarding events in Russia and the messages in the clandestine letters. Often, though not always, of course, there was irritation about the decoding. Sometimes the writing was confusing and difficult to reconstruct. Lenin would become very angry at this. Generally he was calm, but he absolutely couldn't tolerate a bad decoding. For example, a letter would be received. Lenin would ask, "When was the letter dated?" Say it was January 17th. "And when did they receive our letter?" Only Nadezhda Konstantinovna could give the answer to this. She would take out a notebook and say that they had received it no later than the second. "How could they have waited two weeks before answering!" This could drive Lenin into a frenzy, and he would say to Nadezhda Konstantinovna (I remember this very clearly), "Each letter should say in invisible ink, not in code, of course, 'Please reply on day of receipt'." Lenin regarded such delays as virtually a crime against revolutionary ethics. Sometimes Vera Ivanovna [Zasulich] would say, "It's easy for you to talk, but they can't always write in code over there." But Lenin would say, "Go and spread out the paper . . . ;" for him the problem didn't exist. If you didn't demand, nothing would happen. I have never met anyone as disciplined as Lenin. What is most surprising is that, on the other hand, I have known few as undisciplined as Martov. Yet Lenin and Martov were truly good friends. Later, Lenin continued to have good feelings toward Martov, while Martov didn't have the slightest good feeling toward him. I hold Martov largely responsible. I would say that, in a human sense, it wasn't right.

H: What was Vera Ivanovna's role and how did she act?

D: Of course, Vera Ivanovna was a different sort of person from the rest of us. I remember that when I arrived in Munich and my brother said that we would meet Vera Ivanovna Zasulich at the editorial offices, I became terribly excited. It was like an Orthodox believer seeing an icon suddenly leave the inconostasis and come toward him. . . . But she was a very simple and undisciplined person – a living portrait of an old nihilist of the sort that we had not seen in our milieu. Probably, they were all more or less like her in earlier times.

H: What personal differences were there between her and your attitudes toward what you were doing?

D: In the first place, there was the difference in age; in the second, she was much more inclined to romance than I. For me, literature was enormously important; perhaps I knew literature much better than life. But poetry, in particular, was of extremely little interest to me. Probably this was the heritage of Pisarev. She was very responsive to it, and, what is most important, she was embarrassed about this. She made all sorts of attempts to hide it, but it stuck out very prominently, so to speak. Vera Ivanovna was not a regular person, as they say. She was full of all sorts of surprises. What was of enormous importance for her that left its imprint on her whole life was her deep feeling for Plekhanov. I don't know whether they ever were close, but she would have jumped off a cliff for him. There was no doubt about that. In general, she was defenseless before him. She was physically incapable of uttering one word of criticism against him (although she often disagreed with him).

Nowadays, people of the younger generation underestimate the significance of Plekhanov. He was very unpleasant, simply unpleasant, but he was a very important person who was overwhelming in his knowledge and enormous talent for popularizing ideas, his genuine Europeanism, and his knowledge of absolutely everything, so it seemed to us. We were little interested in the natural sciences, but outside of that, Plekhanov knew everything, French literature, French history, art. There wasn't a museum in Italy he couldn't describe in detail. All this made a powerful impression, and, most important, distinguished him sharply from the rest, from Axelrod in particular, who, next to him, was provincial. Plekhanov was a true cosmopolitan European. Axelrod was immeasurably better morally than he, but he was a comparatively small man – a provincial teacher next to a philosopher.

H: Can you describe Plekhanov's personal traits?

D: Plekhanov was a great man with an enormous number of petty traits. I never saw such a combination. You might think that Plekhanov, with all his self-awareness, would not be concerned that, say, insufficient respect was shown to him, but he took offense. His assumption was that he was superior to everything. He wanted this stressed. People were not to argue with him. This is often the case with people who are unsure of them-selves. He was frightfully sure of himself and yet needed to be reassured of his stature. It was strange, but that was how it was. I doubt that there have ever been two people as opposite as Lenin and Plekhanov. Of course, this broke through and had its effect. I would say that Lenin could be very crude as regards Plekhanov, but, to his credit, he was aware of it, and would straighten things out later. It was very difficult for Plekhanov to do this. In general, it was hard for him to admit that he was at fault.

H: In what respect do you feel that Lenin and Plekhanov were such opposites?

D: Above all, Lenin needed nothing for himself. Plekhanov needed a great deal. Not materially, of course. Plekhanov led a very painful, difficult life; he was always in need. In those days the movement was very weak and could not provide for itself. He was a sick man, and was constantly being persecuted, even by the Swiss police. He was deported from Switzerland, which was very hard for him. He lived in France, in Mornais, on the Swiss border. He had a room there, but since he couldn't pay for the gas, it was turned off. And since he had neither money nor credit, it was very hard for him. There was just one store that would give him eggs on credit and I think that for five or six or even eight days at a time he would eat nothing but raw eggs. He had no way of cooking them. Neither did he have any light. And yet he could speak about this without bitterness. But he would speak as if you should understand what kind of a life he had led. I would imagine that if things had been similar with Lenin, he never would have held any-one accountable. Plekhanov didn't hold us accountable, but at the same time he felt we shouldn't forget.

Also, there was a great deal of ego in him, which Lenin didn't have. Lenin had a different manner. Lenin knew, he was convinced, that he knew the truth and that this gave him the right not only to win you over but to make you act as he wished, not because he was doing it for himself but because he knew what was needed. Lenin had this ability to win over and command, and Plekhanov didn't. Plekhanov could attempt conscientiously to win you over. He didn't always succeed and would become angry rather than try to argue more. Lenin didn't get angry; he knew he would prevail. He had an all-consuming confidence in himself. At that time it was fairly harmless. Later, it took on different dimensions and another significance, of course. But neither then nor later, I am convinced, did Lenin do anything for his own personal gain. He was totally unselfish. At the same time, I know that many unselfish people became corrupted to a greater or lesser degree once they gained power. It wasn't so with Lenin.

H: How often did Plekhanov come to Munich while you were there?

D: He came twice while I was there.

H: What was the reason the first time?

D: Simply to meet with the editorial staff; the second time was for preliminary evaluation of the program. That first visit to the Munich branch
of the editorial board involved, I would say, a fairly rotten compromise – a
rotten compromise because both sides were not entirely sincere. The
"young ones" [*molodye*] said that the editorial board should be in Munich,
because it was more clandestine, and so forth.[5] Of course, this was entirely
true. But there was another consideration which was not talked about with
Plekhanov, but only among ourselves. Namely that it was better for us to
be separated. Vera Ivanovna knew this. She was entirely at home among
the "young ones," but she was hurt for Plekhanov and somewhat less so
for Axelrod. Of course, she never said anything to them, but during the discussions she didn't have the courage to support the "young ones" against
Plekhanov. Against Plekhanov she was completely disarmed.

H: Why did you say that the "oldsters" were not entirely sincere?

D: There were various factors; first, Axelrod wanted to be closer to the
Russian movement, while Plekhanov wanted more to leave his stamp on the
entire enterprise. Plekhanov attached enormous importance to the publication of *Zaria*, the theoretical publication.[6] The "young ones" thought that
this was necessary too, of course, but to them *Iskra* was more important,
because they felt it was not only a publication, a propaganda vehicle, and
a collective agitator, but also a collective organizer. Much of the significance attached to *Iskra*, in addition to the fact that it was a national Russian
newspaper, was that it provided a center through which a party could be
constructed. I think that this aspect – the building of a party – was of little
interest to Plekhanov. Probably he felt that he would be marginal in any
case, that he would never return to Russia. For Lenin, Martov, and Potresov, on the other hand, it was of enormous significance.

H: How did Potresov get along with Plekhanov?

D: Not well. Personally Potresov was on good terms with Lenin, and I
think that Lenin was a great influence on him. There is something that I
need to mention, although I am not eager to talk about it. You know that at
the Second Congress [of the RSDRP] there was a great scandal because
Lenin proposed a new editorial board.[7] I don't believe that Martov and the
rest were absolutely right in claiming that this issue was first sprung at the
Congress. The notion was brewing long before it. Both Potresov and Martov
knew about it. I remember well that there were moments when things
seemed impossible with Plekhanov. Then the idea arose of transferring
Zaria to Plekhanov and Axelrod, and we would have *Iskra*. I confirmed this
recently in the *Leninskii Sbornik*, which contains a number of Potresov's
letters in which he writes that it's too bad but that there is no point in constant abuse and perhaps it is really better [to separate].[8] It was another
matter that it was feared that *Zaria* would be ruined after the split. "They
are incapable of doing anything," it was said. There was also a ridiculous
story I remember and have checked. Potresov said, "Let's have Plekhanov
negotiate with Dietz." I remember how everyone laughed. Some negotiations those would be! In any case, this project for separating and regroup-

ing the editorial staff of *Iskra* was not an impromptu move or an intrigue
on the part of Lenin.

H: At what moment do you recall this feeling being the strongest?

D: That is hard to say. For example, Lenin or Nadezhda Konstantinovna would write to Plekhanov reminding him that he had agreed to write
an article for such-and-such an issue of *Iskra*, and that the deadline was
such-and-such a date. Of course, Plekhanov would not submit the article.
With Axelrod, it was even worse. This would drive Lenin mad. But, fortunately, it was not Lenin who wrote the letters but Nadezhda Konstantinovna. And the letters she wrote were not angry but very polite, although
insistent, telling them that, as they knew, this was no way to run a newspaper. Of course, this made Plekhanov resentful and he would write or
come and say (I remember his expression well), "How can I explain to you
that writing an article in haste is no good – it's much more complicated
than that." What this meant, of course, was, "For you, writing an article is
a snap, while for me. . . . " Of course, this was insulting and unpleasant,
and we had to swallow it. Sometimes Martov would allow himself an
unseemly outburst, but Lenin was more restrained. But, for example, in one
Leninskii Sbornik I found a very sharp letter from Lenin to Plekhanov in
connection with the program, without a salutation, that ends by saying,
"You understand that our friendly relationship terminates with this letter."
But later Lenin admitted that he was wrong and Plekhanov forgave everything. This was possible because, at bottom, there was a great deal of
respect and esteem, and perhaps a feeling that we needed each other. But
gradually this feeling began to weaken, and I think that Lenin began to feel
that ultimately, though he didn't regard himself as a "young one," it would
be better if he, Martov, and Potresov could get along without the "oldsters."
You see, Pavel Borisovich [Axelrod] had severe neurasthenia. For years he
suffered from insomnia. Of course, he wasn't able to work much; that was
evident. For the "young ones," though, it was difficult to understand. If you
didn't sleep at night, you could work – and think of what you could do. No
one talked about it, but you felt it, and Lenin felt this way more than the
rest. Lenin himself had all sorts of ailments, but he was able to overcome
them.

H: I would like to dwell on these two aspects of Axelrod's personality:
on the one hand, a great man, attractive, patient, and so forth, and on the
other hand, a man who can't sleep nights and who is simply unfit for work.
How do you explain this?

D: Well, in general there are few monolithic people, and Axelrod was
the least monolithic of all. In this sense Plekhanov was entirely different;
though he certainly had petty traits, he was much more monolithic. Take
the family lives of the two of them, for example. Plekhanov had a wife who
was a doctor, and two daughters, and he made sure to leave family concerns entirely to his wife. She worked and earned some money. His existence might have been meager, but he could devote his time entirely to the
cause which he regarded as necessary and which he felt certain would
bring him recognition. Axelrod had nothing of the sort. To feed the family

he had to run that idiotic *kefir* business.[9] Even so, he probably did even more than was necessary. . . . because he was conscientious and honest. They told him how to make kefir – since he didn't know – that it was necessary to use a culture and to shake the batch up very often. Anyone knows you shake it up once or twice. He would get up five or six times a night to shake it up. You can imagine that anyone would get used to not sleeping after that. That was what happened to him. For years he didn't sleep. He thought he never did at all. Probably he would doze off for half an hour and then jump up and run and shake the batch. So I think he became a habitual insomniac. Partly because he didn't sleep at night, and partly because he was always agitated.

Axelrod was a very good person. Plekhanov thought that in effect he was not bound to his two daughters, though he loved them. Axelrod felt that he had very serious obligations as regards his children and he met them very honorably – he brought them up well. His children were spiritually and politically close to him. (That wasn't true of Plekhanov. It was only toward the end of his life that his daughters began to be interested in what their father was famous for, but they didn't have the slightest interest when they were younger.) In short, Axelrod had thousands of obligations which he had to meet, so he could give only snatches of his time to the party and to the life of thought. This fact always tormented him. He was a man who never had a minute's peace of mind or rest. I imagine that this was the cause of his severe neurasthenia. Perhaps nowadays psychoanalysis would have something more to say about those feelings. For him it was a constant feeling of uncertainty, dissatisfaction, and unfulfilled duty.

Of course, Axelrod was a man of very great intellect, though of mediocre education. He knew the history of German Social Democracy fairly well, but that was about all. Needless to say, he had no philosophical training. I don't think he even knew Marx very well. Perhaps he knew Engels' political introduction better. He was more involved than Plekhanov in the local affairs of Swiss Social Democracy and was close to Greulich and others.[10] He was liked and respected there. Still, he found this life very provincial.

H: Did this feeling of inadequacy which you describe take other forms?

D: Well, I think that he was dealt with rather badly in the Union of Russian Social Democrats Abroad.[11] When the first emigrants arrived, Plekhanov and Axelrod felt that at last there were some fresh recruits, and justifiably assumed that they would be recognized. It didn't happen. Some of the people who came were fairly petty. Plekhanov even made the rather inaccurate generalization that the current generation was mostly small fry, and he turned to all sorts of fault-finding. He laughed at the fact that most of the arrivals had fled, not from political persecution, but to escape military obligations. These new emigrants were not impressive, because they were provincials. They didn't know much, and what they did know did not seem important to Plekhanov and Axelrod, although it was of importance for practical activity in Russia.

Plekhanov's and Axelrod's isolation from Russia was very hard for them to bear. And there was a long period when no one came, except for a variety of students. They were also cut off from the Social-Democratic emigrants [the Union of Social Democrats Abroad – ed.] Their feeling of isolation was very great, and therefore, when Lenin came for the first time he kindled their imagination. They didn't expect that such people were still possible, and both Plekhanov and Axelrod were struck by this experience.

H: How did they react when they met him?

D: Very, very enthusiastically. Plekhanov somewhat less, perhaps, but Axelrod was very enthusiastic. Even before Axelrod met Lenin, he had some notions about the new people, and he had received some of Martov's pamphlets. And when Lenin arrived, he was very excited.

H: Do you recall what topics were discussed when Lenin and Martov came?

D: I think that it all centered around Struve. Plekhanov was of two minds: he felt that Struve could play an important role and that it was somehow necessary to unite with him, but he also felt (as did the "young ones" in general and Lenin in particular) that it wasn't sufficiently clear to Struve that he was nothing compared to Plekhanov. It was tactless and useless to talk about it, but Plekhanov was dissatisfied and took offense . . .

H: How do you know?

D: You could sense it. Much later, Plekhanov could say that at the time we had not demonstrated to Struve how reactionary his views were; Plekhanov never forgave it. I think that in general Plekhanov was incapable of forgiving.

H: But when you were already in Munich, was this entire problem regarding Struve discussed, particularly the relationship with Struve and *Sovremennoe Obozrenie?*[12]

D: The issue had already been resolved; it was clear that nothing had come of it.

H: Why was it clear?

D: Because Struve had been less tractable than might have been expected, and besides I think that Struve (who was generally intractable) felt then that he could manage without the Social Democrats, that is, he didn't have to ride their coattails into the Russian public arena. It was clear, I think, because Lenin, not Plekhanov, played the largest role. Lenin was much less yielding as regards Struve than Plekhanov. Struve's involvement in Social Democracy was more important for Lenin than for Plekhanov, who was in general less interested in the Social-Democratic approach.

H: Something is not entirely clear to me. You recall the famous meeting in Pskov?[13] You know that, according to Martov, both Lenin and Potresov favored collaboration with Struve at this meeting. It was Martov who was generally skeptical and had more objections.

D: I think that this is to be explained by the fact that Martov traveled a good deal around Russia at that time and had met more of the *praktiki* [party people involved in "practical" affairs – ed.] who didn't share this optimism at all, not so much about Struve in particular, as about the Legal Marxists, and what we might call the public figures of the time, generally.

H: Why do you think that Lenin's views and feelings as regards Struve changed, say, before your arrival in Munich?

D: Well, I would say that, first, Lenin was worried. Earlier he had thought that Struve would be more yielding, but now he saw that Struve was pursuing his own line and was not inclined to submit. Secondly, he perceived that Struve was a much cleverer man than he had thought, as clever as Lenin himself. Earlier, he had thought that he would be the clever one and the other would be the fool, but this didn't happen. And third, he had believed that Struve was unlikely to be able to establish his own organization and sphere of activity. He had thought that Struve had no option but the Social Democrats. When Struve arrived, it turned out that he had some other possibilities up his sleeve.

H: How was this perceived?

D: Probably because Struve constantly mentioned his connections in conversations. When he spoke, he would drop a large number of names of prominent members of the intelligentsia and describe them as people at his disposal. There were some misunderstandings; for example, Struve wanted to show that he could arrange everything with Kalmykova as well. But Lenin felt, and not without justification, that he could also deal with Kalmykova. This was not the only instance. Both of them saw that each group had to fight over the same social class, that is, the Russian intelligentsia. I remember Kalmykova's case well, and I think that both were absolutely right. Struve had an enormous influence on Kalmykova and, in a different way, one might say, Kalmykova wanted to be helpful in every way to Krupskaia and perhaps to Lenin. She was not entirely one of us, but she was sympathetic and ready to be of help. There is a legend, a mistaken one, that *Iskra* subsisted on Kalmykova's money. That is altogether wrong, though she did help.

H: You have said that there were disagreements over finances.

D: Well, Struve soon promised fairly large sums. I know that Zhukovskii promised, and he finally gave something.

H: Who was he?

D: I don't know who Zhukovskii was – an *intelligent*.[14] Potresov knew him well. He promised a thousand rubles, and he gave them, eventually, through Struve. Somehow it wasn't clear, but Struve apparently made some attempt to retain these thousand rubles for the common cause and to hand them over only if there was an agreement. Of course, he could collect large sums and lecture, but he wasn't disposed to do so. I remember that there was talk – I have checked this in the *Leninskii Sbornik* and I think that Nadezhda Konstantinovna mentioned it – that both Struve and Tugan-Baranovskii promised five rubles a month to *Iskra*. At that time there was still gold money in Russia and Lenin said, "I propose not to spend this gold half-imperial, but to put it in a little box and pray every day." I don't know whether Struve gave after that, but there were remarks about the half-imperial, humorous ones; we laughed.

H: Was it that Struve wanted admiration?

D: Yes, exactly. But when it came to support, it was thought that he would dish out two thousand, and he came up with a half-imperial. Of course, especially later on, Struve could get even more, because there was *Osvobozhdenie.*[15] He had great prestige.

H: When you arrived, what did Iulii Osipovich say about his opinion regarding this affair and Struve?

D: Well, I would put it like this. Before Iulii Osipovich arrived in Munich, he stayed with me in Yalta after Pskov. Tugan-Barnaovskii was also living in Yalta.

H: Did he also have arguments in Yalta?

D: Not arguments, but discussions.

H: What were the topics?

D: The major one was the Russian liberation movement. Would it be a movement of workers and only workers or would it be necessary to find other ways, involving other social groups that were not necessarily socialist but in the opposition.

H: On an equal basis?

D: Yes. In any case, it was entirely clear, I think that neither Tugan-Baranovskii nor Struve had the slightest intention of conceding a predominant influence to the Social Democrats. Social Democracy, which represented the proletariat and spoke on its behalf, did not impress them, understandably enough, because the Social Democrats in the provinces were scarcely very impressive – even if there were brilliant men like Lenin or even Martov.

H: When you arrived [in Munich] and it was talked about, was it Martov's reaction that all these troubles were to be expected?

D: Yes, he was not surprised, of course. And since he had not been responsible for arranging the agreement, he wasn't as upset. Lenin, on the other hand, had been much more involved, and he was somewhat disappointed. "After all," he thought, "they had twisted me around their finger." Moreover, Plekhanov, either in letters or in conversation, had said, "What did I tell you?" though in fact he hadn't said anything.

H: But you will recall that, even in January 1901, Plekhanov's response to the agreement was favorable, that it should be concluded.

D: Yes, because Plekhanov was little aware of the attitudes among the *praktiki* in Russia. And even more, he had very little notion of the way work in Russia was going and of the underground. He knew what was being done on the surface – legal journals, books, and so on – and that Struve carried weight among the intelligentsia. Plekhanov thought that Struve would be the bridge the Social Democrats would use to reach this public. Martov concluded from the outset, and Lenin gradually, that we were getting nowhere; that they were deceiving us.

*   *   *

H: You would receive articles, and not just from Russia but also from other emigrants. Decisions had to be made; first, whether to publish them or not, second, how much they should be censored or edited. How was this handled, and how did other members of the editorial board in Munich deal with this problem?

D: Well, an article would be received. It might be by a member of the *Bor'ba* group,[16] Smirnov[17] or Riazanov[18] or Steklov[19] . . . First of all, the editorial board knew that these people were terribly sensitive and proud, that they regarded themselves as first-rate, and were very condescending toward those who didn't have the same remarkable past that they did. Nonetheless, the board's attitude toward them was by no means that respectful. It varied. Lenin would be the first to read the article, then he would give it to Martov, and finally it would go to me to look over if there was still time. Then discussion would begin. Lenin always warned Iulii Osipovich not to make remarks on the manuscript, because it might pass through all sorts of hands after, and he would say "Make notes for yourself on a slip of paper." It was very hard to make Iulii do this, but he delighted in reading manuscripts all the same. He usually would also try to correct the style, which was considered very tactless. Potresov did a good deal more of this, and not always well, in my opinion, though he was a marvelous stylist. He had his own notions about how to write. Lenin tended not to find fault with minor points, but he could be very severe and cruel in his opinions. It would be pointed out to him, "Even if you are right, don't forget that it is hardly our aim to set everyone against us. Be something of a diplomat. We can't quarrel with everyone, or otherwise they will say . . ." Lenin did not take this well. But Potresov always tried to take this appeasing, polite attitude. People would exchange opinions and write down their thoughts on separate pieces of paper. I would copy them; there weren't so many. I could figure them out and rewrite them. I would send them off to Plekhanov and he would give them, in turn, to Axelrod. Axelrod usually offered few objections. If he had been there, he could have offered very detailed comments, but it was hard for him to write and there was always such a rush. He would be told, "Don't forget to return it by such-and-such a time," but he could never meet deadlines. Plekhanov, on the other hand, took it very seriously and would send a whole list of criticisms. Very often many realized that Plekhanov's evaluation was correct. Then the whole thing had to be organized. Nadezhda Konstantinovna would handle the correspondence with the author, who would either say that he agreed or say, "I think I will take my article back." That actually happened.

H: You recall I asked you about the extensive correspondence over an article by Nevzorov.[20] Was it necessary to publish it?

D: That was for *Zaria*, not for *Iskra*.

H: Yes, I know, but I am simply citing it as an example. It seems to me that the problem is also relevant to *Iskra*: to what extent should an article be in complete agreement with the view of the editorial board?

D: Don't forget that *Zaria* had to take Plekhanov's opinions into account much more. Axelrod might write sometimes, but that wasn't so important. Plekhanov was jealous about this, you might say. Of course, there was no sense in breaking off relations over the likes of Nevzorov. As for *Iskra*, if an article was not entirely suitable, the problem could be dealt with in Munich. And you could always use the excuse that a letter had arrived late. Plekhanov was, in fact, less interested in *Iskra*. He really believed that he could build a monument not made by human hands to himself in *Zaria*. On the other hand, the "young ones," that is Lenin and Potresov, were dissatisfied with the way *Zaria* was being run, that *Zaria* could be even somewhat boring, and, as I have mentioned, the notion of turning over *Zaria* to Plekhanov arose more than once. Of course, there was a different approach to articles in *Iskra*.

H: But this is precisely the issue: ultimately there were two problems, first to establish and refine a single political line in *Iskra*, and second . . .

D: It would have been a good thing if we had.

H: There might also have been the view that it was necessary to unite and consolidate as a tactical consideration. I would like to know if there were differences of opinion on this issue in Munich, or were there simply personality differences.

D: There was none of that in Munich. Of course, the "young ones" felt that it was necessary to consolidate and reinforce their new strength, but they did not seek this strength among the emigrants. They felt it necessary to attract people from Russia; so the most pressing problem was to get as much correspondence and articles as possible. Both Plekhanov and Axelrod felt that it was necessary to accommodate emigrant forces as well, although the relationship with the *Bor'ba* group was not good, even if it consisted of respected people. In fact, there was a great deal of petty vanity among them. It was unpleasant personal traits more than anything else that hindered joint efforts. If some of the emigrants had been invited to the editorial board of *Iskra*, everything would have been different, but this was out of the question. Perhaps Plekhanov would have gone that far, but the Munich editors would have been absolutely opposed. They treasured their personal union – that they could be informal and always come to an agreement. Lenin could speak for Martov without having heard his opinion, and he knew that Martov would agree. This sense of a personal bond was very strong and played a great role. Now, if someone from *Bor'ba* were to be brought in, you wouldn't get through a conversation. Lenin was very much in favor of extreme simplification of practice, so as to be able to work quickly and clearly. There was the question whether *Iskra* should appear on specified days: ultimately it did not matter, because whenever it came out it would appear in Russia much later. But it was a *point d'honneur* that it appear regularly once a month or once every two weeks – God forbid it should be late. These trivialities sometimes become important. Still, it must be said that the solidarity of the group was exceptional and it was entirely inadmissible that this should end. The cohesion was extraordinary. There was a friendly attitude and a certainty that intrinsically we would always manage to agree. Plekhanov was another matter, and Azelrod was one of the oldsters. Later Axelrod freed himself considerably from Plekhanov.

H: Did Potresov also share this feeling?

D: Yes, Potresov had complete confidence in the group.

H: This question is somewhat out of sequence – it seems that Potresov did not show up every day, like the rest?

D: No, of course he didn't. First, he was a sick man, and second, his family situation was much more difficult.[21] Potresov would come from time to time and could not sit there for four or five hours, as we did.

H: How often would he come?

D: Well, when there was a meeting, he would come to look at the minutes. He could come every day, but in general he lived apart and had his own business. He could not "live together all the time" in that manner.

H: Now I would like to switch to the most important topic which was dealt with at that time, which is, needless to say, the Party program. If my memory is correct, this matter began to be discussed before your arrival; in January, 1901, when Plekhanov and Axelrod were there, Lenin appeared with his old program.

D: Which met with total disapproval among the youth.

H: I think it would be best if we began with the most general aspects. Could you describe how the situation developed, as you remember it from conversations with Martov?

D: Well, the program was read. There were a number of technical problems that are no longer significant but were important at the time. Now we can run off ten copies, but that wasn't possible then. There were only two texts, and people were constantly borrowing to look at them. And again, Lenin reserved the right to make remarks in the margin, while the others, who did not have the right, had to write out their comments on a piece of paper.

H: So they didn't have equal rights?

D: The "right" consisted in that each person had an equal right to speak his mind, at whatever length – it was a pure democracy. As I heard, however, Plekhanov tended to criticize superficially. He was dissatisfied and felt that individual corrections would not improve the situation. He presented a project of corrections, which met with the same repugnance on Lenin's part. But, I doubt that there were profound differences, as I remember it now. In the last analysis, what was the disagreement about? The agrarian program? That was still a fairly touchy issue because of the *otrezki*, which were objectionable to Plekhanov, but had been accepted and were over and done with.[22] Plekhanov, with a great deal of anguish, agreed to it. I can't say what he wanted. I don't know if he himself knew. Certainly he did not favor nationalization. Somehow he was not able to state what he wanted in a way that could be understood by everyone. Plekhanov had the quality, when he expressed himself, of doing so calmly. He knew well what he wanted, and few had this gift. But he had not studied this problem, and I imagine that the aspect which I mentioned, namely the possibility of the development of capitalism, also was very important to him.

H: Could we clarify this last point, namely that the development of capitalism was of great importance to him?

D: I think that it was important to everyone, but to him in particular.

H: Why?

D: Because, in the case of Lenin, illusions were more closely connected to the contemporary scene in Russia; responding to the contemporary attitudes, so to speak, was the pressing problem. Plekhanov slipped easily into abstractions. He didn't know these attitudes and wanted to stick strictly to principles, so he concluded that it was necessary to create the conditions to eliminate all obstacles to the development of capitalism in Russia and thus take Russia out of its unique existence and bring it into the mainstream of Europe. He didn't know and wasn't interested in the attitudes of individual groups or workers. He felt that in the end they should submit.

H: Now let us return to the beginning, by which I mean January 1901, when Lenin presented his program and Plekhanov was dissatisfied with it. What did you hear about his dissatisfaction?

D: I think that Plekhanov's reasons were quite diverse and of varying importance. Sometimes he would suddenly find fault with the style – something which seems insignificant now. But he was always claiming that you couldn't say that, that it had to be be put differently . . . in short, petty considerations. I believe that Plekhanov had one notion: we needed a program like that of all the other European Social Democratic parties. I think that this was the basic idea.

H: When you arrived in Munich, had it already been decided that Plekhanov would write a project of his own?

D: It was already known that, once he had rejected the project, he should write one. I don't know whether Lenin said to him, "Well, write it yourself," or whether Plekhanov said, "Let me write it." In any case, it was assumed that Plekhanov would send in his project for a program.

H: In the conversations in the editorial offices and in cafes and so forth, what did people want the program to state specifically? What was the attitude toward the issue of the role of the proletariat?

D: First, there was a categorical rejection of any self-restraint. Self-restrain was for the liberals; we didn't want it. We would not settle for anything less than a democratic republic.

H: There was complete agreement on this point, of course?

D: Of course! I think that even Plekhanov was convinced of it, although I don't know. The theory of stages of the Economists was alien to him and he ridiculed it.[23] Elementary constitutional guarantees were much more important for him than for us, since simply in terms of age we were more maximialist, if not activist.

H: Did people feel that the proletariat should also have hegemony in the struggle for political freedom?

D: I think that this idea was primarily Axelrod's. Yet he understood it in an entirely different way than it came to be understood later. He certainly felt that, since the Russian bourgeoisie was backward and had done nothing, it would be the task of the proletariat to compel it to act. And once it was compelled, the proletariat would become the dominant force in the literal sense.

H: Yes, but what were your ideas regarding Axelrod's understanding?

D: I think that there was complete agreement. In general, we all had a highly exaggerated opinion of the proletariat's capacity to take the entire matter of the liberation of Russia into its own hands and its own hand alone. Even though we were perfectly aware that the proletariat was still at a very low level of development. The idea was very strong that, even though the proletariat was in fact at a low level, Social Democracy, its representative, was so clever that it could do anything.

H: In these preliminary talks, before Plekhanov's project was received, did people discuss what should be said in the program regarding the resurgence of the *narodniki*? What was the general attitude toward the Socialist Revolutionaries, who were building their forces?

D: Little was said about it, and I doubt that there was a unified opinion. Of course, it was known that the Socialist Revolutionaries were our competitors, and so we needed to be careful. But the attitude toward terror, for example, varied considerably. Some people took a more emotional view. For example, I remember that Martov's remarks about certain acts were quite enthusiastic, and Lenin didn't share this enthusiasm at all. It was a matter of personal opinion, I think, and it didn't go beyond that. Strange as it may seem, Vera Invanovna Zasulich understood that terror could not be applied in doses. This was her main argument – that terror is perhaps a good thing, but terror as a means or method of struggle will absorb all other means. I think this was Lenin's main point; that you couldn't undertake a "little" terror.

H: Now I would like to ask if anyone knew what Plekhanov was writing before the project was received.[24]

D: I couldn't say.

H: Could you describe the reaction afterwards and the general situation once you received it in the mail?

D: I can't remember specifically; I know only that it was received and read and Martov took it home for the night. Nadezhda Konstantinovna was extremely worried that he might lose the letter – God knows what might happen, he might go to a cafe. But he didn't lose it, and spent the whole night reading it and didn't sleep. The next day, after lunch, he came to the editorial offices and began to give his interpretation, disjointedly, jumping from point to point. Lenin also became agitated and critical, trying to maintain order.

H: Lenin had already read it?

D: Of course, Lenin was the first.

H: There was only one copy?

D: Yes – who could have copied it?

H: So Lenin, as the "boss," was the first to read it?

D: Yes, the "boss" read first, although I imagine that the word "boss" wouldn't have appealed to Lenin. Still, that element existed – an unwritten law. He was in fact the first among equals.

H: So he read it when it was received. What did he say? Was there a discussion?

D: Yes, a rather disjointed one. Briefly, Lenin tried to bring some sort of order, but without success, because people knew that later, when Plekhanov and Axelrod arrived, there would be a real discussion, while in the meantime there could only be a general exchange of opinions and feelings. It was rather chaotic, but everyone joined in and you could immediately see that they were fairly united in their [negative] attitude. Vera Ivanovna stood somewhat apart, but in general her attitude toward such issues was not very impassioned.

H: What were people dissatisfied with?

D: The main objection was that Plekhanov's project was entirely abstract. Plekhanov had no notion of who his audience was . . .

H: Did both Lenin and Martov feel strongly this way?

D: Yes, both of them did. They immediately concluded – as if more proof was needed – that Plekhanov was entirely cut off from Russian realities. Sometimes Vera Ivanovna would say coldly, "You were always convinced of it, why do you need additional proof?" But this was incontrovertible evidence.

H: So the great mistake in Plekhanov's program which you detected was that, as far as the workers were concerned, they simply wouldn't understand.

D: Yes, it seemed that these were foreign words and wouldn't ring true to anyone. This was further proof of that complete isolation. Though no one said it, I think that everyone thought, "But *we* know how to talk!"

Sixth interview

H: To begin with, today, I think that we should take up Krupskaia and her mother. What sort of a person was Krupskaia?

D: I would say she was essentially a very good person who generally was good natured and trusting with people. But, needless to say, Lenin had an enormous influence on her and gradually – it virtually happened before our eyes – she came to see a great many things his way. Even when she saw things differently, she always felt beforehand that he, and not she, was right. She really was exceptionally devoted to him, and he knew it and occasionally even deliberately used it, I think. I am jumping ahead, but I am certain that the break between Lenin and Martov was very difficult for her, and she probably felt that Lenin was not always right. But she never would have said a single word in Martov's behalf. She was probably frank with her mother, but her mother felt that, though Vladimir Il'ich was difficult, he came first. Sometimes her mother would say – and she even said it to me – that she did not understand Iulii. "He knows that Vladimir Il'ich has a bad temper, so he should give in to him, but he never does. So, of course, Vladimir Il'ich gets angry and shouts." This was a reflection of her talks with Nadezhda Konstantinovna, who probably also felt that you could give way to Vladimir Il'ich over trivial matters, and Iulii should do it. And it must be said that he went fairly far in that direction, as he says specifically in his preface to *The State of Siege in the Party*.[1] It seemed to him that it was important to maintain unity at least in the central group, and that you could and should make concessions in the name of this unity. Much later, after the [Second] Congress, he recognized that it was these concessions which had made possible the enormous harm that unity had suffered. But this recognition came much later. It fostered Iulii Osipovich's not very justified attitude toward Lenin, his embittered attitude.

For example, you know that a great deal was said after the Congress about Lenin's treachery in proposing that the three "oldsters" not be included in the editorial board of *Iskra*, and that this was like thunder out of a clear sky. This was not true. Certainly, there was talk about it. Of course, they were not "oldsters" as we now understand the term, but it was a different era and a different generation. This was very important. They [Plekhanov and Axelrod] were the people whom life had left very exhausted, and they stood in contrast to the younger people, filled with an enthusiasm that they and Vera Ivanovna [Zasulich] were no longer capable of. For Pavel Borisovich [Axelrod], that old Jewish rationalist, it was hard to be infected with enthusiasm. And it was probably hard for the non-Jew Plekhanov to feel enthusiastic, because he too was a rationalist. The element of romanticism present in the "young ones" was alien to them. This romantic element unquestionably existed – even in Lenin. Martov certainly had it too, though he asserts that both romanticism and mysticism were always foreign to him. In fact, he was a romantic, of course. This problem was frequently discussed, when there were no "oldsters" at the editorial offices and Vera Ivanovna happened not to be there. Then there was talk that it was hard to get along with the "oldsters," and, as I recall, the objections to this were more humanitarian than matters of principle, particularly in Potresov's case. He would say, "How can you remove Vera Ivanovna? Vera Ivanovna who lives for this? So you are going to get rid of her too?" And this was considered a serious argument.

H: What did you answer?

D: We answered what you might expect, "Well, we'll wait. After all, we don't propose to do it right away." In short, the issue was never settled, though it was brought up. But to say that it appeared like thunder out of a clear sky is inaccurate.

H: To return to Krupskaia, was she an intelligent woman?

D: She was no fool. But I don't think that she was very intelligent. There were so many intelligent people that she didn't seem distinguished. She was not talented. But she had something else, a great deal of charm despite her homeliness, and she was a very honest, good person.

H: Did she have any influence on Lenin?

D: No. Of course, he had a high regard for her, but she had no influence. She was entirely under his spell.

H: Did he love her?

D: Of course he did. But in general he was not very erotic. More accurately, his eroticism was awakened quite late and hence when it did it was fairly strong. I don't think he himself recognized how he had always been looking for something in this. But there were many factors that operated against it – the entire atmosphere, which, in a word, was like a bridle that no one ever put on him but which existed. I have no personal impressions of his relationship with Aleksinskii's wife.[2] Aleksinskii claims that there was a romance. Kuskova told me in great detail about his romance with Inessa Armand;[3] it was a very stormy affair. But the family in general was not very erotically inclined. His sisters were cold women; I don't know his younger brother, who was apparently very insignificant. In any case, the family was quite unemotional in this particular respect. I think that Vladimir Il'ich's eroticism was in part suppressed, and, perhaps, in part, it was little developed – it happens that way.

H: What sort of a person was Krupskaia's mother?

D: it seems that she was the widow of an official, not of very high rank, an average intelligentsia family. She had a pension so that she lived on her own money, very modestly. She did not depend on Vladimir Il'ich. She very much loved her only daughter and considered it natural that she should be with her. This was not very pleasant for Vladimir Il'ich, but he accepted it and was always correct. I think, though, that Vladimir Il'ich was very cold to her, and probably it was mutual. Perhaps she felt that a husband should care for his wife differently. Her notions were old-fashioned. She was a person of her time, from a bourgeois-democratic background, and had little sympathy for the whole situation, but accepted it, for what else was there to do. Once she was in the Social-Democratic milieu, she even came to like each person separately to some degree. She was a good person. She often complained, to me and to Iulii Osipovich, that Vladimir Il'ich was stern and had a bad temper, and she would say, "You, Iulii Osipovich, could give in once or twice." Once she even added, "After all, he is your senior." We all laughed that she used the word "senior," but probably she was going on the general awareness that Lenin was senior in some respects, if not in years. I think that this was in the atmosphere of the group. Perhaps this reinforced the latent attitudes which Lenin already had.

H: I seem to recall that Lenin's mother also came to Munich.

D: No, I don't think so. I don't remember that. I think she did come to meet him somewhere in Germany. I knew his mother very well, but that was much earlier, when we spent summers near them. She was a different type of woman – more of a lady, but also adored by her children, who were ready to make great concessions and sacrifices for her. Nadezhda Konstantinovna never made sacrifices for her mother, and they weren't asked for. Maria Aleksandrovna [Ulianova] perhaps didn't demand them either, but it was understood that sacrifices were required and that Mother must be reckoned with. Both daughters were on remarkably good terms with her.

H: Did Maria Aleksandrovna sympathize with Lenin's political views at that time?

D: She was no Marxist, but she had been wounded to the heart by the tragic fate of her oldest son, and the affair had left her with an oppositionist attitude;[4] she felt that she had been greatly wronged by the autocracy. I don't know how her husband would have reacted if he had been alive. It seems that he was a man of considerable character and a great awareness that he was part of the tsarist regime. Maria Aleksandrovna was entirely free of that. It wasn't obligatory for women at that time – not women's business.

*　　　*　　　*

H: I would now like to turn to the feelings and attitudes that were expressed among the editorial board of *Iskra* when Lenin wrote *What Is to Be Done?*[5] First, it seems to me that he wrote *What Is to be Done?* when you were in Munich.

D: He never read unfinished works to anyone. But there were constant discussions on this topic, of course, because this was in essence what we lived on. I don't remember that the idea of spontaneity and consciousness was a major point of interest then. Perhaps it wasn't much talked about, or perhaps I didn't pick up enough. The main thing of interest then – and we were all imbued with it – was the necessity for creating a centralized party. Needless to say, the dictatorial aspect was entirely disregarded then – none of us could imagine that there could be a party that might arrest its own members. There was the thought or the certainty that if a party was truly centralized, each member would submit naturally to the instructions or directives. Of course, there would be avenues for appeal and communication, but insubordination was entirely unthought of. I think that all of us knew the history of the People's Will quite well, and it was quite impressive.

It should be said that Vera Ivanovna tended to be among those who doubted, perhaps because she knew the members of the People's Will better and they were concrete people for her. Probably she knew that these legendary heroes were simply people with all their good and bad human qualities. She spoke much more cautiously. I think that her remarks tended to have more of a moderating effect and were not very influential. Potresov listened to her more than the rest. She was very much liked and respected, but I feel that there was something that linked her more with Potresov than with Iulii Osipovich or Lenin. She had a special little grudge against Lenin, his insufficient respect for Plekhanov, whom she herself didn't always respect. I never knew and don't know now if there was a special relationship between Vera Ivanovna and Plekhanov. It seems strange to me, because he was such an esthete and she was so unesthetic. But I don't doubt that she acted toward him like a woman in love for the first time. You felt it when Plekhanov spoke, I well remember a session of the editorial board in which Plekhanov was speaking about the program. At one point Iulii Osipovich quitely gave me a nudge and said, "Look at Vera Ivanovna." And even though she probably did not agree with what Plekhanov was saying – I can't recall now just what it was – you could see from her inspired face how she yearned for him completely at that instant. And when Lenin said, with a cold face, that it probably wasn't quite so, that one could disagree, it truly enraged her. Subjectively she couldn't handle it. I think that Lenin knew about this and laughed at it. I don't remember Iulii Osipovich laughing at it, but Potresov took it quite seriously. He was more sensitive, perhaps, and he felt that Vera Ivanovna and her attitude toward Plekhanov must be reckoned with. At one point, however, she was definitely close to Deich.[6] It is hard to imagine what she saw in him. Probably Deich was younger and better then, but as we knew him, he was entirely uninteresting.

H: Now I would like to return to *What Is to Be Done?* When I read the correspondence of Axelrod and Plekhanov, it seems to me that they did not feel that it was a historic work. Even Lenin himself made references in writing such as, "Have you read my account of the Economists or have you not had the time as yet?" and so forth. I would like to know the attitude in Munich toward this work and its importance.

D: I think that the attitude was favorable, but no one imagined what was behind the work. Perhaps even Lenin himself didn't imagine – he was pleased that he had cleverly answered the Economists, but he probably didn't bring all the conclusions which could and should be drawn from the work, and which he later reached, to their logical culmination. Perhaps he did not have these ideas yet, perhaps because he thought everyone would come [independently] to these conclusions, in an atmosphere of complete sympathy. It later turned out that his closest friends were against it, and so it was necessary to prepare for a struggle. But I am certain that no one, including Lenin, had this idea then. So it was not that Lenin had cunningly thought it up. Circumstances actually showed that he was capable of a certain duplicity, but at that time, I think, it wasn't there. There was no need for it when he felt himself among people who supported him completely in everything. As for Plekhanov, it wasn't so bad; he could be pushed aside somewhat.

H: It seems to me that he regarded his conclusions simply as guidelines for action which he was expounding freely, but that there was nothing special about them. I would like to treat these concepts more systematically. We have already spoken at length about the organizational notions which everyone shared. Now, what about the concept of professional revolutionaries, which is vividly expressed in this work?

D: It must be said that this notion, or at least a trend toward a centralized organization, was closely linked with another, that was less clearly defined. There was an awareness that the organizations in Russia contained people of varying caliber. There were more and less conscious individuals, those who were more aware of the meaning of the struggle and those who were less aware. These people had to be directed. It must be recognized that no one was averse to this notion. Some felt that directing should be "soft," while others felt that one could also direct [*upravliat'*] strongly, but the idea per se, of directing from a center abroad the people working in Russia, was fairly widespread. The question was how to direct. Of course, correspondence was extremely important. But living people must be directed by living people. At this point there arose the idea of agents, people who would be sent with 25 instructions and who would try to carry out 22 of them, and something would remain.

People had been sent to Russia with instructions before. Some student who was traveling would be asked, if, say, he was from Kharkov, to go to such-and-such a secret address in Kharkov and hand over such-and-such. But this was nothing. To develop the work we needed to have people who could be sent to Kharkov, and to Kiev, and anywhere else. People would be needed who were unencumbered by domestic circumstances. First of all, it would be extremely difficult to be a legal person, because you would be watched and almost immediately arrested. This meant it was necessary to create cadres which would make great sacrifices, renounce normal human life, and make revolution their profession. Members of these cadres would not have a job anywhere, so they would have to be supported. They would have to be furnished with a good passport and then sent, say, to Kiev, and then told to go to Baku. In short, corps of agents, professional revolutionaries, and necessarily illegal people who would risk a great deal – if not their life, their freedom in any case.

Naturally, since these people gave everything that was humanly possible, they had to be given some possibility to operate. This included placing them over the local people, who were unaware of, and cut off from everything. Say, an agent would come with the latest ideas from *Iskra* on how work was to be conducted. Very often he would run into severe oppostion from the local people. Now this would depend on the personal qualities of the *Iskra* agent. One might say, "You're all good-for-nothing," and disband the local committee. Another might not be so emphatic but try to show that the committee was wrong. I can't judge the frequent reproach that the *Iskra* agents criticized the local workers too severely. Perhaps they were conscious of their own superiority, and perhaps they were tactless in pointing out errors. Anti-*Iskra* sentiments and Economism became very much intertwined here.

I think that, in spite of everything, these *Iskra* agents had a great influence and greatly aided the Social-Democratic movement. They probably made many tactless moves, which subsequently aggravated the atmosphere greatly and account for the animosity and factionalism that appeared after the Second Congress. These agents were assigned the task of building a centralized party through the Congress. The Congress had to be prepared, because unless everything that could be done from abroad was in fact done, some committee in Ekaterinodar would send an Economist, while a committee in the Urals would send someone totally worthless. The local people had to be influenced in such a way that they would send reliable delegates to the Congress. Of course, you must realize that everything was done under illegal conditions and that these people were laying their necks on the line for the movement and risking a great deal. No one would receive medals or gratitude for it. At worst, there might be arrests, prison, perhaps exile and hard labor.

I think that the beginning of preparations for the Congress was the most decisive moment as regards a unified *Iskra* editorial board. And, since Nadezhda Konstantinovna handled correspondence with Russia, she probably had a double set of books, so to speak. That is, she would sometimes write letters to Russia that Lenin would dictate and Martov didn't know about, and she probably received letters from Russia that she deciphered and didn't show to Vera Ivanovna or anyone else. This aspect of duplicity, double bookkeeping, and the embryo of subsequent factionalism appeared before the Congress. It was the great trust and friendliness, the harmonious atmosphere of *Iskra*, that kept people from noticing this for such a long time.

H: I am interested in the following. I think that you have correctly described the historical situation in saying that this book [*What Is To Be Done?*] was a polemic against the Economists, so to speak, and second, that it was a kind of cookbook giving recipes, not how to act, but how to build a centralized organization. I would like to know if there was any consideration given to the relationship that Lenin prescribed between different organizations. *What Is To Be Done?* depicts a relationship between an aware minority and an amorphous mass which the minority will use for political revolution. I am thinking of the Emancipation of Labor Group's basic conception that political revolution can ultimately be achieved only though the development of an aware mass workers' party. When one reads *What Is To Be Done?* now, one sees that there was a change, and one might say that the movement took some steps backward in some respects.

D: None of those who opposed this brochure ever made such accusations, so it was not in the minds of the members at that time.

H: But there could be two reasons for this. The first that it was simply not noticed, and the second that others also shared these conceptions.

D: I think that the situation was as follows. On the one hand, in certain groups, which did not include all of *Rabochee Delo*[7] and entirely excluded the Economists, but did include the *Bor'ba* group and certain people from *Rabochee Delo*, it was also felt, of course, that a strong Social-Democratic organization was necessary and that it would be a powerful weapon in overthrowing the autocracy and making a political revolution. There was no dispute about this. If anyone felt it wasn't necessary, they kept quiet, because it was awkward to object to it. Hence it was necessary to create a Social-Democratic party which would struggle for the victory of a political revolution.

There was already occasional talk and debate about the nature of the Russian revolution. That the revolution would be bourgeois was clear to all and there was no dispute about this. Axelrod came up with some rather ingenious constructs showing that the revolution would be bourgeois, but hegemony – we tried not to use this word – would belong to the proletariat which would force the bourgeoisie to be revolutionary. Vera Ivanovna Zasulich was extremely averse to this notion, because, out of purely humanitarian considerations, she was inclined toward cooperation with the bourgeoisie. Bourgeosie of a particular type like Struve. She met with sharp and not particularly respectful opposition to this on all sides, and she became very angry, saying "How are you going to make a bourgeois revolution if you regard the bourgeoisie as the worst sort of scoundrels? Why [*zachem*] should the bourgeoisie go along with you?" Plekhanov would answer professorially, "Vera Ivanovna, you should try to understand that it's not *zachem* but *pochemu*, not the goal but the reason [*prichina*]. The bourgeoi-

sie will go along because it needs this revolution, and not to do us a favor."
He spoke in a calm, didactic tone, which convinced me that this was the
correct Marxist formulation. Not what for [*zachem*], but how come
[*pochemu*]. But it was not at all convincing to Vera Ivanovna, and she protested because she did not want to recognize that she was closer in some
respects to people in educated society. Of course, she was a socialist, and a
very honorable one, but in those times, and perhaps even earlier, she was
probably interested more in political freedom than in socialism.

Plekhanov also felt that the revolution would be a bourgeois revolution,
but somehow he managed to make a connection between the fact that it
would be a bourgeois revolution and that the bourgeois were scoundrels
with whom you should have nothing to do. It was illogical, but even great
logical minds seem to have a certain amount of illogic, and Plekhanov had
never seen a good living radical bourgeois. Even if he had seen people like
Kuskova and Prokopovich,[8] he regarded them as scoundrels because they
decked themselves out in socialist garments but were in reality the worst
sort of bourgeois. Nonetheless, he firmly believed that the revolution would
be bourgeois, and since this was his true inner conviction, it facilitated his
coalitionist and defensist attitudes during the First World War.

H: I would like to return to a point I mentioned earlier. The sequence
was that an aware mass working-class movement would ultimately develop
after the bourgeois revolution, not before?

D: That is absolutely right. The proletariat, as an organized political
party in the European sense, would definitely be capable of taking everything into its own hands only after humane conditions had been created,
that is, only after the overthrow of the autocracy.

H: But before this it would be almost an organization of the People's
Will type.

D: That is not quite right, because the People's Will was not tied to any
mass movement, and this is an important point. We, as a matter of fact,
were Jacobins, with links to the broad masses – this aspect was very real
and played a very prominent part. It also distinguished the future Socialist
Revolutionaries, who also were drawn toward the masses and differed
from the People's Will in this respect. We wanted to think that we would
receive some impetus from the workers' movement and the masses, but in
fact it turned out that we had to lead these masses.

H: This is all well and good, but what were you doing to develop independent action in the workers' movement? How were you building such an
organization?

D: That wasn't a factor.

H: Not at all?

D: We could see that when independent activity developed in one city,
such-and-such economic demands would be issued, while in the next one
the demands would be entirely different. If everyone acted independently,
the result was marking time and there was no movement. The objections of
Rabochee Delo were very easily thrown aside, and they did not affect our
group. How they affected people in Russia is another matter. Probably they

exercised an influence in certain places and not in others, but there were things the *Iskra* people could boast about. There was the May demonstration in Kharkov.[9] This experience seemed to show that, if there was a good committee, a spontaneous movement could take on true political magnitudes; that the Economists were entirely wrong when they said the workers could not be inspired by the idea of political struggle. You could see that in Kharkov they had been so inspired. And this was very influential.

H: Now to another matter. You know that during 1901 there were attempts to unite the various organizations abroad. There was a meeting in Geneva in June, and, as you know, nothing came of these attempts . . . [10]

D: And nothing could.

H: But in any event I have noted in the correspondence that there were varying attitudes at *Iskra* toward these attempts. In short, some people were more opposed than others.

D: I think that the *Iskra* staff, who were younger and not so engaged in the past struggle with the Union [of Social Democrats Abroad] were much less opposed, but they felt morally obligated to yield to Plekhanov. It was chiefly Plekhanov and Axelrod, who demanded subservience and no concessions. Lenin and Martov felt that elementary loyalty required that they support Plekhanov and Axelrod even when in reality they weren't one hundred percent right.

H: Perhaps I am wrong, but it is my impression that at the beginning of 1901 Plekhanov and Axelrod would not have made any concessions for the purpose of uniting the various emigrant organizations. But a few months later the situation was different; Plekhanov wanted to make a few concessions for unity, while Lenin now objected strongly to them.

D: It was only in 1901 that Martov arrived in Munich. Before Martov's arrival, Lenin had already become immersed in the atmosphere of factionalism, even though he had the sincere intention of staying outside of it. But when reality brought him face to face with this controversy, he and Martov felt that loyalty required that they support Plekhanov against *Rabochee Delo*, although their hearts were against it to a considerable extent. As they gradually became involved in the polemics, Lenin perceived that while Plekhanov's [theoretical] accusations against the Economists were not important, in fact the Economists were a more serious adversary than Plekhanov had realized, because they were not adversaries in theory but in practice, in the relationships with the Russian committees. It was at this point that Lenin began to take a harder theoretical line about any sort of understanding, because he feared that it would strengthen the Economist elements in Russia. This aspect was of less interest to Plekhanov. These were the reasons for the change in the front they presented.

In general, Plekhanov and Lenin had different approaches. Naturally, Lenin considered ideological unity very important, and he felt that matters like one's view of Marx were significant. Still, for Lenin this was all secondary, while for Plekhanov it was important in and of itself. I think that in this sense he was more doctrinaire than Lenin, while Lenin, who was

more closely linked to practical work, more readily made certain compro·
mises and more abruptly rejected others.

*   *   *

H: You left Munich at the beginning of 1902, in January, it seems.
D: Yes, after the New Year.
H: And you went directly to Moscow?
D: I spent a short time in Berne, and then I went to Moscow.
H: What were the reasons?
D: I was sent there.
H: How was it decided?

D: Nadezhda Konstantinovna, Lenin and Iulii Osipovich told me in
Munich. This was the plan. Moscow was a very important point, but there
were a great many [police] provocations there. There were frequent raids
and arrests. And since the membership kept changing, there was no defi·
nite line. Later we learned that Khinchuk had settled in Moscow.[11] He was
an *Iskra* man, very reliable in general, but still one who had his own per·
sonal opinions, who was not inclined to obey the directives of *Iskra* blindly.
He had been in exile at some time, and he was a man with a past.

H: What were the points of conflict with him?

D: There were no real conflicts, but there were disagreements. At that
time he had doubts that *Iskra* agents should determine the activity of the
local committees as they did. Of course, unification was important and the
Congress had to be prepared, and this was a serious problem, but the Con·
gress by no means amounted to all the work of a Social-Democratic com·
mittee, particularly an important one like Moscow's. Later Vainshtein,
whom I didn't know then, worked there, and I knew that I would have to
meet him. He was the sort who could readily be an *Iskra* agent.[12]

H: If I remember correctly, they sent you to consolidate *Iskra*'s position.

D: Yes, and more generally so that a suitable person would be chosen
when the time came to select delegates to the Congress. Besides, I think that
there was the idea that I would be given a mandate [to the Congress]. But
it never came to that. Also, because of the arrests, the Moscow group was
very isolated from society: there weren't enough contacts. When I arrived
in Moscow, I had to go immediately to Yalta to meet Gorkii and get leads
and contacts from him. He did this and was really extremely helpful.

H: To summarize your instructions before leaving, then, you were to
establish connections with society and consolidate the position, particularly
to see to it that appropriate people were chosen for the Congress. What did
Iulii Osipovich or Lenin or Nadezhda Konstantinovna tell you about how to
deal with Khinchuk and so forth?

D: First of all, they said not to think of making contacts with workers'
circles. "Your function is entirely different. You must not appear in any
group of propagandists, because you will be immediately caught. Now you
have another task – the Congress." This is very important. Visiting *Iskra*
agents did not involve themselves very much in local work, and this, of
course, sometimes aroused dissatisfaction. In Moscow they would say, for

example, "Since we have so few people, we will put you in charge of a cir-cle." I would answer, "No, I can't." "But why not?" The committee wanted these people to be at their disposal, but it turned out that they came with their own plans and would write letters to Munich rather than be account-able to the committee.

H: What did preparing for the Congress entail, in addition to seeing that the proper people were chosen?

D: I had to find out what the mood was in the Moscow organization.

H: What did this mean?

D: The committee's contact with the workers, the workers' attitudes and the strength of political feeling in the workers' milieu, and how well they were responding. There was already animation among the students. Did this interest the workers? It was necessary to transmit or receive *Iskra* correspondence and to serve *Iskra* and not the local organization.

H: Suppose you found people, perhaps in positions of authority, who were not suitable. What were you to do in this situation?

D: Of course, no one could tell me to try to remove these people. But they would tell me to try to use my influence to fight theirs, to try to create attitudes sympathetic toward *Iskra* on the committee where there might be *Rabochee Delo* people too. I was to show where the *Rabochee Delo* people and the Economists were wrong. I know that I was incapable of that; I wasn't authoritative enough. But I can imagine that some other *Iskra* agent would arrive, say, in Simferopol', might announce that he was disbanding the committee. I could never have taken that step. And in any case no one would have listened to me. But there were such people.

H: Were you the first agent sent to Moscow?

D: No.

H: Who went before you?

D: At the time there was no one, I think, but Glafira Okulova had been there earlier.[13]

H: Before your trip, what was your notion of the political attitude in the committee and did it coincide with the attitudes that you in fact found?

D: When I arrived in Moscow, I saw that we in Munich, on the one hand, had underrated the political animation which had begun in Russia and, on the other, had perhaps overrated it. We had underrated the extent to which a socialist movement was beginning; my impression was of a seething cauldron.

H: An animation in public opinion?

D: Yes. But on the other hand, the involvement of the Social-Demo-cratic organizations was much less than they imagined in Munich. The impressions in Munich were generated on the basis of correspondence written from Moscow. It is natural for people writing about their own activ-ity to unwittingly exaggerate and boast. And in Munich this was taken at face value.

H: What was your impression of the feeling in the workers' movement before your trip, and what did you find?

D: The thing was that Moscow was very atypical in this respect, Moscow had always been a hotbed of provocation; this was a holdover from the Zubatov days.[14] People were picked up very quickly. I think, therefore, that for all the enormous importance of Moscow as a city and an industrial center, the workers' movement was lagging seriously there. I feel that it was much stronger and more influential in Petersburg and even more so in the south, not in Kiev, say, but in Ekaterinoslav and Rostov-on-Don.

H: Before your trip, the editorial board did not expect that the movement would be as you found it?

D: It was generally understood in Munich that Moscow was a weak link in the chain. They accounted for this by the large number of provocations. But preparation for the Congress was considered the main thing. This meant we were to see to it that there were as few Economists as possible. But in Moscow it was felt that this was ludicrous, because there weren't any [Economists]. There might have been a few, but they were outside the organization. Khinchuk, at any rate, didn't know any. The sentiment was entirely pro-*Irkra*. it was clear that organization was necessary, and it was unquestioned and understood that *Iskra* and only *Iskra* could be the central organ.

Seventh interview

H: Did you have a Russian passport when you crossed the Russian frontier?

D: Yes, a Jewish student gave it to me, and I promised her either to return or destroy it, I don't remember, but not to register with it in any case.[1]

H: How did you obtain this passport? Did you know her through the organization?

D: I didn't know her personally; she was a student in the Swiss colony in Berne, not in Munich. Someone (it seems it was Orthodox) arranged it.[2] It was a very common thing and nothing special. I was young, and it was simple for me to go as a student. I don't remember what had been arranged as a secret rendezvous, but in any case the first night I was in Moscow I didn't know where to go.

H: You were not in touch with anyone at this point?

D: No, I arrived and went to my relatives, my sisters-in-law, and saw that my hope that they would be of assistance was completely idle – that there was no way they could help me and didn't particularly want to. This was entirely natural, and I had no grudge against them.

H: This was your husband's sister?

D: One of them; the other was his brother's wife, with whom I had been close because she usually took care of my daughter when I was arrested and so forth. She treated me very well.

H: Had they known that you were planning to come to Moscow?

D: Of course not.

H: So it was entirely unexpected?

D: Yes, I informed no one.

H: And what did you do?

D: I explained that I was an "illegal" and that I could be arrested, and that I would eventually acquire a passport, but that for a while I would need a place to spend the night. Could I stay with them? They had a large apartment. In short, it was entirely possible, but no one wanted to [put me up]. The only thing they did was that my sister-in-law, my husband's brother's wife, agreed that letters could come to her address. I promised her that there would be nothing dangerous in them, and she knew that I would keep my promise. So I now had the problem of where to spend the night.

H: Was it already evening?

D: Yes, I had to go to a railway station and take a trip somewhere. This was a customary procedure (not my idea) – going to a station, buying a ticket to Klin, say, which wasn't far, going to Klin, walking around a bit, and then buying a return ticket to Moscow. The train left at 3:00 a.m., so it was natural to be sitting around the station. It was fairly common and did not arouse suspicion. Of course, you had to arrange it so that you would not always be at the same station, because you might run across gendarmes. There were always gendarmes at the railway stations in Russia. The gendarme might be struck by the fact that he had seen a lady only the day before yesterday and now here she was again. So some change was needed. You could go to Tver', although that was quite some distance.

H: Do you mean that illegals sometimes lived this way for weeks?

D: They could live without an apartment for months. But usually I had addresses of places to spend the night in the city. You could get along for a month in this fashion. My procedure was fairly expensive, because I left my suitcase at my sister-in-law's and, while I could sometimes go to her place to change and so on during the day, I saw that this embarrassed and upset her, so I couldn't do it often. So I would sometimes buy myself a change of clothes, and go to the public baths. In the baths in Russia at that time you could take a room for a ruble and spend a whole hour changing your clothes and so forth at your leisure. This was a great help.

H: [When you arrived in Moscow], what did you do to make contact?

D: It was necessary to get in touch with the organization and to determine what sort of situation I was in – could I obtain a passport, how soon, what about addresses of rendezvous . . . in short, everything that was technically feasible.

H: Whom did you contact?

D: Khinchuk and Vainshtein, and then a pair of students whose names I can't remember now.

H: Did you go to their homes?

D: No, we had secret meeting-places, usually in "bourgeois" apartments. Later, there were often meetings in educational institutions, but at that time it was still impossible, because the university was still closed to women. So that made it more difficult. But there were rendezvous places, say, in the apartment of some doctor. These were the best. You could come as if you were a patient. My sister-in-law, Madame Kantsel, helped me in this respect, because she gave me two or three names and addresses of doctors to use. It was not possible to organize a real secret meeting-place, but you could go there, they would trust you, and you could tell them that they would receive a postcard or letter for you and that you would drop in the day after tomorrow. And of course it was all right. You could also arrange for a meeting there. But I realized that, despite our notions, the Moscow organization was extremely poor in contacts and personnel. They had no links "in society" whatever. This was explained partly by the many recurrent arrests, but also partly because the more radical and sympathetic elements of society had begun to be somewhat mistrustful of people from the organization after the frequent police raids. Some of them saw and read *Iskra*, and they liked it, but since there was a great deal of talk about provocations, people were becoming more and more suspicious. Whereas before some doctor might have allowed you to come and spend the night at his place, he was now more cautious.

It was necessary not just to expand but to organize the network of sympathizers from scratch. I didn't set out to do this, but I soon became convinced that it was a serious problem and that it might even delay all the preparations for the congress I had come to organize. Then the financial situation was very bad. Needless to say, these problems were interrelated. In this respect the Kantsel family helped me somewhat, but not very much. If I had gone to my husband he would have given me money, but I didn't want to, so things were complicated. Then I had to give some thought to what contacts to make in liberal society. Since I was from Petersburg, I had none in Moscow. It was at this point that I thought of going to Yalta.

H: I would still like to discuss what happened before this. Your stay in Moscow before going to Yalta lasted around six weeks.

D: More like a month.

H: Where did you go?

D: I used the railways a lot. Three or four times a week I would go somewhere; then, although my relatives wouldn't let me spend the night, they sometimes helped me to arrange a place. Very soon Khinchuk started to tell me, "You can go to such-and-such a place . . . "

H: Did you have a room?

D: Of course not; I would be given the address of a family where I could spend the night. These places had one drawback, however: insofar as possible, we had to use "bourgeois" apartments, and in those days such buildings had a concierge. The door was always locked and you had to ring; even the residents were not allowed to have a key. Since it was awkward to ring, because the concierge might see, you had to arrive no later than midnight, the time the theaters let out. So you would arrange with the person living in the apartment to meet not far off and go in together. He would ring and they would let him in, of course. This did not arouse any particular suspicion, because it was accepted in this milieu that people would drop in on friends for tea or something after the theater. So this situation wasn't glaringly unconspiratorial. But, of course, you couldn't go to a worker's apartment this way, and this greatly limited and reduced the possibilities. But somehow or other, sometimes well, sometimes poorly, I managed to make my way. I should add that another reason the situation was bad was that, when there was a meeting, you could sit and talk until about 2:00 a.m. if you were registered and had an apartment. But if you were an illegal, you would start to get worried and look at your watch by 11:00, and feel you couldn't leave. In short, the situation made me feel very pressed and nervous.

I remember one incident in particular; I even wrote it down some place. There was a meeting of the committee and an important discussion was under way. I began to worry that it was time for me to leave, but Khinchuk said, "Take it easy, I'll tell you a very good place to spend the night." And, in fact, he gave me an address that wasn't far off. I said, "But what about the concierge?" He answered, "There is an entrance through the courtyard and there is no custodian there, although there is supposed to be, and the gate is always unlatched. So go into the courtyard, up the stairs, through the kitchen," and so on. When the meeting was over, I went to the address, and the gate was latched. I did not dare to ring. I thought to myself that I needed to come up with something, that it was not a catastrophe, that I could go somewhere. There were no all-night cafes in Russia at that time, and, of course, a woman could not go into a restaurant alone. So I decided to walk and think some more. Suddenly I was overcome by such an agonizing feeling of tiredness that I felt I couldn't go on. I had to do something immediately to gather all my strength. As I remember well, I wasn't far from Tsvetnoi Boulevard. That was where the prostitutes walked. I saw a woman who was clearly of that type, and I decided that I would ask her to take me in. I went up to her and said that I wanted to go with her. She probably decided, sensibly enough, that this was a lesbian proposition – "What do you mean, Miss, I don't go in for that." I said, "No, that's not what I mean." I was very insistent and took her by the arm and went, she didn't know what to do. I concocted a really silly story, but one that was fairly believable in those days, that I was a married woman who had fought with her husband and left him. Since he wouldn't give me my passport, I couldn't register anywhere. On the next day I would go to a lawyer. Either she was a passive person or she too was very tired, but in any case she said, "Well, let's go." Without any enthusiasm or sympathy, she gave in to my insistent will.

We went, there was no concierge. Her room was all right, relatively clean. I repeated my story, and she just said, without any great sympathy, "Well, here you are, an honest woman, and you've come to me." I made a few unpleasant remarks about men. We were both tired; she offered me an armchair, a rather wretched one, and then said, "Well, let's go to bed." At this point my courage left me, and I decided that I wouldn't get into bed with her. She said, "You mean you're squeamish?" I answered, "No, not at all." My look was clearly rather foolish and unconvincing, but since she wasn't very interested she didn't try to make any analysis – if I didn't want to, I didn't have to. She got undressed and went to bed, and I stayed in the chair. It wasn't so bad. I had a roof over my head and was in no danger. I fell asleep somehow, and then woke up early and started thinking. I remember this so well because it showed me how much better I knew literature than life. I often had discussed the question of visiting prostitutes with younger acquaintances, but I didn't have any concrete notions about how much such women earned. It occurred to me that she would have gone home finally, but that she might have picked someone else up if it hadn't been for me. How much would she earn, how much should I leave? I didn't have even a rough idea, because I had never asked and no one had ever told me.

My knowledge of literature – French, not Russian – came to my assistance. I remembered the story by Maupassant, a very dramatic story, about a man who decides to celebrate his fortieth birthday by indulging in pleasure, and picks up a woman in Paris. He has no hesitations and spends a fine night, but in the morning, while tying his tie in front of the mantel, he is horrified to see a photograph of his wife with a young girl. The thought strikes him, perhaps without reason, that this young girl might be his daughter. He is shaken and leaves a gold piece, perhaps 20 francs, I no longer remember. I tried, rather helplessly, to figure out how much that would be in rubles. It seemed that it was a great deal of money and perhaps too much. I began to heap scorn and abuse upon myself: what does "too much" mean? How can a value be put on such things? It sounds funny, but then it was very dramatic. Still, I can't remember whether I left three rubles or five rubles – a blue bill or a green one. I imagine I would have been sorry to part with five rubles, but maybe that was what I left. And when I was already dressed, she woke up and noticed that I had left a banknote on the table – not on the mantel, there was none – and she said, very indifferently and half-awake, "It's nothing, you needn't bother." I mumbled something unconvincing and left as quickly as I could. I realized that I still needed to become acquainted with life and not on the basis of Maupassant.

Later I met Khinchuk and told him briefly what I had had to resort to. He was very displeased and said, "But how come, you should have . . . " In any case, it happened. I might be wrong, but I think that this was the final impetus that convinced me to go to Yalta and perhaps make some contacts from there.

H: How do you explain the demoralization in the Moscow organization, particularly in regard to the workers' movement?

D: I think that the main factor was the constant rapid turnover of people in the organization. A positive feature of the Petersburg organization, for example, was that whatever in effect might happen, Stepan Ivanovich Radchenko was always there. Five men might be picked up, but Radchenko remained and in two weeks he would find another five. This was not the case in Moscow. There was no such person. Khinchuk, who dreamed of holding out longer, even said that if he was not arrested for two or three months the movement would become organized. But it didn't. There was a great breakdown. As soon as someone started to visit circles, the fact became immediately known. In addition to provocations, it was natural for a worker to mention to an old friend, a Social Democrat, that a new *intel-*

ligent had arrived, and within five days he would know all the ins and outs of the person in question. I feel that the disorganization of the Moscow group was 99 percent due to the *Zubatovshchina.*

As a result, some outside contacts needed to be established, so I decided to go to Yalta. Gorkii's reception left me highly pleased – it surpassed all my expectations. All my other acquaintances – Vodovozova and the rest – were greatly delighted to see me, but once they learned that I was an illegal, they became very frightened. It was only here that I understood concretely how things had changed. How people from society who were not party members but just sympathetic were afraid. At that time animation had not yet begun in society, but Gorkii said that in Moscow there were a whole bunch of people who were ready to help. He suggested that I first try Skirpupt. Sergei Skirpupt was a very rich man who owned a bookstore and even, as I recall, a publishing house. He lived on the upper floor of a two-story house on the Arbat, while the first floor was occupied by the Krandievskii family. There was Anastasiia Romanovna Krandievskaia, the fiction writer. Heaven knows what her views were, but her work was published in *Russkoe Bogatstvo*. Her husband worked somewhere, and they had children. The oldest son, Seve, was around 14. As I later learned, it seemed that Skirpupt and Krandievskaia were close. There was something irregular in this family. In any case, Sergei Skirpupt (I don't remember his patronymic) told me that he had his own house and that there was no concierge, and he gave me a key so I could come and go as I wished. Of course, I should try not to attract spies. In short, he assumed that I would be cautious. This was a great help to me. Also, Skirpupt gave parties, entirely informal affairs, where people would meet; Sventsitskaia, an older woman who was very sympathetic to the Social Democrats, would be there. Then there were many liberals. Milentovich would come, and various lawyers. I met a great many people there. I found a great deal of sympathy for me personally, and to some extent I was able to use it in the interests of the organization, as I wanted. But it wasn't much, because it didn't last long, and then it was one thing for people to be helpful when they knew that Gorkii was in some way interested in me, but to transfer this trust to someone else was difficult. Still, they did help.

H: What did they do specifically?

D: Well, Sventsitskaia agreed that her place could be a secret meeting-place. This was very important.

H: What exactly was a meeting-place [*iavka*]?

D: A place where once or twice a week, depending on your connections, a member of the organization would be around, say, from 3:00 to 5:00. Anyone who needed to and who knew the password could come and talk to him. Sometimes the passwords were rather meaningless, but the more meaningless the better they seemed because no one would be likely to invent such nonsense by accident. So there would be passwords like, "one jumps, another rushes/'neath the icy haze." No one could come up with that; you had to know it. A message would be sent in code to Munich that if someone came to Moscow there was a meeting-place at such-and-such an address on Tuesdays from 4:00 to 5:00, and this was the password. That was how you could make contact with the organization. And this service was of inestimable value. Later, in Petersburg, there were meeting-places in the cafeteria of the Technological Institute, but a woman could not go in there.

H: And to go directly to someone's place was of course unconspiratorial.

D: Yes, and if he lived with his family it was considered absolutely inadmissible, except in the most extreme circumstances. At that time the telephone was not so common, so it was impossible to call. You had to write, which was always risky. It was documentary evidence. Before May 1 it was decided that we had to print a leaflet. This was something ordinary; there was no difficulty in writing it. But how was it to be printed? They did not even have the necessary connections. I don't mean just that there were no connections with printing shops. But it wasn't even possible to use a typewriter or mimeograph. This service was provided by Skirpupt. He wasn't afraid of his own servants, nor did he feel that it would be a mess. So we were able to do it.

H: He had a machine?

D: Yes. I was not involved, so I don't know how many copies were made, but it seems that 250 were printed. This was a great acheivement then. I delivered them to Sventsitskaia's place, and probably Khinchuk picked them up there. This was considered a great success. To look back on it, of course, 250 leaflets for a city of the size of Moscow was inconsequential, but still it was something, because earlier there had been nothing. When the leaflet was being written, people feared that there would be arrests – there always were before May 1. Khinchuk said, "Why don't you go away for May 1, because arrests are always possible."

I decided to go to Vologda. First, because I wanted to see Savinkov;[3] I still had the illusion that he could be drawn into Social-Democratic work. But in Moscow I was told to go to Tula, where there was an old Social Democrat, Platon Vasil'evich Lunacharskii, Anatolii Vasil'evich's older brother, a more significant, solid figure [than his brother], and very knowledgeable, but very ill.[4] He was paralyzed and stayed in an armchair, because he couldn't walk. He made a great impression on me. A good mind. His wife was very active in the Tula organization. When I visited him, he trusted me completely. I passed on to him what Khinchuk had told me to, and I mentioned that I was going to Vologda and asked if he had any instructions. He said, "Yes, in Vologda there is an insane asylum," and he mentioned its name, "and Doctor Malinovskii-Bogdanov is a psychiatrist there. You should see him."[5] I must add that a sister of the Lunacharskiis was married to Malinovskii-Bogdanov, so that there was a personal connection. "Tell him that we feel that he is staying too long in Vologda, and that he should become an illegal. Ferment is beginning."

When I arrived in Vologda, I asked Savinkov if he knew Doctor Malinovskii, and he said, "Of course I do; do you intend to go crazy?" I said no, I didn't plan to, but I had business with him. I went to see him. Maybe I didn't conduct myself suitably, but in any case he definitely didn't trust me at all. When I said that I had seen Platon Vasil'evich and that the feeling was that he had lingered too long and should become an illegal, he looked at me and said, "This is a strange sort of errand you have undertaken – what reasons does Platon Vasil'evich have for saying such things and for what purpose are you passing them on to me? I don't know you." This despite the fact that I had given him some password. In short, I rose to leave immediately, sensing that at best he regarded me as someone suspicious, and perhaps simply a provocateur. I said that I was sorry, and returned to Savinkov. I spent the night there. It was possible to do that in Vologda. Strumilin, whom I had known from Petersburg, was in exile there.[6] He had a link with *Rabochee Znamia*. And Shchegolev was there.[7] I told Savinkov (and Shchegolev and Strumilin, I believe, were present) what a fiasco I had had. They laughed, saying that you don't always go from success to success. After I left, Savinkov met Malinovskii somewhere and said, "What came over you that you took Lidia Osipovna to be a provocateur?" He became angry and said, "As if I didn't have enough hysterical people of both sexes, you want to make more scenes for me." Even though I hadn't made any scene.

I met Bogdanov many years later, and said nothing to him about it. He didn't mention it either, although he probably had not forgotten. Generally I tended to arouse trust. Often people felt that I was not cautious enough, perhaps, but never in my life did I encounter such unconcealed suspicion. The feeling was unpleasant.

H: What did you find Savinkov's attitude to be?

D: Psychologically he was closer to the Socialist Revolutionaries, and felt that his place was there. He was extremely contemptuous of the Socialist Revolutionaries' program in general, but very attracted to terror. He even tried to tempt me with it. By the way, he said, "For someone like you, with your temperament, there is no place in Social Democracy." At that time I thought it was significant, but I now believe that I overrated it. I was very struck by the fact that E. O. Stentsel mentions in her interview that Savinkov used the phrase "with your temperament" to her.[8] It seems that it was a habitual expression with him.

H: Did he feel that Social Democracy was petty and narrow-minded?

D: He wasn't interested in socialism at all. What was important for him was the overthrow of autocracy. He felt that this could be achieved only by direct action, and that going and speaking to circles was a great risk. I remember that when I arrived in Geneva in 1905 I went to see him at his apartment – there was a prominently displayed copy of *Revoliutsionnaia Rossiia*.[9] I said to him that this was his new passport, and he threw the journal on the floor and said, "No, I am entirely free from passports, but I feel that one can and must engage in terror."

On May 7, Savinkov's brother Alexander was supposed to arrive in Moscow from Warsaw; he was still a student and was formally being sent to the Urals to work; somehow he thought that I was going there as well. I met him, and they arrested us on the street. This was the end of the Moscow saga.

H: I would still like to dwell on Moscow. How was *Iskra* obtained in Moscow?

D: A man would arrive and go to the meeting-place. For Moscow it was considered good if 50 copies came. This made a small package. In the winter a man could hide it under his clothing and not be noticed. He would arrive at the meeting-place, sometimes giving the local man a dreadful scare, and say, "Take me in for the night, don't leave me," and so forth. People were very afraid. But I don't recall that literature was ever lost in Moscow.

H: I would like to discuss the general mood. As you have said, you found some real sympathy on the part of certain people, even if not very much. What political attitudes did you discern in these people?

D: To be frank, I think that the sympathy was not so much the result of the organization's greatness – it didn't have any. It had more to do with the attitude of student society. The students were beginning to stir in Russia at that time. It was not so much the demonstrations. There might be a demonstration today, but there couldn't be one every day. But there was talk in the universities. The professors were saying that the student body was different – not the entire student body, of course, but a small part of it – and that a group of students would accompany a professor down the hall after a lecture, and ask entirely different sorts of questions. They would not ask about the lecture but about political events. There was increased interest in the liberal zemstvo movement. Some considered themselves more radical than liberal, but this was something of a formality. Take, say, a lawyer like Malentovich. He could raise some general political and social issues. Whether he was a Marxist or not was of no interest to anyone. This was not the center of interest. What was important was the feeling that something was beginning in Russia. It was interesting and worthwhile to talk to knowledgeable people. Probably, "knowledgeable people" included the Social Democrats. At that time there were still very few Socialist Revolutionaries, but I think that there was much more interest in liberal society. And we felt that this was very useful. We thought, rather presumptuously, that we could harness this liberal society.

H: Did these liberals in Moscow know about the difficulties between Struve and the Social Democrats?

D: No, I think that they didn't know, or knew very little.

H: During these months, from January to May (1902), do you feel that any significant steps were made toward reestablishing the Social-Democratic organization in Moscow?

D: The situation in Moscow remained chaotic for quite a while. In May, when we were arrested – Vainshtein, Khinchuk, and two students – I don't even know who replaced them. The workers remained the same, although Bogatyrev was also caught and left no successors.[10] Even in earlier times in Petersburg there was a custom, an unwritten law, that each person would designate a successor who would automatically replace him if he was arrested. This didn't happen in Moscow; Moscow was too lacking in people.

H: In this incipient stage, did the Social Democrats with whom you were in contact actually consider themselves *Iskra* members; that they belonged to the organization?

D: Yes, they felt that they belonged to it. But this was more emotional than rational. When an issue of *Iskra* would arrive, it was frequently divided in half; it was a real celebration. These people were ready to learn and accept the formulations without disagreement. Of course, no one would have been prevented from saying that *Iskra* went off the deep end on such-and-such an issue. But it never occurred to anyone to do so.

H: I would like to explore this problem in somewhat more depth. There could be various reasons why, when they read *Iskra*, they felt it to be right.

D: It was taken to be gospel truth.

H: In the first place the attitudes may have coincided. We have already discussed this, and, as you have remarked, there was a common attitude as regards the overall organization, centralization, the political struggle, and so forth. On the other hand, it might have been that the leaders of the organization commanded respect. At that time, what impression did Khinchuk, Vainshtein, Bagaev,[11] and the rest have of the editorial board of *Iskra* in general and of its members?

D: They regarded them as absolutely first-rate. They didn't know any of them personally. Khinchuk knew neither Lenin nor Martov [personally], and, of course, they didn't know anyone in the Emancipation of Labor group. But these people had already become legendary, and part of the legend was somehow transferred to the *Iskra* board. I don't recall the issues, but they gave rise to disagreements. For example, the first terroristic actions of the Socialist Revolutionaries were just beginning then. In Russian oppositionist society, of course, there was always an ambivalent attitude toward terror. On the one hand, it was very impressive, because anyone was ready to admire heroes. But on the other hand, the tragic fate of the People's Will was something concrete, and people naturally felt that it was dangerous to proceed in that direction. There were those who felt that, by stressing the political line, *Iskra* was not disassociating itself sufficiently from terror. But it was very difficult to have unshakeable convictions about such topics: when someone went and risked his life, it still aroused admiration. Not very many raised the question or understood that terror is a means which absorbs all other energies.

I think that among the workers, or for Bagaev in any case, the attitude was one of caution, if not exactly aversion. The reasoning was as follows. In fact, there were very few professional revolutionaries among the workers. I think that this is to be explained not by a lack of courage, but by the fact that it was easier for an *intelligent* to leave his customary surroundings, because he usually had contacts and would not be lost. But for a worker who left his factory (and he could not remain at the factory if he was a "professional") and knew nothing except the business of revolutions, the problem of the next crust of bread, of subsistence, was much more acute and dramatic than it was for the *intelligent*. I think that this was not real-ized then. But now on reflection, it seems to me that this was at the root. There were Babushkin and two or three other outstanding workers for whom the organization undertook certain responsibilities, but they were few. The Russian *intelligent* was a creature without a customary mode of life, a phenomenon that was entirely incomprehensible in Europe, but which was a reality. They had left the bourgeois milieu, on the one hand, and on the other they still had remnants of family ties – a father and mother, or a sister, or someone else who would help. This did not occur elsewhere.

I think that what greatly helped *Iskra* was not so much an ideological or a rational factor as an emotional one, namely its closeness to the Emanci-pation of Labor group, which had assumed legendary proportions. I per-sonally went through two stages. There was a time in my youth, the first period of Legal Marxism, when we expected Struve to provide all the answers. Then I was greatly disillusioned when Struve unexpectedly turned out to represent the bourgeoisie. But this feeling was shared by a relatively thin layer of the Russian intelligentsia [i.e., the Social Democrats – ed.] In sympathetic intelligentsia circles it was regarded as intellectual nonsense – they could get along [with Struve] just fine. Among the workers it was entirely different. In the first place, there was not much interest in theory; Bernsteinism was entirely an abstraction. If you tried to explain that there was both political and economic struggle, it was not linked to Bernsteinism or anything like that, but only to everyday working-class life and reality. Some workers said that the most important thing was to improve the economic situation, while others, the more intelligent, under-stood that this alone was not enough, that political struggle was required precisely so as to wage economic warfare more successfully. And then, at the highest level, it was felt that, regardless of the economic struggle, the task of Russian Social Democracy was to overthrow the autocracy. I think that this was the most important, and more important for the intellectuals than for the workers. Of course, the workers felt the power of the police state more acutely, but I think that, as a whole, they regarded it as almost normal and that the possibility of change was beyond their comprehension. It is difficult to imagine now, but I feel that the district police officer or policeman personified the autocracy much more for the average worker than Nicholas II or the rest. They had never seen Nicholas and had never suffered directly on account of him; he was not something concrete. The local police authorities were what was concrete.

H: To return to this point, I also have the impression that Lenin's per-sonal reputation was not created until *What Is to Be Done?* was published.

D: I think that people became aware of it only after the [Second] Con-gress. The theoretical positions were sometimes offensive, but it was still an abstraction clothed in a very pleasant form. A centralized organization and all that was all well and good, but when people saw that an *Iskra* agent acted in accordance with *What Is to Be Done?* and behaved disgracefully, it aroused disgust in some, and more admiration in others. A well-grounded person knows what he wants. I think that this feeling began to appear only after 1903.

H: I would like to raise one last issue about Moscow, namely, the relationship among the various intellectual circles at the time and the differences in this respect between Petersburg and Moscow.

D: The Moscow intelligentsia was very different from that of Petersburg. The Petersburg intelligentsia was in no way linked to the establishment, such as the City Council and so forth. The Petersburg establishment was extremely conservative and even reactionary, and thus stood entirely apart from the Russian intelligentsia. The Petersburg zemstvo probably was also quite inactive and had no connection with the Petersburg intelligentsia. In Moscow, not only the Moscow zemstvo, but also the Tver zemstvo, the Tula zemstvo, and the Novgorod zemstvo were closely linked to the intelligentsia. But this is not to say that the Petersburg intelligentsia was entirely cut off from oppositionist society. There were several social organizations in Petersburg which had ties to the intelligentsia, such as the Sunday schools. There were also Sunday schools in Moscow, but they were by no means as widespread as in Petersburg. Then there were things like the People's House of Panina, whose services to the Russian revolutionary movement were inestimable.[12] They were considerable at the very outset, and grew as time went on. The Sunday schools did what was later done by the people's universities.[13] True, their level was quite low, and the amount of knowledge they offered was small, but since the teachers began from scratch, it was an enormous gain. I think that the first working- class intelligentsia was created by the Sunday schools. And then there was the Literacy Committee – I don't know where their money came from, probably from certain liberals, but they did a great deal. Students and women in women's programs worked there for nothing. They published inexpensive pamphlets, Korolenko for example, and elementary popular books.[14] This was of great cultural importance. I knew the Petersburg Literacy Committee fairly well; I myself worked there only a little, but my first husband, Doctor Kantsel, was very involved with them. There was a woman named Proskuriakova, a good friend of his, and Fal'berg, and Chernolutskii, who later were very prominent in the Russian liberal movement.[15] They all came out of the Literacy Committee. So there was a world of Petersburg intelligentsia, but it was somewhat different from Moscow's.

H: A point which may be of significance for your activity in Moscow in 1902 is that there were no radical "thick journals" in Moscow.

D: No, there were no such journals at all in Moscow. There was, however, some sort of literary and artistic circle – I don't remember what it was called, which had nothing to do with working-class sentiments, needless to say. Doctors and intellectuals attended it. It was a legal club. They even played cards. But there was always a room where people would meet and discuss something like the last issue of *Russkoe Bogatstvo*. There was no such thing in Petersburg, although there were the Wednesday and Friday affairs at *Russkoe Bogatstvo*. There were also gatherings at *Vestnik Evropy*,[16] although I was never there: this was a more respected, reputable organization; professors would come, but also students and women taking courses, of course. The mood at *Russkoe Bogatstvo* was very democratic; you could go there, and it provided a great deal. People did not hesitate to argue, and when someone's line took a radical turn, Mikhailovskii or someone would say that the matter should be discussed elsewhere. But no one took offense. People who were known to us as student activists, like Kleinbort, held forth a great deal. (Kleinbort was a shallow person in general, but he is remembered in the literature and even published his memoirs.)[17]

In general, the milieu of the radical youth in Petersburg was different from that of Moscow. I think that I can say, without greatly exaggerating, that the Moscow milieu was more grass-roots and in touch with the country, while the Petersburg milieu was more closely linked to literature, which is certainly not the same thing. I think that this is why there was no "thick journal" in Moscow except for *Russkaia Mysl'*[18] – although there might have been some police obstacles as well. Of course, no one read *Russkie Vedomosti*[19] in Petersburg, although it could probably be obtained there. In Petersburg there were long stretches of time when no liberal newspaper was available, one had to read *Novoe Vremia*.[20] There was *Novoe Vremia* and then there was the evening *Birzhovka*, the yellow press. Radical papers appeared occasionally, but they quickly perished. In Moscow there was always *Russkie Vedomosti* and the respectable types read it of course. Later *Russkoe Slovo* appeared[21] – I don't remember when – and it was less concerned with principles but much better journalistically. In Petersburg, however, no one read *Russkoe Slovo*. *Den'* and *Tovarishch* also appeared in Petersburg, but that was later.[22]

Eighth interview

H: Let us discuss the period following your arrest in May 1902. After your arrest, you were imprisoned in the Taganka jail and also spent some time in Butyrki prison. You were in a state of poor health. I would like to begin with a picture of the situation of the prisoners and of life in the two prisons.

D: First of all I would like to point out the differences between these prisons. Taganka was an enormous prison with only solitary-confinement cells. Some cells contained political prisoners, others criminals; and formally they were not supposed to talk to one another. In practice it was relatively easy to communicate by tapping on the walls and even easier to speak through the windows, although you didn't do that right away. In May the windows were all open, because it was hot. The guards did not cause trouble. It was a fairly easy and pleasant way of communicating.

Butyrki prison was entirely different. It was an enormous transit prison with communal cells. People were sent there only when they were about to be transferred somewhere else. In addition to the large cells and enormous corridors, there were four towers. One of them, the Pugachev tower, where I was, was for prisoners who were sick. Another tower, the clock tower, also had three cells on each storey; there were three or four stories, so there might have been nine cells. These were individual cells for men. There were no contacts with the transit prisoners. I can't remember if there was a walk period. It seems to me that there wasn't; I don't remember any place to walk. I think the men were not allowed out for walks either. Perhaps the clock tower was also regarded more or less as a hospital. There was a considerable difference, because there were eight or nine men in each tower, while in the prison itself there were dozens. I think that there were many dozens, probably 80 or 90 or even more than 100 politicals at one time. And the criminal prisoners provided services for us; that is, they would come and clean our cells. In the Petersburg jail we had to do this ourselves.

H: Did the criminals feel that their clean-up duties for you were natural?

D: There was no "sentiment"; it was entirely natural. It was even something of a privilege, and people did it willingly, because we would give them something and share what we had, cigarettes or anything else. I never heard that there were any unpleasantnesses or complications.

H: How did the criminals conceive of the politicals?

D: They had a low opinion of them. I think that the man in the street in Russia thought of politicals as students in revolt. I never heard of a political trying to propagandize criminals. Probably it was difficult, because when a criminal was in a cell cleaning it, the door was usually open and a guard was patrolling the corridor.

H: Could you give me an idea of an ordinary day at Taganka?

D: The day began fairly early with a check. In other prisons you were required to get up for the check, but not in Taganka. Things were still fairly good in those days. Later it changed greatly. On the morning check, an assistant of the warden would come in with a guard and inspect the room.

H: How did he behave?

D: When there was some sort of scandal and someone was taken off to the punishment cell, I imagine that they would not be very delicate. But except for such cases – and they were infrequent at that time – the manner was entirely correct in the European fashion. After the check the slot in the door was open and you were given boiling water. You had to have your own mug or teapot, and the water was poured through this slot. You had to have your own tea and sugar too. All this could be bought at the commissary, and you could put in an order for it. Then there was dinner at 12:00 – again they gave it to you through the slot. I can't remember now how you could obtain an extra helping in Taganka – you had to pay a certain amount for it. It was not starvation rations. There was cabbage soup, with meat, I think, and even kasha. If you had your own butter, the food was tolerable.

After that, you were left alone until evening. In the evening, at 7:00, you were given boiling water or dinner, again a soupy kasha. Then they brought bread. As I remember, it was a big ration of soldier bread, as much as two and a half pounds, so that we could never finish it and would usually give some to the criminals. After supper there was another check, and that was it – after that no one disturbed you.

H: Was there a walk period?

D: In Taganka there was. Each person was given a walk period separately, there was no general one. In the preliminary-detention jail, when you were called out for a walk, there was a small courtyard and six or seven criminals and one political would be allowed out, and then again six or seven criminals. In Taganka it was different. They simply let you out for 15 minutes or less. It depended upon the number of people in the prison. You could sit outside for a while. The courtyard was partitioned into small sections. Still, you could get out for a walk every day.

H: What about reading?

D: There was a fairly good library, because many prisoners left their books when they departed.

H: Could you go to the library yourself?

D: No, never. There were notebooks, sort of like catalogues, and you could ask for them. Some of the more intelligent criminals worked in the library, and one of them would bring you a notebook. You would tell him that you needed such-and-such a book, and he might say, "It seems it isn't available, but I will bring you such-and-such, if you like." But mainly people had their own books, which could be brought in. If you had visitors, you could get books, and you could use the criminal workers to send books to such-and-such a cell. Though formally it wasn't allowed, it was generally tolerated.

H: How often could you see people?

D: For me it was very seldom. I was an illegal, so I didn't give my real name right away. As a result, I couldn't write home for a while. Then my father could not come. In short, none of my family came. Relatives of my first husband, Kantsel, did come and visit, but very seldom. Once his brother, a doctor, came from Baku; my daughter lived with him and his wife. They brought my daughter to see me. I left the child when she was three, and now she was about five. Of course, she had become unused to me, but they conscientiously tried to tell her about me. She didn't have the faintest idea what to say to me. She said, "Know what, they built a new mortuary at our place." She had picked up all the interests of her uncle and aunt. Their hospital was their exclusive concern, and evidently the most frequent topic of their conversation. I didn't know how I should respond.

In general, I had few visitors. But others who had more relatives could have visits once a week. I, at any rate, never had visits across the screen, because the investigation was already over by then. But usually, during the investigations, it was the same as in the preliminary-detention jail: there was a special room with two parallel screens running the entire length. Visitors would come, and a police officer (usually one) would walk up and down the "corridor" [between the two screens]. But if you talked very quietly you weren't heard because the room was fairly noisy. This was called an open meeting. I was allowed a private meeting because my husband's relatives brought my child when the investigation was over. I had extremely little satisfaction from such meetings. Of course, everything depended on who came.

H: How did you find out who was in the prison?

D: Usually, when a newcomer was brought in, for the first few hours he would not know what could and could not be done. The daring sorts would shout out the window, "I'm so-and-so, I was brought in today." This could be done most easily in the summer, of course.

H: And what would he say through the window?

D: That he had been arrested today on the street. If he was an illegal, he would not give his name. He would ask who his neighbors were. People would answer. You would find acquaintances that way. That was how it was with Skirpupt. He understood that he was arrested because of me, since I was constantly spending the night at his place. If a person didn't have the energy to declare himself, the criminals would help. It was established fairly quickly who was where. I don't know whether the authorities made use of these conversations. But these were still the Zubatov days and the regime was not very strict. Perhaps it was also important for Zubatov to familiarize himself with the general mood, although, of course, he understood that the politicals would not reveal any secrets.

H: So you would speak through the window, someone would recognize your voice, and you could talk. But how would you become acquainted with someone you didn't know?

D: It might go like this: "You a newcomer?" "Yes." "When were you arrested?" "The day before yesterday." "On the street?" "Yes. And who are you?" "I'm Mikhail Bagaev." "Where were you arrested?" "In Nizhnii Novgorod." "For what crime?" "No crime, but I am an accessory in such-and-such an affair."

H: In the summer you used the windows, but what about winter time?

D: We would communicate by tapping. When you got used to it, you could communicate very rapidly and at length. It was certainly simpler to use the windows, because often an entire group would become involved, not just two people. But even in the winter you could talk in some detail. There was lots of time. It became much more difficult when the guards interfered, although it must be said that they interfered little. You could tap on the wall, but it was better if you tapped on the pipes, because that way it could carry beyond your immediate neighbor.

H: And everyone knew the code?

D: Yes, everyone.

H: How did it work – 1 for A, 2 for B . . . ?

D: It was like a table: A – 1; B – 1,2; V – 1,3. It repeated at the sixth letter, so that E was two A's.[1] I imagine that the administration might have listened in and also took part, so any real secrets could not be talked about. But there was a great deal that could be said. There were devotees who could tap out entire poems.

H: Were you allowed to write?

D: You could buy notebooks and pencils. As I remember, I had pen and ink, and perhaps a pencil. It was understood that when you left prison you had to hand over all your material for inspection. But I don't remember that the inspection was very rigorous.

H: Did people write memoirs?

D: Not memoirs, when you didn't know whether or not you would be able to get them out. I don't think so. But some of the younger people would write lyric poetry. I was never guilty of this, though others were. Some wrote outlines of works. To tell the truth, there was nothing tragic about this stint in prison. There were very unpleasant interrogations, but they were only unpleasant – there was no torture or anything like that. But Zubatov himself did the questioning. Ultimately, however, you could say, "I refuse to give testimony," and that was it. Probably there were punishments on occasion, but I never experienced them.

H: You eventually gave them your correct name?

D: Yes.

H: Why?

D: Because not to tell and remain unknown meant to have no hope of receiving letters and so on. I had no reason to hide it. I could have remained unknown, but then I would have been entirely isolated and would have no visits or letters, and couldn't write either.

H: What did you eventually say in your testimony?

D: My entire testimony came down to five lines, because I only admitted that I had come illegally and had lived in Europe. They asked, "Where did you live?" "I don't wish to give such testimony." When I had my encounter with Zubatov, he said, "You are young and basically healthy; it's too soon for you to be buried away; so be more pliant and you may be freed." In a fairly indefinite way, he hinted that, if I were more tractable, gave information, and so forth. . . . At this point I became infuriated and threw an inkwell at him. I later wrote to Iulii Osipovich about it, and this letter can be found in the *Leninskie Sborniki*.[2] There was nothing tragic about it – I threw it and that was that; I didn't hurl myself at his feet.

H: Did Zubatov often do the questioning himself?

D: Very often. At that time he was frequently present at interrogations and, it must be said, he was quite successful and obtained a great deal. The situation is still strangely misunderstood. There was a former member of the Bund, Mania Vilbushevich, now living in Israel, who was arrested and interrogated by Zubatov. He convinced her that her activities were a waste of effort on her part, that he understood the situation of the Jews very well, and that some sort of cooperation was needed. She was freed very quickly and organized a movement that was oppositionist but not revolutionary. I never heard about her again and thought that she died long ago, but I recently read that her eightieth birthday was celebrated in Israel with a great deal of hullabaloo. They forgot that she worked for Zubatov. It was quite a scandal at the time.[3]

H: What was your impression of him?

D: He was by no means a fool, and not at all arrogant. I think that many yielded to his persuasions.

H: How and why?

D: He would say, "I know all the shortcomings of our system as well as you, and probably better. A country of this size you won't change in five minutes. Of course, you're young . . . you think that one-two-three and that's it. But things aren't done that way. "Of course," he would say, "Our government knows this as well as you and I. Tradition is important, and then there are various elements in the country. This sort of shrill opposition causes only harm and interference. In your own interest – and, of course, I am not saying that you should change your interest – you should struggle, but in a different way. Improve your material circumstances. I can well understand that, and don't consider it a great misfortune. But if you shout, 'Down with autocracy,' it cannot go unpunished." This was the sort of thing he would say, and there were people who were susceptible to it.

H: Did he try it with you?

D: He was somewhat different, more subtle. He began by saying, "You are a young and sick woman, and you have a child. Think not of yourself, to say nothing of your parents, but remember that it is hard for children. You have a daughter, and, as her mother, you should think of her." I listened with a bored expression. How could I argue with him? Then he continued like this: "I only want to try to persuade you. Here you have ruined your life, possibly forever. Is it worth it? The matter can be remedied." Of course, I don't guarantee that he used these words, but this is what he meant. "You say that you were abroad. Were you abroad the whole time?" "Yes, all the time." "I don't think so. Did you travel to Yalta?" "No, I didn't." "What do you mean, you didn't? With whom did you meet? Well, if you don't want to say, you don't have to. But when you were abroad, what did you do? Did you carry out any instructions? What instructions?" This was his line. Finally, he started to say, "Stop saying 'No' all the time – tell me everything." This was the gist of it. The manner was nice and not at all aggressive.

H: How did you know who he was?

D: The interrogation was conducted officially – a police office was present and a record was taken. It stated that so-and-so was present, and that so-and-so conducted the questioning. He didn't hide the fact. He signed the record and asked me to sign. It seems to me that I didn't sign, though maybe I did.

H: What were the conditions like in Butyrki?

D: It was entirely different. It was also rather free there, because there was less surveillance. And the jailers and guards were not on every floor. Taganka was a civilized prison in which you could ring and someone would come. As I remember, you couldn't ring in Butyrki – you had to go to the door and shout. This was stupid, because we were supposed to be a hospital ward. But that's the way it was. The people were not seriously sick. If someone had a severe illness he was transferred to the Litovskii Fortress, where there was a real hospital. I was there in 1906 – but no, the Litovskii Fortress was in Petersburg. Probably there was a hospital in Moscow where people were transferred.

H: You said that people were not confined to their cells?

D: In the hospital ward, one cell would contain women, the next men. Depending on your cleverness, you might prevail. Say, for example, a man, not a woman, needed to go to the toilet. You had to knock on the door, and a guard would come and unlock the door and let you out. At this point a clever fellow might try to get into another cell. If the guard was agreeable, he would say, "OK, go ahead"; then you could take a chance on staying and talking. You could also communicate by tapping, and this was not interfered with in any way. In addition, the cell doors always had a slot, which was supposed to be closed all the time. But there was a peephole, and, with some skill, you could open the slot yourself. You could talk through the slot, since the doors were very near each other. But you could not hold a general conversation. You couldn't let yourself be heard in another corner, but you could talk quietly to your neighbors.

H: Which people were with you in Taganka?

D: Khinchuk, Vainshtein, Bagaev.

H: I believe you have said that you became acquainted with Bagaev in jail.

D: He was from Nizhnii Novgorod.

H: How did you meet him?

D: Through the window – "Are you a new neighbor?" "Yes." "What's your name?" I don't remember if I told him then what my name was.

H: But were all your talks through the window?

D: Through the window in the summer, and then by tapping. I always tapped lying down.

H: What did you learn in this way?

D: It was interesting for me, because Bagaev was a very well-educated worker; there was a great deal that was interesting and new to me in what he said. Particularly when we could talk through the window. Needless to say, I was way ahead of him in some respects, and he found our conversations on the history of the movement useful. But much of what he said about working-class attitudes and capabilities was new to me. Apparently he had been very influential among his fellows.

H: What was his history prior to this time? What did he tell you?

D: He didn't talk about it readily. He was married, and apparently his wife was much more educated than he. He never graduated from any institution, but he was quite literate and read a great deal, a self-educated man.

H: He was a worker in Nizhnii Novgorod?

D: Yes, he was a metal worker and apparently good in his specialty. But if you compared him with Petersburg workers, you could see enormous gaps. The Petersburg metal workers (I knew only a few) had not completed any formal education, but many of them went through the Sunday schools. This provided them some more or less systematic instruction. Bagaev had none of this. As regards geography, for example, he could easily say that Spain was located . . . God knows where . . . I don't remember if he actually said that, but it was entirely possible. He had no systematic knowledge, but he had read a great deal and educated himself. Naturally, he never read Marx, and probably felt no need to do so. But he had worked his way somehow through Beltov's book, although much of it was incomprehensible to him. He found out about the Emancipation of Labor group through Beltov.

He had been involved in a circle with some members of the intelligentsia. Much of his education was picked up in revolutionary circles, and thus it was entirely unsystematic.

H: In Nizhnii Novgorod?

D: There was an underground movement in Nizhnii Novgorod, although it was not very extensive; there was a group of intelligentsia that had certain contacts abroad but which changed constantly because of arrests. Bagaev had met a great many intellectuals who frequented these circles in Nizhnii Novgorod. Of course, these contacts were rather haphazard, and superficial, but he managed to pick up a great deal. He was keenly interested in knowledge.

H: What was his revolutionary activity?

D: He was an organizer of the underground in Nizhnii Novgorod. He was involved in the local party, took part in all the decisions, and discussed how to prepare strikes and demonstrations. If literature was received, he would distribute it.

H: So probably he was the first educated worker with whom you became well acquainted.

D: I had known Babushkin in Petersburg; he was an outstanding worker. And I had gotten to meet a few other workers from Petersburg. The Petersburg worker was a very advanced type; I never met a single such worker in Moscow. Bagaev was very unusual, I think.

H: You said that there was a great deal that was new for you in his outlook.

D: In the first place, I had thought that I had a fairly clear notion of the Russian working-man's life. But from talking with Bagaev I found out that this wasn't so. Not merely had I not fully taken account of the workers' painful material situation, but I also had not realized the extent to which they were subject to all kinds of arbitrary acts on the part of the police and the factory management. We all knew about police repression and could feel it acutely, but I must say that even the Jews in Petersburg and Moscow were not as dependent on the whim of any policeman or constable as the workers. I had been angered by what the Petersburg women weavers had told me about the factory management. The picture was dreadful. But the police situation was not brought up much, though probably this was due to my own inability to make inquiries. Now, there was a great deal that was new to me. I formed a concrete picture of life in a provincial town for those who enjoyed no privileges, and the picture was a terrible one. But, and even more important for me, Bagaev characterized for me the worker's attitudes. He himself was very political, but he thought that such attitudes were not all readily accessible to the workers. He was one of those who said that economic agitation was much more intelligible for the workers than political agitation. Of course, any worker would understand if there was a demonstration and workers were beaten. After this they would much more readily listen to purely political discussions, but otherwise this did not happen spontaneously. If you were to say that the material situation was dreadful, that was something that any fool understood.

H: But were Bagaev's political conclusions about the line that the party should take in accord with *Iskra's?* Did he have his own opinion about disputed issues, in particular that of the political and the economic struggles?

D: He unquestionably had arrived at the conclusion that, on balance, it was necessary to pursue a sharply political line. Even though it might not be successful today, he agreed that this was the only way to introduce political ideas to broad sectors of workers. This was the basis for his sympathy for *Iskra,* which he was able to read, though not very regularly. He usually listened to our conversations sympathetically. He attempted to modify my negative attitude toward the Economists saying that the situation was not so black and white, and that what they said had some grounds and should be understood. But opportunistic attitudes were fatal, and must be overcome.

H: From what Bagaev told you about life in Nizhnii Novgorod, did it seem as though there were workers or intelligentsia there who pressed for the Economist viewpoint?

D: Of course there were.

H: Many of his comrades?

D: At that time those involved in the movement could be counted in dozens, not hundreds. I think that it was a fairly frequently debated issue – not to exaggerate.

H: How did he explain the Economist viewpoint to you?

D: He said that every worker in Russia felt the weight of all the horrors that resulted from the workers's situation. To this I would reply, "Yes, of course, but what is horrible is not just the abysmally low wages, but also being without rights." He would say, "That's true, but consider this: if I am poorly paid, I can talk things over with the workers in my shop or factory, and together – in the usual way, by going on strike – we can manage to get wages raised. My own and other workers' lack of rights is not a problem that can be eliminated by our own efforts. Much greater masses are required to do this." Furthermore, in the awareness of the poorly educated worker, I think the chief enemy was not tsarism in general, but the local police officer. It would have been very easy to organize a group of people to go and beat a policeman half to death. Of course, the workers understood that this was a means of struggle and rejected such direct methods in the name of "political struggle." On the other hand, they had no possibility of organizing political struggle on a large scale and didn't know how to go about it. They understood that this could not be done by workers' hands alone. In short, a broader front was needed, but how could this be approached? Well, there were the students – they could always offer support. The zemstvo activists – this had just begun –but the workers had neither the confidence nor the desire to work with them. I think that, at the root, there was a feeling of complete helplessness and hopelessness about achieving anything through their own meager resources, so it was better not to try. But, closer to hand, if one could organize one's shop and the next one, one might get the wages increased from 11 kopecks to 15 kopecks. I think that this was at bottom – of course, there were very detailed and extensive discussions.

H: How did Bagaev conceive of the aim of this political struggle – what was to be changed and how?

D: I think that, in the outlook of the time, the aim was to push for a democratic republic by overthrowing the autocracy.

H: Did he understand the concept of a bourgeois revolution?

D: No, I don't remember conversations on that topic.

H: Did you discuss the participation of the liberal bourgeoisie in the struggle and how it might be possible?

D: Yes, it was talked about, although we ourselves had a rather negative view of Struve and the rest. The view was that the liberals, of course, were capable of oppositionist activities. But while we wanted revolutionary activity that would lead to the overthrow of autocracy and the establishment of a democratic republic, the liberals were not interested in this. Against this they upheld the notion of a limited autocracy and a constitution, which didn't appeal to us at all.

H: Did he specify at all what the results of this revolution would ultimately be? Would it be within the framework of a democratic republic, or a bourgeois regime?

D: No one even dreamed that there would be socialism within our lifetime.

H: I would like to dwell at greater length on the literature with which Bagaev was familiar. You mentioned Beltov . . .

D: Beltov's was a legal book. I don't believe that Bagaev read the "thick journals" at the time, for example – I don't know that he did. But there were legal books, like Lissagaray's *History of the Commune*, a small book of around 200 pages, which he had read and had some idea of.[4] He also had read about and had some notions of the French revolution. But he got the most in terms of content from illegal literature.

H: What else did he read?

D: He had never seen *Zaria*. Something which he had read, of course, which was very much in vogue and not so difficult to get, was Tun's *History of the Revolutionary Movement.*[5] Thus he had some notion of the Russian revolutionary movement. Naturally, he was primarily struck by the romantic and heroic aspects of the movement. He regarded himself as a Social Democrat and hence an antinarodnik. But I doubt that he knew much about the details of the *narodnik* movement.

H: Why did he regard himself as a Social Democrat?

D: Because the Social Democrats worked among the proletariat and their attitude toward the peasantry was one of equanimity, if not exactly disparagement – they expected nothing good of them.

H: And he didn't either?

D: No, and, naturally, he knew more about the peasantry than I.

H: What was his attitude toward terror?

D: At that time there wasn't any; his attitude toward the earlier terror was reverential. The romantic and heroic aspects had an influence on everyone, because a twenty-year gap separated us from that period. Sometimes I would tell him what I knew from reading about the People's Will – it was a very interesting topic.

H: But that was later?

D: Yes, after the assassination of Bogolepov, at the end of 1901 or the beginning of 1902.[6]

H: It was talked about?

D: Of course – everyone knew about it. It was in the legal press. What stunned everyone about the Bogolepov affair was the high-handed manner of drafting students into the army. I think that his assassination aroused some sympathy in a fairly broad sector of society.

H: What was Bagaev's attitude toward it?

D: That it was extraneous, but a good thing. Terror was not an immediate issue, and it was natural for a student to assassinate a minister who had conscripted students into the army. But what did it have to do with us? It wasn't tied into the overall picture of the current revolutionary struggle, so to speak. It was something we liked, but which was essentially entirely unrelated to us.

H: Did you notice that he had any notion about the plan to create a nation-wide organization?

D: I think that he had some misgivings that the intelligentsia would largely dominate the workers in such an organization. He understood that this issue was not one of principle. But ultimately he felt – although I don't recall whether he actually said this – that "a person like Khinchuk is someone serious who you can get on with, but others are different, you know." Probably there were also young students in Nizhnii Novgorod who had not been very tactful. Perhaps he had personally experienced some supercilious attitudes on their part. Still, his attitude toward the intelligentsia was very guarded. He felt that you couldn't get along without the intelligentsia, but things must be arranged so that the workers did not completely become slaves to them. He was afraid, given the need for centralization and the impossibility of democracy in any organization under the tsarist regime, that it would be much more difficult for a worker to make his way in such an organization than for an intellectual.

The workers understood that the intelligentsia, particularly the present-day intelligentsia, lived badly, and sometimes no better than the workers themselves, but the *intelligent* was essentially not tied down; if things didn't work out in one place he could leave. If he was young and unmarried and had no family, he could move from Nizhnii Novgorod to Kazan. The worker, on the other hand, had nowhere to go. If he did not feel comfortable in his surroundings, he could step aside and become entirely passive, but he could not actively rearrange his life. How could he get away from his family? He was much more tied down to his external situation. I think that, like many other workers, Bagaev exaggerated the independence of members of the intelligentsia. Of course, it was great compared to the workers, but still I think Bagaev exaggerated the difference.

There was the matter of becoming an illegal. Formally one could, but who would take care of one's family? Not everyone was able simply to abandon his wife and children – they would be lost. The party could not be counted upon for support. Naturally, people were greatly tied down and restricted by this.

H: Who were Bagaev's heroes in the Social-Democratic movement? Who would he ask you about?

D: He would ask me about my life in Munich, about the editorial board of *Iskra*, and about each member separately, and listened avidly to what I had to say. I would tell him about Zasulich or Plekhanov, and he would be tremendously interested, of course, because what had been an abstract notion for him was now filled with some content. He had no notion of all of Lenin or Martov. It was only at this point that he formed one. I talked about *Rabochee Delo*, and he was terribly interested.

H: Was he familiar with the arguments used by the Economists abroad? Had he seen any issues of *Rabochee Delo* by then?

D: I can't recall that he had; perhaps some issue had passed through his hands. Of course, there was all manner of pamphlet literature. It was colorless and frequently quite untalented, but it offered something. And formulations in *Iskra* were clear, so he had some idea.

H: But *Iskra* was the sole base of this knowledge?

D: Even though there were many issues of *Iskra* that he missed, it was his major store of knowledge, and he regarded it as most important. When he read Beltov, he felt that it was a revelation to him.

H: Did he explain in what respect?

D: This was true for a great many people – for the first time Marxism was presented to the Russian reader not as some incomprehensible abstraction, but as something directly related to the workers' cause. Somehow he had acquired and read Plekhanov's *Socialism and the Political Struggle* and *Our Differences*.[7] Perhaps not all of it was comprehensible to him, but it was part of his store of knowledge. I think that from reading Plekhanov he – for certain – and probably others perceived the real link between the Russian workers' movement and the European movement – that the Russian movement was an integral part of it. This was a prominent factor in his criticism of *narodnichestvo* – that people felt blindly that something separate could be done in Russia. In reality the strength was in unity, and we were as much the brothers of the Spanish workers and others as of our own Russian workers. I think that the idea of internationalism came to him primarily from reading Plekhanov.

H: Was it of great importance?

D: For him its importance was extremely great.

H: Did he ask you many questions about the working-class movement in the West?

D: Of course he did. In this respect I was fairly well-equipped to answer. Much of what I said was very interesting to him. He was impressed by the degree of organization in the working-class movement in the West – the extensive funds, trade unions, organizations, real strength. For him this was in effect a new world. He had heard of it earlier, but through me he could put together a fairly concrete notion of how it looked. It seemed to him that it opened up great prospects.

H: Let us go back to the topics of conversation you had during this period in Taganka and Butyrki: there was the issue of centralism, as well as the issue of the Economists and the extent to which the workers were sympathetic to them.

D: It should be said that all the conversations in our milieu remained more or less in the sphere of party politics and party tactics. Sometimes someone would try to recall some verses, or something like that, but that was infrequent. Kugushev [a fellow prisoner] was amazed when I told him what narrow people we all essentially were.[8] In the first place, we were city people; in the second, we were narrow. His involvement with nature was extremely important – for us it virtually didn't exist. This was when I first understood what few roots we Social Democrats had in Russian society. We were a little corner, a very respected one, but without firm ties to the mainstream of the Russian people. But in our conversations, of course, we would try to catch any little bit of information [about the party] – what so-and-so had said, whom so-and-so had met, some little bits of information from abroad. It was all crumbs.

*   *   *

H: I think it would be useful to describe how you became involved in the hunger strike.

D: The story is rather comic, but not without interest. We had been wondering impatiently for a year when we would be sent off to Siberia. The conditions were not harsh, but we wanted to be at liberty. Each of us thought that, as soon as we arrived, we could escape right away. Others said that families could go along, and so forth. So the question of our departure was a major one. At the same time, there were discussions and arguments through the windows, involving a great many people, about the disagreements with the Bund. They were about the Bund's insistence on a federation with the party [i.e., on the Bund's autonomous organization within the party – ed.]. Its rationale was that, since the Jewish proletariat had its own particular problems, it should have its own organization. At that time Lenin was saying that the Jews could achieve nothing by themselves. The Bundists replied that this was all true, but since they had special problems, they needed a special party. I should add that the factor of youth was very important; we were fairly lightheaded. At one point I said that if a special.position meant a special party, then, comrades, there should be a special women's party, because we women no doubt had special interests. Probably people laughed at this; I can't even remember.

Some time later, when the question of our departure again arose, someone said, "They'll send us off one way or another, but it seems that the women will be sent separately, and that's bad." "What do you mean, separately?" We had counted greatly on being able to see one another. I can't reconstruct what the day-to-day sequence of events was, because no one had told us that we were being sent off. But soon people were saying that we wouldn't go, and a hunger strike was decided upon. This was fairly easy to decide. Don't forget that we had been in prison more than a year. (It was already late summer, probably August 1903.) Our state of mind was not exactly calm and philosophical. "We're declaring a hunger strike – the hell with you, we've had enough!" And people started to refuse food. "No, I am not having any of that garbage." "Well, who cares? If you don't want it, you don't get it!" We still accepted boiling water for tea and drank water, because hunger strikes without water, as sometimes happened, were very agonizing. It lasted two or three days. In Taganka prison, when a hunger strike was declared, an assistant of the warden, not the warden himself, would come and ask what the demands were, and you could tell him. If the strike continued, an assistant procurator would be called in, because under the tsarist regime the prisons were administered by the Ministry of Justice.[9] The assistant procurator was supposed to determine what was going on. In this case, when the assistant procurator came into my cell, I more or less mumbled something, like a complete fool, and couldn't state anything articulately. He gave up and went to talk to others. In a word, he didn't understand anything after his visit. The question was, how the entire affair had started.

H: Why didn't you simply explain to him what you wanted?

D: No one had told us about the strike, so it was rather confusing. I too was surprised. I was told: "Why are you surprised? It started with you." "What do you mean, me?" "You said so." "I never did." "What do you mean, you never did?" At this point someone whispered to me that we had in fact begun by talking about special interests, and the entire picture was reconstructed. Then there arose the question of how to end the hunger strike. Someone was empowered to tell the administration that we were calling it off. I am not very certain, but I think it was Khinchuk – I don't remember very well. I should add that I was not so sick that I couldn't move. Still, the strike had an effect on me. I felt very awkward and somehow responsible for the entire affair and would have been grateful for a change of scene. I called for the doctor and told him that I was not feeling well. I always could, because my health was always rather poor. The doctor said I could be transferred to the Pugachev tower. I answered, "If that's possible, please do." So I was transferred.

H: Did you explain to your comrades that it was for your health?

D: They all knew and were very concerned about me. I was in fact weaker than the others. And the whole affair did not improve my health. I still had tuberculosis, although it was not severe.

H: So you were transferred to Butyrki?

D: Yes, to the Pugachev tower.

H: How long did you remain there?

D: I think that it was until spring – part of the late summer and part of the winter of 1903 in any case.

H: And you went directly from there to Siberia?

D: No, I returned to Taganka, and they dispatched us from there . . . without any trouble.

H: Now, could you describe how you went from Taganka to Aleksandrovsk?[10]

D: Well, they put us in railway cars [to Usole].

H: This was approximately at the end of the winter of 1903?

D: Yes, perhaps it was even spring. I am almost certain that when we went from Usole to Aleksandrovsk prison, a distance of around 30 or 35 kilometers, it felt like spring. Everyone was expected to go on foot, but there was a wagon for those who were ill. Very many people were happy to go on foot; there we had a day's rest. We covered the distance in two days.

H: Perhaps we could begin with a picture of life at Aleksandrovsk. You have said that the situation was exceptional.

D: We were no longer under trial; we were "administrative" exiles. Next to the transit prison was the Aleksandrovsk Central Prison, which contained people who had received hard-labor sentences in court and been deprived of rights. They were a special category, and the administration dealt with them differently. We were half-free, and in fact the administration felt somewhat guilty, because there was a custom (not a law) that when a person was sent into [administrative] exile he should be sent soon, because there was no point in being in prison when there was no trial. This was at the time of the Russo-Japanese War, and transportation was very disorganized. We had been in prison a damn long time, and therefore they tried to give us an easy time, fearing that otherwise we would start something. So they didn't oppress us. And then, the regime was an easy one, I feel. Inside the prison there was a wooden barrack, which was open all day. You could sit there, or you could go to the kitchen, or you could sit in the courtyard; there were no guards beyond the walls. This meant a great deal. The windows had gratings, but in the kitchen they didn't, and everyone congregated there. Whoever was in charge of cooking was dissatisfied that people were always hanging around the kitchen. "Why do you always sit in here?" "We like to." Eventually someone figured it out. It was because it had been so long since we had seen windows without gratings.

H: And, of course, it was very easy to talk there.

D: Yes, you were entirely free to do so, and you could read or debate. No one had anything they had to do. Those who wanted to do something did, and those who didn't, didn't. Because people had been in prison for so long, they would readily drop serious work to talk. Everyone was interested. I don't have any bad memories of the place. The regime was so easy that you could escape. Sergei Osipovich and Konkordiia Ivanovna did.[11] It wasn't a bad prison.

H: Under the circumstances, with a great deal of freedom, was the life of the prisoners organized? Did you have a chosen leadership?

D: No, though there was a *starosta* who dealt with the warden. We did our own cleaning, cooking, and other services. Besides that, we were free.

It must be remembered that there were people from all parts of Russia here, so it was very informative. For example, there were people from Odessa, where working conditions were entirely different. There were people from the Jewish Pale where a broad movement had already emerged, and people were arrested who were totally uninvolved in party work. For example, Jewish butchers, who didn't even speak Russian. It seems that they had organized a strike, not against the government but against their own fellow Jews. They had been arrested and sent to Siberia. They were ordinary Jews, but they had interesting things to say.

H: Approximately how many people were there?

D: About 70 to 80 in the men's section, and 15 or 20 women. It was not exactly comfortable, but we were young and didn't pay much attention to that. Of course, everyone wanted very much to escape from this communal life into his own little corner.

H: You have said that you met more of the elite of the Social-Democratic intelligentsia there than ever before.

D: Yes, a great many, especially the party activists. They were brought from all parts of Russia. And since there was nothing else to do, people talked about their lives and thus became acquainted with one another and with party work. This was all very informative.

H: Perhaps it would be useful to describe what was unexpected for you when you first got this first over-all picture of the movement.

D: For me personally, it was the considerable amplitude in the development of activity that was unexpected. I had always lived in a more uniform party milieu. There were figures of greater prominence, but they were all party intelligentsia. The differences were purely quantitative, not qualitative. At Aleksandrovsk I encountered the most diverse levels of development, and yet all those people were Social Democrats. This was unexpected, because I also perceived that the general intelligence was not very high, particularly among people from the provinces.

H: And you had expected more?

D: Yes, but it wasn't tragic.

H: Let us briefly discuss the political events of that time. Was the resolution regarding the Socialist Revolutionaries known in prison?[12] It is not clear to me, but it seems that you were in prison at the beginning of 1904, so the resolution had already been passed at the [Second] Party Congress.

D: At Aleksandrovsk there was already some information about the party congress – not documentary information, but it was known and talked about obliquely. In the first place, it was known that the Bund had left the party.[13] There were many Jews who were associated with both the Bund and the party, at least in fact if not formally, and it was a great shock to all of them. Secondly, there was the matter of the Socialist Revolutionaries and the attitude toward terror. I think that there was a great intellectual aversion to terror in our Social-Democratic milieu, but emotionally it commanded respect. So Plekhanov's sharp disassociation from it was a shock.

H: Did many people disagree with him?

D: Yes, many. Because earlier, they had thought that it was important for us to make a unified front with the Socialist Revolutionaries. If we now shut ourselves off from them, we must still recognize that there were sympathies toward them among the working class, and so it was risky. This was talked about a great deal. I think, however, that there was a fair amount of cowardice. People did not venture to condemn the resolution, but they felt somewhat uncomfortable with it.

H: Why was it not condemned? Because Plekhanov commanded such respect?

D: Yes, of course, and then there was the vote of the congress.

H: In any case, there were certain reservations about this resolution which attempted to describe the SRs as a bourgeois phenomenon?

D: It was felt that the Socialist Revolutionaries were socialists and that the entire Russian experience showed that this movement could become as powerful as the proletarian movement. And even more, because Russia was a peasant country, and the SRs had greater access to the peasant masses. The main objection to terror was as follows: even assuming that the Socialist Revolutionary party was in fact a very good one, it would undermine its own foundations, because, if it set up a "combat organization," this sort of activity would eliminate everything else. All efforts would be concentrated in that direction.

H: But could they accept the notion that the Socialist Revolutionaries were bourgeois?

D: That was very difficult. When you see people who are going to their deaths you still have to feel some bond with them. We didn't exactly see bourgeoisie going to their death. So the Socialist Revolutionaries were somehow distinct. It must also be said that some, though not all, of the acts of the Socialist Revolutionaries made an enormous impression and were very revolutionizing. The assassination of Plehve definitely evoked a response on a national scale.[14]

H: Were there people among the Social Democrats who had the courage to express their doubts about terror?

D: Of course there were, but they spoke about it very guardedly.

H: What do you mean guardedly?

D: They condemned it, but not categorically – they had reservations. This was extremely important.

H: I would like to clarify something. You were courageous people who had already been in prison; Plekhanov couldn't do much to you . . .

D: It wasn't that we were afraid of repression, but we didn't want to disagree with our beloved leaders. We trusted Plekhanov more than we did ourselves.

H: What rumors did you hear about the party split at that time?[15]

D: It is very difficult to say, because they were different and contradictory. Some said that there was a real split, while others said that it was not exactly a split as yet.

H: But in any case it was known that there were disagreements among Lenin, Plekhanov, Axelrod, and Martov.

D: It was known. I, for one, was very bewildered: how could this have happened? It was hard for me to imagine.

H: And you tried to discuss and explain it?

D: It was so unexpected. When people began to talk about it, they claimed that Lenin had been saying more or less the same thing from the very beginning; they asked why was it said now that "the news came like a bolt out of the blue." There is an element of truth in this. Lenin might have been mistaken or he might have begun to draw logical conclusions, while Martov or other Mensheviks . . .

H: You were saying that there was such confusion and lack of understanding that even Ezhov supported Lenin when he first heard about the split.

D: He favored the Bolsheviks, but for a very short time.

H: It interests me that you said that Lenin ultimately drew logical conclusions from his long-standing premises. Does this mean they thought Martov and company did not agree with these conclusions?

D: They did not always agree. Martov, in the preface to *State of Siege*, also says that he let a great deal pass, even when he did not agree, and never spoke up because he felt that unity was the most important thing. Later, people maintained that Martov had been saying the same things as Lenin; if he didn't protest, he must have agreed. When Martov screamed bloody murder, they said: "But why now? You should have shouted before." There was a great deal of confusion and uncertainty. People were very much lost. The *Iskra* group which had seemed so firm, united and monolithic, now seemed to have disagreements in its midst which for some reason had never appeared before. And they had come forth all at once in this dreadful form. This caused a great deal of confusion. Still, I identified myself as a Menshevik fairly soon.

H: This was before you left Aleksandrovsk?

D: No. As yet there was not enough information and we vacillated.

H: And others?

D: I think that the attitude was more or less general. A little later, in Olekminsk,[16] Glafira Akulova, Teodoróvich's wife, was very definitely pro-Bolshevik.[17] She also had no actual ties, but attitudes definitely linked her to them. Then there was Uritskii, who was definitely a Menshevik.[18] And Shipulinskii[19] and Popov[20] were all Mensheviks. Still, since there was no practical activity, all of this should be understood . . .

H: At this point the Russo-Japanese War had been going on for several months.

D: This was the topic of very extensive discussions. In the first place, there were discussions about "defeatism" and "defensism" which absorbed us a great deal.

H: What attitudes were there?

D: In general, defeatist attitudes were very widespread in Russian society, and not just among the socialists, during the war. Even the liberals felt, and we felt even more so, that tsarism would not survive the shock if Russia was decisively defeated. So there was no reason to be defensist. But the thought flashed through some people's minds of volunteering for the war. In that way you could be freed immediately. I recall Avram Ginzburg saying, "Do you think it makes sense to volunteer for the war? You would be freed immediately, and you could propagandize at the front," and so forth. I was definitely against it, and he didn't insist very much. But I remember that such attitudes existed.

H: Was it expected that the war would bring the revolution closer?

D: Yes, definitely. People even had exaggerated hopes that the collapse would be immediate and that tsarism would not survive it. We in Siberia could not perceive how the workers felt, because we were cut off from them. But there were constant rumors that the soldiers were inclined to defeatism and didn't want to fight at all. This was not even out of political considerations, but because the autocracy was so totally unprepared; it was helpless and incapable of doing anything, so there was a great deal of bitterness.

H: Did you discuss what tactics should be used?

D: No – how could we, since we were cut off from any activity? There was no concern about tactics. We simply waited for someone to tell us something, and then we would express our attitude, positive or negative. There was nothing else to do there except to discuss. So we discussed everything, the important and the unimportant. There was talk about the Bund's break with the party. This was a rather painful topic; we really didn't know what stance to take: yesterday they had been comrades and closely linked to us, and now today they were aliens. It shouldn't have happened that way, but it turns out it had to. There was a great deal of mutual irritation. The Bundists talked fairly freely about antisemitic attitudes in the Russian part of the party, which was generally unfair. Still, it wasn't exactly conducive to a friendly atmosphere.

H: Did it mean that you ceased to call the Bundists comrades?

D: No.

H: Did you stop calling the Socialist Revolutionaries comrades?

D: There was no rule, but in any case it wasn't as before, If some news was received, you would think about whether to tell them or not. It was silly, but so it was. A sense of alienation appeared.

H: And, up to this point, you had shared your life in Aleksandrovsk prison with the Socialist Revolutionaries?

D: The comrades all lived in one commune and shared everything.

H: How far did the conflict go?

D: We were more or less open in our discussions. When letters were to be passed on, finally they all were; but you might say that now it took an effort. No one left the commune. There was a smaller commune that split off, but that was over an entirely different issue.

H: What was it?

D: It had been resolved that everyone would hand over their money to the commune, and we did this very conscientiously. But there were two people from Odessa, a husband and wife, whose names I can't remember, and they had a child. Their behavior wasn't entirely correct. They kept their own finances, which wasn't so dreadful, but such issues assumed great proportions in prison. There was a meeting, and a lot of unpleasant things were said. I, Savinkov, Avram Ginzburg, Anna Rozenfeld, Boris Tseitlin, and someone else whose name I can't remember, split off and formed a small commune.[21] We said that we wanted to have nothing to do with the large commune, because they had not acted in a comradely fashion. It didn't last very long, however; there was some affair, a scandal, which resulted in the decision of all the prisoners not to submit to the demands of the administration. We went out into the courtyard and refused to enter the barracks. I don't remember what the issue was. At this point, someone cautiously asked Avram Ginzburg if the small commune would take part in the protest. He said, "What do you mean? Of course we will." So we were all together again. Then Kurnatovskii solemnly announced that he hoped that, since everyone had shown true comradely feelings, and so forth, that there would be no further talk of a separate commune, and everyone started to embrace – it was a very touching scene.[22] This was the end of the small commune.

Ninth interview

H: I would like to begin with your journey from Aleksandrovsk prison to Olekminsk.

D: We traveled on a barge, a large flat-bottomed boat [*pauzok*] that floated downstream. It had no motor or anything of the sort. There were both criminals and politicals on board, and in general the conditions were not too bad. Perhaps they were bad, but since we all understood that we were going to be relatively at liberty, we were fairly patient and put up with the minor inconveniences.

H: How many people were there?

D: I think that there were around 200. The barge was huge, of course. It had a large deck and then there was an area like a hold. The women, men, and criminals all slept separately in the hold, but we were not locked in and could spend the entire day sitting on the deck. The weather was good, so there was no problem.

H: This was in July 1904?

D: Yes. It was summer, the weather was good, and the landscape was gorgeous. The main thing was that we were heading for "freedom," so there was a really festive mood. We were out in the air and the sun for the first time after a long stretch in prison. There were guards, but they did not interfere – there were no checks or anything of the sort. When we reached a village or small town, we would stop and some of the criminals would get off; they were being sent to the Verkholensk district and elsewhere. No new prisoners got on, so the numbers dwindled. Usually the local peasant women would set up a small bazaar. They sold provisions, eggs, and other items. Generally we ate dry food – there was nothing hot. But there was tea, because on deck there was a sort of small stove with a fire and a container for boiling water. We met various exiles along the way and learned the news. For example, we heard about Plehve's assassination in Kenenst. Of course, this event was of enormous significance – it seemed as though the revolution would come tomorrow.

H: Did people shout the news to you?

D: Yes, the exiles shouted it as soon as we approached the bank: "Plehve has been killed, by order of the Combat Organization of the Socialist Revolutionaries."[1] We were simply ecstatic. The effect was the same as if we had been told that there was a revolution, because Plehve was for all of us the embodiment of oppression and hatred. It was a tremendous thing. At the same time, there was much that was funny about it, because, in the midst of the general rejoicing, the Socialist Revolutionaries were saying, "Now you applaud, but before you were claiming that we were bourgeois democrats." They shouted "Why are you applauding? It wasn't comrades [*tovarishchi*] but misters [*gospoda*] who did it." This was trivial, of course, because in fact everyone was equally enthusiastic.

Not everyone realized it, but the thought flashed through some people's minds that we were entering a new period, that something had changed in Russia if it had become possible to assassinate Plehve. At some place further on, a guard tried to stop us from doing something, some petty thing, but we said that we wouldn't leave the bank and get onto the deck, so they called up some other guards. Larin behaved very aggressively here. This seemed funny to everyone, because he was an invalid and totally disabled, but he was very brave.[2] We all linked arms and said that we wouldn't go, and he did too. The guards laughed, saying "Look, look, he too doesn't want to go." In short, the mood was rather good-natured. The whole affair amounted to nothing, because we gave in, got onto the deck, and in the end arrived at Olekminsk. It is 2,000 kilometers from Irkutsk to Olekminsk; we traveled more than a month, I think, and arrived in August. It might have taken five weeks.

If I were to tell all the details, people now would say that we had a bad time, but I don't remember it as hard and no one else did. It was pleasant, because we were headed for freedom. We were all young, and we figured that a new life was beginning for us now. When we arrived, we were met by local exiles. There was a fairly large colony there, as we knew. We were immediately told where rooms were available for us, and so on. So we were very well received. It was immediately apparent that Uritskii was in charge of everyone. He was not a leader, but an authority. Anything that involved the exiles was to be taken to Uritskii; he could handle anything. He asked me and Savinkov, "Well, do you want to be together? I have rented a house for you on Taiganskaia Hill."[3] There was a little hill by that name. In short, quarters were found for everyone. He said that we had to go to the district police officer the next day, because he had to record how many people arrived and to check the lists to determine how much money we were to get. We received something like 17 or 18 rubles a month, and that was a fair amount of money. You couldn't live on it, but it was basic. I remember one detail that struck me. It was a small detail but one that was very characteristic of the time, of Siberia, and of these people. Savinkov and I arrived at the district police station and sat and waited. We were told that the officer was busy and that we should wait. As we were sitting, we heard someone talking with the officer, and saying, "And the same noblemen who kissed the hand of Louis XVI cut off his head afterward." We were greatly amazed that someone could talk like that to an officer. It turned out that Teodorovich was there and that, in reply to some admonitions on the part of the officer to the effect that it was better to give in and so forth, he cited this maxim. This shows what the "alignment of forces" was in general. In Petersburg, in the Okhrana, or anywhere in Russia, you couldn't say such things, of course. But in Siberia the relationship was different, and the exiles were treated entirely differently. Since sometime before, the exiles had been called "state people" [*gosudarstvennye*], because it was felt that they were "state" offenders. And they remained "state people." The name became, if not a rank, a characterization, and rather a respectable one.

H: It impressed people?

D: Yes. For example, there was a story about some little girl. Some exiles returned and they had a little girl. She was asked, "Is your father Jewish?" She answered, "No we're state people." It was a natural answer because they had lived beyond the normal Russian divisions into classes and religions. We lived beyond general laws. We had no great rights, but still had a special status.

H: Could you briefly describe Olekminsk?

D: Olekminsk was a district town that consisted of one street running along the Lena River. There were no stone houses, only wooden huts, but good huts. It was a tidy, nice town. Olekminsk stands where the Olekma River flows. On one side of the Olekma was Olekminsk proper, and on the other side was the village of Spasskoe. Exiled *skoptsy* lived in Spasskoe.[4] I think I told you that by old Russian laws, the *skoptsy* were regarded as a pernicious sect and exiled to Siberia. They lived separately, on the other side of the Olekma. The government tried in general to isolate them from the bulk of the population, because the *skoptsy* were supposed to be constantly trying to seduce people into their sect – and it seems that this was in fact true. So the government had reason to try to isolate them. The *skoptsy* lived very well. They had their own houses, also of wood, of course. But they had something that no one else in Siberia did – small gardens. The Siberian peasantry was not partial to garden plots. There was forest all around so why bother? But the *skoptsy* fenced off their houses and planted small gardens. They even planted flowers. Curiously enough, they planted only flowers that did not smell. *Skoptsy* cannot tolerate the smell of flowers. It has something to do with their physical condition.

The *skoptsy* didn't receive payments. But they probably had a mutual-assistance arrangement and help from Russia. They were all involved in small trading. They had a shop, not in Spasskoe, but in Olekminsk, so they would walk there every morning to trade. This was generally forbidden by law, because the *skoptsy* were supposed to live where they were registered, but they would go every day, and the situation was tolerated until the police officer was in need of money. If he was in need, he would round them up

– "What are you doing here?" Then he would throw them in the clink and, two hours later, would come and agree to let them out and take two or three rubles. There were both men and women there. When some new convicted woman *skopets* arrived, she would be offered lodging with one of them. This was with the agreement of both the administration and the *skoptsy* themselves. One of the *skoptsy* would take her in as a "sister." How far their relations went, I don't know. No one knows. They were generally very discreet. But the *skoptsy* lived decently, more decently than the Siberian peasants, or *cheldony*, as they were called.[5] They lived better. They had various books and read. They were more cultured than the average Siberian peasant. They also maintained more contact with Russia and their people there than was usual for a Siberian in such a remote place in those times.

H: What was their political orientation?

D: Generally they were dissatisfied with the government. But there wasn't any differentiation beyond that. In general, they were religious people. They spoke so reluctantly about their attitudes and business that it was almost impossible to ask. But I can't imagine, for example, that any Siberian peasant would have been interested in cameras, particularly at that time, but the *skoptsy* had cameras. Even in the cities of Russia, cameras weren't very common. Probably the *skoptsy* got them from friends, likeminded people in Russia. I should mention that there were *skoptsy* in some very wealthy merchant families in Russia, and probably they helped one another. There was a great deal of collaboration and mutual help among them in general.

H: And how did the exiles live?

D: There were around 20 of us, and we didn't live badly. Each of us could rent a room or even a hut. For example, Savinkov and I were in a small house, a big hut, so there were two rooms. When the stove was going, it was warm, but you had to know how to start it. The first time we tried, we were almost overcome by the fumes. You have to know when to close it off, which is tricky. No one put any limits on us.

H: What did you do?

D: We read a lot and worked. Savinkov and I, in particular, took up photography. I had a remarkable album, which was lost, with pictures of all the exiles; people who had completed their terms, say, in Kolymsk, would stop off in Olekminsk. Some people, like Teodorovich and Shipulinskii, gave lessons. The local people, like the police officer, were very happy to have their children taught by an exile. In the first place, the exiles were the only true intelligentsia, and second, you could count on learning French or German from them. In general, the exiles stood well with the local people. There were some young Jews, Bobinskii, Khinoi, and others, and this was a new element among the Siberian exiles.[6] It was too plebeian and could ultimately lower the exiles' prestige. In these remote places there still existed the old notions of the lords, the *bary*, who were immeasurably higher than the local people both materially and in general. So now there were these new exiles, the mass exiles.

There were five Jewish butchers who themselves did not know why they had been exiled to the Iakutsk region. The local police officer in their village had become angry at them and sent them off to Siberia at the first opportunity. It seems that there was a strike. They spoke Russian poorly. I tried to work with them, although I knew Yiddish very poorly. I read the Erfurt Program with them.[7] Whether they understood, I don't know. But it was serious work.

In general, there was considerable self-education and mutual assistance, and I think that many people learned a great deal. It was a kind of school. There were many books. When an exile left, he wouldn't take his books with him, but leave them with the colony. Also, we were constantly receiving journals and the like. The mail came once a week; now I remember, it was on Wednesdays. It came on a boat. We would receive a week's worth of newspapers. By 1904–1905 there were already some new liberal and democratic newspapers, like *Pravo*,[8] *Nasha Zhizn'*,[9] and so forth. There was a lot of information. I remember an argument I had once; I said that I customarily began reading the newspaper with the lead article. Uritskii objected that he always began with the chronicle, because the chronicle contained the latest events. Generally we were quite free, there was a great deal of time, and there were many opportunities to meet one another. It was a fairly easy time. There were also family people there, who also were well set up.

H: I would like to discuss some individuals. Perhaps we could begin with Uritskii. How do you picture him as a leader?

D: For example, as regards everyday affairs, I once said that I would like to be able to ride horseback. He said that even there that could be done. But how? Two days later he went off somewhere and brought me a man who had a horse. Then he went to the local priest, who for some reason had a lady's saddle, and so I could indeed ride horseback. In general, whatever you needed, Uritskii could arrange. His connections were enormous. If a local person was in difficulty or had complaints against the authorities, he naturally went to Uritskii who would give him advice and assistance. He had a great deal of influence.

H: How long had he been there when you arrived?

D: He had been there around four years, since 1901 or maybe even 1900. He had been sent for eight years, and had served a great deal of it. He escaped later, anyway, but he lived there a very long time.

H: What was Uritskii's career before his exile?

D: He was a prominent Social Democrat in Kiev. I don't think he was outstanding – he was a Social Democrat of average education. I can't say what he knew about Marxism; I never had reason to think he knew a lot. On tactical matters, of course, he always had an opinion, and a correct one, and could defend it. In general, he was a good practical Social-Democrat type, who, I think, would not lose his head under any circumstances.

I don't think, although I don't know for sure, that he was a brave man. If anything ever frightened him he would never have showed it. He wanted to appear as a strong person, but he wasn't. The fact that he was constantly training himself to be strong had a very great effect on his whole makeup. I was having a lot of trouble at that time, and he was a great help to me and very open. We were on very friendly terms. He definitely had some sexual defect, some kind of impotence which he carefully tried to hide and cover over with a great energy, strength, authoritativeness, and so forth. I was not the only one to note that this show of strength was very affected. I think that his joining the Cheka was one of the manifestations or one of the consequences of this internal split.

H: What was his political orientation then?

D: He was a Social Democrat, politically inclined and in favor of *Iskra*. The term "Menshevik" was not yet current then, because the distinction was just beginning, but in any case he had no Bolshevik attitudes at all. Much later, Trotsky said of him, "Look at how Uritskii waddles like a typical Menshevik, you can see that he has no backbone" (he did always walk with a sway). This was Trotsky's opinion of Uritskii, and I think that many shared it. But people underrated the fact that, despite his sense of weakness and inferiority, he had great will power that he could exert to conceal it. And this was a big factor in his entire political career, I believe.

H: On the basis of what impressions or information did you come to know, or think that you knew, the cause and nature of the split between the Bolsheviks and Mensheviks?

D: All of our information was fragmentary. For example, I don't recall that we ever got hold of a single issue of *Iskra*. We had no printed matter, only individual letters. Someone would receive a letter from Kharkov, say, written in an Aesopian language, and we would have to figure out what it meant. In short, the information was not distinct and intelligible.

H: How did you conceive the split?

D: Each person used his own views as a starting point. It was known that *Iskra* had very much favored a rigorously centralized organization until recently. People recalled *What Is to Be Done?* which many of us had read and probably had a fairly clear idea of where it could lead. And people debated, probably with some confusion sometimes, using arguments that followed logically from the views expressed in *What Is to Be Done?*. There was a great deal that was abstract in this. Purely emotionally, I felt I should side with Iulii Osipovich, of course. But it was very hard to justify this attitude at the time. I think that people do not appreciate the smallness of the group that had a clear understanding of the meaning and importance of the split – even among those involved.

H: But your main feeling was that Martov was ultimately right?

D: It was primarily emotional, but I felt that I had to support him. And many others felt the same way. Martov was poorly suited to be a leader. He was not the type. But he had an inexhaustible charm that attracted people. It was frequently difficult to account for why they followed him. He himself said, "I have the nasty privilege of being liked by people." And, naturally, if something like a schism occurred, Martov would be noble, Martov would be honorable, while Lenin . . . well, Lenin's influence was enormous, but still . . . For my own part, it was very tragic to have to say that all my sympathies for Lenin (which were considerable) were based upon misunderstanding. I simply couldn't reconcile myself to that.

H: You were disconcerted?

D: Yes, very much.

H: And your main feeling was that it was a misfortune?

D: Yes.

H: And that it might be a misunderstanding?

D: No, not that. But I kept telling myself one thing – not to be too hasty in declaring where I stood. I had to learn what was going on first. The situation was entirely unclear. It was only through separate letters that we learned. One person would tell a second, he would tell a third, and the third would write to some exile. This letter would then be recopied and passed around. There were a great number of distortions, and much that was entirely incomprehensible. The main thing, on which we all agreed, namely the building of a centralized party, now turned out to have two possible results. And you had to choose one or the other. And that was hard. The choice was particularly difficult because centralization could go to such extremes that some 18-year-old *Iskra* agent could arrive and disband a committee consisting of 17 graybeard workers – this would be a scandal and a disgrace. If such things had really happened, there would be a scandal and a disgrace, but did they? In the underground, this lack of clarity, this vagueness in accounts of events plays an important part. I think that virtually none of the exiles arrived in Russia and said, "I am a Menshevik," or "I am a Bolshevik."

You should remember that a broad movement began in January 1905.[10] And the issue arose of how to relate to it. People asked what the difference in attitudes on the part of the Mensheviks and Bolsheviks would be. And they managed to guess fairly accurately. The Bolsheviks, of course, would be one hundred percent opposed to the Gapon movement because no party leadership was involved in it. And probably the Mensheviks would try to join this movement and have some influence on it (and there was some proof of this).[11] When the Shidlovskii Commission met, we could already follow this in the legal press, because we received newspapers.[12] Some, like Teodorovich, said that it was thoroughly disgraceful. And even Shantser was very much opposed – you can't get involved in Zubatov organizations and things like that.[13] But Uritskii said, "Hold on, if it is a mass workers' movement, we belong there." So there was a sometimes distorted, and sometimes half-correct, understanding of the tasks of the party.

H: What was your personal view?

D: Personally, I overreacted to it. It seemed to me that we had already entered the revolution. It was really as if a bomb had exploded. In Petersburg, nearly 200,000 people were going to the tsar, and things like that. We understood that Zubatov's policies were involved, but still . . . it seemed that maybe these 200,000 were going to the tsar today, but since they were received as they were, tomorrow they would be Social Democrats. In short, it seemed that it was already the morning after the revolution. And later it turned out that it was still being postponed.

H: Was your opinion related to the differences between the Bolsheviks and the Mensheviks?

D: No, that was not a factor. We learned the details of what happened on January 9th on the 22nd or 23rd, probably, or even the 24th. And by February 2nd I had already escaped. I felt it was impossible for me to remain longer.

H: I would like to return briefly to the Gapon movement and to your conception of it, and the prospects you saw in it.

D: We learned about the Gapon movement, of course, not from private letters but from the newspapers. So, with certain limitations, our picture corresponded more to reality. If someone had written in a letter that 200,000 people were involved, we wouldn't have believed it. What a wild story! But if it was in the newspapers, it must have happened. This was the first time in the history of the Russian labor movement that such a powerful and widespread movement had somehow been created.

Of course, no one knew that Gapon was an agent then. But it was clear that Gapon was being used by the police. This explained why he was permitted to have these unions, or "sections," as they were called. I think that the orthodox Social Democrats, who tried not to become involved in these sections, still had the feeling that they should try to operate from within. But then it was said that it was better not to meddle, because you would have to take some responsibility if you did, and there was nothing you could do. There were various opinions on this issue. We heard rumors that Petersburg workers were putting pressure on influential Social-Democratic acquaintances of theirs – "Why don't you come to the section?" "What for? They're all police fronts." "What? No!" They stood up for them a lot. This created a very difficult situation for party-minded people, an isolation from the working-class milieu with which they wanted to fuse. This was a very important aspect. Later, after the massacre, when it was announced that there would be elected delegates and so forth, people who were more sympathetic to the Bolsheviks said that it was a trap and you should not take part. But others, who gave more importance to participation in the mass movement, said that it was true that this element existed, but you still had to be with the workers at this time. Of course, it was a very difficult situation, even morally. Word of it reached the exiles in letters and later, when I was in Russia and emigration, it was the most frequent topic of discussion.

H: From what you have said, I have the impression that at the end of January 1905, when the news appeared in the papers, you really felt that a revolutionary period had begun.

D: Not just that, but that the revolution itself had begun and that its results would come tomorrow – you couldn't wait. We were wrong about the timing, but this opinion was fairly widespread. It seemed that life could never return to its old course after this.

H: How did you conceive this forthcoming revolution?

D: We talked about it a lot, constantly. People had a great deal of time on their hands, so there was every opportunity to spend time speculating.

For example, it was very frequently said that here was the revolution, there will be a representative regime and an elected parliament, and how large will the Social-Democratic faction be? There were two opposite opinions. Some felt that the entire population would favor Social Democracy – who would dare say that they weren't for the Social Democrats? That was how we thought.

H: But who in your circle felt that way?

D: I think that the younger ones all did. I, for example, was a skeptic, because I was sure from before that it would be a bourgeois revolution. It was impossible to conceive that the biggest party in parliament would be a socialist one. That was what went through my head. But there were bolder sorts – Teodorovich, if I remember correctly – who felt that, bourgeoisie or no bourgeoisie, we would have the largest faction and we would pass all sorts of social legislation and the like. The maximalist attitudes which were later a factor in October 1905 were already present in embryonic form.[14]

A frequent topic in exile was . . . well, we formulated it differently then, but now I would put it like this. We instinctively understood the backwardness of the Russian revolution – the autocratic regime, the backward nobility, and so forth. But, on the other hand, we felt and tried to convince everyone that, for all the backwardness, despite the fact that Russia had something approaching 100 percent illiteracy,[15] a proletariat that was very aware and on a high level was being created and it would be the vanguard in the revolution. This was of course Plekhanov's idea, which we knew very well. But what Plekhanov did not say and we arrived at by ourselves was that, on the one hand, there was to be a bourgeois revolution, but, on the other, the bourgeois revolution was to be made by the proletariat. Consequently we will do things differently somehow. We had a very harmful and widespread notion that the Russian bourgeoisie was rotten and venal and the like. That did not correspond to reality, but there was such a notion. On the other hand, there were people with some elementary consistency who said that if the revolution was really to be bourgeois and could only be bourgeois, what sense did it make to develop and intensify maximalist attitudes in Social Democracy? Why create a thinking proletariat if it is to act on orders when the revolution comes? This was a dreadful contradiction. This view was held in common with the Economists, although we didn't understand it at all at the time: if the revolution was really to be bourgeois and a bourgeois political party would lead it, perhaps it would be better for the workers to try to improve their economic situation, rather than get involved in politics. A great deal was said on this topic, but no one would give you a direct answer, and say, "Well, then, there is no point in stimulating the proletariat's development."

H: Since you had a clear picture of this dilemma, did you arrive at maximalist conclusions or not?

D: It varied a great deal. The same person would vacillate, saying one thing today and coming up with something else tomorrow. There was no stability in attitudes. But these issues were constantly in vogue and this was what people wracked their brains over.

H: You just gave the Economists' line in the arguments. How was the maximalist political line set forth?

D: It was felt that the proletariat would have hegemony, of course. Seeing this, the bourgeoisie would eventually come to its senses and would also be politicized. But since we had started first, the proletariat's party would be the leading party, and of course it would set up a democratic republic, an eight-hour working day and all sorts of freedom. It never occurred to anyone that the party of the proletariat would want to nationalize an industry, for example. That seemed thoroughly impossible, since we knew for certain that we would have to pass through the stage of capitalism.

H: Did anyone have the view that, since the party of the proletariat would be in the majority, it should remain in political power? Was that talked about?

D: No. It probably existed subconsciously, but the feeling was that there was still time to think about it.

H: Because it was known that it was entirely unorthodox?

D: I think so. There was a sort of block, and this thought was avoided.

H: In looking back over these attitudes, how do you account for them?

D: We only sensed the following: on the one hand, there was the backwardness of Russia, while on the other, it was necessary for the proletariat to enter the political arena. If you were to be consistent, you should not be a Social Democrat – or, if you wanted to be a Social Democrat, you should do everything possible to raise the social and revolutionary level of the proletariat. And if you succeeded in doing it, it was clear that people would then want to achieve something. But here they placed a period. Were we to take power solely to make a bourgeois revolution? I well remember that, in Munich, even before my trip to Russia, Struve was constantly discussed, and I remember how angry Vera Ivanovna [Zasulich] would get when the Russian bourgeoisie was derided as being rotten and so on. She would say, "What do you want – if the bourgeoisie is so rotten, what would it want to make revolution with you for?" To this Plekhanov would reply – and I will never forget his answer – "Vera Ivanovna, remember once and for all that the question is not what for, but why." It seemed that he had said the last word and made everything perfectly clear. But in fact there was nothing clear about it. Why would the bourgeoisie make revolution? Because it could no longer stand the autocratic regime itself. But what for? Who asked about aims! It was pragmatism. And Plekhanov's answer seemed like the ultimate wisdom to me.

*   *   *

H: Could you describe the circumstances of your escape?

D: It was fairly easy. It was largely a matter of money, because escape was very expensive – 2,000 kilometers by horse. Kugushev sent money for me to some address.

H: Who was Kugushev?[16]

D: I had been in Butyrki prison with him, and he was good to me. He sent money. I don't remember how much, but it was a lot – something like 2,000 or 3,000 rubles. The arrangement was as follows: there were gold fields not far from Olekminsk, and you could get things there that you couldn't get in Olekminsk. There was a lot of loose money there. The main thing was that if an exile was suddenly to buy a *vozok*, that is, a closed sleigh, everyone would immediately know. You had to buy one where it wouldn't be found out. Savinkov went to the gold fields and bought a sleigh, which was then to be delivered. Uritskii gave some address. Then he bought and brought me a Siberian fur coat, which goes over your winter coat, and the right boots, because the cold in February was dreadful. Then he bought a revolver – I needed it like a hole in the head, but it was felt that, if a person was escaping, he needed a revolver. I wasn't afraid of guns, but still there was no point in having it. It was a good Browning. And then – and this is a dramatic detail – Savinkov bought one for himself as well and told me, "I bought myself a present with your money." "Well, so what? What do you need a revolver for?" He later shot himself with it. So everything was provided – the coat and the boots, and the sleigh was delivered to some friend of Uritskii, a Iakut. Uritskii arranged for everything. I remember there were discussions about how to do it. When Iritskii and Shantser went to Teodorovich, there was a meeting, and Shipulinskii was there. Shipulinskii had served out his term and was returning to Russia. They asked him if he would agree to take me along. Teodorovich and Shipulinskii were not very happy about it, but Shantser and Uritskii were very insistent. People didn't refuse to do such favors, and Shipulinskii agreed.

H: So everyone wanted to escape?

D: No, not everyone. Teodorovich's wife had just had a baby, and he didn't want to leave her. And then, it was a fairly risky enterprise, and escaping in the winter was difficult. So there wasn't exactly a waiting line. It was easier to escape by boat when the river opened up. If some valuable person had expressed the desire, I probably would have given him my money – that was the usual thing to do. But there were no takers. Uritskii had a Iakut acquaintance who lived where the road ran, near the post station. It was about 30 kilometers from Olekminsk. Shipulinskii had received an "open order," as it was called, for one post horse – when an exile finished his term, he was given a piece of paper that gave him the right to one horse for nothing. But, of course, you wouldn't get very far on one horse. Uritskii went with me to this Iakut's place, and we took the sleigh down to the post station, and, since Uritskii had connections and acquaintances, they assumed that we were exiles returning in a sleigh. Shipulinskii said that he had an order for one horse, but that we wanted three and would pay for two of them. If I remember correctly, it was three kopecks a kilometer. "But why do you have an order for only one? Who are you?" "I'm Shipulinskii, and this is my wife." "Why didn't they give you an order for two?" He said, "We're not married." The attitude toward this was open-minded. It was all the same before God.

H: His wife remained behind?

D: Her sentence was for five years, and his was only for three, so she remained. After that station, we traveled together. Shipulinskii got into the sleigh with me, and we said that we wanted to travel day and night. And we really did. We would stop at stations – we had our own provisions – for hot water, drop some of our *pel'meni* into the water, eat, drink tea, and push on when they had changed the horses. We traveled like this for ten days, day and night. The cold was terrible, it wasn't an easy journey. But when you are young and going to freedom, everything is very easy.

H: How far was it from station to station?

D: Thirty or 40 kilometers.

H: Could you describe the trip from one station to the next?

D: You would arrive and say that you needed horses. There were people who unharnessed horses and there was always a coachman on duty who would take the next stage. And there were horses. You always changed horses. Of course, you had to tip them – it wasn't obligatory, but in practice you had to do it. This stimulated enthusiasm greatly, because if there was a blizzard the coachman might say, "Why go in a blizzard like this?" If you said that you would make it worth his while, he would agree.

H: It is hard to imagine that you could travel in so much snow.

D: Since the cold was so severe, the snow was not loose, so the ride wasn't bumpy. But there was a lot of rocking, and you could sleep.

H: But it was cold?

D: You wore a winter coat and over that a Siberian coat, which was of reindeer top and bottom. It was nearly impossible to turn around.

H: And what was the road like?

D: We travelled on the Lena River – there was no road to Usole, and then to Ust-Kut, I think. By then there was a road, then we went to Irkutsk by post.

H: The stations were on the river shore?

D: Yes. There were always a few huts around the station, where people lived. There would be a store and a little settlement, sometimes a larger one. Life existed only along the river out there.

H: How far did you go along the Lena?

D: To Ust-Kut, where the Kut River flows into the Lena. After that, the road ran over ground, not over the river.

H: How was this possible in winter?

D: The road was in good shape in winter – it was February. But by the end of March, say, and in April you could no longer travel over the river, and as yet the boats couldn't get through. The impassable period lasted six weeks sometimes, and it was impossible to go anywhere then.

It was ten days to Irkutsk. We had some addresses in Irkutsk. The Tsukasovs. Shipulinskii and I went. The first thing I said was, "I want to take a bath, because I haven't changed clothes in ten days." The next day they bought me a ticket and I left on an express train. I didn't go as far as Moscow, but turned off somewhere – I was in Russia by this time. It was only when they sent a telegram from Irkutsk to Olekminsk that we had arrived that people stopped hiding the fact that I had gone. But there was no danger by then. If they had found out earlier, they would have immediately sent a telegram down the line and arrested me. But it all went quite well.

H: Did you have a passport?

D: I had one, a bad one, but it was a passport.

H: Where did you get it?

D: It was sent to me in Irkutsk. No, in Olekminsk.

H: Who sent it?

D: Our people. It was not a very good one. I was afraid to register with it.

H: What do you mean "our people"?

D: People from the organization, from *Iskra*.

H: But how did you get it, if you were not in correspondence with them?

D: There was no direct correspondence, but I had letters from my sister, Nadezhda Osipovna. She took it from there. I didn't write abroad, since it would have been too risky. They sent it to my parents. Then they sent a package to me in Olekminsk, and the passport was concealed inside a book.

H: You didn't stop anywhere in Russia?

D: I stopped somewhere; I don't remember where. Then I went to Vilno, where I met Sergei Osipovich, and he arranged for me to cross the border.

H: And you went directly to Geneva?

D: Yes, it was all very simple. I spent a few days in Berlin and wrote from there to Nadezhda Osipovna in Kharkov, and she sent me money. I was there a day or two, not for long.

H: Were you able to talk with Sergei Osipovich?

D: Yes, of course. He was already a firm Menshevik and worked with the Menshevik part of the party. But he couldn't talk much and wasn't up to it. He wanted rather to get rid of me, so as not to be caught.

H: So you arrived in Geneva without much additional information about the situation in the party, and so forth.

D: I found out where Iulii Osipovich lived and looked him up, and we talked. Later, he said, "Now we'll have lunch in such-and-such a restaurant, where all our friends get together." I was greatly astonished to see Martynov there – how could it be? He ws an enemy when I left. I saw from the way people talked with him that he was really one of us. For me, this metamorphosis was completely incomprehensible.[17]

H: You arrived in Geneva approximately at the end of February 1905?

D: It was probably already the beginning of March.

Tenth Interview

H: To begin with, I would like to know how Martov and your other comrades in the movement explained the reasons for the split between the Mensheviks and Bolsheviks to you when you arrived in Geneva at the beginning of March 1905.

D: When I arrived, I was thoroughly bewildered. The first thing that was said to me was, "Read the literature that has appeared during this time, and familiarize yourself with the history of the breakup and reconstruction of the editorial board of *Iskra*," that is, Plekhanov's departure from the board, and so forth.[1] There was a good deal of literature. I read everything conscientiously, of course, and a great many questions arose in my mind. You can judge the situation by what I said to Iulii Osipovich: "You know, I still think that I should drop in on Vladimir Ilich [Lenin]." He was unhappy with this. He didn't say, "Don't do it," but rather, "Well, if you want to breed misunderstanding, then go ahead, of course." Since I didn't want to breed misunderstanding, I didn't go, though I felt at the time that it wasn't very correct in a human sense. I must add that I heard only very one-sided explanations.

H: What literature were you told to read about the situation?

D: Iskra, first of all. Then, if I remember correctly, there were all sorts of leaflets and pamphlets, and a summary of the [Second] Congress. I think that the minutes of the congress had not yet appeared – no, they had, but the version was a poor one. But I read it all conscientiously.

H: Could you reconstruct your impression after you read this literature?

D: I wouldn't insist on it, but I now have the impression that the nature of the disagreements was in fact very unclear to all the participants in the affair. People did not think things through, and I feel that the principal reason was that they all felt themselves to be members of one party. There was no interest or desire to show that a joint effort was impossible. All sorts of scathing remarks might be made in polemics, but, as far as I remember, there was no feeling that those who followed Lenin should be regarded as enemies and people who were cut off forever. Again, I wouldn't insist on it, since I personally didn't experience all the commotions at the congress, but I think that the people who considered themselves Bolsheviks were probably less remote or alien to me than the *Rabochee Delo* people had been in their times. The *Rabochee Delo* people had been "enemies" – in quotes, of course, but still enemies.

I think that my personal attitude toward the Bolsheviks was not unique. This is borne out by the fact that, very shortly afterward, in May 1905, there was the Geneva Conference, which was almost simultaneous with the so-called Third Congress in London.[2] Gutovskii, a Siberian delegate, went to the congress as a Bolshevik. Then he came to Geneva, and he was fully accepted there.[3] So there was as yet none of the discord that appeared in 1912 and later, although, of course, very harsh things were said in polemics. I think that Martov felt very greatly alienated from Lenin, but that this is to be explained not so much by political differences as by very bitter personal feelings. When a person so restrained in his feelings went so far in friendship to meet Lenin halfway, and when he saw that he had been mistaken as regards the moral aspect of Lenin's actions – such a person could never blame himself for his mistakes, but rather the person he was mistaken about.

H: You have said that, after you read the literature, you had a great many questions, because the situation still wasn't clear. What were these questions?

D: First of all, there was the major issue of the makeup of the editorial board, which as I sensed then and am certain now, had an entirely different meaning than we all thought at the time. I said, and I say again, that it was not a *coup de foudre*. This had been talked about a great deal. Of course, Lenin noticed that the "youngsters" were prepared to do without the "old-sters" under certain circumstances, and thought he could make use of this situation.[4] But I feel that it was only at the last moment before the [Second] Congress that it had become clear to Lenin that the makeup of the board was very important in terms of who was to control the party. If the Central Committee was in the service of the board, then the board should clearly be uniform and free of extraneous elements. Possibly Lenin had perceived this [earlier], but I don't think so. In any case, the reaction at the congress itself was rather an emotional one – it's a disgrace to get rid of old comrades suddenly like that. But I think that few people at the congress understood how significant the issue of the editorial board and the Central Committee was in Lenin's conception.

H: When you put this question to Martov, did you say that, after all, there had been similar discussions in Munich before the [Second] Congress and that it had also been said that Plekhanov and Alexrod could not be worked with properly and that they were cut off from Russian reality, and so forth? How did he account for his emotional response to the congress and his complete opposition over this issue?

D: It was natural for Martov. He said, "So you felt that Vera Ivanovna could be pushed out?" "No, of course not. I'm only saying that it was talked about." [During these early discussions in Munich] we were in that unhappy situation when two people are saying the same thing, but not always meaning the same thing. We said these things, but we had something entirely different in mind [than Lenin], because the notion of an all-powerful editorial board and an omnipotent Central Committee wasn't even discussed. I see it all in a different light now. Our objections all had relative merit: I had become used to being very trustful, and I don't want to conceal the fact that I voluntarily relied upon Martov's opinions and attitudes a great deal, although he by no means forced me to do so. Of course, the new situation was entirely different, because such [dependencies] assumed different proportions.

H: It was an entirely different situation because it meant Lenin's control over the party?

D: Not only Lenin's; it meant control over the party by a party center. Whether Lenin would manage to seize power was another issue, but even if he didn't succeed, Martov felt even in 1905 that such control was unacceptable, that is, centralization to such a degree that the party would be at the disposal, or, to put it primitively, at the service of a central agency. Naturally, the party should be centralized and all those committees and local workers should think somewhat as did the editorial board. And it would be natural for a central agency to subordinate the party's will and opinion to itself. But I think that, given the closer contact with the people from Russia during the congress, many became aware that those people were not such nincompoops after all – they also understood something. If we were to give orders to them, God knows where it might lead. I think that this notion, which arose at the Third Congress, was something new to many people.

H: Did you raise the question directly: "Why did you think when you read *What Is to Be Done?* that it was all well and good, but now you have a different opinion?"

D: I didn't formulate it like that, naturally. But there was much talk about it, and Martov realized it and stated it in print: "Yes, I overlooked a great deal in Lenin's views, because I thought then that unity of our leadership was most important. And if Lenin went too far, it wouldn't be as hot to eat as it was when it was served." (These German sayings were very much in vogue among us at the time.)[5] But my talk with him was not an interrogation – I myself was groping to try to figure out what was going on. For me there was a great deal that was entirely incomprehensible emotionally. In general, I think that the emotional aspect was very prominent in both cases.

H: Could you describe this emotional aspect more specifically?

D: That is very difficult. It involved the fact that, despite all the differences that we saw, in the various positions which we took, each of us still felt that the period of *Iskra's* founding was one of the most important and fruitful in the history of Russian Social Democracy. And this colored all our recollections in a certain way. For example, Iulii Osipovich said – I don't remember if it was then or later – "Well, is it pleasant to be made a fool of?" "Of course not." "Well, I've been made a fool of." I can't say for sure that he was speaking of precisely this issue, but there was certainly that sort of unpleasant feeling regarding the differences with the Bolsheviks. I didn't experience it myself, but others encountered some extremely unpleasant and unscrupulous manifestations of the fight during the congress. For example, our Gusev was held up for the fact that he put together some list of people that the Mensheviks allegedly proposed for the Central Committee, but which in fact didn't exist.[6] A pamphlet, *Regarding One "Unworthy" Action*, was even written about this.[7] Of course, it was only later than I learned about it all.

H: What else?

D: I can't remember it all. It is probably . . . no, it probably isn't in the literature. But it was talked about a great deal. When Dan came after the Congress, he wanted to see Lenin and Lenin wanted to see him because he counted very much on his joining the Bolsheviks. The first thing that Lenin said was, "Before talking to you, there is this secret dossier which you should become familiar with." It was a notebook filled with absurd and ridiculous bits of scandal, purely personal, involving Martov and Ekaterina Mikhailovna Aleksandrova and a number of others.[8]

H: What sort of scandals?

D: Intimate matters, absurd things. It was considered a good weapon in proving why the Mensheviks were a bad lot, while the Bolsheviks were all right. In the human sense, it was on a very nasty level.

H: Was it about morals and the like?

D: Yes, morals and personal relations.

H: Who was sleeping with whom?

D: More or less. This was unwonted in our milieu, and therefore Dan decided not to talk to him – "If you feel that it is necessary for me to become familiar with this dossier, then there's really no point in talking to you." Martov surely knew about this dossier – it is mentioned in *Regarding One "Unworthy" Action* – because comrades of his who knew it probably told him. In short, in addition to political differences, there had been a great deal that was disgusting in a human sense, both during the [Second] Congress and afterward. It had been largely smoothed over, by 1905, because there is a time for all things; the boundaries became more or less established and people naturally began to seek a political basis to attach political content to the entire affair.

I think that the main point of the disagreements was conceived of at the time as follows: the party is something new in Russia, and the proletariat is insufficiently prepared for its outstanding role, which thus falls to Social Democracy and the intelligentsia. People must be directed, but who can do it? First, there was this group of staunch revolutionaries, and then there was talk even earlier about professional revolutionaries. This was not a new term, but, to be entirely frank, it commanded a great deal of respect. In my mind – and not only in mine – it drew us closer to the heroic period of the Russian revolution and the People's Will. For example, when they asked Zheliabov at his trial what his occupation was, he answered, "Revolution."[9] In our time we didn't talk like that in interrogations, but, of course, his answer made a tremendous impression. But the reality was different and often the behavior of the "heroes" was not pretty. For example, there was the affair of Liadov who apparently received money for a trip to Russia and squandered it in a rather dubious place.[10]

H: Yes, in a brothel, but that was in 1902.

D: Yes, but it somewhat spoiled the image of the heroes of the revolution, of course. The image was very much marred by the Bauman affair, in which a comrade committed suicide because of him. That was in Orlov in Viatka province – a rather nasty story. There was talk about it.

H: I think it would be appropriate to retell it.

D: It happened before the congress. Bauman later died very tragically – he was hit by a stray bullet in 1905 and thus became one of the heroes and martyrs of the revolution.[11] I knew him fairly well. He was, beyond a doubt, a very charming man. I don't know what his talents were – perhaps they were many, but he never had a chance to reveal them. He was a cheerful, intelligent person, moderately well-read, and he made a very good impression on the workers, though he wasn't much involved in workers' circles. I don't know whether he was a good speaker, because he never had the chance to speak in public – it wasn't possible then. I also don't know if he could write, because where was he going to do so? He might write a leaflet, but that didn't mean he was a talented writer. It was evidently assumed that he had many such qualities, but the poor fellow didn't have the time to show them. He could draw rather well, not as an artist, but simply as an amateur. He was a cheeful, rather derisive fellow, and was enormously successful among his women comrades. Bauman was in prison for a rather long time, like the rest, and was exiled to Orlov in Viatka province. There was another Social-Democratic exile there named Klavdiia Prikhodko, and the two of them apparently had an affair. Later they broke up and went their separate ways, both of them remaining in Orlov. There was another Social Democrat in exile there, Mitrov, one of the technical experts, and he became friends with Klavdiia and helped her out, since she was very depressed. They took up with one another; I don't know if she married him formally, since such things weren't very important then.

Bauman liked practical jokes, and he didn't always understand that certain topics were not suited for such joking. He began to crack jokes about Klavdiia Prikhodko. Apparently she was expecting a child and he drew a caricature which everyone immediately recognized – Klavdiia as the Virgin Mary with a child in her womb, and a question mark asking who the baby looked like. In short, it was pretty malicious, on the verge of being indecent. She was apparently very distraught, and committed suicide, hung herself. Needless to say, this caused great indignation. I don't know whether there was a formal "comrades' court," but the opinion was that Bauman should leave the revolutionary movement. He served out his term, or perhaps he didn't, but in any case he decided to leave. He offered his services to *Iskra* as an illegal agent, and at the same time a group of exiles in Orlov wrote to *Iskra* in Geneva to say that this person could not be tolerated in the revolutionary movement, and so forth.

There was much controversy between Martov and Lenin over this issue, with Vera Ivanovna and others taking part – I don't know who else, because I wasn't there. Lenin insisted that it was a private matter that did not concern us. Martov felt that it was certainly a private matter, but that we were greatly lowering the prestige of the organization by taking such people into our confidence. There was a great deal of talk about this, but no definitive split over it. I think that it was frequently recalled after the split in 1903 and probably the Bolsheviks were repeatedly reproached for feeling that they could work with such people. The affair was soon forgotten, however, because Bauman was arrested, then freed from jail by a revolutionary mob and killed in a demonstration. After that, nothing more was said. I mention this to point out that very often purely personal facts which could be evaluated in various ways gave rise to disproportionate reactions.

It should be said that, while we were a political party at that time, besides that, or in addition to that, we were a group of people that were exceptionally closely linked. And we were linked, it seemed to us, not only by our political program but by an entire world view, something that was impossible for an European political party. Why should Social Democrats in England or Germany care whether so-and-so lived with his wife or not?

Among us, this was important. If someone left a wife and child penniless – as happened a thousand times in German Social Democracy, where there were other means of protecting this abandoned woman – it became a momentous event among us. These family, friendly, and human concerns must always be borne in mind in speaking of our party. Of course, it all changed greatly after 1905.

H: For the record, I would like to ask in regard to the Liadov affair whether there was a debate over his personal morals and whether he should remain in *Iskra*.

D: No, that wasn't even discussed. Naturally, it was said that here someone had gone to Russia illegally and had ended up without money, but there was no talk of removing him. Lenin said, and rightly enough, "We are not an institute for young ladies of gentle birth." It would have been very hypocritical, because we all knew a great many people who visited these establishments. There was no need to drag in morals and exaggerate the whole issue.

H: Did Martov insist in 1905, when you spoke to him, that Lenin had a moral approach that was ultimately entirely different from that of the Mensheviks, and that this was one basis for the split?

D: In no way was that a basis of the split. You remember that in Gogol's *The Inspector General* the hero Khlestakov has a servant named Osip, who says, "Even a piece of string can be useful." It was frequently noted that, for Lenin, as for Osip, everything could be useful – even a man who was a piece of trash could be useful; in business anything can be useful. It was discussed in these terms, but not as an explanation for the disagreements. And still this inclination to use people who were not first-rate or genuine did exist. It became much more important later on, when there were the expropriations and so forth; then, disagreement reached such a level, that the moral issue could exert a great influence on political activity.[12] But in 1903, this hadn't happened yet, and these problems never went beyond a small circle of people.

H: When Martov talked to you personally and made comparisons with articles in *Iskra*, what points did he emphasize, particularly at the beginning, as the basis for the disagreements?

D: That is difficult to say. The basic issue, of course, was what the Mensheviks spelled out later on: control from below [*samoupravlenie*] in the party,[13] self-government on the part of people engaged in such dangerous work from which they derive no benefit, but simply risk their necks. If you were to put people in such a position, you had to give them the feeling that they were acting of their own accord. They could be advised, but they could not be told what to do, which was what the Bolsheviks and sometimes even the *Iskra* people did. But a great deal depends upon the way you look at it. I don't think that anyone had been reborn by the time the congress began; rather, each one was developing those features which had existed before the congress, in their rudimentary form, but had not interfered with the overall work. At some later point, these features could no longer be tolerated. But, I repeat, there was no feeling at this time that we could never act in common with the Bolsheviks . . . no one said such things. But in 1911–1912 they did.

H: At this point you were in Geneva and, in the new situation, you found people such as Martynov in the Menshevik faction. No doubt you had some questions about this.

D: Of course. I became very much attached to Martynov later on, but [at the time] the impression was stunning. How could it be that Martynov was suddenly a friend? But people answered, rather sensibly: no one is born perfect and he had rethought a great deal; after all, you can't deny that he knows a great deal. Indeed, he knew and read a great deal, though rather unsystematically, I feel. In his orientation, Martynov was an extreme leftist. He probably longingly dreamt that, if he had lived during the French Revolution, he could have been a Marat. He was a maximalist in theory but extremely petty bourgeois and helpless in practice. I think he concealed his helplessness by the extreme nature of his views. He adapted very quickly, and radically rejected all of the errors of his *Rabochee Delo* days. No repentance or confessions were required of him – no one said to him, "Remember you wrote such-and-such." There was no interest in that.

It was in 1905, a year of great political ferment that did much to separate us from the Bolsheviks. Liberal activists appeared on the scene – not just Struve, who had been one of us so recently, but also a great many new people who became national figures to some extent, much more so than the Social Democrats, it must be said. There was Miliukov,[14] Petrunkevich,[15] a great many people. The rise of the liberal movement greatly intensified the idea of revolutionizing the zemstva in any way possible. In particular, there were organized banquets.[16] The Mensheviks – I can remember it, it was in 1905 – called upon the local committees and activists to take part in them and to unfurl their slogans, "unabridged" slogans, as they were called, regarding a democratic republic and so forth. There were constant clashes and polemics on this issue. The Bolsheviks felt that attending these banquets meant to debase the role of Social Democracy. At most they thought you should go to spoil and expose the banquets. This gave rise to very heated debates among the Mensheviks. It was something entirely new.

At that time the Mensheviks were starting to feel that they should leave the confines of their closed circle of the "underground." The phrase "leaving the underground" was to become popular much later, but it began, I think, in 1905. On the other hand, I feel that many Mensheviks understood the dangers of excessive rapprochement with bourgeois democrats. I think that this feeling was very strong in Lenin. He feared that this bourgeois element would inundate and drown the first shoots of a proletarian [revolution]. Lenin, more than anyone else, had a healthy and correct awareness that it was important, for the success of the movement, to concentrate attention on oneself, not necessarily even sympathy, but attention. To make people talk about you. This was because he felt that it was necessary to reach the awareness of those beyond the confines of the world known to us. If we showed that we knew the real truth, the broad masses of the population would follow us. Therefore we should not mingle with the limited and cowardly bourgeois democrats. I think that the Mensheviks were not afraid of doing this, and we considered it important to associate with the democrats (this was Axelrod's idea), but that it was also important to make them move faster and farther in their demands. At the time this was identified, rather incorrectly, with the idea of hegemony [of the proletariat in the bourgeois revolution].

H: I would like to return to the editorial board of *Iskra*. I would like to reconstruct more concretely what the sessions of the new [Menshevik] *Iskra* were like, as we have done in the case of the Munich board. When did you begin to participate, how did the board operate, who was involved, and so forth?

D: In Geneva we had our own rented premises. The police conditions in Geneva were such that it wasn't necessary to be conspiratorial. Mail would arrive at various addresses. Kabtsan[17] would collect it and bring it in, and we would all read it, rather unsystematically; Iulii Osipovich was constantly hanging around, and Fedor Il'ich [Dan] and Martynov. To imagine it exactly, you must remember that all of these people were involved in only one thing – revolution. After getting up in the morning and having coffee, there was only one task – going to the editorial offices. Later, nearly all of us would go out to lunch together. In Geneva, Koltsov went home to eat, but since the others didn't have a real home, we would go to a restaurant. There we would talk during lunch.

H: Did the editorial board meet every day?

D: Of course – there was no other business.

H: Let us begin by listing those who were constantly involved.

D: Martov, Dan, Zasulich; Axelrod wasn't in Geneva.

H: He was in Zurich?

D: Yes, but he came fairly often; it was a short trip and not too expensive. I don't remember that Plekhanov ever came. Sometimes, when there were discussions, it was necessary to go to Plekhanov's home. Don't forget that, in those days, there were no telephones, so you couldn't call and ask – you had to go and find out.

H: Of those involved in the editorial board, you have mentioned Martov, Dan, Zasulich, Axelrod . . .

D: And Martynov and Koltsov. He was not a board member, but he was a constant participant. As I recall, although I wouldn't insist on it, both Dan and Martynov were not formally members of the board, but this was of no importance. Their opinions were held in the same regard.

H: What sorts of arguments were there in these meetings of the editorial board? I know you have said that it was very democratic, each person talking the floor and so forth. And was Potresov involved?

D: Potresov did not live in Geneva proper, he lived outside the city, and his wife was sick. He frequently didn't come. I don't recall any formal voting, and I don't think there was any. For example, Martynov, say, would write an article. I don't remember typing any of his, though I would have been the one to do it, in six copies. But in any case, everyone was supposed to have read the article when it was discussed, so it would be passed from hand to hand. Sometimes the author would pick up his manuscript and partially read it aloud if some objection was made – "You say that such-and-such is necessary . . . " "No, I don't say anything of the sort," and he would pull the manuscript out of his pocket and read a part. It was perfectly proper and permissible for anyone to make remarks, such as, "This isn't very well written, it would be better to say it that way." I don't remember that there were any objections to this. If it sounded better that way, it sounded better, and that was all there was to it. The atmosphere was not very formal.

H: Was it friendly?

D: Yes, absolutely friendly.

H: And were there arguments sometimes?

D: Very often, particularly since there were debaters like Martov around.

H: What were the main topics?

D: A thousand different things, sometimes trivial matters. But very often there were extensive and fruitful debates. A very serious issue was whether it might be better to be in Vienna than in Geneva. I can't say exactly, but I think that this was because of the Potemkin mutiny.[18] It was very important to determine the limits of our opportunities. There was a feeling in the air, as the Bolsheviks urgently stated, that everything was virtually ready – almost as if we only needed to give the signal and there would be a general military insurrection. No one said it in this grotesque form, of course, but the danger of overrating the possibilities of the socialists was a matter of practical importance. The Bolsheviks wrote that it was necessary to form workers' detachments and to furnish them with arms. Where could the weapons be obtained? Well, from sympathetic soldiers. It was even said – though I don't recall it was written about in the newspapers – that it would be worthwhile to make attacks on barracks, once the agreement of the soldiers was secured. But somebody said, "How do you know that there are weapons in the barracks? There is hardly likely to be an arsenal in every barrack." Then it was said, "Well, all right, suppose you seize 200 rifles, but they don't shoot by themselves – 200 rifles require 2,000 rounds of ammunition." This sounds funny now, of course, but it was not funny them.

H: Who took the more optimistic attitudes toward all of this?

D: Martynov, who felt, mainly because of his temperament, that everything was ready. Martov didn't feel that way, and Dan still less. Martynov was ready to leap into the fray.

H: What was Potresov's view?

D: I think that Potresov already felt to a considerable extent that the would-be bourgeois democracy would have "hegemony," not the proletariat at all. But he was very cautious in stating this – not because he was afraid of saying something heretical, but because he himself wasn't too sure.

H: Were there discussions of this issue?

D: Yes, many.

H: Who spoke out against Potresov's opinion?

D: I remember the content of the debates very well, but I don't recall now who said what. In essence, we were in a very contradictory situation. We were all agreed that the revolution in Russia was belated, because of the autocratic regime and so forth. It was belated also because the bourgeoisie was insufficiently organized. The main force in the country was the sterile, reactionary, and uncomprehending gentry, on which the autocracy, the bureaucracy, and the like rested. And it was under just these circumstances that the bourgeoisie had begun to think politically, and the proletariat had greatly outstripped it. Plekhanov was the first to express these thoughts. Plekhanov felt that the proletariat was the moving force of revolution in Russia. There was his well-known phrase, "If revolution comes in Russia, it will occur and will triumph as a workers' revolution."[19] Catchwords of this sort were very much in vogue. But then the notion arose – though in a very restrained form, like a question that has not been thought through – that if the revolution would triumph as a workers' revolution, then the proletariat would seize power – no, they didn't say power, rather victory. But what would they do the next day, after we had won? This was a very serious question.

H: What was the answer?

D: People got hopelessly confused here. We should prod the bourgeoisie; its left-wing elements would eventually come to their senses and organize and create the most advantageous conditions for the development of the proletariat and so forth.

H: This was the general formula?

D: With various nuances, this was the content of all the discussions.

H: I understand, but I would say that even Lenin would have expressed it in this same general form, particularly if you emphasize that the proletariat would be the most active element and that the framework of a bourgeois revolution would be best for the proletariat. I would like to determine the following: when this general formula was discussed at the sessions of the editorial board, what were the various conclusions that were drawn and the various views held?

D: That was the problem – these thoughts simply fermented in everyone's mind, but no one could formulate them. For example, sometimes the following question would arise: if the revolution will in fact be made by the bourgeoisie, were we correct in following Plekhanov's advice and creating a working-class party? What exactly was the point in doing this, if the party is to withdraw respectfully at the decisive moment and turn everything over to the bourgeoisie?

H: Who posed the question in that fashion?

D: Dan did, and Martov's position wasn't very different. The idea of a bourgeois revolution in backward Russia wasn't always clearly formulated, perhaps, but it stood behind virtually every issue. At that time even Lenin was under the sway of this idea. I can state categorically that the question of power was not raised. I don't remember any discussion to the effect that the proletariat should take power into its own hands.

H: So Martov and Dan, with whom you were closely associated at that time, posed this question. But if I were to pose you the question in such a form, it would mean that I have doubts on the issue.

D: But the question might be raised not because people had doubts, but because Russian realities raised questions on precisely this plane. There was ferment – insufficiently developed, perhaps, but real – in Russian society, on the one hand, and among the proletariat, on the other. It seemed to us, though we might have been mistaken, that the proletariat was maturing quite rapidly. It was beginning to set certain aims on more than a local scale. But I think that the issue of the necessary connection between economic and political action was not raised among the workers. Except for the Anarchists, who had no influence among the proletariat, no one proposed to the workers that they seize plants and factories. I think that the Russian workers understood fairly well that they might seize something today, but what would they do tomorrow? I would say the proletariat was unprepared for thinking about problems of government. Such concern with the functioning of the state was rather poorly developed even among the Western socialist parties at the time, I think, and it was altogether absent for us. Everyone knew perfectly well that a bad bureaucracy ran a country badly, and that, though the bourgeoisie that was coming into being was probably more capable, it did not particularly value the development of the country either because of its own economic interests. But attention was not focused on this problem, and it was not thought through. The main task, which seemed like an absolutely necessary solution, was the overthrow of the autocracy. Not a change in the entire social system, but the overthrow of this absurd institution.

H: During the editorial sessions, as you have said, Martov and Dan were saying. "The proletariat should win freedom, it is the most aware element in Russian society, and so on, but we are faced with the situation that, after political freedom has been won, the proletariat should stand aside."

D: The issue was not formulated in that way – that the proletariat was the best, most aware, and so forth. The aim of the proletariat's efforts was to overthrow the hated, entrenched, bureaucratic, autocratic system. It would succeed in doing this. There was a formula to the effect that we must immediately elect a Constituent Assembly. We could take cover under that, and then the elections would show where the real strength was. There were the most varied opinions on this issue. For example, Potresov said that if the Constituent Assembly was to have a five-member socialist faction, he would be very satisfied. "What do you mean, five? We'll probably have a majority!"

H: Who said that?

D: It was fairly widespread, I think. Many based their opinions on what they knew about their own town. For example, Aronson, if he had been there, would have recalled the situation in Vitebsk.[20] In his mind, the workers, members of the Bund and others were the most genuine force in Vitebsk, so naturally they would be in the majority.

H: Were Martov and Dan sympathetic to this view?

D: No! Neither Martov nor Dan would have permitted themselves to think that way, because they knew, they knew for sure, that after the autocracy was overthrown there would still be a bourgeois system and it would be necessary to strengthen it, and how could the proletariat be involved in this? This was repeated, to some extent, in 1917, when they were in fact in the majority and could do nothing.[21]

H: Who at the time thought that Social Democracy would be in the majority?

D: I think that Martynov was firmly convinced of it. This was his view not because he knew the conditions of Russian life better than others, but because his head was full of all sorts of accounts he had read about the French Revolution. I think, and I am not ashamed to admit it now, that as people we were much more out of books than out of real life.

H: What did Plekhanov think?

D: Plekhanov felt, naturally, that this was all nonsense. But he was made to defend himself – "But after all you said that we must try to develop [the bourgeois revolution]. No one pours water into a bottomless bucket."

H: But was Martynov completely alone in his optimism?

D: To a greater or lesser degree, probably, it found some sympathy.

H: With whom?

D: I can't recall exactly now, but no one laughed at it. It was something that could be argued about.

Eleventh interview

[Eds.: Lydia Osipovna and other Menshevik leaders moved to Vienna in August 1905 to be closer to the Russian border. They remained in Vienna until the issuance of the October Manifesto, a few months later. Lydia Osipovna was impressed by the huge demonstrations in support of universal suffrage in Austria in which she and other Mensheviks took an active part. She recalls:]

I vividly remember Victor Adler giving a speech.[1] There might have been 30,000 people on the square and no microphones. He spoke in a very loud voice, but it was still a human voice. I am certain that, except for the 500 people who were standing near him, no one heard it. But I can state categorically that the entire huge crowd was completely gripped by his speech, and thought and felt in unison. A few words would carry across, or someone would pass them on. But the feeling was definitely universal. I never experienced it anywhere else again. Even the Petersburg meetings, which were very stormy, didn't have the same kind of mood. I don't remember loudspeakers in 1917, but I think that no one heard and no one listened. Everyone arrived with his mind already made up. When Lenin spoke from Kshesinskaia's palace, he was a great success, of course.[2] I don't know if anyone heard him, but they knew in advance what he might say. In Vienna it was somewhat different. It was the first time that the Viennese workers had heard such free speech, and it made an enormous impression on everyone. I think that it taught all of us something because we lived with the idea that we had to repeat the European revolution.

[Eds.: From Vienna, the Menshevik leaders also followed anxiously the events in Russia – the Potemkin Mutiny, the rising strike movement – reading all the accounts that appeared in the European press. Cut off from the revolutionary tide, they found themselves in the role of distant spectators. Then came the news of the October general strike and of the issuance of the October Manifesto.][3]

H: Could you describe how you, Martov, and other members of the board heard about and reacted to the news of the general strike and the October Manifesto?

D: From the newspapers. No Russian newspapers arrived, but there were European papers like *Arbeiter Zeitung* and *Berliner Tageblat.* It was exclusively from newspapers, because there were no letters. You can imagine that we lost our heads entirely. It is very difficult to depict now, because it was mostly inarticulate noises: "We must go right now . . . " The question was how to leave immediately. A very serious matter was what to do with the archives. I remember that Kabtsan and I packed them up; I don't know what ultimately became of them – we sent them to Geneva.

H: And you took the train?

D: Yes, via Berlin; I don't know why. I had some false passport, but it wasn't important.

H: What were your intentions in going?

D: Simply that we had to be there.

H: And you all went together?

D: Three of us went to Berlin, Iulii Osipovich, Fedor Il'ich [Dan], and I. There was still no communication with Russia, so we waited some two days and then went. Iulii Osipovich went several hours later, because he wanted to go through Vilno for some reason. He had a passport, to be sure, an old expired one. In general, there were no difficulties at all.

H: And what was the situation when you arrived in Russia?

D: It is difficult to say. It was fairly strange and unusual. We arrived in Petersburg, and went to my parents' apartment while Fedor Il'ich went to the hotel Severnaia Gostinitsa. Later he told me that he had been asked for his passport; he told them to go to hell, and no one was surprised. He used to say that it was much more difficult to move into our apartment than to cross the border, because my mother was quite astonished . . . what was going on? She had known Dan's family from way back; his parents were the same sort of Jewish bourgeoisie as mine, and she knew very well that Dan was married and had children. So it seemed peculiar to her. But when I said that he would live with us, she didn't try to argue; she only asked that we take two adjacent rooms. When I came home the next day, I noticed that the door between the rooms was shut and a dresser had been put in the way. I asked the chambermaid who had seen to this, and she said that the old Missus had done it. I told Iulii about it, laughingly, but he said not to bring it up, because Mother was sick and feeling so poorly. So I didn't try to protest. Dan and I moved the dresser aside without saying anything to mother. Probably the chambermaid said something to her, since two days later the dresser was back in place, and we decided not to argue.

Vladimir Osipovich, who had been in the south, arrived a few days later. He brought his wife and said, "This is my wife." And Sergei Osipovich also said, "This is my wife," and everything was fine. My mother, who was very sick, died soon after, and I started to run the household. Three or four months later we were searched – I don't remember what it was about. The "days of freedom" were over. I should add that Vladimir Osipovich's wife did not have the right to live in Peterburg; she was living on a false passport. We registered her, and that was all there was to it. When the police came, I said that we had to tell Father that Vera was called something else. She was Natal'ia something on her passport, so if he was asked he should know what to say. I said, "Father, Vera does not have residency rights, so she registered as such-and-such." He answered that we should have warned the nurse about it. (We had our old nurse living with us, Vladimir Osipovich's wet-nurse.) I answered that Nurse had known for a long time. Father said, "So Nurse is trusted, but I'm not." He was terribly offended. I said that it wasn't a matter of trust, but rather that we didn't want him to be upset. He said, "So why is it all right to upset Nurse?" In short, he was terribly offended, but he said everything he was supposed to. As regards Konkordiia Ivanovna Zakharova [who was not Jewish – ed.], Father asked Sergei, "Do you propose to convert so as to get married?" Sergei answered, "No, nothing of the sort." "How can that be?" "Well, that's the way it will be. I don't think it's necessary to convert." On one hand, Father was glad, of course, that he didn't intend to convert, but on the other hand it was improper toward a woman. Although it seemed normal to us, he felt that there was something incorrect about this, but he in no way interfered. In this sense he was a remarkable man – I don't know another one like him.

H: So you were all together?

D: Yes. It was a very large apartment, although somewhat dark, and we soon found an even bigger one so that we could all be together. My two younger sisters, Margarita and Evgeniia, were also at home, while my older sister, Nadezhda Osipovna, was in Kharkov, so she didn't live with us. There were no political troubles of any kind; the troubles were entirely domestic.

Father never permitted *Novoe Vremia* to be brought into his home. He felt that no decent person should read that paper. But we told him, "You do as you please, but it is absolutely essential for us to read all the newspapers, including *Novoe Vremia*." When in the morning the servants brought all the newspapers that were appearing then, Father was very shocked. But he felt that his children were now grown up and could read anything they wanted. But this meant that he – and he considered himself a Jew – would have that antisemitic mouthpiece on the table in his home. We said that we didn't read the anitsemitic articles, but that this was an influential political paper. Still, he was unhappy. Since we had to exchange opinions, constantly, there would be political discussions in the morning over tea. Whoever reached the dining-room first would take the paper and read it, and then say, "You know what?" Fedor Il'ich, who liked to drink his tea in peace and read the paper, but not talk at the same time, would reply, "How can I know, since you have taken the paper?" Then I had to instruct the servant to bring three copies of *Novoe Vremia*, so there wouldn't be fights over the paper. Father said, "Do I have to put up with this too? Just three? What will happen tomorrow?" I told him that there would be no more and that in any case it wasn't such great financial support for Suvorin. He didn't protest, but it seemed to him that it simply wasn't done.

Very soon, the newspaper *Nachalo* began to appear. I think that Dan, Martov, and Potresov were formally part of the editorial board, and I believe that Trotsky was too. But Parvus wasn't, I am certain.[4] Parvus was very friendly with Trotsky, and they tried to publish a small newspaper. I think it was called *Russkaia Gazeta* – I don't recall now.[5] They pursued an entirely separate line in it. It was their paper, and no one could interfere. They started to preach the idea of permanent revolution, very forcefully and not in a very popular form.[6] The practical significance of this was that, in their opinion, the state of ferment which we found in Russia should be pushed higher and higher in an ascending line. This view certainly didn't win much sympathy from Martov. As for Dan, I would say that his attitude was not only more tolerant, but perhaps more positive as well. In contrast to our usual ways, this difference of opinion was of a very peaceful nature – there was no cooling of feelings. It was discussed, of course; our entire life had become exclusively "political" – there was talk every day about it.

H: Did you have a newspaper office?

D: We rented a large apartment on Nikolaevskaia – I no longer remember exactly – which had almost no furniture. I recall that Iulii Osipovich would write articles every day, always on the windowsill, squatting or kneeling because there was no table. The manager was Sergei Nikolaevich Saltykov, and all the money that there was was given to him, but it wasn't much.[7] Fedor Il'ich reproached him for the fact that nothing was set up, and that it wasn't a matter of money but rather a certain pessimistic attitude: Saltykov was so convinced that it would soon be over that he didn't want to spend money on tables and chairs. There was an element of truth in this, and in fact it was all over very soon.

H: So Trotsky took part; but Parvus, you say, was not active . . .

D: He was very active in *Russkaia Gazeta* and it was all the same premises, although there was another printing shop. The newspaper in effect became a sort of political center where various people would come and talk about this and that and the other. It was important to Trotsky and Parvus to be there all the time.

H: So it was Trotsky, Parvus, Martov, Dan, Sergei Osipovich, Vladimir Osipovich . . .

D: And I . . . Vladimir Osipovich less so, because he was more involved in the local organization. And Dan and Sergei Osipovich also. Later, Potresov was there every day, but not from morning to night, like the rest.

H: Who else?

D: Martynov. We always divided ourselves between *Nachalo* and the Soviet of Workers' Deputies. There were evening sessions there. I can't recall what building they were held in, but you could always go there. You had to go and elbow your way in and listen to what was being said. I wonder now what we lived on – I can't find an answer now. No one had any job or income, but somehow we survived.

In particular, we didn't have to worry about the apartment, because Father paid for it. He was by no means a wealthy man. Nor did it occur to any of us to chip in for household expenses. He took it all upon himself.

H: Could you describe a typical day at the end of October and the beginning of November?

D: In the morning we would finish reading the newspapers . . .

H: Which ones did you read?

D: All the ones that were being printed. Before *Nachalo* came out, there was *Novaia Zhizn'*, and we had to read it too.

H: Did other people come to your father's apartment to take part in the discussions?

D: No. As soon as we finished with the papers, we would all split up, either to go to the editorial office or to the Soviet of Workers' Deputies. I don't recall anyone coming.

H: And you usually went to the newspaper office?

D: I had no function there, but it was a natural place to go to. Then there were some very difficult days when my mother was seriously ill. Then she died, and there was the funeral. After that, I had to take responsibility for the household. You couldn't simply leave everything up to fate. So again I was involved in domestic work.

H: What were the conditions? The political line?

D: I can't say that I realized at the time, but in thinking about it later, I am reasonably certain that this was perhaps the first time that we faced the issue of how to continue our work. And it was clear that we no longer had the possibility and necessity of "using" existing worker organizations; rather we needed to work with them. Now, in recalling individual details, I think that it was a watershed. It was the first time that the issue had confronted a fairly broad circle of people. We became aware that we did not have the right simply to "use" such phenomena as the workers' movement. It was in 1905, I think, that this attitude finally emerged in our group. For example, I noted a remark in Sapir's very interesting study about the link between Menshevism and *narodnichestvo*.[8] He says that we inherited the notion from *narodnichestvo* that we should "serve" rather than "use." I also sense this feature, but I don't ascribe it at all to *narodnichestvo* – it was of an entirely different origin.

The fact is that for the first time we came face to face with reality, with large-scale phenomena, in the light of which each of us separately, and our organization as a whole, felt proportionally a very small quantity. Before October 1905, on the other hand, many of us could and did feel, more or less definitely, that we were the source of history, while everything else was simply material for history. Now it turned out that this material had "grown up" and became an independent phenomenon. Probably the workers used our abilities and readiness to serve them: the phenomenon had become a commanding principle, and not simply material to be used. We were not so clearly aware of all of this then, but subconsciously the awareness was probably there. I think it is an interesting question.

H: Did you discern different shades of opinion between Dan and Martov over the Trotsky-Parvus notion of permanent revolution?

D: Among the Mensheviks in general there were different attitudes.

H: Specifically, this issue was reflected in the question of the tactics used in November and December in the strikes. There was the strike in support of Poland, and then the economic strikes. I would like to know if there were disagreements within the editorial board of *Nachalo* over the issue of these strikes as against the tactics of joining forces with the bourgeoisie, and what discussions and debates took place within the board.

D: All of this was discussed, of course. For Potresov it was clear – and this was later repeated many times – that Russia was suffering mostly from inadequate development of capitalism; that Russia had not yet truly entered the capitalist era. Yet, of course, it was perfectly natural to strike for an eight-hour working day, and there was a great inclination to achieve this by force. Potresov was against this, which was very unpopular. [People would reply:] "To you gentlemen of the intelligentsia, of course, this is a tenth-rate matter, but for the worker it is the most important thing." Potresov used the following argument: "Instead of making our struggle easier, we are making it more difficult. We should struggle against the autocratic regime, but we are encouraging an alliance between the regime and the bourgeoisie, and the bourgeoisie is perhaps the only class that can provide a truly sound foundation for the tsarist government. The government is so stupid that it has underrated the bourgeoisie up to now and has tried to rely on the gentry, an absolutely muddle-headed class, and we, so to speak, are correcting its mistake and are pushing the bourgeoisie into the arms of the autocracy." There was a good deal of truth in this, but it was very unpopular. But, ultimately, it was absolutely pointless and senseless [to speak against strikes] because the voice of reason could not be heard in such an emotional atmosphere. The issue of strikes was decided now not by the editorial board but by the Soviet of Workers' Deputies.

H: Did the members of your group, the editorial board of *Nachalo*, try to establish a common position on these issues so as to maintain such a position at meetings of the Soviet of Workers' Deputies?

D: No; the whole thing lasted only a very short time, so nothing was consolidated. And then no position was obligatory. However much you might try to force or induce Trotsky not to write that he was for permanent revolution, you couldn't succeed. If Trotsky wrote some article, you might get him on some trivial point, although he wasn't particularly yielding, and the article would appear in the same form that he had submitted it. It is very possible that if this period had lasted longer than two weeks, everything would have settled down – that is, either one tendency or the other

would have become consolidated. But everything was unstable and in ferment. I was probably at the Soviet Workers' Deputies every day. I don't
remember a single objection to the demand for an eight-hour day. Probably
it was difficult to object.

H: So Potresov's position was expressed only in what he said within the
board?

D: There was an all-day meeting. People sat on the windowsills, on the
floor. I remember well that there was an expression in vogue to the effect
that Struve was speaking through Potresov's lips.

H: Did no one support Potresov?

D: I wouldn't say so. Martov was closer emotionally to Potresov than
Dan was at this time. Dan was very infected by "Trotskyism"; Martov, who
could not dissociate himself from this rationally, was emotionally adverse
to it, but he had not yet formulated his objections in a definite form. For a
time he felt himself to be so far from the official line that later he refused
to go to the Stockholm Congress.[9]

H: You said that there were also personal motives?

D: There was his personal relationship with Liubov Nikolaevna Radchenko, which did not turn out well, and this depressed him.

H: What specifically were his doubts regarding the Menshevik official
line, and how did he express them?

D: I think that Martov had his own line. Martov had very strong bonds
with the West, unlike Potresov, whose roots were much more purely Russian. Martov's Russian experience was largely drawn from the Western
region, and moreover, he conceived of the Russian revolutionary movement
as an extension of the European one. He regarded the development of Russia as extremely closely linked and subordinate to the general development
of Europe. At that time capitalism was still healthy and strong – European
capitalism – and the eight-hour day had not been introduced anywhere and
[the idea of a socialist revolution in Russia] simply seemed to him like a
violation of any orderly scheme. How could it suddenly pop up in Russia?
I think that Martov was more afraid of the "elemental forces" in Russia
than others, who still thought, rather naively, that the Russian proletariat
had already "matured." Martov already understood that this was impossible. He writes in his memoirs that when he traveled from the border to
Petersburg, the first impression that struck him and stunned him was the
expression of antisemitism.[10] A country where pogroms were possible –
here were forces to be afraid of. He was not infected by Jewish feelings,
but, simply, he couldn't be indifferent to any violence or outrages committed against the individual. If such "elemental forces" were not met with a
genuine rebuff, how could one trust them? I think that this was approximately his scheme of things, and he talked freely and at length on this
topic.

H: How did Dan counter these arguments?

D: Dan somewhat overrated the strength and potential of the proletariat. It was so self-evident that ours would be a bourgeois revolution that
there was no argument over this issue. But, of course, the bourgeois system

might reconcile itself with the eight-hour working day. Capitalism could exist with an eight-hour working day. It seemed to him, therefore, that his view was very realistic. Then, like all the rest, he regarded the liberal bourgeoisie as "rotten," but he still probably felt that, whether it was rotten or not, it understood what was good for it and so would not immediately throw itself into the arms of the autocracy.

H: In what way was he sympathetic to Trotsky's ideas and attitudes at that time?

D: Well, in a more active demand for an eight-hour day. This was of enormous importance for the workers then. Of course, the theory of permanent revolution had many aspects; an essential one was undoubtedly the issue of a possible and fairly imminent transition from capitalism to socialism. I don't think Dan shared this view. But this was only just taking shape, because in 1905 no Russian Social Democrat could talk seriously about socialism. Don't forget that Parvus was a German, not a Russian Social Democrat, who had grown up in the midst of German conditions which were considerably in advance of Russian ones.

H: But can it be that even in 1905 people discerned, in the theory of permanent revolution, the aspect of power and in particular the participation of workers in the political power? It seems that this aspect was already clear in Trotsky's views.

D: Even earlier, I think, Parvus used the phrase "workers' government." For Parvus this was an entirely specific, immediate demand. I think that this did not enjoy any popularity at all among the Mensheviks. But Dan was definitely somewhat inclined in this direction. His sense of the state was stronger than any of the other Mensheviks. For him, the interests of the country had great importance, and if there was to be a country [*strana*], then there had to be a government. But Dan, who unfortunately did so much to create a coalition with the bourgeoisie later, did not have enough respect for this same bourgeoisie at this time. The interests of the country, therefore, had to be entrusted to some sort of reasonable workers. He understood, of course, that no reasonable worker was about to work eleven hours in the name of the good of the country. Therefore it was first necessary to show the worker that he could actually improve his situation, apart from all theories and attitudes, and give him the possibility to do so. In general, Dan felt – and this was a Menshevik idea – that you could learn something only in practice, only by actually taking part in all public functions. It was necessary to make an enormous jump from our amorphous, illiterate, spontaneous forces, and this couldn't be achieved by any sort of "club" work. Therefore, some sort of violence had to be committed on history – make it rear up on its hind legs, as Vera Ivanovna Zasulich said. How could this be done? In precisely that way. That is why I think Dan had certain sympathies in this direction.

H: Let us take up the Soviet of Workers' Deputies. My first question is, what was the attitude toward it; in particular, how did you define this strange thing and how to relate to it?

D: Well, the idea was current among the members of the *Nachalo* board, and thus among the old members of *Iskra*, that, while the Soviet had risen apart from us and without us, it represented to some extent our notion of worker self-unification – part of Axelrod's idea of a workers' congress.[11] In reality, of course, it appeared in somewhat distorted form, but it was the same idea, and we took comfort in this.

H: How was this "distorted form" conceived of at this time?

D: Because it was very chaotic, needless to say. The dimension of rationality, which the Mensheviks always valued, was not very prominent. And it seemed that there was less purposefulness than the Menshevik scenario called for. Elemental forces overtook Menshevik rationalism. So you had to take account of this. There were various attitudes on this issue. Some people, like Martynov, said, "Down with rationalism; let's join the elemental forces." Martov found the elemental forces appealing, but being himself very emotional, he insisted on a more rational approach to political victory. Don't forget that this was all unusually complicated by the struggle with Bolshevism. There is a very interesting connection here, because the competition with the Bolsheviks frequently distorted Menshevik life as well. Nothing develops in a vacuum or empty space, but rather takes shape through objections, obstacles, and so forth. The Bolsheviks posed enormous obstacles. They began by completely denying the Soviets, because they, and Lenin in particular, had trememdous distrust for the elemental forces, which was not shared by the Mensheviks. But, of course, you can't say that the Mensheviks were entirely free of this either. You have to be fair. Later the Bolsheviks were prepared to recognize the significance of the Soviets, but under the condition that the Soviets recognize the dominant role of the party. This was very difficult, because the Soviets included representatives of all the other parties as well. The Socialist Revolutionaries were weak, but they were there nonetheless. It made no sense objectively to try to prove why they should recognize this political party as dominant. Everyone recognized it was not Social-Democracy or even the workers who had organized the strike. The Union of Unions played an enormous part in it.[12] The railway union was the only union in which bourgeois elements had an influence, perhaps a greater influence than the workers. But they had more than influence, because they were more intelligent and intellectually above the workers, so they had more possibility to communicate among themselves and to act according to a plan. But there is another element which has yet to be clarified. A very prominent element in the Union of Liberation was the Masons, who acted according to a definite plan which they told no one about.[13] This organized, planned movement was unique, because the leading forces, the socialists, had much less capacity to come to an agreement and act according to plan.

As it turned out, the "elemental forces" were much stronger than the leaders of the railway strike, who very soon became somewhat mistrustful or apprehensive about how far those forces might go. Therefore the aims which the Union of Liberation set for itself differed greatly from those of the other more poorly organized elements. The Union of Liberation and the

Union of Unions certainly wanted nothing to do with permanent revolution. They felt that you could and should wrest some concessions from the autocracy and achieve a constitution, which would markedly improve the general state of affairs in Russia. [But] they were very much concerned for the state. They wanted Russia to be a strong and powerful state eventually, and naturally they did not want the development to be only in favor of the workers, who might demand an eight-hour day today, and then a degree of social security tomorrow which would be beyond the capacity of the fledgling state. But that was what the Bolsheviks were striving for. To some extent, this also determined the Mensheviks' statements. On the other hand, they spoke to the Soviets as being completely non-party-minded; on the other hand, the party should win primacy in them. This was later repeated in the struggle around the trade unions – the unions themselves were all right, but if they recognized the primacy of the party . . .

H: It seems to me that you have dealt with only one side of the picture – the other side is that the Bolsheviks also regarded the Soviet as something which could be turned into an instrument of power. In this respect they were somewhat more correct than the idea of the Workers' Congress . . .

D: Which was generally very vague, and diffuse.

H: Now, what was the Menshevik attitude about the Soviet as an instrument of partial power: what it could and could not do?

D: Don't forget a very important element – that the railway strike was the source of everything. This was where everything began. It was necessary to eradicate all traces of arbitrary autocratic rule, but to keep one's feet on the ground of the current capitalist system. The class struggle should be kept within a legal framework. This wasn't talked about much.

H: But how did all this affect the attitude of the Mensheviks toward the Soviets as an instrument of power?

D: The Soviet had turned out to be, one might say, ungrateful. It had arisen as a result of this original railway strike, from which everything had sprung. But then it had greatly infringed upon the representation of the intelligentsia. These railway engineers were saying, with great indignation, that they had been treated like swine, in effect. None of the Mensheviks had foreseen any indignation on their part, because we were still very much under the sway of the idea of "using" them. Then there were people like Potresov, who had a very high regard for intelligence and awareness, and became somewhat frightened: how was this institution to manage the state, if it wasn't really interested in many of the aspects of the state which were so important to him? For example, everyone was in favor of complete freedom of the press. But, in essence, the Soviet's entire concern for culture ended there. If it had lasted somewhat longer, they probably would have presented various cultural and educational demands – improvement of education and so forth. But this issue was left completely untouched. For Potresov and many others these aspects were of great importance.

H: On the basis of the fact that the Soviet was irresponsible and chaotic, did Potresov feel that he could not imagine the Soviet as an instrument of power?

D: I don't think he formulated it in that way, but that was definitely the sense of it. I don't know if you could find any indication of it in his writings from that time, but this was the import of his and Vera Zasulich's attitude, I think.

H: We have been talking about Potresov. What were Martov's views of what the Soviet could or could not do as an instrument of power?

D: For local affairs the Soviet was in effect the instrument of power, of course. All sorts of matters were addressed to it, and somehow it tried to resolve them, whether it could or not. But it was all confined to fairly narrow local issues. You could ask the Soviet for assistance in clashes with management. Workers would come and ask that the decisions of their bosses be declared invalid. And how many cases were there when the Soviet mandated workers who had been fired to return to work? Of course all this was good for a few days, because management would exert influence, and so forth. In any case, though, the Soviet was reckoned with in such matters. But there was not a single case in which the Soviet actually interfered in state affairs. It could interfere only by means of protest. For example, the strike over the events in Poland. It all ended rather badly. And it probably couldn't have ended otherwise, because the Soviet, despite all its enormous power, didn't take power. The police were afraid to take them on, but the army . . .

H: I would like to clarify the following: what was the extent of the difference in the appraisal of the Soviet's capacities among the members of the board?

D: That is very difficult to determine, because it was all so extremely short-lived. There wasn't even the opportunity, in terms of time, to interpret and formulate this question, so that very frequently the arguments were over the events of the day and it was only after it was all over that people tried to generalize. People groped their way along. They made demands, and it turned out to be possible to do something about them. They wouldn't have been at all surprised if it had been impossible. Everyone lived under the enormously enthusiastic emotional spirit after the strike and the victory of the strike. But when the government was bold enough to arrest them, as you know, protest turned out to be utterly powerless and impotent. And if it had happened five days earlier or two weeks earlier, there still wouldn't have been any more protest.

It was at that time that the idea – which the Bolsheviks so feared – the purely Menshevik idea of a push toward *samodeiatel'nost*, toward free and autonomous activism, spread. It now took on a more specific form and became more concrete and comprehensible. But I think that the Bolsheviks were right when they said that this alone wouldn't get you very far. You definitely needed a firmer organization, and since the organization needed some kind of directing movement or force, it was hard to argue against the view that this force could only be provided by a centralized and organized party. In short, the debates between the Bolsheviks and Mensheviks returned again to the starting point. With new trimmings, perhaps, but it was essentially the same thing.

H: Now I would like to take up the following issue. As we know, even before you arrived in Petersburg, there were very strong tendencies toward unification between the Bolshevik and Menshevik organizations. I would like to know how this was expressed. What was the situation during these weeks and how did the members of the *Nachalo* editorial board view these tendencies?

D: In the first place, I would assert that there was as yet no clearly formed awareness at that time that two Social-Democratic parties existed. Of course there were tactical and other disagreements, but not two parties. The party was united. This feeling also came from below. For example, I just reread Volskii's book, *Encounters With Lenin.*[14] He writes that Lenin was convinced even much earlier that what was needed was power, power, and more power. I don't argue with what Volskii writes, of course, but I feel that it is greatly stylized. From his own words you can see that Lenin himself has departed from this a great deal. And he thinks that this was because he did not meet with sympathy among the Bolsheviks. This is possible, but in any case I feel that there was no clear-cut awareness that there were two parties. And Lenin was also definitely involved in the push for unification. No one had the boldness to begin to advocate a schism – it was psychologically impossible. You can see the extent to which it was impossible from the fact that, when the newspapers were shut down and *Severnyi Golos* appeared, they decided to issue it as a joint mouthpiece.[15] Even Potresov didn't think it possible to protest and say, "I won't take part in such a paper."

H: But apart from this, what specific forms did these tendencies assume for you?

D: Of course, in emigration we had to deal with more advanced people who had a clearer picture of the disagreements that existed and were able to read between the lines in all the resolutions, something that was entirely impossible for the rank-and-file Social Democrats in Russia, who took everything at face value. And, perhaps, the exigencies of the day were more important for practical workers than purity of principle. This is why it was even impossible for them to comprehend what the argument was about. Everyone wanted the same thing. I think that this was very widespread among the rank-and-file workers. I also think that the Soviet of Workers' Deputies in fact included many people who were sympathetic to the Bolsheviks. This didn't keep them from protesting against the Bolshevik demands for party primacy and the like. I think that the Bolsheviks were in the same situation as the Mensheviks – the unexpectedness of all this, the absence of contacts and opportunities for influencing the masses, who were sympathetic but in whose awareness everything came out somewhat different than among party people.

H: What specific incidents do you recall about your first contacts with these attitudes?

D: For example, there was an Armenian Bolshevik who played a great role in the Soviet, Knuniants.[16] Knuniants later became one of the most brilliant Mensheviks. He was a Bolshevik and was well known as such, but in the process of working with the Soviet, he saw that if you really wanted to remain with the masses you had to join the Mensheviks. What many Bolsheviks were saying about party primacy was entirely alien to people who worked among the workers. Exactly the same thing was repeated in the development of the trade-union movement. This idea of the party running the show in large organizations was never widely recognized in Russia.

H: In addition to Trotsky, what other specific part did the members of the *Nachalo* board play in the activity of the Soviet, and how was it expressed?

D: As I recall – and I hope that I am not mistaken – none of the party people had a specific function in the Soviet. But party representatives had the right to be present and speak at sessions. They didn't have a deciding vote, but that wasn't so important then. I know that Dan frequently spoke in the Soviet although he was not on the Presidium.

H: Did Martov try to also?

D: Martov spoke much less frequently, since it was difficult for him on account of his throat – he had trouble speaking in large meetings. And then his manner of speaking made his speeches rather hard to understand. He had to get extremely excited and in a complete rage in order to be able to talk freely and simply. Generally, his sentences were very complicated and intricate. He also had a bad manner of speaking – he would do so without a definite plan. In the course of speaking he would think, express a thought, and then digress from it. It could be interesting, but it made him very hard to listen to for someone who wasn't used to it. Dan, on the other hand, always spoke without any notes, yet he knew in advance what he would say. I know that he made notes for himself, but he never looked at them. So he formulated beforehand what he would say and what he would keep quiet about.

H: Was Sergei Osipovich involved?

D: No, he was busy with other things.

H: And Martynov?

D: Yes, very frequently. Martynov was attracted to it. He had not been in Russia for many years, so for purely practical reasons it was very important for him to be among simple Russian people. This was the first time in his life that he had been in touch with such masses.

H: And Potresov never?

D: No, I don't recall. But Vera Ivanovna Zasulich was there, and they greeted her very warmly. But she was very bashful.

H: Along what line did the people who were actively involved – Dan, Martynov – try to influence the Soviet?

D: I think that they, although Dan less than the rest, definitely felt it necessary to introduce some restraint. I realize that this was so unpopular that people couldn't make up their minds to come out and say it. So whoever might have expressed this opinion was extremely cautious. It was a rather rare situation to appeal to the masses and not have to urge them on farther. They themselves were prepared to go as far as possible. Rather, you needed to restrain them. This is why it was so unpopular.

H: Now I would like to return to the relationships with the Bolsheviks. My first question is: what do you remember about contacts and conversations with the Bolsheviks over approximately these six weeks?

D: I think that there were no negotiations even in emigration, though we saw each other constantly there.

H: But now you were in Petersburg and great events were taking place. Both sides ultimately felt that there were disagreements, but that they were still in the same party. It seems to me that it would be natural to have contacts to see if there was a possibility of creating a common political line.

D: There was one general arena, the Soviet of Workers' Deputies. Some Bolshevik, I can't remember who exactly, got up and said that a proclamation should be issued that the Soviet recognized the primacy of the Social Democratic Party. This was rejected. A whole bunch of people spoke out against it or in favor of it. The session ended with no acceptance of any kind of declaration. But it was natural to continue talking about the issue after the session was over, perhaps simply because people would leave together to catch the trolley home.

H: Was the creation of a combat organization discussed?

D: As far as I recall, there was no talk about that in the sessions. There were conversations.

H: What kind of conversations?

D: For example, the strike, the last tragic days before the Moscow uprising. Some people said that we could halt the dispatching of the Semenovskii Regiment, not politically, which we were incapable of, but purely technically. There was a suggestion to sabotage the railroad line. But these discussions were not in open session, of course, and perhaps not all the Bolsheviks spoke about this. But many felt that it could be done. Before doing it or not doing it, though, there was talk about whether it was necessary. It was here that political motifs began to appear. "Perhaps you can in fact interfere, but then what will happen? Who will support you? The Semenovskii Regiment will certainly be backed up by the entire army and then the entire power of the government, and who will support you?" It was tragic, but it was all said in a peaceful and conversational vein, not practical. I think that the Bolsheviks already understood that, despite all the outward strength of the Soviet, it in fact had no power at all. Of course, they might say, "You are responsible for this," but this was just talk and had no practical significance.

After the Soviet was arrested, there was a long debate about how to respond. The Mensheviks felt that moral protest was of great importance; the Bolsheviks felt that, while the moral aspects had their importance, you had to apply force. But this was easier said than done. They were told, "You are always dealing with groups of three or five or something like that –

where are your forces, what can you do?" In short, when the Soviet was arrested, as you know, there was no protest and everything came off as if it were entirely usual.

Then a second, illegal Soviet of Workers' Deputies was formed. Parvus was the chairman. I was his secretary. It was a very pitiful spectacle, because what yesterday had been a powerful institution – the Soviet of Workers' Deputies – immediately became an underground group which had to meet in some apartment – in the working-class districts, not in bourgeois apartments. Or in schools, 40 or 50 people might meet. It was still felt that the police would not risk going into these districts and arrest you, and in fact there were no mass arrests. And then there was talk about how to prepare a response and, in particular, how to prevent the dispatching of armed force to Moscow. Even people who didn't believe in the reality of it took it as a kind of moral obligation.

H: Where did the idea of organizing a second Soviet come from?

D: It came from below. Elements were found in each major enterprise – no one knows how they were chosen, but they said, "I'm the representative of such-and-such a factory."

H: And what was discussed?

D: Chiefly how to aid the Moscow uprising. There was a rather comical ocurrence, which I perceived as extremely tragic, namely that all sorts of adventurers came and said that there were possibilities for action. Rutenberg, who had not been arrested with the first Soviet, became active again and brought someone who had invented some chemical compound that, if sprinkled on a policeman, would supposedly make him lose consciousness immediately so that you could grab his weapon. In this way you could build up an entire cache. Parvus was extremely partial to this idea; he liked it a lot. As the secretary, I was in a very difficult position, because, on the one hand, I had to keep the minutes about this, but it was dangerous and impossible. In a word, it was all idiotic. Someone suggested – and I can't say who – that we should try an experiment, and ask for the powder. It was at this point that I began to insist that we couldn't experiment on the premises, because suppose we were all to lose consciousness. And they instructed someone to take the powder and its applicator and try it on a cat. They found some cat and blew the stuff on its nose, but the cat just shook itself off and left the room. We wasted two evenings on that. This is indicative of the level to which this powerful organization had fallen.

H: To return to the Moscow uprising [which began on December 10 – ed.], what did you know and expect?

D: We knew that the Petersburg Soviet had been arrested [on December 2 – ed.]. There were Soviets not just in Petersburg but in various other cities, and they continued to exist, but what could they do? They thought that they could again foment a strike, but nowhere were they able to. This was extremely significant at that time, and even later it was thought about. What could you do on the basis of such "unorganized" organization? And, of course, it was like grist for the Bolsheviks' mill, and they said, "You see, we warned that nothing could be done without a centralized group acting according to instructions."

H: Until roughly what time did the underground Petersburg Soviet exist?

D: Until Parvus's arrest; probably in January. It lasted about a month.

H: And what did it discuss in addition to the idea of obtaining arms?

D: There was nothing else. Earlier, the workers' deputies would number 80, sometimes even 120. They would meet, and everything would be right and proper. In the underground you would have 13 to 15 people at a meeting and they would turn around and glance – the feeling was entirely different. There were no parties and no regular meetings. You couldn't record the proceedings. People would simply come, exchange opinions, and decide whether to make experiments. Things had broken down, and of course, no one had the desire to write the history of the collapse.

Twelfth interview

H: Let us continue with the major event of December 1905: the collapse of the Soviets, the suppression of the Moscow uprising, particularly in connection with the absence of any significant errors in its behalf and the absence of a response on the part of the working class. How were they and their historical significance explained?

D: That was an agonizing question, of course. Lenin, for example, immediately went to Finland. None of our people left. The atmosphere was not one of terror; organizations continued to function, although not very actively. There were workers' circles, and probably they continued to exist. I don't recall if leaflets were issued, but I don't imagine that it was possible. Of course, we no longer had the control of the presses that we did during the brief period of the "days of freedom." You couldn't stick your head into the printers and say, "Print this." But in any case, there was no atmosphere of terror. People were not handed over to military tribunals, but to civilian ones, and it lasted a very long time, they were defended, and so forth. As we know now, it was not at all like what happened in Moscow.

H: But in December and January, what opinions were expressed?

D: Many "prudent" people – and this word then began to be used without any respect, indicated someone who was strong on hindsight – understood that you should not go too far. I think that the defeat, as always happens, threw many people a long way back. But it was not an entirely typical picture of total collapse. Leaflets and meetings were still possible. There was even the idea that there might be a general strike.

H: How did Dan explain what had happened?

D: By the fact that the proletariat was unorganized. This was an idea which was important, in various ways, among all the Mensheviks, and it runs like a leitmotif through the entire period. The Mensheviks understood perfectly well that, on the one hand, the Russian revolution was extremely belated, while on the other hand, it was premature. The overthrow of the political structure, as it existed in Russia, clearly would have required a national assault. But to favor an all nation movement meant largely to reject an independent line – what was called the hegemony of the proletariat. We might think that we would force the bourgeoisie or the liberals to be very active. They were no fools either; they wanted to be active in their own interest. These contradictions were certainly perceived by everyone, and particularly among us. I think that this was used to explain all the lack of success.

H: Did Martov explain what had happened in terms of the lack of organization of the proletariat?

D: Yes, lack of organization on the one hand, and, of course, the objective – not subjective – inability to create a general national movement, toward which he personally felt no attraction.

H: Were there any different nuances in this polemic regarding the explanations for the failures?

D: Of course. Doubts had begun to arise regarding the correctness of the intelligentsia's behavior. What was later called "change of landmark" [*smenovekhovskie*] attitudes. The first seeds of this were sown at this time. "Look what the intelligentsia had gotten us into with its maximalism. If they had been more humble at that time, something might have been gained."

H: Who expressed these thoughts?

D: Potresov was entirely free of them, but the people around him, former Social Democrats, were all imbued with these attitudes.

H: At the end of 1905 and particularly at the beginning of 1906, Plekhanov already advanced the explanation that it was the maximalism of the socialist intelligentsia that had frightened the bourgeoisie – they had simply scared the bourgeoisie off with their tactics, particularly the Bolsheviks. This was the explanation for the lack of success. In reply, Lenin expressed the opinion that the cause of the failure lay in the fact that . . .

D: The forces were not organized.

H: And, of course, he accused the Mensheviks of having made the mistake of feeding the proletariat all sorts of illusions instead of preparing it systematically for an armed uprising.

D: Lenin said – or, more accurately, he repeated – that, apart from any ideology, any successful uprising had to have technical preparation. And ultimately it was not so important that the proletariat should comprehend the situation, but that it should know how to handle weapons. The issue was technical.

H: And to organize an uprising, without illusions or wasting effort on things like strikes and so forth. So the result was two entirely different conceptions of what happened. I would like to know how did these two entirely different orders of explanation affect the perspective of the Mensheviks regarding the revolution?

D: At this point the relationships between the Mensheviks and Bolsheviks began to come into play very decisively. Of course, it wasn't that all the Bolsheviks thought in a certain different way. But, to judge from the embryonic attitudes, the Bolsheviks already felt sincerely that we had suffered a defeat, and that we ourselves were partially responsible, because we weren't adequately prepared for the blow technically. In short, they tried to shift everything onto technical problems, and, accordingly, reaffirmed their previous negative views of any sort of evolutionary development. This was a factor during the First Duma elections.[1] They said, "To hell with the election campaign. Boycott it and nothing else, because we have to prepare for the final blow."

The Mensheviks were more reflective. Of course, by no means everyone realized that, after a short interruption, we were entering a new period of the Russian revolution, one which was scarcely as brilliant or vivid or, in particular, as rapid in tempo as the events in October. By no means all the Mensheviks felt this way; there was still a very wide range of feeling. But all the subsequent attitudes were conceived at this moment. I think that the so-called "liquidationism," that is, a negative attitude toward the underground, took final shape at precisely this time.[2] Menshevik party workers became convinced that to rely only on small organized groups of aware Social Democrats who were entirely within the orbit of the Central Committee or even the RSDRP as a whole meant to condemn oneself to a very narrow, closed sector, and if you were really to think in terms of any large revolution you had to get out of this underground organizational framework. There was great attraction for broad social organizations without a limited membership.

It was here, I think, that there was a sharp swing away from Plekhanov toward Axelrod. Until then Axelrod had only spoken vaguely about the Workers' Congress, which was all very unspecific and poorly understood. He himself formulated it badly. In any case, now, the rudiments of these attitudes first yielded some results. This viewpoint was given a decisive rebuff by the Bolsheviks, of course, and even, I think, by many Mensheviks. There was a certain party patriotism that we were all more or less imbued with. So, naturally enough, it was not easy to reconcile yourself with the idea that the dominant line would not be the consolidation of the RSDRP but a loose inchoate organization which could attract a very large number of nonparty and not completely conscious members of the proletariat with only leanings in our direction. I think that this later yielded enormous results, but it began to be discerned even in 1905. The fact was that in Petersburg – and I know only about the Petersburg Soviet – the activity created enormous illusions. It was indeed an extraordinary experience to observe how, where yesterday there had been nothing, there had appeared, as if by magic, a powerful organization that was capable of anything. Until December 3 it seemed that it was capable of anything; on December 4 it turned out that it was capable of nothing. Few people recovered from this shock immediately, and, I feel, this still exerted a considerable influence on some people during the preparations for the Stockholm Congress.

H: Now let us concentrate on the period from January until the middle of April [1906], when the Stockholm Congress began. I think that we can discern two points which are extremely pronounced in the reconsideration of earlier views. One line is that of Axelrod, as you have already noted, and "liquidationism" in general. Axelrod states directly that now the issue should not be revolution, that there is no revolutionary situation at present, that it would be a long time in coming, and that during this period, you should foster independent activity on the part of the proletariat, organize the party on the basis of a Workers' Congress, and so forth. This means that he was not linking the idea of party reorganization only with the assumption that the present moment was not a revolutionary one. The second line was that of Plekhanov, who criticized the Moscow uprising, saying that it was unnecessary, particularly because it had frightened the bourgeoisie. We have already talked about this. Let us take up these two points: how did those people with whom you were in regular contact during these months, Martov, Dan, Potresov, and Maslov respond to these issues?

D: Permit me to formulate again the basic positions of the Mensheviks, because it may be useful. Although I can't say that he stated it in exactly this way, the gist of what Axelrod was saying was that under no circumstances should we return to the underground; we are entering a new period, all this talk about who is a party member should be thrown out because there is no point to it, and anyone who wanted to work for the liberation of the proletariat, well, go right ahead. Even if this was right, what was to be done with the organization, which, after all, existed? There was a current expression (the accusation was made that Gorev, who became a Bolshevik later, had said it) that everything should be disbanded. Axelrod didn't say that, but he passed over in silence the issue of what to do with what remained of the party – to maintain an independent existence or to merge into the broad-based open organizations. In contrast, and, perhaps, precisely because of this, Plekhanov became more and more imbued with party patriotism. And he stressed this view, which attracted a great many Mensheviks as well as Bolsheviks, because for people who had worked in some organization it was natural to consider that form of organization important.

H: Now I would like to take up a point on which Plekhanov and Axelrod were more or less in agreement, it seems – namely, that a revolutionary situation no longer existed.

D: Here another factor began to come into play, one which also distinguished Axelrod from Plekhanov: Plekhanov clung very much to the idea of a general, universal [*vseobshchaia*], nationwide revolution. For him it was extremely important not to burn the bridges between the proletariat and the other progressive social groups. Of course, Axelrod never said that he didn't give a damn about this, but he placed his emphasis elsewhere [on the development of a mass workers' movement, capable of independent initiative – ed.]. This was of great importance in practice, and in particular it was a strong factor during the election campaign, which still had to be carried on. To be sure, Social Democracy, and the Menshevik faction as well, was scarcely unanimous in opposing the boycott, and this must be taken into account. The attitude was different from that of the Bolsheviks, but this [support for the boycott] existed, because you can't escape your illusions in 24 hours – it is a fairly lengthy process. And the process ran its course differently for different people. In particular, Martov took longer to come to a definitive conclusion and a definite analysis than Dan. He needed more time to make a definitive analysis of the so-called "current moment."

H: Let us now consider Dan, and then return to Martov and the doubts which he had about Dan's line. How would you describe Dan's viewpoint during these months, before the congress, about the revolutionary situation?

D: Dan had no illusions whatever in this respect. He understood that we had come to the end of an era and that the form in which we entered the next depended on a thousand different conditions. He later gave a good deal of weight to the view that Social Democracy should enter it as an organized entity, so he was less enthusiastic about so-called "liquidationism." Although he attached much importance to semilegal and open organizations, he very much favored keeping the party organization intact. In this respect the liquidators never regarded Dan as entirely one of their own. They felt much more that Martov was closer to them. After the series of shocks which Martov had experienced in the Second Congress and the break with Lenin, he was more ready to depart from the party line in the narrow sense. He always advocated the idea of the party in the broad sense of the term, but he was much less a partisan of the organizational aspects. Dan, as someone who was more practical technically, considered it very important to have some sort of party apparatus at hand.

H: What did he think had to be done to reorganize the apparatus?

D: What had always been done, propaganda, agitation, setting up a newspaper – nothing special.

H: What was his attitude on the issue of unification with the Bolsheviks during these months?

D: I can't remember anything that I could be sure of. The idea was very popular. During the period of the Soviet, this idea welled up very strongly from below – there were no grounds for two parties. But I no longer encountered that attitude after the Moscow uprising, as I recall. It seems to me it wasn't there, because the methods of action began to differ markedly by then. The Bolsheviks began to overemphasize the technical and combat aspects, which was something alien to the Mensheviks. We were convinced that we didn't need this, and that it didn't offer the slightest possibilities. It seemed entirely fantastic. Don't forget that we had entered the revolution of 1905 with certain illusions as regards assistance from the military – the Potemkin mutiny and so forth. So the Mensheviks had attached some importance to technical capacity as well. It had turned out to be sheer illusion. And the Mensheviks, to a man, felt this very keenly, particularly after the Moscow uprising. They simply eliminated these hopes from consideration.

H: Preparation for the Stockholm Congress were under way. What did Dan expect from the congress?

D: Since it was felt that there must be a great deal of disillusionment and disagreement with the Bolshevik notion of the "current moment" in the provincial organizations and among the Social Democrats in general, there were hopes that the party majority – the organized elements – would favor the Mensheviks and give them the majority. Dan expected a majority and thought that it would naturally happen as the provincial Social Democrats would elect Mensheviks rather than Bolsheviks to the congress. And that is what happened. Then, once the Mensheviks had the majority in the congress, the congress would naturally elect a body, like a Central Committee, with a Menshevik majority. That turned out to be utter illusion, because the Bolsheviks, though they were a minority on the Central Committee, immediately organized as an independent entity and took a more or less contemptuous attitude toward all the resolutions of the combined Central Committee.

H: Then, in essence, Dan conceived of this entire undertaking as a chapter in the political struggle between the Mensheviks and the Bolsheviks.

D: Yes. He figured that the Mensheviks, through the apparatus of the Central Committee, would be able to exert an influence that would sober up the mass of the party from a variety of Bolshevik prejudices. But, in fact, this wasn't what happened. They didn't even try to create a common organization. I don't recall any talk about creating a joint newspaper. Perhaps there were such plans, but I don't remember any such thing.

H: Did Martov say anything on the issue of unification?

D: He was very passive and didn't interfere much. Perhaps I am mistaken, but for him the issue didn't exist. And to be carried away by it? Hardly! It was all very abstract: it's always better to unify than not to unify, but on the basis of what views? In this respect the difference of attitudes toward the "current moment" were so striking that there could be no illusions about the possibility of unification. The Bolsheviks in general, and Lenin in particular, were still talking about groups of five or ten; in other words, they talked politics in terms of arithmetical technical units. This was very foreign to the Mensheviks in general, particularly Martov. What kind of unification could there be? And as for political problems, there were enough of them too. The debate was rather long as to whether we were going from a revolutionary era into one of reaction – this continued until 1911 or 1912 – or whether we were on the eve of a new, much bigger, and more violent outburst.

H: This issue is reflected specifically in the attitude toward the election campaign during these months and the kind of tactics that were needed. Perhaps we could discuss the various individuals separately and their attitudes toward the elections. Let us begin with Dan.

D: From the outset, Dan was against the idea of a boycott. This view wasn't recognized, and it was necessary to fight for it. I think that the attitude among the Mensheviks was overwhelmingly negative. It changed definitively only when it became clear that, in the elections in the Caucasus, only Mensheviks were elected, and this proved a tremendous political force. This fact seemed much more convincing than all the arguments in favor of a boycott, because, when people talked about involvement in the campaign, they said that it was silly to waste effort and to maintain the illusions, since nothing whatever could come of it. But suddenly it turned out that in the Caucasus something did. An abstract idea became immediately embodied in flesh and blood.

H: But before the elections in the Caucasus, before the congress, was everyone's attitude negative? What disagreements or different nuances were there?

D: And here the amplitude [of disagreement] was considerable.

H: Who was more in favor?

D: Dan was for involvement more than the rest. But he wasn't strongly convinced either. He expressed himself very cautiously; the idea was still unpopular then. But gradually, as the revolutionary illusions were overcome, people began to see that, apart from the miserable, pitiful public life that was our lot, there was the election campaign and involvement in the Duma. Then the maximum that was desired was to use the Duma. There was no talk of maintaining any specific political line there, but it seemed that it might be an arena where things could be exposed. I imagine that various attitudes were involved here too: some were ready to expose the government, but others were prepared to expose the bourgeoisie. This definitely existed. And it was a very slow process even for the Mensheviks, who were after all the most European of the Russian socialists. It was very hard for them to adapt to legal political life, in the basically deformed institution that the State Duma was. I think, though, that ultimately both the First and the Second Duma did a great deal to help all of Russian society, and the Mensheviks in particular. The Soviets were very powerful, but you couldn't learn any parliamentary procedures there. But during the time of the Duma some notions could be gleaned of how to act within limits established by the law, and on the basis of these laws, to work for the cause.

H: With whom were you constantly in contact? Was Potresov still in Petersburg?

D: Everyone was in Petersburg. But Potresov was not the sort of person you run into every day. He was entirely incapable of that, both because of the state of his health and in general. But we frequently met with the others, of course. In Petersburg we couldn't all spend an entire day together, as we had in Geneva. In Petersburg many people had to face the problem of earning something – you had to live on something and serve or work somewhere. So life in Petersburg became quite different from what it had been in emigration. This, Martov found very hard to adapt to, incidentally, because never in his life had he worked or kept a regular routine. He was a person totally alien to everyday life.

H: How did people adapt? What did Dan do?

D: I might be wrong, but I think that Dan didn't work. He still had some small means of support, because he had received an inheritance, and I think that he had a party salary. In other words, we got by somehow. I worked. And then, our family – in particular Martov's situation – was unusual because my father was still alive and provided some sort of shelter, so that a variety of financial problems didn't exist for us. We all lived together, so it wasn't so hard. But, outside of our family circle, the problem of how to lead a legal life was a very serious one for a great many people.

H: For whom?

D: Everyone – Martynov, for example.

H: And what did he do?

D: Nothing; he lived very badly, because he was someone who had never been able to care for himself. And many people were in this situation. Maslov was a legal person and was paid something for his books, so he could arrange some sort of life.[3] But this was a very serious problem that the emigrants faced for the first time. This topic of the change from rootlessness to an everyday mode of life has not been explored anywhere. The Russian intelligentsia was outside of everyday life for a long time and in a great many ways. But the situation reached its extreme among the emigrant and party intelligentsia.

H: There are two aspects of the problem of unification which I don't understand very well. The first is that, if already in December 1905 a majority of the Mensheviks – I am thinking of Martynov and similar romantics – conceived of the Stockholm Congress and so forth as a chapter in the factional struggle, as an opportunity to strengthen themselves and gain control, then it would seem logical to me that two platforms [at the congress] would be just fine. Because on this basis you might gain a complete victory, whereas if you twisted everything around . . . is this not true?[4]

D: No, it isn't. It was important for the Mensheviks to gain a majority in the central institutions. But, in addition, it was just as important to formulate a clear understanding of what was happening. So there was hardly complete unity – it was a very shifting majority that the Mensheviks had. And then the Mensheviks always valued the ideological aspects more than the purely organizational and technical ones.

H: So there was another issue, as you say, namely, that of achieving a consensus in the party, particularly among the rank and file.

D: Yes, to gain the possibility of exerting a correct influence in the party. Capturing the central apparatus was not as important as setting the party on the correct path. And since the party was organized democratically, this could be done only if the majority accepted this conception.

H: And this result would require a great deal of discussion and clarification so that the voters could get their bearings. Again there was the problem of enlightenment and education.

D: Don't forget, you are overlooking the fact that, after the setbacks of 1905, there was a great deal of disarray in the party ranks, even among the organized members. As always destructive elements began to appear after the defeat. For example, the issue of expropriations from banks came up – it wasn't something only the Bolsheviks thought up. A great many people who had been disciplined party members yesterday slipped into the attitude of favoring expropriation, because of the great need that existed. It seems that the party was virtually on the point of extinction, particularly because of the lack of funds. Until 1905 the party had received relatively large amount of assistance from nonparty elements. This ended after 1905.

The bourgeoisie no longer wanted to help. It was necessary to find other sources to live on. Of course, the organized mass of the party was not as strong and didn't have the capacity to exist on membership dues that foreign parties did. It was an absurdity; it was impossible. I don't think that there was a man alive who paid membership dues as a regular member. It wasn't possible. Expropriation was a tremendous evil, so it was natural that a good deal of attention was given to it at the Stockholm Congress. And the Mensheviks regarded it as a great victory of theirs that it was definitively prohibited. But the prohibition scarcely meant much, because the Bolsheviks still practiced it anyway.

H: I wonder if you could summarize the Menshevik attitude toward the party and party unity after the Moscow uprising.

D: I would formulate it as follows: The process of formation of the party was a unified process, though it assumed at times various forms. I think that the basis of the Menshevik party was the notion of a party organized in the European manner. You know that I do not agree with many comrades nowadays who want to derive Menshevism from *narodnichestvo.* I consider that to be entirely inaccurate. Rather, the Mensheviks went too far in the other direction – toward Europeanizing the party. After 1905 the idea began to take shape that the party should leave its small cells, particularly the clandestine ones, and should become an organism that rested on a fairly broad base. In 1905 there was the illusion that this could be arrived at through the Soviets. Then, when nothing remained of the Soviets, the idea appeared gradually that a fairly broad base could be created through the election campaign and our own deputies in the Duma. This idea was at the foundation of Menshevism, but few people perceived it in the same way.

Now, many years later, it is important not to forget an emotional aspect which is not very important on the scales of history but was a factor in people's awareness. After 1905 it was necessary to eliminate the streak of romanticism which always exists in an underground party. Of course, it didn't disappear immediately, because our party didn't become legal immediately.[5] Perhaps it never did become legal. But the romanticism disappeared. It is easy to be a romantic when the entire party numbers 200 people and you know each of them, and not just them but their mothers, fathers, and so on. It was like a large family. This was tremendously important, but this element gradually disappeared. Romanticism gave way to a fairly sober reckoning, a necessary one, of a variety of real circumstances. This process of shedding the past was by no means easy, and people are aware of this in varying degress. I recently reread a pamphlet by Martov – an unimportant one, without any historical value whatever – that he wrote after the congress in 1903. He says, among other things, "We can have as many disagreements as we please, and very great ones. But the issue of the moral attitude toward the party cannot be modified. It is given once and for all and is obligatory for everyone."[6] In this absolute form, this could have been said in 1904, of course, but in 1917 or 1922 the issue was on a different level, which couldn't be allowed for in party talks. It was enormously important for Martov, and he was alone in this respect. He even drew an incorrect conclusion, though it was prophetic. He says that, once you begin to be too tolerant because of personal relations, of the moral flaws of a party member, you will end up by taking the Degaevs into the party.[7] He didn't know at the time that this was prophetic, because Lenin tolerated the provocateur Malinovskii.[8] This is interesting in both its psychological and emotional and its historical and party aspects. The emotional aspect can't be used as a point of departure, but it can't be disregarded either. To really understand this – not just to conceive of it logically, but to become steeped in it – you must bear this in mind. Now it is difficult to imagine the shock suffered by the Social Democrats, in particular the Mensheviks, after the collapse of the revolution of 1905. These shocks were tremendously important in Russian Social Democracy.

H: I would like to return to the question of what people thought could come of unification.

D: I will tell you something which may seem heretical. I know that, for myself and a great many people around me, there were emotionally no real proponents of unification with the Bolsheviks. Everyone said and realized that a unified party was better. But whether, deep in their hearts, people believed in the possibility – doubt about this grew steadily. In 1903 there might have been no awareness as yet that there were two parties – I even said that *Rabochee Delo* was more of an enemy for me than the Bolsheviks. Unification was talked about so many times. But a real yearning for unification of the Social Democratic leadership, I think, did not exist. It wasn't that we wanted factions, but we felt more "at home" in the existing situation.

2
Boris Nicolaevsky

Plate 3. Boris Ivanovich Nicolaevsky, early 1920s
(courtesy of Boris Sapir)

Plate 4. Boris Ivanovich Nicolaevsky, circa 1960 (courtesy of Alexander Rabinowitch)

First interview

N: I'll begin with my family. My father came from a long line of priests. He told me that seven of his ancestors had been priests (in the province of Orel); he was the eighth. My paternal grandfather, the priest Mikhail Ivanovich, died of cholera in, I believe, 1872 (there was a severe epidemic in 1871–72). He left behind four young children, a daughter and three sons. My father, the eldest, was eleven or twelve at the time; he and his brothers all went to a parish school and then to seminaries. My father graduated first in his class in the seminary – in 1880 or 1881.

H: How was he able to pay for his education? What funds were available?

N: Government funds. With respect to these, the situation was difficult. Conditions of life were hard, but the clergy did have a means of mutual aid. When a man came of age, he either had to enter the priesthood or go into the army. The central provinces were overloaded with priests, so that one had to marry some priest's daughter to obtain a parish – acquire it along with a bride. My father didn't want to do this – he had already fallen in love with my mother, the granddaughter of a State peasant from the province of Vologda. They were self-sufficient peasants, well-to-do. My mother's father, Pavel Krasnoborov, had been at one time a prosperous contractor working in railroad construction but later was terribly impoverished. I believe there were four children, three daughters and a son. They made ends meet by renting out rooms, taking in boarders in Orel. My mother acquired only an elementary education but she read a great deal.

H: She went to a parish school?

N: No, a public school in Orel. Later on she and my father decided to move to another town. During the seventies the network of churches had expanded considerably and many church schools been founded, mainly in the regions then under colonization near the Urals and beyond the Volga. My father went to Ufa – at first to check the prospects. He was very well received there. He was a good student, intellectual, and the local bishop promised him a parish. He went back to Orel, married my mother, and they moved to Ufa.

H: I am curious to know how they met.

N: My father studied in Orel, my mother lived there and attended the church attached to the monastery. She has written about this in her memoirs, about how my father walked her home after vespers, struck up an acquaintance, and would come to visit her family.

After he moved to Ufa, the "laying on of hands" rite,[1] as it was called, was performed and soon after my father obtained a position in the town of Belebei. At that time Belebei was a very, very small town; it's by no means large today, but it is the regional center of the Bashkir Republic. In those days it had a population of slightly over 3,000 and was one of the most backward towns in the province of Ufa. The very name of the town is Chuvash. The Chuvash, who are descendants of the ancient Bulgarians, had gone through a great decline culturally, deteriorated to a very marked degree. There was dire poverty in the several Chuvash villages in the vicinity. (Trachoma was rampant among them.) Belebei was an old Chuvash settlement, and its town population consisted of Russians and Tatars – roughly two-thirds Russian, one-third Tatar, and a handful of Chuvash. There were also many landowners, members of the old nobility, throughout the area. Not far off were the Bunins, descendants of the main branch of the Bunin family that lived during the reign of Alexander I. There were others, but they were severely impoverished. At the time, the province had no zemstva; not even the self-government that existed in the central provinces. Belebei had three churches: an old one, another that was built later, and, lastly, a cemetery chapel. It also had a public school, a parish school, a post office, and a hospital.

H: Did it have a library?

N: The library was built during my time. Probably in the latter half of the nineties. We often went there, it was located across from our house.

The town was divided by a little river – actually by two little rivers that flowed through and divided it into three parts. In the central part, there was the old church, the treasury, the prison, and a large market square for the bazaars that were held on certain days. There was no railroad. It wasn't until the mid-nineties, probably in 1893–94, that a railroad was built a short distance away, about 10 versts from town. Before that, I remember, things were dirt cheap – you could buy 100 eggs for 7 kopecks. When the railroad began operating and eggs were shipped out (the Tatars bought them up cheaply and exported them), people got terribly indignant. The price jumped to 20 kopecks a hundred.

H: What type of work did the Russian population do?

N: Peasants lived throughout the surrounding area. The town people had kitchen gardens and planted some crops – that was the usual practice. There were also many district officials and members of the nobility. None of the homes belonging to the nobility were in the section where we lived. They were on the other side of town. I used to go there and visit, had friends in the district.

To the left of our house was the home of the town doctor, Iakov Nikolaevich Sokolov, who was married to Maria Vasilevna, the daughter of a Bunin. To the right, the house belonging to the other priest, Saltykov. After that came the gardens, the park, the fire tower, and the building housing the local government offices. And it was in this building that the library was opened. When I first started taking out books in the early nineties, after the famine (I was then five . . . seven years old), I used to get them from the public school. Then this library was opened.

There was a large, very broad roadway that ran through town. It's hard for me to picture it now, but as I remember it from my childhood, it seemed almost endless. Suffice it to say that people rode along the middle of this roadway in carriages driven by horses with bells. There was a distance of at least 100 meters, perhaps even more, between this roadway and our house. In front of the house was a narrow sidewalk; after that, ditches for draining water from the spring rains; further on, a large, vacant stretch of land; and right after that, the roadway. On summer evenings we used to play skittles and catch and do round dances in that vacant area – it was a very broad stretch of land.

In one direction the road led to the center of town. We lived on the outskirts, not far from where the Tatar section of town began. It was inhabited completely by Tatars, some of them very prosperous. It had a Tatar mosque and a so-called *madrasa* school – that is, a school attached to the mosque, where they taught language in the old-fashioned way and read the Koran. I had many friends among the Tatar children. To be sure, we waged "war" with them. I remember that the drainage ditch on the corner, near the Sokolov's house, served as our trenches when we fought against the Tatars. Recently, I met one of my classmates here in America. He recalled that I had deserted the Russians and gone over to the Tatars. And I, too, recalled the incident – remembered how they had mistreated the Tatar children, several of them ganging up on one child. There were battles between us and the Tatars; we threw stones and fought, but it was considered unfair for several children to attack one.

H: Which groups of people in town were your father and mother friendly with?

N: My father was a priest, and in the beginning the bishop who appointed him (I forget his name) was very fond of him. I remember the stories about his coming to Belebei and stopping at my father's. His visits involved considerable trouble, but they were also a great honor. Later, in order to earn more money, my father took a job as a teacher of catechism in the public school and became very friendly with the director, Stanislav Antonovich Dvorzhitskii, who was from a Polish family but had become Russified, Orthodox. Apparently, he was a very good organizer, a very cheerful, obliging, well-mannered person who was on friendly terms with everyone. And it was with him that my father established his closest relationship. His children were our close friends. His daughter, Valentina, who married Tsitovich, a Land Captain,[2] was a good friend of mine. She was graduated from the *gimnazium* but didn't continue her education. The son, Petr, went to the university. What became of him, I don't know, I've lost track.

On the other hand, we were also friendly with the Sokolovs, the large family of Dr. Iakov Nikolaevich Sokolov. Sokolov was a very fine organizer, a very cheerful, lively fellow. He bought a large plot of land and planted a garden. Safoterova, his wife's mother, also lived with the Sokolovs and had a son, Safoterov, who taught at Kazan University. He would come to visit the Sokolovs and also do some work on the land, plant things in the garden – mostly flowers. There was no fruit in Belebei. Even apples couldn't withstand the cold weather there, the severe winter frosts and wind: and so apples were brought in from other areas. I remember that my father's brother, who worked on the railroad in Orel province, visited us and brought a case of *antonovka* apples with layers of sawdust in between them.

My father tried in all sorts of ways to acclimatize apples to our garden. He loved gardening and was forever seizing on different plans. We had two gardens and a large kitchen garden. My father grew mounds of berries – cherries, raspberries, gooseberries, currants – but he could never manage to grow apples. He did have an apple tree that blossomed several times but once, as I recall, the blossoms were killed by the late frosts. Naturally, we did a good deal of farming; we had several horses and cows, and my father also set up a kind of small menagerie with two wolf cubs, a bear cub, and an owl. I remember that he set the owl free, but since it had become domesticated, it came tumbling down in the neighboring kitchen garden after it flew off. Some boys attacked it there. It had struck someone with its beak and they beat it with stones. We managed to rescue it but by then it was too late. Such was life in those days!

My father associated mainly with teachers. I scarcely remember any of the local clergy visiting us. There was a psalm reader who lived on the second floor of our house (the back part had two stories). I think his name was Ivan Grigorevich. But he was an absolutely colorless person and I remember nothing about him. The neighboring priest had no interests; he drank a bit and had a large family, many children, Mikhail, Aleksandr, all of whom entered the clergy. The people who met at my father's were teachers – teachers from the public school. At one time, I remember, their meetings were held regularly. I was probably four or five years old at the time.

H: Did they meet at your home?

N: Yes, but they alternated. Sometimes they met at my father's, other times at Dvorzhitskii's. I remember the meetings that were held at our place. They didn't play cards, the usual form of recreation then, but held some kind of discussions, read things. My father was interested in public life. He was a subscriber to magazines and newspapers, but a strange sort of subscriber. He used to get *Niva* [Field], a weekly magazine with illustrations and a literary supplement. Subsequently, he received the journal *Russkaia Mysl'* [Russian Thought]. This was one of the most interesting journals – liberal, *narodnik* in its policy. At that time the editor was Goltsev, a man with a very democratic outlook. Extremely progressive authors were published in the journal. I remember having their pieces read to me. I myself hadn't learned to read yet. At the same time, my father also received the newspaper *Svet* [Light], a vulgar, right monarchist paper, published by General Komarov. It was patriotic, nationalistic, if you will, Pan-Slavist. The chief enemy was England. The paper was alway writing about Afghanistan, about the need to conquer India. Later, I remember, the newspaper supported the Boers against the British.

But I also remember the books my father had in his library. He had the complete works of Ushinskii.[3] The first edition of Ushinskii's works had just come out and my father ordered it. He also had religious books. I recall that he had books by Father John of Kronstadt with whom he even corresponded regularly. I vaguely remember that for some reason the meetings that the teachers held displeased the authorities. A denunciation had been made, and they were forced to discontinue them. I think I was six . . . eight years old at the time.

H: You were born in 1887?

N: Yes. We had a large family. My sister Aleksandra was two years older than I; my brother Vladimir a year and a half younger. My next younger brother, Vsevolod, died when he was still a student at the *gimnazium*. Then there was my brother Mikhail, my sister Natalia, and, finally, my brother Viktor, who was born in 1998 or 1897 and was my godson.

H: Could you briefly describe each of their careers?

N: My sister Aleksandra was graduated from the *gimnazium* in Samara. My father sent us both to the *gimnazium* there – sent her to the girls' *gimnazium*, me to the boys'. After graduation, my sister became a teacher in Ufa and joined the SRs [Socialist Revolutionaries]. I had been the first to join the revolutionary movement; she was more cautious and restrained. But we were always together. Later, in 1907–08, she shifted her allegiance and joined the anarchists. In the Urals, it was fairly common for people to switch from the SRs to the anarchists. My sister married Nikolai Pavlovich Fedoseev, a rather prominent anarchist, and they lived in Kharkov. She is now in Moscow.

Vladimir was a year and a half younger than I. He attended the Ufa *gimnazium* but didn't finish, since he was forced to flee. He, too, had joined the Social Democrats and, like all of us, participated in the movement of *gimnazium* students in 1905. He joined a fighting detachment, took part in the resistance of the railroad shop workers in 1905, and had to flee. Those who didn't were arrested. My brother and I met in exile; he, too, was sent to the province of Arkhangel. In 1908–09 we lived together in Pinega, where he married Rykov's sister.

H: Was he a Menshevik then?

N: In the provinces, among the lower rungs [*nizy*], the factional divisions weren't as clear-cut as in the center. There were Bolshevik-conciliators, Menshevik-conciliators, and conciliators who were allied with neither faction.

H: But what did he consider himself to be?

N: In Ufa he was a Bolshevik. In exile he had already adopted a "conciliationist" attitude, and after his release he was active as a Menshevik. He became a member of a cooperative in Krasnodar (then Ekaterinodar) and had a family – three children. I went there from Baku to visit him in 1912. Naturally, he remained a Social Democrat and participated in legal work, but he didn't take an active part in the revolutionary movement. For that matter, no organized movement existed at that time. When preparations were being made for the August 1912 Conference,[4] I made a trip throughout the entire northern part of the Caucasus, and I found no trace of an organized movement. By this time, in any case, my brother had become a Menshevik; and he was a Menshevik in 1917, when he participated in the resistance against the Bolsheviks. He was in danger of being arrested but Rykov, who came to Ekaterinodar in 1920, took him to Moscow.[5] They lived together after that and were eventually arrested together [during the Stalin purges of the 1930s]. And both of them perished.

The next of my younger brothers, Vsevolod, died when he was a student in the *gimnazium*. Mikhail was born after him. In 1905, when he just began studying at the *gimnazium*, he was probably eleven . . . twelve years old, which means he was born in roughly 1893–94. He was graduated from both the *gimnazium* and the Medical Faculty of Kazan University and became a provincial doctor. Later, in 1932, someone wrote to tell me that he had volunteered to work as a doctor in the Kolyma Mountains. I was sent photographs he took there and his letters. I don't know what became of him, I've lost track.

H: Was Mikhail never active politically?

N: He had leftist inclinations, but he wasn't politically active.

H: Did he identify with any party?

N: I'm not certain. Natalia was a Social Democrat.

H: She was born approximately when?

N: Probably in 1895–96. During the First World War she served at the front as a nurse; after that she participated in the Social Democratic organization at Orenburg. When I was there, she was handling administrative details, working as the secretary. She married Ponomarev and they moved to Moscow in 1921. I've lost track of her now.

The next of my younger brothers, Viktor, was graduated from the *gimnazium* in 1917 and joined the Bolsheviks. He was a volunteer in the Red Guards,[6] fought at the front, then was sent to the Military Academy of the General Staff, and took part in the assault on Kronstadt.[7] The whole contingent of officers from the Academy was sent out for the assault. When he returned, he visited me in prison and told me that he had come despite the orders of his political cell, which had forbidden him to see me. I later learned that he had been subjected to something like a trial and been acquitted. Later, he completed the General Staff Academy, was sent as a staff officer to Turkestan, and died there. His wife later visited my mother, who wrote and told me that in Turkestan my brother had started some campaign against abuses. His wife, like him, had been a Communist, a member of the Komsomol. She charged that they had deliberately eliminated him as a troublemaker, had contributed to his death. She had a son. I don't know what became of him.

Of the sons in my family, I was the shortest – the oldest and the shortest, and I was almost six feet tall. I remember that in 1918 my brothers and I met by chance in Moscow; Viktor came back from the front and Vladimir arrived from Ekaterinodar. People in Moscow were going hungry then. Vladimir brought several round loaves of bread and lived at Rykov's place. Rykov was also going hungry then; he held an important post, was chairman of the *sovnarkhoz*,[8] but at the time he still had romantic ideas, and he may have had even less bread than I. My brothers and I would walk down Tverskaia Street and I'd be the shortest. The three of us made up a tightly knit group.

H: Now let us go back to your childhood.

N: One of my earliest recollections has to do with the year of the famine, 1891–92. When I try to recollect the past, this is the starting point for me: up to the famine, I remember very little, have only the usual childhood recollections. But the famine is part of my early recollections. There were many starving people roaming the town. Starving peasants came into town with their children and stayed there, living out on the roadway without a roof over their heads. Efforts were made to get them to leave, but they refused to listen. The police drove them away. They would go from house to house begging for something to eat. The gates of our house were locked and the wicket gate closed, but we always felt obliged to open up and give the people some food. Soup kitchens had been set up in town, and my father bought meal tickets which the peasants had to present. But they would come to us and ask for still more bread. And so I was always running to the kitchen for some bread without asking permission. There were a lot of inquiries, considerable talk [about the famine]. On the whole, we knew the countryside well.

H: How did people explain the famine then?

N: We all knew that there had been a terribly dry summer, a drought. The social aspect of the problem was not yet clear to me. I was less than four years old at the time, so this is perfectly understandable. Still, I remember wondering about the need, the poverty, about why the poor harvest and the drought had had such a devastating effect.

I remember that at this time my mother read us – that is, me – stories (I had just started learning to read). She read me children's stories by the *narodnik* writers Kruglov and Zasodimskii,[9] stories about poor children living in oppressive conditions. There were several children's magazines at that time. We received *Detskoe Chtenie* [Children's Reading], the magazine that was the most distinctly *narodnik* or, to be more precise, *narodoliubivyi* ["people-loving"]. And we liked it best of all. The arrival of each issue was an event. I made my mother read it to me; later, I myself gradually learned to read.

H: And what impression did these readings make on you?

N: I had heard many stories even before this. We had a nursemaid. She used to tell me a lot of stories. And my family made many trips to the countryside; we had a coachman and our own meadow which we leased. I was struck by the poverty, the sight of ragged little children always going barefoot. We also ran around barefoot but we were made to put on shoes, whereas these children went barefoot in the fall, in the mud, the cold. Naturally, we felt great sympathy, concern, which grew with time. There was never a time when I wasn't concerned about this. My father always spoke about such poverty with great compassion. He reminded us that after his father's death his own childhood had been almost as bad. He never spoke contemptuously of the poor as though they were beggars but, on the contrary, always with a note of sympathy. And he instilled this attitude in us all from the very beginning.

H: When your mother spoke about this, when she answered your questions, was her concern for this suffering prompted by religious feelings? How did she put it?

N: Her concern was simply humanitarian. Naturally, we observed religious rites and lit Easter and Christmas candles before the ikons. In addition, I remember that somewhat later, probably when I was six ... eight years old, my father conducted services in the cemetery chapel. The standard service was offered in the regular church, whereas the cemetery chapel was a little church where about ten ... twenty religious believers came for matins when they visited the graves of their loved ones. The services had to be performed in the district beyond the town. My father would get up and wake me (sometimes I got up even earlier and woke him) and we'd set off together. I remember that he still didn't let me handle the reins, but I proved to him that I knew how. We returned home after the service. Of course, it had a powerful effect on me – the semidarkness of the church, my swinging the censer to fan it. At times, it seems I even put on a surplice.

H: On the whole, what role did religion play in your childhood?

N: It did not play a great role. There was never any element of religious fanaticism. I simply never recall hearing that religion was supposed to inspire fear, that people feared the terror of punishment, the Day of Judgment. My father was a religious person with normal, intelligentsia views, perhaps even with a shade of free-thinking. I remember the conversations I had with him. The first ones dealt with history. My father was a catechism teacher, and I have never forgotten his attempts to reconcile Holy Writ – the creation of the world in seven days – with science. I remember that when I was in the *gimnazium*, there was a priest in the first form who later became a leader of the local Black Hundreds[10] in Samara; in explaining the creation of the world to us, he insisted on this business of seven days. I got up and said: "But, Father, learned people say ..." His reply to me: "Sit down, learned person." He didn't believe an explanation was necessary, but my father did. And his explanation amounted to the interpretation of religion which is generally accepted today: that in ancient Hebrew, a "day" did not designate a day in the literal sense but an entire period; that the history of the world breaks down into seven periods (Archeozoic, Palaeozoic, etc.); and that all this fully accords with the scheme of the creation in seven days. All this was fairly elementary, but the age I lived in was that way. It was almost seventy years ago.

H: I'd like to dwell a bit on an important point. Up to the time you entered school at the age of six-seven, were the feelings and impressions you had – particularly about the peasants' suffering and, perhaps, the injustice involved – were these bound up with religious explanations?

N: No, they weren't. My father didn't go in for that sort of thing. Nor did my mother. She was no less of a freethinker than he. In the world of the clergy, my parents were exceptions; they stood apart from the rest.

H: Did you develop an interest in religion before you entered school?

N: Not a genuine interest. I remember that when I was still very little, I had my mother read me all the stories in the Old Testament. But I regarded them as stories of the everyday life of ancient people – to some extent, as heroic tales. I simply liked them. But I developed an interest in the natural sciences while I was still very young. My first book was a work on astronomy. I read it when I was probably no more than eight . . . ten years old.

H: You started school when you were six or seven – that is, in 1894 or 1895? Could you describe the school for me?

N: It was a public school that included six grades. The first three grades were preparatory classes. They were followed by classes in which trades were taught – workshops. The school offered training in metal work. In any case, after the third or fourth grade, one could go on to the *gimnazium*. For me it was a transition to the *gimnazium*.

H: Were the pupils a fairly democratic group?

N: I don't remember any children from the families of the nobility. Normally, they didn't go to our school. I don't even remember the children of our neighbor, the doctor, attending. In general, the pupils were from the petty bourgeoisie in town, from the families of officials, and the poor. I remember terrible poverty among some of my friends. We were supposed to wear uniforms, but I remember that they went to school without them and the director pretended not to notice. Naturally, the teachers wore regular uniforms. Everything was regulated by the Ministry of Public Education.

H: And only boys attended?

N: Yes.

H: Peasants' sons as well?

N: I can't remember now. I recall that there were many Tatar children. There were one or two Jews in the school, and I remember my relationships with them. It was at this time that I first became acquainted with Jews. Naturally, the usual remarks were made – that they had crucified Christ, etc. But these weren't made in earnest, didn't offend. I used to visit a Jewish boy in my class. I remember his Passover; it was the first time I saw Jews dressed in the traditional clothes they wear at Passover. I remember all the conversations, the interest this had for me.

H: From roughly 1895–98, what impressions did those years in school create – particularly with respect to the development of your own conception of the world? What impact did the school have on you?

N: It is difficult to determine. I don't think anything happened during those years that was a landmark for me. They were a continuation of what I had felt since childhood: love and concern for the people, feelings I did not explore in any particular depth.

H: What were your interests in those years? You told me that you had become interested in the natural sciences and had already gone to the library to take out books on astronomy. What did you read?

N: The library came later, at the very end of the nineties. In 1896 I remember reading the magazine *Detskoe Chtenie*. I read it regularly, reread it from cover to cover; I also went over the back issues for several years. I was interested in travel, of course, fascinated by it. I read the magazines

Vokrug Sveta [Around the World] and *Priroda i Liudi* [Nature and People],[11] which were published then. Adventure novels – Fenimore Cooper, Gustave Aimard, etc. – came somewhat later, during my first year at the *gimnazium*. In the earlier period, what intrigued me was, if you will, "adventure geography," travel books, Jules Verne. I remember that I was particularly keen on astronomy and pounced upon books having to do with the stars. It stands to reason I didn't understand everything I read. I realize now that I couldn't have understood Flammarion's *Pictorial Astronomy*. But, apparently, I grasped something from the drawings about the main points.

H: Were you interested in history?

N: Yes, but not to the same degree. I was more interested in the sciences. As for who exerted any real influence on me, I couldn't say. There was little apart from the questions my father put to me. When I asked my father about something, he wouldn't give me a direct answer, wouldn't explain, but would ask me a question that forced me to think.

H: Did the interests you developed at this time create a skeptical attitude toward religion?

N: I wouldn't say that I had a consciously skeptical attitude toward religion.

H: Doubts?

N: Not doubts, but religion was simply pushed into the background. I simply don't remember having any specific doubts. I've thought about the question and tried but simply been unable to recall experiencing what people call the anguish of awareness. I didn't experience this. And I think the same was true for us all. Our closest friends and neighbors were the Sokolovs. Their uncle, Safoterov-Kazanskii, who came to Belebei and was a doctor at the hospital, had some sort of professorship. He didn't propagandize or offer explanations, but made passing remarks and asked questions that started one thinking. And so all the religious notions simply vanished. The Saltykovs' neighbors had a nephew, Chanov, who was then finishing his studies at the seminary or, at any rate, was in the upper forms. Sometimes he would say things like: "Is God omnipotent? Yes. But could he create a rock so heavy that he himself couldn't lift it?" This was the kind of primitive, freethinking philosophy indulged in by seminary students.

H: I'd like to go back a little and discuss your feelings of love for the people. Could you tell me a bit about how these developed during this period? Were there other things apart from the famine of 1891 which contributed to your outlook?

N: There probably were. I believe that from the very start, from our earliest childhood, we interpreted everything from this standpoint. Our nursemaid told us what a bad master she had as a little girl. And I remember that once, when we went berry-picking in a field on an estate about ten ... twelve versts away, we were told there were many watchdogs on the premises. And one of the peasants said, "Well, that's so, but when the old master was alive, things were so bad here that the dogs lived better than the people." But this, too, didn't impress me as some sort of discovery. We accepted it as the normal thing, another corroborating fact.

H: Was your attitude toward the people reflected in your attitude toward the authorities? How did your family regard the authorities? What did they represent in your life?

N: The authorities for us meant the district police officer. Authority meant the chief of the military detachment. But the latter was an unfortunate man who had a hunchbacked daughter. She had fallen when she was a little girl, injured herself, and remained a hunchback, was practically the only one in the town. We didn't regard the man as though he were an authority. As for the police officer, I can't even recall now what he looked like. We didn't relate to these people in the usual way.

H: If you had negative feelings, were they focused on the nobility?

N: I didn't experience those either. My impression was that they represented the past. (The master had died but the dogs remained.) And it was [a past] that was vanishing. None of the families of the nobility in our region were thriving. They had all had their day. And this provided additional background for my love for the *narod;* it developed in this setting.

There was a young fellow who did have some influence on me, a coachman from the neighboring village who worked for us for several years. He told me a number of things, spoke about the countryside in fairly good terms, said that it was fun living there. "Ah," he'd say, "I'd like to go there for the holidays and have myself a good time. But will your father let me off?" He was a young, robust fellow. If you ask whether I felt an element of protest, indignation . . .

H: Or simply of disorder in the world . . .

N: It wasn't a question of disorder, but a sense that something had to be changed, that a more humane attitude toward people was needed. That was obvious. But there was nothing sufficiently concrete to take hold in my memory, to arouse indignation.

*   *   *

H: In 1898 you went to the *gimnazium* in Samara. Did your father do the customary thing in sending you to the *gimnazium?*

N: In the world of the clergy it was, if not a revolutionary act, at least an act of defiance. My father said he was the eighth priest in the family and that was enough; he didn't want his son to become the ninth. He had wanted to break out of that milieu, but he couldn't; for the sake of his family for a variety of reasons, he had had to become a priest. But he told me to take a different path.

H: And you yourself wanted to?

N: I must say that I didn't want to become a seminary student. I had no knowledge of what a seminary was like, but I knew seminary students – our neighbors' sons, the Saltykovs. On the other side of our house lived the Sokolov children, *gimnazium* students who were two . . . three years older than I. The Sokolov children went to study in Kazan, where they lived with their uncle Vasilii Nikolaevich Sokolov. They came back and told me that Kazan had three *gimnazia*, and a university, and this and that. I can't remember what else they mentioned then, but I was terribly impressed. Naturally, I wanted to be a *gimnazium* student.

H: If it was unusual for your father to send you to the *gimnazium*, wasn't it even more exceptional for him to send both you and your sister Aleksandra?

N: Yes. She should have gone to a diocesan school where future wives of priests were educated. Not even all of them, by far. A priest who sent his daughter to a diocesan school was considered a man of culture. Those who sent their daughters to the *gimnazium* were complete exceptions.

H: And how did your father explain this?

N: I don't recall any conversations about this; in sending her to the *gimnazium*, he undoubtedly was operating on the same plane of thought as he had with respect to me. He wanted to break loose, to be emancipated.

The very prospect of becoming a priest, I imagined, meant the sort of life that neighbor of ours, Saltykov, lived. There were endless quarrels with him, all sorts of incidents. We never had any conflicts with our other neighbor, Dr. Sokolov, although it would have seemed there were more grounds. Our window faced their garden and this, of course, was awkward for both them and us.

H: There is the question of material conditions . . .

N: It stands to reason that as a doctor, Sokolov was better off financially. But I don't think that even this played a role. Our financial situation was not at all bad. At first my father had additional income from his work as a catechism teacher. Later, he bacame an inspector of Church-parish schools and was paid a decent salary – 75 rubles a month.

H: When you discussed the issue of your future before you entered the *gimnazium* . . .

N: We didn't discuss it. My father decided. He said that I would be better off, have broader horizons. And his decision was accepted.

Second interview

H: Could you give me a general picture of what Samara was like as a city and what the *gimnazium* amounted to when you went there in 1898?

N: I first visited Samara in the spring of 1898 when I went there to take the examination. I took the examination in the old wing of the *gimnazium*, a large three-story building on Zavodskaia Street, which was lined with stone buildings. In the nineties, Samara (you, of course, know its history) was a major commercial center whose growth had been particularly rapid because the Samara-Zlatoust Road and the Orenburg Road to Turkestan had been built there. Samara amazed me in every respect. I remember staying at a hotel and being served a bottle of lemonade and this, too, was a novelty. So was the Troitskaia Hotel which was located near the Troitskii bazaar (a big market); there was also a second-hand market, and small shops, and bazaars. Not far from the *gimnazium* building was the Volga with a garden laid out above the banks. There were steamboats sailing; I saw them for the first time in my life. Samara had a large theater. We didn't go to it, but I saw the building. In Belebei, we didn't have any stone buildings except for the public school and the hospital, which also wasn't very large. But in Samara there were three, four-story buildings and large shops.

My father, of course, said: "Do well on the exam and don't put us to shame; there are many students competing." I was disconcerted by this, frightened. I can't say that I passed the examination brilliantly, but I passed, and the teacher immediately said "Well, of course you've been accepted." Later that evening I was informed officially that I was on the list of those accepted.

When I search my memory, I find that it was the Volga which made the greatest impression on me. I had read about major rivers but had seen only our Usen, which was no more than a little stream. My father loved to go bathing; without fail, once or twice a week on summer evenings, we would go bathing. But also everywhere, the water was so shallow we could wade across.

H: You returned to Samara in the fall of 1898?

N: I passed the examination, came home for the summer, and in the fall my father took me to Samara and registered me there. Akimov, the teacher in whose home my sister had been living, was transferred that year, and she had to move to the boarding house attached to the girls' *gimnazium*. I was lodged in the one connected with the boys'. It was situated beside the Volga in a three-story building that had been donated to the *gimnazium* by Kozhevnikov, a former student who, I think, had later become a city judge.

H: How was the boarding house connected with the *gimnazium?*

N: I really don't know. The boarding house was under the authority of the *gimnazium* and the *gimnazium* inspector had charge of us. There was a special supervisor, various supervisors.

H: What was the atmosphere like? Was it a happy life or did you find it oppressive?

N: Naturally, it was oppressive. I was used to a great deal of freedom. Still, it wasn't particularly bad. I was absorbed with my studies, had many friends, and interesting conversations. Until the death of my father, none of the events of my early life stand out in particularly sharp relief.

H: Can you recall and describe in somewhat greater detail what the *gimnazium* was like?

N: I began telling you about the boarding house. It had three floors with about 20 boarders on the top two. The younger ones lived up above, on the third floor; the older ones on the second. Each boarder had a small desk. There was also a general study hall and a small library, mainly of the classics: Pushkin, Lermontov, Gogol, Turgenev.

H: Did it have a large dining hall?

N: There was a large dining room downstairs, where we were summoned by the bell. I lived in the boarding house for four years and there were almost four changes of supervisors; and each one left his imprint on the place. But there wasn't one for whom we could feel any real affection.

In any case, their relationship was not that of pedagogues. Not one of them impressed us.

The boarding house was on the shore of the Volga. You walked out the door – and there it was. Naturally, there were Gorkii-type characters to be found there: stevedores and all sorts of drifters. We later learned that there was a brothel a few blocks away. Formerly, this brothel had the distinct advantage of being fairly close to the [old] *gimnazium* building. You just had to walk up two blocks. But when the *gimnazium* was set up in the new section, near the Cathedral of St. Nicholas, which was practically at the other end of town, you had to walk very far. There was a horse-drawn tram in town but the drivers, of course, wouldn't take us.

H: Did the boarders attend different *gimnazia?*

N: There was only one *gimnazium* then, but the boarders were from different forms. Samara had a *gimnazium*, a *Realschule*, a school for railroad engineers, an agricultural school, and, later, a business school. It also had a theological seminary and a girls' *gimnazium*. A second boys' *gimnazium* was not opened until later.

The boarding house was comparatively shabby; it charged 15 rubles a month, and that was very little. The food they served there was nothing to boast about. You were always left feeling hungry, underfed. If the students weren't able to buy some additional food, they were famished. There was constant talk among us about the supervisor stealing. Virtually our first impression was that the cook was stealing such-and-such from us, the supervisor such-and-such. If I'm not mistaken, the supervisor during my first year was some retired deacon who had lost his job. In the second year there was a fellow we nicknamed Dracula.

H: Were there riots, unrest, because the students were fed so poorly?

N: There was real unrest only once, when they fed us rotten meat. But there was constant dissatisfaction, and the students were always demanding more food. There was talk, but nothing came of it.

H: Roughly what sort of food was served?

N: We were served breakfast, dinner, and supper. The worst part was that from breakfast at 8:00 a.m. until dinner at 4:00, we had nothing to eat. At first they gave us three kopecks for rolls, but later this was discontinued, and we went hungry. In the morning, we had a glass of tea with milk and a small roll. For dinner: soup, roast meat, and some dessert, usually *kissel'*. For supper we generally had porridge. The meals were always insufficient, the portions small. On Sundays there was pie; it was always good and I have the fondest memories of it. But it only served to whet the appetite.

Needless to say, there were all sorts of escapades. For example, after evening roll-call at the boarding house, some of the students would sneak out. Roll-call was at 8:00; after this, the place was closed down, and the students would bolt – the older ones, of course. The whole boarding house knew, there was always talk. The students would be caught, and there'd be all kinds of incidents; there were expulsions for this. Of course, we all sided with those who had fled.

In the morning, of course, there was the prayer. That official prayer, and the necessity of having to chant it at the very start of the day, aroused a sense of revulsion in us all. "Ah," we'd think, "The prayer . . . how can we avoid going, how can we get away?" And we had to be on time for the second prayer that was chanted in the *gimnazium;* we weren't allowed to come late. This enforced prayer was extremely repugnant.

Later on I went to a new *gimnazium,* a good one, that had been constructed out of solid material. It had been under construction for some time with funds allocated by Samara merchants. Apparently, though, there had been some loose spending. A teacher of Greek, who was one of the people involved in the construction, had built his own house at the time, and it was said he had used public bricks. When he appeared in the corridor, muffled shouts could be heard: "He stole bricks!" Only scraps of information about this got through to us, but these, of course, did not enhance the teacher's authority.

H: From what classes of society were the students in the *gimnazium?*

N: This became clear gradually. The town also had a boarding house for noblemen's sons. Samara was an ancient Volga "nest of gentlefolk," where the nobility were distinguished by a certain degree of independence. They had built their own boarding house, but many of their children attended the *gimnazium.* A classmate of mine was an Aksakov. His father was a Land Captain as well as a landowner. There was also a bank director's son in the school.

H: Let us now discuss the development of your social views and the view of your classmates during this period.

N: As for myself, I had two lines of interest from the start. I mentioned that while in Belebei I had become interested in the sciences. In Samara I devoured books: I read, studied, made notes. I remember I had a large notebook listing all the astronomical distances, and I memorized the names of the constellations. On the other hand, my interest in poetry, liberal democratic poetry, awakened in the first form. I started with Pushkin. The dormitory had a small library with the works of Pushkin and Lermontov, and in my early years there, what appealed to my sympathy and interest was the poetry of rebellion. I also remember being very keen on chess in the first form. Chess was a great passion of mine that lasted for two years. In the second form, I recall, I was overjoyed when I beat our class preceptor at the dormitory in chess. He considered himself a great chess enthusiast; I played badly, of course, yet I beat him.

H: What I would like to know, first of all, is whether the teachers stimulated your interest in poetry, particularly, as you say, in the poetry of rebellion.

N: No, I wouldn't say that. Konstantin Andreevich Rylov, a Russian language teacher of mine, who was a very likeable person, did have some impact on me. He read Chekhov's short stories well. But from the standpoint of my interest in poetry, he wasn't a factor. On the whole, it's difficult for me to specify the people who did influence me. I remember that I was carried away by Nekrasov; had enormous enthusiasm for his works, but I don't remember anyone stimulating this interest. Naturally, I had talks with people. I remember we had a coach who tested us. After preparing our lessons, we had to review them with him at night before going to bed. He was a student in the sixth form of our *gimnazium*. I no longer remember his name but I recall – this probably happened while I was in the second form – that I was forever telling him about the poems I had read and memorized; and he warned me: "Watch out, Nicolaevsky, you're going to end up in the Peter and Paul Fortress!"[1] By that time I was already familiar with the fortress, knew about it from the works of the Decembrists and from Nekrasov.[2] In the second form I was already reading the memoirs of the Decembrists. I had to hunt for them, there weren't many available at the time. By 1898–1900 I already knew a great deal. I remember that in the third form we had a new history teacher, Aleksandr Ivanovich Pavlov, a man with an actor's face who had come to Samara to make a career for himself. He had a rich wife, played at being a liberal and, by means of innuendoes, recounted various episodes from Russian history, going no further, of course, than Nicholas I. He ended up by becoming an inspector and our persecutor, first expelling those of us, like myself, who had talked to him at great length and confided in him. That occurred in 1903.

H: Which events before the reign of Alexander II brought out his liberal views?

N: Peter I and the murder of his son; all the palace revolutions of the 18th century; and the Decembrists. The Decembrists attracted attention at a very early stage, and he was fascinated with them. He didn't offer any full-scale, complete accounts but allusions that stimulated our interest. Usually what would happen was this: He would talk (he loved to talk and was a good narrator) and make some sort of allusion. And no sooner had he finished an episode than there would be a barrage of questions.

I had read very little illegal literature; in the last analysis, there was none to be had. I first came across illegal writings when the icon of the Holy Mother of Kazan or Kursk, which was later blown up, was brought to town in 1900. It was winter, probably late November: there had been many blizzards and a great deal of snow had fallen. As I recall, we were walking along the main street in town, Dvorianskaia, when we saw a shop window used for announcements and noticed some sort of leaflet lying there. We had heard about these but hadn't yet seen any. With extreme effort, which involved committing an act of vandalism, we forced the wire gate, got the proclamation out and began reading it. It dealt with the icon, asked whether it wasn't the height of stupidity for people to revere such a thing. I later met and became acquainted with the author, Mikhail Vedeniapin, a "realist" who was older than our group.[3] He had written the proclamation. At the time he had already completed the *Realschule*. His nickname was Shishiga. (In the North, *shishigi* means various types of demons; there are little *shishki*, big *shikyny*, and *shishigi*. They have different temperaments.) In 1906–07 when we were in prison, he and I became friends. He was the same Vedeniapin who was convicted in 1922 in the trial of the SRs.[4]

H: What impression did the proclamation make on you?

N: A great impression. I remember that I read it before we had to go and kiss the icon, and recall how it affected me. I didn't want to kiss the icon. I must say this was nothing new; earlier, too, religion had not aroused any great piety in me. But the proclamation impressed me as the first free word I had hear, a statement in which the writer had dotted his *i*'s, called things by their proper names. And what he had to suggest did not offend me. I remember that the proclamation had been drenched by the snow, that we dried it carefully, outlined in ink the letters that had become wet and blurred, and read it, passing it from hand to hand. I wanted to keep it but somehow it got mislaid. We had many talks about it. This happened when I was midway through the second form; by that time we had a group of students who could talk frankly with one another. We also read Nekrasov and gave each other his works to read. At this time, too, I was suddenly carried away by Mayne Reid and Gustave Aimard.[5] Naturally, I read all their works. Gustave Aimard was also a revolutionary writer; he described South American revolutionists who had struggled, gone to battle, etc. Which meant they were people under the same sail as we. At that time, everyone was moving under the same sails, and what mattered wasn't the way the wind was blowing, but the direction in which your sails were set. The political attitudes of the day were such that we searched everywhere for like-minded people. I can even recall Krestovskii's poem, a reactionary thing.[6] But what do I remember of it? "Our eagle – heraldic, double-talking, double-headed, orthodox – is to blame for it all."

H: As I understand it, your main spiritual nourishment in those days was Pushkin, Lermontov, and Nekrasov.

N: Mainly Nekrasov. Our *gimnazium* library didn't have his works. I found them at a friend's. I remember the first time I came across his works in the public library. Samara had a good public library which had been founded with the help of exiles and given a good, solid start by the local liberals as far back as the seventies. Lenin took books out there. A librarian, Vikenteva, the wife of one of the members of the circles in Samara in the early nineties, looked after us. For some reason she was without her husband at the time. Another woman was the director of the museum. The library and reading room were on the first floor of a big building, the local museum on the second. Samara had a good regional museum with a fairly large collection in the natural sciences, and I remember that it was precisely to see this that I went to the museum during my first days in town. The collection was very large. I can't say that I became friends with the director of the museum, but I felt attached to her and asked her all sorts of questions.

On the whole I had an enormous thirst for knowledge that went in all directions. The instruction in the *gimnazium* gave us little satisfaction. We studied Latin. Greek was usually given in the third form. But as we jokingly used to say: "The Greeks retreat before our advance." After we moved on to the third form and had been studying Greek for a few months, the course was cancelled because the first Vannovskii Reform transferred it to the fifth form.[7] Yet when I had gone on to the fifth form, Greek was shifted again; so we never once had to be examined in the subject. In general, regarding the reform, everyone recognized that the old program was bad; yet everyone, on down to the teachers, said the situation would have been better had the reform been a good one. And this fostered disrespect for the program.

The instructors we had were nothing to brag about. The only one who impressed us was K. I. Shidlovskii, an old Latin scholar and a truly erudite man. But we didn't have him for our Latin instructor; we had a poor Latin scholar, and I must say he didn't inspire confidence. As for the foreign language instructors, in the second form I took German with a mediocre, frivolous, ignorant fellow, some sort of functionary who had come to town. The only *gimnazium* instructors about whom I have any pleasant memories are that fellow Rylov and Inspector Spasskii, a likeable person, though not one of our teachers. The director was Ilia Nikolaevich Reznikov, who compiled and published collections of sayings of great people. Reznikov was unquestionably a good, honest man but decidedly not a pedagogue, and totally unsuited to the task. The *gimnazium* had a new building but an incompetent faculty.

H: I would like to go back in time again and have you describe your social attitudes by the end of 1900. First, I'd like to know what poems of Nekrasov's you had read.

N: The ones I remember best deal with the Volga. "The Volga in spring . . ." The river was right there before us, we'd run down to it and go sailing, our favorite amusement. Life in Samara centered around the Volga. Everything about it attracted people – from a commercial standpoint and from that of everyday living. And it was beautiful. "I remember the lights above the Volga . . ." I no longer recall what I read besides Nekrasov.

H: Which of his works did you read?

N: All of them, almost all. Naturally, I read those poems, and *Knight for an Hour, The Pedlars*, and *Who Can Be Happy and Free in Russia?* I wanted to find out what had been deleted, what all those lines of dots were. I'd make inquiries, guess about the words these dots concealed. Later, I began to collect verse. It was probably in the third form that I started a notebook where I copied the poetry that interested me. By then I had begun making a systematic survey of all the writers and compiled a list of the civic themes in their works. I also read the periodicals.

H: What social attitudes did you draw, say by the end of 1900, from your reading of *Who Can Be Happy and Free in Russia?*

N: In the third form my feelings were love of the people and love of freedom – nothing more concrete than that. I think that at the time I still had not heard anything about the debate between the Marxists and the *narodniki*. I remember nothing about this. I had not yet read the *narodniki* with serious attention. I'd merely begun, glanced at them.

H: But you got an impression of them from your reading of Nekrasov?

N: No. of course, I was familiar with the names of Chernyshevskii and Uspenskii, with those of all the writers, but I had no clear conception of them as figures yet. I hadn't read Chernyshevskii's *What Is to Be Done?*, and didn't until much later.

H: But had you formed some notion of the movement "to the people"?
N: We had heard about it. The librarian and museum director had told us a few things about it. They'd say: "You young people are nothing but kids, but those were men!" Samara was a city with the type of Russians whom Chirikov had characterized as "aliens [in their own land]."[8] It had a large colony of former exiles who had returned to Russia and settled in the city to repair their situation, earn some money, etc. *Samarskii Vestnik,* which was the first Marxist newspaper in Russia, was published there.[9] At the time, of course, I knew nothing about such things. Those "foreigners" were there, but I learned of this only later. Krzhizhanovskii lived there; Artsybushev arrived later.[10] I found myself in this circle, began to establish connections with these people in the winter of 1902–1903, a time that was linked for me with the twenty-fifth anniversary of Nekrasov's death. A Nekrasov memorial celebration was arranged; the *gimnazium* students were permitted to go and all of us did. Nekrasov's works declaimed on stage made an even more powerful impression than they did in book form. And students turned up who had been banished [to Samara] for participating in disturbances. They stood out by the nature of their conversation and their vitality, and we – the older generation of *gimnazium* students – were drawn to them.

It was at this time (December 1902) that I made my first acquaintance with a person who was involved in the revolutionary movement. Somehow, during a conversation, he came out and said: "If this interests you so much, fine; let's go over to my place." When we got there, he took a mirror off the wall, pulled out the back panel, thrust his fingers in, and pulled out a pamphlet. It was some sort of Social Democratic pamphlet. I was wondering whether it might be Plekhanov's pamphlet on Nekrasov, when he said: "Here, read it."[11] And, of course, it was that very work about what one wasn't permitted to discuss, yet had to know. I think it was the first pamphlet of this nature that I obtained. No, that's not true. Prior to this, of course, there had been others.

By the end of my second year in the *gimnazium,* or the beginning of my third, a group of us gathered who were not identical in our convictions, but shared the same mood and were drawn to Nekrasov. It wasn't exactly a passion for Nekrasov that bound us together, but the love of the people, the love of freedom. How did this manifest itself? There wasn't as yet a real circle. Each one read things in his own way. There was Lev Nikolaevich Kreiner, whose father was the chief of the Ussuriiskaia Railroad. Lev's mother, Maria Kuzminishna Kreiner, had separated from his father, lived in Samara with her son and looked after him. They had a small apartment and I often went there to visit. Then there was Vladimir Kotelov. His mother too had separated from his father and lived alone with her son. And it's possible that this situation affected the children's outlook. I know from history that many people have been influenced by broken home lives. There have been fewer instances of people from stable families joining the movement than from broken homes. Beginning with Herzen, this has been the pattern. Herzen doesn't write about this, but there is no doubt that this tragedy . . .[12]

H: What was Kotelov's background?

N: His father lived in Kazan and was, I think, a lawyer. Then there was Kazachenkov; his father was a bookkeeper in some local firms. Then there was Liubimov. He, too, was from the provinces, from some small district town. He received room and board for some work he did.

H: You mentioned that one of the students was the son of a merchant. Who was this?

N: Kostia Larin, the son of a merchant from a village near Samara. If you like, I can simply describe all the students in our circle. Lev Kreiner, a lively, sociable fellow with a poetic nature, stood out from the group. He read avidly and widely and wrote with facility, but his writing was very superficial. He and I were expelled from the *gimnazium* together in 1903 as the most dangerous. Kostia Larin was also expelled. So was another fellow, Balabanov, who was also the son of a merchant, a small merchant from Buzuluk. There was also another fellow in the group – Volodia Orlov. If I am not mistaken, he was from the nobility, but from the service nobility. I saw him in 1905; he did not take an active part in the movement. Many of the students came from the nobility and the *raznochintsy*.[13] But the noblemen's sons remained aloof and by the third form our circle was, in fact, the center of the class.

H: Your circle consisted of about seven or eight people?

N: Yes.

H: How many students were there in the class?

N: Thirty. What provided a bond between us was that we played lotto together. We really loved the game and used to play during recess. Then, in the spring of 1901 or 1902, we went on all sorts of trips. I was very keen on the natural sciences, and near Samara there were deposits of chalk and limestone, as well as various types of ammonites and delatynites, etc. I remember that in the third form I was carried away by my excavations and by my assembling collections. A geological expedition was doing work in the area and there was a big laboratory affiliated with the zemstvo board. It was headed by Preobrazhenskii, who was still quite young at the time.[14] Later, he bacame an academician. After he had observed my interest, he gave me permission to come and work in his laboratory in the evenings. Parts of the time he helped me; at other times, he would tell me to go work at it myself, and I did. He had literature there and a fairly good collection of well-preserved fossils and stones of the various Samara periods: the Cretaceous Period, and others.

H: You mentioned that by the third form the lines of demarcation had already been drawn between the different groups of students.

N: They had been there all along. I should note one other thing that, apparently, played a role: during this stage, an age difference of a year or two was of major importance. In the aristocratic circles the students were already involved in all sorts of romantic adventures – not always of the nicest kind. There were also several Jews among us, two who were in our class. One was Levka Nikiforov; the other was Gurev. He was longing for this kind of experience. He was three or four years older but had been left back several times so that we caught up with him. Somehow he latched on to us, but sexual adventures and commercial matter occupied him. He had already begun thinking about going into business and wondered whether it wasn't time for him to leave school and find work in a store – which, I think, he did. I can't remember now for certain. I have to organize my recollections of these events (I have a fairly tenacious memory) and reestablish the dates on which they occurred.

Through this entire period, I was fascinated with the Cretaceous, the hunts for stones and fossils in the area, and imbued with enthusiasm for poetry. My friends used to tease me by calling me "scientist," "astronomer." But they did so in jest. Neither I nor any of the others had nicknames. We all called each other by our first names and were very friendly. Leva was a particularly good friend of mine; then Kostia Larin. He was the first one to go abroad and when he returned, he brought a whole carload of [revolutionary] literature with him.

H: The picture so far is of a group of people who gravitated strongly toward Nekrasov and had personal likings for one another. Do you feel that during these years, say at the age of thirteen, that these five or six people had already begun to build a collective life, that they were eager to organize a group?

N: No. I wouldn't put it in such definite terms. We were a company of friends. Groups of friends were constantly being formed in the *gimnazium* – through personal attraction and general attitudes. But by 1902–1903 we had already begun to form groups along clearly defined lines. I should say that our class was somewhat more rebellious than the others. We made several attempts to obstruct the work of the school. We got hold of some chemicals, poured them in the teacher's inkwell, and he went charging out of the room with a roar.

H: How would you explain this rebelliousness?

N: I don't know, and I wouldn't venture to say. Balabanov was a great rebel. The mores of the Volga region were making themselves felt. There was another rebel in the class – Boris Sokolov, whose mother was a surgical assistant, and father a surgical assistant in the local hospital.

H: I see, then, that the overwhelming majority of these people were from the plebeian intelligentsia, several of them sons of merchants.

N: Small merchants. In the small towns where they had their businesses, merchants were social climbers.

H: What I would like to know is this: Before the turning point came, was there conflict between the plebeian and aristocratic elements in the class?

N: It was definitely noticeable in the second form. They had a different set of interests and were drawn in different directions. They tended to look down on us as a rowdy, unserious lot who were being carried away by something, and made noise. And we regarded them as a bunch of lousy aristocrats. That situation was clear.

What also made an impact was that our class was not isolated from the others. There was an older class, and a younger one. The older students were in the fourth form. I was in the third. In the older class, too, there was a whole group of students who joined the movement: Sashka Popov, Lenia Ilin.

H: Did the older class influence your group?

N: To a certain degree, but not directly. They didn't concern themselves with us. They had their interests; we had ours. But we knew one another. We became closer later, in the third and fourth forms – that is, during the second year of our acquaintance. When I try now to think of what activated our gradually mounting interest, it seems to me that it was the student unrest and the arrival of students who had been banished as a result.[15] A whole group arrived in 1901. The year 1902 marked the next period, when the influence of the students was considerable. I remember several of them, recall someone like Pavel Vasil'evich Bekenskii being in the revolutionary movement.[16]

I was keeping busy in that laboratory, not understanding a thing, only spoiling material. But then Preobrazhenskii's brother came. He was a student who had been exiled for participating in the 1901 disorders in Moscow. A significant date! Apparently he arrived in the spring of 1901. He was a poet. After he and I had a talk, and he learned that I was interested in poetry, he invited me to his home and read me his verse. I remember something of it: "What does the coming day have in store for us?/Perhaps not the freedom we have long awaited?/ Perhaps not the liberty for thoughts to come?/O, the days to come are dark indeed." This kind of thing, of course, was very primitive, but in those days it made an impact on us. The main thing was that Preobrazhenskii's brother told us what sort of meetings they held, what kind of leaflets they issued. He himself was no revolutionary. He was a fine person, an *intelligent* who wanted to do scientific work. But he had an elementary kind of revolutionary outlook, and this attracted us to him.

During the evenings the "old man" (he really wasn't an old man, he was twenty-five) would drop into the laboratory. So would Vasilii Konstantinovich Klafton, the secretary of the zemstvo board. He had been a student in Kazan, a member of the circles of the late eighties. (Later, he was the chief leader of the Kadets in Samara; still later, one of Kolchak's ministers.) Preobrazhenskii would always come and tell me the news they had received about the movement. He'd talk to me and I'd always ask questions. He said it was too early for me to get involved; that I had to work in geology, study, prepare myself, lay the groundwork for a future. And he was right about all this.

H: I would like to ask you the following question: When did the plebeian section of your *gimnazium* class form a separate circle?

N: I don't remember now. It's difficult for me to distinguish between the third and fourth forms. In the fourth form we were still trying to obstruct the work of the school. We scattered some hydrogen sulfide and drove everyone out of the *gimnazium*. But it's possible that we held meetings during the spring of 1902, we definitely did during the fall of that year [that is, at the beginning of the fifth form].

H: How did these get started?

N: The plan for them originated with Kreiner, who thought we should issue a journal. He was usually carried away by a variety of projects, and inspired many of us. His mother considered him very able, with poetic inclinations, and to some extent, she encouraged him. I should mention one other thing that happened at the end of 1902 or 1903. My sister, who was two years older than I, graduated from the *gimnazium* in 1903. She lived in the dormitory attached to the *gimnazium* and had a number of friends among the girls there, all of whom joined the movement. I was the link for them. I used to go and visit my sister every week. I'd tell her about all the things we did and ask her about her group. She was very, very interested in it all but was discreet, reserved. In the eight form, the girls in her *gimnazium* exhibited considerable freedom. My sister asked me to bring my friends over and she introduced them to hers. As a result, when the meetings began to assume more or less definite form, my sister attended. And she wasn't the only girl present; by this time our circle consisted not only of students from the boys' *gimnazium* but from the girls' as well.

Prior to this we also held readings in an apartment, read Pisarev there. The readings were held at Kreiner's, in an apartment he and his mother rented. We always felt much freer meeting there. We were received warmly and served tea.

H: Who would come? Kotelov? Kazachenko?

N: Kazachenko came during this period but left our circle the next year. His uncle went blind. And Kazachenko, who had been well off up to this point, became very poor, was literally reduced to kopecks. He had to work a great deal, fell behind the group.

H: Did Kotelov attend the readings?

N: Yes, Volodia came. So did Sasha Sokolov, Venia Liubimov, Kostia Larin; they, Kreiner and I made up the group.

H: And it was Kreiner's idea that you read together?

N: He managed to get hold of a library card. *Gimnazium* students weren't allowed to sign for library cards, were forbidden to take out books. We had to get them in someone else's name. Kreiner's mother signed for a card and we often went to get books. I remember all the books that I liked – a world history and others. All of them were taken out on her card. Her apartment was transformed into a constant meeting place. She lived fairly close to the *gimnazium*, and we could go directly there from school (Kreiner would even run home to have lunch). The apartment became our headquarters and our meeting place; it definitely had by the fourth form, perhaps even the third.

H: And you met regularly?

N: We met almost every day. We had classes in the *gimnazium* until three or four o'clock and met at five. At half-past six supper was served at the dormitory and we had to be there. But between five and half-past six I would run over to the apartment; and quite often they had me stay for supper. We used to have readings there on Sundays. I can still remember those

Sunday scenes. We'd sit and talk. I can't say that we had any real system, a clearly established routine.

The fall of 1902 was a very painful time for me. I had been living in the dormitory on a government stipend, but that year Inspector Stavskii, who had helped arrange things for me, was transferred, and I was left without a stipend. Kreiner's mother offered to have me come and live with them, and I did during that year. We lived together in one room and my older sister would come and bring her friends. Quite a few *gimnazium* students joined the group later; at first there were two or three. I don't remember who the first ones were. And we began to meet regularly on Saturdays. We didn't go to vespers on Saturdays, as we were supposed to. We didn't go to mass. It was a whole tale how we slipped away. The secret was to go over to the *gimnazium* and leave some trace of our presence there – some article of clothing on the coat rack; then we'd dash off. But before we could get out of the building, we had to race across a field that was within the guard's vision. If he caught sight of you, you'd spend the coming Monday in the detention room. Nonetheless, I'd take off. What else was there to do there?

We began reading a variety of subjects, half the reading dealt with literature that was mixed, to some extent, with sociopolitical ideas. Pisarev's and Dobroliubov's works were not circulated at the library; they had been removed. Strangely enough, I remember that you could get Chernyshevskii's works there. His articles had appeared unsigned in the nineties, and you could get his *Essays on the Gogol Period of Russian Literature*, whereas both Pisarev's and Dobroliubov's works had been removed, and we had to obtain them in devious ways. There was a seminary student, the son of a local priest, who had all their works and gave them to us.

H: At the meetings in Kreiner's apartment during this period you read Pisarev's and Dobroliubov's works aloud?

N: I only remember reading Pisarev's. What we had did not amount to a real circle, but a series of readings. I can't remember exactly what we read, but I think we read some work on natural science. [Pisarev] was a good popularizer, and we were fascinated with this. I made the group read Timiriazev's *Life of the Plants,* and we conducted experiments with starch solutions, etc.[17] But this, too, didn't last long. Natural science wasn't the basis for our remaining a group, but it was a beginning. And it was a result of my influence; I tended in that direction.

H: In terms of your outlook on the world, did you consider yourselves realists?

N: Of course, but I don't remember using the term. For us, it meant students from the *Realschule.*

H: What terms did you use?

N: It's hard for me to say. I think "democrats."

H: Did you feel that your grasp of the world, your propensity for natural sciences, implied a distinct point of view?

N: We had far less understanding than that of what was going on around us. We were simply living a life we found exciting; we raced off in all directions, were interested in everything. Preobrazhenskii was right when he said we were spreading ourselves out too thin.

H: Were you interested in history at this time?

N: Yes, and even somewhat earlier. I don't remember how it happened, but in the second form I became interested in our Bulgarian ancestors, the Volga Bulgars. The museum had an entire display case of excavations from the ruins of ancient Bulgaria, and I read everything I could find in the library on the Bulgarians. Some literature on them had appeared in the forties. Some professors at Kazan University wrote about them for the *Journal of the Ministry of Public Education* and the *Reading Library*.[18] I read through all this material, and when we began issuing a journal I wrote an article entitled "On the History of the Bulgarians." It was my first article.

H: Did the revolutionary movement in Russia and the West, the French Revolution, interest you?

N: I should mention that Kreiner's father had been arrested once and this, apparently, was the beginning of the rift between his parents. His mother had no great respect for the revolutionary movement, and to some extent, her attitude affected us. She said that the brochures we were reading were nonsense, that illegal literature lacked seriousness. She'd tell us to study and read – read Pisarev, Dobroliubov. But she thought the brochures lacked interest. We managed to escape from her influence somewhat later. But at the time it affected us in precisely the way she wished.

H: What about the Decembrists?

N: That was different. Maria Kuzminishna respected them and the romanticism surrounding their exploits captivated us all.

H: Had you read anything about *narodnichestvo* [Populism] by this time?

N: We hadn't done any serious reading. Though I can't say for certain, it seems to me we knew nothing about *narodnichestvo*.

H: I'd like to spend a little more time discussing the readings. What works did they include?

N: I remember our reading the poet Minskii, whose new book – *Alma*, I think it was – was published then.[19] I must confess that it had no interest for me whatever. He was a Symbolist poet who was completely outside of my orbit, and I didn't understand his symbolism. Levka was fascinated with Nietzsche. Maria Kuzminishna was urging him on. My sister became interested in this, in problems of personal happiness.

H: What other new writers did you read that year?

N: Pisarev, Pomialovskii, and Dobroliubov – I read them all that year.[20]

H: I would like to talk now at somewhat greater length about the journal you decided to start when you were in the fifth form, in 1902 and the early part of 1903.

N: We probably began discussing it late in 1902, but I'm certain that it was February by the time the first issue appeared. If I'm not mistaken, we printed a total of three issues. These didn't contain anything that was purely political, but with the exception of my article on the ancient Bulgarians of Kazan, they reflected an oppositional mood – opposition of the vaguest, most indeterminate kind. You can judge from the first issue. It didn't contain anything revolutionary. We each contributed. Leva wrote sketches, a Gorkii-type scene about the second-hand clothes market. All of us, of course, were very keen on Gorkii. I wrote about the Bulgarians; people laughed at my article. Vladimir Orlov turned out to be the poet, wrote symbolic poetry. "From the Creation/to the present/our poor spirits chase after life/later they will rest." Pretentious, worthless stuff.

During this time a new teacher arrived: Dmitrii Ivanovich Godnev, a literature instructor. He was the son of Ivan Godnev, a professor at Kazan University. Dmitrii Ivanovich was a very likable fellow. He arrived right after he had married and graduated from the university. We were his first students. He exhibited considerable affection and interest in his relationships with us and mentioned me in his memoirs. He didn't last long at the *gimnazium*, was kicked out even before us. He and I had become really close friends, and we parted with great emotion.

H: What did you discuss with him?

N: Literature – literature in a very humanistic light.

H: Did he introduce you to some of the new writers?

N: By this time we were already familiar with them and had read Gorkii even earlier. During this year, we turned up some of the works of Andreev and Skitalets. I think the first volume of the anthology *Knowledge* [*Znanie*] had already been published.[21]

H: What impression did Gorkii make on you? Why were you so fond of him?

N: Because his rebelliousness corresponded to our own mood. Samara was his home town. Gorkii was a Samaran. Everyone there knew that he had published in the Samara newspaper, had walked down the same streets. I personally had a strong interest in science and undertook to master the subject, to collect material, etc. And this was fused with my interest in poetry, with a decidedly humanitarian outlook on life. One could sense that the country was headed for a fight; and since I had a fairly restless nature, why shouldn't I have liked him? I'm oversimplifying, of course, but I think that what I have said is fundamentally true.

Third interview

H: We have arrived at the time when you and your friends started a journal. What other activities were you involved in during that time, in the early part of 1903?

N: Apart from our group, I began to attend Social Democratic circles at this time. I made contact with the exiled students. When I think back on my own development, I believe that by the end of 1902 I already considered myself a Social Democrat. Why I did is not clear to me. I hadn't read anything in particular that influenced me, but the general atmosphere was such that we were drawn toward the party and were constantly talking about it. And I had, of course, seen the legal Marxist journal *Zhizn'* in which we had read Gorkii in 1901, when the general mood was as I have described it.[1]

What made a great impression on me was the first strike we witnessed early in 1903, the bakery workers' strike in Samara. For several days we went without rolls or bread. There was an enormous amount of discussion. I remember that I tried to become acquainted with the striking bakery shop workers and was terribly disappointed when I discovered that they were most ordinary fellows, who understood nothing. But through the students I made important contacts, and in the early spring (in March or April) a circle of students from various educational institutions in Samara was formed where people gave talks on political economy. It was one of the typically higher level circles for the intelligentsia organized by the Social Democrats. I was the only member of our group in such a circle.

H: Who delivered talks there?

N: If I'm not mistaken, the circle was led by Pavel Vasil'evich Beken-skii. He was a sympathizer who later left the movement and became a doctor. I myself did not have occasion to meet him later, but I knew about him. He worked as a doctor in one of the towns on the Kama River, somewhere near Izhevsk or Botkinsk where he had been born.

H: Did the people who spoke on political economy attempt to expound Marx to you?

N: Of course. They treated the theory of surplus value and the social structure of society in a Marxist vein. To a greater degree, I think they may have interpreted these according to the views of Bogdanov, a recent arrival on the scene whose ideas were being cited by everyone.[2] At the time, all this was new to me, and economics still did not engage my interest, though I became somewhat interested in it later. There was a fellow by the name of Petr Kuzmin, whose father owned a grocery store.

H: Who was this Kuzmin?

N: He was a Social Democrat, later a Bolshevik.

H: Was he, too, a student at this time?

N: Yes, a student at the *Realschule.*

H: He was about 18?

N: Yes, 18 or 19. He was completing his studies at this time, was in the last form. Later he joined the Social Democrats and played a prominent role among the Bolsheviks. He was something of a bum, and drank a bit. I don't know the circumstances surrounding his death, but he died while still very young, in 1918 or 1919.

H: Did these talks on political economy make a great impression on you, strike you as something vital?

N: I was fascinated by everything. Fascinated by the revolutionary movement and its literature – the only literature I read – and the debates I listened to. I remember that Lenin's *What Is to Be Done?* arrived at this time.

H: Did you read it?

N: No, I merely saw a copy. It appeared in the summer of 1902 and there were only one or two copies available. I saw how eagerly people read it and was told: "This is some book! Some book!" It revealed all the secrets, and so I was still too young to read it. I wouldn't understand anything.

H: What, in fact, did you read at this time?

N: Of the *Iskra* publications, I read Martov's *The Workers' Cause in Russia* and *The Red Banner,* and Tun's *History of the Revolutionary Movement.*[3] I can see now that I was being caught up in the revolutionary movement, caught up with history; that clearly – perhaps before I myself was aware of it – I was being pulled in this direction, that of historical analysis. Even more so, during my stay in Ufa. Samara did not have a good library; its revolutionary literature dated from an older period.

H: What else did you read while you were still in Samara?

N: It's difficult for me to single that out now. I had already seen the first issues of *Iskra* and *Revoliutsionnaia Rossiia.* I don't recall seeing *Osvobozhdenie* in Samara, but I brought home the revolutionary literature we did have, and we all read it there. I recall that Maria Kuzminishna, who remembered the literature of the eighties and nineties and had tried to prove to us a year or two before that the present-day revolutionary literature lacked seriousness, now had to admit that it was far more serious than she had thought, and she was clearly impressed with it.

H: I would like to dwell a bit on the manner in which you developed a conception of yourself as a Social Democrat. Perhaps we should go back in time a little. In the last interview you told me that you first encountered one of the university students in December 1902. Was it through him that you met other students?

N: Through several people. This student gave me my first illegal brochure. I remember that it dealt with Nekrasov. During that same autumn, though, I also met with other students and with that fellow Preobrazhenskii, who had been banished for participating in the student movement. A good many students turned up, and we all took an interest in them.

H: Were there any from Kiev University?

N: No, they were Moscow students. But there were also students from other universities – Preobrazhenskii was from Iurev and there were students from Kazan. The disturbances in Kazan were small; nonetheless students had been expelled from the university there. Kazan was our university; the *gimnazia* were attached to educational districts, and our district included Kazan. It was usually assumed that the students from the Samara *gimnazia* would go to Kazan University.

H: These students, naturally, told you about the agitation in the universities. Did they also consider themselves Social Democrats?

N: No. However, Pavel Vasil'evich Bekenskii did. We knew he was connected with the party.

H: So he was the first who spoke to you in a clear-cut, straightforward manner about them.

N: I knew about the Social Democrats' existence before this and I myself wanted to become one, even before I met them.

H: For what reason?

N: I knew they were a revolutionary party, and represented the working-class movement. The main thing that impressed me was that they were the party of the workers' movement, and a very strong, influential party. At the same time, what doubtlessly made an impression on me was Gorkii, whose "Song of the Stormy Petrel" we all knew by heart. Shaliapin had not been in Samara, but he appeared on the scene at this time, and every seminary student considered himself a potential Shaliapin. At every party some seminary student would get up and sing: "In the steppe/a lonely eagle sits/enchained . . ." It was the romanticism of the poor seminary students, and of the barge-haulers [*romantika . . . bursatsko-burlatskaia*]. Gorkii's world fused with that of the seminary students.

H: When did you first learn about the existence of the Socialist Revolutionaries?

N: At roughly this same time, I learned that there was another party – the Socialist Revolutionaries – who were drawn to the peasantry.

H: When you made your initial choice, you knew this party existed?

N: I knew one SR – a fellow by the name of Veniamin Pavlovich Bulatov, a writer from the Sormovo factory.[4]

H: When did you meet him?

N: Early in 1903.

H: And he told you something of the SRs?

N: Yes, but only in general outline. He was a young fellow, a very fine worker. I can't remember now why he failed to impress me, since the SRs were regarded as the party that had adopted the *narodnichestvo* of the seventies and eighties, and I already know about them. Terrorism did not impress me. At one time I had the greatest awe of the *narodovoltsy*, that is, of those who perished after assassinating the tsar.[5] But this method of action didn't impress me, didn't strike me as sound. I pounced on old journals at that time, got hold of them in the library and the reading room, and looked through complete sets covering the years that interested me.

H: What were you searching for in these journals?

N: Some clues that would help me gain an understanding. I was very interested in the movement of the seventies. At this point, too, I developed another friendship with a *narodnik*, a woman from a teacher's college. My acquaintance with Veniamin Pavlovich Bulatov relates to this period, but it was a minor episode in my life, since he left very soon on one of the first steamers and went to Saratov.

H: One reason why he failed to impress you, then, was that you considered the approach futile?

N: Yes, though at the same time I felt great personal sympathy for these people, perhaps because it seemed that they had sacrificed themselves to no purpose, unwisely, that they might have achieved greater good. Terrorism didn't impress me, whereas the workers' strikes did – very much. And when the first strike took place . . .

H: But you had already begun to consider yourself a Social Democrat even before this strike. There appears to be another side. I remember you told me that when you were still a very young boy, your father showed love and concern for the people, an interest in the life of those in the country-side. With respect to the issue of the peasantry versus the working class, what influenced your feelings?

N: I wouldn't even venture an explanation, and I don't think I could have explained it in those days. I think I was groping for what seemed to me most effective, what would yield the greatest results. Later on, too, I never had a negative attitude toward the peasantry. On the contrary, from my earliest involvement with Menshevism, I was criticized because of the outlook on the peasantry held by a number of Mensheviks, particularly Dan, who felt clear-cut aversion for the peasantry. Dan, of course, exacerbated the conflict. I never shared such feelings. I did not oppose the peasants to the workers. I considered the workers an independent force, but not a force that ought to be at odds with the peasantry. I never felt that. And, later, I settled down in Ufa and reread all the *narodniki* back to Nikolai Uspenskii and Levitov.[6] I reviewed all of them in the *narodnik* writings of the seventies.

H: The last question on this subject. Was there a time during 1902 and 1903 when you wavered between these two parties?

N: No, more likely I did in Ufa. But I will discuss that later.

H: If you were able to compare the two types of experience – the discussions in the circle on political economy and the impressions made on you by the strike – which would you say had the greater impact?

N: I couldn't say. They represented completely different planes of experience, and they didn't contradict, but complement each other.

H: I'll put the question to you another way. Let us focus on the circle. Did you experience a need to develop a comprehensive outlook on life, a systematic world view?

N: I'm afraid that if I answer yes, I will be projecting backward what occurred later. It came from the gut. I had to join this camp; truth was to be found there. The fact that I would take part in the movement had been clear to me even earlier, practically from my first years in the *gimnazium*, when I was searching in Nekrasov's writings and elsewhere, searching for something solid and serious. And in this period, I began to have this feeling. It was the working-class movement and the Social Democrats. I was fifteen years old at the time, so it would be an exaggeration for me to say I seriously raised the question of a world view.

H: Apart from discussions of political economy and theory of surplus value, what other topics were dealt with in the circle?

N: All sorts of issues. After a lecture, there would usually be discussions that led to talk about political issues of a general nature, the situation of students. I remember that at this time there was talk about that strike. On the whole, the circle had few meetings. It was supposed to meet twice a month, but it got started late – I remember that we had already changed to summer clothes by then. By May I had left town. In May we were also busy with various field trips, so that the circle held no more than three meetings.

H: Which of the discussions do you remember most vividly?

N: At the first meeting Bekenskii talked to me about general tasks. At the second or third (the last meeting), Kuzmin attemped to lecture on surplus value. And he was very unsuccessful. That was my impression. I remember that as I listened to him talk, I felt he was confusing issues and was somewhat embarrassed on this account, since he had undertaken to lecture and was doing such a poor job of it. Apparently everyone else felt so too because his talk didn't produce any real discussion. Bekenskii glossed over it and we moved on to something else. There was talk about whether the students shouldn't form a union. We made a groping attempt to determine whether we could form an organization of students. Though ours was a Social Democratic circle, we also discussed the question of whom to invite as members, and everyone agreed we should enlist whomever we could. I think there were people in the circle who weren't even clearly confirmed in their views as Social Democrats.

H: You said that at the first meeting Bekenskii lectured on general tasks. What did he say?

N: That everyone was uniting; that we, too, had to unite and to study; that we had assembled this circle on the instructions of the Social Democrats; and that we had to unite, study, and decide what had to be done. What we needed, he said, was organization. It showed the influence of *What Is to Be Done?*

H: Had he nothing to say about bourgeois revolution, political freedom, etc.

N: No.

H: With regard to the strike, you told me that even if the bakery shop workers failed to impress you, the strike itself did. In what respect?

N: We were attracted to the proletariat because of our political mood and the kind of literature we had read, but we, of course, did not know the proletariat. We wanted to find out what that strike was all about. We were also reading Gorkii at the time. He had bakery workers in his "Twenty-six Men and a Girl," so the striking bakery shop workers eventually fused in my mind with Gorkii's characters. However, there was really nothing romantic about what we had witnessed. Our mood was romantic, but there was nothing romantic about the way each of the workers interpreted that strike.

H: Did your circle plan to do something about this strike or not?

N: No. I can't understand why I didn't take any of the members of our group there, can't remember the reason for this now. I don't even remember taking Leva there to meet anyone. He made contacts on his own. He also became friendly with the son of Vasilii Petrovich Artsybushev, an old revolutionary, and introduced me to the boy.[7]

Vasilii Petrovich Artsybushev's son was our age, and we struck up an acquaintance with him right on the street – that is, Leva did. He had a great facility for meeting people and getting into conversation with them, was an intelligent fellow. I don't know how he started the acquaintance, but he was simply thrilled at who he had met – a very interesting son – his father a famous revolutionary. So that's how we met Boris Artsybushev-Shekhter.

His mother's name was Maria Petrovna Shekhter (his parents weren't officially married). He didn't attend either the *gimnazium* or the *Realschule,* but was, I believe, educated at home. I fail to understand how his father could have been so nonchalant about things that he gave his son no formal education. Nonetheless, the boy was our equal culturally and was greatly attracted to revolutionary literature. He impressed us.

H: Did he consider himself a Social Democrat too?

N: Yes. His father and mother were both Social Democrats, so it was only natural he should become one too. He lived half a block away from us.

H: You said that he formed the link between you and the bakery workers?

N: No, he told us about the strike. A proclamation about the worker's demands had appeared, and I'm almost certain we got it from him. It was from him that I learned who the important figures in the strike were. Samara, Samara! It was a spring that was tumultuous from any point of view. The inspector of our *gimnazium* had been transferred and replaced by the history teacher, that careerist Pavlov. From the start he began tightening up on the *gimnazium,* and he was particularly hard on me and Kreiner. We were told that at a meeting of the academic board, he had said he could take over the *gimnazium* but couldn't guarantee law and order unless he were free to tighten the reins. We had indulged in some obstructive activity in school. I was studying chemistry and I brought some chemical which we poured into the inkwells (not just in our class, but in others) and it released hydrogen sulfide vapors in the air. We were dismissed. It was still spring when this happened. Keep in mind that this was the spring of 1903, the time of the Kishinev pogrom, the Zlatoust strike, and shortly afterwards the assassination of the governor of Ufa.[8] So that almost every week there was an episode that caused agitation, aroused unrest.

It was at this point that Pavlov talked about expelling us. I told you that we were expelled, but so were students from other classes. During this period, students were expelled from the next form, the sixth, the group headed by Aleksei Sapozhnikov, an SR. And there was the group run by Leonid Ilin and Aleksandr Popov. They were a year older. We were in close touch with them after we left the *gimnazium,* in 1904 and 1905. By that time we were one group, whereas in 1903 we had just come to know one another. It was precisely in connection with this unrest that a society of *gimnazium* students was formed. It stands to reason that everyone sympathized with us; several students from the girls' *gimnazium* were also members!

H: How did the other students show their sympathy?

N: They questioned us at length. Naturally, we hadn't as yet rendered any real support to the bakers' strike, but the two things were connected. We felt we had to work together, come to an understanding. I don't remember whether any seminary students were there. There were students from the boys' *gimnazium,* the girls', the *Realschule,* and the business school. And there were students from a school for surgical assistants, an old school from the seventies; also from the teachers' seminary.

H: Were there student disorders?

N: No real disorders. Things never reached the point where we under-took collective action, had speeches, demonstrations, or rallied under flags. We knew that we were in a precarious position, that they wanted to expel us. I remember trying to be more cautious. I even went to my class precep-tor to explain myself but he behaved badly. There was a different atmo-sphere in the *gimnazium* in 1903, a change that was apparent also in gov-ernment circles. With the resignation of Vannovskii,[9] came an attempt to tighten controls. In short, the only person who interceded for us was God-nev, a young literature teacher who later published his memoirs about this episode.

H: When were you expelled?

N: I wasn't officially expelled. The school authorities, you see, had come to a decision: to suggest to the parents that they themselves withdraw the children to avoid formal expulsion. From our groups, Kreiner and I and, I think, Balabanov were removed. I'm sure Larin was, because he went abroad. Kreiner went to Moscow.

H: What did you do during the summer?

N: I went to Ufa. A completely new period for me began in Ufa. I had the address of the Social Democratic meeting-place and a recommendation to Gardenin, whose family was well-known in Ufa. The eldest son, Sergei Fedorovich, was a trade representative in Stockholm. He, too, was from the student circles. The next youngest brother, Boris Fedorovich, had been dis-missed and did military service that year. The next, Mikhail, was a class-mate of mine when I was in the sixth form. The boys also had a sister whose name I can't recall.[10]

H: Your mother?

N: Was already in Ufa. She moved there after my father died; she found a job as a guard in a government store.

H: And you lived at home?

N: Naturally. My sister had finished school and found a job as a teacher in Ufa.

H: Did she, too, consider herself a Social Democrat?

N: No, she joined the SRs. In Ufa she defined herself as an SR. There was an old established colony of SRs in Ufa. It included Vasilii Viktorovich Leonovich, Angarskii, and Viktorov, who was something of a poet from the Petersburg *People's Will* circles of the nineties.[11]

Leonovich's wife, Marie Vasil'evna, was the sister of Tsimmerman-Gvoz-dev, a Social Democrat. He was from the *Samarskii Vestnik* group and had the Samara tendency for oversimplification. He tried to prove that despite their negative features, the kulaks and usurers represented a progressive factor in the development of rural Russia.[12]

Now I must move on to discuss Ufa. I arrived there full of anxiety about my fate. I had doubts whether I would be able to enroll in the *gimnazium*, even though my two brothers were studying there and were fine students. They were in good standing, but some information about me must have gotten through, and the director either was skeptical about me or wanted to show that he had the upper hand. He was a good person. After the revolution of 1917 I had occasion to meet both him, Matveev (the director of the Ufa *gimnazium*) and Pavlov. They made entirely different impressions on me. For the Ufa director, I felt nothing but gratitude. He was strict and demanding, taught Greek, and was a real expert. He gave me bad marks because I happened to have been in Samara at a time when Greek was totally neglected. Despite all the trouble in the school, Matveev conducted his class in such a way that he managed to impart a basic minimum of knowledge.

H: Did Matveev accept you unconditionally?

N: Unconditionally, but only in the beginning. Later he even issued me a warning. I remember that he summoned me to his office in the *gimnazium* on the day of my arrest and asked me questions, like "What sort of things interest you?" Something of that order. Had I been more experienced, I would have realized that something had gone wrong and that this was a warning. But I didn't understand. Although I wasn't annoyed with him, I failed to understand why he was interfering in my affairs.

H: You were there in the sixth form?

N: Yes.

H: When you entered this class, were you interested in establishing connections with the students there or had you already begun to gravitate toward other groups?

N: From the start I had no interest in the *gimnazium*. It managed to exert some hold on me simply because I knew I had to behave myself and complete my studies.

H: And you made contacts with the students in your class?

N: Through my brother. He was a year younger than I and was in the next form. He lived in the boarding house for *gimnazium* students and introduced me to his friends. There were also students from my class there, but it wasn't until the fall that I got to know them. I spent the summer months completely under the sway of revolutionary attitudes. Through Gardenin I became acquainted with a number of other people in Ufa during this time – people who were acknowledged as members of the local party committee.

H: Let us concentrate now on that summer and on your activities in Gardenin's circle.

N: Gardenin was a member of the Ufa Committee, which at this time consisted chiefly of members from the zemstvo board:[13] Petr Nikolaevich Grigorev, and another fellow whose name I no longer remember. I became closest to Boris [Gardenin's second son]. He and Sergei Fedorovich also introduced me to people in the zemstvo board. I wanted to obtain some part-time work there, to earn a little money, but things went badly because Gudz, the head of the statistical department, had just been exiled. But I remember that I rummaged through their library and found the journal *Novoe Slovo*,[14] which Struve had edited in 1897, and *Nachalo*, which was published in 1899.

H: What articles did you find of particular interest in *Nachalo* and *Novoe Slovo?* Articles on economics?

N: Not particularly. What appealed to me most was poetry, and I remember all the verses I read, those dealing with the social issues. I was interested in articles on literary history and, at times, in some of the reviews. But economics had only slight interest for me.

H: So it was the literary part that specially appealed to you?

N: Yes, the historical-literary part. I remember reading an article signed with one set of initials and a second followed by another set. Later on I learned that this was Martov's article on Russian *narodnik* literature. Then there was an article in *Nachalo* by Potresov.[15] Economics did not interest me. As for the unrealistic economics proposed by Levin-Ilin, I remember seeing his articles, but I confess I didn't read them.[16]

It was at that time that Gardenin introduced me to the Akhtiamovs, a very interesting family. They were Bashkir Tatars, aristocrats, *intelligenty* who had joined the liberation movement. The younger generation was represented by the sons Ibragim and Ibniamin Abasugudovich. Ibragim was already an experienced party worker, a more serious, responsible fellow than Gardenin.[17]

H: What did you discuss with him?

N: I asked him questions, listened to what he had to say. Through him, and particularly through his brother Ibniamin, I gained access to Ufa's large library, a good library with old underground literature. Of the periodicals published in the seventies, it held the *Chronicle of the People's Will* [*Vestnik Narodnoi Voli*],[18] and Burtsev's *Over a Hundred Years,*[19] which I had dreamed of finding. It also had the memoirs of Dragomanov which had been published abroad.[20]

During this time I also read a great deal about the Decembrists and about Novikov; about that period.[21] When we began to issue a journal in Ufa, we, well, I wrote an article for the first issue on the history of the revolutionary movement in Russia, and in this piece I began with the pre-Decembrist period.

H: Could you tell me what picture you had formed of the development of the revolutionary movement?

N: I can't say, because I hadn't developed one. I accepted the general conclusions Plekhanov offered in his introduction to Tun.[22] I studied Tun's work very closely. It provided further illustration.

H: I would like to dwell on this point somewhat. The picture Plekhanov gives of the revolutionary movement is that its entire development amounts to a straight-line progression ending with Marxism. What was your view? Was there a continuum of development, an unbroken line from A to Z, that culminated in Social Democracy?

N: I'm afraid to attribute to that early period the views I formed later, those I presently hold. I think I had fewer fully formulated ideas than sentiments in those early days. But it stands to reason that I concluded Social Democracy represented the culmination, the crowning point of the movement. I should say that during this time I became acquainted with the local democrats in town who exerted a certain influence on me. They impressed me.

H: In what way?

N: I told you that I was opposed to terrorism. I wasn't opposed to it on moral grounds, but from the standpoint of expediency. Because of the act committed in Ufa [the murder of the province's governor after the Zlatoust strike], terrorism became associated with the working-class movement. Later, when I met Leonovich in prison, we had considerable opportunity to exchange ideas. I already knew Leonovich's life story. He was considerably older than I and greatly impressed me. I studied the *narodnichestvo* while I was in prison and indulged in rather oversimplified ideas about the workers' movement being the polar opposite of *narodnik* socialism. But I had some doubts. Were our constructs altogether sound? It wasn't exactly that I had a *narodnik* outlook, but that from the start, the correctness of the *Iskra* group's attitude toward *narodnichestvo* had not always impressed me; those articles, saying the *narodniki* are called Socialist Revolutionaries because their socialism isn't revolutionary and their concept of revolution isn't socialistic [*sic*]. This seemed to me too scathing a comment.

But during that autumn [1903] I considered myself a Social Democrat. I established solid contact with Sergei Gardenin and the SDs and was in particularly close touch with Grigorev on party issues. The SDs were in favor of forming a general union of students. At the time, a general student union had been formed in the south of Russia. The plan and program for it had appeared in *Iskra*. It was traditional in Ufa for a union to consist of both SRs and SDs. And although *Iskra* got the upper hand, became predominant, people's attitudes remained what they had been. I remember that the SDs didn't offer any particular resistance to my sentiments and interest in the SRs. They brought me SR literature when I was in prison [a few months later]. I read the complete set of *Revoliutsionnaia Rossiia*, which I had obtained from them.

The first circles were formed in class . . .

H: Did you assume the leadership in this?

N: Yes, I was the organizer. But shortly after the start of the year, arrests were made: Gerdenin and Petr Nikolaevich Grigorev were arrested in November and December. I remember that Gudz, the fellow from the zemstvo board, was exiled at about this time – probably in August. The democratic committee was arrested, and I remember that when this happened I had no hesitation about what to do. I invited Ibniamin [Akhtiamov] into our *gimnazium* circle, even though he was half-SD, half-SR.

H: Could you tell me more specifically how this circle was formed?

N: Once again, what I have to say may be strictly my opinion, but it seemed to me that everyone must have had the same general attitude as I. And I must say that I very seldom encountered any rebuffs. I happened to share a bench in the *gimnazium* with Vasilii Gorelov, who may have been a year older than I. He had no revolutionary ties whatever. I think his grandfather had been a soldier, his father had served in the army under

Nicholas I and then became a railroad conductor. Later on, Gorelov and his father arranged for me to travel free from Ufa to Samara. From the first words I exchanged with Gorelov, I made no attempt at concealment and told him I was a revolutionary. He, in turn, asked me a good number of questions, expressed sympathy and interest. And he became the first candidate for our circle. Later, he was one of the central figures in the Ufa [Bolshevik] Combat Organization, one of the two people who commandeered the train from which 300,000 rubles were seized. When he and I met later, he told me the whole story. It's a story that has yet to be written down.

H: It occurs to me that when you wished to form such a circle, you had to decide whom you could and could not appeal to as prospective members. How did you resolve this?

N: I started my conversations with all the people I approached by trying to sound them out. And to indicate that I sympathized with the revolutionaries, I would quote from a poem by Pushkin, or Lermontov, or Nekrasov. I hardly ever got a negative reaction. Naturally, it happened sometimes. There was one fellow, Zelenskii, whom we feared. We believed he was acquainted with the family of the Zelenskii who was a captain in the cavalry. And so we were rather intimidated by him.

H: Weren't you afraid of persecution, that someone would tell the administration?

N: No, I never experienced such fear.

H: You felt that the mores of the *gimnazium* students were such that even those who didn't sympathize with you would never inform?

N: Nine out of ten students were either active or passive sympathizers. I found out through my brother what students were saying. He was in the fifth form and lived in a boarding house (I was in the sixth form . . .) One could find out more about people in the boarding house; students had closer personal friends there and talked about each other. So that I knew who was inclined one way or another. The Ufa *gimnazium* had a more democratic student body than the one in Samara. I don't even recall there being any aristocrats among them.

H: I would like to clarify something. You said that nine out of ten students were actively or passively sympathetic. With respect to the other ten percent, didn't you feel you had to set things up in such a way that they wouldn't find out?

N: It stands to reason that I didn't talk with them, but I never went so far as to take special precautions.

H: Weren't you afraid they would inform?

N: No. One fellow, Voznesenskii (the son of the town architect, a very prosperous man) was unlike the students who usually joined circles. He was a gallant, became an officer. I had talked freely to him and we printed our proclamations at his place. When be became an officer and was stationed in Samara, he joined our military organization. He wasn't an active worker, but he contributed money. The feeling of comradeship in the *gimnazium* was very intense. I don't remember anyone deliberately giving information against us, not even the sons of the nobility. They fought with us but kept the battles between us.

H: Was there a sense of generational solidarity?

N: Yes, and solidarity within the class. There was a sense of solidarity in the *gimnazium* as a whole – that of students against teachers.

H: Now let us get back to the circle. I would like to ascertain whether there had been other circles in the *gimnazium* prior to this and, if so, whether you knew about them?

N: I knew about the heroic period in the history of the Ufa *gimnazium* which ended in 1901. Shurka Serebrovskii, who later became a prominent Soviet figure, was there at the time.[23] Legends circulated among us about that heroic period, which I heard about for the first time from Boris Fedorovich Gardenin, who was two years older than I. Attempts had been made to form circles, though not in my class.

H: Was there a circle in Boris's class?

N: No, I don't know of other circles in existence at the time. I don't think there were any.

H: In the *gimnzaium* as a whole?

N: I think that once we had established a circle in our class . . . we drew two students from the seventh form who were a year older. Boris Fedorovich Gardenin gave me their names and addresses. We became a general student organization.

What I have been describing lasted from October (or November) 1903, until January 1904. I was arrested in January, so that the circle never assumed final form. But it did hold meetings. I don't recall now where they were held. There were four people, in the circle . . . No, five or six – *gimnazium* students. It was at this point that the seminary students entered the picture. They were organized in Ufa, had circles and a *narodnik*, SR, organization. We made contact with them, very close contact. The SRs were fine fellows. Subsequently, we established connection with the girls' *gimnazium* in Ufa, where there were girls from Belebei such as Marusia Bondareva, who was in the seventh form.

H: In terms of background and outlook, how would you compare the members with students who did not join the circle?

N: I don't know, but the fact is that almost all of them remained in the revolutionary movement. Vasilii Gorelov, Genadii Gudkov, Vasilii Zakharov, and Boris Nemvitskii, a Bolshevik who is still alive today. He wasn't in our circle but we knew about both him and the revolutionary Ivan Kadomtsev, who was in another section of our class. Among the Ufa *gimnazium* students there was also Chaikin who was an SR, eventually a member of the Constituent Assembly. He, too, wasn't in our group but we knew about him. There were several other people, one being Vinius, another surviving Bolshevik. In general, the Ufa *gimnazium* gave a great deal to the revolutionary movement. Almost our entire circle joined the Combat Organization. Ivan Kadomtsev functioned as the chief of staff – in 1905–1906, the period of their campaigns. Although I myself had nothing to do with the Ufa Combat Organization, I'm very familiar with it because Gorelov, who was one of its chief military leaders (along with Kadomtsev), gave me a candid account of the organization.

H: What was the political outlook of these people like before the circle was formed? Had they already begun to identify themselves as "politicals"?

N: I think we brought into the circle people who were trying to become active politically. When I try to explain to myself why I made no attempt to enlist Kadomtsev or Chaikin, with whom I had become acquainted, I think it was because we took in people who needed to be made active. Not all the people in the circle were Social Democrats at this time. Undoubtedly some were still wavering.

H: Between the SRs and SDs?

N: Yes. More Socialist Revolutionary literature was available to us. After the party committee was arrested, we lived on literature furnished by the SRs.

H: What material did you deal with in the circle?

N: Ibniamin [Akhtiamov] started with Lavrov's *Historical Letters.* We discussed our obligations to the people, etc. This aroused dissatisfaction and bewilderment among some members. But they came.

H: What grounds were there for their dissatisfaction?

N: They said this literature was too old. I don't remember the word "dated" being used, but something like it. And someone commented that the themes were far too *narodnik* in character. Yet, we agreed that we had to take up this material and discuss it, since it involved many issues that were of general interest to everyone. Our organization was a general one and the unifying tendency was strong. And the SR center was larger than ours, the SD.

H: When you speak of the "center," what do you have in mind?

N: We established a center, a society of students. We did the preparatory work during Christmas and created a center that included students from the boys' and girls' *gimnazia* and the seminary. It was the center for a union of the student youth of Ufa. We decided to issue our first journal, which I edited. I published the first issue, which contained a political lead article written in a southern vein.[24] It dealt with the need to unite all revolutionary socialist youth and stressed that we young people, who understood the significance of events, had to become active participants. My article concerned the early history of the revolutionary movement, the pre-Decembrist period. It was a big article. I was arrested the day after I delivered the issue. It came out after we had published a proclamation about the creation of the union. It also mentioned that the journal would appear. At this point I had reached the height of my enthusiasm for collecting poetry of social protest. I made the entire group work on this, had them look through old journals in the main libraries, the boys' and girls' *gimnazia*, and the seminary. I accumulated an enormous pile of notebooks with excerpt from the writings of these poets. Marusia Bondareva was living in the dormitory then and the enitre class did work for me there, all of them copying verses.

H: Did you describe the purposes of your organization in the proclamation?

N: Of course. I said that it was a union of student youth and that, considering the events that were developing, we, the young people, had to take a stand. Naturally these were stock expressions. But to a great extent we lived by stock expressions in those days. They corresponded to our political moods.

H: Still, I would like to clarify the following. Did the proclamation state, in one form or another, that a union of socialists was to be formed? That a distinction would be made between those who were or were not Social Democrats, and that non-socialists wouldn't be included in the organization?

N: I don't think this was made so emphatic and clear. Our job was to unite for the revolutionary struggle. I think that a unifying tendency had taken hold of us at the time. Many people joined the youth organization, and this corresponded to the mood of those in our midst.

H: But I would like to get a better idea of how far the unifying tendency went. *Osvobozhdenie* had already appeared at this time, and you undoubtedly had read it.

N: We had seen individual issues of *Osvobozhdenie*, but we didn't read it regularly. We did read *Iskra* on a fairly regular basis at this time.

H: I know you felt the *Revoliutsionnaia Rossiia* represented your *publika*. Did you also feel this was true of *Osvobozhdenie?*

N: I couldn't say. I was in Ufa, I repeat, for a short period of five . . . six months that was taken up with fairly active work and a good number of talks. I should say that in Ufa I found myself in the midst of an old group of *Narodovoltsy*. There was Koslov, the representative from the Steamship Insurance Company "Nadezhda," who had been implicated in the Nechaev Affair and exiled.[25] He settled down in Ufa, had a big house, and had been a subscriber to the old journals. He had *Russkaia Mysl'* and complete sets of *Otechestvennye Zapiski.*[26] I was permitted into his home and read all this material. He had a daughter and a son, Mikhail, a student who was arrested and exiled.

H: Was there a time during these months when you and your comrades felt that the issues being discussed concerned not only a political but also a social revolution?

N: We definitely knew about the existence of the minimum program and about the fact that our minimum program was strictly political. We and the SRs had no quarrel about the minimum program. They justified it in a different way. Their program was based on subjective attitudes and needs, ours on objective possibilities. But I don't think, the difference penetrated our consciousness. We were aware that we concurred in thinking a program had to exist, that we were not building socialism at this time but merely representing a class. This, roughly, was how the matter stood.

H: Now, in terms of the points of the minimum program: At this time you, on the one hand, read *Revoliutsionnaia Rossiia* and, on the other, *Iskra.* What can you say with respect to those points of the minimum program, such as the question of *otrezki* (cutoffs) versus socialization of the land, on which the two clearly conflicted?

N: I should tell you that the SRs' program had not yet been written at this time. It was printed in 1905 and adopted at the January Congress of 1906. If you read the articles in *Revoliutsionnaia Rossiia*, you'll see that they differ in their points of view. There are articles by Novokreshchenov and others by Peshekhonov which formulate the issue in entirely different ways. The SRs and SDs shared the political program of the day. The SRs were more interested in and well-disposed toward the peasantry, were oriented more toward this class. Why should the one have contradicted the other? As I review the issue now, I see that it had to be analyzed, had to be debated, but that there was absolutely no need to have it exacerbated in the way that *Iskra* did. And *Iskra* did exacerbate the issue. My explanation is that from Lenin's point of view, his tactic was completely sound. Since he had no chance of waging war against the powerful enemy, autocracy, he intensified the feelings of struggle against an enemy which, though a possible ally, was closest at hand and easy to conquer – the Socialist Revolutionary movement.

H: For you, in any case, and for those of your comrades who were still wavering, these disagreements were of no great weight?

N: No great weight. I remember there were discussions about them, remember people defining their sympathies as SR and SD, but this had no great significance. Its representative, I repeat, was Pavel Nikolaevich Grigorev, with whom I worked closely. I simply do not remember any objections from him.

H: Prior to your arrest in January 1904, had you heard anything about the split [of the RSDRP]?

N: We had heard about the Second Congress but not about the split.

H: Were you informed about and interested in the disagreements that had arisen prior to this, particularly with the Economists?

N: No, and I knew nothing about the working-class movement, was not a witness to these.

H: Apart from reading and discussing Lavrov, did the circle take up any other material?

N: No. There were very few sessions – three-four at the most. And my interests were devoted to establishing a general organization and to preparing the issue of that journal. I was also the one who printed it.

H: Your circle had established connections with other groups – the seminary students, the girls, etc. When you look back now, do you feel there was some difference in outlook within these different groups?

N: I think the differences were slight. I remember all sorts of details, some of them quite comical. When we went to see someone in the girls' boarding house, we had to identify ourselves. I'd say I was the girl's cousin. But when my brother went and was asked what relation he was, he replied, "I'm her cousin's brother." I think the seminary students may have been older, and they were more serious, more concerned about the immediate future. The girls were very young and gay, always laughing and asking us to visit more often. It goes without saying that all sorts of romantic ideas were stirred. There were a great many among us who were would-be cousin's brothers.

H: On the whole, what were your relationships like with the girls?

N: There was a great deal of romantic feeling. Perhaps some actual romances came of all this, but they were just beginning to develop. Our relationships with the girls generally had an air of tenderness and friendship that turned into infatuation. But we were, after all, sixteen years old.

H: Were your relationships with the girls colored by ideas you had inherited from the Nihilists? I am referring to the concept of equality of rights.

N: Equal rights for women? That was obvious to us. We didn't debate such things ... we never even questioned whether anyone could have doubts about such elementary matters. If a person did, if he thought in the manner of the *Domostroi,*[27] he would never have found his way into our circle.

H: What I wanted to establish was this: Were there ideas about forms of behavior and relationships that you had inherited from the *narodniki?*

N: Of course. We adopted in full those that were suitable to our revolutionary milieu. They constituted the very air we breathed. Whatever failed to accord with the idea of justice was unthinkable. Justice was what mattered to us – mattered more than anything else.

Fourth interview

H: Tell me how did it come about that you were arrested?

N: I mentioned Kozlov and the fact that he had an enormous library. I was always going to his place. I borrowed several years' issues of *Otechestvennye Zapiski* and *Delo* to read.[1] I very seldom encountered his son Mikhail. The daughter, Zinaida, was the one who took me into the library. But it happened that Mikhail was arrested and our proclamation was found when his place was searched. Later on, at the end of 1904, when the whole affair was over, and I was called in to sign the record of the case, I read his testimony and was appalled to learn that he had said he got the proclamation from me. I think he was the person who wrote it. He himself said that he was the author. I remember that I signed the case record and went to see his sister, with whom I was on good terms, and told her about it. "It's impossible," she said. "You must be mistaken. It's impossible!" I went back to the police official thinking that perhaps I had made a mistake. I simply had to reread his testimony. But the police officials started to argue with me, saying: "By mistake, you were shown the testimony of such-and-such a person; but now you want to read this. If something happens to him, you'll have to answer for this." They wouldn't let me read the testimony, but that technique convinced me. So I went back to the Kozlovs and had it out with them. It was a great tragedy. Mikhail was an SR and his entire family had held a very prominent place in the Populist movement. Everyone treated him with respect. What he had done was to commit an act of intolerable and inexplicable betrayal. The proclamation was in no sense a threat to him. If he said he found it on the street, he would have spent two or three weeks in prison at the most. Later on, I learned from the documents that it was after he had testified that the inquiry was sent to the *gimnazium* director, asking whether a certain Boris Nicolaevsky was a student there. It was after this that Matveev called me into his office and had the talk with me which I failed to understand, which I thought was totally unwarranted interference in my affairs. It was, in fact, a warning, an attempt to put me on my guard. He couldn't tell me this directly, a fact I could well appreciate later when I read the documents on my case. Consequently, when I met him in 1917, I was so moved that I was on the verge of confessing my love for him. I told him how much I respected him.

My arrest took place, I believe, on the evening of January 24, 1904 (Old Style). This date is memorable for another reason in that the trial of the Zlatoust workers was to begin on my first day in prison. They were convicted of disturbances, attempted violence, etc., and executed. This was quite an event in prison.

The police came to arrest me during the night. I heard the bell ring. As usual, I had cleared the place of all the literature. We usually sealed it in a small jar. A great deal of snow had fallen, and I hid the jar in the snow. But one or two brochures had been left behind. Then I was arrested.

The first thing that struck me after the arrest was that the prison was overcrowded. Owing to this, I had been put in a large cell not generally used for prisoners under interrogation. It had windows overlooking the courtyard, across from the exit gate, and I could see the large groups of Zlatoust workers being sent off to court, returning from there, and I would see the demonstrations they staged.

I was in this cell only for a day or two; then I was placed in solitary confinement. I should mention that the Ufa prison had two buildings with solitary confinement cells. The new one had, I think, twenty cells; the old one, which was called the old apiary, had six or seven. At first I was confined in the new building, which was also full (a cell had been cleared out for me). I was acquainted with a number of people there – among them, that fellow Vasilii Viktorovich Leonovich, a very prominent SR who later became a member of the Socialist Revolutionary Central Committee. Later, there were a number of workers whose voices I could hear, including that of Khaustov (later a [Menshevik] deputy to the Fourth State Duma).[2]

I remember that Leonovich, being an experienced inmate, approached the little window of my cell that first evening. He was on good terms with the guard, who permitted him various privileges. He asked me how things were going. I wasn't acquainted with him, but he knew about me from his wife, Maria Grigorevna Tsimmerman, the sister of Roman Gvozdev-Tsimmerman. Leonovich asked: "What message should I transmit to those outside?" I asked that I be brought things which, owing to my lack of experience, I'd failed to take. I'd taken very few books. Leonovich loaned me some.

H: How did you feel about your arrest? Were you expecting it?

N: On the whole, I was prepared for it – psychologically prepared, but I didn't think it would happen so soon. I regretted that a great deal had been started and then abruptly came to an end. But I was fully prepared psychologically. I had read the directives issued by the SDs on refusing to testify, and so the arrest didn't shake me. I remember that I was taken to my first interrogation about two weeks after I arrived. There the following scene was performed. I came in and saw the gendarme from the police administration (I don't remember his name). He was a colonel whom the townspeople called "Pug-dog." He was a small, snub-nosed fellow who really did look very much like a pug-dog. He tried to appear very severe. The prosecutor was also there. And since I was young, still a complete greenhorn, he tried to exert . . .

H: You hadn't yet reached seventeen?

N: No, I had just turned sixteen. One disturbing thing happened that really did startle me. Shortly before my arrest I had written a letter to Boris Gardenin, with whom I had a secret understanding. He had started a student organization in the *gimnazium,* and after being expelled, he volunteered either for the artillery corps or the field engineers in Kiev. I had received a greeting or a note from him and sent him a reply containing the following sentence: "The work begun by you is proceeding well." My reply had been intercepted, and during the first session, the prosecutor asked: "Is this your handwriting?" "I don't know," I replied. "Come now, this sentence here, 'The work begun by you is proceeding well.' Did you write that?" "I refuse to testify," I replied. At that point they tried at length to pressure me, to persuade me to talk. Following that, I said: "I refuse to sign the record of such an interrogation." "Just you wait!" said the prosecutor. He summoned the gendarme and said: "Take him back to prison!" As I was leaving the room, he added: "And tell them he is not to have any cigarettes." Like a schoolboy, I replied: "Thank you, but I don't smoke." I paid dearly for that remark. For quite some time they refused to let me have any parcels or books. For probably two months I lived, so to speak, exclusively on prison rations and with a limited number of books. I remember writing a statement protesting this treatment and threatening to go on a hunger strike. At Easter the ban was lifted. They brought me an enormous parcel and books I had received, and then the books began coming. Until then, I read what the prison library had to offer. It was in prison that I read the Bible for the first time.

H: You told me that you had no trouble arriving at the decision not to testify. Yet prior to the interrogation you did not know whether to reply to questions or how. What, then, determined your decision?

N: I knew all along what I would do. My decision was not to testify. As long as there was no objective evidence against me, it was possible for me not to exacerbate my situation. All they had found at my place was one proclamation. I could easily have said I'd found it lying around in the *gimnazium.* I suspected they had some evidence but was in no position to judge. So when I went to the interrogation, I expected I'd get some indication of how to act, that they'd indicate they had something on me. And when I saw that they had the letter to Gardenin, and that he'd been arrested, I realized that my testimony could jeopardize his position. But it was evident by then that they didn't expect anything from me, and so I refused to testify and no longer went to the interrogations. And so, I repeat, the first month and a half or two – until Easter 1904 – were fairly difficult for me, but then things opened up and I received piles of books.

H: A few more questions about this. Prior to your arrest, had you discussed the quesiton of how you would behave if you were arrested?

N: It was generally agreed that we would not testify – this was a promise people made to one another when they had just met and become acquainted. Shortly before this the Social Democrats had issued a directive on the refusal to testify. The SRs, too, accepted it. I remember that Gershuni had made some very impassioned statements about this in *Revoliutsionnaia Rossiia*.[3] It was an axiom. By the time my arrest came I was psychologically prepared for it.

H: Fine. The last question. During the days right after your arrest, how did you feel? Uplifted?

N: On course, somewhat uplifted, for I had become part of the cause. But it was also disagreeable to think that I had been caught. Why had I left that proclamation? Still, it had become clear to me that I would soon be arrested. Later on, when I was allowed to have visitors, people told me Maria Grigorevna Leonovich's remark: "Well," she had said, "it's clear that he would have been arrested soon in any case, that he'd already been uprooted from a normal student life."

H: In their memoirs, Martov and several others mention that one's first arrest brings a feeling of heroism. Did you, too, feel this?

N: Martov had been arrested ten years earlier, in the early nineties, when there was a different atmosphere. With us, I repeat, things were simpler, clearer, more elementary. We were trodding a well-worn path, had no Americas to discover. We had read a great deal already. I, in particular, had read all the prison literature I could lay my hands on. I knew how I had to act, knew what to expect.

It was far simpler, the kind of heroism that was part and parcel of the daily life of someone who had chosen this path. It was an everyday kind of heroism I felt. It enhanced my mood, gave me a certain moral lift but didn't involve any high-flown rhetoric.

H: What this arrest meant for you, then, was that it completed your education as a revolutionary, that you were no longer a boy.

N: I think this is undoubtedly what I felt, though not in such a conscious, well-formulated fashion. I had expected my arrest at any moment and it had come. It was an ordinary thing. It meant I had to go on, that there could be no wavering.

Towards Easter, or somewhat before that, I was moved to the "apiary." I was moved and isolated because I used to talk to prisoners in the adjoining cells in the evenings. I was put in a large cell. The adjoining cells were empty and I had no contact with other prisoners. I remember being brought an enormous pile of books. My sister was then a confirmed SR and she brought me some literature she had obtained – – mainly from the SRs though some from the Social Democrats as well. I remember reading Struve's *Critical Notes* and Lenin's *The Development of Capitalism.*[4] Prior to this I had no books. I had issues of *Novoe Slovo;* I read all the Marxist journals, including *Nachalo* and *Zhizn'.* I was brought *Russkoe Bogatstvo* and the *Znanie* edition of Kautsky's *The Agrarian Question,* though it was missing the entire second part, "The Day After the Revoluiton." At the same time I received copies of *Russkoe Bogatstvo* for the year 1900, which contained Chernov's "A Type of Agrarian Capitalistic Revolution."[5] I enjoyed this. I was brought what I requested but my requests ranged rather far and wide. I remember reading all the *narodniki;* Uspenskii, Zlatovratskii, Reshetnikov, Lipkin, Koronin. I read the complete works of Pisarev and Dobroliubov, and a great many journals.

H: What impression did you get from reading this legal Marxist and *narodnik* literature?

N: I became more determined in my views as a Social Democrat. I remember that after I left prison I called myself a Social Democrat. Strictly speaking, I had done so even earlier, in the *gimnazium,* but now I was more set in my views. It's difficult to say how this manifested itself. I remember that after I got out of prison, I had a meeting with a representative of the SR Committee. I remember that we arranged a meeting in a park on Sluchevskaia Hill. By the time we met, though, there was little to say, since I had already become a Social Democrat.

H: What did you find most convincing in the Marxist literature you read?

N: That it dealt with a mass movement. I had always pounced on articles concerning German Social Democracy. German Social Democracy definitely impressed me.

H: Because it was serious?

N: It was serious, was precisely what would reconstruct human society, what I would define now as a force of cultivation and enlightenment. I remember that I was especially influenced by Kovrov-Grossman. Kovrov wrote about the cultural role of Social Democracy.[6] I was already studying history through literature; through the writings of the *narodniki* I studied the history of Russian social thought. And I combined this with Kobichevsk's articles on the history of Russian censorship and the history of Russian literature. I read all this material. I also read Andreevich – that is, Evgenii Andreevich Solov'ev, who wasn't exactly a Marxist.[7]

H: What about Plekhanov?

N: Yes, Plekhanov's works were brought to me in prison, the first edition of Beltov's [attack on the *narodniki*].

H: And what impression did this make on you?

N: Less than I expected. I was somewhat put off by the excessively sharp polemical tone. I had always felt definite attraction, interest, and sympathy for the *narodnik* struggle, and I didn't understand how one was to reconcile it with these arguments. It goes without saying that I was a revolutionary, but I was a revolutionary who was involved with a mass movement and had always been drawn spontaneously to it.

H: Were you impressed with the treatment of the agrarian policy and the political mood of the peasantry that Chernov offered in his articles?

N: Chernov, you see, offered more factual data than any other writer on the history and formulation of the agrarian question and the International. And this greatly impressed me. But Chernov himself struck me as a man who had arrived at a crossroads between *narodnichestvo* and Marxism and, in fact, he had.

H: His conclusion about the political mood of the peasantry didn't seem convincing to you?

N: I don't remember whether he dealt with this in these articles. In any case, I must say I was not one of those people who embraced Marxism because I felt the peasantry was passive. Even before I went to prison, I had come to think that participation by the peasantry was possible. And the movement of 1902 made an enormous impression on us.[8] We had all come to reject the myth that the peasantry would react passively to what was happening in the cities. The one point on which I questioned Chernov's analysis was whether the peasantry could become socialistic. I didn't agree with his view. I thought the peasantry was still too, I wouldn't say conservative but unenlightened culturally to embrace socialism, that the city was the arena for socialism. But as I mentioned before, I never adopted an anti-peasant outlook.

H: Did you find unacceptable Chernov's new synthesis?

N: These were questions which had to be discussed and given more thought, and I remember that I was overjoyed to find his article "In Defense of Labor Theory of Value" in *Zhizn'*.[9] His article on labor theory of value is worth reading. In the final analysis, labor theory of value is *the* fundamental thing. I can't say that I understood this at the time, but I was approaching such an awareness. Labor theory of value is important in that it proves the basis of humanism for the social sciences. One could improve upon the theory, but all bourgeois authors who reject the labor theory of value are, essentially, engaging in a rhetorical battle against humanism.

H: Had you also read the realists of the sixties at this time, particularly Pisarev and Dobroliubov?

N: I think that the simplistic realism of the sixties was very much to my taste. I remember being greatly impressed by Evgenii Andreevich Solov'ev's brochure on Pisarev's life.[10] Pisarev's prison letters to his wife, which Solov'ev cites, demonstrate the soundness of a rationalistic approach. This is very simplistic, of course, but it appealed to the mood of a sixteen-year-old. I think that in many respects, my outlook was determined by the quantity and quality of the material I could obtain. I wasn't able to get any of the writings of the nineties. In the long run, even *Novoe Slovo* offered very little, nothing but sketchy material. But I studied the writers of the sixties and seventies in a thorough, *gründliche* fashion.

H: It's not yet clear to me what it was in this conception of the world that impressed you. Was it the aspects you have touched on or the emphasis on a need for a scientific world view?

N: I think it would be a mistake for me to try to define this more precisely. As far as I remember, what I felt then was chiefly a spontaneous attraction. I clearly remember being profoundly impressed by an article on the educational work of German Social Democracy. And the primitive rationalism of the Pisarev-type men of the sixties had a real impact on me.

H: Which of Pisarev's works did you read? All of them?

N: Yes, all six volumes [of his collected works which appeared in the 1890s].

H: Were you in sympathy with his attitude toward literature?

N: My friends and I had, of course, discussed this earlier. We knew that Pisarev oversimplified and we recalled Nekrasov's remark that "Von Deviderskii smells worse than a chamber pot." So we weren't impressed any longer. But the spirit itself, the approach to art in terms of practical utility was precisely what struck a responsive chord in us. You have to take it this way: there were not precise, clear-cut formulations; there was a tendency which allowed attitudes to take shape; there were basic ideas that appealed to us. In any case, the emancipation of the country had come about in this way, and each of us was thrilled by it.

The SRs conceived the idea of service to the people. I remember conversations I had with SRs, people like Diagelev and Tretiakov, who later embraced terrorism. I didn't share these people's ideas of service, of the need for sacrificing oneself. In the long run, we understood that we were going to make a major sacrifice, but it was not to be done for the sake of sacrifice. For us it was part of the process of struggling to seize power. Bogdanov distinctly emphasized this idea later in the discussions that appeared in his *Red Star* [*Krasnaia Zvezda*], and in its writing it is bound up with empiriomonism – that is, with an oversimplifed version of Marxism.[11] As I see it, empiriomonism oversimplifies, rather than complements or improves on scientific materialism.

We did not think in terms of service, but in terms of the struggle needed to improve the structure of society, so that all of life, including one's own life, would be better. But for us, all this was illuminated by socialist ideals, by the necessity to work with the working class. Then the struggle for political liberation, for Lenin's program – an idea we had firmly adopted – would lead directly to and become fused with the struggle for a socialist program. There you have a simplified version of our thinking at this time.

H: How many months did you spend in solitary confinement?

N: I was in solitary the whole time, for five and a half months.

H: Being in solitary confinement meant you had no opportunity to talk to people?

N: I conversed with other prisoners by tapping. But for a period of time I had no one to "tap" to. Then one day I suddenly, unexpectedly, heard a noise; someone had been brought into the next cell. I knocked and got a response, though it didn't come through very clearly. Then the sound became more audible, since there was an air-hole there, and I heard the man say he was a worker, that he was being detained there. This is an interesting story, a very important story. He was a Petersburg worker from the Griboedov-Pavlov plant and had become an agent provocateur in the Social Democratic workers' organization. The Ufa Police Department had found themselves up against a Social Democratic workers' organization that they couldn't crush, and asked to be sent an experienced provocateur. He arrived in late 1903 or early 1904. I wasn't involved with the workers' organization, so I had only cursory, indirect information about this. He began to conduct operations in Ufa as a provocateur, a malicious provocateur; that is, he made an accusation against a worker who was under suspicion [in the SD organization] and fanned this suspicion without cause. The man had simply left his circle, but he was accused of provocation and killed. This agent and Izvekov had organized this murder.

And so, there I was in prison, confined in the cell next to this fellow. And he talked to me. I think he wanted to trap me too through some kind of provocation, because he was a vicious agent. He and Izvekov were sentenced to a convict labor gang. He was shipped off to prison and escaped from there, was the only escapee who disappeared without a trace, was never caught. And I remember him strictly by his voice, never even saw his face, though I may have caught a glimpse of him during the exercise periods. I don't understand whether he engaged in that provocation on his own, without informing the police, who denied they had knowledge of the affair, or whether he had acted with their consent and in so doing gotten himself arrested and sent to do hard labor, thereby instilling demoralization in the ranks.

Except for the encounter with this provocateur, my life in prison took a normal course. I read a great deal and remember that my sister was forever cautioning: "Don't ruin your eyes!"

H: Given the condition in which you were confined during these months, I assume you weren't able to obtain any information about the split in the RSDRP?

N: No, I wasn't. We learned about the war [with Japan]. Everyone talked about it, but we had no news of other events. The assassination of Plehve, which occurred after my release, left everyone in a state of agitation.

H: You were released in July 1904?

N: About the 10th of July I was released on bail pending a final decision on my case. It was to be reviewed under the new law which was introduced then – the Statute on Punishments. I was charged under Article 132, "possession," not "distribution" of illegal literature. The prosecutor's office decided that I was to be released on bail in the custody of my parents – that is, my mother. But my release was complicated because of some incident and I was forced to spend the night in the police station. But by the 11th or 12th, in any case, I was free, and I immediately became immersed in party activities. Former *gimnazium* students, the older generation of them, invited me to a Social Democratic meeting. The committee was also there.

I had met Gardenin and Petr Nikolaevich Grigorev in prison, but I don't believe I saw them after I was released. It was the *gimnazium* students who invited me to this gathering and then took me to a meeting held with the SRs, with Marina Prokof'evna.

H: What did you discuss?

N: The assassination of Plehve. Plehve had kept the entire country tense over one issue – the war; yet at the same time, things were being shaken loose from within. This became apparent right after Plehve was killed. One sensed that the same level of tension could not be maintained. I don't remember whether anything was written on this in the press. The new organs, *Nash Zhizn'* and *Syn Otechestva*, made their appearance only in October or November, probably in late November.[12] It was during October–November, too, that the demonstrations began. December was the period of the meetings – the "banquets."

H: Was there a sense that revolutionary activity had begun?

N: The feeling, I think, was that something had to be changed. The government itself lacked confidence. Over two months passed before a new minister was appointed. The tsar, it seems, did not attend Plehve's funeral. This was taken to mean that the supreme power was dissociating itself, undoubtedly dissociating itself from Plehve. Something had happened! (By the way, it is my belief that Lopukhin had authorized the murder of Plehve in agreement with Witte.)[13]

H: And the war was going badly?

N: Yes. During the period I'm speaking of, the country had just suffered its first defeats, but these very first defeats had made an impact. Meaning was attached to every trifle; people wanted defeats. It would be hard to say who didn't. The mood of the people had crystallized; to be more exact, it had from the very start. This became obvious after Plehve's assassination; people spoke candidly to one another. And during those three months I spent in Ufa . . .

H: You were there from roughly July to November?

N: No, I left earlier. I think I left in the latter half of September, which means I was there slightly over two months – two and a half at the most. While in Ufa, I was summoned to the Police Administration. The procedure there was such that minors, those under the age of seventeen, had to appear before a special commission which would determined whether one had acted in sound mind. It was strictly a farce, and one was even subjected to abuse there. Naturally I was judged to have acted in sound mind. I had decided to go to Samara. Ufa was a far less populous, far less commercial town that had no newspapers of its own, and it was harder for me to earn a living there. I had already decided to look for work in this field, and Samara had two newspapers.

H: I'd like to return to the split and ask you one more question. What had you learned about it?

N: I had learned the details, a great many, I believe. I think that I had already learned of the formation of the Bolshevik Committee – the Bureau of the Committee of the Majority – because while I was in Ufa, Ogarev had gone to a conference in the Urals and brought back information on how the work was going and what individual workers were doing.

H: What did you conceive to be the cause of the split? And, in general, how was it taken in your milieu?

N: I interpreted the split to mean only one thing: that the minority had refused to submit. This produced a very bad impression on everyone. Because once there was a majority, one had to submit. If one didn't agree, the thing to do was defend one's views. If people had been denied the right to defend their views, we would have supported them, but since the minority rebelled and broke discipline [we stayed with the majority].

H: And how were the disagreements conceived?

N: The disagreements were viewed as related strictly to the party rules as focused on the organizational question.

H: Everyone in Ufa felt that this was the case?

N: In the circle in which I moved. And it was a typical circle – particularly for that period.

H: During these three-four months, what were the other major topics of discussion?

N: I became involved with the organization, met with a lot of people and had many discussions. But I didn't formally join the organization because I decided to leave town, not remain in Ufa. Since I was under surveillance, I had to apply to go to Samara. I did. And it was that fellow Vasia Gorelov who arranged to have his father, a conductor, take me to Samara in the baggage car. This was in September 1904, either the 29th or 30th of September. I hadn't been in Samara for a year and a half; it had changed a great deal.

Fifth interview

H: As our last interview ended, you mentioned that Samara had changed a great deal during your absence. Could you describe the impressions you formed of the mood of the Samara intelligentsia when you arrived there in late September 1904?

N: I was first taken to a commune located not far from the prison – on Orenburg Street, I believe. There were many such communes of *intelligenty* and semi-*intelligenty* in Samara. I should point out that earlier, during my days as a *gimnazium* student, we knew there was a school in town for railroad engineers but hadn't made any acquaintances with the students. On this occasion, however, I found myself in precisely this milieu and encountered two groups: students from the mechanical engineering and agricultural schools. It was about this time (apparently in 1902–1903) that a large agricultural school was built at the Kinel' Station in Samara. It graduated lower level agronomists and was filled with young people, mainly students from peasant backgrounds. The railroad had been instrumental in founding the engineering school, which for the most part trained people to become skilled workmen, railroad engineers, etc. During the winter of 1903, and particularly in the spring of 1904, there was massive unrest in the educational institutions that offered technical training. It had begun in 1902–1903 when they were founded.

H: Apart from the school for railroad workers, were there others that offered technical training?

N: No. There were, I think, two or three public schools which we knew about when we were *gimnazium* students. On this trip to Samara, I did not find a cohesive group of students from these schools. They were attended by the plebeian elements of Samara, students from the lower middle class. I did not notice an appreciable number of them catching the spirit of 1904–1905, though some individuals did.

In general, [the students of the technical schools] were valuable, particularly at this time, the fall of 1904, because they had just been cast up from the lowest strata of society. Some of these students left town and returned to their homes, but others remained and settled down in Samara, where there were several communes. The commune in which I found myself had both engineers and agricultural workers, and both groups played a great role in the liberation movement.

H: What were their social backgrounds?

N: The railroad students were from the urban petty bourgeoisie. (What figured largely in the lives of the lower middle class [in Samara] was the fact that mustard seed could be grown in the surrounding area; these people made a living by planting and making mustard.) But some of the people in the commune definitely were from workers' families. There was one fellow, Razumnik Nikolaevich Dmitriev, who drew particularly close to us and became one of the leading figures in Samara in 1905. His father, who was from the petty-bourgeoisie and had done a little work for the railroad, had enrolled him in the engineering school. It appears that from 1902, perhaps even early 1901, the working-class youth of the engineering school had established ties with the Social Democratic organization. The engineering school produced a smaller but more active group of workers than the agricultural school.

The agricultural students were a much larger group and were, in the fullest sense, what are termed proletarian *intelligenty* – people with little education who craved knowledge, wanted a better life, greater skills, a higher standard of living but who had encountered obstacles the first step of the way. I was told that the agricultural school in Kinel' tried to create living conditions like those in the seminaries for impoverished students. The students lived in cold boarding houses where they were badly fed and suffered from inadequate heat. Over the poor food and poor heat, large disturbances broke out during the winter months in the early part of 1904. I think some of the incidents were caused by the failure to replace broken window panes for long periods of time, and for other reasons. But, as always, the underlying cause was the mood of general dissatisfaction.

The students in the schools were from peasant families, and they craved education. Those in the province of Samara were slower to feel the need, but the desire was stronger among the peasants in the provinces of Ufa and Viatsk. The Viatsk zemstvo set up its own printing press, and after 1905, when it acquired somewhat greater rights, it achieved one of the finest records for promoting democracy and education among its members.

H: What, would you say, had influenced these groups? Where did their desire for knowledge come from?

N: In the province of Samara the peasantry – that is, isolated individuals – had been gripped by the movement of the seventies. They remembered the propagandists and were always talking about Sofia Perovskaia.[1] I became interested in these old people and used to get into conversation with them. One old man who was brought to me had known Perovskaia and Solov'ev.[2] Apparently, he really had known them, though it often happened that people said Perovskaia's followers had been there when, in fact, the person in question turned out to be some other propagandist. The important thing was that a legend had developed around Perovskaia, who was the tsar's assassin – a sympathetic legend that bathed her in an aura of martyrdom and love for the people. This was the case mainly in the prosperous villages along the Volga. The center of the area was Absharovka. There the person chiefly responsible for the cultural work of the *narodniki* was an SR – a well-to-do merchant in the small *narodnik* settlement that had been established here, and he later raised all his children to think along similar lines. The improvement that commerce had produced in his standard of living had not cut him off from the peasantry but made his outlook more typically peasant and populist [*narodliubivyi*].

What I have said about Samara province held true of the neighboring province of Saratov. There the agricultural school in the little town of Nikolaevsk became a center for Social Democratic propaganda. We found it easier to engage the interests of *intelligenty* of this type, who were aligned into groups; among the students who were expelled from the Kinel' School in Samara, most joined the Social Democrats – spontaneously, of course.

H: What you have been describing is the mood of the countryside. What was the picture like among the workers?

N: I began to get a sense of the workers' circles somewhat later, in January 1905. I had become acquainted with them when I arrived, but I must confess that I didn't want to enter into this life. I had the secret address of the Party Bureau of the Eastern Central Committee, where Dubrovinskii was at the time. I was personally acquainted with him. Aleksei Feodorovich Ogarev had come from Samara to talk to him about me. He was a major figure, a man who played a very significant role and was known under the pseudonym "Leo," as a "conciliator."[3] He was a very skilled organizer, very adept at selecting people. Despite the directive Lenin had issued then, Dubrovinskii proposed to put out a newspaper. He had set up a printing press in Samara, and he put me to work selecting material for the review of domestic events. At the same time, I did a little work in statistics to earn some money and rented a room. So, all this means that while I knew workers' circles, I had broken away from them, was moving in different direction.

It was at this time that I wrote my first articles. I remember going to the *Samara Courier* [*Samarskii Vestnik*]. There were two newspapers in town:

the *Samara Gazette* [*Samarskaia Gazeta*] and the *Samara Courier*. The *Gazette* was an old paper that had been in existence for probably twenty years, and it was staffed with *narodniki*. Vasilii Viktorovich Leonovich was working there at the time; so was Alesha Sapozhnikov (he was a year older and had been in the sixth form in the *gimnazium* when we were in the fifth). And Izmalei, the only member of our entire group who joined the *narodniki*, was also working there. These people didn't want me. Since I was drawn toward Menshevism, they didn't want me to join the staff and said they had too many people working for the paper already, that I should go to the *Courier*, a new paper that had just begun to publish. So I did, and I was very well received there. Nikolai Nikolaevich Skrydov had been asked to become editor. His sister, Natasha Samoilova, was a well-known SD at this time,[4] and he later became one himself, but he never became a vituperative party-type man. I remember he said to me right away: "Write about Ufa." And so I wrote first about the Ufa library and the reading room there. This was the first thing of mine to appear in print. Later, when I wanted to switch to historical themes, I wrote a long article about Shelgunov, in a fairly primitive fashion.[5] I wanted to work in this area, but I had been thrown off the track by the youth movement that got under way after 1904.

Later on I learned that the youth movement had been organized by the Liberationists [*Osvobozhdentsy*], who became involved in all sorts of legal societies. They had penetrated the parents' committees, which discussed the situation in the schools and were very much in vogue then – were people's way of saying: "We insist that our voice, the voice of the parents, be heard." The student youth, to be sure, and all those who had recently left their school benches but still felt like students, were interested in these committees. On the 18th of November, it seems, a meeting had been arranged (a general meeting of the members of the pedagogical committee) to discuss what I think was the issue of the curriculum. The meeting was held in the zemstvo board building, and I made my way upstairs to the balcony. Down below were the mothers, fathers, and spectators. One after another, they got up and said: My opinion, as a parent, is such-and-such. My opinion, as a mother, is such-and-such. At this point Nikolai Ivanovich Konovalov, who had just been released from prison, stood up in the balcony and said: "And now listen to our view, the view of the students who have recently been expelled!" And he began to talk. The president rang the bell for order, but he went on to make some remarks – what, I don't recall. I remember that after this, he asked us to leave the meeting to protest the denial of his right to speak. And we all left. We went out on the street and started a demonstration. I should tell you that Nikolai Ivanovich Konovalov later became a major provocateur in the Bolshevik Petersburg Committee.[6]

After Konovalov had made his remarks, we all walked out. The zemstvo board was located two houses down from the house in which Kuzmin lived, where our first circles met. On the other side of the zemstvo board was the police station. We came out of the building, intending to go left, away from the police station, but Konovalov led us to the right – towards it. We got past the police station safely but no sooner had we done so than firemen or policemen began nabbing and seizing us. I must confess I got away successfully, but about an hour and half later, I decided to go back to find out what was happening. I went to that fellow Kuzmin's place and was arrested on the spot. I was released fairly soon after but still managed to spend about a week in prison, and this had a disrupting effect on me at the time. The demonstration we staged was not a party affair, but I know that Konovalov got into trouble because of it.

H: What sort of slogans did you shout at the demonstration? "Down with autocracy!"? Others?

N: "Down with autocracy!" – yes, yes. There was nothing special about the demonstration, it was the usual sort of thing, Mention of it was made in *Revoliutsionnaia Rossiia* and *Iskra*. I got out of prison at the very end of November or the beginning of December. It was the period when the "banquet" campaign had already gotten underway.[7]

H: Since the "banquet" campaign made for certain changes in political attitudes, etc., I would like to focus on the impressions you had formed before this – specifically, your impressions of the political attitude of people in the circles, the communes of young people you mentioned, and the party circles with which you were in contact.

N: As for the party circles, I had become acquainted with them through that Dubrovinskii at this time. He set me a quota of work and told me not to spend too much time in local party circles, that he would give me work. There was an episode involving Dubrovinskii: In the middle or latter half of December, he travelled to the center to attend a conference – negotiations – of the Central Committee and was arrested in early January at the apartment of Leonid Andreev, at the time when the Central Committee was arrested. The arrest of the committee was a major event in the history of the Party in that it was the "conciliationist" Central Committee. The two people who were left – Krasin and one other – reached an agreement with Lenin and convened the "Third" Congress [where only the Bolskeviks were present – ed.][8]

H: On the whole, did the Social Democrats in town consider themselves Bolsheviks at this time?

N: I think so, but strictly in the sense that the Mensheviks did not submit to the majority. What I told you earlier about us was typical of all. There were no Mensheviks; that is, persons who would have declared themselves Mensheviks. I remember that in December, when I spent a week in prison, I became acquainted with a number of people. The Samara Committee of 1903 was imprisoned there, and I met Voevodin, one of the Bolsheviks who is still alive today.[9] At the time, he had not yet become a Social Democrat. He wavered between the SRs and SDs, vacillated. While I was in prison, he and I got to know each other and became quite friendly. He was released during this period and moved into an apartment with me, lived there for a while after he got out of prison. I remember the conversations we had. Naturally, he had already been drawn to the Social Democrats, but he still had not conclusively defined himself as one.

H: Would you say that this wavering between the SDs and SRs was characteristic?

N: I must say that it was characteristic of this region. There was a Union of Social Democrats in Ufa, another in Perm, and another in Saratov. We were all friendly with the SRs, but we were all SDs.

H: As for the young people who emerged from the technical schools, what was their political attitude like?

N: They were revolutionaries. How did their activity express itself? They were mobilized to paste up proclamations; when proclamations were issued, people had to go around and paste them up. So all these people would take their sacks and little bottles and set off on an excursion. I took part in one of them, along with Razumnik Nikolaevich Dmitriev. He had already become a party worker, had brought proclamations with him (some of them he had distributed in the commune), and we all set out to paste them up. Everything went well, of course, since there were no guards in the city at night, only old men working as watchmen, who were themselves afraid of being attacked.

H: In what circles travelled the SRs in Samara?

N: The SRs were in circles connected with the Samara newspaper [*Samara Gazette*], they were on the staff and had solid ties with the zemstvo employees. For instance, they had that same arrangement in Absharovka, as I later learned, where there was a small village center for propaganda. People from neighboring villages would come there to see that rich fellow, with the storehouse of literature, and would take some to give out. I'm not certain, of course, but I think they had more contacts in the rural areas than we. Later, in 1905, when our work in the countryside expanded, we encountered SRs everywhere. A zemstvo employee, a teacher, a doctor, a surgical assistant – all these people had joined the SRs and became their mainstay. So did that shopkeeper-*intelligent*, who represented a fairly typical phenomenon in that the rural bourgeoisie were not grasping, at least not at this time; in any case it was a group that was not self-seeking.

H: Now, during this same period – that is, in October and November 1904, apart from the young people you have described, what was the social background of the SD membership? What impression did they make on you?

N: I got to know the Samara SD Committee a littler later, toward the end of December or the start of the new year – mainly during the early part of the year when the zemstvo campaign had begun. Vladimir Mikhailovich Pototskii was on the committee then. He was a chemist, whom I knew from the zemstvo, and had helped me a great deal with my experiments. He was one of the chief propagandists of the organization. Subsequently there was Boris Pavlovich Pozern, who later joined the Bolsheviks and played a leading role among them. He became one of Kirov's assistants, and, as a Kirovite, he was shot later during Ezhov's reign of terror.[10] There were also two Georgians on the committee. I think that David Kapagadze, who organized a printing press, was among the people on the committee. But I came to know these people later.

H: Were these people generally *intelligenty?*

N: Yes, the group of worker intelligentsia joined later in the spring and the summer.

H: I would like very much to know what relationship the Liberationists had to Social Democracy – ideologically and socially.

N: A Liberationist sometimes turned out to be a moderate liberal, sometimes a radical, but an individual who operated within the framework of the law. There was Deushin, who was from a *pomeshchik* family in the zemstvo; also Piksan, who was well-known at the time. He was a teacher who had come to the district. Dmitrii Ivanovich Godnev, the literature teacher, also belonged to this group. So did Preobrazhenskii, the geologist, as well as his brother. Similarly, Klafton, secretary of the zemstvo board. There were few contacts with this group. I had some as a journalist. But they did not have a newspaper; our group did, and so did the SRs.

H: The general impression I get is that these people represented an older and more affluent group. Is that true?

N: True, they were a bit older. Yes. And they were more affluent in the sense that they were people with status; social status. No one in our group had any status except perhaps one fellow, Vladimir Mikhailovich Pototskii. There was also Boris Pavlovich Pozern, whose father owned the largest pharmacy. He led two lives: one in the Pozern Pharmacy, the other in his underground work, where he came wearing a worker's cap.

H: Very well, let us start discussing the banquet campaign.

N: The banquet campaign in Samara, you see, started relatively late. After we had turned the meeting of the Parents' Committee (in late November) into a demonstration, parents' committees were no longer permitted. And so people rebuked us saying: "Because of your stupid demonstration when you shouted a few times and got yourselves beaten up, we've lost the chance to explain the state of affairs, etc." Naturally, all this was true, we were a bunch of kids. But the mood was such that we couldn't sit still. This mood manifested itself at the first meeting, the first meeting of the zemstvo campaign in Samara.

The large banquet was held at the end of December in the Zhigulevskii Brewery, a picturesque location, a central beer hall, very good beer of course, and a very fine, newly built house and garden – all this was rented for the meeting. A mass of people crowded in. Plans had been made about who was to speak. Petr Voevodin, who had just been released from prison, addressed the meeting. He and I arrived together. He made a few remarks that went something like: "We are workers . . . I have just come to you from prison . . ." etc. We had to set ourselves in contraposition to the people at the meeting; psychologically one sensed the need for this. And so Voevodin went on to say: "While you do nothing but make speeches, we are preparing ourselves in earnest." In addition, you know, men were being sent to the front,[11] and so mention of the war was interwoven with the message of our proclamation; it contained a statement that began: "Now that you are a soldier and going to the front, keep in mind . . ." It was a brilliantly written *Iskra* proclamation. (Later, proclamations arrived in great quantities and were reprinted. I still recall the appeal to the soldiers. I remember Martov's proclamation.)

Only one banquet was held and soon afterwards news came of the "January" strike in Petersburg.[12] It shook us all. At the time I took care of proofreading. The *Samara Courier* did not yet have its own printing press and type was set at Levinson's press, the largest in town. As a proofreader, of course, I knew all the workers, and it became clear that quite a number from theirs and other circles were our people. And so the telegram arrived with news of the strike in Petersburg. We too had to strike. The first strikes started at Levinson's printing press. We went to stop work at the neighboring presses. The typesetters and employees at the *Samara Gazette* didn't want to strike. "Why?" they asked. "It will be better for us to print, what we say will be spread. This is essential." But we overcame their objections. At the provincial printing press, where state workers were employed (this was government service) they somehow dissuaded us, deceived us into thinking they would quit, though in fact they didn't. In the evening of the same day or the next day, we held a meeting to discuss how to organize workers' strikes. I worked out the plans; they came little by little. There were several steam-mills, three or four mills owned by Shapovalov, Lebedev's small factory which, I think, was right next to the commune, the Zhuravlev factory on the bank of the Volga, the depot, and, most important, the railroad shops. There was little industry. At this time we still had not established ties with the shop assistants. But we decided we had to stop work, to shut down Lebedev's factory.

H: This was in mid-January?

N: It was after January 9, not on the day we received the telegram but more likely the following day.

H: Now, in addition to the people on the Committee, who else took part in this?

N: There was one member of the Committee and five or six of us. There was Razumnik Nikolaevich Dmitriev, myself, Pet'ka Voevodin, then Chernyi whom we called, then two workers from this factory, Egor and Aleksandr Korostelev, who later played very important roles among the Bolsheviks.[13] They were splendid fellows. I got to know them quite well and became friendly with them. They were quite young, skilled in their professions and were very sturdy material. We decided to force our way into the factory, since we had heard that the workers there would not strike. We had to go and disrupt things there.

So a plan was worked out. A meeting was held at Aleksandr's father's apartment. Since work began at 4:00 a.m., we stayed overnight there, and in the morning we all went off together. As workers, the Korostelevs had [identification] numbers. They went in and we pushed in after them. They made their way in and blew the whistle. The workers ran out into the yard terrified. Voevodin made a few remarks, saying that in Petersburg this, that, and the other thing were happening and that the workers should show their solidarity and go together to the gates. I remember that we had already gone out on the block when Cossacks appeared at the other end of it and darted toward the factory to stop us. We brought work to a standstill. But work was stopped only at Lebedev's factory. The mills didn't stop working, nor did Vaganovskii's Brewery.

H: In general, what was the mood of the workers like when they learned about the shooting of Gapon's demonstrators?

N: They were all shaken and their mood was one of protest. I remember that when the workers at Lebedev's factory were told people had been killed, they screamed: "It's impossible! Impossible! What are they, beasts? What committee was in charge?" But all this was uttered quickly, very quickly and passed over within a few minutes so that we could get out of the factory and avoid being arrested.

H: Up to this point, the workers were not prepared for this?

N: At the Lebedev factory, you see, there was a small circle, but one could count only on three or four people in it. And it was the Korostelev brothers who were the most active, the most energetic. I remember the others, since I knew them all, but they did not impress me, whereas the Korostelevs made a fine impression. I saw them often.

H: Could you describe in general the development of the strike movement in Samara after January 1905?

N: The strikes were of a fairly broad nature. Almost all of the printing presses, railroad shops, steam-mills, and small factories that existed then went on strike. The students responded to the call, and there were a mass of amusing incidents. I remember a strike in a girl's *gimnazium* where the students started out by demanding a Constituent Assembly and ended up by demanding that the dampers on the stoves be changed, because they were being poisoned by the charcoal fumes. This type of reaction was seen not only in Samara but everywhere.

Samara was the center of the Eastern Bureau of the Central Committee [of the Social Democratic Party], and information arrived there from all the cities of eastern Russia. The problem everywhere was one of combining the political with the economic movement. In the final analysis, these were the first strikes in eastern Russia that aroused the working class as a whole. Everywhere the most elementary economic demands were advanced. And there was some indication that the political demands had receded into the background. This was at odds with the sharply political mood in the Party,[14] but in all probability it made sense, because it was still too early to proceed with political demands against the tsar in factories that were full of soldiers. But there were clashes between workers and local SD committees.

In general, the test showed that the workers' mood was sympathetic and vaguely expectant but that they were still listening and watching to see what was to come. During the following months – February, March, April – the groups lobbying among the workers were in a state of heightened agitation. It had come about in this way: The basic cadres of the organization, the "activists" as they are now termed, consisted of *intelligenty* and semi-*intelligenty*, people who had been thrown out of the agricultural school and the *gimnazia* after the agitation of the preceding years, and who were now drawn into the periphery of the organization and took all the work upon themselves. Almost all of them were Social Democrats, very few joined the SRs. Groups of us in different districts of the city would rent apartments for a period of time, often not even settling into them, in order to arrange workers' meetings. The apartments were used three or four times, after which the police would appear. But there were few arrests in Samara, since special conditions existed there.

Not long ago Naumov's reminiscences were published here.[15] Naumov was a Samara nobleman and a dealer in a Moscow multimillion dollar firm. He brought those millions back with him, built a palace, and was very conservative, a man of militant conservatism. In his reminiscences Naumov speaks about the governor of Samara province, Zasiako, saying he was a captive of the local liberals. The local merchant class was very liberal. It included the Batiushkov dynasty, major corn merchants who exercised enormous authority and knew everyone. When some dignitary came to town, gatherings were held at the Batiushkovs. Avksent'ev, for instance, delivered a report there.[16] Outstanding people courted them, people like Khadrin, a prominent millionaire (he built himself a real castle), who was later a member of the Kadet Party. During this period everyone was under the influence of the Liberationists and sympathetic to Social Democracy and this exerted an influence on the administration. The chief of the city police was a fairly decent fellow, who was waiting for his pension. He tried to keep things calm, didn't create any incidents and lived peacefully.

There was an opposition party within the police which, in spite of the police chief, wanted to crush the revolutionaries in town. The vice-governor was one of those militant conservatives of the old type, and he became friendly with Naumov. Later, it became known that the entire reactionary campaign in Samara, all the attempts to take reactionary measures stemmed from this group. Naumov provided money and a split was created within the police. During the summer this played a major role in the life of the local organization. But at this time [in early 1905] it had only just begun to make itself felt and did so mainly in that there were no systematic arrests in town. The city was a center: the printing press of the Samara Committee operated there; so did the press of the Eastern Bureau of the Central Committee; the organization in town functioned regularly, with only chance arrests that either resulted from a denunciation or occurred during a demonstration.

The campaign carried out during these months had the effect of preparing people for the events of May, for the May Day strike and the May Day demonstration. Naturally, we did not understand that to summon really broad segments of the population to strike, one had to confront them with the question of their economic situation. Our proclamations were political. Everyone's mood was ultra-political, although now this political "rhetorics" reflected more consciously than it had in January the necessity of economic improvements. I don't recall the May Day strike but I remember that there was a large meeting outside the town at which speeches were made. In the evening there was a small gathering in the Strogovskii Garden (that was the town garden), after which a night demonstration was staged. That took place along the block when the police swooped down. Several shots were fired. The police dashed to one side, then Cossacks came darting in. There were several clashes and then people dispersed. There were no wide-scale arrests, only a few. We knew all the police. Among them was Robchev in plain clothes, who tried to make his way through to see who was leading. I caught sight of him, grabbed him and threw him out of the lines. On the following day they came to arrest me; there was the face-to-face confrontation with that fellow from the police station.

H: This happened on roughly the 2nd or 3rd of May?

N: Yes, the day after the demonstration. The police officer asked that fellow: "Do you know this man?" He replied: "It seems he is the one who grabbed me by the collar and threw me out." The prosecutor, who clearly didn't sympathize with him, said: "None of this 'it seems.' Be exact." He hesitated, hesitated, then said: "I can't take this sin upon my soul . . . say whether it's him or not." Then he said: "There's no point in this." I was released. Of all those arrested, only three or four people were detained. They had been arrested on the scene.

Thus, I was released after two . . . three days. But during this time the town had struck. The strikes began after this jolt, started in all of the small workshops. Our group remained intact, and we wrote out all the demands for the striking workers. Naturally, we could and did insert everywhere the demands for a Constituent Assembly and all the rest, but this was mere decoration. The workers reacted sympathetically to this, but did not really pick it up. Naturally, they did not talk about dampers as the students had in the girls' *gimnazium*. Their talk had to do with serious economic demands, but were of the most shallow kind (that they be given overalls for work); yet it reflected the actual state of affairs. I remember that all this lasted for about a month. The newspaper did not come out for about a month.

I remember that at the end of the month Dmitriev and I put together a report for the newspaper. It presented all the demands, filling two typed pages. This was an exceptionally interesting document. It summarized the demands from each shop. There were, for example, several icon-painting shops where old men daubed paint on icons. And these people went on strike . . . The strike spread to the very lowest strata. There were many small handicraft enterprises in the city, usually consisting of ten-fifteen workers. And there were even small mills, steam mills, with ten . . . twenty workers, which were considered industrial enterprises. They were handicraft industries which we had not taken at all into account. The workers in these small enterprises were aroused by the May strike movement in Samara and joined it.

H: What I would like to ask, firstly, is how were the demands established? What was the relationship between your group and the workers?

N: The workers came to us. Everyone in the city knew us, and they would stop us on the street and ask us to come over. Or they would come to us and we would write the demands for them. We wrote the demands and they decided on the order – usually in the course of negotiations with the administrators.

H: Did you formulate these demands or did they give them to you?

N: They told us what the demands were and we provided the formulation. Many of the workers didn't even know what to demand. In these cases we had considerable influence. We aimed for the level of our minimum program, but the workers, of course, specified items. No minimum program could have predicted their demands, since they were far too idiosyncratic. The strike was a success almost everywhere, not fully, but almost everywhere. One could say that everywhere, without exception, the bosses were forced to make concessions. Until then the working day had not been standardized in many places; now fixed working hours were established. There were cases in which workers appealed to the Factory Inspector who pointed out that although this did not fall under the law, one nevertheless had to take into account the old law which was intended for larger enterprises. Consequently, the nonstandardized working day, in which people worked from dawn to dusk, was eliminated *de facto* at this time. . . . And a whole number of other changes occurred. Relations were too outdated to avoid undergoing change. This was virgin territory.

H: In general, how did workers respond psychologically?

N: At this time, I did not observe any antagonism toward the intelligentsia. There was great dissatisfaction after December [1905], which manifested itself by people leaving us to join the SRs and the anarchists. But in the period I am speaking of, it was the reverse: everyone was drawn toward us, great waves of sympathy poured in from the most unexpected segments. But during the summer an organized attempt was made to mobilize resistance [to the revolution] among the lowest strata. This had become clear by June and July.

I recently found several proclamations concerning the attempt by the police to organize the Black Hundreds. All this material was collected by us. One fellow among us, Sashka Balkanov, was the son of a police inspector. His father was up on all the police activities and he was enlisted into the Black Hundreds organization "to kill revolutionists and Jews." His son was aware of all this and kept us informed, and the proclamations we issued were based on his information. When one looks back at these events a very interesting thing emerges: the fight was for the support of the most unenlightened strata of the population [*obyvatel'shchina*].[17]

There were rumors that Black Hundreds groups were being organized on Sokol'nitskaia and Il'inskaia Streets, that they were organizing among the *gorchishniki* (this was a term used in earlier times to refer to the people who dealt in mustard seed that they planted on the edge of town). What happened was that the Black Hundreds tried to mobilize the lower middle class, the home owners on the outskirts of town, against the revolutionary movement. But these homeowners had other interests; their own children were bound up with workers' enterprises – in factories and on the railroad, and some of them had already attended various schools. And it was through these ties that they came over to us and that we gained control of the street.

The upshot was that by the end of the summer the Black Hundreds did not dare to appear in these outlying districts. Naturally, there wasn't a sign of policemen on duty. The street was ours. I can't imagine, can't recall a time when our outlook didn't reign supreme on the street from the latter part of summer on.

The latter part of summer – I have already singled this phase out – was the time of the Black Hundreds' attempt at an attack. There was a small crisis in town – something had gone wrong with the grain freight traffic and quite a few of the bakery shop workers were unemployed. (The stevedores had already become our people.) There were rumors that they [the Black Hundreds] were bribing and trying to bind people together in the taverns near the Troitskii Bazaar and that there might be a pogrom. But there was no real pogrom, nothing like it, only one scene: There was a fellow among us who had arrived in the fall – Grisha Prigornyi.[18] He had been at the "Third" Bolshevik Congress, where he had been elected a candidate [member] to the Central Committee. He was a native Siberian, but looked like a Jew. And as he was walking along there was some sort of scuffle; he was shot at and shot back. He had a small revolver. As we watched we didn't believe that he was shooting, but the cartridges actually had been fired. This was the only incident I recall resembling a pogrom at the time. [At that time also] a "public committee" was formed which registered as a self-defense organization. The public committee included Artsybushev, a Bolshevik and members of the Eastern Bureau of the Central Committee. He had very extensive ties in bourgeois circles as well, was an old revolutionary, a Blanquist of the seventies who had been in Siberia, then held a post in the bookkeeping division of the railroad. A group there formed the *okhotnicheskaia* artel, which was an artel of accountants with whom people deposited savings, etc., and had very extensive connections. There was Aleksandrov, whom I knew slightly. At one time in the past, he had ties with the revolutionaries. These people were from old Marxist groups in Samara, and they had started this public organization to avert pogroms.

H: They had already done so by the spring?

N: No, this came about later, when workers on the steamboats became unemployed, at the end of August and in September. They went to the *okhotnicheskaia* artel and gave them information about the state of affairs. The most important thing was that a local artillery brigade, which had come from the Far East, made its appearance here. It was headed by Colonel Von Galin, a very interesting figure, a man of German descent who had become completely Russified and was very influential among the officers. He declared that he would not tolerate a pogrom, and he joined this committee in which official representatives of the Social Democrats, Socialist Revolutionaries, liberals, and stock-exchange committee participated. Kritskii, the chief of the city police, gave a report to this committee and Von Galin participated in its activty. "I am not participating officially," he told the committee, "but I will help you in every respect." And the following happened: A home guards detachment was put together quickly and I found myself temporarily acting as its chief. Many of the students from our schools were

involved, comparatively few workers were. The strength of the organization lay not in us but in the fact that artillery officers appointed by Von
Galin were on duty at the police stations. We patrolled the streets. We
worked out a password with Von Galin and the guard on duty. If anything
happened, we had the right to summon guards with this password, and
they would race over to the scene of the action. This was in September,
prior to the October days.[19]

I remember a conversation with this Von Galin. For some reason the two
of us had remained together in a room. I was approaching eighteen at the
time; he was a man getting on in years; over forty, approaching fifty. I said
to him: "I ask you, as a revolutionary: Why are you not against the tsar?"
He replied: "Forgive me, but how old are you?" "I'll soon be eighteen," I
told him. "In a few years you'll think it over," he said. When I was working
in the archives in Petersburg later, I came across his name there. He had
attended the artillery school there and in the latter half of the eighties had
been in a Social Democratic circle, in one of the three that existed there.
Von Galin was among those who had been prosecuted for this business,
who were not exactly suspended but detained on suspicion. It had had an
effect on him. "When I was your age everything seemed simple to me then
too," he said to me. During this period [in 1905] he played a major role.
Through their connections the Black Hundreds found out about this, and
he incurred great hatred, was arrested. Later on I read that Von Galin had
been sentenced to a convict labor gang. At this time it was unheard of for
a military man, a colonel, to be reduced to the ranks and sentenced to a
convict labor gang. It seems that his case was reexamined and he was
resentenced. I didn't see any more material on this. In any case, this was
one of the most interesting episodes in that it showed how we drove the
Black Hundreds away from the lower strata who lived in the outlying areas
of Samara; and how, thanks to this officer, the leaders of Samara put an
end to that movement. All the officers were behind him.

Now as for organizational developments. The SD organization in Samara
was a joint one, in which there were both Bolsheviks and Mensheviks. I
have found documents here which prove that at one time there were three
Mensheviks and two Bolsheviks – or, to be more exact, three who were
opponents of the Bolshevik Third Congress and two who were for the official Bolsheviks. There was also a separate Menshevik organization. [Its
organizer], Vladimir Trapeznikov, an old Social Democrat of the nineties,
had been one of the pioneers of Social Democracy in the Urals, in Viatka
and Perm'. But the Bolsheviks of that time and even the Mensheviks were
against the split. Consequently, separate organizations were considered
very undesirable. The Samara organization in 1905 was a unified organization, which later elected two delegates to the Stockholm Unification Congress, and both voted for the Mensheviks and returned home as
Mensheviks.

H: At this time, how did people in Samara interpret the various conflicts between Mensheviks and Bolsheviks?

N: I should say that in 1905, in the beginning, there were no typical disagreements. There were disagreements about party rules, about who was a member of the Party. There were disagreements as to whether there should be greater or less organizational discipline, organizational strictness. We, of course, were in favor of discipline, of strictness. The fact that the Mensheviks had not submitted to the decisions of the Second Congress had had an impact on us. Our relations with the liberals, I think, played a certain role, but not such a major one. I don't think the Mensheviks were opposed to criticism of the liberals. They were always for it, and criticized them no less sharply than the Bolsheviks – even more artfully.

H: What Bolshevik or Menshevik literature did you receive at this time?

N: I had a great many contacts. The literature was received through me, and I was often the first to read it. I remember that the first issues of *Proletarii* were brought in by Kostia Larin when he returned from abroad, and he left them with me.[20]

We had seen the central organs. But if one considers the polemics (the Leninist zemstvo program and the *Iskra* plan with regard to the banquets had already appeared),[21] I would say that in essence there was no great difference between the critical statements of Bolsheviks and Mensheviks. The Mensheviks said one had to take a critical stand in order to jolt the liberals into taking liberal action; the Bolsheviks – to expose treachery. This was the kind of nuance that was difficult to distinguish. All the more so, since criticism was always turning into exposure.

It was the chance to influence the young that presented us with a field for massive work. The SRs did not have young people. Only among the seminary students was the SR influence fairly strong. The SRs, in fact, had more contacts in the villages and a greater sense of the mood that prevailed in the countryside, yet only once did they issue a leaflet directed mainly toward the peasants, explaining their position. The mood [of the countryside] was keenly felt among us, as well. We had to reckon with the countryside – all the workers said this, too. The petty bourgeoisie on the outskirts of town were bound up with the countryside, but there were also real peasants who came to us. And when they did, they always asked for something to read. About the time when the campaign for the May strike had started among the lowest classes, the work with the peasantry started too. I know this because Razumnik Nikolaevich Dmitriev was the initiator and the leader of it. He was the first to begin discussions with the peasants at the bazaars, became involved with them. They would spend evenings sitting in the taverns, not drinking beer but consuming a great deal of tea. He later went out to see them in the villages. And it was with these visits that the Samara countryside organization [of Social Democrats] began, only later did the committee sanction it. The September conference in Samara – combined Bolshevik and Menshevik – dealt with the work among the peasantry. Dmitriev was the Samara delegate to the conference.

What else took place during that summer period? Great events occurred in Moscow; there was an uprising in the fleet, and I remember that at the time we received word from the Central Committee telling us that we definitely had to respond, to show our support. We were issued an order to work out a plan for a six-month celebration of the events of January, to end the celebration with a strike. If an additional leaflet had been issued, summoning people to this strike, it could have come off. Workers struck a great deal, very readily. But, in essence, the movement developed according to its own internal laws. And these internal laws were mastered by the masses – not only the workers but all those around them. There were students who were with us [the Social Democrats]. And there was one, common home guard of all the students. It was fairly well-armed independently, and it had taken shape with the support of the population, the support of the elders.

[Eds.: The dramatic events of 1905 culminated in the general strike that reached Samara on October 11, through the railroad telegraph and the local Union of Railroad Employees and Workers.[22] The strike brought with it a period of intensive activity and raised hopes high of an imminent collapse of the tsarist government. Samara's Liberationists, SRs, and SDs (Nicolaevsky among them) worked together to organize strikes and demonstrations. Large public meetings were held at the Samara "People's House" at which speakers of all three parties addressed crowds of workers, soldiers, and townspeople. Although most of Samara's SDs, including Nicolaevsky, saw themselves as Bolsheviks, and accepted Lenin's call for a "popular insurrection," they wholeheartedly supported the strike. They also followed the example set by the Mensheviks in St. Petersburg, reported in the SD press, and set out to organize the small Samara working class into trade unions (about 10 of them had already been established by early December, including a separate, "proletarian" Union of Railroad Workers). In regard to the question of a union's political affiliation, The SDs again upheld the Menshevik position, favoring "neutral," nonpolitical unions. "On this question we spoke in Menshevik prose, though we did not know it," said Nicolaevsky.

On December 4, acting on the instructions of a messenger from the Petersburg Soviet, the SD leaders of Samara's trade unions established a Soviet of Workers' Deputies. The Samara Soviet was short lived, "did not play any role," and its dispersal by the authorities on December 11 provoked no protest for several reasons: the SRs had been against its establishment from the outset; relations with the Liberationists had been cool ever since the SDs had turned their attention to trade unions; and neither the workers nor the generally supportive artillery unit could be roused to action. Nicolaevsky tried to explain this paralysis:

> Samara was a small town. Even smaller as a working class center. In October, [the workers] seized it because the government was lost. There was a strike. Now, the strike did not frighten the government – the trains kept on running, the same sappers [who had struck in October] were forced to work, and they worked. There was a strike in the center [of Russia], [but] the news from Moscow was not good.

In St. Petersburg nothing happened. By itself, Samara could not play any role.

During the early months of 1906, the Samara SDs continued to promote trade unions, but supported the boycott of the Duma elections, and turned their attention to preparing an insurrection in the army. It was Nicolaevsky's involvement in this "military" work that brought about his arrest on April 23, 1906.]

Sixth interview

H: During our last interview we began discussing your arrest and how, on the basis of talks you had with people in prison, you came to define yourself as a Menshevik.

N: Naturally, that didn't come about quickly. I was arrested, I believe, the evening before the First State Duma convened. At the time, I recall, I had been in a military organization.[1] It consisted of myself and one other person, and we had to do all the work ourselves. I had arranged for a meeting with some soldiers and had to hand them proclamations.

H: Yes, you told me about this.

N: I went to the street where I was to distribute the leaflets, and I was arrested. Since I had the leaflets tucked into my trousers, and wasn't searched on the street – merely had my pockets rifled there – nothing was found on me. I was taken to the police station and from there to prison. At the police station I managed to destroy the leaflets, so there was no evidence. Nonetheless, a soldier testified that I had had revolutionary discussions with him and given him proclamations. As a matter of fact, I had not yet given him any proclamations. This was the first time I had been instructed to bring them. Nevertheless, the soldier's word served as evidence. What counted most against me was that when I was arrested, I refused to give my name and address. (I shared a place with a friend and didn't want to compromise him.) Therefore I was said to be withholding information. This was an aggravating circumstance and I was not let out on bail. My trial date was pushed up. I was brought to trial in the fall and given the usual sentence – exile to Siberia. But since I was a minor, under twenty, my sentence was commuted to two years' imprisonment, with time deducted for the period I had spent in preliminary detention. In making that decision, the court also took into account the fact that I had served most of that detention period in a prison rather than a fortress. I remember that I spent a total of sixteen months in prison.

In the beginning, though perhaps only during the first few days I spent there, the Samara Prison, as the slang expression had it, was "nailed tight" – run according to a strict regime, and prisoners not allowed to associate with one another. (The period I'm referring to corresponded roughly with the opening of the Duma.)[2] During those first few days we staged a protest, and the warden put in an appearance. He was a man named Orlov who had been the assistant warden of the preliminary detention . . . no, of the transit prison in Petersburg. He said he knew Gapon well. He agreed to our demands with no hesitation, and we were allowed to mingle freely with one another. The "elders" had the right to go wherever they wished in the prison. I don't recall who the SR "elder" was at the start; later it was Vedeniapin, who figured in the trial of the SRs [in 1922]. From the beginning, and perhaps until the very end of my stay there, I was the "elder" for the SDs.

H: Were these elders elected?

N: Yes, but the fact is that many prisoners were transferred, so that generally people who remained there longer became "elders." By the fall, I was already an old-timer, and so it was more or less natural that I had been elected.

The prison was an extremely interesting place; a mass of arrested people had been brought there – peasants, soldiers, comparatively few workers. After I had been there a while, it became a big transit center, and enormous detachments of prisoners arrived there. (We, the "elders," had the right to go into the transit wing.) And later on – imagine what happened then! From the early part of May or June [1906] there had been unrest among the soldiers in town, also among those on the military base. Under the influence of this agitation, the soldiers on the base were planning to come into town and liberate the prison. I remember that the warden showed up and that at night the "elder" woke us and said: "I have just come from a meeting with the soldiers, and they are planning to liberate the prison. We have to organize things so that there will not be any clashes, no bloodshed." [Then the warden said] "I'll do whatever you say." Well, we stayed up all night drinking tea and waiting for them. But they didn't come. For some reason they postponed it and did something else.

But to return to the political aspect of things. Two factors influenced me . . . above all, the phenomenon of the so-called *druzhiny* [partisan bands]. One could meet a good many people who had taken part in partisan actions.[3]

H: Was this the first political fact that influenced you?

N: I wouldn't say it was the first, but I believe it had a considerable impact on me. With respect to it, quite a few impressions are interwoven in my mind. There were several SRs in the Samara prison, outstanding fighters. I had discussions with Vedeniapin and Sergei Nikolaevich Kalistov, later with Frolov, the worker who assassinated Blok, the governor of Samara province. Frolov was one of the very workers who had broken with us SDs [after December 1905]. Later, when he was sent to do hard labor, be became a major figure and apparently a very strong person morally. In the prison there were also many *agrarniki* [landed peasants], who had staged a rebellion after the dissolution of the First Duma. There were members of *druzhiny* that had been equipped with dozens of rifles. There were . . . the three Zubkov brothers, one of whom had been wounded in the leg. All these people were executed – shot or hung. The peasants were dealt with very harshly.

All the people from the Samara *druzhina* – a Bolshevik fighting unit – were brought into the prison. Boris Solovskii was one of the men in this group. That is, he was listed as Solovskii on his passport, though I believe his name in fact was Iakubov. He was a very nice young fellow from Perm', but he'd been lured into this activity. Pavel Melnikov – whose earlier pseudonym had been Ganer – used to come and try to dissuade these people from fighting. He had been a member of the Siberian Union since 1902–1903, was a Menshevik. I saw him for the last time in 1919, in Krasnoiarsk, visited him then. His real name was Nazarenko. On explicit instructions from the [Samara SD] Committee, he used to come to the prison to try and prove to the people from the *druzhiny* that they should desist from fighting. He was investigated, dragged into the case, and sentenced, as a fighting man, to hard labor, though, of course, he had nothing in common with the *druzhiny* members. There were many personal tragedies; several fine young men were shot or hung.

At this same time, the Ufa *druzhina*, a well-organized unit, widely expanded its activites. Its foundation had been laid by the group I myself had created earlier. I used to receive information from these people – they would simply come and visit me in prison. Later, in 1907, immediately after my release, I went to Ufa. And subsequently, while I was passing through Omsk, Vas'ka Gorelov, who had been a member of the Ufa *druzhina* and was one of my best friends, told me in great detail the whole saga of that *druzhina*. It has not been written up at all in the literature, but I must tell you that it constitutes one of the most colorful pages in the history of the partisan fighting. Our circle in the *gimnazium* formed the nucleus of the group. Later on, in 1907, and particularly in 1917, the entire group held firm as Social Democrats; every one of the people I knew in it – Gorelov and Zakharov and Gudkov – repudiated Bolshevism. So did my brother. They became Mensheviks on the basis of their experience, even though it had included some very effective partisan operations. The three Kadantsev brothers came to head the organization.[4]

H: You say these people gave up Bolshevism in 1917?

N: By 1917 they had. Their repudiation of it constituted a long, but very interesting saga; they left gradually, for various reasons. In 1907 Gorelov told me all about the life of the group – a friendly, happy one. In essence, it was a group which, among its valiant exploits, performed acts of expropriation. Mikhail Kadantsev and Vasia Gorelov got involved in these and held up two mail trains, one near Ufa and the other along the Dema River.

H: Did these take place in 1906?

N: Yes. They seized 300,000 rubles from one of the trains and 40,000 from the other. Gorelov described how he and Kadantsev carried out one of the operations. After they had leaped onto the train, Gorelov killed the guard, the only victim in this incident. Then they seized the money and jumped off the train. Everyting had been well prepared and they got away.

There were, I repeat, many good aspects of these adventures. But, basically, according to Gorelov's account, they managed to unhinge these people, so that from the standpoint of the movement, they were lost. None of them were content to do normal political work, they found it boring. And among those on the fringes of the group, there were all sorts of scandals involving money. This was true even of those in the very center. After they had seized the 300,000, they divided it and hid it in various places. One large bundle – it appears to have contained 70,000 rubles – disappeared. And this poisoned the atmosphere in the group. Who had taken it? There was practically no information to be had. Yet someone had stolen it. Only a few, including the culprit, were in the know because, I repeat, these people held together as a group, and no one was betrayed during the arrests. Still, the theft had a demoralizing effect.

As for smaller groups such as the Samara *Druzhina*, there were several fine workers in it, perhaps the best people among us, the most active, the most resourceful. That fellow Solovskii – Iakubov – was a splendid man. During one of the *druzhina* operations, he had a bomb in his pocket. He fell and slipped and the bomb exploded in his pocket. It was a weak, trashy pocket bomb, but it mangled his leg. He was brought into our prison before being operated on. The operation was done in the prison. A good doctor was found, and the operation was said to be a success, but he lost his leg. And in his case this personal tragedy was interwoven with a romance, with many things.

In short, because of the impact all these sagas had on me – I can no longer distinguish specific episodes – I was strongly repelled by "fighting operations." In 1905. . . .

H: Was it simply that you felt it had moral . . .?

N: I felt it was corrupting the movement, that is, was dangerous, harmful, call it what you will. At the time, perhaps, I wasn't able to formulate my impression, but I had distinctly negative feelings about this.

It was precisely at this time that the Second Duma convened – the Second Duma, which provided the first example of a European type of socialist propaganda and socialist activity. Naturally, Tsereteli's speeches made a profound impact.[5] Everyone in that prison regarded him with more than reverence. He had won everyone over. What wasn't written about him! The right-wing press was malicious. Nonetheless everything written about him was suffused with such enormous respect that the man became a charismatic figure. And it was this contrast between partisan activity and its consequences, and political activity which, despite all the circumstances, opened a wide path – it was this which primarily determined my quest. I did a great deal of work in prison, read a great deal.

H: What did you read?

N: On the one hand, you see, I was fascinated by the history of the revolutionary movement. All the literature published on it had found its way into the prison by then, and I read and studied it. On the other hand, I made a determined effort to acquaint myself with the movement in Europe. I did not know any foreign languages, but I read and reread everything that appeared in Russian on the Western European movement. It was against this background that I formed a fundamental impression of Tsereteli on the one hand, and of the partisan movement. I embraced the views of Tsereteli and from that point on my attitude toward him was quite special, had already become so.

H: I'd like to go into this further. Which of your readings and discussion influenced you most?

N: I had discussions . . . I had several clashes with Bolsheviks, who were angry with me because my attitude was so negative. True, the people who quarreled with me were not "fighting men." With the latter, with Boris Solovskii, for example, I was always on good terms and perhaps influenced him to some degree – in 1917 he sided with the Mensheviks. Later he went over to the Bolsheviks again, rejoined them. But for him, who had lost his leg, it was strictly a personal affair. During this period [1907] he abandoned Bolshevism. There were many ardent young people there, or more precisely, followers of the Bolsheviks. I can't recall now what our major quarrels were about. But there were a good many.

Pavel Nikolaevich Kolokolnikov was there.[6] He had come to Samara to investigate the partisan activities. He was a member and agent of the Central Committee.[7] Later I learned that he and Akim (Leon Goldman) had been sent to the Urals to clarify that episode involving the expropriation, and the fate of the money. The point was that the people from Ufa had turned over part of the money to the Bolsheviks. It had been received by Ismail Samber, who died in 1920 or 1921. It was said that it had been turned over to the center, and this gave rise to the legend that the money had gone to the Central Committee. There was even some indication of this in the literature. . . . In actual fact, not a single kopek reached the Central Committee. The money came to Lenin. He, of course, was a most honest man, and so it was out of the question that he had appropriated the money for himself; once he had received it, he must have passed it on. But rumor had it then that something improper had been done. The two men sent to investigate were arrested. They were arrested in Samara, with no evidence against them, and Kolokolnikov was soon released. I had a good many talks with these men, who wanted to arrange my escape. I'd always had a great love of adventure, and so I agreed to have them make the arrangements. But with respect to the escape, the [Samara] Committee argued that this was utterly absurd, particularly an escape involving the likely use of armed force, when I was facing only a light sentence. This was true. When Kolokolnikov, who was present at the session, learned about my state of mind, he was amazed.

Knowing the role he played in the trade union movement – he was Secretary of the Petersburg Central Bureau of Trade Unions – I repeatedly asked him how matters stood. I was interested in this aspect of things. I wanted to know what the state of affairs was in Petersburg. (I am referring to the period prior to the Second Duma – Kolokolnikov had probably been arrested in November or December.)

Gorev also came to see us.[8] By this time, it seems he had already left the Bolsheviks. Yes. He'd been a Bolshevik at the Tammerfors Conference,[9] which means he came to see us in December 1906 or January 1907. It appears that before the elections to the Second Duma,[10] before the London Congress,[11] his name was listed among those who had signed the Menshevik Theses. In any case, he was no longer an orthodox Bolshevik, was an agent of the Menshevik Central Committee. I heard a great deal from him about what was transpiring. What he had to say was supplementary and played no role except for his remarks about how the trade union movement was developing. The unions were developing at an intensive rate in Petersburg in 1906, particularly the unions of metal workers and printers. Kolokolnikov maintained that given the conditions in Russia, there was no possibility of creating [a trade union movement] and cited examples to prove this. Naturally, he didn't always insist that what had been accomplished was far from sufficient, far from what could be done in Germany, he conceded that a little progress was possible. His remarks, too, made an impression on me.

H: What did you know at this time about Akselrod's ideas? Were you at all familiar with them?[12]

N: I was familiar with them but, of course, hadn't read everything he'd written. I was very much in sympathy with his ideas, though I must confess I didn't believe in the likelihood of their realization. What least appealed to me then and later about Menshevism was its disdainful attitude toward organization. I had no doubt about the need for a policy distinct from that of the Bolsheviks. But I believed that whatever the policy of the party, the party organization must be kept intact. I followed this line always, scarcely ever shifted from it, and I think that in the provinces people shared my feeling. For example, when I got out of prison, I traveled quite a bit through the Urals and Siberia and with respect to this [matter of organization] generally found precisely the same line of thinking.

H: I would like to go into this somewhat more deeply. Are we talking now roughly about the period during the spring and summer of 1906?

N: It was more likely the fall of 1906 and spring of 1907.

H: After the dissolution of the First Duma?

N: After the dissolution of the First Duma.

H: But, to put it concretely, what did you know then about the Mensheviks' political line? And on what sources was your information based? You have already commented about Tsereteli and his policy in the [Second] Duma.

N: We all knew about Tsereteli and his policy in the Duma, had precise details about it. We received the newspaper, read it regularly, and discussed all the issues. But our information wasn't limited to what we read there. We regularly received all the writings put out by the illegal press, all the reports on meetings of Mensheviks, as well as material from the SRs quasi-legal press. And we had all the collections comprising *Soznatel'naia Rossiia.*[13]

There were SRs there who were under especially strict regime. After that attempt had been made to arrange my escape, I too was placed under a strict regime – but only for a short time. Because after my arrest, I'd been a prisoner in a fortress, and the position of such a prisoner, even one transferred to a prison, was more privileged and favorable. I remained in contact with those SRs I mentioned and developed a personal friendship with them, perhaps a closer one than with any SDs during this period. I simply can't recall a single SD whom I was close to then, I decidedly wasn't on close terms with the Bolsheviks who had been brought in along with Demian Protopopov. I was particularly friendly with Vedeniapin, since he became the "elder" for the SRs, and I for the SDs. We had a great deal of work in common: we received the same sorts of packages and distributed the same type of literature, so that we did develop a personal relationship.

H: Were you aware at this time that the Bolsheviks and Mensheviks differed in their evaluations of the mass movement, particularly the trade union movement.

N: We had departed from the principle of *partiinost'* in trade unions as early as 1905.[14] I read you quotations from my correspondence (a somewhat abridged form of it) where, even in 1905, I had argued that the requirement for party affiliation [of trade unions] wasn't appropriate for conditions in Samara, generally didn't hold for them, that conditions there were, in this respect. . . .

H: Did you attach much importance to this in your political outlook?

N: I think that at the time (although it had a psychological impact on me) I wasn't that conscious of it, because there were far more arguments concerning tactics in the Duma. It wasn't that we favored agreement with the Kadets. I remember being impressed then by a kind of parable which went like this: You know the characteristics of the different nationality groups. Supposing you were to ask a member of each what he would do if he were the tsar. You'd ask a Ukrainian, and he'd say: "I'd like to sit on the stove, eat lard and smear myself with lard." A Gypsy: "I'd steal a pair of silver candlesticks and make a dash for it." A Great Russian: "I'd stand at a crossroad and give each person that came by a punch in the nose." This did not leave me with the impression that criticism [of the Kadets in the Duma] was unnecessary but that it was rather like a punch in the nose. Perhaps my reaction shows the influence of the SRs. I had not so much an affinity for Populism, as a respect for the SRs' romanticism, a respect which, as I told you, I'd had from an early age. The personal encounters I had with SRs in the prison strongly reinforced this feeling, because they were very good people – especially that fellow Vedeniapin, an ideal person, and Mikhail Ivanovich Symbin, a statistician. Symbin was much older than I but we became close friends. Later on he was a member of the SR Central Committee. He was the first to leave them, to go into scientific work. He established a scientific method for studying permafrost and made quite a name for himself in this sphere. There were several other people with whom I became friends. In general, I repeat, I had closer personal relationships during this period with SRs than with SDs. In any case, I felt that the critique of the SRs should be more serious. I remember our debates. We received some new collections of articles; I think they were entitled "On Various Topics," put out by the SRs. They were edited by Chernov. I was particularly struck by Chernov's polemics with those on the left, with Tagin and Trotsky. Still, my attitude toward Bolshevism was determined by some facts which became known to us. I knew a great deal. Recently I corresponded with Aleksinskii, who indicated that he had not known that a conspiratorial Leninist troika existed. I simply couldn't believe this! Compared to him in those days, I had been a mere boy confined in a provincial prison. Yet even I knew of this. True, the situation in Ufa was quite special. But this alone does not explain things. After all, we'd begun having frank, major discussions in prison.

H: Were there major discussions regarding the Stockholm Congress?[15]

N: No. We did not meet any of the people who had been to Stockholm. The Stockholm Congress, and the resolutions it adopted, showed that those people were not keeping pace with reality – the resolution prohibiting the creation of a parliamentary group in the State Duma if socialist deputies were elected. We learned about the resolution after the socialist faction had already been formed. During the period of the First Duma, we seemed to be living in a state of intoxication. It was during the decisive days of the First Duma that we stayed up that night waiting for the soldiers, thinking that it was merely a matter of minutes before they would come and liberate us. Clearly, we had lost our sense of equilibrium.

H: Did you know anything about the land question?[16] About municipalization? And if so, did it have an impact on you?

N: Yes, the debates about this made an impact on me, a very strong one. We knew the Bolsheviks had failed to reach a consensus on this issue, that only a negligible minority supported Lenin's stand on the nationalization of the land, that essentially Rozhkov's point of view – that private property must be divided – had triumphed. And that only because of Lenin's attitude this viewpoint had not been officially sanctioned [by the Bolshevik faction].

H: Where were your own views about this question?

N: I was for municipalization, precisely because there were many different regions, and it was impossible to prescribe one course of action for them all. This was, if you will, a matter of necessity, though I realized it only later – the necessity of proceeding to decentralization in Russia. At the time, you see, we were centralists. We had repudiated the idea of autonomy, repudiated it for the Caucasus, repudiated it for the Ukraine. Yet, considering the uniqueness of the different regions, objectively there was a great need for autonomy. Hence I did some work on the legal situation [pertaining to the land question] in the Urals, and it seemed to me that special rules on land reform had to be introduced there.

H: Now let's turn to another issue. You have remarked, stressed, that you were opposed to boycotts and that this was one of the main reasons why you defined yourself as a Menshevik. In addition, you said you had some conception of the issues at stake with respect to the political affiliation of unions. And that you had already raised the question of the Social Democrats' rapports with the SRs and the Kadets. Toward which of the two did you gravitate more?

N: Less toward the Kadets. The Kadets were not a significant force in Samara. I told you that in Samara it was the *meshchanstvo*, lower middle-class people, who played a major role in 1906–07. They did so under the influence of the Social Democrats but they themselves were not Social Democrats. In order to keep them in our orbit one needed to have a more flexible

approach politically to the question of unions. This was even more important with respect to the SRs, because in the area near the Volga they represented a major force, the countryside was SR territory. Recently I came
across memoirs by Skitalets, who mentioned Obsharovka, all the familiar
places. I was in prison with Skitalets's brother, a teacher, with a great many
SRs. And my personal sympathies for them were interwoven with political
ones, or to put it more precisely, already then my political evaluation of the
role played by the SRs in the Russian countryside influenced my personal
attitude toward the SR *intelligenty*. That's the way it strikes me now, and I
think I am not mistaken. I think it was true then, though of course I was
not aware of it at the time. I should tell you that when I got out of prison
in Samara I was not yet twenty. I got out in early July . . .

H: Did you known much about the conflicts which, as you have noted,
took place during this time – conflicts concerning elections to the Second
Duma, the danger of the Black Hundreds, and the question of electoral
agreements?[17]

N: Yes, of course, it was this problem that raised the issue of the
Kadets. We had to avert the danger of the Black Hundreds; everyone
agreed on this. There was no sympthy for the Kadets, there was no question
of that. The position of electoral agreement with the Kadets was a particular conclusion from the general premise of the need [to mobilize] for a
struggle against the Black Hundreds.

H: Yes, I understand. But on this point did you fully support the viewpoint of the Mensheviks?

N: Yes. We followed the course of the elections very closely. I remember that I compiled notes and made various tabulations on them.

H: I find it somewhat difficult to visualize all this. In 1905, for you and
many other young people Lenin was a hero, isn't that so?

N: Who?

H: Lenin.

N: Lenin was what?

H: I asked whether Lenin had seemed to you a heroic figure in 1905.

N: Yes, particularly since I had heard about him from people who
knew him in Samara. But I wouldn't say that Lenin in particular was a
heroic figure for me. I was very interested in Martov, in . . .

H: As early as this?

N: Yes, of course. I knew as much about Martov as about Lenin. I knew
that his articles had been publised in *Novoe Slovo*. I managed to find issues
of the journal.

H: In prison?

N: No, I had bought them before I was arrested. I had complete sets of
Novoe Slovo, Nachalo, and *Zhizn'*.[18] I bought all these before I was arrested.
I even bound them. I regret it now, because I used very good binding. Well,
. . .

H: Why did Martov impress you?

N: Because of his historical approach. He always dealt with historical
themes. These figured very largely in the articles he published in *Novoe*

Slovo. And it was the historical approach that interested us most of all. In Lenin I did not sense the historian. I would not say, and never did, that Lenin was a hero to me. No, this was never the case.

H: So that you never went through a major process of disillusionment?

N: No, no major process of disillusionment. I should tell you that in this period generally, particularly in Samara, there were no borderlines or walls between factions. I cited you an example of how we, knowingly elected both of those delegates – Bolsheviks . . .

H: Yes, I know. You had discussed this in prison.

N: In prison this was a continuation of a natural process of develop- ment for me. There were more Social Democrats than SRs in the prison. Our self-definition was Social Democratic. And to a great extent I was ori- ented toward the European workers' movement. I remember studying all the information that was available about the movement in the west. I remember that for me America was like a newly discovered country, and that the first articles by that fellow James on America, which appeared in *Otkliki Sovremennosti*[19] made a great impression on me.

H: With respect to the workers' movement, what did you read?

N: In a real sense, scarcely anything. *German Social Democracy* had begun appearing at this time, but I didn't read all the issues. During this time, too, Paul Louis' book on French Socialism was published,[20] and Zorge's on the American workers' movement.[21] Naturally, there was also Brossard on the French Revolution. More had been published on revolution than on the workers' movement. It goes without saying that I read all the material that came out. I also obtained a copy of Ellis's book, which had appeared then – *Letters on the Workers' Movement in Germany.*

I should tell you that there was a wealth of journal articles to be found in Russian, and I became interested in what turned out to be an old field of endeavor. I later learned that by the 70s or 80s it had become traditional to compile collections of books on a particular subject by using articles cut out of journals. I myself started doing this. Old journals and books could be obtained for next to nothing in the market. From the time I was a *gimna- zium* student, some book or other printed work would catch my eye as I was passing the book stalls, and I would try to figure out the real name of othe author, of these "Kartsevs" and "Mazaevs." When I was still a student in the Ufa *Gimnazium*, I learned there was a dictionary of pseudonyms and checked it out of the main library.

H: In general, what was it that commanded your respect? Was it the spectacle of a massive, aware, workers' movement?

N: Yes, it is difficult for me to distinguish now what I read then or later. In each volume of *Russkoe Bogatstvo* there was something worth reading; in each volume of *Zhizn'* all articles proved interesting. I read and retained all this. It was a long road to an education, but it paid off.

H: Can you recall what Menshevik literature you read at this time? Which articles made a particular impression on you?

N: Of course I can. I remember A. N. Potresov's article on the State Duma. I think it appeared in the fourth volume of *Otkliki Sovremennosti.*[22]

It was one of the first articles I read. Subsequently, I was greatly impressed by the polemics surrounding Kautsky's preface "The Motive Force and Prospects of the Russian Revolution."[23] Even earlier, of course, by the time we demarcated our stand from that of the SRs, the necessity for a bourgeois revolution had become axiomatic with us. Kautsky's brochure set forth – correctly, as I see it now – the great limitations in our formulation of the question. Martov's reply which, I think, was not published in *Otkliki Sovremennosti* but in *Otzyvy*, or in *Otgoloski*, aroused a great deal of discussion.[24] I can't recall now what other articles I read during this period. . . . Later on I read some minor ones. I remember that article on America and one on . . .

H: But were Potresov's the most significant?

N: Potresov's, Martov's, and the polemics with Kautsky. Lenin translated these. We received a pamphlet of Lenin's containing a preface in which he expressed triumphantly, about this. . . .

H: Did you know anything about Trotsky's ideas at this time?[25]

N: Yes, of course, all of us were familiar with them. His *Preface to Civil War* was fundamental to an understanding of his position at this time.[26] When we were still at liberty, we had already become familiar with the particular nuances of Trotsky's writing in 1905. I had not yet seen his *Russkaia Gazeta*.[27] I read it much later. With respect to Trotsky's position on the debate about whether maximalism would erupt if the revolution triumphed, opinions fluctuated in the Menshevist camp. I liked Trotsky very much. His polemics "Mr. Peter Struve in Politics" and "In Defense of the Party" . . . I remember his incisive criticism of Prokopovich and Kuskova.

H: Had the Mensheviks completely repudiated the idea of permanent revolution?

N: We were drawn to Trotsky as a fine publicist but were not in sympathy with his political ideas.

H: Had you already read Lenin's "Two Tactics"?[28]

N: Yes, I read it when I was still at liberty.

H: What did you think about it?

N: It was probably late in the summer of 1905 that we received copies of "Two Tactics." Prior to this we had had fundamental debates about the "Third" Congress and the [Menshevik] Conference.[29] Gutovskii had been one of the delegates of the Siberian Union and had attended the "Third" Congress."[30] He passed through our midst like a meteor. He was the first to return from the "Third" Congress. He made a speech [in Samara] and the very next day raced off to Siberia. Two or three days later Maksimov arrived. When he learned that Gutovskii had left, he told us it was very important to issue reports so that Gutovskii would not "capture" [the party organization] in Siberia. Then he himself set off there.

H: When you read "Two Tactics", what impression did it make on you?

N: It's difficult for me to say now. At the time I read it I considered myself to be in the Bolshevik camp. Nonetheless, "Two Tactics" didn't make a great impression on me.

H: It didn't?

N: In any case, I can't recall now what it was, possibly because there had already been too many disputes.

H: In any case, by the time you were imprisoned in 1906, had you completely repudiated the idea of the dictatorship of the proletariat?

N: I had. I was very impressed with the need to work with the peasantry. I felt a very strong affinity for the peasantry. I believe that one of the major faults of Menshevism was its anti-peasant attitude. This conception of Dan's that the peasantry was progressive socially but reactionary politically – I believe that in Russia, where eighty-five percent of the population consisted of peasants, such a conception bound Menshevism hand and foot, so that it could not progress politically. In order to expand democratic activity, we first had to achieve democracy for the peasantry.

H: When you look back now, do you think that in 1906–7 during the period of the First and Second Dumas, you repudiated Bolshevism because Lenin's conception was no longer relevant? And that you thought it lacked relevance because a revolutionary situation no longer existed? Was this the case?

N: I don't think so. Naturally, my attitude toward the Bolsheviks was negative, but I did not have a factionalist approach. After all, when I came to St. Petersburg, I published my impressions of Siberia in a Bolshevik publication edited by Lenin, *Vpered.*[31] While I was in St. Petersburg, Lenin expressed a desire to make my acquaintance, and we met.

3
GEORGE DENIKE

Plate 5. Iurii Petrovich Denike, January 11, 1908 (courtesy of Boris Sapir)

Plate 6. Iurii Petrovich Denike, circa 1960 (courtesy of Boris Sapir)

First interview

H: Could you describe your family background, and the place where you were born?

GD: First, I have to say that I was born in 1887, on a day that was to become famous, November 7, the day of the October Revolution.[1] I was not born where I had to say I was, the provincial capital of Kazan, because there was some misunderstanding in my papers, but in a tiny village in the province of Simbirsk, Korsun or Korsun' – I don't remember exactly. I was a few months old when my parents moved away. My father, Petr Mikhailovich Denike, was a judge. He came by his name entirely by chance. Only much later, after his death, did I learn what it was all about. I and my five brothers (particularly the older ones) were troubled because while on our mother's side, there was a grandfather, grandmother, uncles, and aunts, on our father's side there was nothing at all. Once someone with the same last name of Denike came by, but it was apparent that he was no relative of father's. Actually, the situation was similar to Herzen's or the composer Borodin's. (I found this out only after my father's death.) He was the son of the Kazan marshal of the nobility, Osokin, and his mother was the landowner Kasianova. My father was born in 1855. At that time divorce was virtually impossible in Russia, or involved extremely humiliating legal proceedings. So long before that, and long afterwards, there existed so-called civil marriages. My father's father had left his wife, but could not obtain a formal divorce. He was semiofficially married to Kasianova. The trouble was with the children; it was extremely difficult to adopt them formally. As a result, a father was bought for them, so to speak. For a certain sum of money my grandfather secured the agreement of a watchmaker named Denike to recognize my father as his son. I learned later that my father had a brother and sisters, and that they were adopted by someone else. I don't know the details of my father's childhood or youth, but his real father seems to have cared for him.

H: He did not live with him?

GD: No, that was impossible for some reason. I don't know just how it was arranged. In any case, he graduated from the same *gimnazium* in Kazan which I was graduated from much later. He then completed the Law Faculty of the university, and began a typical career as a judge. When I was born, he was a district member of the court. His career began very successfully, and then, because of circumstances, went no further. He was transferred to Kazan but always remained a district judge. He reached that level when he was less than 30 and was never promoted. Perhaps I will now say why, but I did not hear this from Father, who was a very reserved person and never said anything about himself. When he was still in Kosmodemiansk, where I spent the better part of my childhood – from two to nine – the judicial administration became displeased with some minor functionary, and asked my father to fire him. This functionary had only a short time to serve before retiring on full pension. My father did not obey the instruction and permitted the man to finish serving and retire quietly. The result was a kind of persecution of my father by the higher-ups. Although I learned of this later, I mention it because I believe it played a big role in the way I developed. My father was not political at all; I never heard him discuss politics. But remember that he was born in 1855 and graduated from the university in 1877 to 1878: that was the generation of Russian jurists who were the product of the Great Reforms, with extremely lofty ideas about the duties of the representatives of justice.[2] This characteristic of my father surfaced when I was around nine years old. I remember, there was the Dreyfus case, which, strange as it may seem, affected my whole life in many ways. Very intelligent accounts of the proceedings were being printed in some Russian newspaper (*Russkoe Slovo*, I think), and different things captivated us, in particular the open speeches, which were rendered quite completely. My father, who was generally a very reserved person, literally boiled with indignation, because he immediately sensed a miscarriage of justice. He and I would discuss the accounts, and I think that the notion of law, on the one hand, and of the violation of law resulting from such things as antisemitism, on the other, left a very deep mark on my entire later development.

H: You were about nine?

GD: Yes. It was when we were living in Kosmodemiansk. I don't remember now when *"J'accuse"* of Zola appeared.

H: That was in 1897.

GD: I was then ten. It was very strange: in Kosmodemiansk, where we were living then, no one had ever seen a single Jew. But I remember that there were two mysterious creatures, one visible, the other invisible. The first was a correspondent; he actually existed: he was seen and he was feared. He was a harmless enough fellow, who wrote for some paper, but it was known that he was a correspondent, and this meant he was a person to beware of . . . "look, there goes the correspondent." That was the first thing that really intrigued me. The second was that there never had been any Jews in the town, and yet I heard all around (not at home, of course) that the "yids" were guilty of everything. The "yids" were hated by people who had never seen a Jew. But that is another matter; what is important for my relationship with my father and his influence on me was what one might call his passion for justice.

I would like to fill out the picture in two other respects. When I was graduated from the *gimnazium* and asked myself the question, "what next?" my father said, "I do not wish to influence my children's choice of the path they want to follow. My only wish is that none of them become a lawyer." I asked why, and he answered, "Because lawyers are people, who, for money, will say one thing one time, and something else the next." The second conversation in this connection occurred when I was weighing various possibilities and my father said, "Why don't you enter the Institute of Engineers of Ways of Communication?" I said, "But, Father, they are all bribe-takers!" That was well known. My father answered, "But that is precisely why it is important that honest people, who would fight bribe-taking, should go there." I think that this gives a good idea of what might be called the moral-political side of my father's influence.

H: Besides this abhorrence of illegality and injustice, did your father have any philosophical views? What were his social and cultural attitudes? What writers influenced him?

GD: I must confess that I know nothing about that. But his library was quite a respectable one and typical of the intelligentsia milieu. Of course, all the Russian classics were there. My father also subscribed to the journal *Vestnik Inostrannoi Literatury* [The Courier of Foreign Literature], which gave the collected works of foreign writers as appendices.

H: Which ones in particular?

GD: Zola, Maupassant (who strangely was called "Huey" in Russia at that time), Sir Walter Scott, Dickens, and so forth. Doubtless, he read. But, as a district judge, he was virtually the only judge in his region except for justices of the peace; he had to work a great deal, and spent little time with us. But he doubtless read. I don't remember exactly what, but he knew German, while my mother knew both German and French. Beyond that, he played the piano. He was not a good pianist but played competently. I think that this is about all I can say about him.

H: Did you ever have political talks or discussions on social topics with him?

GD: He was very reserved about political questions. Even when I was involved in the movement and was arrested once, then a second and third time, he never said a word to me about it. He clearly did not wish to have the slightest influence.

H: Did he read aloud to you when you were little?

GD: No, but my mother did.

H: Let us now turn to your recollections of your mother.

GD: From my mother, there was an entirely different inheritance, although both my parents came from middle nobility. My father, as ostensibly the son of some watchmaker, was not at first a nobleman, though later he reached the necessary rank and received a title of nobility.[3] My mother was straight from an old and renowned noble family. Her maiden name was Glinka. She was not directly descended from the composer Glinka, but my great-grandfather, that is my mother's father's father, was Sergi Nikolaevich Glinka, who played a small role in the War of 1812, receiving the title of First Home Guardsman. He wrote patriotic propaganda. His memoirs were published, and there was a genealogical table which went back almost to the twelfth century. The name Glinka was Polish; in Poland there were various Glinkas. The name also exists in Slovakia, and I suspect that the Slovakian Glinkas are the same family. It is that branch that the direct descendants belonged to; the so-called Smolensk branch. My great-grandfather's brother was the poet Fedor Nikolaevich Glinka, whose fame rested basically on one poem, "Moscow": "Glorious city, ancient city, in your confines you contain," etc. So these were the descendants; they are mentioned in Pushkin. By the way, the name was also known in court circles, because one of my grandfather's brothers was the godson of a Grand Duke; I believe it was Michael Pavlovich, the brother of Nicholas I. They were also distantly related to the second, morganatic wife of Alexander II. So, in short, they were aristocracy. Such things could happen then! It was an interesting combination. On the one hand, an aristocratic family, and on the other a succession of scholars named Glinka. There was my uncle, my mother's brother, and then there was a Glinka who was a kidney specialist; in short, it was a combination of a predilection for science and an aristocratic background. Of course, there were no landed estates at all. How that came to be, I don't know.

But this side of the family influenced me not so much through my mother as through her father. It is very curious, but that's the way it was. He did not study any science, he was a bureaucrat with a definite inclination toward adventures, not the romantic kind. He was one of those mid-nineteenth century bureaucrats who went off to organize the Ural region, which had only recently been incorporated into the Kremlin state. There was an episode in his life that drove him insane toward the end of his life. I will mention it, although it is not of great significance for my biography. But it is very curious. Administrators who had served several years in the Urals received a piece of land, which they greatly valued because there was a chance that gold might be discovered on it. My grandfather obtained such a plot and, after a while, forgot entirely about it. Later, when he was around 80, my family was in very difficult circumstances, because, as I mentioned, my father's career had stood still. At this point something fantastic occurred. Somehow he found out that gold had been discovered on his plot of land, and that his sister had forged his signature and sold the land. He sought out the owners to prove that he had never signed it away and initiated a legal proceeding that was absolutely hopeless, because more than fifty years had passed and the transaction was covered by the law of limitation. He did not become entirely insane, but had delusions and hallucinations. Nowadays we would say that it was acute paranoia.

But that is, so to speak, incidental. My grandfather played a large part in my life. Though he was not a student of science, he was a passionate reader, in particular of history. And read endlessly. He died at the age of 84 or 85 and never wore glasses, despite all he read. He explained this by saying that he never used any lighting except stearin candles. He would sit in his room and read with a stearin candle on the table. We only had kerosene lamps in our room in the small town, but he would not read by their light. Later, when there was electricity, he wouldn't read by that either. And he read an incredible amount. When he came (which would be for a few weeks each year), he would go every day to the public library, which, as I recall, was quite respectable. I was his favorite grandchild and always asked him questions. He was very willing to talk to me and would take me with him when he went to the library. There I would read anything that was at hand. I was six or seven at the time. I read Pisarev, Belinskii, and anything else. I remember that I would walk along the street and wonder, "What does it all mean? Turgenev [probably means Belinskii – ed.] says that what is reasonable is real and what is real is reasonable." And I would ask each acquaintance who passed by why this was the case? Why? What does it mean? It is real, really exists. But Turgenev said what is real is rational. This was a curious thing but it helped to develop a passion for reading in me, although later this passion became weaker because of rationalistic principles. In my childhood and youth, however, I read an incredible quantity and, of course, too early! Why, when I was only 11 or 12, I had already read all of Dostoevsky, all of Turgenev, and what's more, several times. And I read at a rate that I am now entirely incapable of. I remember, for example, that I read Dostoevsky's *Crime and Punishment* from cover to cover in one day. I was ten at the time, probably, and we went to bed fairly early. In this way I accumulated a great store of something which, if it wasn't knowledge, was at least akin to knowledge. I think that it influenced me. And since Pisarev, Dobroliubov, Belinskii, and Mikhailovskii passed through my hands, they prepared the way for a particular political orientation.

H: But did your grandfather have any definite influence on your outlook?

GD: As I already mentioned, he was a great patriot. He began to read *Novoe Vremia* while it was still a liberal newspaper. Until 1905 he followed the entire evolution of *Novoe Vremia*. By 1905 he was already a reactionary and an antisemite. Then he suddenly underwent a complete reversal and became a passionate anarchist, you might say. He did not have any positive program. But a hatred of the tsar and of autocracy appeared suddenly like a revelation. On this ground, he was completely at odds with his only son, my uncle, who was a general and professor in 1905 and at the beginning of 1906. My uncle maintained his monarchist convictions, and when my grandfather made a derogatory comment about the tsar, Uncle said, "Poppa, please don't talk about the tsar like that!" To which he answered, "Well, I forgot that I was speaking with a bureaucrat. I am speaking with a bureaucrat!" "Papa, I am not a bureaucrat, I am a scholar!" You see, it was eccentricity, but still interesting. The late Dan accused me of a tendency toward adventurism. Perhaps this adventurous spirit (of which there was no trace in either my father or my mother) was inherited from my grandfather with his peculiarities – if, of course, there is such a thing as heredity.

H: And your mother?

D: It is difficult to say, although she was and remains an active woman in my eyes. I inherited a great deal from her. But, of course, this may be my own conceit or partiality. I think, rightly or wrongly, that I received from her what I regard as my ability to think and reason calmly, even in highly critical situations. She remained calm and logical even in the most tragic situations. She suffered deeply, but externally she always appeared tranquil and premeditated. Their marriage was exceptionally happy. I don't remember, I don't think, a single instance when either of them said so much as a sharp word to the other. And after my father's death, if one of her sons would say something sharp to her, she would say, "Your father never spoke to me like that." After my father's death, she wanted to commit suicide.

H: When did he die?

GD: In March 1914. When he died, I was not with him. I was in Moscow. I arrived later, and my brothers told me that he had died. My mother, for some reason, kept her composure. My older brothers knew that she wanted to commit suicide. They had talked to her about it, and afterwards she said "Very well, I will stay alive if you promise to stay with me." We all promised, and therefore I moved from Moscow to Kazan and finished my university studies there. The most striking thing which she said to me later, and she said it in an entirely placid way, was, "You see, I don't know whether or not God exists. Is there a life after death? But there must be, because if I had no hope of ever seeing Petia (her husband) again, I could not go on living, and I must live for the children." This was said without any anguish or dramatics. It was entirely calm reasoning behind which extremely deep suffering lay hidden.

H: How old was your father when they got married?

GD: They were almost the same age, 25 or 26, I think. I forget. There was a family legend to the effect that, soon after they married, they were both walking down the street when a mullah, a Tatar holy man, approached them (Kazan is 40 percent Tatar). He was so touched by the sight of them that he stopped and blessed them in the Moslem fashion. The legend was that this extra, Moslem blessing added to the family's happiness.

H: What was your mother's education?

GD: She was graduated from a women's *gimnazium*, the same one where Aleksander Fedorovich Kerenskii's father taught Russian.[4]

H: He was an inspector?

D: Yes, later. It was the Marinskaia Women's *Gimnazium* in Kazan. One other thing should be noted. Among the Russian intelligentsia there were various orientations: German, French, and, within a narrower circle, English. This was also the case in Russian science. As a rule, Russian professors traveled constantly. Those who were not involved specifically in Russian disciplines as a rule went abroad every year. Some would go primarily to France, others to Germany, still others to England. Professor Kustov, my teacher, went to all three. In our family, on my mother's side, there was a certain French tradition. It is a curious coincidence – since childhood I had a particular love for everything French. Possibly this was because I learned the rudiments of French, so to speak, from my mother. I learned to read French and could speak French somewhat. Later, while reading the memoirs of my great-grandfather, Serge Mikhailovich Glinka, I learned that in childhood he was so taken by everything French that he convinced himself that he was not the son of his parents, but a French child. I think that it was in the family, though I didn't recognize it for many years. I should add that this genealogical tree made no particular impression on either me or my brothers. It was said there that some ancestor saved some Polish king while he was hunting, and was made a nobleman as a result. Heaven knows when that was, perhaps the twelfth or thirteenth century. It was interesting. But unlike a distant relative through that same great-grandfather from a different line who is still alive and completely imbued with stories of ancestral glory, my brothers and I had none of that. Naturally enough, however, there was a very strong interest in music. To be related to Glinka, the father of Russian music, was sure to stimulate interest. Moreover – and this was also a family legend, no doubt, since we were not direct descendants – I was alleged to look very much like the composer. I looked at portraits, and noticed no resemblance.

H: How long had your father and mother been married when their first children were born? There were seven children in your family?

GD: I was the third. I think that the oldest son was born a year later. He died ten years ago. He was a professor – a specialist on the history of Eastern art – and a symbolist.

H: So he would have been born in around 1881?

GD: No, I was born in 1887, so he was born in 1884. My second brother was born in 1885. Then births every two years, the next in 1887, then 1889, then 1891. Then there was another gap.

H: The oldest brother was Boris?

GD: Yes.

H: And the second?

GD: Petr. Then Dmitrii in 1889, Sergei in 1891, Vsevolod in 1894, and a daughter, Mariia, in 1897, who died while still a girl. There might be some mistakes in my reckoning. I was born in November, and two of my brothers in December. There was two years' difference.

H: Of these children, who, in addition to you, became a revolutionary, and specifically a Social Democrat?

GD: My older brothers were Social Democrats, or socialists in any case. Petr, in particular, was involved in socialist circles. This is perhaps worth noting, because the Bolshevik literature, particularly that of the 1920s, includes various descriptions of my involvement in such-and-such a circle or in such-and-such an event, where in fact there was nothing of the kind. I believe that they are referring to my brother Petr. Moreover, unlike the rest of us, he was a classicist, so to speak; he studied in a *Realschule*. Dmitrii, on the other hand, did not become a socialist. He was born in 1889, so that in 1905 he was still a *gimnazium* student. He was very musical; played the violin, and was not interested in politics. Vsevolod was a socialist but did not become a Social Democrat. In 1917 he became part of a special group of independent socialists forming in Kazan. I believe that, in terms of intellectual quality, they were the most outstanding group in Russia. They were the flower of the young teaching staff of Kazan University. Those who survived were all more or less brilliant scholars.

I should add that my brothers and I set a kind of Russian record, because three, or in effect four, of us became university professors: Boris in history of art, I in history, Vsevolod in law, and Petr was on his way to a professorship at the Military Medical Academy in Petersburg. So one family gave four future professors. This points to a certain tradition, because, despite the absence of philosophical or ideological conversation, the intellectual level in my family was high. It was certainly not a philistine environment.

H: In what year did you enter school?

GD: First I became a normal *gimnazium* student.

H: Prior to that, did you study at home?

GD: Yes.

H: Until around 12 or 13?

GD: Up to the age of ten. Students were normally accepted into the first form at ten. But I took the examination for first form when I was still nine, which wasn't strictly supposed to be. But apparently I made such an impression that I was assigned to first form. At that time, however, we were not yet living in the provincial capital, and they didn't want to send me, so in effect I was ten when I entered the *gimnazium*. But I went straight into second form.

H: Did the teachers you had at home have an influence on you?

GD: Not a great deal. Doubtless our teacher had a touch of liberalism. I don't know the facts of his life, but, in hindsight, on the basis of some subsequent general impressions, I would guess that he was one of those teachers (and there were many) who were sent off to small towns because of their freethinking. As far as I can recall, he was more than just a humble district schoolteacher. He could not have had a definite influence.

H: This is a peculiar question, but I am basing it on my personal experience. When you entered the *gimnazium* in around 1897, did you display any interest in social problems? Of course, a boy of 10 has had no social experience, but there could already be some inclinations toward social problems.

GD: I had no such inclinations the first two years. At that time I dreamed of becoming a missionary. Until the age of 12, I was very religious, although I did not particularly like church or the ceremonies, which I didn't care much about. Somewhere or other I heard a passionate sermon by a missionary priest, and I thought the idea of missionary work very attractive.

H: What was the situation at home?

GD: It was formally religious, but there was no special piety. So I think that it was simply my own emotional attitude. I don't recall any special religious influence.

H: What did becoming a missionary mean for you?

GD: I don't know what it meant. Going somewhere, preaching something to someone, to change into something, and the rest.

H: So it was like, for example, the Red Cross or social service?

GD: I don't believe that I had a clear notion. To stand there – like this monk or priest whom I heard – and to convince people of something good . . .

H: How would you describe your first two years in the *gimnazium?* Were the boys quiet, energetic, or undisciplined?

GD: They were average. I was not particularly quiet. I had a trait then which remains even now. In speaking to another, the *gimnazium* students always used the informal form thou [*ty*]; I always kept my distance. Mother was constantly mentioning this. I was the only boy in the *gimnazium* who always used the polite form *vy*. It was like that with me. It was very hard for me to enter into too-simple relationships. And with the *vy*, I had very friendly relationships, though it has always seemed curious to me, even now, that a boy of 10 or 11 should have such gentlemanly manners. I should add that in this respect I was similar to my father. I conclude from this that his real father did in fact influence his upbringing, because once my oldest brother said, "I think that our father is a prince – look how he walks!" He was tall, approximately the same height as I am, and had very good manners, that is, manners that could come only from a very good upbringing, and his father had doubtless paid attention to that.

H: Could you describe your first two years in the *gimnazium?* Your relationships with the teachers and students?

GD: My relationships with the other students were very correct, but I kept my distance. Beginning in the third form, I had a peculiar friendship with a real character. He was the German teacher, Baron, a well-educated German who had written a German-language textbook. He had a penchant for funny little facts. He was always taking some word as an example and speaking of linguistic origins (which awakened in me a great interest in linguistics). But he was highly eccentric, and would make utterly fantastic comparisons. I remember one: "*Lisitsa* in German is *Fuchs*, which comes from the Greek *alotex.*" I asked "Aleksandr Dimitrievich, how can that be, *alotex-Fuchs?*" "Very simple: *lotex, otex, Fuchs....*" This made a real impression on me. But, in general, I can't say that any of the teachers had a great influence on me then. This was to change later.

H: Did you have friends with whom you were spiritually close?

GD: No, there was the distance and therefore more an element of loneliness.

H: Now, when you were between 10 and 12, what was your relationship with your older brothers like?

GD: You see, there were six of us. And six brothers naturally divided into two groups: the three older ones and the three younger ones. And they referred to each other that way. I was always very close to my two older brothers. There was a kind of friendly competition between me and my oldest brother. I would immediately want to know whatever he knew, though he was three years older and hence three forms ahead of me in the *gimnazium*. So, he was studying geometry, and although it was early for me to learn geometry, I had to know the same things he did. So I spent several days devouring an entire textbook. And then, in a friendly, good-natured way, I would ask him something, and he would say such-and-such, and I would say, "You are taking a year to learn this, and I will know it in three days." Yet, our relationship was very good. Petr and I, on the other hand, tended to play together more. Most of our games were rather strange. We would run around the room together and imagine that there were Indians or savages or that we were on an adventure, and so forth. One of us would say something, the other would then add something, and so on. This was before we entered the *gimnazium*. In the *gimnazium* we studied, and there was no more of that. I have deliberately separated the first two years, because an important change occurred after that. Still, there is one thing about these first two years in Kazan that I should mention. My second year in Kazan, my father was transferred to Simbirsk from Kosmodemiansk. In the spring I had the measles, and then an inflammation of the lungs. It was one of the most pleasant experiences I had ever had, because I had never been sick. I fell asleep. Sometime later I woke up and saw my mother standing next to me. How could it be that she had traveled from Simbirsk to Kazan in a single night? There was no direct way; the trip by railway involved a transfer. It turned out that I had been unconscious for eight days and was critically ill; my mother told me later. My father's reaction was extremely unrestrained – when the news arrived that my life was in danger, he became very upset. My mother said that it was the only time she ever saw him cry. I never suspected that I was in danger. I simply fell asleep and woke up, and saw that there was ice on my chest and my mother was standing there. It was like a miracle to have appeared overnight. I slept for eight days. They fed me my favorite foods. I didn't go to school and could read: I clearly did some crazy things, for example, lying in bed I read Dostoevsky's *The Idiot* five times in a row.

H: This was approximately in 1899?

GD: It would have been the spring of 1899. I cannot say precisely how this affected me, but I am convinced it agitated me a great deal. I cannot even now explain why I wanted to, but I did read *The Idiot* five times in a row.

H: Your parents then moved to Simbirsk? In 1897 or 1898, therefore, you had already begun to live in the *progimnazium?*

GD: No, my grandmother, my mother's mother, took up residence in Kazan, and thus we lived in Kazan together. So the situation remained more or less as before. When my father was transferred, my parents did not want to move us and disrupt our education. They let us finish the year in Kazan, and then brought us to Simbirsk. That was when I was in the fourth form, in 1899 to 1900. This year marked a sort of watershed, because I became acquainted with a boy in my class, whom I got to know. This acquaintance without doubt had a great influence on me. He came to a very dismal end, but that is not so important. His last name was Znamenskii and his mother was a very original person. I met her only a few times. She gave a very courageous impression. I later learned that her father was a prominent Socialist Revolutionary. The father was of the middle land owning class and nonpolitical; he led a very disorderly life. The mother transmitted her heritage in differing degrees to her children. So I got to know this boy who had already read various "liberation" writers with awareness and was in some circles. He didn't introduce me to them right away, but suggested that I could participate the next year. But the next year I was already in Kazan. It was here that revolutionary ideas and the aim of changing the existing order first appeared before me in concrete form. And there was another thing, in an entirely different direction, which made an enormous impression upon me at that time and played a prominent role in my life: for the first time I went to a concert, and what a concert it was! Joseph

Hoffman came to Simbirsk.[5] It was incredible. I am self-taught. I began to take up music in the craziest way. Somewhere I found an old book of music and started to play, getting lost, of course, and muddling through somehow. I retain some of the methods of this period of mad musical passion even now. These were two big impetuses in different directions, but neither was ever lost. The two persisted through life. Perhaps you could say that there were three, the third being related to the subsequent influence of revolutionary politics. So the influences were revolutionary politics, art, and science; each occurring at a different period of my life. In this respect, the year in Simbirsk, 1900 to 1901, when I was in the fourth form, was extremely significant.

H: This fellow Znamenskii . . . did he call himself a Socialist Revolutionary at this time?

GD: He was involved only a short time. Many decades later I learned what actually happened. While still a boy, he became a drug addict, and apparently never finished the *gimnazium*. He didn't follow me, but for other reasons, moved to Kazan, so our friendship continued for a while. But we were going in different directions and he had to drop out of the *gimnazium*. He was visiting brothels. He would drop out of sight for several days, living in brothels. So our acquaintance was short-lived. But in Simbirsk, our acquaintance was a great influence on me.

H: How did this pivotal year specifically affect your reading, conversations, and so forth?

GD: At this point I should mention another aspect, because two influences overlapped at this point. In essence this was the only serious influence a teacher had on me, as far as I can remember. When I returned to the fifth form in Kazan, my mathematics teacher was Nikolai Nikolaevich Parfent'ev, a rather unique person. His name is mentioned in the Soviet literature and doubtless in the *Great Soviet Encyclopedia*. He was unusual even in his external appearance, because he was of Sartish origin – a tribe in Turkestan. While a *gimnazium* teacher, he was a Privat-Docent at Kazan University, and this happened but rarely. During these years my abilities were clearest in mathematics. I have mentioned how I was carried away for a few days by geometry, and so forth. He began to notice me and often, when classes were over, we would walk together and talk. He was a socialist, as I learned later. But he made no attempts to influence me politically or to talk about politics. We talked about various things, primarily scientific subjects. He once advised me to read a collection of articles by Ernst Mach which had appeared in Russian translation.[6] And Mach had an entirely unexpected effect upon me, the reverse of what happened to most Mrxist It was Mach who made me a Marxist. In the first place, I began to think about the economic principle of thought, about the form of knowledge and thought. At that time I could already read German and knew Mach's *Mechanics* (I don't know when I obtained it), where he demonstrates the development of the ideas of mathematics and applied mathematics in accordance with new observations and experiments. These were the absorbing ideas which attracted Marx's attention in his time. In what sense,

I don't know. But in Marx's notebook, which Riazanov later gave me to read, there is a comment about Mach to the effect that he began to realize that something as pure as mathematics or applied mathematics is related to politics. And when I first encountered Mach's thought, I felt the same as Marx. Probably I was the only case of reverse development, but this played a prominent part in 1905 to 1906.

It is hard for me to make precise chronological distinctions, but I want to note one more rather strange trait. My relationship with my parents was always excellent. Well, sometimes, as a boy I would say something bad and my mother would get angry. But from the time that I left Simbirsk for Kazan, I felt a stubborn desire to be independent. Life at home began to weigh heavily upon me because of the concerns I had there. The idea would not leave me, that I should earn enough to be able to live independently if necessary. And throughout school, I was always first, a straight A student. It was customary for the teachers to give work to the better students and to recommend them as helpers or coaches for the less capable or younger students. Beginning in the fifth form, I began to take on lessons. And it was really so that I could live independently if necessary.

H: What did this mean for you? Was it social conscience?

GD: I think that it was a further development of my need to have a distance between myself and people. There have been extremely few cases in my life in which this distance has not been kept. Take the Mensheviks, for example. Most of them began to use *ty* even in Berlin – Lydia Osipovna [Dan], Rafail Abramovich,[7] Boris Ivanovich [Nicolaevsky], and so forth. My relationship with the late Dubois was particularly friendly, but this was a unique exception, so to speak.[8] I could count the exceptions on my fingers. Of course, I exclude the German Social Democratic Party, where the informal usage was the customary form of address. There, friend or not friend, even bitter enemies would use "thou." There are long-standing traditions in France, for example, where members of the same profession, such as lawyers, address one another informally. The reason for my behavior could perhaps be determined through psychoanalysis. If this had been the result of personal friction with people, it would be another matter, but this was not the case. Thus, as soon as I graduated from the *gimnazium* I left Kazan so as to be able to live alone. I had a buddy who was an engineer, and there were two or three other such cases, but aside from that I didn't desire to be with people. I don't know, but can confirm it myself as an inherent peculiarity of mine.

And this peculiarity, incidentally, explains why I didn't participate in any of the *gimnazium* circles. I had a cousin by the name of Nikolai Ivanovich [Dankerov], a somber-looking fellow, tall – much taller than I – and older, probably eight years older. Doubtlessly eight years older – when I entered the *gimnazium*, he had already graduated from it. In effect, he was the most prominent figure in the Kazan Social Democratic organization which at first was, so to speak, a general Social Democratic organization and subsequently a Bolshevik one. I'm referring here to the years prior to 1904 . . . years of development for me, during which I spent a good time reading, as

I had no need to work. Later I formed the opinion that in such a prerevolutionary period, apart from the conscious development of thoughts, ideas, perceptions, and of certain political convictions, some element beyond rationality is at work. It was as if there were revolutionary bacilli in the air, and without people having any real grasp of things, without any revolutionary formulations that registered as intellectual convictions, a rebellious mood and sense of expectation had developed and spread from one person to another. I can't say that I had already become deeply interested in the workers' movement, in strikes, and so forth. But in any case a kind of excitement, expectations, and a [psychological] need for change had set in. In the summer of 1904 my cousin decided I was sufficiently adult and mature. Even before this, I should tell you, he had discussed ideas with me and given me various book concerning Marxism, so that I already had some conception of it. The books confirmed what I considered correct in the ideas of Mach. In 1904, my cousin gave me the first volume of *Das Kapital* to read. And later, during the summer, when we were at our dacha, he decided it was time I did some work. And he began to tell me about the illegal organization [to which he belonged].

At this time the banquets started (this was in 1904; I was now in the eighth form of the *gimnazium*.)[9] I began to attend the banquets, and found myself moving into a different circle of ideas.

And now I want to explain why I didn't participate in any of the *gimnazium* circles.

H: Yes, that's precisely what I wanted to ask . . .

GD: I didn't participate because from the fifth form on I was in close contact with people considerably older than myself who, so to speak, satisfied my need for social and political interests. I don't know . . . but I think, am almost certain, that there were [student] circles in my *gimnazium.* I simply knew nothing about them, took no interest in them, because whatever needs I had in this regard were satisfied, on the one hand, by these older people, and on the other, by my cousin and the friends who often came to visit him, including the theoretician Vladimir Viktorovich Adoratskii[10] . . . I was associated with people so much older than myself that during this period of 1904 to 1905, I – just think, a student from the eighth form of the *gimnazium* – was invited to a "coalitionary" conference of public figures attended by socialists, several professors, several lawyers – and an eighth-form *gimnazium* student. It's possible – I am not certain, I can't remember precisely now – but I may even have had a disdainful attitude toward the *gimnazium* circles. I used to meet regularly with professors. Just imagine, Parfent'ev was not just a *gimnazium* teacher but Privat-Docent of a university. Then there was a physics teacher, with whom I was not on such close terms as with Parfent'ev, but who also was not simply a physics teacher but an exceptionally broadly educated man . . . Thus, I bypassed the usual phase of development, attended the banquets in the winter of 1904 to 1905, and after that gradually began to carry out various party assignments. And since by that time the organization had become distinctly Bolshevik and I knew only one Menshevik in Kazan, a rather hysterical type, we were then operating under the impression that there was really but one major party current.

H: I would like to pause now and discuss the following points. You remarked that during the summer of 1904 you were influenced by circles of older people – thanks to Parfent'ev and particularly to Dankerov. Secondly, you mentioned your own reading. Let us talk a bit about what you read during that period. You mentioned works on political economy and the history of the revolutionary movement. Apart from the impression Mach made on you, which you have already commented on, what works influenced you?

GD: During this period I read hardly anything about economics or the history of the revolutionary movement. I had great interest in books, not only in Mach's writings, but I can't readily come up with the titles of books I read . . . I don't recall them . . . About this time there was another eccentric fellow in Kazan who used to go around dressed in a strange cloak. He set up a small publishing house and translated from the German a pamphlet by the physiologist Ferberg. I can obtain the title for you, I have it written down somewhere. Later on he ordered for me (his business didn't bring in a profit) a translation of Mach's *Analysis of Sensations.* I started to read it but work on the translation was interrupted by the revolution. I also read a great deal about the history of revolutions.

H: What topics particularly interested you?

GD: In time the French Revolution became my predominant interest. I remember reading Aulard.[11] Naturally, everyone read him. And later . . .

H: When you read Aulard, had you already read Michelet?

GD: No, I hadn't.

H: Louis Blanc?

GD: I had read part of his book. After that, I devoted a good deal of my reading to the current literature in all the thick journals. Paradoxical as it may sound, the Marxist *Pravda* began to appear.[12] I think that with the exception of Mach, nothing I read exerted a great influence on me.

H: Did some fantasies about the French Revolution, about its heroes, say, particularly strike your imagination?

GD: No.

H: This was not a major factor?

GD: Perhaps . . . I felt an affinity . . . Naturally, here Aulard played a role . . . Those of my comrades who were nihilists [i.e., read nihilist literature] became more Russian-oriented. Yes . . . Then there was philosophical literature. My cousin included it in the preliminary work he assigned to me, said it was . . . obligatory for everyone. Then I read Franck's *History of Materialism* and I read Kant . . . At this time a German woman had started a book business and sold works in German (the local stores had only works in Russian). I bought books at her place, began to read in German, and at this point I came under a truly great influence. I read practically all of Nietzsche. His works made an enormous impression on me.

H: What specific ideas and conceptions did you draw from him?

GD: I can tell you that for a time it was as if I was possessed by Nietszche. For example, "I teach you not love for your fellow man but love for remote objects and symbols." I still remember this even though I haven't reread Nietszche since then. As for other philosophical writings . . . I read Descartes . . . read the history of philosophy.

H: Did you feel the need to try and construct a systematic world view? Or did you simply read individual works the ideas of which you found interesting at least from a critical standpoint?

GD: I didn't have a need for a systematic world view. No.

H: And did you feel that this attitude was entirely proper?

GD: Yes, although afterward I went through a brief period of orthodoxy . . .

H: Was this after you read the works we discussed?

GD: Yes. I became an orthodox Marxist after I read the first volume of *Das Kapital* . . . and then Kautsky, and the other teachings of Karl Marx . . .

H: Did the history of Russia hold great interest for you?

GD: Of course, although I was especially drawn by the West.

H: And what did this signify, this particular attraction of the West?

GD: Well, interest; I was drawn to the history of ancient Greece.

H: What had you read about the history of the workers' movement?

GD: Some books in translation. I can't recall the titles now.

H: Apart from the titles of the books, what ideologies, ideas, events interested you?

GD: I simply don't remember at all.

H: Had you read Babeuf? *The History of the Commune?*

GD: I can't say when I read *The History of the Commune.* Later on, but I can't say just when. It's one of the books that made a profound impression on me. Then I became interested in syndicalism.

H: This early?

GD: Yes, but the French form of syndicalism. I had read a book about it, I don't recall who the author was. Then I noted certain curious phenomena which attracted my attention. (Things like this generally intrigued me.) For example, as a matter of policy, in the French syndicalist unions the higher administrative organs customarily had an even number of members – six, eight, etc. – to avoid having close majorities. A total membership of five, say, might well split 3 to 2, but a membership of six would have to split by at least 4 to 2 for there to be a majority. This sort of thing made a great impression on me. Subsequently, in another sphere, I came into contact with a set of completely new terms for dealing with many issues.

H: I want to concentrate now on your attraction toward Marxism. What aspects of Marxism most appealed to you?

GD: I think it appealed to me on various levels. Undoubtedly, owing partly to the affinity I felt for Mach's ideas, what mattered most to me was economic materialism and the idea, bound up with it, that in Marxism we had found a method on which to base, solidly and scientifically, our desire for – and the possibility of attaining – a distinct ideal. By the winter of 1904 to 1905 the Marxists among us had already started debating, not simply along Bolshevik-Menshevik lines, but on a more theoretical level, particularly when there were encounters between Social Democrats and SRs [Socialist Revolutionaries]. By this time some of the Social Democrats adhered to the view that Marxism was not a theory but a method. I was inclined to accept this viewpoint. What I found hard to digest was dialectics. Dialectics in this form seemed laughable to me.

H: But what made an impression on you? Was it the interpretation by Marxist theory of political and economic phenomena? You told me that even before the summer of 1904 Dankerov had given you Marxist literature to read or instructed you to do so.

GD: Yes, he had advised me to do that.

H: Apart from the first volume of *Das Kapital*, what Marxist works did your cousin give you? Plekhanov's writings?

GD: Yes, in particular *The Development of Capitalism in Russia* and *The Monistic View of History.*

H: Did he give you issues of *Iskra* to read?

GD: I didn't start reading *Iskra* until 1904 or 1905.

H: What about the period before this – when he began to advise you?

GD: I can't exactly say. He talked to me about party work, about joining an organization. It was in the summer of 1904, probably, that we had those talks. And then came a period which was limited, mainly, to the banquets (only a few of them were held in Kazan). And there were, so to speak, semilegal discussions, in particular a discussion between Social Democrats and SRs, which instilled in me a very negative attitude toward the SRs, mainly because the SRs [in Kazan] were not only weak but politically embodied the crudest type of SR mentality with their use of florid expressions and the like. Well, they weren't serious people. I can't say that . . .

H: But let's go into the period before 1904. You mentioned Beltov, mentioned *The Development of Capitalism in Russia.* You hadn't read any of Martov's pamphlets?

GD: These were illegal . . . I was afraid I'd be arrested . . .

H: So then, did your cousin discuss your reading with you?

GD: Yes. These talks didn't take up a great deal of time, but . . .

H: What ideas did he try to instill in you? I would like to know more about Dankerov. What sort of person was he?

GD: Above all, he was called a great conspirator. He never spoke at meetings. He did organizational work. He undoubtedly had decisive influence within a narrow circle of the party committee. Adoratskii had already become a theoretician. He literally worshipped Dankerov – and to such a degree that it became laughable. Like a monkey, he imitated Dankerov's manner of speaking and behaving. So you can see that Dankerov was always highly respected.

H: Was he about 26 years old at this time?

GD: Yes, 25 or 26. And he did something which I later realized had certain significance. He collected money both for the party organization and for the assistance of political prisoners – set up a kind of political Red Cross. Through this he made his way into a liberal bourgeois milieu to which he imparted Social Democratic ideas, a fact that is not without historical significance. He wasn't the only person to do such things, but I think he exerted great influence. He was a medical student, and since he was quickly arrested . . .

H: At Kazan University?

GD: Yes, so that his studies dragged on for a very long time . . .

H: Was he still a student at this time?

GD: Yes.

H: Wasn't he expelled?

GD: Temporarily.

H: Prior to this time, prior to the summer of 1904, had you also studied with Adoratskii?

GD: Yes, I think so. We were close relatives, were related through my mother's side of the family. And our families were very close. He visited us frequently and I used to go to his house almost every day. I remember that often he wasn't at home, and that when he returned he was always gloomy, sometimes even a bit rude. He actually managed to come up with a theoretical justification for his behavior. He pointed out that everyone has moods, sometimes good, sometimes bad, and said: "I want to be in a good mood all my life. Hence I transmit my bad mood to my environment."

H: Was Adoratskii also a student at this time or had he already completed his studies?

GD: He'd already completed them.

H: Did he also have talks with you? And if so, on what subjects?

GD: Yes, he used to talk . . . He talked more about music. He played the piano.

H: There is one last point on which I'd like to dwell. You said that when you read works on French history, the "history of the movement" had significance for you. Was this because you felt drawn toward the Russian workers' movement? I'm referring not only to the abstract ideas you derived from reading Marxist literature but to an emotional involvement. Did you experience this or not?

GD: No, at the time I didn't. Firstly, I should add to what I said about France that . . . This has to do with the French Revolution. Namely, that the history of the peasantry, particularly in the eighteenth century – in the works, say . . . of Karelin – this did interest me. As for phenomena of Russian life, I developed a keen interest in the lives of vagabonds. This didn't come about through Gorky's influence, although in one respect I felt it, but as a result of my own personal experience.

H: Concretely, what did this mean?

GD: I'll tell you how it happened. One evening as I was walking down a street in Kazan, a beggar approached me. I wanted to give him money. At first he took it. I don't know how much . . . no great sum . . . I simply don't remember. Then he said to me: "It's not money I need so much . . . Could you spare some underwear?"

Second interview

H: Now we will discuss the revolution of 1905 in Kazan. Beginning with the "January Days," what impression did they make on you?

GD: January 1905 is also a good starting point because of an episode which, in my opinion, was very typical of those times. In addition, it was of particular importance. After January 9 in Petersburg there was increased ferment everywhere of course, including the universities. There was a large meeting at Kazan University. I earlier mentioned Parfent'ev, my mathematics teacher, who was at the same time a Privat-Docent at the university. He did something entirely out of the ordinary: he came to this student meeting and declared his solidarity with the students.

H: When was this?

GD: In January 1905. I am not certain of the date; it might have been in the first few days in February. At first it seemed as though there would be no repercussions. But not long before our *gimnazium* classes were over, prior to the final exams, we learned that the upshot of the Parfent'ev affair was that he was fired from the teaching staff of Kazan University. Although it cannot be said that all my fellow-students had revolutionary inclinations, there was enormous indignation. At the very end of classes, I organized a general meeting of all the students in my form, delivered what was probably a very impassioned speech, and made a proposal which was adopted. We declared a strike, and unanimously voted that if Parfent'ev did not remain a Privat-Docent at the university, we would refuse to take the final exams. This was in May, before the final school-leaving exams in the *gimnazium.* Since it was the eighth and last form, there was a great risk for the *gimnazium* students: if they did not complete their studies, they would be unable to enter any higher educational institution. On the other hand, the refusal of an entire class to take the final exams was regarded as an incredible scandal both inside and outside the *gimnazium,* so that the strike produced an enormous impression.

I was not let in on the details of the talks which were conducted between the administration of the *gimnazium* and the Ministry of Public Education, but the result was that the *gimnazium* director called me into his office and said that he had clarified the situation and gave his word that Parfent'ev would remain a Privat-Docent. On the basis of this solemn promise (and I believe that the director acted entirely in good faith), I believed him. We called off the strike and agreed to take the final exams. But we were duped, as was the director, no doubt, because two or three months later Parfent'ev was tranferred from Kazan to some remote town where there was a *gimnazium* but no university. A Privat-Docent did not have a steady salary, so that his income as a *gimnazium* teacher was the basis of his existence. In other words, Parfent'ev was not formally fired, and in this sense the promise was kept, but he was in effect removed from the staff of Kazan University. In essence, my recollections of the *gimnazium* period terminate at this point, since these final examinations in effect marked the end of my schooling. Aside from a period of a few months in the second half of 1905, it was only much later, in several years, that I returned to university studies.

Immediately after the *gimnazium* exams, I devoted myself entirely to party and political activity, beginning with the transport of *Iskra* from where it was received to the distribution point. I will mention one humorous episode. I would conceal a large package of *Iskra* under my shirt and calmly carry it about the city. Once, however, I apparently took too many copies, because, as I was walking along Gornaia Street, my belt broke, all the copies fell out, and the wind scattered them. I was able to collect them with the assistance of a policeman, who evidently hadn't seen where they had been and had simply decided to assist a young man. What was unpleasant for me was that after this episode I could no longer hide them under my shirt and had to cross the whole town carrying a large package of *Iskra* in my hands.

H: I would like to ask, first, who persuaded you to concentrate all your efforts on party work after you graduated? Or was it your own decision from the beginning?

GD: There was no one who could have influenced me in this respect. I cannot even say that my cousin did. History, circumstances and, of course, my already established convictions, were what influenced me. In the Kazan organization, there were no people who could have had a serious influence upon me. There were people who subsequently played a fairly prominent part, such as Lozovskii, who became a central figure in the international Communist trade-union movement. But, in 1905, I remember him primarily because, when several people would get together for a convivial evening, he would sing Jewish religious songs, and he sang very well.[1]

H: Another question in this respect: I recall that you said that the Kazan Social-Democratic organization was a Bolshevik organization in 1905. Did it not matter that *Iskra* was Menshevik at that time?

GD: It did not have the slightest importance, not the slightest! It was always a great delight when a shipment of *Iskra* arrived, and we distributed it as we would have distributed Bolshevik publications, which didn't arrive during those months. In general, this was in accord with the overall mood. At that time, all the members of the party organization (although I can only speak confidently about the Kazan organization) continued to regard themselves as members of the same party as the Mensheviks. It was only a difference in opinion. As I already mentioned, there was a Menshevik girl, not at all a serious person (how or why she became a Menshevik I don't know), who would come to meetings and speak . . . It was all one party, but, well, so-and-so had such-and-such a bias. . . .

H: How did you regard this split and the difference between the Bolsheviks and the Mensheviks at that time?

GD: Doubtless it was a very one-sided view, because, although current Bolshevik literature did not reach us, we became familiar with writings like Lenin's *What Is to Be Done* and *One Step Forward, Two Steps Back*. Later, since the makeup of the organization was Bolshevik, some representative of the central organization would come from time to time and deliver a report.

H: Do you recall who these people were?

GD: I cannot, because they were all anonymous figures. I believe that Stroev-Desnitskii came once, or in any case I met him then, but I don't recall if he gave a report.[2] They were all Comrade What's-his-name, or something like that! Heaven only knows who was who! If you met one of them again by chance, you wouldn't know who he was. There are a number of people about whom I still can't say who they were. A few I knew fairly well, such as Comrade Nikolai, who came to Kazan and was fairly prominent in the organization there, and later in Petersburg after the revolution [of 1905], he was a writer. I learned that he was Konovalov, a provocateur, a fact which was discovered after he committed suicide in 1911. But many of these people were forgotten and our paths did not cross a second time. In any case, I should say that none of the people who came to Kazan made any great impression on me. On the other hand, all the information and interpretation of disagreements, it later became clear to me, was presented in a very simple and tendentious form.

Here a psychological aspect comes in. In general, I feel that two factors (which are not always taken into account) were involved in the original split between the Bolsheviks and Mensheviks. One was the influence of local conditions. It was natural that where there was an established Bolshevik organization, new members became Bolsheviks, and where there was a Menshevik organization, they became Mensheviks. So there were a lot of random choices. Or more precisely, there was no choice. You joined what was there. The other factor was psychological. And I would not claim that I ever thoroughly overcame this psychology completely. On the Bolsheviks' side there was logic. Even if it was sometimes primitive, it was usually rigorous. You might say unilinear; the path from the premises to the conclusion was always entirely clear. If you more or less accepted the premises, you would arrive at the same conclusions. With the Mensheviks, there was always some sort of interference, so to speak; unexpected and not easily understandable factors would intervene. Even then, that is when I was a very young man, I could not understand a concept of revolution [the Menshevik one] according to which we should struggle, overcome, achieve a provisional government, and then not participate in it, leaving it to others to rule the country. This always seemed highly artificial and abnormal, so to speak. I will say frankly, I still have not freed myself from this view. With the Bolsheviks, however, everything was quickly reduced to an extremely clear form: an armed uprising, a provisional government, a constituent assembly. Later, logically enough – because the proletariat constituted a very small part of the population – the provisional government was to be a democratic dictatorship of the proletariat and peasantry. This scheme was attractive to me and to very many others. As a result, there was no need for self-reappraisal in 1905, the more so in that the split with the Mensheviks seemed like a temporary situation. I believe that everyone was certain that, as soon as possible, there would be a unification congress, and party unity would be restored. Virtually no one had an idea of the deep roots of the disagreements, which became apparent only later. It is said that they were clearly perceived by Axelrod, and that Trotsky had something to say about them, but this didn't reach us.[3]

H: How let us return to the Social-Democratic organization in Kazan at that time, in the spring and summer of 1905. What did it amount to?

GD: First, as might be expected, it was entirely Bolshevik in organization. It was headed by a committee, which had never been elected by anyone. It had arisen in some fashion, and when it needed to increase in size, did so by cooptation. Theoretically, the members of the committee were not known to the organization. Neither then nor later could I determine the makeup of the committee at the time I was working in the organization. Because of my relation to Danker, I knew a committee member, and later one or two more through him, but the overall composition remained unknown to me. But the members of the committee were divided according to function. There was an organizer, and a person in charge of propaganda or agitation. Sometimes these were in the charge of one person; sometimes there was a division [of responsibilities]. There was someone in charge of shipments and receipt of correspondence, and someone in charge of illegal printing or hectographing. Of course, each leader of a given sector was known to a small group of assistants chosen by him. For example, the one in charge of agitation would be in contact with the agitators, naturally enough. Very soon, however, things ran of their own accord. Essentially, everyone did as he wished, because events developed so tumultuously that it was necessary to react quickly. I don't remember that we ever received directives to say such-and-such, or to explain such-and-such in such-and-such a way. It was left up to us, so that, despite the strictness of Bolshevik principles, there was a good deal of independent action. I recall, for example, that there might be a person who handled some technical matters, but I don't know whether he was a committee member. Perhaps he was not a member but was designated by the committee for special functions. This was the general structure. And there were extremely few meetings of the members of the organization. In case of a special problem, for example, the unmasking of a provocateur or traitor, the committee would call together, by invitation, a number of people, by no means all the party local [members]. They were picked and invited by the committee.

H: Among what sectors of the population of Kazan did the organization find support?

GD: The workers and part of the intelligentsia. And certain professions were particularly easily involved. These included pharmacists and dentists, which can be explained largely by the fact that both groups were Jewish.

H: What about the workers?

GD: There were some, but, in my experience in 1904, I cannot say that there was any prominent worker. They were simply raw material to be worked with in groups or at May Day meetings, when they demonstrated. Later, in summer, when everything became much simpler, a meeting was set up somewhere out of town of several dozen workers. This was entirely a workers' audience. Most of the party apparatus, however, was of the intelligentsia. But some of those who arrived from elsewhere, such as Lozovskii, had been workers.

H: What did you do, in addition to transporting *Iskra?*

GD: The transport of *Iskra* lasted a very short time. After that I was an agitator among the workers.

H: Could you describe your impressions as an agitator? What were your successes, or lack of them? In particular, what were your impressions of the intellectual and psychological contacts that you had with your audience?

GD: That is fairly difficult to reconstruct. The contacts were essentially rather meager. For me, at any rate, party or organizational life proceeded as follows: a group of, say, four to six people would form, purely on the basis of friendship, out of the organization. These people would meet constantly, talk a great deal, and discuss current events. The party apparatus which was involved in setting up meetings would say that on such-and-such a date at such-and-such a place there was to be a meeting, with an anticipated audience of several dozen or perhaps a hundred workers, and that rapport needed to be established. So, without any special instructions, things would be handled of their own accord. Sometimes certain people would handle them, sometimes others.

H: What topics were brought up at the meetings?

GD: There were two topics, of course. The first was the overthrow of autocracy, and the second was the future, the socialist ideal.

H: Could you describe the second? In particular, what did it mean for the workers?

GD: I had a more definite line of argument later in Petersburg, when it was frequently necessary to speak right at the factories, amidst the tools and machinery. It was a very simple line, which could be instantly grasped. Here they are working together, creating a product by their joint collective efforts, and who is bossing them, who is exploiting them? The owner! The capitalist! That is why the workers live very badly. The capitalists live very well! Then the workers themselves would conclude, naturally, that all those who work should share in the fruits of their labor more or less equally, and that they should organize for this to come about. This primitive form of socialism was very readily grasped and required no special proof. Republican propaganda was sometimes more difficult, because, well, there was, perhaps, a semi-mystical conception of the tsar. There was still fear and cringing before the tsar. As for universal, equal, direct, and secret suffrage, this was not a rousing topic. It was a subject of propaganda, not agitation. The distinction between propaganda and agitation was drawn fairly clearly. Propaganda was discussions in small groups. It was more businesslike and peaceful.

H: Were you in such a group?

GD: I did not have my own circle, but I would speak on occasion. Not more than that, especially in the summer, when we were not confined to indoors and there was pressure for agitational work; we had to agitate, arouse, stir, and so forth.

H: Until when did you remain in Kazan?

GD: Only until August. Then I moved to Petersburg.

H: What events come back most vividly in the period between January and August 1905?

GD: It is difficult for me to distinguish specific events. But various rumors or communications came to us from different quarters – about waves of strikes and so on – that created a powerful impression that we were "on the eve," that we were awaiting a revolutionary outbreak.

*   *   *

H: Under what circumstances did you leave Kazan?

GD: I would say it was because at that time I decided that for a Marxist it was natural to become an economist. Economics was very weak in the Russian universities. I don't recall what year it was, but some years prior to 1905, Witte, who was then Minister of Finance, organized a Polytechnic school in Lesnoi, a suburb of Petersburg, which had four faculties or divisions as they were called: electrical engineering, shipbuilding, economics, and some other one. This school, which was entirely independent of the Ministry of Public Education and was under the Ministry of Finance, was, one might say, more liberal than the other higher educational institutions. Here Witte's personal ambitions played a part, I believe. The school did in fact have an outstanding teaching staff. It was not easy to be admitted. But my record was unimpeachable – a gold medal and straight A's – and no exams were required for the economics division. In short, I was admitted without the slightest difficulty. Classes were to begin August 15. The school was virtually in the country, several kilometers from Petersburg. The students had very comfortable dormitories with individual rooms. And there was a good library.

For a short while, I went to classes, but even in September my chief concern was meetings, either in the school itself or in the city. It was the same at other educational institutions. This was something new; no one thought then that such actions could be forbidden, or that there could be arrests. At the meetings, there were mostly students. On the one hand, they would invite or bring in workers; on the other hand, some professors would sometimes speak or enter the debate, usually Kadets. This was somewhat later. For example, I debated Petr Struve there. I might add, I vanquished him completely. I suspect that he spoke more knowedgeably than I, but not in the spirit of the times.

H: Where did you live in Petersburg?

GD: At first in the dormitory of the Polytechnic Institute.

H: That was somewhat outside the city?

GD: Yes. But, even though I had a secret address in Petersburg, the wave of meetings required rapid organization of relatively large cadres of participants, and this was, obviously, virtually beyond the capacity of the organization. As a result, I lost contact with the organization. There was only one meeting at which I spoke independently, so to speak, without any mandate from the organization.

H: Where was this?

GD: In the Technological Institute in Petersburg, I believe. Someone came up to me and asked, "Comrade, you are obviously a Bolshevik, aren't you?" I said, "Yes." "And you are affiliated with an organization?" "At the moment, I have lost contact." "Well, you should join the board of agitators." So I ended up on the board of agitators. By then it had become impossible to study at the Polytechnic Institute, because it was necessary to appear not only at educational institutions, which was fairly burdensome in itself, particularly during a general strike when it was necessary to travel a great deal on foot; but now, in addition, I belonged to this board of agitators and also was specially assigned to the Narva district. This was where the Putilov works were. The thought of making the trip on foot from Lesnoi was inconceivable – it took a long time even by trolley. So I rented a room in the city itself.

H: Do you remember who was in the College of Agitators?

GD: Well, I remember Schwarz.[4] Again there were pseudonyms – Comrade Gavrila, Schwarz knows who he is, but so I didn't know last names. There was also Comrade Makar: a very interesting person, yet I never learned who he was. We met very rarely. Generally we would go to some specified location and receive orders: go to such-and-such a place. This soon took an entirely different form, and I am coming to serious history here. By the second half of October, the nature of the work had changed entirely, as a result of the formation of the Soviet of Workers' Deputies.

H: Perhaps you will get to this, but I would like to know your impressions of the background of the general strike of October.[5] Was it within the framework of the discussions of the board of agitators?

GD: I intend to talk about that. There are two aspects: the strike and the formation of the Soviets. On the basis of what I remember, I can state categorically that, although the Bolsheviks in Petersburg were at first against the strike and took a negative view of the Soviet, we, the rank-and-file workers, and everyone I knew, were either unaware of this or disregarded it. Together with the Mensheviks we called for a strike and for the election of Soviets. The party administration was more or less won over, and there were absolutely no disputes between the Bolsheviks and Mensheviks at that time. The overall conception of revolution remained, and was reiterated. But we were dealing with current tactical problems, the overthrow of autocracy – the time was coming for it, the wave of strikes was increasing, and so it had to be turned into a general strike. There was one very large meeting in the largest auditorium of the Polytechnic Institute. It was completely full; there were probably 1,500 people present. The Menshevik Vainshtein spoke, under the pseudonym of Zvezdin – a brilliant orator. We applauded as enthusiastically as the Mensheviks. He was opposed by the jurist, Professor Vladimir Matveevich Gessen, a Kadet, also a very good speaker.[6] Not knowing either Vainshtein or his party pseudonym Zvezdin, he said, "This brilliant speaker has said such-and-such and such-and-such, and yet I have my doubts. . . ." We of course supported Zvezdin in everything, completely disregarding the fact that he was not, so to speak, one of us, but a Menshevik. I cannot answer for all the people with whom I worked, but in the fairly wide circle in which I was active, this was the way it was. All disagreements were forgotten, and everything was concentrated on the present immediate problem, and that problem was conducting a general strike. And then, at some moment (this idea somehow cropped up and spread), to call for the formation of a Soviet, to elect deputies to the Soviet of Workers' Deputies. We visited the factories, and later became extremely angry at the Socialist Revolutionaries because they seemed more partisan than we. Even at that time there were reports in the newspapers about meetings, and we would learn that, after I had been in the Putilov works, in such-and-such a shop, had a resolution passed about electing deputies to the Soviets, and left, these damned Socialist Revolutionaries had come and had a resolution passed about the land [question] in accord with the SR program, and were proud of their huge success.[7] There were stormy and often rather curious scenes along these lines. Some years ago I reread what was printed in the contemporary press, and became convinced beyond a doubt that the Bolshevik organization first tended to be against a general strike, which it regarded as inopportune, premature, and remained suspicious of the Soviet.

H: I would like to ask about the level that you were at. Did you discuss matters with representatives of, say, the Petersburg committee, or with higher levels of the party or the Bolshevik organization? Do you recall discussions of the problem of a general strike around October 9 and 10, on the eve of the strike?

GD: We, that is our groups of agitators, dealt only with one representative of the Party committee, Comrade Makar. Possibly, Nikolaevskii or Schwarz know who he was; in fact, I never did really know if he was a member of the committee. Perhaps he was a member but had his own opinion, since at that time discipline was less important, but, in any case, there were no traces of the official Bolshevik line on the strike and the Soviet. It seemed of so little importance that, for example, someone might emphasize that the Soviet was not an agency of revolutionary self-government, but an auxiliary organ in the revolutionary struggle, so that, in any case, it must not incorporate any elements of power! I, at least, and those whom I met and spoke with, paid no attention to this. It seemed to us that what happened was perfectly natural: the Soviet of Workers' Deputies became in fact the center, and as a result, as I already indicated, our work was completely redirected.

H: Tell me about this.

GD: It changed as follows. Each revolutionary party, and Social Democracy was still regarded as two parties, so that it was the Bolsheviks and Mensheviks on the one hand and the Socialist Revolutionaries on the other, placed 30 workers each at the disposal of the Soviet of Workers' Deputies to carry out its assignments. I remember, though it needs to be checked, that altogether there were 90 of these workers. The Soviet met very often. The practice was that all these agents of the Soviet would attend its sessions. Decisions were made – calls to strikes, or simply some kind of resolution. For example, during the printers' strike there was a debate in the press about whether the strike should extend to the revolutionary press or not. Or, there would be the question of how to react to some lockout that was allegedly in preparation. Our task was, if a decision was made to take some action – to organize a demonstration or declare a strike – to go from factory to factory early the next morning and to call for the decision to be implemented. Sometimes we would discuss what had happened with the appropriate deputy, and clarify the meaning of this or that resolution, or when there was no specific call to action, sometimes we would simply go alone. From this moment until the arrest of the Soviet, all the activity was entirely concentrated on the Soviet and subordinated to it. Most of us, myself included, were arrested together with the Soviet.

H: Were you specifically assigned to factories or districts?

GD: As I said, I had [responsibility for] the Narva district, and especially the Putilov works, enormous works! Once I spoke there together with Comrade Trotsky. It was a very interesting episode, and one which almost ended unpleasantly for me. There were open-hearth furnaces at the factory, and a so-called open-hearth shop, whose workers were the rawest and politically most unenlightened (a fact I at first didn't know). Usually the strategy of conducting a meeting was as follows: one of the representatives of the Putilov works was Poletaev, a prominent worker, who was later to be a member of the Duma, and we would meet him and go into the plant with him.[8] Like here it was necessary to go through a checkpoint and display a badge; this was all arranged in advance. And so I spoke in this dingy shop, and at first everything went very well – I talked about various things. The workers seemed to like it, and there were approving remarks. But, because of my lack of experience and ignorance, I did not reckon with the psychology of this meeting, and cited the words of the *Internationale*. "No one can save you – neither God, nor tsars, nor heroes." Then things became wild. "So, he is against God and the tsar!" The crowd rushed toward me. I was standing on some sort of platform and continued to stand there, completely at ease. They stopped before me, then dispersed. Poletaev came up to me and said, "Good man! If you had not stayed calm and had taken to your heels, they would have killed you for sure!" In short, it was a serious matter. How could we deal with people who would not permit attacks on God and the tsar? The affair was discussed at various levels of the organization. I don't remember the details, but Poletaev spoke about it in the Executive Committee of the Soviet. They decided to send me there again with Comrade Trotsky. A large meeting, including workers of the open-hearth shop, was arranged for early in the morning.

Since there was no possibility of getting to the Putilov works early enough, Trotsky and I spent the night in Poletaev's apartment. Spent the night does not mean sleep. We talked the whole night without stopping. No one even thought of going to bed. Poletaev acquainted us in detail with the general feeling. Then the conversation gave way to various recollections.

Trotsky, in particular, told a fairly funny story. . . . Later, we went off to the factory. I don't recall other details. I remember that I said something after Trotsky. Poletaev opened the meeting with some introductory remarks which I have entirely forgotten because they were overshadowed by Trotsky's stunningly brilliant speech. Trotsky began by speaking of the existing order that ruled the country, of the people's lack of rights. Something needed to be done. He explained what democracy was, universal suffrage, the parliamentary system, and so forth. I listened and became excited. I sensed he was approaching the question of the tsar. And he did come to it. He said that there would be a parliament and elections. But who would head the government? Who headed it now? The tsar, Emperor Nikolai Aleksandrovich! Then, unexpectedly, he continued: the tsar, like all of us, is born of man and woman. He has two arms, two legs, one head – let him be like the rest, let him be called Mr. Nikolai Romanov, that will be enough for him! And the crowd roared, "Enough, enough of him!" At the Putilov works, monarchism was killed by this speech of Trotsky. It was fairly primitive, but the device, under the circumstances, was brilliant. Obviously, he had weighed and taken account of everything he had been told regarding the intellectual level and education of this portion of the workers. Once he had finished this educational and political speech, so to speak, we had to carry on with something. I said something to the workers, persuading them to do something, but I have entirely forgotten it. What I remember is only the night with Trotsky and his speech. And at that time I was a Bolshevik, and he was a Menshevik!

H: I am interested in one aspect of the Soviet's activity and of the workers' attitude which has remained fairly obscure: this is, of course, the question of economic strikes and the real attitude toward them on the part of the Bolsheviks and Mensheviks in the Soviet, and the leadership of both factions. What impressions do you have? Was it a spontaneous wave of strikes, and if so, to what extent?

GD: My overall impression is unclear. In general, however, the situation was as follows. There was a constant pressure from below toward organizing both political and economic strikes. The Executive Committee, however, was trying to hold things in check. Curiously enough, Trotsky was particularly skilled in doing this. He had a gift for proposing very moderate tactics with very resounding revolutionary rhetoric. When there was a strong trend toward organizing a bigger strike or some big demonstration which was forbidden and, it was feared, might lead to forcible repression and bloodshed, but which the Executive Committee did not as yet feel itself strong enough to oppose outright, Trotsky argued, and successfully argued, that the proposal should be rejected. But he did not say that we were not yet strong enough, and so forth. He used a completely different approach, namely, that it was all a provocation by the government, which regarded the moment as most favorable for them. We were not passing our resolutions, he continued, for the government's convenience. The proletariat would call for revolutionary action at a time when it felt it necessary, and not when it suited Mr. Witte. These were essentially moderate views phrased with a great deal of revolutionary glitter. Trotsky was not yet the chairman of the Soviet, but he spoke very often. Lenin spoke, but only once that I remember, and for some reason I was not present – either there was some assignment, or I simply couldn't spare the time. When I first saw him then, I remember clearly how he sat quietly and inconspicuously, looked and listened. The impression was that he wanted to comprehend as clearly as possible what these workers were like – what kind of people they were. It was clearly new for him. Later I met him personally.

H: When?

GD: In November. He spoke at a meeting of the Bolshevik faction. It was a large meeting; all the active members of the Petersburg Bolshevik organization were there. I would very much like to check what I remember about this meeting, since I remember certain details very well, but I have found nothing about it in the literature (though I can't say I know the literature exhaustively). Lenin gave a report on the agrarian question. (It is interesting that several months later Lenin proposed the nationalization of the land.) As I recall, what he said at that meeting was a great surprise to me (and not only to me). Of course, he primarily criticized the Socialist Revolutionary program, but at the same time he held to these cutoffs [*otrezki*] of the old Social-Democratic program.[9] And he mocked what the Socialist Revolutionaries were saying: "You have come up with crumbs and bits and cutoffs! Oh, but in reality it is a very important and serious matter." In other words, it is my recollection that, at that time, November 1905, Lenin had not yet revised his agrarian program. I am not certain of this, but perhaps some former Bolshevik who is still alive was at that meeting.

H: What about the specific question of the eight-hour working day, which, of course, was a principal issue in these economic strikes? Did you receive instructions indicating how this matter was to be handled, and so forth?

GD: No.

H: You have mentioned Vainshtein, Trotsky, and Lenin. What other figures, particularly Mensheviks, do you have impressions of from this period?

GD: I remember when the first prominent "foreign exiles," Vera Zasulich and Deich, returned. They were received triumphantly at a session of the Soviet, at the very beginning of its activity. As I remember, Trotsky gave the principal welcoming speech, and then there was some Bulgarian who entirely forgot that it was Zasulich and Deich who were being honored and who went on and on about Plekhanov and the affection that the Bulgarian proletariat had for him. He spoke Russian with a strong accent, and it was all about how the Bulgarian proletariat read, knew, and loved Plekhanov. This was all confusing and had little to do with Zasulich and Deich. But it was even worse when Viktor Mikhailovich Chernov greeted them on behalf of the Socialist Revolutionaries. His was a very unpleasant speech which angered us all, because his greeting went like this: "Today we are honoring Comrades Vera Zasulich and Deich, who are eminently worthy of this. But, comrades, we must not forget that it was not only they, the Emancipation of Labor, and the Social Democrats who were the revolutionary leaders. There was also the People's Will!" The rest of the speech was entirely given over to the praise of the People's Will and the Socialist Revolutionary party. So, his praise was rather peculiar. Still, he was applauded, of course!

H: What about the editorial board of *Nachalo,* aside from Trotsky, that is, Martov, Martynov, Dan, and so forth?

GD: I don't recall that any of them spoke in the Soviet. I had no contact at all with them at that time.

H: In general, in these months prior to the dispersal of the Soviet, did you notice any differences in the attitudes of the Bolsheviks and Mensheviks toward the Soviet as an institution or toward the organization of the working class?

GD: For us, the rank-and-file, or noncommissioned officers, so to speak, there was no difference. The Soviet was ultimately directed by the Executive Committee. Probably there were disputes within the committee, but they never got outside. The Bolsheviks had Bogdanov there, who was not a public speaker. I do not remember him speaking. Knuniants often spoke under the pseudonym of Petrov. Trotsky was there from the Menshevik side. Insofar as the work of the Soviet was concerned, there was complete agreement then. Perhaps they fought before the meetings, but it certainly wasn't noticeable!

We would go to hear Trotsky's speeches. I heard his address on permanent revolution, and it was remarkably beautiful.[10] What was terribly appealing, as I have noted in my memoirs, was his description of revolution spreading from one country to another and so forth. We Bolsheviks really liked this, and we applauded. On the next day, though, it was difficult to recall exactly what he had said. He was enormously successful wherever he spoke, even if he had no supporters there. He played an important role in the Soviet. It was natural that after Khrustalev's arrest it was he, Comrade Ianovskii [Trotsky], who became chairman.[11]

H: Does this absence of disagreements also apply to the trade-union movement? Were there any doubts?

GD: None. I was the speaker at the meeting at which the tailors' union was founded. I explained what a trade union was, why it was important, and so forth. The several hundred tailors who were present, who came from all over Petersburg, agreed and decided to organize a trade union.

H: Was there any question about whether the union should be party-affiliated or not?

GD: No. I don't believe that any of us gave it any thought. To us it was simply self-understood that any workers' organization would be under Social-Democratic influence. I would have been astonished to learn that there was any friction, say, between an organization and the Soviet or between trade unions and the party. To me, this would have been competely crazy. For what reason? Why? It must be kept in mind that this was a hurricane, a maelstrom, and that it wasn't necessary to sit and think. I am surprised that I or anyone else was able to read much at that time. But I even read things that I had not read before. For example, Bernatskii, an economist and professor at the Polytechnic School (who was a Menshevik Social Democrat at that time and subsequently a minister of one of the White governments), lent me *Die Neue Zeit*.[12] I fear that the library of the Polytechnic School lost several issues, because when I was arrested my apartment was searched and they were confiscated. I don't know whether or not they were returned to the library.

H: What were your impressions of the Social-Democratic press at that time? What publications did you read?

GD: Well, *Novaia Zhizn'* and *Nachalo*, of course.[13]

H: What were your impressions of the former?

GD: I would say that *Novaia Zhizn'* was more interesting and definite, on the one hand, and, on the other, that it caused some confusion. The confusion was that, unlike the usual Bolshevik straightforwardness, there was unclear talk about a union of Bolsheviks with mystics and metaphysicians – Minskii and others. I remember that I visited a very mediocre writer named Gordin with whom I had become acquainted earlier, because he was the husband of the daughter of the proprietress of the bookstore in Kazan where I would buy books. When I came to Petersburg, I would visit him. One evening when I was there the writer Gusev-Orenburgskii was present. (He wrote stories chiefly about the life of priests.) I don't know if he was a party member, but in any case he was regarded as, and considered himself, a Bolshevik. On that day an article by Lenin had appeared in *Novaia Zhizn'* (the article can be found in his collected works); it was an indirect answer to the Menshevik attack to the effect that the Bolsheviks were involved with all sorts of people, religious groups, and so forth. Lenin wrote that the party was opening up, entering the public arena and, naturally enough, could not be narrow and rigid in its composition. Its doors should be open to all and its membership could include religious people and metaphysicians and the like. There was nothing awful about this – we would digest it all. We staunch Marxists have strong stomachs! Or something like this. The subject of this article was brought up, and Gusev-Orenburgskii, who was probably a religious man, was completely enraged, and shouted, "I've had it, I don't want to be a product of Lenin's digestion!" I, of course, did not think as he did. I thought that there was something strange about the matter but didn't think it important. I guess I felt that otherwise there would be no newspaper, no money, etc. It was only later that this became a part of my general impression of Lenin's boundless opportunism.

H: What about *Nachalo?*

GD: My memory is not clear. I think that the Socialist Revolutionary paper was perhaps the most literate.

Now I will try to remember which of the prominent Mensheviks I saw at a distance, so to speak. I heard Sofiia Moiseevna Zaretskaia with whom I was to become very friendly much later.[14] It was on the day that the manifesto of October 17 was proclaimed, when the entire city became a single meeting. The crowd was enormous. There were tens of thousands on Kazan Square in front of the Kazan Cathedral. There were several of us. I remember Comrade Gavrilov (whom Schwarz knew well, I believe), someone else, and myself. We tried to speak but it was impossible to talk loud enough. Then a young, robust, and fairly stout woman some years our senior, appeared: it was Comrade Anastasia Nikolaevna, and she spoke in such a sharp metallic voice that it could be heard anywhere in the square. I later learned that she was Sofiia Moiseevna Zaretskaia. She was a first-class agitator and a very clever woman, not a mere demagogue. Trotsky was effective that day, but he contemptuously tore up the manifesto. That was hardly a Menshevik thing to do.

For us in those times, who do you think represented Menshevism? Not Martov and Dan. It was Trotsky who stood for Menshevism. So this Menshevism was not 24-carat gold or pure water. Trotsky lectured publicly and to the party about permanent revolution.

H: What else do you wish to say regarding 1905 prior to your arrest?

GD: Perhaps one of the episodes of the arrest itself. The arrest is not interesting in itself. The entire Soviet was arrested. But there was a curious conversation . . .

H: But how were you arrested? You were at a session?

GD: Yes, at a session of the Soviet in the Free Economic Society. Soldiers came, surrounded the premises, seized us and took us off to various jails.

H: But you expected this, of course?

GD: Not so suddenly. But Khrustalev-Nosar' had already been arrested, and then I was arrested the day before when I arrived at the Putilov works. It is true that I was detained only overnight, but a record of evidence was drawn up since a revolver was found on me. I stated that I had never fired it, but proceedings were instituted and I was later sentenced, and so forth. Almost immediately after I was freed, I went to the Soviet and was arrested again there. To characterize the mood, I might mention a curious conversation. In addition to myself, there were fairly prominent Bolsheviks; I remember Pavlovich-Krasikov and someone else.[15] The conversation was as follows: Well, we are being arrested, but it is unimportant since we will be freed by the revolution. It is a pity only that we will be in prison until it is all over. And someone raised the question, "Well, but when we are freed from prison the revolution will be over, there will be a Russian republic, and so forth. But what will we do?" It was an odd posing of the question. It was a real Bolshevik ideal way to pose the question! The question was not how we would work in the workers' movement, but what we would do next [for the Revolution]. One of those arrested, Liadov, said, "I think that we will have to go to China and make revolution there. All we know is how to make revolution!" Here was a curious awareness that we were essentially good for nothing else, though it was not stated directly in this fashion. This was the basic premise, the background of this curious exchange. On the one hand, we were totally optimistic about complete victory in the near future. But, on the other hand, we felt that there would be nothing for us to do then.

Third interview

H: Last time we stopped at the point you were arrested, at the last session of the Soviet. Today I would like to take up the period from your arrest until about the autumn of 1906, when you had already left the Bolshevik party.

GD: I think it would be well to mention some details about the arrest of the Soviet of Workers' Deputies. The Soviet met in the building of the Free Economic Society, in a hall which was a sort of balcony connected to the second floor of the building. The chairman of the Soviet was not Khrustalev-Nosar', who had been arrested earlier, but Trotsky, under the pseudonym of Ianovskii. The Soviet was arrested before the beginning of the session, but while the Executive Committee of the Soviet was meeting. A very substantial number of soldiers had been mobilized for the arrest. So they appeared and surrounded all the deputies, those in the Soviet downstairs and the entire Executive Committee upstairs. After a few minutes, which were obviously used for a hasty discussion of measures in connection with the arrest, Trotsky came out onto the balcony and said, I think I can render his very dramatic statement verbatim: "Comrades! I transmit to you the resolution of the Executive Committee: don't name names, don't give evidence, destroy everything that can be used for personal identification." The voice of one of the members of the Soviet came from below: "Comrade Ianovskii, I have a check, what shall I do with it?" "Keep it! They won't steal it from you!" he said, with majestic contempt and a gesture toward the soldiers standing behind him with rifles and bayonets. That was one aspect. Another detail that was typical of the mood of the times involved the Bolsheviks. I spoke with several of them: as I recall, Mandelshtam-Liadov, Pavlovich-Krasikov were there. They said, and we were generally in this mood, "Well, they'll put us in jail, which isn't so bad, because the revolution will eventually free us. But it is a pity that the revolution will be over and won without us." It was a half-serious, half-joking conversation, but it was characteristic that some of the relatively prominent Bolsheviks were absolutely certain that we were on the eve of total victory of the revolution. I think that this element played a considerable part in the organization of the armed uprising in Moscow, which occurred about two weeks after the arrest of the Soviet.

I learned about what happened afterwards only from notes that were sent to me in jail, since I was allowed to receive parcels and various things. They would send me cream-filled pastries and there was always a little rolled-up note in a small tube inside the cream with news in tiny handwriting about what was happening in the world. Of course, this sort of information was hardly adequate. I knew about the course of the Moscow uprising almost daily, but very little about what was happening within the party. At that time the grounds for unification were being laid within the party; it took place some months later. There was a discussion, and a very sharp polemic, about the attitude to be taken toward the State Duma. The

Bolsheviks took the position that the Duma was to be boycotted at all stages. As I recall, the Menshevik position seemed to me even then to be too intricate and irresolute. As far as I can remember, it amounted to this: that since the elections were multi-stage, we should become involved and try to mobilize the masses in the first stages, and then see what happened. On the basis of later discussions, I reached the conclusion that the formulation was not entirely sincere. In fact, the Mensheviks, or at least their leaders, were for the elections, but this seemed so unrevolutionary that they worked out this intermediary position.

Meanwhile, I was in jail in Kresty Prison until mid-March. After my release, I wasn't able even to renew my contacts with the organization, because I was arrested "administratively" very soon after I was freed. On the eve of the arrest of the Soviet, I was supposed to speak at a meeting at the Putilov factory. When I arrived there and tried to get in, using the badge which admitted the workers, I was arrested. They detained me only one night and let me go, but they confiscated a revolver which, frankly, I had never used – I never fired it once. For illegal possession of a weapon I was sentenced administratively to three months, but I was released somewhat earlier in connection with the opening of the First Duma. This was not a legislative but a kind of police matter. So when I was arrested this time, I was not in prison but at a police station, and I had a lot of contact with the outside. There was a curious reason for this, that has nothing to do with the working-class movement or the Mensheviks, but is of some interest for characterizing the state of affairs at the time. I was treated with extraordinary deference: I was allowed to have any visitors I wanted, not only at visiting times but at any time at all. I couldn't account for this liberalism. Later, a woman visiting me explained. My father was a State Councillor, a fairly high but not really high rank. In my arrest record, however, "Privy Councillor" had been written by mistake. Thus I was taken as the son of a very high official and they regarded it as their duty to give me all sorts of privileges and attend to me in every way. I wouldn't say that my confinement in the police station was particularly pleasant as a result; in fact it was extremely unpleasant in many respects, but at least I didn't suffer greatly. Once I was at liberty, I immediately renewed my ties with the organization.

This was at the very end of April, 1906. In May I began to work for the Bolshevik press to some extent, but the month of May also turned out to be very interesting and of great consequence for my future development and fate. I should recall that, even as a *gimnazium* student, as I have mentioned, I had become interested in, and enthusiastic about, Mach, Avenarius, all these schools of thought – it was my mathematics teacher, Parfent'ev, who first gave me the impetus. Later on I read *Essays on a Realistic World View*, most of whose authors were Bolsheviks and yet also Machists, empirocriticists, etc.[1] At the time of the revolution, I was working on the Russian translation of Mach's *Analysis of Sensations*. A young man who had just become a student, and a Bolshevik besides, and who was an enthusiast of Marxism and empirocriticism, was something rather sensational. People such as Lunacharskii, Bazarov,[2] and Bogdanov, whom I could walk with and who could talk with me not only about narrow party or political issues, but about philosophical topics as well, became very interested in me and I saw all of them a great deal. This gave me access to the leadership itself, because Bogdanov, as Lenin later said in a letter to Gorkii, was his right-hand man. . . . At the same time, still entirely under the sway of Bolshevik views, I dashed off the brochure *Where Are the Kadets Leading the People?*, which was of course written in a very Bolshevik spirit. I presented the manuscript of this brochure and Bogdanov read it. This was in May 1906. Bogdanov's comments were not just complimentary, but really enthusiastic. The brochure should have been printed, but it wasn't for the same reason that prevented Lenin's brochure entitled *The Treason of the Kadets* from appearing.

I don't know to what extent this interesting episode so characteristic of Lenin at the time is known, but I know all the details. Lenin was constantly predicting a deal between the Kadets and the tsarist government. I remember an enormous meeting in the People's House of Panina where there were speeches by such luminaries as the People's Socialist Miakotin and the Social Democrats Lenin and Dan.[3] Although there were disagreements, there were no public polemics between Bolsheviks and Mensheviks. Each of them upheld his own viewpoint, without emphasizing that he was polemicizing, say, Dan against Lenin or Lenin against Dan. But the most spectacular moment of this meeting was this: Lenin was speaking against Miakotin, and he said, very typically, "Citizen Miakotin! You say that the Kadets are honorable participants in the liberation movement. They conduct negotiations with the government but won't make a deal with them. And I ask Citizen Miakotin: "What are negotiations if not preparations for a deal, and what is a deal if not completed by negotiations?" A very effective point, and one which no doubt made an impression. The main interest of this meeting for me, though, and I think not just for me alone, was the colossal suggestive impact of Lenin's unique brand of oratory. It was not particularly beautiful or eloquent; he spoke abruptly, more with a certain rhythm, with enormous strength of will. The result of the meeting was that, after various speakers, including Dan, had expressed different opinions, Lenin introduced his resolution, which was unanimously adopted by the thousands present. No doubt there were people there who were more in agreement with Miakotin or Dan than with Lenin. But Lenin won them over. This episode was very revealing for me. Even now, perhaps, I very much disagree with many others in my estimation of Lenin, precisely because I saw the forcefulness of his personality directly, as well as its weaknesses, which I became acquainted with very soon thereafter.

But something else happened then that also turned out to be important. I was writing the pamphlet and going to meetings. Lunacharskii liked very much to be co-speaker with me, and we would go together for instance, to debate against Petr Struve and were completely victorious, of course. Petr Struve was annihilated by the bursts of our oratory. I often met with Bazarov – whom Lenin regarded, in his last years, according to Gorkii, as the most intelligent man he had ever met – and his conversations with me were very valuable. Least of all did I think of the simple fact that in order to live you need to have something to live on, and by about June I was completely broke. I could have obtained some money from home, since it was agreed that, as a student, I should receive some support, but I was ashamed to ask my parents for money to finance my Bolshevik activities. But except for pittances I got for short articles I wrote for some provincial newspaper (the name of which I can't remember) I had no other source of income. And the time came when my comrade Pinkevich from Kazan (I mention his name because it comes up later) and I, who lived together in one room, had to pay the rent, and we literally didn't have a penny. We wandered around Petersburg trying to find friends who could lend us money, but didn't find anyone. We returned dejectedly, and precisely because I was dejected, I was looking at the ground and saw a wallet on the sidewalk which turned out to have some money in it. I counted it up and said, "This is exactly the amount we need to pay for the apartment, plus another 60 kopecks. Let's hire a carriage with it!" So we spent those 60 kopecks on a carriage, and used the rest to pay the rent. But it was quite clear that we couldn't go on living like this, because the next day there was nothing to eat, even though at that time in Petersburg you could eat very cheaply, for pennies, at the People's House of Panina, but we didn't even have that. At this point I had a stroke of luck. One of my comrades in the Bolshevik organization, named Domantovich, a nephew or cousin of Kollontai,[4] and rather wealthy, rented a summer house in Terijoki and, once he found out what my situation was (we were on very good terms), he invited me to live there, where I was given free room and breakfast. For a number of months, it was my only meal.

What is interesting, though, is something else. All the prominent Bolsheviks either lived in places in Finland near Petersburg, or else they came there all the time on visits, and meetings would be arranged. For example, Kamenev lived in Kuakola, and Mandelshtam-Liadov and Lunacharskii at one time lived in Terijoki. So there was constant association, and I was regarded (not only by Lunacharskii, Bogdanov, and Bazarov but also, through their recommendation, by others) as a highly promising young Bolshevik. True, I didn't get together with Kamenev, who lived in Kuakola, though I saw him a few times. When he came to the summer place from the editorial offices of the Bolshevik paper, he would put on slippers and spend the whole day indoors, so that the whole time in Kuakola he wasn't at the shore (the Gulf of Finland) once, although it was ten minutes away on foot, at most. The impression he made on me was of extreme laziness. Perhaps I'm mistaken; I must be, since he was educated and erudite. But I became more or less friendly with a great many other Bolsheviks, such as Mandelshtam-Liadov and Goldenberg,[5] and then later Liashchenko and Steklov. As a result, this is what happened: for some reason, Mandelshtam-Liadov told me that a very important meeting of the leadership of the Bolshevik faction was to take place at his summer house. Mandelshtam-Liadov himself was very factionally minded. Of course, he was very hostile to the tsarist government, but this hostility was only tertiary. The Mensheviks were the main enemy. Once when we were out walking in Terijoki and spotted a group of Mensheviks who were also out for a walk, he said, "I hate them from the bottom of my heart." The Kadets came second, and then, well, the tsarist government came third. He was not particularly interesting as a person, but my acquaintance with him was.

H: How did this hatred express itself and what was it focused on?

GD: That the Mensheviks were opportunists, not revolutionaries; that they were sabotaging the preparations for an insurrection, and did not participate in it; that their evaluation of the situation was all wrong; that all they dreamed of was to make something like a common bloc with the Kadets, and so on. As I remember Liadov, he was rather primitive in his thinking. He treated me very well and did something rather unusual, and maybe not altogether legitimate – he invited me to his summer house to this important meeting of the Bolshevik leadership group. For some strange reason, I can't recall who all participants were; they were very few, seven or eight.

H: This was after the issuance of the Vyborg manifesto, you think, after July?[6]

GD: It was August 6, I remember the date precisely, and in a moment you'll hear why. Lenin was there, Rykov was there, Bogdanov, Goldenberg, Liadov, and Comrade Demian-Teodorovich, who much later under the Soviets was the Minister of Agriculture. The question under discussion was the approach to be taken in the elections to the Second Duma. The speaker was Teodorovich, Comrade Demian, who, entirely in the spirit of the Bolshevik line, said that a revolutionary situation was crystallizing, that a new wave of revolution was growing – the usual argument given then – that the complete passivity of the peasantry after the dissolution of the First Duma was due to the fact that the peasants were then totally engaged in field work, but that when this was over, there would be a strong reaction. He was one of the most vigorous proponents of this point of view.

H: Was he a Leninist?

GD: In words. But the most vigorous proponent of this was Vladimir Savel'evich Voitinskii.[7] Perhaps I'm getting somewhat ahead. There was a curious episode around the dissolution of the Duma . . . I remember it when I mentioned Voitinskii.

H: We can return to this.

GD: As I mentioned, I think that Lenin's pamphlet on the treason of the Kadets was not published. When a resolution on various issues was passed in the First Duma, Lenin decided that a deal had been made and went off to a summer place not far from Petersburg, to write the pamphlet. While he was writing it, instead of a deal being reached between the Kadets and the government, the Duma was dissolved, and so neither his nor my pamphlet ever appeared. I saw Lenin at that time through the window of a train going through Terijoki, where I was at the time. He was on his way to Vyborg, for the conference, and, moreover, there was a conference of revolutionary parties in Terijoki that was very clandestinely set up – it was dark in the hall, deliberately so, and there were prominent personalities seated behind the table, including one representative of the Socialist Revolutionaries (Azev, as I learned later). At that time the Bolshevik faction had prepared an appeal that called for a general strike.[8] The text of this appeal was given to me to take to Petersburg to hand over for printing and dissemination. I arrived in Petersburg and went to the place – it was in the suburbs, beyond the Nevskii gates, at the Semenovskii Railway Plant. There was a certain door I was supposed to enter. It was nighttime, around midnight. When I reached the door, I found it closed and with soldiers around it. So I was on the street with the text of the appeal in my pocket. There was no transportation back to the city by this time; the last local train had already left. I was supposed to spend the night there and then get to Petersburg with the appeal in the morning. What should I do? Wander around the streets? There was a risk of getting caught, since I saw a patrol that was stopping people. Fortune, or rather misfortune, came to my aid: a huge fire started nearby. I and many others hurried over to the spectacle and I spent almost the whole night helping to put it out, completely certain that I would not be searched and arrested. After that, I arrived in Petersburg on the first train, I handed over the appeal, from which nothing came. Later, I met Vladimir Savel'evich Voitinskii, who said "It's good that you've arrived, we need someone like you. Go to Shlisselberg immediately. There are a gunpowder factory and a dynamite factory there. Organize a group of comrades immediately so that, as soon as you hear from Petersburg that the insurrection has begun, you can seize these factories and blow up the railway." I was not yet 19 at the time. Vladimir Savel'evich, who gave the orders, was just a year or two or three older. But everything was quite simple and clear. I went there and got everything ready. Then I sat and waited, and, finally, since I hadn't received either the agreed-upon message or, for that matter, any news at all, I went back to Petersburg to determine what had happened. I learned that the call for a strike had had no impact, no one had gone on strike and the country was completely quiet. In short, I need not return to Shlisselberg, seize the factories, or blow up the railways. At that point Voitinskii explained to me (in justifying his philosophy, which he characterized as "subjective idealism") that in actuality events occur in people's consciousness and that the dissolution of the Duma had not yet reached the consciousness of the peasants, that we must wait some number of months, but that future prospects were splendid. Teodorovich's report was more or less in this spirit. Lenin listened quietly and kept silent.

H: Now let us return to the Bolshevik conference in August.

GD: Others evidently found that this was irreproachable, entirely correct, and I think that, as usual, Lenin's opinion was the one most waited for. Lenin began something like this: "Comrade Demian has spoken marvelously! Fascinatingly! Splendidly! Captivatingly! It's only a pity that he is all wrong!" And at this point he said, "Comrades! In Tammerfors, in December, I was against the boycott; you were for it. The majority was for the boycott, and in December 1905 I gave in to you. On August 6, 1906 I won't give in to you. It's time for us to stop being boycottists!" And he made a fairly long speech in which – and this was typical of him – he constantly repeated the phrase "It is time for us to stop being boycottists!" Like a leit-motif. His conception (and I don't know to what extent it was sincere) was like this: "Of course there will be an insurrection! Comrade Demian said the end of September or October, but why so late? Perhaps much earlier? What sense is there for us" – and here, I think, his argument was not sincere – "to carry on a debate with the Mensheviks, on the eve of an insurrection, about whether or not to boycott the Duma! Our position should be: 'Comrade Mensheviks! You are against boycott, and we are against boycott! But what is your position about armed insurrection?'"

I think that his position wasn't sincere because at this point a development took place that was one of the starting points for my break with the Bolsheviks. Lenin first came out in favor of a preelection agreement with the left revolutionary parties, the Socialist Revolutionaries and the Trudoviki.[9] When the Mensheviks formulated their position, which allowed for an agreement with the Kadets to a certain extent, Lenin decided that the position of "no agreements with anyone!" was politically advantageous against the Mensheviks. When the Mensheviks, including Martov, reminded him that he had been in favor of an agreement, he stated categorically that this was an insolent lie and that he had always, and from the very beginning, been against any kind of agreement. This bore very little resemblance to his earlier idea that we should come to an agreement with the Mensheviks on this issue. I was very upset about this and went to Bazarov and said, "Vladimir Aleksandrovich, what is this? Lenin used to be in favor of an agreement!" Bazarov replied, "It was in the same chair you're sitting on that Vladimir Ilich demonstrated the necessity of an agreement." For me, this was a completely shattering blow. The incredible shamelessness, not just of changing one's position and of denying that it had been different, but of violently accusing those who had accurately reminded him of his position of lying! I wouldn't say that this finished Lenin for me then, but any deep admiration and respect for him were liquidated, essentially for moral reasons.

But, in addition to this, there was another episode. After the dissolution of the Duma, and under the impression of the complete calm and lack of response in the countryside, I began to doubt that the revolutionary process would develop further. At that time – I can't remember whether it was before August 6 or right after – I went home to Kazan for a short visit. I went because I was very tired and had received some money from home – they had sent it on their own initiative. Since I had gone hungry so long, I needed to restore my strength. I went from Petersburg to Leninsk by railway, and then from Leninsk by ship to Kazan. It was a pleasant trip; there were many stops at stations along the way where the peasants would sell food cheap, and there were many passengers of all sorts. Not a single fact, a single conversation, or a single observation suggested anything but the restoration of complete calm in the country. And I had the same impression in Kazan. When I returned to Petersburg, I again talked about this with Bazarov, who, as I said, was very intelligent and erudite. I visited the public library and read the current literature, particularly newspapers of an economic and financial type. I read, took notes, gathered data on the situation in various factories in various areas, and arrived at what for me was the indisputable conclusion that the economic crisis – on which the Bolsheviks and Social Democrats had counted so much – if it had not been liquidated altogether, was in the process of rapid liquidation. This had been the conclusion Bazarov had drawn. Meanwhile the "leadership group" of the Bolsheviks, that is, Lenin and the leading Bolsheviks – there was formally no Bolshevik Central Committee, the Central Committee was common to the entire party[10] – put together a thesis which began with the traditional "constantly deteriorating economic situation and deepening economic crisis, etc., all indicate that we are on the verge of a new upsurge in the wave of revolution." And the conclusion, as I recall (I never saw these theses in print; perhaps they will appear in the new edition of Lenin's Works), was that because of this forthcoming insurrection, the Social-Democratic party (the theses were supposed to become the common party position) should take up the purist revolutionary position: it should not boycott the Duma elections, but take part in these elections pure in its principles, without any agreements.

H: You know, I've never seen this in the literature, and yet I've read everything that Lenin had to say about agreements, and I have never noticed a complete rejection of any agreement.

GD: In a moment, you'll see how genuine, so to speak, my information is. At that point I sat down and wrote my countertheses, which Pinkevich also subscribed to. My countertheses made a concession, not entirely sincere, to the dominant tendency. They stated that the crisis was not getting deeper, but, on the contrary, was being liquidated, but that nonetheless, some new upsurge of revolutionary attitudes could not be entirely ruled out. To exploit this new upsurge and have the possibility to make a stand for some position (in general, I did not have in mind the final victory of the revolution), the working-class party must not act in isolation, but ally itself as closely as possible with other parties – the Socialist Revolutionaries and the Trudoviki (I didn't go so far as to say the Kadets). A meeting of the Bolshevik faction in Petersburg was held. Lenin wasn't there; he was in Finland at the time. The party theses were presented to this meeting.

H: Do you remember where it was?

GD: I don't recall . . . in one of the higher educational institutes, perhaps the Technological Institute. It was still possible then. Anyway, it was in Petersburg itself.

H: Who was present?

GD: The representative of the leadership group and the leadership's speaker was Goldenberg. There were 150 or 200 people present, at least, and my theses were presented. (I had presented them earlier, so they were already known to the leadership.) After Goldenberg's report, setting forth the official position and the conclusion that there should be no agreements (it's hard for me to fix the date, I think it was in September, but I don't recall precisely), I gave my presentation with the conclusion that there should be agreements with the SRs and the Trudoviki. Then there was a debate in which Pinkevich supported me. Goldenberg scoffed at us, saying, "Here are two young comrades who have imagined themselves to be Marx and Engels; as Marx and Engels correctly concluded in their time that the revolutionary situation was over and said so in such-and-such a document, these two now want to play the same role. When we told Vladimir Ilich of their position, he observed, 'These comrades have lost the last remnants of Marxist principles.'" In short, there was a complete rout, with the overwhelming majority voting against us.

This in itself would not have been of major consequence, except that a few days later both of us, Pinkevich and I, were informed that we were forbidden to present our point of view at general party meetings. Schwarz broke with the Bolsheviks at this time over the issue of party and factional discipline. He had been talking with a comrade and was told: "The last time, of course, the faction adopted the opposing decision, and you don't have the right to advocate your views." This prohibition in the name of factional discipline was completely intolerable for me too. The question then arose of what to do? I made no formal declaration about leaving the faction – and couldn't have anyway, because the faction didn't exist formally. I could have left the party, but I didn't want to. The only way you could stay in the party and not be in a faction was by not formalizing the fact. Although I was on very good terms with individual Mensheviks, I wasn't at all attracted to Menshevism at that time, and was not in agreement with the Menshevik position. My theses reflected a position on very many points – I can't remember them all of course – that differed from the official Menshevik line. At this moment, fortunately, a comrade came from the Lugansk organization to recruit people because there was a serious lack of party workers there. Both Pinkevich and I went to Lugansk, and this ended the Bolshevik period of my life. Here we can put a period.

H: What was the difference between you and the Mensheviks at that time, in November 1906, or how did it express itself?

GD: I think that, first, there remained the old psychological repugnance to positions I felt were always half way, inadequately defined, not spelled out. Second, since the moral element was very important for me, I should say that, although the Mensheviks didn't show the kind of amoralism that Lenin did, still in their polemics and debates there were things I didn't like. . . . After the Unification Congress, speeches reporting on the congress were arranged. They usually took place in institutions of higher learning, and two-hour time periods were the ones generally allowed. The sessions were set up in such a way that first there was a detailed report, in some cases by a Bolshevik, in others by a Menshevik, and then normally someone from the meeting, say after a Bolshevik's report, would propose that the comrade Menshevik be given more time. For instance, the norm might be five minutes, but he would be given ten or a quarter of an hour.

I was present at a report by Lenin. He spoke for over an hour. It was chiefly about the agrarian question. Then there was a resolution that Comrade George should be given time to rebut. Comrade George was Vladimir Osipovich Levitskii-Tsederbaum, who began to speak at a frenzied tempo, terribly agitated, terribly heated. Ten minutes passed, then fifteen, and the meeting started to become uneasy. People were saying, "Others need to speak." Not listening, he went on and on, and finally someone said: "The speaker must allow time for the concluding remarks." Lenin got up and said, "It's all right, comrades. To answer Comrade George, I need only five minutes." It was demagogy, but very clever demagogy. A few days later I went to a speech by Dan. Lenin was in the auditorium. After Dan's speech, someone got up and said that Comrade Lenin was there and proposed that he be given not five minutes but somewhat more – I don't remember how many. Dan said that he was absolutely against this, that there should be equal rights. The issue was put to a vote and the overwhelming majority resolved to give Lenin more time. At that point Dan got up and said, "I can't stay at a meeting in which comrades are divided into haves and have-nots and Lenin, an *intelligent*, is given more time than worker comrades who would like to express themselves. Therefore, I am leaving." It was clear to everyone, alas, that Dan was simply afraid of a polemic with Lenin, and had resorted to an extremely cheap polemical device instead. This was a single episode; I can't say that I hated the Mensheviks the way Liadov hated them. I had friendly relationships with some of them which were to be renewed many years later.

H: With whom in particular?

GD: Especially with Ermolaev.

H: What sort of person was he?

GD: An intelligent man who could think calmly and critically, one of the very few people in our milieu who could see what was actually going on and was not simply living in an imaginary world. He and I talked a good deal, and we concurred in our sharply negative attitude toward factionalism – on my part with respect to the Bolsheviks, and on his part not exactly with respect to the Mensheviks, but in general. So the conclusion that I drew was that I would leave the Bolsheviks but not join the Mensheviks; I didn't need either one. I needed to work on reorganizing the party and make it nonfactional. Since Ermolaev had the same attitude, it was completely understandable to me why he became of one of the three leaders of Liquidationism later on.[11] The process had begun as early as 1908.

H: Now let's return to the most important events. We could define the situation as follows: in November or December 1905, the first shocks of the wave of revolution were dissipated. I would like to know, within the framework of the suppression of the revolutionary wave, the changes in attitude that you and your comrades experienced. Perhaps the primary issue is one we have already discussed, namely participation in the First Duma. So at that time, at the time of the elections, when the official Bolshevik position was one of boycott, did you have any doubts about it? And, if not, what sort of future prospects did you perceive?

GD: There were no doubts before the dissolution of the First Duma. There was a conviction, a faith – probably universal among the Bolsheviks – that there would be a new wave of peasant insurrections, that one had to prepare for it, and that the entrance of the working class into revolutionary action must be timed so as to convert the new wave into an armed insurrection.

H: How would you summarize your explanations, before the dissolution of the Duma, of the defeats of 1905?

GD: Lack of coordination and organization, the fact that the various outbreaks had been scattered, irregular. Some towns jumped the gun, so to speak. For example, the Petersburg Soviet was like a second government for some time, but it didn't have the physical power to maintain its position. We had an organization working among the soldiers that assured us that such-and-such regiments could be completely counted on, like the Semenovskii. And these same "reliable" soldiers arrested us and were then sent to Moscow to quell the uprising. So it was apparent that the agitational and organizational work was in fact not of the necessary caliber, and this had to be rectified and the next wave had to be prepared for better. But then doubts arose: the lack of a reaction to the dissolution of the First Duma, and then a conversation I had with one of the leaders of the Trudovik group (there are times when my mind goes blank, and although I know his name perfectly well, I can't recall it now) who had traveled about Russia a great deal and told me about how the punitive expeditions to suppress the outbursts of insurrection had affected the peasantry. He told how they had created an atmosphere of fear and oppression among the peasantry, and he gave an example: it seems that a punitive expedition was sent to a village, where there had been an uprising. The local police authority was a war invalid, one-armed or one-legged, or something like that, and the peasantry, so recently in revolt, was not only blindly submissive, but would bear it patiently when he, angry at someone, beat him with his crutches. I remember that these talks made an enormous impression on me and, combined with the total passivity of the peasantry, they didn't allow for much consolation in the thought that field work would soon be over, and that the dissolution of the Duma would affect the peasants' consciousness. What's more, it was not altogether convincing psychologically and somewhat too metaphysical.

H: Now, as for the Unification Congress and the information you received about it – in particular on the basis of these speeches that both the Bolsheviks and the Mensheviks made – what were the aspects of the decisions of the congress that made an impression on you? In particular, what about the elections and participation in the elections – what possibility did local organizations have to decide the issue? In April or at the beginning of May, how did you perceive this issue?

GD: By then, the issue had already been resolved by life, so to speak. When I was set free, the elections had already taken place and the Duma had already convened, and I, like many other Bolsheviks, was very happy that there were Social Democrats in the Duma, God knows what kind, to tell the truth. I was fairly close to some of them.[12]

H: Did you meet with the Georgian deputies at that time?

GD: No. As for the overall impression, of course, there was happiness over the unification, something which changed very rapidly, largely as a

result of the speeches, and the impression that the unity was purely fictitious; that the difference between the factions was not eliminated but
rather had become more firmly crystallized.

H: Before August, did you think that the fault lay with the Mensheviks?

GD: I wouldn't say so. There was a good deal of intolerance on both
sides. As for the resolutions of the congress, the primary issue was the
agrarian question.

H: Did this seem like an important issue to you?

GD: Yes, a decisive one. One of the conclusions drawn from the past
was that the failure of the first wave was due to the lack of common struggle of city and countryside, that is, the working class movement in the cities
and the peasant movement.

H: What was your attitude toward the position of the Mensheviks and
the Bolsheviks in this regard?

GD: I must be a primitive thinker, because I still can't understand
"municipalization."[13] It was sort of an attempt to have nationalization of
the land and yet not to have nationalization, a kind of intermediate form
with guarantees, that didn't seem very realistic. The two other positions,
division into private property and nationalization, were more comprehensible. Partially under the impact of Lenin's very convincing arguments, I
leaned toward his program.

H: How did you explain nationalization? Were you convinced by Lenin's arguments that it could be reconciled with the development of capitalism? Did all this seem convincing to a Marxist?

GD: It's difficult for me to reconstruct the attitude exactly, but the main
approach was not what decision was more Marxist or more rational for the
future, but how to approach the peasantry – what program could be a
mobilizing force for them. Division into private property could be such a
force, but there were objections to it. Nationalization of the land, on the
assumption that the land belongs to no one, the land is God's, could also.
"Municipalization" couldn't mobilize anyone for anything.

H: Did you discuss this with the Trudoviki whom you knew, that is,
Lenin's program?

GD: No.

H: So you were of the opinion that nationalization could revolutionize
the countryside, that there was the notion among the peasantry that the
land belongs to God?

GD: This is what Plekhanov had talked about at the Second Congress,
I think – the guarantees against restoration – that with the division into
private property and the formation of petty land-owners, these land proprietors would become a bulwark of reaction.

H: At that time you were fairly close to the first generation of Bolshevik
cadres, so to speak, such as Lunacharskii, Bogdanov, Bazarov, and so forth.
I would like to know a little more about your impressions of how their political opinions, their Bolshevism, and their philosophical outlook came
together: that is, what was the point of coincidence between all this empiriocriticism and Bolshevism?[14] I'm not thinking of the abstract reasons they

presented, but psychologically, what are your impressions of this type of Bolshevik in general?

GD: I don't think that a connection can be established between empiriocriticism and Bolshevism. I think that the coincidence was more or less accidental in a certain sense, at least for these people. What was it that distinguished this group – a rather large number of people among the Bolsheviks from the corresponding party of the Menshevik intelligentsia? I'm not referring to all Bolsheviks or to the professional ones, so to speak, headed by Lenin, but to the group that included Bogdanov, Lunacharskii, Bazarov, and Goldenberg, and later Polskaia-Iurevskaia, who were close to them in some respects. These Bolshevik intellectuals had a broader educational background and broader interests than most Menshevik intellectuals. I remember that there were conversations of the sort, "Well, let's compare. Who has more prominent people?" and they would enumerate: the Mensheviks have so-and-so, the Bolsheviks . . . I remember, Lunacharskii's wife, Anna Aleksandrovna, nee Malinovskaia, who was Bogdanov's sister, said, "Well, could the Mensheviks have a genius of the stature of Bazarov?" And in the anthologies that appeared, where problems of realistic world view were so important, the Bolsheviks predominated almost without exception.

H: Perhaps I could phrase the question as follows: What did it seem to you then, and what does it seem to you now, caused these elements to gravitate toward Bolshevism?

GD: That's a question that I have given a lot of thought to. In most cases, with one very important exception, I think that it was a matter of temperament. The exception, and a total mystery to me, is Bazarov. I can't understand at all why Bazarov was a Bolshevik.

H: This is something I would like to know for myself – on the basis of your talks with Bazarov, Lunacharskii, and Bogdanov, what were their views about the Mensheviks, aside from the fact that they were not very brilliant people?

GD: We talked very little about the Mensheviks in these conversations. There was always the view that they were people with tortuous thought processes and a fear of coming to final conclusions. The Mensheviks didn't manage to come to a fully logical conclusion from their position in any direction. Nor could they bring themselves to say, "Now we, as an independent force, are very small; we should merge with other elements, and so forth, into a unified bloc."

H: Would it be correct to say that they seemed too bound by dogma?

GD: As regards Marxist orthodoxy, the Mensheviks were more dogmatic than the Bolsheviks or Lenin at that time. You know the correspondence with Plekhanov over *Novaia Zhizn'*.[15] Lenin made a philosophical deviation without worry, and Bazarov, of whom Lenin had such a high opinion, was extremely unorthodox. I remember the conversations and some things that astonished me in various spheres. For instance, Bazarov would say, "A person is worth so much. But there is a weak point – it doesn't explain prices. There is no way to derive from it why prices are what they are and not something else." He also had very interesting notions about the future prospects of socialism itself. He literally said, "Of course, perhaps a political revolution should be a seizure of power, but it is entirely incorrect to think that there will be a revolution, and then the building of socialism. The transition from feudalism to capitalism was a process that lasted a long time, and it will take a very long time – though perhaps not as long – for capitalism to be replaced by socialism." Or, for instance, Bazarov's idea (with a somewhat disguised but polemical commentary on Lunacharskii): "Why should we expect a flowering of culture and art and so forth, as soon as capitalism turns into socialism? Look at the roots of great art and painting and music, and you will see that they were religious roots. To have a new flowering, a new great art, we must find stimuli that are similar and equal in their ability to inspire as the religious motifs which inspired artists and musicians in the past."

Do these thoughts sound like Bolshevism? I always wondered, but I never happened to ask, "Vladimir Aleksandrovich, how did you get involved in this?" I could not understand it at all.

H: Did you discuss any of these issues? First, that you were confronting a lengthy process – economic, cultural, and so forth – and that this should occur within the framework of the dictatorship of the proletariat and peasantry, reflected in the character of the Provisional Government, and so on. And more generally the issue of power and the interaction between political power and social processes?

GD: Yes, but we conceived it quite differently – the lengthy phase, during which the process of building socialism would be completed. It would be a dictatorship of the proletariat and peasantry which would continue until the convening of a Constituent Assembly, and after that, precisely because of this dictatorship of the proletariat and peasantry and the opportunities for influence it provided, a true democratic republic would be set up: capitalism would be maintained but with very strong footholds for the struggle for socialism within the framework of a democratized capitalistic Russia.

H: I know that this has not been discussed in the literature, so I would like to find out to what extent it was discussed in conversations and to what extent the topic was of interest. Several stages were visualized: the Provisional Government, then the Constituent Assembly, then, on the basis of the Constituent Assembly, a democratic republic. What government would there be in this democratic republic? For instance, what role would the Social Democrats play in it?

GD: This question could not be posed, because the nature of the future government depended on the make-up of the Constituent Assembly. That was why I mentioned the conversation on the night the Soviet was arrested: these Bolsheviks, and fairly prominent ones, felt that there would be nothing for them to do in Russia for a long time after the revolution was victorious. Why? Because they were not suited to organic political activity, but were professional revolutionaries. And then a democratic system would be set up, but one that preserved capitalism, and a period of parliamentarianism, parliamentary conflict, et cetera.

H: Now let us consider this issue from the other side, namely the Menshevik conception, which we could define as follows: as soon as there is a Provisional Government, we should go over to the opposition. This was not the exact conception in 1905, but . . .

GD: But that was how it was generally understood.

H: By you as well?

GD: That was how we understood the Menshevik position.

H: Did you approve of it?

GD: No, and I can tell you why. We felt that the makeup of the Constituent Assembly would depend on the nature of the Provisional Government, and it would be possible for this government to use its power to carry out a number of necessary and useful reforms. I'll illustrate for you how it was expressed specifically. What did the Bolshevik conception of the dictatorship of the proletariat and peasant mean? The mobilization of the peasantry. If this mobilization was around a program of nationalization and the Provisional Government took the appropriate stance and agitated in this direction, the chances would be much greater that the peasant majority in the Constituent Assembly would carry out nationalization. If there was no slogan or program around which to mobilize, either no uniform majority would appear or some other solution would go through – but not municipalization under any circumstances.

H: Now I want to return to the question of factional discipline. It was ultimately over factional discipline that you left the party, and Schwarz left at the same time. This is my question: how could brilliant intellectuals like Bogdanov, Lunacharskii, and Bazarov, who were not particularly disciplined, how could they support factional discipline? Did you talk about it?

GD: I only talked with Bazarov, who agreed with me, but my conversation with him was before I wrote my theses. It had never entered my mind that there could be a prohibition, as a matter of factional discipline, from presenting a point of view at general party meetings. For me it was still *the* party, and a factional meeting was only preparatory. An issue would be decided at a general party meeting. When I talked with Bazarov, I never envisaged such a prospect, and, as far as I remember none of them spoke up; they kept quiet. Of course, the attitude toward Lenin played a part, a great part. Lenin's authority was colossal, even when people recognized his shortcomings and did not agree with him over particulars.

H: How did Lenin's authority express itself, say in relation to Bazarov?

GD: Bazarov? I would say it was a mystery to me – such a critical thinker and yet so inconsistent that I simply don't understand . . . I would have to know more about his biography.

H: What was your general impression as to why Lenin commanded so much respect among these people?

GD: I think that the question could be framed as it was clearly framed by some people much later. I remember a conversation with Abramovich, much later, after the October revolution, and one that I won't remind him of. It was at the time when there was a struggle between Lenin and Trotsky over the trade unions and so forth. It might seem strange now, but Abramovich expected Trotsky to come out on top, and generally maintained that there was no comparison – Trotsky, a far more brilliant personality and a man with a totally different education, and so on – Abramovich always felt that, if the revolution was victorious, Trotsky would be at the head of it. I said to him, "Rafail Abramovich, if you, or any Bolshevik, had asked me in 1905 who would head the Provisional Government if the revolution should be victorious, I and many others would have answered Lenin without a moment's hesitation. No one thought that Martov might have headed the Provisional Government." A leader! Perhaps it was that these not completely orthodox Marxists evaluated the significance of a leader in a different way.

H: Do you think that we have taken up everything before November, or do any other items remain?

GD: I think that there is one point worth recalling: it is important for the future. Namely, I should mention my conversation with Ermolaev. At that time, the summer and autumn of 1906, there was complete stagnation in party life at the grass roots. I don't know if this has been described in the literature. I was then a member of the district committee of the Nevskii district, the most important working-class district of Petersburg, together with the Narvskii; there were railway workshops and the Semenov and Obukhov plants, a huge number of works, a very high percentage of them organized. But no one came to party meetings or they came in tiny numbers. We tried to set up circles but nothing came of it – there was total apathy. And I remember that I begged to be given some other work, but it happened that the District Committee consisted of five or seven people, I think, with a Bolshevik majority of one. I said, "I can't continue doing this, I feel completely purposeless, nothing can be done, I go to meetings that don't meet." But I was told, "No, you can't leave." "Why?" "If you do, you will be replaced by a Menshevik in the elections, and they will have the majority." At that time my relationships with my Menshevik colleagues were excellent, and we talked about it. They also said that it was about the same with them, that they wanted to leave but were told they couldn't because the Bolsheviks would be all the stronger.

H: What Mensheviks were there in this district committee?

GD: Ermolaev, I think, but I don't remember precisely.

H: There is another issue we should discuss, I think. Among the higher-ups, there were these factional struggles, which took on rather nasty overtones in the autumn – Lenin's party trial, all the squabbles, and so forth. But at lower levels, say in this committee, what were the relationships like?

GD: Excellent.

H: In your talks with these Mensheviks, how did you explain the factional struggle, its meaning, and so forth?

GD: I don't think that the understanding was deep enough. I have a vague recollection, I can't say from where, of a phrase bandied about, something like "No, we must build a new party without Lenin and without Martov." A major aspect of this factionalism, of course, was the effect of emigration.

H: Would it be correct to say that the rank-and-file members of the Petersburg organization had had enough of this?

GD: Yes, and there was another aspect that is very important in historical perspective: an enormous reluctance to return to illegal forms of operation; illegal work was disliked.

H: Can you say something more about relationships at the grass roots?

GD: It was similar to what is expressed in a Ukrainian proverb which runs something like this: "When the lords fight, the fur flies on the peasants." So to some extent, I would say, the conflicts transferred to Russia from emigration were aggravated.

H: I recall a conversation between Sablinskii and Schwarz. What bothered Schwarz at the time, and what he now regards as the basic reason for his break was that the attitude toward the working class movement on the part of the Bolsheviks was too authoritarian. To what extent do you feel that this was widespread?

GD: I don't think it was.

H: You don't think, say, that in this district committee, aside from the sense of despair about the apathy of the workers at this time, there were disagreements about the line to be stressed or the type of activity to be involved in, particularly as regards the legal movement?

GD: The question wasn't posed specifically, but people yearned for an open movement, because by then it was necessary to reduce activity to very narrow forms, if not to go over to illegal work entirely.[16] This was felt to be a painful response, of course, and people yearned for those open forms – as I said, the reluctance to return to illegal activity was very great.

H: What specifically do you recall about this? My first question – it may sound simply funny – is this: was Axelrod's idea of a Workers' Congress of any interest?[17]

GD: No.

H: Was it talked about?

GD: Well, somewhat, but it was seen as something fantastic and confused.

H: Now, you know that the first signs of the spirit of Liquidationism appeared in the Menshevik organization at this time.

GD: I think that they were only very rudimentary.

H: How did this express itself?

GD: Without any specific plans, there was the thought that something else, other forms must be found, that there was nothing in the current forms, complete stagnation.

H: There were considerable efforts in 1906 to form legal trade unions – to what extent was this of interest?

GD: In the narrow circle that I was in, we were completely apart from this. All our activity and party life, over the weeks that I was in the district committee, amounted to futile attempts to arrange at least some kind of meetings, organize some circles, and so forth. I don't remember a single success.

Fourth interview

H: Last time, we stopped at November 1906, when you went from Petersburg to Lugansk and left the Bolsheviks.

GD: Yes, I went with a comrade to whom I was very close, Albert Petrovich Pinkevich, who, as I told you, had rebelled against the Bolshevik line with me, and had also been forbidden to speak at general party meetings. For us the opportunity to go to Lugansk was a good way out of an intolerable situation. Frankly, the offer was made without an awareness of the circumstances, because Lugansk had one of the strongest and most solidly Bolshevik organizations and if the local committee had been informed of our conflict we scarcely would have received the offer.

H: What specific work was entrusted to you?

GD: Nothing specific. They needed agitators and propagandists. In many respects, Lugansk's situation was quite exceptional, something which is scarcely mentioned in the literature as far as I know. Above all, something that amazed us when we arrived was the complete freedom, you could say, that still prevailed there. Of course, there was a committee with clandestine meetings, of which no minutes were kept, but you could go to any meeting and speak completely openly. The entire town knew the Social-Democratic activists. My involvement began like this: I had just arrived in Lugansk and had yet to make contact with the local committee when I learned that a meeting of shopkeepers had been arranged on the day of my arrival or the next. I went straight to the meeting, thinking that it might be somewhat risky, and asked for the floor and spoke. One of my future comrades, who had yet to learn of my arrival, came over and began to talk to me: "What's going on, you should get in touch with the committee." I said to him, "That's why I came, I just haven't been able to do it yet." We went around to the factories and spoke, and there was no question of anyone getting arrested. You can tell how widely known we were from one funny thing that happened. I was walking along the street when I met a total stranger who had obviously heard me a few times. He greeted me very joyfully, called me "comrade speaker," and, as a token of his sympathy, gave me a present of some pickles. It is something very curious and calls for an explanation, of course – why could this situation exist in Lugansk, why was it what one might call the freest place in all Russia at the time? There was something quite unusual in Lugansk. There was a large plant there, the Hartman locomotive works, a branch of a large Saxon company. The plant had a trade union that was unusual by Russian or even European standards. It was organized not by professions but by a principle well known in America: it was an industrial trade union that encompassed all the workers of the factory. Unfortunately, I can't recall now how many workers there were. By Russian standards, the plant itself was very advanced and, naturally enough, as a locomotive works it had a large number of highly skilled workers.

H: When had this trade union been organized and who organized it?

GD: I don't remember exactly. It was a fully established organization by then. I'll tell you about the people in this union. The Bolsheviks in the Lugansk organization had mixed feelings toward this plant. On the one hand, it was a reservoir of party members, and a very rich one. I need mention only one name: one of the workers prominent in the Lugansk organization then and later in the history of the Bolshevik party was Voroshilov, who was Comrade Volodia in the party.[1] On the other hand, the presence of the union and the tendencies that were naturally associated with it alarmed the Bolsheviks. They didn't like the trade-unionism it represented. In fact, this union [*soiuz*] was usually called a trade union [*treidiunion*].

This union was important not only for the workers' movement and for the party organization; it also loomed large in the social life of the entire town. I remember one incident. That winter there was virtually a famine in part of Russia (I don't remember exactly where, but I think throughout this region), and collections to aid the hungry were taken up everywhere. Lugansk was in Ekaterinoslav Province and there were appeals there as well, of course. I remember that the chairman of the trade union of the Hartman workers appeared third or fourth on the appeals, right after the governor and the bishop. His name was Voloshinov, I think, but I'm not certain. The impact of the workers' organization on the life of the entire town – which later was shown when a Lugansk person was elected to the Second Duma – affected all of the conditions of our work, right up to our arrest. We were arrested under very peculiar circumstances, Pinkevich and I, in March 1907.

As I mentioned, the organization was Bolshevik and the split was not yet total, with some Mensheviks taking part in the organization. Pinkevich and I arrived with the aim of organizing a nonfactional center. This was an idea that was fairly popular in the party in general then, I think both among the Bolsheviks and the Mensheviks (to the extent that it was expressed): that we must reorganize and rebuild the party; create a party without Lenin and Martov, since many ascribed the sectarian tendencies within the party largely to the personal characteristics of the leaders. A representative of this "unifying" tendency at this time was Trotsky, who on many issues was closer to the Bolsheviks than to the Mensheviks (to whom he formally belonged), and the Bolsheviks dubbed Trotsky's position "the swamp." So we thought that we would try to create something similar and then link up with Trotsky.

H: So you had this intention before you arrived in Lugansk?

GD: We didn't know the working conditions in Lugansk or the physiognomy of the organization, but we thought and talked about it, especially on the trip from Petersburg to Lugansk which lasted eight days because of snow storms and snowdrifts. We got pretty hungry, because we were stranded in snowdrifts, I think, for three days, and ate up everything we had taken along for a shorter trip. Then all the passengers on that ill-fated train had nothing to eat, and quenched their thirst with snow. So during such a long trip, of course, we talked a lot, but there was no definite plan, because ultimately the specific shape a plan would take could only be worked out in contact with people. To bring changes in the character of the Lugansk organization, what we needed was not just a few people – such people could probably be found in any organization – but to get one of the strongest Social-Democratic organizations as accomplices, and in this we were successful. We succeeded through long conversations with individual people, and one of the prominent activists of the Lugansk committee who came over to our position was Klementii Voroshilov. In a moment, I'll tell you what resulted, and why this great victory turned out to be utterly fruitless. I remember that Lugansk was in need of agitators. There were no effective agitators there. Now Pinkevich and I were first-rate. The need for agitators was acute because of the coming election campaign [to the Third Duma], and this was taken very seriously in Lugansk. The attitude there toward the Duma and the elections wasn't so scornful. Again, I think, this was related to the peculiar nature of life in Lugansk and its effect on the Lugansk organization. Furthermore, there was a change in Lenin's position and so the position of the Bolshevik faction changed too. I think this was finally confirmed in January 1907, when agreements and common lists with the Trudoviki became permissible in the first stage.

H: It seems to me that this depended on local decisions.

GD: Yes.

H: When was it allowed?

GD: It was allowed then, and at voters' meetings in provincial towns agreements with the so-called bourgeois parties were considered permissible and took place.

H: That is, with the Kadets?

GD: Yes, the Kadets, even with non-party people, more or less, even with not always very liberal electors. In Lugansk we had an agreement with the Trudoviki who virtually didn't exist, and the entire burden of the election campaign lay upon us in the Social-Democratic organization. So the presence of agitators was a very important issue, the more so because the candidate problem was very complicated. Voroshilov, who would have been the most natural candidate (although he didn't have a brilliant mind or great education, he was a very powerful speaker, an energetic and strong-willed man, and an important figure in the trade union), could not be entered, because he had been tried and convicted earlier, and had been deprived of electoral rights. So there was an issue of the candidate to be chosen as an elector at the beginning. A very curious struggle was waged over this. One of the workers in the Hartman trade union was a Jew named Friedkin, whom I met and came to know quite well. I should add that, even among the Petersburg worker intelligentsia, I never met as intellectually gifted a worker as Friedkin, and he was a brilliant speaker as well.

H: He also worked at the factory?

GD: Yes, he did, and he was one of the members of the trade-union committee and very important there, but he had one drawback from the point of view of the party organization: he was not a party member. His candidacy, which seemed extremely valuable to me, would have elected to the Second Duma a man who could speak entirely on the same level as all those brilliant orators in which the first two Dumas were so rich. I doubt that there was ever a parliament in the world that had such a high intellectual level as the first two Dumas, where there were so many luminaries. But, as I mentioned, the obstacle was that Friedkin was not a party member. After many long conversations, I became convinced that he was definitely a socialist, definitely a Social Democrat, but didn't like the party organization. I decided to push his candidacy and, with Pinkevich's support, I waged a struggle within the organization. I got them to agree that provided Friedkin became a party member, which he did, they would enter him in the list of electors. This was a great victory. As I recall, the city of Lugansk chose seven provincial electors, of which the majority (five, I think) were Social Democrats.[2] I think that no other place had a higher proportion of Social-Democratic electors than Lugansk. So we went to the meeting of electors at Ekaterinoslav in a very strong position. At this point, though, something happened which has left me with extremely bitter memories. The Mensheviks had a clear edge in other organizations of the Donets Basin and Ekaterinoslav province. They also figured that they would be elected to the Duma, and their candidate was Belousov, also a worker.[3] I don't have a clear notion of what became of him later; the impression he made on me was that of a very mediocre man. On the other hand, Friedkin made a very powerful impression on the Mensheviks. Their first response was ecstatic. Then, as was quite clear to me, they became frightened. And although they knew – and didn't conceal it – that he was not a true-blue Bolshevik, it would clearly be extremely unpleasant for them to have a brilliant Bolshevik candidate and a very mediocre Menshevik candidate – vastly inferior to Friedkin, at any rate – elected from Ekaterinoslav province. Naturally, I don't know everything that happened behind the scenes, and even then there were some distressing accusations by our side against the Mensheviks, but the fact is that, on the eve of the deputy elections, the Mensheviks came to us and said that, although they wanted him, Friedkin wouldn't do, because we would have to vote together with bourgeois electors, and they claimed that these electors wouldn't vote for a Jew. We had the impression that it was not the bourgeois electors but the Mensheviks, who were virtually all Jewish, and who raised the issue. But this can't be proved.

H: The votes of the bourgeois electors were needed to obtain a majority?

GD: Yes.

H: And when you say "bourgeois," you mean not the Kadets but simply individual progressives?

GD: Yes. In the last analysis, we couldn't elect anyone with our own votes, but there was a coalition against the extreme right, and in general it was entirely necessary.

H: I would like to establish one point – when the coalition was formed in Ekaterinoslov province – was there a leftist bloc of this sort in Lugansk?

GD: It was formed in Ekaterinoslav. The electors met in Ekaterinoslav three days, I think it was, before the elections. Three days of very intensive negotiations.

H: As you know, in Petersburg, and on the higher levels of the two factions, there was a sharp struggle over this issue of coalition, with whom it was permissible to coalesce, and under what circumstances. Were there debates between the Bolsheviks and Mensheviks in Lugansk over this issue?

GD: In the centers, chiefly Petersburg and Moscow, they needed formulas, like the struggle against the danger of the Black Hundreds. I can't say that it was true everywhere, but in Lugansk, at any rate, no one talked about it. The situation was much simpler. We didn't want reactionaries from the right to be elected and the more or less liberal and progressive common-sensible people didn't want it either. It was entirely natural for us to agree to promote as many nonrightist elements as possible, if not all of them. But we didn't succeed with Friedkin. As I said, we had the suspicion, which we couldn't prove, that this was concocted by the Mensheviks. In 1917 I obtained some indirect proof. In one of my visits to Petersburg, I met one of the Mensheviks who had been in Ekaterinoslav province at the time; I think he worked in Iuzovka, but I'm not sure. I never knew his name, and didn't learn it in 1917. He said to me, "You know, a couple of years after the elections, Khinchuk came to us from the central committee.[4] He got to know Friedkin, talked with him, and then gave us such a tongue-lashing for keeping him out of the Duma." So this was recognition that our suspicion was at least justified. The more so in that it was not very pleasant that we knew, and the fact couldn't be hidden, that the Mensheviks were in contact with the bourgeois partners the whole time, without involving us. So the relationship that developed wasn't exactly gratifying. But Lugansk, which had produced a majority of Social-Democratic electors – it was a majority, as I recall – had the right to send one of its electors to the Duma, something our comrade enemies didn't deny. Since Friedkin had been eliminated, we had to propose the candidate who was chosen, Ivan Nikolaevich Nagikh, also a worker of the Hartman factory. He was a good fellow and not stupid, but totally insignificant, and, as you would expect, played absolutely no role in the Duma. Thus the campaign, which had cost so much effort, energy, talk, and preparation, ended in complete failure. But a victory of a different sort followed it.

H: I would like to take up one point about Ekaterinoslav, the meeting of the provincial electors. Did the bourgeois progressives who were in the bloc agree that there should be two Social Democratic deputies?

GD: No. There were about ten deputies from Ekaterinoslav province. And the agreement was, of course, that there would be more Social Democrats. Probably there was some bargaining, but I don't remember this. They were all very loyal. There were engineers from factories, lawyers, more or less liberal businessmen. I had the impression that their attitude was in fact loyal, and that they had no bad feelings about any of the Menshevik comrades. Now, two deputies were chosen from Lugansk, one Social Democrat, Nagikh, and a bourgeois deputy, Selenov – I don't remember what his occupation was. Upon our return, a large banquet was held at which both the Social Democrats and various other people spoke. Allowing for the fact that it was a staunch Bolshevik organization even then, this was a very unusual event.

H: And Selenov designated himself in the Duma as a Kadet or a progressive?

GD: A Kadet, I think, I don't recall. That could also be checked.

H: But, at any rate, the Bolshevik organization in Lugansk wasn't worried.

GD: By then there had been a major change in the organization.

H: I imagine that's what you want to talk about now.

GD: Yes. The situation within the Lugansk organization was played out on two levels. One of them was very unpleasant. That was simply a nasty personal squabble that was so uninteresting in and of itself that I have even forgotten how it arose. The Lugansk Bolshevik organization had no printed mouthpiece, but there was a newspaper in Lugansk, *Donetskii Kolokol* [The Don's Bell], that appeared two or three times a week, and was the private undertaking of a Menshevik in the organization named Rozlovskii. Naturally, this created some tension with the Bolsheviks. One of the chief Bolsheviks in the committee was Samoilov; he and his wife were known under their party names Anton and Natasha. (She was later a fairly prominent Bolshevik figure, and he, as far as I was able to find out later, was a lawyer and worked subsequently with the Cheka somewhere, after 1917.)[5] Not only were they both very ardent Bolsheviks, but Anton, particularly, was extremely excitable and high-strung. Some kind of scandal arose between him and Rozlovskii, with insults and so on; an arbitration court was set up; and I, unluckily, had to be the chairman. It was a nightmare, because each meeting of the court ended with the start of some new dispute. Anton and Rozlovskii were both temperamental people, and the sessions turned into wrangles with savage accusations, one against the other, so that I had to terminate them. Then there was new round of new statements, one by Rozlovskii another by Anton, who demanded the investigation of some accusation that had been made in some session of the court. In short, it was a complete nightmare, and if there was a pleasant side to my impending arrest, it was that I felt that at least I was free from involvement in the court arbitration, and I made a promise to myself never to be involved in one again. But there was another development that was more interesting and important, I think – the elections to the Party Congress.

H: The Fifty Party Congress in London?[6]

GD: Yes. Now, Pinkevich and I had the ambitious idea of keeping Bolsheviks from Lugansk from going to the congress, and to go ourselves. It turned out that our opponents within the Bolshevik committee were Natasha and Anton Samoilov. Voroshilov and others came over to our side, and the committee elected Pinkevich and me as delegates. We needed only to be confirmed by the members of the organization, which no one doubted; as far as I know, the members in the minority, and an insignificant minority at that, didn't even plan to speak and were reconciled to the idea. But, of course, it was a slow process. In the interval between the committee's decision and the meeting of the organization, Pinkevich and I were arrested, on the same night. I was still somewhat naive at the time and couldn't figure out the weird circumstances of our arrest, which were entirely incomprehensible. We were not arrested by the Lugansk police; suddenly some *okhranniki* arrived from Ekaterinoslav.[7] In addition to Pinkevich and me, two minor Menshevik members of the organization were arrested; none of the staunch Bolsheviks were.

H: This was approximately in February 1907?

GD: In March. Before our arrest, we already sensed that this period of exceptional freedom for the times in Lugansk was coming to an end. So there was a discussion among us, Pinkevich and myself, and the comrades in the organization in general, to the effect that after the congress, we would not be able to continue to work in Lugansk, because of the prevailing conditions, for we, who were the most conspicuous, were literally known to the entire town, including the police in all its forms, of course. So a scheme was hatched that was sometimes practiced then – an exchange of delegates after the congress. For instance, if delegates from one place could not return to their own organization, they would go to another, and delegates from there would replace them. I wrote to the secretary of the Kazan organization about this. Bernheim, the secretary of the Kazan Bolshevik committee, who was later known in the Bolshevik party under the pseudonym of Batinskii.

I sent the letter in code, as was the practice, with a clandestine address. When I was interrogated for the first time after being arrested, they showed me a letter from Bernheim which he had written and signed himself, not in code and not to a clandestine address. Moreover, soon after my arrest, I was called out for a visit. I went out, and guess who I saw on the other side the screen – none but the secretary of the Kazan committee, Bernheim! Of course, there were observers present, so I couldn't ask him, "How could you possibly do such a thing?" We greeted each other very amiably, and I simply asked him, "What are you doing?" "I came to Ekaterinoslav on business, and learned that you had been arrested, so I decided to come to Lugansk and see you . . . ," and so forth. I came to the conclusion, which later turned out to be completely wrong, that he had turned traitor. Now I am absolutely convinced that it was a Bolshevik maneuver, that other people from the Bolshevik committee, maybe that same future Cheka member Anton, to whom our intention of swapping had been no secret, had communicated to the Kazan organization that some "unreliables" were planning to go there, and to stop them if possible.

And this was the reason for the letter, which could only fall into the hands of the police. The Lugansk police did not react to the letter, and the arrest itself was so much out of line with local practices that the Lugansk procurator, or more precisely the assistant procurator, who came to visit us in jail, was indignant at the arrest and declared that he refused to initiate any action since he saw no evidence of a crime. True, it was established that we were both members of the Bolshevik committee, but, although I don't remember exactly what the legal situation was then, the procurator felt that there was no legal basis for prosecution. He refused to prosecute, something that could have taken years; so the case was handled only administratively and ended very easily, with simple banishment to my home town under police surveillance. It never could have entered my mind then that such a Bolshevik maneuver was possible. Now I am certain that this was the case; I can find no other explanation because Bernheim was not such an idiot as to correspond like that. On the other hand, there was not even the slightest hint that he was a turncoat, either on the basis of his subsequent activity or from any of those innumerable lists of [secret police] agents that were discovered in 1917. But, if it was a planned maneuver, it was fully successful, because after Pinkevich and I were eliminated, the candidate elected to the congress was Voroshilov, who for all his softness, returned to the fold and went off to London with some very Bolshevik sounding pseudonym. Natasha Samoilova also went there. This circumstance was very significant for the fate of Voroshilov.

H: I would like to go back at this point. When you and Pinkevich arrived in Lugansk, you had the idea of creating a non-factional center, and this had a considerable influence on the organization and on the exchange of views within it. But we have yet to discuss the substance of this episode, and particularly the changes that took place. Could you tell me specifically, then, about the influence that you two, as "nonstaunch Bolsheviks," had in the organization regarding factional struggles, forms of organization, and so forth?

GD: Well, all our work was aimed at changing the character of the organization, because, as I said, our task was not simply to recruit a few people but to get the entire organization to occupy a middle position. As I conceived it, the organization would declare that it no longer had any relation to the Bolshevik faction and was taking such-and-such a position, say, aligning itself with Trotsky. It was not so much a matter of formal declarations as of changes which should effect the selection of delegates for the congress. This was the strategy, so to speak, and it was fully correct and successful. Now, how was it done? Through constant discussions. I should say that purely personal influence played a major part. I won't characterize myself, but Pinkevich was – I don't remember if he was in his last year or whether he had just graduated from Kazan University – in any case he was a geologist and a brilliantly gifted man. I later met the professor he worked and was very friendly with, and the professor was very distressed that so brilliant a person had given up science, since he regarded him as his successor and so on. Pinkevich ruined his scientific career by getting involved in politics. Although the professor was himself a liberal, he felt that geology was vastly more important than working in a Social-Democratic organization. On our side, then, there was a factor of considerable intellectual superiority, which soon had an influence on our position. Perhaps because of my own temperament, I got together with people on a personal basis even more easily than Pinkevich. We were so esteemed and admired that, for instance, we were invited to the sessions of the council of the trade union and our opinions were very much heeded. And in individual conversations – most of them were with Voroshilov – we talked about the impossible situation of a party supposedly united while at the same time there was a split; that this weakened the party, and that the major factors in the split were not far-reaching ones of principle but less important factors. The more or less intellectually developed workers were quite receptive to all this: they were not attracted to intellectual squabbles, and were very sympathetic to those intellectuals who did not involve themselves in such squabbles but were sincerely and thoroughly opposed to them.

H: Was this an important theme in your conversations; that is, differences among the intelligentsia that the real workers were not sympathetic to?

GD: No, never in that form.

H: And, in general, was this divergence between the intellectuals and the workers sensed; that is, did it appear a good reason for a change; were the workers dissatisfied about it?

GD: To some extent they were, of course, but it was not formulated like that, and perhaps not even recognized distinctly. As much as possible, I'm trying to express their vital concepts and notions. To take the Bolshevik committee, the key figure was Voroshilov. I can't even remember some of the faces of some of the worker members in the committee. They also had a voice, if you like, but Voroshilov was a striking figure, with a great deal of influence among the workers, so that the degree of influence of the committee on the workers and its success as regards recruitment depended primarily on him. Now, there were two pairs of intellectuals, Pinkevich and I on one hand, and the Samoilovs on the other. I wouldn't call the Samoilovs outstanding, but they were educated people, and not at all stupid.

All the rest, as I recall, were workers; I don't remember any other intellectual. But these intellectuals were outspokenly factional, and, alas, these things also play a role. Anton had an unpleasant character; he was irritable, inclined to be insulting; so that in addition to everything else, the chance element of sympathy, purely personal human appeal, was much more on our side than on theirs, although Natasha had a much more attractive character than her husband, even while she too was very staunch. And then, when this squabble began with its endless arbitrations and savage and hysterical outbursts on Anton's part – now I can't even remember the petty things that were involved – we had on our side a definite intellectual superiority, personal sympathies, and a superior position that drew people toward us. It was only later that Voroshilov became such a factionalistic Bolshevik; about all he was was a Social Democrat. The first sign of progress in the organization was that it ultimately agreed to propose as a Duma candidate a man who was essentially not a party member (although he had been admitted to the party and promised to be a disciplined member), and who was the foremost representative of the trade-union line. This also disturbed me somewhat, but I figured that his other qualities so much outweighed his trade-union slant that it could be lived with, and the Bolshevik organization, after some resistance, ultimately agreed. The whole affair did not unfold very fast, although now, when you recall that it all happened in one winter, it seems that the winter was quite eventful. In fact, there were many long conversations, attempts at persuasion, explanations, and so forth.

H: I have one more question on this issue. Besides the argument that there was just one party and that factionalism weakened it, and that personalities were a major factor, and so forth, was there dissatisfaction over the Bolsheviks' tactical line or program? That is, were there any issues of principles, more or less, which could be worked on?

GD: To some extent, I think so, yes.

H: What were they?

GD: I didn't have a clear picture of what had happened earlier, but my impression is that Lenin's initial position of "no agreements" was not popular, and this is understandable, especially in view of the conditions in Lugansk. Our people there felt themselves to be so strong that they could succeed in getting a deputy elected. But if they were to maintain the purely negative position of "no agreements," it was all futile – no one could be elected, nothing could be achieved, and probably even Social-Democratic electors wouldn't be elected. Although there were no serious Trudoviki there, to go into the countryside and appeal to people to vote for worker candidates was unthinkable. And since we were working entirely in the town, which was preponderant in the district, and the Trudoviki, with their connections were appealing to the peasants to vote for the same list of electors, success seemed almost guaranteed. Again, none of it was spelled out in distinct formulations, but I simply can't remember a single point at which anyone defended the position of "no agreements" to the end.

H: Well, what about the concept of exposing the Duma – Lenin's position?

GD: It was unimportant.

H: It wasn't brought up or supported or anything like that?

GD: It simply wasn't mentioned.

H: Regarding the Bolshevik tactics, aside from the issue of agreements, was the attitude toward the Duma a factor?

GD: There were no serious disagreements in practice. . . . I told you, right after my arrival, before I had made contact with the committee, I appeared at a meeting of shopkeepers, and my speech – completely independently of its relation to any particular tactical position – aroused great sympathy from the committee members at the meeting. I convinced the shopkeepers that they were proletarians and had to unite with the workers, and not with the bourgeoisie. Everyone was in agreement on these things, and it was such issues that made up practical work. On the way to a meeting, we wouldn't even have to agree how to present the issue of tactics in the Duma or any other thorny issue; it was all definite and concrete. . . .

H: Within the committee, was there disillusionment about the revolutionary slogans and possibilities, the preparation for an armed insurrection, and so forth? Were there traces of the autumn of 1906?

GD: If so, very few. You mentioned "exposure of the Duma." Now try to imagine a concrete situation. I would go to a pre-election meeting to persuade people, say workers, to vote for Social-Democratic candidates. So that they would expose the Duma? No, I would say, so that they would defend the workers' interests.

H: That's fully understandable.

GD: It would have been so unrealistic.

H: But what I have in mind is this: when you talked among yourselves, in the committee or with Voroshilov, or with other workers in the committee, could you discern any disillusionment with the Bolshevik line or leadership, aside from issues relating to the factional struggle between the Bolsheviks and Mensheviks?

GD: There was a disillusionment which, I think, cannot be explained by the factional struggle, but was in this context, so to speak, its concomitant. There was a definite reluctance to return to illegal work, particularly in Lugansk. The result of this was that both policy and tactics should be that legal opportunities should be preserved as much as possible. So it was only in this respect, if you like, that there was Liquidationism. For people like Pinkevich and myself, it was simply an aversion to the underground that made any prolonged return to illegal activity simply impossible.

H: As regards the activity of the trade union, were there any conflicts in the committee before your arrival, or did you sense any dissatisfaction with the Bolshevik leadership for underestimating the importance of worker self-organization?

GD: None. The Bolshevik leadership was careful enough not to take a definite position against trade-unionism, because, if they had done so, they would have completely lost the workers. I would like to compare the material situation of the Lugansk workers as opposed to workers in other places. I have no statistical data, but I saw the conditions of their life and, naturally, the Lugansk workers lived much better than others. I'm prepared to say that it was almost immeasurably better than that of workers in Kazan or of most of the workers in Petersburg – the way they dressed, for instance. Something that is particularly important is that they were a part of society; like the banquet that honored the Duma deputies – there were many Hartman workers there. The presence of this very strong worker center made an impact on the workers of other, smaller enterprises, so that the direct and major advantages that stemmed from this trade-unionism were absolutely indisputable. To simply condemn it would have been suicide on the part of the organization. So the line was different – at least among the party members of this group. They could form their own idea. "Yes, of course, it's a good thing, but we mustn't forget that it's not something solid as long as capitalism still exists, and that a really complete change can happen only under socialism," and so forth. The irritation that existed with respect to trade-unionism was expressed only within a very narrow circle. It was a fact of life that couldn't be disregarded.

I will give you a humorous example of how far this freedom extended. I had not yet given up music at that time – I still played the piano. With all my wandering, I hadn't played for a long time, but I simply had the urge to find a piano somewhere and play a little. I got to know one of the party comrades who had a music store. So one day, without any hesitation, I went to his store and sat down and played. I even remember that I played Beethoven's *Moonlight Sonata*. When I finished, I went out of the store and a man came up to me and said, "I heard you playing. You see, I have a Romanian orchestra and we're missing a pianist, so I would like to ask you to play with us." Not all, of course, but many of the passers-by knew what I did, and it would never have entered my mind that you would have to go and hide after playing, nothing of the sort. We would go out onto the streets, meet there, have conversations on the street, things you could no longer do in Petersburg.

Also, while in Ekaterinoslav the relations with the Mensheviks before the electors' meeting had been tense, in Lugansk both Pinkevich and myself were on very friendly terms with the local Mensheviks and with Rozlovskii, the editor of *Donetskii Kolokol*. In January, at the time of the Reichstag elections in Germany, I wrote "Correspondence from Berlin about the Elections" – this sort of thing was very common.

H: Besides Rozlovskii, what other Mensheviks were there in Lugansk?

GD: Two or three young men. Rozlovskii had a sister who was also a Menshevik, and there were two or three young men who were nice people and good comrades, but nothing special.

H: And were your good relationships with them typical? Did other Bolsheviks have the same experience?

GD: I think so, except for the Samoilovs.

H: What about the political attitude of these Mensheviks?

GD: Roughly the same as mine. In general, the split was felt to be a burden, more so in that it was difficult to justify it at that time. Besides, the split existed in fact, but not formally and this was a distressing situation. On the one hand, the party was united, while on the other hand, one part of the party followed one set of directives, the other, another.

H: Did this also bother them? When you talked with Rozlovskii, were there points of disagreement?

GD: No. You see, our visits to Rozlovskii's were a form of relaxation. There were friendly, lively conversations; sometimes, well, to call it a carousal would be too harsh and exaggerated, but people drank somewhat, danced sometimes. Since Lugansk was part of the Ukraine, the dances were the rather wild Ukrainian ones. There were people who had absolutely nothing to do with the party organization and who were not at all socialists. It was "social life" in the English sense of the term, without social problems. To a considerable extent, of course, there was also talk, particularly about what to write and print in the newspapers. The paper was published in a loyal spirit, so not only did no attacks on the Bolsheviks appear, but in general there was nothing that would constitute a separate line, contradictory to the general one, because the general line in Lugansk was Bolshevik, due to the makeup of the committee. Well, Bolshevik, but with the difference that it had very much faded.

H: But Rozlovskii regarded himself as a Menshevik at the time?

GD: Yes.

H: And did you talk about it, that is, on what issues did he feel that there was a different line that he supported, which seemed important and understandable to him?

GD: I would say that the sharply emphasized Bolshevik line of armed uprising was completely alien and repugnant to him. But this issue had lost all practical importance by the time I arrived in Lugansk. Since Lugansk was in a way a special case, as I have said, and since, aside from some correspondence with Bazarov, I had little or no contact with the center, I would have been very interested if anyone could have shown or explained to me exactly what, at this time, the differences were. Of course, the Mensheviks had a tendency, even in the first stage, to make agreements with parties as far away as the Kadets; but for us in Lugansk, this was of no practical importance, because there were no Kadets there. For us it was quite sufficient to make agreements with some colorless people who had the merit to be known as Trudoviki and could appeal to the peasants who, again, were with them not out of conviction, but out of instinctive sympathy to the Trudoviki as representatives of the peasantry. Therefore, our list of elector candidates was not just a worker but a worker-and-peasant list, and this was the reason for its considerable success.

H: My last question is this: of the Mensheviks whom did the party workers prefer?

GD: They didn't know anyone. None of the Mensheviks ever came to Lugansk.

H: Well, what about reputations?

GD: Essentially, only one name was widely known, Martov's. As for Axelrod, there was only a hazy notion.

H: And what about such things as the Workers' Congress and all that?

GD: That was already in the past. Ultimately, most if not all of them realized that things in the rest of the country didn't at all look as they did in Lugansk.

H: Very well, let's move on. So you and Pinkevich were arrested in March 1907 . . .

GD: And by a strange coincidence, I spent 110 days in jail, just like the first time. But legal proceedings weren't initiated and I was administratively sentenced to two years in my home town under police supervision, and forbidden to leave. But I would like to say something about my experience and impressions outside of purely party life. After all, there are things that you know but which really become palpable realities when you experience them. For example, the fact that although the Donets Basin formally belongs to the Ukraine the working-class population is not Ukrainian but Russian and Great Russian. Even knowing that, I was really struck by the fact that I never heard a single word of Ukrainian in Lugansk itself. When I went around to where the workers were, as I did fairly often, no one ever spoke Ukrainian. But when I encountered a non-worker, peasants or petty bourgeoisie, it was sometimes difficult to make myself understood. It was a striking contrast between the town and industrial population in general, and the peasantry.

Then there was something to which the inhabitants of Central Russia, while they knew the general circumstances, were completely insensitive and didn't attribute much importance. I'll give you a striking example: there existed then the so-called Ekaterinskaia Railway – and it still exists – serving chiefly this basin with its branch lines. Who in Russia didn't know that bribery existed? But it was only there that I saw striking examples of this kind of fraud. I was a so-called professional, which meant that I had a salary from the party organization, and when I traveled I was given traveling expenses. Something that struck me immediately was that I would be given not the entire cost of a railway ticket, but half the cost. Why? For a very simple reason. You didn't go and buy a ticket at the ticket-window, you simply got on the train. No matter what, no one ever collected tickets. The conductor would come through and collect money, half the price of a ticket, and put it in his pocket. I saw this several times, and the scenario was always the same. The conductor would run along the train shouting that after such-and-such a station there would be a check. The train would stop at this station, literally all the passengers would get off and stand in long lines to buy tickets to some other station. The inspector would pass through, and everyone would have a ticket. I knew fully well – how could he not know – that it was a strange coincidence that all the passengers on the train had tickets to places two or three stops ahead. So he was obviously involved, but still had to maintain appearances. For me it was a very valuable experience, because both then and occasionally now, in talking to people more or less of my own age who lived through those times, I see that they have no notion that even then, in 1907, in many parts of the country at any rate, life had become thoroughly rotten. For me it was one of the elements of the hopelessness that I fell into after the Lugansk experience.

H: My next question is this: what is your opinion regarding the Menshevik influence in other parts of the Donets Basin, in particular Ekaterinoslav province? In particular, what accounts for the predominant influence of the Mensheviks at this time and even later, especially in the Donets Basin and Ekaterinoslav province?

GD: In many cases I'm inclined to attribute it to almost chance factors. One place would happen to have organizers who felt one way; elsewhere there would be organizers who felt otherwise. But once a Bolshevik or Menshevik organization would form, the newcomers would naturally [follow]. As regards my observations in Ekaterinoslav province, this is completely inapplicable, because I never met any strong Menshevik personalities who could have made gains for Menshevism through personal influence and their own actions. So something other than chance factors must have been important, and probably even decisive. Again, this would have to be checked against objective data, but I think that chief aspect was . . . it was only happenstance that the Lugansk organization did not become Menshevik. There was the trade union, there were tangible opportunities for improving the situation, and therefore the Social Democrats who counted more than the rest on economic struggle, on the possibility of economic improvements, and on practical achievements which could be gained through the development of self-organized worker activity, that is, all the things that in most cases distinguished the Mensheviks from the Bolsheviks, particularly at places where there was a dense concentration of workers, could create a predisposition in favor of the Mensheviks. I don't know, but I should add that I didn't feel that there was the kind of poverty in Lugansk which I sensed in other places. I lived in the apartment of a railway employee; they ate very well, the apartment was quite decent . . . and when I went around and spent the night in different places, I wasn't aware of poverty.

H: What other places in the province did you visit during this time?

GD: I was in Iuzovka several times; it has some other name now, for a while it was Stalino, but they have changed it again. It was a village that grew very rapidly, suddenly arising around some factory – I forget what kind of factory – that belonged to an Englishman named Hughes. There were nice houses and apartments for workers, but the strongest impression that remained with me from Iuzovka was that I got stuck in the mud in the street and barely managed to get out. It was an unpaved street, and there was such an unbelievable amount of mud that I got stuck, I floundered around for a long time, and finally had to use my arms to help myself crawl out.

H: Was Iuzovka a metal working center then?

GD: Yes.

H: And were the Mensheviks predominant?

GD: Yes.

H: What were your impressions of these Mensheviks in the Donets Basin and their attitudes?

GD: I can only judge from one side. The local Mensheviks I encountered were very factionalistic. . . . Still it didn't go so far that they would hinder me, say, as a member of a Bolshevik organization and Bolshevik committee whom they regarded as a Bolshevik, from operating in their sphere of influence. In fact, there were invitations, they needed an agitator and so on in Iuzovka or Karnatorovka, more frequently in Iuzovka. Of course, something that's very hard to judge is whether there was any influence of foreign capital, which was strongly represented in the Donets Basin. For instance, if you ask why the Lugansk trade union was generally on pretty good terms with management, it may be because the enterprise was German, and in Germany credit norms of relations between union and management were entirely natural. And it was already 1907, when the German trade-union movement was already highly developed.

H: Do you think that it was easier to put forth economic demands under these conditions?

GD: I think so. For example, in Kazan there was complete lawlessness, even later. The labor inspection was more decent, but . . .

H: When you were there, what forms did this trade-union trend take concretely? Did the members take part in strikes then?

GD: No. There weren't any at that time. There had been earlier. The workers didn't regard themselves as pariahs, and this is something that is always a consequence of trade-unionism.

H: But what did the union do, and what were its specific demands when you were there?

GD: Issues of wages, regulation of working hours, the usual economic politics of trade unions.

H: And were there negotiations over these issues?

GD: Yes, but during my time I don't recall any severe conflicts; negotiations were always conducted along more European lines.

H: Very well, let us stop here. I think that our next chapter will be Kazan.

Fifth interview

H: Last time we stopped at the point at which you were released from the Lugansk jail and returned home to Kazan under police supervision. This was about the end of June or the beginning of July of 1907.

GD: I should say some more about my decision to go to Kazan, because I think that the motives that determined my decision were not unique to me but expressed the feeling of many people, in any case of a considerable number of party workers. The choices were to submit to the sentence, that is to return to Kazan under police supervision, or to go over to illegal work and continue party activity. When I was packing before leaving Lugansk and saw the state of my clothes after several months of wandering, I remembered some lines of a Gorkii piece – and these lines were to haunt me later on – "I went in search of sun and fortune; naked and barefoot did I return. And in my wanderings, I wore out hope and clothes." The last line about wearing out hope and clothes literally corresponded to how I, and, I have no doubt, many others felt at this point. What was important, of course, wasn't the clothing, it all had to do with the hope. The middle of 1907 was the point when it became completely apparent that all hopes and expectations had collapsed, although, of course, they had been very exaggerated ones.

It was not so much a matter of personal disillusionment. Most important was what it involved. If all our predictions had been so inaccurate, if what we had expected had not, to such a striking extent, come to pass, the question then arose as to whether the premises on which both the Bolshevik and Menshevik predictions and hopes had been built were erroneous. This inevitably led to a reexamination. Another change that occurred, with others as well, was a growing opposition – or to put it more bluntly – an aversion to illegal forms of operation. It was not merely that such work was completely fruitless and unnecessary. But, on the basis of my own experience, it was simply painful to recall the way human relations were under illegal conditions. It was a strange paradox, and one that was even more tragic for the Socialist Revolutionaries than for us. On the one hand, people supposedly lived in close comradely atmosphere; on the other, they, in fact, didn't know each other at all. This is the only way you can explain how easy it was for police agents and provocateurs to penetrate the underground work. What psychological blindness there had to be in people who collaborated closely with Azev over a number of years not suspecting his real role! And then once the exposes began, they refused to believe them and stubbornly resisted recognizing who he was.

I think that this psychological blindness was an inevitable consequence of the conditions of illegal activity. The comradely closeness was still extremely superficial from the point of view of human relations. This was sometimes revealed even in the period of joint activity, for example by the form that relationships between the Bolsheviks and Mensheviks sometimes took. And it was confirmed much later with regard to people whom I theoretically admired a great deal, and later learned absolutely disgusting things about, like the case of Comrade Nikolai whom I knew in Kazan and met in Petersburg and who turned out to have been a provocateur for a number of years, something that came out only later, in 1911, when he completely unexpectedly committed suicide. That is, it had not been revealed, but some question had been raised. And it was only after 1917 that he and many others who were regarded as true and reliable comrades were revealed to be provocateurs. But this was in the way of later confirmation. Even at that time, however, you felt that illegal activity created entirely abnormal conditions for human relations. I simply couldn't think, to put it crudely, of getting back into that quicksand. I wouldn't say that it took a lot of deliberation – it was almost self-evident that I wasn't going back to illegal work.

H: Were there any particular aspects of your experience that made such a painful impression on you?

GD: There was one occasion in particular. It was in Kazan in 1905. I didn't talk about it, and then later on I was somewhat sorry that I hadn't. There was a comrade whom everyone liked very much, an able, lively fellow named Sapetov. He did something that was entirely unexpected – he tried to commit suicide by poisoning himself, but he didn't succeed; he was treated and recovered. But it didn't stop there. People watched him, and they took a gun away from him. Now Kazan was not far from the Volga. You could get to the river by trolley. I saw him on the trolley. I went with him, and asked him directly, "So, are you going to drown yourself?" He admitted he was. I said, "Listen, I'll make you an offer. I have a revolver. You tell me what's going on, and if I conclude that you really should do away with yourself, and you don't change your mind, I'll give you the gun. You won't have to deceive anyone or flee from anyone, and you can shoot yourself right here and now."

He agreed. So that we wouldn't be bothered by anyone, I bought two tickets for the steamship from Kazan to Samara. We both, incidentally, had close friends there. During the trip I heard his confession. Here was someone about whom there were absolutely no suspicions, but it turned out he was an agent. And he told me how it had happened. Once, after he had been arrested, he was interrogated – in Rostov, I think – there was a remarkable Okhrana investigator there who was supposed to have simply hypnotic abilities and was particularly talented at getting people to make careless revelations. Sapetov said that the colonel's pressure in the interrogation led him to make some unguarded remarks and he was caught. This was the usual method. They would say, "You have to work for us now, otherwise we'll expose you." And he talked about the torments during the two or three years when he was forced to write reports and had to do them well, and how he had to try hard not to actually be a traitor at the same time. And, indeed, no one suffered because of him. He would make reports about activities, but if he mentioned people it was in such a way that they couldn't be caught. He simply couldn't tolerate the situation and decided to commit suicide. It was a great emotional drama, so to speak. And here was someone who hadn't been exposed and was not the object of suspicion. He could have easily continued this life. But I was able to convince him that there was no reason to end his life, that a way out could be found.

Of course, he couldn't remain involved in party activity under the circumstances, and that was best for him because he wouldn't have to disclose things about the movement. He was really an extremely dedicated man. And since he couldn't just up and leave, the organization had to be told everything about the situation. So I made the appropriate report, and a meeting was called. I don't remember who was there: the members of the committee, beyond a doubt, probably all of them. But there were also some others, probably some of the influential comrades. Sapetov was not there. He was no longer admitted since he shouldn't be allowed to see the clandestine members of the committee and the others. I described his whole situation. Then one of the members of the organization – and possibly also of the committee, I don't know exactly – named Kulesha, completely calmly, as if it went without saying, said that it was clear what had to be done – kill him. This kind of flippant attitude to the question made me furious. I delivered a very passionate speech. I succeeded in winning the comrades to my point of view, and they decided only to have him expelled, excluded from all activity, without any punitive measures. But I was shocked by this flippancy. Its a curious coincidence, though perhaps not completely accidental, but some years later this same Kulesha, who at the time was a university student, was graduated and moved from Kazan to Ekaterinburg, and was killed there – he was shot by the local procurator out of jealousy. He was going after the procurator's wife, so he was the one who got the death penalty. Sapetov's life, of course, was shattered completely. He became a minor journalist. They still didn't leave him alone. After 1905 the Okhrana kept pressing him and he dodged and tried to wriggle out. Perhaps he didn't always succeed; I don't know. But the fact that some people, at any rate, absolutely lacked any understanding of the complexity of such situations, requiring exceptional heroism to be endured, was something that amazed me.

I would like to relate two other incidents, although I am rationalizing my attitudes at that time somewhat, of course; they weren't so clearly related for me then as became clear later, in hindsight. How were we most radically mistaken? Primarily in that we were unable to foresee the responses of different strata of the population. We formed an abstract notion of the proletariat as a permanent and continuously revolutionary element. As I formulated it in my reflections and conversations with others, the workers were seen as ready to go to the barricades at the drop of a hat, which in fact wasn't true. All of them tired, their attitudes changed or they fell into apathy. We saw this after the dissolution of the First Duma. Even worse, even more profound, was our misunderstanding of peasant psychology. There was no understanding of what only later, in the period of Liquidationism, was expressed in the Liquidationist literature, by Potresov in particular: the deep penetration − even into proletarian psychology − of what we contemptuously call *meshchanstvo*, petty-bourgeois prejudices, and so on. In short, we failed absolutely to understand and evaluate human psychology, and this was related to the experience of illegal activity.

I didn't have a clearly articulated conception of this then, but the implications for me were clear. I would go to Kazan to enter the university and study psychology. Now, according to the ideas of the time, and of the milieu that I knew, at any rate, the basis of social psychology was individual psychology; and the basis of individual psychology was physiology. Physiological psychology already existed then, and it was not just in Wundt that I read about it. So the choice was fairly clear − I would enter the natural-science division of the Faculty of Physics and Mathematics and specialize in physiology. It was a completely logical decision.

H: I would like to dwell on one issue. In your written memoirs, you also note that at this point your relationship with the Bolsheviks had deteriorated on the basis of your earlier experience and that your impression of the Mensheviks in jail in Lugansk was not very favorable. So the idea of working with the Mensheviks was as repugnant to you as that of working with the Bolsheviks. What happened with the Mensheviks in your experiences in jail?

GD: I must correct you − I had no contact with the Mensheviks in jail. The contact with the Mensheviks, which tended to be antagonistic, was in connection with the Duma elections, but I can elaborate somewhat . . . The revolution hadn't followed either the Bolsheviks' or the Mensheviks' calculations. I am prepared to admit that the Mensheviks were less in error, but there is no basis to assume that their line was completely correct or that they understood the true state of affairs. [When we were released from prison,] we were dominated by an idea that could be formulated in simplified fashion, like this: "Above all, we are all inadequately educated, and in many respects profoundly ignorant − the most important thing now is to study!" So I reached the logical conclusion that I should go to the university and study psychology on the basis of physiology! And that's what I did. Although physiology did not begin in the first year, I became involved with some new colleagues and people whom I met at the university, and decided that there was no time to lose − that I should choose physiology, along with a solid grounding, and so forth. At that time in Kazan University, and probably elsewhere, there was an interesting phenomenon, something I have never seen mentioned in the literature. Special groups or circles would be set up under the guidance of a professor. For example, there would be, say, a history group – not a seminar or something official, but simply a group of students who would meet and invite a history professor to direct them. And it was the same in other fields. So I organized a physiology group, and we invited Professor Samoilov, an outstanding physiologist, to be the leader. Curiously enough, incidentally, his answer was surprising: "Me? The leader? I can't lead anything, and I should tell you that I wouldn't respect an organization that chose me as its leader!" But we persuaded him that he could be of assistance. Before these negotiations were over, however, I was asked to produce a certificate of trustworthiness, and since I was in no position to do so, my university studies came to an end at this point.

H: I have two questions regarding this two-month period: first, did you encounter other young former revolutionaries who had returned to the university at this time?

GD: I couldn't say. I think that I did (what a cautious way to put it – "I think I did")! I simply didn't know, and I wouldn't find out, whether they had been involved in party work.

H: Did these study groups take the place of earlier political groups? Did political groups no longer exist among the students?

GD: I think that they didn't exist in their earlier form. What remained from the organization was a small group of young people, very young Bolsheviks, and a few older ones. But no organization in fact existed, because every attempt to resurrect the organization was rapidly put to a stop by arrests, something that no one could understand then. Only in 1917 did we learn that the long-standing secretary of the organization – a most reliable person, who had never aroused the slightest suspicions in anyone – had worked continuously for the Okhrana for around ten years, and very cunningly, in such a way that no one found out, turned in one set of members after another. As a result, the Social-Democratic organization was not restored in Kazan until 1917. There were attempts, and there was a small but very interesting (as it turned out) group of Bolsheviks, interesting because Molotov was one of them. Also Victor Tikhomirov, was subsequently prominent, and Arosev.[1] (The leader of the group, who was somewhat older, died recently in New York – he was one of the directors of the Amalgamated Clothing Workers' Union, a rival of Dubinsky's Ladies Garment Workers Union.)

In Kazan, however, the question simply didn't arise for me of trying to resume underground activity, the more so because, as I told you, I had a very strong inner aversion to it. My situation was that I wasn't allowed to study in the university. I had to wait two years, until at least the autumn of 1909, to be allowed to return to study in return for good behavior while under police surveillance. So no party work, and no university studies. What was left? Self-education, so to speak: reading and observing life in general. I tried very hard to get to know people from the most diverse and unusual strata of the population. I had virtually no contact with workers and couldn't have, because if I tried to start acquaintances with workers, it would have naturally aroused suspicion, without being of use to anyone but myself; and for me the benefit would have been offset, probably, by not getting a good recommendation. It still aroused suspicion to try to meet workers. Peasants could be observed, and I tried to do this at the *dacha* in summer. What's more, I became interested in unusual cases and professions. At one point I became acquainted, and I think I can say made friends, with people like circus artists.

At that time I had a problem that brought out how little we understood about people (it never entered my mind that there could be such cases). It was a curious situation that had great significance for me. There was a circus act called the "death leap," in which the performer would jump from a considerable height – some dozens of meters – into a narrow pool ringed with fire. An absolutely horrendous scene. I learned – I read about it or someone told me – that, literally without exception, all circus performers who did this ultimately died from it. And it would happen fairly quickly – fifty or sixty such jumps and a mistake would happen. There was no halfway: either you succeeded and hit the water, or you died. I was shocked by this. I had to understand how it was possible for a human being to do this, knowing that it was not for very long and that he was doomed to death. I got to know this circus performer. We spoke very frankly, and I discovered that there were two reasons for this paradoxical situation. His pay was good, and he saved money. He led a modest, proper life, and didn't squander money. He lived decently, but without luxuries. And although he knew that all those before him had died, he still hoped that he would be able to save enough to retire before it was his turn. This kind of direct experience was as good as reading Dostoevsky. He viewed his life quite calmly and rationally. But what sort of a person was he, and how should he be regarded? A proletarian or a petty bourgeois? It seemed that there were very strong motives in people which worked entirely outside of the categories which seemed absolutely essential for us. And, along with this, there was a development that had begun earlier, namely, I became an adherent of Jaures. This was a time of heated debates on the issue: a brochure had appeared containing speeches by Guesde and Jaures. Of course, all those with orthodox views, both Bolsheviks and Mensheviks, were on Guesde's side. I was on Jaures's. Otto Bauer came twenty-five years later.

H: What did this mean for you specifically? Was it social patriotism?

GD: No, it didn't have to do with social patriotism, but rather with the importance given to emotional and moral factors. It appeared insufficient to appeal to material conditions. In part, it was essentially the same development as in the young Marx – the significance of alienation and an appeal to the emotional and moral world of people. I don't know to what extent it's true, but someone told me – and I was terribly pleased by it – that my oratory was very similar in nature to Jaures's in his early youth (later it became quite different). That was on the one hand, while on the other there were political feelings. The automatic rejection of participation in bourgeois government also seemed unsatisfactory to me. And I was inclined to see some truth in this criticism of German Social Democracy, even though I was not yet familiar enough with it. This was the combination – more real activism, not agitational activism but activism in practical politics, and allowance for moral and emotional and, more generally, psychological factors.

H: And these thoughts of yours were consonant with your work for a local newspaper?

GD: Yes, in part, because I was entirely in favor of these "small deeds." It wasn't enough to just sit and think about the way things should be – at each point you had to do what was possible.

H: What was your psychological state; were you depressed at this time – the end of 1907 and the beginning of 1908?

GD: Yes, for a short time. In general, though, my life in Kazan was burdensome because of purely personal experiences which I will not mention, since they are in no way related to our topic. Then there was another thing that made life in Kazan very distressing. Kazan was one of the worst centers of malaria in Russia. It was an outrage that very much encouraged my tendency to become involved in small deeds. There was a stagnant lake in Kazan with a ditch that led from it – simply unbelievable, with foul water and all sorts of miasmas. It was known throughout Russia and considered so important that in order to transfer to Moscow University (which wasn't always easy), it was enough to say I had malaria and needed to leave Kazan, and the doctors considered that I had to leave Kazan so it wouldn't become chronic. And, of course, my occasional attacks of malaria didn't make life easier, and my mood would be affected at these times. But I couldn't say that my depressed mood lasted very long.

H: I want to ask a more general question. During these two years, were you working for a newspaper that I think was called *Volzhsko-Kamskaia Rech'*?

GD: Yes, *Volzhsko-Kamskaia Rech'* [The Volga-Kama Word], and later *Kamsko-Volzhskaia Rech'*. I didn't stop working for it until 1917. I wrote either from Moscow or from Kazan.

H: And did you think about the prospects that you personally and Russia in general were facing?

GD: Well, of course I thought about the future, as did many others, and not just socialists! I would say that the dominant view, mine and many others, was that no revolution could be expected in the near future, but the country couldn't avoid a revolution in the long run. No one said how many years it would take, of course, but whether it was 10, 15, or 20 years, it wouldn't be endless at any rate. We didn't believe that the tsarist regime was eternal. And it was not just Social Democrats, but also party unaffiliated people, liberals, and even some on the right, people with entirely different sentiments.

One very interesting example was Alexander Fedorovich Kerenskii. I got to know him very shortly after I arrived in Kazan. Kerenskii was married to a Vasil'ev, a cousin or niece of those Vasil'evs with whom I became acquainted (and one of them died in New York very recently, just two weeks ago). It was an exceptional family; I knew the Vasil'ev brothers and sisters. Both brothers were outstanding. The father, Vasilii Vasil'evich Vasil'ev, was a prominent mathematician and in particular a philosopher of mathematics – he was internationally famous. Even under the Soviets he was elected chairman of the International Congress of Philosophers, in 1928, although the Soviet government didn't let him attend. He had a considerable reputation in those days. Moreover, he was a political figure, a Kadet member of the State Council. His father, the grandfather of my Vasil'ev friends, had been the founder of Chinese studies in Russia. It was a very interesting and exceptionally highly cultured milieu. Kerenskii was married to the niece of Vasil'ev the mathematician, so he was the cousin of my close friends. They had a small estate near Kazan. I mention this because it was a very interesting circumstance; if I have the time, I will write something about it sometime. These Vasil'evs – not the one who died here, but his brother – had a sort of informal circle, people who would get together at their place nearly every day. And it was an extremely intellectual and interesting group, people like Vasil'ev himself, Nikolai Aleksandrovich Vasil'ev, a doctor, philosopher, and poet who went crazy and then died. It was a dreadful story, I was very close to him. In summer, this intense cultural life continued at their estate – they were always inviting people there – some professors from Moscow University, and I would visit too. Every year Kerenskii came to spend some time there.

I must say that, in this society, Kerenskii did not make an impression of being very cultured or intellectual. This was before he became renowned for his involvement in the proceedings of the Lena goldfields incident.[2] He was a young Petersburg lawyer, with experience as a Socialist Revolutionary, and although he never told me (I know it from his relatives, or rather his wife's relatives), he was already absolutely convinced that there soon would be a revolution and that he would head it. So his relatives (not in my presence, but among themselves) would refer to him as the "president of the Russian Republic." I think that this detail is of great interest for Kerenskii's subsequent fate. The question that always comes up is how he could occupy such a position. I think that a major factor was his firm confidence that it would be he, that he would achieve it. When evaluating future prospects, he was much more optimistic than the rest. Particularly after he was involved in the trial and gained some renown, and became a Duma deputy. He was one of those optimists who could bide his time.

What is psychologically important here is not how a person evaluates future prospects, but whether he lives expecting revolution or has put off the idea for the time being and lives on a day-to-day basis with current problems – trying to find a place for himself working for a local nonparty or multiparty coalition newspaper, exposing abuses, or taking part in that remarkable educational coalition called the Society of People's Universities which was widespread in the country. It conducted educational activity, and many intellectuals, brilliant scholars, took part. This was the sphere of "small deeds" to use the old phrase. It was one solution. Some of the former activists, like the Socialist Revolutionary who was collaborating on the same magazine I was, had about the same feelings. Others went entirely in the opposite direction, like the Bolshevik Tarasov-Rodionov. It never would have occurred to me that Tarasov-Rodinov was really a Bolshevik. He had been a comrade of my brother in the *gimnazium*, then he had gone to the university. I don't know whether or not he had graduated. And what did he become enamored of at this time? There was a whole spate of regional exhibitions and fairs in Russia, in different places or different regions, like Kazan, or along the Volga or somewhere in Siberia. And he loved to get involved in organizing these exhibitions, financing them, gathering advertisements, and so forth. It wasn't merely that he liked it, of course, he also made some money, but he was enthusiastic about it.

H: I have another question. You note in your recollections about Kazan that your colleagues on the newspaper were politically diverse: two Social Democrats, one former Bolshevik . . .

GD: The Bolshevik I mentioned today, Orlovskii – I don't know his real name.

H: Yes, and former Social Revolutionaries, one Trudovik.

GD: Yes, the makeup changed somewhat. At one point, a Trudovik was the editorial secretary, and the secretary was in fact the editor, since the editor was a "dummy editor," that is, the one who would go to jail.[3] The newspaper didn't entirely pay for itself. It was financed by liberal bourgeois, and its management was dominantly Kadet.

H: I would like to know what these political designations represented for you at this time. The joint activities would indicate that they didn't make much difference, but what about conversations and the like?

GD: Political designations were very unimportant in practical matters, so the fact that I was a Social Democrat didn't shock anyone in this circle. The main point, namely, that the overall orientation should be toward overthrow of the autocracy, was generally held. And the main day-to-day activity consisted of attempts at reform and the struggle against abuses. I forgot to mention that, soon after I arrived in Kazan, I was invited by some young Bolsheviks who remained to work with them on the other local paper, *Volzhskii Vestnik* [The Volga Messenger]. This was before I began to work for *Volzhskaia Rech'*. I refused and went to work at *Volzhskaia Rech'*, and for this reason they wanted to exclude me. Molotov and some others had already left, and those that remained behaved very stupidly and got involved in a highly unpleasant affair – I don't know to what extent it affected their future. Specifically, Kazan was the first city where there was a major trial involving the military commissary. And, strikingly, the supposedly legal Social-Democratic newspaper *Volzhskii Vestnik* maintained a very strange position, defending the military. It turned out that they had received money from the commissary to subsidize the newspaper. It was like Lenin's principle: money doesn't smell! When the affair came to trial, there was a great scandal. Of course, this wasn't typical.

H: What else can you recall about your Kazan period?

GD: I would like to mention something I have already brought up. It affected others as well as me. The character of the universities had changed, and the proportion of students who wanted chiefly to study had greatly increased. I think, and I'm fairly sure, that those who had been principally involved in politics a few years earlier tried to concentrate on their studies. It was a kind of sublimation, but for me and others, particularly in my Moscow period as we will see, it wasn't limited to trying to gain what we call concrete knowledge. We had a keen interest in art, literature, music and so forth. For the newspaper, I didn't just write practical articles, exposes of the military commissary, and articles about the provincial zemstvo. I also regularly wrote literary and theatrical reviews, and worked very hard in this sphere. This whole period has been talked about as the Silver Age, the flowering of symbolist art, and so forth. All this happened, but it was all in the capitals. Actually this was a period when progressive and practical activity developed, as Stepun confirms in his memoirs. He was a philosopher and involved in these circles.[4] For example, I was very much interested by *Vekhi*.[5] Stepun traveled about Russia giving lectures, and he was struck by the fact that while *Vekhi* was a constant topic of conversation in Moscow, there was much agitation about it there, no one knew anything about it in the provinces; people were entirely uninterested. This was the true situation between 1906 and the war – not at all the way it is depicted. Yes, it was the Silver Age! My friends and I used to sit around and read the Silver Age magazines and poetry. But the realistic and secretly radical collections like *Znanie* were much more widespread, of course, and played a much greater role.

H: How important and significant did you regard your work involving the exposes of the provincial zemstvo, and the commissary trial?

GD: I regarded it as something very sound that yielded results. Now, the Kazan commissary trial was the first, but it was not just a legal proceeding. Purely by accident, because I played a considerable part in this, I met an exceptional man – not exceptionally gifted, but absolutely exceptional. He had gone to work for the commissary with the utopian hope of being some kind of healthy influence – not to steal, but to combat thievery. Nothing had come of this directly. But I obtained from him some extremely interesting and valuable material regarding abuses, which I then published in the Kazan paper. Later this led to a series of trials across all of Russia, and it had a certain practical effect. I think that, although the commissary wasn't entirely cleaned out, it was still not as rotten during the World War as it had been, say, during the Russo-Japanese War. So I had the feeling that I was involved not just in a certain kind of intellectual activity, but in something that could be of practical importance.

H: As for your activity regarding the zemstvo, which you've mentioned, did you try to expose its activity?

GD: Yes, but here the exposes were entirely different. They weren't exposes of abuses. The zemstva varied; some were liberal, some conservative, some reactionary. The Kazan zemstvo was very reactionary. I wrote critical accounts of provincial zemstvo assemblies. In doing so, I primarily unmasked their class nature. I know that its participants were dreadfully angry with me. I was told that in the zemstvo I was called "a bastard, but a clever bastard."

H: The zemstvo was dominated by the gentry?

GD: Yes, very much so. There were also more liberal elements. But what did "more liberal" mean? The district marshal of the nobility in Kazan, Baratynskii, was an Octobrist. A very decent man, of course. Later he was a member of the Third Duma. He gained a certain renown there for finishing a speech with the appeal to the government: "We will persistently wait!"

H: As you know, in the zemstvo elections, at the beginning of the Third Duma, there was a sharp shift to the right. But I have the impression that at the beginning of the Fourth Duma there was something of a leftward tack, at least in the cities. Do you know of such changes in Kazan?

GD: Perhaps. There's a name that escapes me – one of the Kazan deputies was a minister in the first Provisional Government. I think that was the case.[6] But elections were fairly infrequent. Then a Tatar, Maksudov, was elected. He was not a very pleasant person, but relatively liberal and a Tatar in any case. The shift toward liberalization was fairly evident in the Kazan city government. Specifically, it was the merchants who supported the paper. They made up the liberal parts of the City Council, the majority, and though it was never a clearly defined majority, still, they managed to extend their influence, and for this they needed a newspaper. It made no difference to them, say, that I wrote a long feature on the occasion of Marx' birthday. Perhaps they thought, "So let him throw bombs, its none of our business. What's important for us is to influence city politics and get results." An objective indication of this is that the mayor they elected was Baronin, a former judge or jurist, at any rate, who had gained a standing among the more liberal elements of Kazan society. So that when the tsarist regime was overthrown in 1917, be became mayor without any serious opposition.

H: What year did they succeed in doing this?

GD: Before the war, in 1912–1913. So there was slow progress, and I think that this was a reflection of fairly rapid developments in the country. Of course, the city government didn't get around to a constitutionalist stand right away.

H: In 1912, I think, this was fairly widespread, particularly in city governments. My last question for today is about the background of your moving to Moscow. When did you decide to go?

GD: I decided to as soon as I was free from open surveillance, the autumn of 1909, and I began studying in Moscow in January 1910. I ran into a problem that is usual in many places, including the United States. I sent an application to Moscow University, and the reply never reached me. I eventually gave up hope and went to Moscow. Why no answer? And there I was told that an affirmative answer had been sent back in August; they gave me the exact date. I had to wait for the new semester, and so began only in January 1910.

H: Had you lived for these two years in constant expectation of returning to the university as soon as possible?

GD: Yes, but not to study physiology, because I had gradually become convinced that it was a dubious way of reaching my goal. I had been reading literature on social psychology, and it was fairly obvious that I was hardly going to gain an understanding of social psychology and social conditions from physiology. I had to take an entirely different tack. It was a choice between economics and history, but the choice was made for me because economics had been reduced to a minimum in Russian universities. Except for the economics department in the Polytechnicum, there were no special faculties of economics. Returning to the economics department of the Polytechnicum was complicated, because my credits had been cancelled, so that I would have to begin at the beginning, and it was doubtful whether I could get in. So I was left with history, and I entered the history division of the Faculty of History and Philology in Moscow.

H: Did you decide to go to Moscow because the faculty of history there attracted you more? Why Moscow rather than Petersburg – because the historians seemed more brilliant?

GD: No. I myself don't know exactly why it was Moscow that drew me. Moscow was better known than Petersburg in the provinces, and in many respects it was the center. Petersburg was more democratic, Moscow more artistic. There was another, purely coincidental matter: in Moscow there were performers whose acquaintance I had made. All the actors and musicians I knew were Muscovites. So when I went, I was insured a group of friends. I planned to concentrate on Russian history, and for those who wanted to do this, there was an enormous attraction in Moscow, namely, Kliuchevskii. Unfortunately, the year I entered the university was the year that Kliuchevskii stopped lecturing.

H: Did you intend to become a professional historian? Had that already been decided?

GD: Yes.

H: Who influenced you in this respect?

GD: No one. Well, in part. One of the members of the informal group that met in the home of my friend Vasil'ev was a professor of ancient and modern history – a frequent combination in Russian universities – namely, Mikhail Mikhailovich Khvostov, the father of the Khvostov who is now a historian. (The son, Vladimir Mikhailovich, I used to call Volodia.) But he wasn't a decisive influence. It was not a special decision on my part to concentrate in Russian history. The way I imagined it was that I would first study Russian history thoroughly for several reasons. Briefly, I wanted to see life through the historical facts, and this was easier for me in Russian history. I had not yet been abroad. This prejudice, or whatever you want to call it, has remained with me until now. I always feel distressed when I must study countries I have never been in.

Sixth interview

H: Could you say a little more about your reasons for deciding to go to Moscow?

GD: I can add that Moscow was much closer than Petersburg to Kazan and to the Russian provinces in general, not only geographically, but also in the way it influenced provincial intellectual life. It is not by chance that the sisters in Chekhov's *Three Sisters* yearn to go "to Moscow, to Moscow!" But I had my own reasons, which I have already mentioned briefly. While still in Kazan, I had made a circle of acquaintances in Moscow, a particular kind of circle that greatly influenced my Moscow life and made my student years there quite different from what they had been in Kazan. In a sense I can say that, beginning in January 1910, I led a kind of double life: I lived in Moscow during the academic year, while in my free time I would invariably visit Kazan, so that every year I would return for a few months to my Kazan life. In short, I had a Moscow life and a Kazan life.

I worked for the Kazan newspaper, writing what were then called feuilletons on literary topics and the literary events of the time, and also articles of a more publicistic nature. Working for a provincial newspaper was something important for me, because my family's material circumstances had substantially changed. In the first place, my father had moved, with only a slight increase in salary, from smaller towns to the provincial capital, where life was much more expensive, and besides the family had grown. My sister, the youngest in the family, had died by this time, but there were six sons, so my parents simply didn't have enough money, and we older children had to think about earning our own money, something I had begun to do while still in the *gimnazium*. Later, I not only paid my own way, but helped out the family as much as possible. So the issue of earning money was a very important one for me at the time and, in going off to Moscow, I firmly intended not to take anything from my parents, but rather to make my own way.

It was then, while working for the Kazan newspaper, that I began to write theater and music reviews fairly regularly in addition to the longer articles. As a result, I made a great many acquaintances. I've never reread what I wrote, so I don't know what my writing was like, but there is some objective proof that my reviews were all well received. The Moscow theater magazine *Rampa i Zhizn'* [Stage and Living], where I knew no one, neither the editor nor any of his collaborators, sent me an offer to become their Kazan correspondent. Provincial correspondents were not paid any money, but in some way there was the understanding that if I should turn up in Moscow they would be very glad to take me on. So in Moscow I already had a partial solution to my money problem. Then I had already been introduced into certain artistic circles. I had met and become acquainted with actors and musicians while in Kazan, and with only a few exceptions they were Muscovites. I went to Moscow with the feeling that I was not simply drifting into a large city where I wouldn't know anyone, but that I already had some acquaintances, and friendly relations with some of them. When they learned that I was moving to Moscow, they said, "First off, you'll need to find a place to stay, so please" – typical Russian hospitality – "come straight from the station to our place, and you can live there until you find a room."

Particularly attractive was the fact that I had gotten to know opera singers, including Stanislavskii's sister.[1] She was a coloratura soprano, an extraordinarily musical person, but with so squeaky a voice (to put it disrespectfully) that she couldn't make a career out of it. She had money (her family, the Alekseevs, were rich) and at that time was married to the famous tenor Sevastianov, who became her agent and entrepreneur and organized an opera company in which he too sang. They were in Kazan for one season, a few months, and I got to know them quite well. They were extremely friendly people, and this opened up all sorts of possibilities, though not as many as I imagined, because it turned out that Stanislavskii's relations with his sisters were extremely cool. But still, it was something that helped me out, because soon after I arrived in Moscow, this sister of Stanislavskii's proposed that I tutor her two sons. And as you can imagine, Stanislavskii-Alekseeva didn't pay the kind of fee that I usually got for teaching. For about two years, this and my very modest earnings from *Rampa i Zhizn'* gave me more than an adequate income, in students' terms. (At that time, for instance, students from relatively well-to-do families received 25–30 rubles per month for living expenses, while I earned 70–80 rubles. That is a big difference.) Later, when another new magazine started up, and I had made something of a name for myself in Moscow, my earnings rose to as much as 300 rubles a month, which was about as much as my father received as a judge. But that was later.

These [various connections] affected the whole quality of my life very much, the more so as I had privileges not available to very many people. For instance, as a theater critic, I could go to anything put on by the Moscow Art Theater, the Malyi Teatr [Small Theater], or any of several concert series. And at that time, the theatrical life, particularly the musical life, of Moscow was extraordinarily rich. It was about the same in Petersburg, but my impression was that Moscow was slightly more prominent: partly because in addition to the regular orchestras there were people like Koussevitsky, who subsequently became the conductor of the Boston Symphony, and who was married to a woman from a very wealthy merchant family. This is a curious example of the "enlightened merchant class," which was free of prejudice to the extent that a woman from this milieu could marry a Jewish musician. It's very interesting, and was by no means a unique instance. He organized his own orchestra, and though he was still a very mediocre conductor at that time, he was able to assemble an excellent group of musicians, to invite first-rate soloists, and to act as a patron of the arts. For a number of years he not only performed everything that Scriabin wrote (he subsequently broke off with him), but he also published his works and thus influenced the entire character of musical life. I realize that this subject is rather remote from Menshevism, but I feel that all this was important to me. Living in Moscow, I was able to go to concerts free as a writer for my magazine, and I heard almost all the giants of the time: the violinist Kreisler, the cellist Kazantsev, the pianists Busoni, Hoffman, to mention only a few of those who came to Moscow almost every year. So life in Moscow wasn't just life in the capital, it was, in a certain respect, life in an international center. I might add that on one occasion, on a trip to Petersburg, I saw an exhibition entitled "One Hundred Years of French Painting," which greatly affected me, because up to that time I had been entirely insensitive to painting. I used to go the Tretiakov Gallery, but didn't understand what it was all about. Neither the "Wanderers" movement, which was dominant at that time, nor that of the "World of Art" which was fresher, made virtually any impression on me.[2] But French painting was a revelation; I finally understood what painting was all about. And this again broadened my circle of acquaintances in another direction, because I cultivated friendships with a number of artists who had steeped themselves in the modern trends, especially the French.

If you take account of all these circumstances, and you add to this diversity of interests my work on scholarly subjects, which I kept up with, I think you will understand that I had very little time left over for party contacts. And, frankly, I didn't look for them at the time, because the main thing in my life then was studying and learning as much as possible about all sorts of fields – theater, music, literature.

H: What kind of literature attracted you most at this time?

GD: What I have to say about this can correct the characterization of this literary period, particularly in the emigre literature, where the "Silver Age" is recalled in such rapturous terms. You get the impression that this was an era when Russian literature was dominated by so-called Decadence, Symbolism, and the various trends in poetry represented by Briusov, Balmont, Blok, Andrei Bely, Vyacheslav Ivanov, and so forth. I am absolutely convinced that this view needs correction. These literary preferences were confined to a very narrow circle. The great majority of the Russian reading public was primarily interested, as before, in traditional realism, or in literature which went beyond realism but did not involve the strongly religious and mystical tinge associated with the Silver Age. To be sure, Leonid Andreev, who sometimes went beyond realism, as in *Life of a Man* or *Tsar Hunger*, was enormously popular. In general, though, people like Bunin and Kuprin were more typical of the prevailing taste, as was Maksim Gorkii with his distinctive "vagabond novels," [although] his popularity had declined somewhat.

H: Is that how you would now describe your own tastes at the time?

GD: No, I belonged to a middle group that was highly catholic in this respect, particularly avid for different things. Already in Kazan, in the circles I frequented, we devoured one thing after another. We read the decadent symbolist journals like *Vesy* [Scales] and *Skorpiony* [Scorpions], and also followed the collections such *Znanie*. What I want to repeat is that the conception of the Silver Age doesn't correspond to the tenor of the time. I have already mentioned in my recollections of Kazan that I think the most characteristic features of the period between the revolution of 1905–1906 and the revolution of 1917 were "piecemealism" – the emphasis on relatively minor issues and so-called small deeds – as well as a keen desire to learn about, and understand Russian life, which seemed immense in its magnitude and sweep. The literature that so described this life was much closer to the prevailing mood. I remember that I, as well as others, were profoundly impressed by a piece by Sergei Vetsenskii, whose title I can't remember – that was the first work of Russian literature to depict a farm and farmers after the Stolypin land reform.[3] It was a kind of revelation. It was another piece of life for you to learn about, and you would hardly have learned about it from Briusov's *Flaming Angel*. The themes of the works of the Silver Age made very little impression on those without mystical inclinations. What's more, I had the feeling both then and now that this mysticism was, to a considerable extent, false and affected. For instance, Valerii Briusov was a supreme cynic – he could become a faithful Communist if there was any advantage in it for him. There were exceptions: Blok was very much admired, and at one point there was some enthusiasm (which even I shared) for Igor Severianin. But that was idle chatter – not the Silver Age, though very spectacular. He was interesting because of the technical brilliance of his verse. For the rest, I and people with my inclinations were interested in everything and everyone. Western literature was not particularly important at that time. To be sure, French literature was always well-known in Russia. Anatole France, Paul Bourget were read. And I tried to read French. As far as I recall, there was nothing in English or German literature that produced a sensation.

H: You have just observed that you belonged to a group with catholic interests. Could you distinguish and define the groups somewhat more precisely, in particular, the group to which you belonged who regarded themselves as realists and so forth, and those who did in fact regard themselves as belonging to the Silver Age?

GD: That's not easy to do. What I have in mind is people who thought more or less as I did, since we didn't form a defined group. I think that, first, this range of people with broad interests included students and young academics with scientific concerns. In the last analysis, the overwhelming majority of academic people and intellectuals in Russia at the time were positivists (to use the term broadly, not in any precise sense), people who were not predisposed to mystical poetry.

H: What about you personally? After you learned that physiology didn't provide a direct approach to social psychology, that is, at the time that you went to Moscow, what did positivism come to mean to you?

GD: First, I continued to regard myself as a Marxist, though a heretical one.

H: In what respect? How did positivist and Marxist beliefs combine in you?

GD: Well, I didn't believe in any supernatural or unnatural interference in human affairs and in history in particular. Since you mention physiology and social psychology, I should say that I was already basically an agnostic, since I regarded it as quite possible that at some very distant time natural science and physiology would be able to explain the processes of the human brain. But this was regarded as something quite remote. If we wished to study psychology, therefore, we had to begin at the other end, not by analyzing brain cells but by observing (either directly or on the basis of historic material) the thought, emotions, and experiences of people.

H: What philosphers, social thinkers, historians, made the greatest impression on you at the beginning of your Moscow period?

GD: Nietzsche was already passé. I was very much impressed by Bergson, although this somewhat contradicts what I just said.

H: What works in particular?

GD: Two works of his. In the first place, *The Dual Roots of Religion and Morals;* second, of course, *Creative Evolution,* and this has always remained with me. I was particularly struck by Bergson's thought that religion arose only among people, and that it is impossible for animals, because animals do not comprehend that they will die.

H: And did Bergson also make a big impression on your contemporaries, or was it only on you?

GD: I think that he did, but only on a few. He was translated, but not widely read. Many people could read French, as I could, although I read *Creative Evolution* in translation. Then there was a book by Lévy-Bruhl which was widely circulated, I think *Les Fonctions mentales de la société primitive.*

H: Now let us get more deeply into the matter. To what extent were you assimilated into student society? Of course, your situation was exceptional, in a sense.

GD: I wasn't assimilated into it. But there is another interesting circumstance: the student milieu was in a certain sense a society of people in disguise [*zamaskirovannye liudi*]. For instance, that fellow Varlam Aleksandrovich Avanesov who managed the magazine *Rampa i Zhizn',* and whom there was no reason whatever to suspect of the slightest political activity. After the October Revolution he turned up as the First Secretary of the All-Russian Central Executive Committee of Soviets. Or take another young man, Osovskii, an artist – I don't remember now whether he was still a student at this time – it turned out after 1917 that he was an old Menshevik. It never would have entered my head – or his – to begin any sort of political discussion. Or again, I got to know a certain family, brother and sister, through musical interests, and they turned out to be Social Democrats too.

H: It was only later that you learned this?

GD: Yes. I had a very close friend, again chiefly on the basis of musical interests. We shared quarters. Because of my relative wealth, I could afford luxuries such as two spinet pianos and a lot of music, and we used to play four-hand piano music on the two pianos. He himself had no political interest, but later, when we were already good friends, I visited his family in the south of Russia. I learned there that his older brother was a prominent Bolshevik, and in exile.

H: How do you explain this?

GD: I have no explanation for it. Still, I strongly suspect that in many or most cases it was simply the result of a desire to safeguard one's life. This fellow Varlam Aleksandrovich Avanesov worked because he needed to earn money, of course, but in most cases I think it was (as with me) a result of the fact that legal opportunities were relatively hard to find, and that illegal activity was unattractive. And I would add that the kind of practical work I engaged in Kazan was much less possible in Moscow. To take me as an example, I could write about zemstvo affairs or the excesses of the commissary for the Kazan paper, but it never would have entered my mind in Moscow to go to *Russkie Vedomosti* and say that I wanted to write a commentary on the sessions of the provincial zemstva. There were people there who had been dealing with zemstvo issues for decades, and they would have regarded me as an impudent kid who was sticking his nose in where he wasn't supposed to. I think that many of these people, like my musical acquaintances or those whom I met at the editorial office of *Rampa i Zhizn'*, like myself, organized their lives around art and the like to a considerable extent. This fellow Osovskii, for instance, would come into the office with a large folder full of drawings of actors or singers, and he would be paid two or three rubles for them. That was how he managed to get by. I always chatted with him; he was very nice. What point would there have been in my talking with him, an artist, about political problems? I would talk about his drawings and similar things

So you see, it was a kind of life led in disguise. In some cases, like Tarasov-Rodionov's, whom I mentioned and wrote about, there was a real enthusiasm for more than just making a fair amount of money – he was really involved in these regional fairs and in gathering advertisements for them. He had the interesting job of traveling about the country, meeting all sorts of business people and the like, and using his eloquence not for summoning the masses to the overthrow of the autocracy, but for getting people to place advertisements for the fairs and sending their exhibits. So the motives were rather complex and diverse.

H: What did you learn at that time about radical elements and political groups in Moscow? Did you have any contacts at all?

GD: In the first place, there wasn't a single occasion when anyone at the university – Bolshevik or Menshevik – attempted to recruit me. Still, I wasn't a regular student, so that if any group existed, they arose in some manner that was unknown to me. With one major exception, I don't recall anything resembling political propaganda within the university walls. There's something here that's quite unclear, and I think it would be interesting to clarify it. There was no serious danger whatever in revealing one's views, and in the case I'm going to describe to you, those people who were openly Bolshevik didn't suffer for it at all. When Tolstoi left home and died, for example, the response in Russia was something that is hard to imagine – you had to see it and experience it to understand what Tolstoi really represented for everyone, people with all sorts of views. The universities ceased to function for several days – and not just in Moscow, but everywhere else, as far as I know. There were continuous meetings and gatherings, with thousands of people! And, curiously enough, no one spoke out, at least at the few meetings I attended, on behalf of the Socialist Revolutionaries or of the Mensheviks. Two persons spoke on behalf of the student faction of the Bolsheviks at a meeting in the university. I don't know if there was a faction or if these two or three people constituted the faction. But in any case, they spoke on behalf of the Bolshevik faction and introduced a resolution in the name of the student body of Moscow University, proposing to send Sofia Andreevna Tolstoi a telegram expressing indignation that she had driven her husband, a great man, into leaving home. I became completely enraged. Rather than express indignation, I said, we should kiss the hand that had copied out *War and Peace* nine times over! I completely won them over. But this was the single occasion I witnessed at the university when two speakers spoke out on behalf of the Bolshevik student faction.

H: Let us now discuss more fully the university, your own studies, the orientation of student life. To begin at the beginning, did you remain a student until the outbreak of the war?

GD: Until later; I was graduated in 1915. In 1914 I moved away from Moscow and transferred back to the University of Kazan. My father died in March of that year, so I returned to live with my mother – especially since my younger brothers had to be supported. I was in Moscow from February of 1910 until May of 1914, with regular visits to Kazan.

H: Was there an evolution of student attitudes over these three and a half years?

GD: My general impression was that the student body of these years, and more generally after the revolution of 1905, was much less interested in current politics; those who were active in 1905–1906 probably differed only slightly and felt a much stronger pull toward their studies. I wouldn't even say that there was a pull toward science, though this did happen, but rather a desire to study and to obtain a more or less solid preparation for life. Literally, no one whom I met saw any prospects for revolution, as did Lenin and the official Bolsheviks.

I still hadn't decided definitely whether I would specialize, and, if so, in what kind of history. In Russian universities history was usually divided into two parts: Russian history and world history. Since there was not any overabundance of professors, world history was usually divided into two parts, as was the case in Moscow. The division was a rather interesting one: ancient history was combined with modern history, so that, for instance, Vipper in Moscow, and Khvostov (later my teacher) in Kazan, gave courses on ancient Greek, Roman, or Near Eastern history, and also taught the eighteenth to the twentieth centuries. The other subdivision was medieval history which didn't exist in Moscow, but did in the provincial universities, like Kazan. Medieval history was combined with the history of the Slavic peoples.

One of the proseminars I registered for was on Russian history, taught by Professor Kizevetter.[4] It was on the historical views of the early Slavophiles. I must say that I never experienced anything in the university that was more brazen and outrageous than Kizevetter's proseminar. He was a political figure, a prominent Kadet, and also wrote theater articles for *Russkaia Mysl'*, I think. He was a brilliant lecturer and always ended each lecture with some striking phrase. I only attended one lecture because after that I had no desire to hear him. It was about Paul I and ended with a story about Emperor Paul being told that lampoons about his Imperial Majesty were being circulated in Kharkov. Paul's response was, "Find the guilty and punish them appropriately, and destroy the city of Kharkov," and it was only his death, which followed soon thereafter, that saved the town from destruction. The tale was striking, but you can't say that it was very historical.

In his seminars, Kizevetter would give students some article or part of a book, by one of the Aksakovs or someone like that, to be discussed at the next sessions.[5] And while the students talked, he would sit there yawning or cleaning his fingernails – it was entirely obvious that he didn't care at all and was completely uninterested, but was there because he had to be. I made some remarks that differed somewhat with what he had said about an excerpt I had read, and his reply was, "I don't agree with you and that's that." He didn't feel it necessary to convince me or explain to me why he didn't agree. Later, I stopped going, but I passed the exam.

The other seminar was entirely different. It made an enormous impression on me and, I think I can say, on my entire life. It was taught by Protopopov, a privat-docent and specialist on the Middle Ages. He was a drunkard, and generally led a very unhappy life, but an unusual person nonetheless. He had married a completely uncultured woman, evidently she had been a servant-girl (a frequent occurrence). He volunteered for the war [in 1914], though as a privat-docent he hardly needed to, and was soon killed. Perhaps it was his own form of suicide. Protopopov was definitely a very gifted man. His seminar was titled "The *Leges Barbarorum.*" I don't remember now which *Lex* he chose specifically, but he would give a student an excerpt and ask him to read, without any preparation whatever. The student would do so, and then he would ask, "Well, what can you say on the basis of this excerpt? Do you feel anything in it that reveals the life of the time?" I found this method absolutely fascinating. In this way Protopopov would create, first, an atmosphere of intensive work, and second, a manner of approaching sources which I have continued to regard as the only proper one. So this proseminar of the *Leges Barbarorum* captivated me and left a profound impression.

Mikhail Mikhailovich Karpovich (whom I didn't know at the time, because we were in different fields, but who was in the same faculty of Moscow University at the same time) later told me that no seminar at Harvard, to say nothing of the Sorbonne, was ever on the same level as at Moscow University.[6] World history had some brilliant exponents at Moscow University. First, there was Vipper who regarded himself then as a Marxist and Social Democrat, but who turned out to be a monarchist after 1917 and wrote a little book in praise of Ivan the Terrible.[7] (He felt that the nasty Russian people could be governed in no other way.) After the Bolsheviks took power and his house in Moscow was municipalized, he went to Riga and was there when Riga was incorporated into the Soviet Union. He reworked his book about Ivan the Terrible somewhat, received a Stalin Prize for the new version, and lived to be more than 90, a highly esteemed Soviet historian.

H: In what forms were his Marxist and Social Democratic views expressed at that time?

GD: They were expressed quite strongly in his lectures and books (though I didn't pay particular attention), and in a very keen interest in economic developments, something that was characteristic of all Russian historians virtually without exception. I account for this by the fact that historians in tsarist Russia were extremely confined in the area of political history; they didn't have the right to say much or even to know much. For instance, it wasn't known in Russia before the revolution that Peter III was murdered, that Paul I was assassinated, or how the death of Nicholas I happened – it seems that the circumstances remain cloudy to this day – to say nothing of certain characteristics of the tsars and other important figures. I never managed to hear Kliuchevskii, but people still had lectures with the words, "There were many widows and orphans, many sick and feeble-minded on the Russian throne; all that was missing was an idiot. Eventually one appeared." In the printed course notes, of course, this wasn't included. That was Kliuchevskii with his enormous renown and very moderate views.

As far as I can judge, economic and social history were more important than in the West. In an article published in a *Festschrift* for Kliuchevskii (this was during my period), Struve wrote that we had learned Marxism from Kliuchevskii, who himself was not a Marxist at all, of course.[8] The historians of Russia and those like Petrushevskii[9] who wrote on the Middle Ages focused primarily not on so-called pragmatic history, but on social and economic history – not to speak of Vinogradov, who had returned to Moscow when I was there.[10]

Then there was Vipper, who was known as a man with definite political views. For Petrushevskii he was a very great authority. When the Kasso affair occurred,[11] and several dozen professors in Moscow were forced into retirement, Petrushevskii asked Vipper for advice: "What should I do? Leave or stay?" "You should leave, of course," Vipper said, and Petrushevskii, like many others, resigned. But Vipper didn't leave. Petrushevskii himself later remembered that he asked him, "How come you didn't leave?" "Listen! It was a bourgeois-liberal demonstration! But I'm a Social Democrat! That's not our method!"

H: We have been discussing your scholarly and artistic interests. Now, in the years 1911 through 1914 there was also a political and social life which became particularly animated after the Lena events and the beginning of the Fourth Duma. What were your impressions of this political and social life, and to what extent were you interested in it? What particular figures in it were of interest to you?

GD: I would like to emphasize that, despite the nature of my life in Moscow, I was hardly apolitical. Not at all! My sphere of interests was outside the university and consisted almost entirely of the artistic and literary circles I was in contact with, but it can't be said that these people were entirely apolitical. In general, they were liberals, with more or less Kadet inclinations, with one exception. The exception was Aleksandra Nikolaevna Lebkovskaia, who was an actress herself in her youth, then stopped per-

forming and became the wife of Lebkovskii, the actor and director of the
Malyi Teatr. She was one of the acquaintances I made in Moscow. Lebkovskaia was from a landowning family in Kazan province; it turned out we
had acquaintances in common. Her husband had her perform for several
months in Kazan, and she returned several times. I met them not as a critic,
but through mutual acquaintances. She was one of the outstanding and
leading figures in the movement for women's emancipation. I should say
that this was a constant topic at the time. She was a feminist, and combined
this with general political interests. On the other hand, she was also something of a Theosophist, which I openly and impudently ridiculed. There
was always a circle around her, of young people primarily, where all sorts
of purely political issues were debated. It was very fatiguing for me and
doubtless aggravated my ailment, because she was a night person. She
didn't sleep at night, only during the daytime – there are such people, as
you know. So her circle would generally go on the whole night. I must say
that she was really a woman of rare intellect and manner of thinking. I
mention this as one example of something more general – that this life of
circles or groups always remained a significant part of Russian intellectual
and political life.

H: If I understand properly the nature of your life from your accounts,
it seems to me that there was a process of pluralization, in your life at any
rate, so that political aspects didn't coincide with the scholarly and artistic
ones. It seems to me that the nature of the groups and circles in your life
were constantly changing, and that they were all different groups that did
not combine political, intellectual, and esthetic interests. Am I correct in
assuming these processes of pluralization?

GD: Yes, but it needs some modification. You must allow for the fact
that though public discussions were very popular, they could hardly be
political discussions. Acute or urgent political problems could not be discussed publicly.

H: I don't fully understand. In the 1890s, for instance, in the Free Economic Society you could discuss political issues, although in theoretical or
abstract form, of course, like the debates of the Populists and the Marxists.
This situation remained the same, didn't it?

GD: No.

H: Why not?

GD: I think that it was a consequence of the direction of interests in a
certain stratum. For example, the meetings of the Religious and Philosophical Society became particularly popular after the revolution [of 1905], at
least among the intelligentsia of the capital, in contrast to the prerevolutionary discussions in the Free Economic Society.

H: Yes, but it seems to me that, in the last analysis, it was legally possible, and that in 1912–1913 and the beginning of 1914 the legal opportunities were greater than in the 1890s. Is this not true?

GD: I don't see any evidence for it in terms of these public discussions.
There were several reasons. In the first place, there was less interest, and
second, people became more cautious. But I cited the example that you

could speak out on behalf of the Bolshevik faction at a meeting at Moscow University without any repercussions.

H: Well, what about the election campaign for the Fourth Duma in the fall of 1912?

GD: Another era was beginning then.

H: So your impressions refer to the period before the Lena events?

GD: The Lena events played an important part, but, as I recall, it was the Balkan Wars rather than the Lena events that really caused a major activization of political thinking. At least in my circle, the Balkan Wars were talked about a good deal more than the Lena events.

H: Very well, so it is your impression that there was more or less an absence of intense public political life, until, say, the end of 1912 or the beginning of 1913, and then there was a turning-point.

GD: Yes, but I don't recall public meetings about the Balkan Wars either. To sum up, however, I would say that what basically predominated at that time was the "enlightenment spirit."

H: Could you describe to me your political interests and contacts before 1912?

GD: Yes, but again I should mention that I spent a few months out of every year in Kazan, so that I again became involved in a milieu that had remained politicized to a considerable extent, but whose politics were chiefly oriented toward what I have called "small deeds," concrete practical issues.

H: Was this aspect also characteristic of your life in Moscow?

GD: Only in cases such as the small circle of people around Lebkovskaia were political issues mentioned, and relatively little in this period. Something that was renowned throughout Russia was the Literary and Artistic Circle in Moscow. We rather uninformed provincials had a very idealized notion about it – that it was a remarkable center of cultural life and the like, where lectures and talks were given regularly. I should say that, when I got to Moscow and started to go there, I was very disillusioned, though some of the talks were very interesting, and then there were other things. I recall a talk by Stepun, a philosopher and a very interesting man in general. He was already important in philosophical circles. What was his lecture – a public lecture – about? About an actress! This was my first contact with Stepun. It was very eloquent. Obviously, it never would have occurred to him to discuss a philosophical or religious topic, not to speak of a political one. But I was mainly disillusioned by what I saw, namely, that the so-called cultural life of the Literary and Artistic Circle was simply a false front. What the flower of the intelligentsia chiefly busied itself with there was card games. It was essentially a gambling club. And there were scandals there. Now, in hindsight, there is a tendency to idealize this period very much. Perhaps I am biased in this respect; I attribute much more importance to small deeds, to the practical outlook and political realism that was developing at the time. The more affected side of cultural life was not perceived so much, and in retrospect seems a sham.

Seventh interview

H: Today let us take up some specific social and political issues. From everything that you have told me, it seems that the Third Duma was of no interest. What about the Stolypin land reforms?[1]

GD: Of course, that was of interest. I mentioned the impression that Sergei Vetsenskii made on me personally, as regards the farm issue. Naturally enough, this was of interest and it stimulated, if not exactly debates, at least an exchange of opinions, as I recall. There were hardly many people who had a clear notion of what it meant or what it could lead to, but it was a new development, and this doubtlessly made it interesting. My own impressions from that time have been very much obscured by later thoughts. I sensed partly, but in a very vague manner, something that I thought of much later; I didn't sweepingly condemn the Stolypin reforms, as some did. I saw a lot of shortcomings in them, of course, but I had the notion that they might lead to some political crystallization of the peasantry. I later thought that everything depended on the Socialist Revolutionaries and the group of People's Socialists and Trudoviki that were more or less close to them. Their role was very unfortunate for they organized the peasantry in the name of socialism, something that was entirely alien to peasants. What Russia needed was a solid proprietary-peasant party. But there was no formula for it. Still, there was a vague feeling that the reforms weren't simply as disgusting as they were regarded in some circles, and in particular Vetsenskii's account gave the impression that there was something important and valuable in them. That some sort of new people would appear.

H: That they would foster economic development? Political differentiation of the peasantry? In what respect?

GD: That the peasants would become less benighted.

H: Let's return to a specific aspect, namely Stolypin's death.[2] Did you have the feeling that the government was coming apart?

GD: Yes, to a certain extent, and not just because of this. You see, politics penetrated in various ways. There were things like the commissary trials – which were not just fraud on the part of a certain category of people but something that involved government participation to a certain extent. It was organized thievery, evidence that the regime was thoroughly corrupt. There were not immediate revolutionary prospects, but very many people were convinced that things couldn't go on like this indefinitely, and that somehow a new revolution would eventually occur. For some, however, like Kerenskii, there was a deep conviction that revolution was very close, and he had definite ambitions of playing a decisive role in it.

H: Now, I know already that Social-Democratic politics did not particularly interest you at this time. But to what extent were you still linked to the Social-Democratic movement at this time? I'll give you some specific examples: first, the Menshevik "Liquidationist" tendencies, as expressed in *Nasha Zaria*.[3] Did you read this journal at the time?

GD: I read the collections that appeared at the time,[4] I read *Nasha Zaria*, and it generally corresponded to my own outlook. I must say, though, that my strongest impression from *Nasha Zaria* came from Bazarov's article about Tolstoy, which Lenin later attacked.

H: Does this mean that at this time, before the autumn of 1912, you began to regard yourself as a Menshevik? Or a "Liquidator"?

GD: I was definitely a "Liquidator;" I couldn't say that I regarded myself as a Menshevik. To describe my state of mind in general : I was potentially a Social Democrat. I had the feeling that there was no place for me anywhere in party work in whatever form, but I did feel subjectively ready, should something happen, should some prospect open up, to resume a place in politics. And, of course, if you consider my entire evolution since that time, that was what happened.

H: Did you have any contacts with workers' clubs at this time?

GD: My contacts with the masses were of an entirely different nature. It was in connection with the actress Lebkovskaia. She was the chief organizer of a "people's theater." These were theatrical groups that formed in small towns and larger villages, and they chiefly consisted not of peasants, but of workers. I think that the diversity of the working-class intelligentsia is something that has remained entirely unnoticed (probably it was not of any great significance). It was something very unexpected. In one village they put on a play by Ostrovskii – *Woe to Him*, I think. The actors were all workers, and they definitely had a great deal of talent. How surprising that in a small village they would become interested in the theater and suddenly become actors. This "emphasis on enlightenment" was very strong, at least for me in any case.

H: But your interest did not extend to workers' circles?

GD: No.

H: Why not?

GD: I don't know, I never thought about it.

H: Very well. After the Lena events occurred, the response involved some fairly large demonstrations, isn't that right? What were your impressions and those of your contemporaries?

GD: The main feeling was indignation! But it was not yet related to any hope or expectations of revolutionary developments – indignation strongly tinged with a feeling of impotent rage. Possibly it was the first stage in the reappearance of a revolutionary mood.

H: Could you elaborate on this somewhat?

GD: The main thing was indignation that the loathsome government had done something incredibly disgusting, and that it had been absolutely impossible to stop this despite the fact that there was the Duma and so forth. There was no strength to do it.

The impression of the Lena events was a strong one, of course, but it was driven into the background, [as I said earlier], by the Balkan Wars. The first Balkan War[5] began a few months after the Lena events. At that time, of course, few people could follow the complex of European international relations that were linked with the Balkan question. But one thing stood out: a widespread mistrust of Austria's policies. I spent the summer of 1912 in Kazan, as usual, and was again actively involved in the local paper. I now recall that there were a great many discussions on this topic, and the editorial secretary – in effect, the editor of the paper – regarded himself as a specialist in matters of foreign policy. He was particularly vehement in his critique of Austrian policy, and I remember how we laughed when he began one of his lead articles by saying, "We have already pointed out to the Austrian government. . . . " We made a joke of it – "What sort of government is it if it even disregards what's written in the Kazan newspapers!"

This attitude toward Austria was then linked – consciously for some people, instinctively for others – with a fear that the situation might lead to open conflict, that is, to war. This was very alarming, because the memory of the catastrophic Russo-Japanese War was still fresh in everyone's mind. As I will explain later, my view of the war and that of the people I was in touch with, was in no way related to the idea that the war might be "progressive" and hasten the revolution. On the contrary, the notion was very alarming. With some effort, I can recall the overall tenor of the discussions that I heard or was involved in. Opinions were quite diverse. Many people had a sentimental notion that our brother Slavs were involved and that, with respect to Austria and Turkey (because relations between the Balkan states and Turkey soon became strained), Russia could not be indifferent – that she should side with the Balkan states and give them assistance. Although I don't recall specific statements that we should go to war for them, I believe that the attitude existed.

H: Did you share it?

GD: No, and I was sharply attacked for this. I was one of those with different attitudes. Of course, we were sympathetic to the struggle for liberation of the Balkan people, but didn't feel that Russia's policy should make war inevitable. In a sense you could say that the people who shared my attitude – and perhaps it was even the predominant attitude – were pacifists on this issue. Moreover, there was the complicating question of which brother Slavs Russia should support. There were two orientations, a Bulgarian one (vigorously supported by Miliukov), and a Serbian one. I was interested in the issue, and I studied and read the literature. I am not sure when Derzhavin's pamphlet appeared, supporting Miliukov's viewpoint, but I read it at the time or even earlier.[6] I was generally inclined to a Serbian rather than a Bulgarian orientation; in any case, Miliukov's reasoning didn't convince me. It was this concern and alarm about the situation in the Balkans that were foremost among political interests. There was definitely sympathy, particularly during the First Balkan War when the Balkan states all fought together against Turkey. There was a certain enthusiasm. For instance, my cousin Danterov, who was a doctor, and one of my older brothers who had completed medical training volunteered as medics. There was no other way to go since Russia was a noncombatant, but such assistance [was possible].

H: Did your cousin or brother regard themselves as Social Democrats at the time?

GD: No. My brother was not active in general, though my cousin had been the major figure in the Kazan organization. [Subsequently] he left the Bolsheviks and didn't return in 1917. He remained a socialist, but his disillusionment with underground party work, in which he had been more involved than I had ever been, was even stronger than mine. (He was about eight years older than I and had begun party work much earlier.) He once said, "No, I was a Bolshevik for so long that I couldn't become one again!" But he remained a socialist, and kept up with the literature and so forth. It was a situation that was widespread, as became apparent in 1917, when numbers of people who had left (and I include myself) promptly returned to the mainstream of Social-Democratic work, like war horses at the sound of a bugle.

[But to return to the matter of war.] My cousin's impressions were alarming: they gave a somewhat different notion of war which played a great role for me – namely that the war would be conducted in entirely new ways and would cause great destruction. Right up until the last minute, virtually until the First World War began, I felt more or less that it couldn't happen, that so much had been invested in Europe and such a level of civilization reached that the states of Europe could not take the insane step of deciding to annihilate centuries of labor to be found on every patch of land.

Now here's a question that interests me and that leads to observations of a different sort; namely, why, even though war was recognized as possible and likely by many people, were there no expectations, as far as I can remember, that it would be a revolutionary factor? My explanation, which perhaps isn't definitive, is roughly this: we constantly thought that the future revolution, which we imagined in the fairly distant future, would be a bourgeois revolution. This was Lenin's point of view, too, something I learned much later, of course. He wrote to Gorkii that there would be "Kadet capitalism" in Russia instead of "Octobrist capitalism," and so forth.[7] We had experienced the relative powerlessness of the working class and the peasantry. Therefore the bourgeois revolution was associated, as in Lenin's formulation, with the idea that the bourgeoisie would play a much more important part.

In this respect my observations, at any rate, offered absolutely no hope. I remember that I had read at the time about the "law of three generations." You know it was formulated in reference to the development of the German bourgeoisie: the first generation creates something, the second continues and maintains it, while the third is no longer interested and dissipates what the preceding generations have created. Through some chance encounters, I began to pay careful attention to the Russian bourgeois merchant or merchant-industrial dynasties. I saw a number of them in Kazan who were associated with our paper. These were Kazan bourgeois with political interests, including a few members of the Kadet party, but generally involved in local affairs and city politics. They were least of all similar to the classical bourgeois, the bourgeois of the third estate, who knows his own strength and wants to achieve political power corresponding to his real strength. There were a number of cases, particularly in Moscow, when members of the bourgeoisie essentially lost their bourgeois character. Among them were many of the bourgeois patrons of the arts. The classic example, of course, is the Alekseev family, which Stanislavskii and the Moscow Art Theater came from. The whole family was that way – only one brother, Vladimir Sergeevich, carried on the business, and it was a heavy cross for him to bear. He hated it. I remember that the sisters could never forgive Stanislavskii for his egoism in dumping all the management of the business on his brother, who was very talented and sometimes, as a kind of vacation, would work as an opera producer. Then there were all the celebrated art collectors; the Shchukin collection of Picasso and Matisse was regarded as the best in the world.[8] There were many such collectors. I don't want to go into all the examples.

H: But why your feeling of hopelessness?

GD: This was one category of these people. But the other category – what might be tentatively called the third generation – lacked any will to power or even, to a large extent, interest in economic activity. I am thinking of a Kazan merchant family, the Tikhomirovs, whom I recently wrote an article about for *Novyi Zhurnal* in conjunction with the fiftieth anniversary of the first *Pravda*.[9] The first *Pravda* – and this even the early Soviet literature attests to – was not founded on working-class nickels and dimes, as was later asserted, but on Tikhomirov's money. Aside from one older brother, who handled the family business, all the remaining children, one after the other, became Bolsheviks. What kind of bourgeoisie was this? To the extent that they became politically involved and actually revolutionary, they joined a party that was antagonistic to the bourgeoisie. This was not unique; there were a good number of such Bolshevik merchants.

Then there were people who got out of the family business altogether. I met some of them. In this respect I noticed something that markedly affected my perspective. There was an extremely wealthy, multimillionaire family, the Stakheevs. The father of the Stakheevs, whom I knew, was a very simple person, almost a *muzhik*, a man of great range and enterprise. He had made millions in shipping and the grain trade. His principal holdings were estates and land along the Kama. He was supposed to be very stern and severe (he had already died by the time I got to know some of his children), yet you could find a portrait of the old man in virtually every cottage in the villages along the Kama! From my point of view at the time, he was an exploiter! I saw how grain was traded on the piers along the Kama, how the price was dictated to the peasants, and how they could add so many kopecks per pud and so forth. And yet they regarded Stakheev as a benefactor! You see, during the famine of 1891, Stakheev had opened up his storehouses to all the famine districts, telling the people to come and take as much as they wanted. And to each peasant who came for bread, he said, "You see, you won't die, because I have grain. Don't forget! And when you have grain to spare, bring it to me!" In this way he had brought a huge part of the Kama region into his commodity trade and built an enormous fortune. However, of his children, only one was seriously involved with the business, though the rest had something to do with it. One son, who lived by himself in his Kama estate, received his share of the profits, didn't want for anything, and concerned himself only with music. He ordered a Steinway piano from America which came all the way to the Kama river station without mishap, but when it was being unloaded the gangway broke and the Steinway ended up on the bottom of the river. It was a curious state of affairs. What was *this* bourgeoisie like? It was a kind of premature parasitism, like that of the French aristocracy before the French Revolution.

I knew one Moscow family that I had met on a steamship on the Volga. There was a widowed mother, and two children. The mother was still involved in the family business in some way. The children were interested in absolutely nothing except the pleasures of life. So I wondered, who ran the business? It turned out to be some fellow who sort of hung around them. I visited them. It was a lovely apartment, and they had two cooks, one Russian, one French. So we have here a very interesting sociological process. In substance, the old Moscow merchant class of Ostrovskii had died out. It was a class that had had a certain strength. The next generation – and I think that on the whole the course of the revolution confirmed the fact – was entirely powerless and unsuited to an active role in the revolution.

But there was another type, it seemed to me – a new and entirely different type of bourgeoisie. It would be difficult to verify this now, because this development was cut short by history. Who in fact ran the family business? An overseer, a hired manager. These were very clever people, who ultimately swindled and plundered their employers. It happened with the Stakheevs. So I at least perceived an entirely different line of development.

H: What was that?

GD: The formation of a more active and at the same time tougher bourgeoisie, both agrarian – from the Stolypin homesteads – and in trade and industry, but made up of these new managers rather than of the old dynasties.

H: What did all this mean for your expectations regarding the future?

GD: The conclusion I drew for myself was that I needed to graduate, remain in the university, and prepare for a teaching position, not in Moscow but in Kazan, where I went after the death of my father in March 1914.

H: What about the country as a whole?

GD: I think that the predominant mood – and, incidentally, it was recorded in the resolutions of one of the Bolshevik conferences much later – was that the country would gradually move toward a new bourgeois revolution.

H: What were your impressions about the development of the working-class movement in 1913 and the beginning of 1914? What struck you about it, and what did you notice in particular?

GD: It was evident, of course. But I didn't pick up that much, because what was known at that time was much less than what became known later.

H: Why?

GD: Because the press couldn't discuss it so freely. I should perhaps insert a comment about the situation of the press, one that contradicts the prevailing notion that there was no preliminary censorship after 1905–1906. Formally there wasn't, but it did exist. It wasn't true for the major newspapers in the big cities or of the largest newspapers in the provinces, but other newspapers, particularly those that sought to be informative, were actually forced to ask that censorship be instituted. As a special favor, preliminary censorship would be instituted at the request of such-and-such a newspaper. It was very simple: the authorities would confiscate the issues of a paper; the first time they would close it down, the second time they would fine it, and so forth. The newspapers couldn't survive. I remember one such case that was most unfortunate for me. I went to see some acquaintances in Pskov in 1909, a time when a Social-Democratic newspaper was published there two or three times a week. I met with the editor, and it happened that his wife was an acquaintance of mine. He was glad to meet me and asked me to write something. So I wrote two or three articles but, after the third, the newspaper was shut down and the editor was sentenced to several years in prison. I was shaken by it. I was used to Kazan conditions, where it was less dangerous, because if an article went beyond certain limits, the censor, who was appointed voluntarily, would simply strike it out, and that was all. But in Pskov there was no such agreement about voluntary censorship; an offensive article would be printed without being given to the censors, the newspaper would be shut down, and the editor jailed. Incidentally, I have encountered an absolutely firm conviction among the students of this period that progress was such that preliminary censorship didn't exist. And yet in many cases it did, and the press remained very constrained. As before, you frequently had to write in so-called Aesopian language. The censor might be more or less liberal, but he was still there.

H: To return to the labor unrest of the period, was it not a phenomenon of paramount importance for you?

GD: It came close to being so in the summer of 1914, the more so because the wave of strikes and demonstrations in Petersburg coincided with the arrival of Poincaré. Poincaré heard the *Marseillaise* and supposedly – it might even be true – thought that it was being sung in his honor. I don't know if anything about it was printed in the papers.

H: Yes, it was. What about the situation of the Social-Democratic party on the eve of war in 1914? What were your contemporary impressions?

GD: At that point I was out of contact. After my father's death the family had nothing to fall back on, and since it would take some months for his pension to come through, my principal concern was to earn money to support not only myself but my mother and younger brothers. So it was a period when family matters took up most of my time.

Of the people who remained, Adoratskii comes to mind. He was a staunch Bolshevik, a friend of Lenin who held an honored place after the revolution. And yet he got married – before my eyes, he married a daughter of the proprietor of the largest clothing and fabric store in Kazan! It still seems strange – this bourgeois daughter marrying such an ardent, staunch Bolshevik! But I should recall, as I said, that there was in fact no organization in Kazan.

H: I would like to simply give you a list of events and find out what your response was. For instance, there was the split within the Social-Democratic faction in the Duma in the autumn of 1913.[10]

GD: It didn't make any impression. In general, the attitude toward the Duma, beginning with the Third Duma, was mainly scornful.

H: Even the Fourth Duma?

GD: The Third and Fourth Dumas had no authority. But there was the memory of the first. There were major political demonstrations I witnessed in Moscow in 1910. One of them was the funeral of Muromtsev, the first Duma president. It was something unexpected. The size of the crowd that followed in the procession was simply unimaginable! It was definitely a kind of demonstration! It was not just the Social Democrats or the Socialist Revolutionaries or the Kadets, though all three groups were there, of course. But there must have been hundreds of thousands of people there! It was enormous! It was one of the most gigantic demonstrations I have ever seen. And soon afterwards there were mass expulsions of students from all the universities and Kasso's purge of Moscow University. I don't know, I never studied the issue, but perhaps there was a relationship between the furor in the university and Kasso's measures. It would be interesting to find out.

H: The Beilis affair?[11]

GD: Oh, yes, that made a very strong impact, but again I should say not upon everyone. My reaction was very strong, particularly because the Jewish question had been a painful one for me since childhood, in connection with the Dreyfus affair and my father's attitude toward it. But, apart from that, there was another factor. I don't remember why, but I gradually began to feel that antisemitism was growing in the population – specifically, in the circles of the intelligentsia, even the Kadet party. I can illustrate this with one example that applies to the whole country. There were two lines in the Kadet party, one represented by Miliukov, the other by Iosif Vladimirovich Gessen [who was Jewish – ed.]. If Gessen's adherents mentioned Miliukov, they would call him "Pavel Nikolaevich," while many of Miliukov's adherents would say "Es'ka Gessen." It was a contemptuous form with a clear hint of antisemitism. But my reaction to the Beilis affair was very strong, and, of course, it disturbed a great many other people. Later, during the war, I met a clergyman; this was at the time that there was an uproar over the fact that the Germans were bombing the Rheims Cathedral. And this clergyman, a very old man, stated that a country in which the Beilis affair could happen had no right to be upset over the bombing of a cathedral. I think that this example was not unique. There had been something disturbing and conscience troubling – one of the most striking events.

H: What about the Malinovskii affair?[12]

GD: Well, that came to light much later. And of course, after the Azev affair, which had been felt very acutely in its time, the Malinovskii affair was hardly special. Something that was very upsetting, and entirely incomprehensible at the time, was the episode involving Nikolai Konovalov, a Bolshevik whom I knew well. After the first.revolution, he wrote for *Russkoe Bogatstvo*, although he was a Social Democrat and a very ardent Bolshevik. He traveled around Russia and wrote sketches – then suddenly he hanged himself! It was all incomprehensible and strange. Later it became known that he had been in the service of the Okhrana the entire time.[13] Of course, we all knew that there were plenty of provocateurs and traitors, and that even the Socialist Revolutionaries had been done in by Azev. But the Social Democrats had the comforting feeling that, well, "It couldn't happen to us." Those people, the thought ran, were a terrorist organization, highly clandestine, where people worked together without knowing who the others were.

At the same time you have to keep in mind that the basic attitude toward the tsarist regime was antagonistic and that there was a clear sense that it was not simply bad or reactionary, but rotten as well. One manifestation of the riot was the commissary trials, something that I became passionately caught up with. You see the way political responses came forth every time that there was something to latch onto. Otherwise there would be nothing. As for the working class, my attention was focused not so much on the workers' movement, as on legal proceedings between workers and their bosses which were clearly prejudiced against the workers. There were infuriating instances, such as when a Bolshevik who was well known to me, a brother of Vladimir Voitinskii, acted as the bosses' representative against the workers. Everything was so mixed up!

H: Since you mention the question of the working class, to what extent was your attitude drawn to such issues as the workers' health insurance movement, the new insurance law, and the Duma debates regarding freedom of trade union coalition in 1913 and the beginning of 1914?

GD: They affected me very little. At that time I was more interested in French syndicalism than in problems of the Russian working class movement.

H: In what way were you concerned with French syndicalism?

GD: As a particular variety of socialism. The fact that there were organizing principles that differed sharply from ours. For example, the principle that governing bodies should always have an even number of members. For instance, six people, rather than five or seven, so that it wouldn't be a matter of decisions of the majority over the minority, but rather of agreement on the part of all the members. And then, my great enthusiasm was Jaurés. There were debates between Jaurés and Guesde; I was on Jaurés' side. I also became involved with theoretical problems, matters relating to dialectics and historical materialism. As regards my love for Jaurés, it had to do with the importance of the moral factor.

H: As an autonomous force in the victory of socialism?

GD: Yes, but after that the question arose quite naturally, why dialectic development should stop at socialism? After all, contradictions could arise in socialism too! And there was yet another kind of observation, one that had not yet led me to any definite conclusions. Kazan was about one-third Tartar. The Tartar quarter was entirely isolated, so to speak, but I had contacts with Tartars, and one of my cousins married a member of perhaps the most progressive Tartar family in Kazan. Through these contacts I perceived that a large part of the population of the country was still living at an extremely low level of civilization. The Tartar intelligentsia had just started to form. And the Tartars themselves lived in complete isolation.

H: My last question is this: did the war come when you were in Kazan? What was your first response when the war began – what did it mean, what would happen? And, in particular, what should your attitude be?

GD: My response was a mixed one, like all of my wartime experiences in general. I wouldn't call it a burst of patriotism. But when Austria presented its ultimatum to Serbia and so forth, there was a virtual hatred for Austria. I remember that, to some group of people or other, I recited Tiutchev's poem about the occasion when Austria had sent some prince as a representative to the funeral of Nicholas I: "Begone, begone, thou Austrian Judas from his funeral bier. . . . " At the same time, there was an almost total certainty that the war would end in defeat, and [this feeling] provoked an ambivalent attitude: on the one hand the desire that the cursed tsarist regime be overthrown, and on the other, a painful sense that this would be a time of great and terrible misfortune. This mood was very widespread. I remember that, at some country meeting-place, a zemstvo official (someone by no means left-wing) said, "Well, they say that Courland, Lifland, and so on will be taken from us, which is unavoidable, but ultimately it won't matter a lot, because so much more will remain." That was the attitude.

Then, the editor [of the Kazan newspaper] told me, "Listen, we need accounts of the war. Would you like to become our military commentator?" I thought it over and it seemed very attractive – it was the opening phase of the war, and I became vigorously involved. I prepared; I read military literature and strategy and all kinds of books about various kinds of armaments. I studied maps throughout the war, and right up until the October Revolution I was chiefly writing military commentaries. They made a big impression on some people – the fact that I would be so audacious as to decipher the truth when a defeat was camouflaged in the official communications. They would say that our soldiers had occupied new positions to the west or east of such-and-such a locality, so I explained what that meant. Incidentally, I signed my reports with just the letter D. Someone jokingly called me Colonel D, and the rumor went out that my reports were written by some colonel on the General Staff. One fine day the editor said to me: "I have to talk to you." I had just written something particularly brash. He said, "Listen, you have to be more restrained. I was summoned by the censor, and he stated that he should have cut out these articles by Colonel D a long time ago. He said the only reason he didn't do it was because of a request from military headquarters saying 'For heaven's sake, don't stop him, it's the only way we can learn about the real situation at the front.' "

H: What was the response of your friends in the first days of the war?

GD: In my university circle, the response was generally very patriotic. Some also held the conviction that Germany could scarcely hold out for long. I remember vividly an argument with my advisor Khvostov who said, "Germany? Where will she get supplies? She can't run the whole country on ration books!" I said, "That's just what she'll run on!" Others were very alarmed, but there were no specifically defeatist attitudes at first. I know, but this was mainly later, that there were various individual feelings; a desire to see the regime defeated but not to see the country defeated, at least among some of those Social Democrats who became Defensists later on.[14]

H: Of course, you knew about the declaration of the Social Democratic faction in the Duma. What was your attitude toward it?[15]

GD: I had my own point of view on the issue. The question was discussed, usually in connection with votes for credits and German Social Democracy, and both people with a socialist orientation and others as well were upset by their betrayal of their convictions. I never saw it that way. My point of view was that no large party that aspired to become the government could take upon itself the responsibility for the defeat of its country. Our people in the Duma, as I naively thought then, might think that the danger of their being responsible for the country's fate didn't exist for them – they could permit themselves the luxury. You find the same point in Marx, incidentally, in his correspondence with Engels. I remember this issue was hotly debated. I said that I couldn't blame the German Social Democrats. I felt that a large party – and they were the largest party – couldn't follow such a policy [voting down war credits].

H: And you yourself felt that it was impossible to abstain from voting for war credits?

GD: Yes, where the voting was important. Where it didn't matter, you could vote as you pleased. In this respect, my point of view was a cynical one, for I was sympathetic to the vote of the [S.D.] Duma deputies [against war credits].

H: In what sense?

GD: As a demonstration without practical significance, but which underscored the opposition in principle.

H: As for your expectations, you said that you anticipated defeat. Did this mean that Russia would probably be defeated, and that this would bring about a new bourgeois revolution?

GD: I was extremely pessimistic on this issue. I expected a revolution, particularly later on. It is not true that no one expected revolution in Russia. By the end of 1916 it was a widespread expectation. I remember a conversation with one Social Democrat who lived part of the time in Kazan and had returned there for some reason. He said, "Well, we are headed toward a revolution." "Yes," I said, "I'm convinced we are heading toward revolution and I feel that it will be an enormous misfortune." Revolution in the country would be the same as devastation. I remember that, even earlier, my cousin Danterov, who was a military doctor, came and described the incredible devastation at the front.

H: When was this? In 1915?

GD: In 1915 I no longer had the slightest doubt that the war would end in utter military catastrophe. The railways were completely disorganized, while the mood in the army was dreadful – there were alarming stories about people going off to be killed with only enough cartridges for a few shots . . . simply murder. They made a horrible impression. I was profoundly pessimistic in this respect, and, after a brief hiatus in 1917, I returned to this attitude of pessimism.

Eighth interview

H: I think we can proceed directly to the revolution itself. Of course, you were in Kazan at the time. Perhaps we could simply begin with your personal recollections. How did the news of the revolution reach you? What impression did it make? What were your immediate reactions to the events when you learned of them?

GD: First I would like to say something about who I was when the revolution began. It is important and, I think, necessary in order to obtain a clear idea of how I reacted to the revolution. During the war I not only wrote military reviews but also completed my university studies. I had been retained at the university to study to be a professor. Naturally, I won't go into details of what this entailed. I will mention only that studies ended with the so-called Master's examination. Each future Master, and Candidate as well, was to prepare a certain number of topics in various areas of history – ancient history, medieval history, modern history, Russian history, etc. I don't know if it was by accident or by a predisposition on my part, but the topics that I chose (in conjunction with the professor) included two in ancient history that were the same in several respects. One topic was on Hellenism, the other on the Roman principate. In the course of working on these topics, I became very much interested in a problem that arose in connection with the deification of monarchs. At that time there appeared an extremely interesting German study that presented facts that were new for that time, from which it was evident that the practice of deification began in the Roman Empire before there were any emperors: specifically (and this was new to me and to many others), in the Near East, altars were raised not to a particular Roman personage but to the Senate of *populoque romano.* It was the deification of the Senate and the Roman people. This showed me how new authority is sanctioned. In working on this, I perceived the outline of my future dissertation, which would not be purely historical but rather historical and sociological in nature. I had a chapter title that I still like: *Arcana Imperii* ["The Mysteries of Authority"]. I stress this because the problem of the formation and sanctioning of a new authority haunted me, one might say, throughout the revolution. I should also note that Max Weber lay entirely outside of my field of view. I couldn't even say how much he was known in Russia at the time. I think he wasn't known at all yet.

So, without any knowledge of Weber, I arrived at the concept that authority is sanctioned either as traditional, or through deification by religious sanction, or as democratic power through democratic election, or, finally, on the basis of compulsion and force. This was my theoretical approach in those years. Much more than others, I watched how authority takes shape and, in particular, I keenly sensed the elements of a growing anarchy, the lack of organization of a new authority, and the disorganization of the elements of authority that existed at the time of the revolution. Clearly this colored my views. I won't exaggerate by saying that this approach was constantly on my mind, because there was such a huge number of current and changing impressions, experiences, and all kinds of work that there just wasn't time.

Now let me move on to the onset of the revolution itself. At that time I still had occasional attacks of malaria. A few days prior to the revolution, I had an attack, so I didn't go to the editorial office but stayed home. But news had already come that things weren't quiet in Petrograd. There was a tense mood of anticipation. At that time, I generally felt, as I have already mentioned, that revolution was inevitable or at any rate highly likely. But I didn't expect it to come tomorrow or the day after. The point in time was an open question as far as I was concerned. I don't remember exactly how I learned that a revolution had occurred in Petrograd. Then, of course, I got dressed and hurried to the office. What I learned (and Voitinskii mentions the same thing in relation to Irkutsk in his memoirs) was that a telegram had been received from Bublikov.[1] This telegram, which for some strange reason has been forgotten by many authors, played an enormously important role. Without it, probably, it would have been a much more difficult and complex process to carry out the revolution throughout Russia. The telegram announced that a new government had been formed.

H: What was Bublikov's position at that point?

GD: He was the Commissar of Railways. He sent a message to all railway stations throughout Russia, over the railway telegraph rather than the ordinary one, that a new government had been formed in Petrograd, the Committee of the State Duma, and so forth.[2] Thus people were confronted with a *fait accompli.*

H: So the telegram was transmitted to all station-masters.

GD: Yes, they told the newspapers and so on, and also the authorities of all kinds. Then feverish activity began. It's hard for me to say how and when; it all seemed to take form by itself – a Soviet of Workers' Deputies and a committee of public safety were established, by the majority, not just the socialists. Revolution had always been linked with what was known one way or another about the French Revolution. But no one gave a nationwide go-ahead to form committees of public safety, and yet they were formed everywhere. At first, of course, it was primarily the students who reacted quickly.

The military commandant in Kazan at that time was General Sandetskii who was infamous throughout Russia for his cruelty. In the period after the revolution of 1905 and 1906, when there were court-martials and the like, he was ferocious, putting pressure on judges and demanding the death penalty. By this time he was a sick old man, with a progressive form of paralysis, and, as I later learned from a doctor (Professor Vishnevskii, who subsequently became famous under the Soviets), Sandetskii's life was being maintained artificially with daily injections. He was absolutely bestial. Almost immediately, news came from somewhere that Sandetskii was mobilizing troops to suppress the revolution in Kazan. A huge meeting took place at the university, and it was announced that Sandetskii intended to fight. It was decided to take to the streets immediately and to summon the people to a large demonstration. I was so conservative – I think it had to do with my general approach – that I gave a long speech against it. I said that it couldn't bring anything except unnecessary bloodshed and a period of anarchy. I did in fact dissuade them. Instead an attack on Sandetskii was organized, and he was arrested. What followed is connected with the Committee of Public Safety and the Soviet of Workers' Deputies.

H: I'm interested in the mood of the students at this point. To what extent was it politically defined?

GD: I don't think that it was politically defined. Something happened then that I experienced myself and that I observed among many others. People, including former Social Democrats, who had gradually moved away from political activity in the interval between the revolution of 1905–1906 and 1917, had taken up various professions. These were students whose once intense political interests had virtually atrophied by the time that the news of the overthrow came. I remember that I said of myself – but with reference to others as well – that I felt like an old war horse who hears the sound of the bugle.

Then a revolutionary headquarters formed, almost by itself, and people converged there. I was there too, literally every day. The headquarters was in the courthouse, in the office of the assistant barristers, that is, young lawyers who had not yet become full-fledged attorneys. All sorts of news and rumors came there from everywhere, and some preliminary measures were taken. If my memory doesn't deceive me, it was here that the idea of a Committee of Public Safety arose, because these young lawyers knew something about the great French Revolution, and it was a natural thing to think of. The workers, of course, formed soviets. That was evident; it didn't even occur to anyone that it might be otherwise. And as for the other social elements in the revolution, well, they formed the Committee of Public Safety.

H: What do you mean by "other elements"?

GD: Not the workers – the intelligentsia and progressive bourgeoisie.

H: Of course, this wasn't a unique phenomenon, was it?

GD: Yes, almost everywhere.

H: My first question is to what extent did the idea arise independently? Did you learn that the same thing was being done in other cities?

GD: I think that it was entirely independent. It happened everywhere simultaneously.

H: So the idea was that the progressive elements should set up a Committee of Public Safety to defend the revolution. I simply want to make a comparison with 1905, when this didn't happen. To what extent was the feeling articulated that the power was dual?[3] Also, what do you mean by "progressive bourgeoisie"? And what about the division of power between the Soviet, which included only socialist elements, and the Committee of Public Safety, which included progressive elements of the bourgeoisie – did it correspond to the general mood? Was the situation more or less clear in this way?

GD: It wasn't entirely clear, but people were aware of it to a certain extent. The picture will be clearer if I sketch the situation in concrete terms. What happened was that the government immediately appointed provincial commissars, including one for Kazan. The Provincial Commissar – I don't think that he was a Kadet, but in any case he was relatively liberal – was Plotnikov, the chairman of the provincial zemstvo board, and he automatically became the chairman of the Committee of Public Safety. Now, to establish a good working relationship between the Committee of Public Safety and the Soviet [Council] of Workers' Deputies, the same person was elected vice-chairman of the Committee and of the Soviet. The result was that there were two instruments of power, the Soviet and the Committee. Each of these organizations had a vice-chairman, but he was the same person, namely me. I was Comrade Vice-Chairman in both places simultaneously. So there was a personal tie which was intended, as people were more or less explicitly aware, to prevent friction between the two organizations and mitigate the division of power.

H: Besides the Commissar of the Provincial Government, who became the chairman, and yourself, who became the vice-chairman, who else was on the Committee?

GD: There were doctors, lawyers, liberals, and zemstvo people. There were a few other elements – Kadet elements of the bourgeoisie, and many young university people – docents.

H: How many socialists were there besides yourself – Socialist Revolutionaries and Social Democrats?

GD: There were very few Socialist Revolutionaries. But there were many socialists, because university youth had formed – if not a new party, a new independent group of socialists. The group was fairly strong and, incidentally, my cousin, who had once introduced me to the Bolshevik organization (although he was already a doctor and outside the university), also joined this group of independent socialists.

H: What did this mean?

GD: There were people like my cousin, who told me flatly "I have had enough of being a Bolshevik, but you, for heaven's sake, will you still join up with them?" They wanted to create a socialist organization not burdened with the Social-Democratic heritage of the past, which was no longer popular.

H: Did they regard themselves as Marxists?

GD: Most of them did.

H: Did they think that they could be a bridge between the Socialist Revolutionaries and Social Democrats?

GD: No, because, you see, the situation in Kazan was rather strange. The Socialist Revolutionaries had negligible influence among the Kazan intelligentsia, with one exception: there were some in the student body, because one of the professors of Russian history was a thorough-going Socialist Revolutionary (although he couldn't fully say so). In any case, the fact that he was a Socialist Revolutionary made an impact.

H: Were there people, say, in Petrograd with whom these independent socialists personally identified?

GD: No.

H: Were they involved in the Committee?

GD: Yes. There were also Kadets and liberal elements that were close to the Kadets.

H: In particular, then, it reflected the conception and fact of dual power, if I understand you correctly.

GD: Yes, and at first it worked very well. I was on excellent terms with the chairman of the Soviet. And since soldiers were immediately brought in,[4] the chairman was an officer, a pleasant fellow and not a bad speaker, but unsuited to be an administrator. As a result, all the administrative functions fell to me. I was on very good terms with the Provincial Commissar and the chairman of the Committee, Plotnikov.

H: When were soldier deputies first incorporated into the Soviet?

GD: During the very first days.

H: Was this discussed?

GD: No; it seemed entirely natural at the time. Kazan had a huge reserve garrison. There were 40,000 soldiers there at the time of the revolution, mostly in the immediate vicinity. Later on I read in the Bolshevik literature that the Kazan garrison consisted of 35,000 soldiers at the time of the October Revolution. It's hard to say how accurate these numbers are, but they're not contradictory, because at the beginning a small body of soldiers was sent to the front, and later some simply deserted and disappeared into the countryside.

At this point I think that I should mention some items that made a strong impact on me. I mentioned that we arrested General Sandetskii. The responsibility for this was assumed by the recently formed Soviet. Then the following chain of events unfolded. We received a telegram from Aleksandr Ivanovich Guchkov, the Minister of War of the Provisional Government, demanding that General Sandetskii be immediately released and restored to his post. We replied that he had been arrested to avoid bloodshed, and that he was sick and senile. Guchkov disregarded this and sent us a sharp-worded ultimatum: release Sandetskii and restore him as military commander. We decided that it was absolutely unthinkable. By this time, I had also learned of his progressive paralysis. So we decided to send a delegation directly to Guchkov in Petrograd, to try to convince him to appoint a new commanding general. Three men went, with myself as the head of the delegation. We arrived in Petrograd on March 15, I think, and I used the occasion to renew my Social-Democratic contacts with both the Mensheviks and the Bolsheviks, but more of this later. As for Guchkov, we didn't have to persuade him. As soon as we entered his office, he rose, came to greet us, and began to shake our hands, saying, "First of all, gentlemen, many thanks for the peaceful and firm way you established Soviet power in your area!" Despite his earlier insistence, he didn't mention Sandetskii's name in the conversaion. I think it would be accurate to say that I was shocked. I wondered what kind of authority we were dealing with. Guch-kov, who enjoyed the reputation of being very strong, had immediately capitulated at the first rebuff, completely disregarding a considerable loss in prestige. (Much later on he had a completely unexpected part to play in my life. Thanks to him, I avoided a concentration camp in Germany, even though he didn't know me personally. But that was much later. Boris Iva-novich [Nicolaevsky], who had extensive connections with extreme right-wing groups in Germany, was the intermediary in this case.)

Then I had a short talk with my old acquaintance Aleksandr Fedorovich Kerenskii.[5] Our conversation only lasted about three minutes. There were handshakes, mutual congratulations and exclamations like, "So much to do! I'm being torn to pieces! Excuse me now, let's try to talk some more later on . . . Goodbye!" The people who were "tearing him to pieces" were in the Soviet. The Soviet was complete chaos, complete disorder. The Exec-utive Committee sat in continuous session. No one at all asked me who I was or anything like that; I simply walked right into the room where the committee was in session. I listened to what they were saying. One delega-tion after another from various military units were arriving to hail this new authority. As soon as a new unit arrived, the same person, Vladimir Savel'-evich Voitinskii, would go out and deliver a speech. I heard it I don't know how many times, and it was always the same: "Comrades, first of all I salute you on behalf of the Executive Committee of the All-Russian Soviet of Workers' Deputies . . . ," and so on . . . "Hurrah! Long live the Revolution! Long live the Republic . . . the Constituent Assembly . . . ," and so forth. There were a few old acquaintances there. Then I went to the editorial offices of *Pravda*.

H: Did you have any chance to talk to anyone in the Soviet itself?

GD: Talk? What talk was going on?

H: Wasn't it more or less like a meeting?

GD: The atmosphere was somewhat more heated, you might say. So I arrived at the editorial offices. First of all, there was my old friend Abram Gert, or Gertik, who was married to Abramovich's sister. He had been in charge of the technical division at *Pravda* before. We were glad to see one another; it had been a long time. He worked in a room which people passed through on their way to the editors' office. The editors at the time were Stalin and Kamenev. I didn't know Stalin personally, and had very little notion of who he was, but I was well acquainted with Kamenev. Then the following scene occurred. Kamenev entered. I couldn't tell whether Kamenev recognized me or not, because he walked without a glance straight past Gertik, with whom I was sitting, right into the editors' office. I wondered what was going on. I had no sense yet of the internal situation. Gertik said, "Yes, he won't be around long! When Ilich [Lenin] comes, he'll get rid of him right away!" So I learned that within *Pravda* itself there was intense hostility to *Pravda*'s own position, which at the time seemed to be a more or less reasonable one.[6] But this little episode indicated to me that Gertik was speaking with complete certainty. They already knew exactly.

And there's something that I couldn't at all explain when it happened. While I was still in Kazan, a Bolshevik pamphlet with a proclamation arrived that was completely contradictory to the *Pravda* line. I assume that it originated from the Petersburg group that included Shliapnikov, Gertik, and Molotov. It spoke quite specifically of the seizure of power and "all power to the Soviets."[7] And, to boast a little, I remember that when I was shown the pamphlet in the lawyer's chamber in Kazan, and people were horrified and asked what it could mean, I simply read it and said, "Well, so that's the way it will be." They looked at me in horror. Still, I wasn't completely certain. But on this visit to *Pravda* it became clear that Lenin at any rate wasn't upholding the same line as *Pravda*.

H: Did you talk about anything with Gertik?

GD: The conversation was more or less about what he had said concerning Kamenev and Lenin. I asked him what was going on. He said that he didn't know, that Lenin didn't share the line of Kamenev and Stalin at all. And yet at that time, perhaps a little later, the Bolsheviks in Kazan as well began talks about unification.[8] But it was already clear to me from the conversation that this was not to be and that the *Pravda* line was temporary, and I was convinced that if Lenin was in complete disagreement, that was the way it would be.

H: Did Gertik say anything about Stalin?

GD: No. At that time Stalin was almost the last person on people's minds.

H: When did you meet Stalin?

GD: At the editorial offices also. He said to me, "The main thing now is to end the war. Germany isn't our enemy – China is! The yellow peril! We will have to fight against China." He seemed a very nice fellow, completely self-taught. To sum up my impressions of my visit to Petrograd, it was more or less like a visit to a madhouse, a *first* visit.

H: Did you meet with any Mensheviks?

GD: Strictly speaking, I spoke only with Voitinskii, who was in fact already a Menshevik though he perhaps hadn't yet formally switched.[9] He left me somewhat disconcerted by saying, "Iurii Petrovich, I'm now convinced that I'm not a politician. I am a technician of revolution! And I have decided to become a technician of revolution with Tsereteli's politics."[10]

H: You didn't visit the editorial office of *Rabochaia Gazeta* at that time?[11]

GD: No, not yet. We hadn't established formal relations at that time. I don't remember now, but I probably met with someone – I had some acquaintances. I didn't meet with Tsereteli in any case.

H: What about the left Mensheviks, like Sukhanov, Steklov, and the rest? Did you meet with them?[12]

GD: I saw Steklov, who was an old acquaintance. I didn't know Sukhanov. But in general, it wasn't possible to really talk. So that was my first visit to Petrograd.

H: What impression did you return with?

GD: A painful one. Later on I will talk about my attitude toward the dual power. But now, since I have described one madhouse, I should mention another one, this time a real one. This happened a little later, soon after my trip to Petrograd. Near Kazan, perhaps half a mile from the city limits, there was an insane asylum. An insurrection took place in this insane asylum. It was organized by the attendants. The leader was an attendant in the security ward – for the violently insane. And not just the security ward, but the security ward in the criminal section. It happened that the principal instigator of the riot was named Pavlov, a name that was to come up a lot in Russia. He mobilized these violent lunatics and, under his direction, they beat up the doctor. The attendants assembled and took over from the entire medical staff. They elected a director and doctors from among themselves.

H: Very democratic!

GD: Yes, they made their own revolution on elective principles. There was complete confusion in town. What was to be done? In the meantime we received a telegram. Someone had already informed Petrograd about the situation. And one of the newspapers, either *Novoe Vremia* in Petrograd or some Moscow paper (but in any case a more or less counter-revolutionary newspaper) wrote that anarchy reigned in Kazan, that 3,000 inmates of the insane asylum had revolted and were marching on the city. I contacted Provincial Commissar Plotnikov. He said that the situation was terrible, and that something had to be done. Couldn't troops be sent to the asylum? I said, "Listen, there's no need to send any troops. I'll go there myself!" "You will? But let me give you an armed escort." I said, "Just a coach and driver, nothing more." "You can't mean it!" "I said just a coach and driver, nothing more!" I got in the coach, drove to the asylum, and walked in. "Who are you?" "The vice-chairman of the Soviet!" That aroused some respect. "Where are you going?" "I wish to see Mr. Pavlov of the security ward." They looked at me and let me in. Some doctor grabbed me and told me about the atrocities, saying "For God's sake, don't go, they'll kill you!" I went on and met Pavlov. An extremely nice fellow. I said to him, "You have misunderstood 'elective principles.' You can't go about it this way, with patients electing doctors and so on. It's done differently. Now we have Soviets of Workers' and Soldiers' Deputies. You should restore the doctors and the director to their posts. The attendants should meet, choose a delegate to the Soviet, and write him a mandate, as it's called. Then we will talk to him about what to do next . . . " I said that a Constituent Assembly would be set up later on for all of Russia. He was very pleased. And that was the end of the lunatics' revolution.

H: Was he merely an attendant there?

GD: Yes, an attendant in the violent ward, and absolutely uneducated. A few days later he came to see me at the Soviet and told me proudly that the meeting of attendants had elected him to the Soviet of Workers' Deputies and to all Constituent Assemblies! This was the end of my acquaintance with the Second Insane Asylum. Unfortunately, the First Insane Asylum wasn't so easy to liquidate. Of course, there was an endless number of petitioners of all sorts and the like. Have I told you about the officer's wife?

H: No.

GD: I recounted this incident in some article in *Novyi Zhurnal.* It made a great impression on me. And, if you follow the story from the perspective that I sketched at the beginning, you will see why. At one point a lady came to see me. Not exactly elegant, but a middle-class lady, very well dressed, probably with a *gimnazium* or secondary education. I received her, and asked what she wanted. She said, "Well, I am the wife of Captain So-and-So in the army. My husband is in Rybinsk, now, not in Kazan. And I have learned that he has taken a mistress." I asked her, "Is it that he's left you without resources?" "Oh, no, in that respect he's been very good, he sends me money every month. I can't complain on that score." So I said, "Excuse me, but then it's not clear to me what you want from us." "What I want? I want you to order my husband to drop his mistress and return to his lawful wife!" I said, "I'm sorry, but we can't do that." She looked at me scornfully and said, "What sort of authority are you if you can't even do that?" I thought to myself, "Yes, evidently we'll have to wait for such an authority that even this will be possible."

Arbitration commissions took up a great deal of time. We had strikes, chiefly because wages were fantastically low. We will have to speak about this later, because the situation was becoming worse and worse as a result of inflation. We had to get, through talks and negotiations, some sort of tolerable minimum wage, which generally meant a three- or four-fold increase in wages. Each time, there would be protracted negotiations between representatives of the Arbitration Commission and representatives of the workers and employers. In general, this whole first period went off fairly well; all this was settled. The permanent chairman was there too, but I was frequently present and sometimes acted as chairman myself. There was a great deal of work of all kinds. In terms of general political perspective, the issue of dual power was attracting more and more attention and debate. Our position in the Soviet was that, so as to maintain some unity of political line, we would clarify, interpret, and impel the Soviet to confirm the decision of both the [Petrograd] Soviet and the Provisional Government.

H: I don't understand.

GD: A peculiar form of democracy existed. Decisions of the Executive Committee, or even orders from the Provisional Government, were regarded as not necessarily binding (not *de jure* but *de facto*) until they were confirmed by the corresponding local agencies. Moreover, the Committee of Public Safety soon disintegrated somehow of its own accord, and the entire function of confirmation fell to the Soviet.

H: What do you mean that the Committee soon disintegrated? Over what period of time?

GD: I think it was by mid-April. The Committee had no real power. It carried out a number of reforms – a new Procurator was appointed, and the police was replaced by a militia, something that meant a great deal. One of the few Socialist Revolutionaries, a young lawyer, received instructions to organize a militia, and he was its chief. But it was the Soviet that had some resources; the Committee of Public Safety didn't have any. So the Chief of Militia was soon in the position that he operated under the Soviet and on the Soviet's instructions. Sometimes, for the most fantastic reasons, people would come running to the Soviet to say that a counter revolutionary coup was being prepared. "Why? Where?" Little slips of paper saying "They're all liars!" were spread throughout the city. Clearly in preparation for a counter-revolutionary coup. People came from all sides bringing these little slips. The Chief of Militia began an investigation. It turned out that the local cinema was about to show a picture called "They're All Liars." Now, this is just amusing. But it took hours of discussion, receiving people, work, and then investigation. Initially no one thought of the cinema. And we had a primitive police organization. All the former policemen had been dismissed and the new ones were incompetent. So there was a day of panic in anticipation of a counterrevolutionary outburst.

Then there was the conflict that ended in Miliukov's resignation.[13] I wasn't certain of this at the time, but it was said that I was the first to raise the issue of a coalition government in the Social-Democratic press. Perhaps I wasn't objectively the first, but I was the first subjectively, because I raised the issue on the basis of no one else's thoughts but my own. I regarded the situation as entirely impossible, and I had some hope that the formation of a coalition government would put an end to this dual power.

H: Where did you publish this?

GD: In the local Kazan newspaper. It was a curious newspaper. It consisted of two parts – the first, the *Izvestiia* [Transactions] of the Kazan Soviet of Workers' Deputies, and the second the organ of the Kazan Committee of the All Russian Social-Democratic Party of the Mensheviks. So clear and indisputable was our [Menshevik] predominance in the Soviet that no one was at all shocked that the *Izvestiia* of the Soviet and the Menshevik organ were in the same newspaper.

H: Was your article before or after the Miliukov incident?

GD: I think that it was a few days before.

H: You stated that at the end of March and beginning of April you unhesitatingly regarded yourself as a Menshevik Social Democrat. When did this process of self-definition take place?

GD: After my first visit to Petrograd and to the editorial offices of *Pravda*, it was clear to me that there would be no unified party. At first there was the thought that it was possible, and, as I said, the position taken by *Pravda* reinforced it. On the other hand, there was that mysterious leaflet – and I have yet to find any clear evidence about where it came from. But then Tikhomirov, the same one who had financed the first *Pravda*, returned to Kazan and resurrected the moribund Bolshevik organization. And he held some talks about unification, in the sincerity of which I didn't believe.

H: In his personal sincerity?

GD: Yes. I had the feeling that it was a maneuver to detach as many people as possible from us. I also didn't believe in my own sincerity in these talks. So that was the nature of the process of self-definition. It didn't mean that I perceived Menshevism to be what it had been before. I continued to regard myself as a Social Democrat. I felt that the independent socialists [in Kazan] were a highly qualified, perhaps too highly qualified, group of talented intellectuals who had no chance whatever of any success; so the choice was between the Bolsheviks and the Mensheviks. Looking closely, I rejected the Bolsheviks completely. Besides myself, there were many other former Bolsheviks; at least three-quarters of our Menshevik organization consisted of former Bolsheviks. There never was a Menshevik organization in Kazan – just some of these back-door Mensheviks.

H: When did this happen? In March?

GD: Either at the end of March or the beginning of April.

H: What were your impressions about Menshevism in Petrograd? What were its political and programmatic tendencies and to what extent did you yourself identify with any of them? So what did it mean to you to be a Menshevik, say before the May Conference?[14]

GD: That we were democrats first and foremost.

H: Socialists and democrats?

GD: Yes. In general I agreed with Tsereteli's speeches. It was only later that I got the distinct impression that he and virtually everyone else were living in a fantasy world, not a real one.

H: But what about you in April?

GD: That still hadn't happened. The situation was very complicated. First, I had attached myself to a particular party, like all the rest. Then we took the position of the Defensist rather than the Internationalist wing. We will need to talk about that more; it is a basic issue. In general, we regarded ourselves as obliged to maintain a particular line. For instance, I wrote what I think were quite convincing articles about how the elections to the Constituent Assembly should be run; about universal, equal, direct, and secret suffrage, and about proportional representation. At first, you almost didn't think about it. It was only later, having understood and seen it all in the conditions that prevailed in Russia, that both direct elections and proportional representation appeared absurd to me. But at first, there was neither the time nor the breathing space to analyze such fundamental problems. There was the general line, as it was called, of Revolutionary Democracy[15] which enjoyed some sympathy, though less and less as time passed, and this line had to be maintained.

H: So in April, when you had to declare your position, you didn't use the term "Revolutionary Defensist"?

GD: No, I don't think so. That was later.

H: Now it seems that we can delineate three elements. You have already said something about the issues of unification of the party and of a coalition government. The last issue, of course, is that of war and peace. In April there was the whole affair with Miliukov and the Dardanelles – already with the Soviet's appeal for a peace without annexations and indemnities.[16] What was your attitude about all this?

GD: I had the firm conviction that the continuation of the war meant the destruction of revolution. But that it was impossible to end it.

H: But what did this mean?

GD: At that time, in April, it meant primarily just what I said. Later another aspect became involved. I didn't think that a general peace could be concluded.

H: Why?

GD: Because, although our information about the outside world was slight, I didn't think it possible that the allies would agree to a peace. Abramovich, for instance, seems to have forgotten completely what the situation was. It is true that America had entered the war,[17] but there was still no evidence of her involvement and we didn't know much about it. Abramovich does correctly point out that America's involvement was almost entirely ignored, but this was something that was objectively quite correct rather than a shortcoming: America's involvement meant only some material aid that was not of decisive importance. It was a period of rout. The Russian Army was entirely shattered and disorganized. Germany's position at the time was very strong – the possibility of a German victory was very real, or so it was imagined. So conclusion of a peace could mean only a separate peace with Germany. And most of us were convinced that this would mean the liquidation of the revolution, the restoration of tsarism, and the like.

H: Why?

GD: We regarded it as utterly impossible that Germany would foster a democratic and independent Russia. It would be a Russia with a figurehead tsar, to use a later expression, almost a German protectorate.

H: And you thought, of course, that there was no way out?

GD: Later, in the course of conversations I had in Petrograd, I learned of another concern. I don't recall exactly who it was, probably Sofia Moiseevna Zaretskaia, who said that we couldn't end the war at all, because conclusion of peace would not mean the end of war. And she was very close to the upper circles. I think that she or someone else who held more or less secret information said that conclusion of a separate peace would lead to an invasion of Russia by allied forces. So there would be war in either case. At the time I didn't know more precisely what this meant, but perhaps it was because, as I was to learn only from Kennan's book, Japan had offered to send 12 divisions.

H: But no one knew this, of course.

GD: Yes. Of course no one knew, and later it was denied. But I remember that I was told definitely that if a separate peace was signed, an invasion would follow immediately, though this was in June or July. It wasn't talked about in April.

H: But in the period before the May Conference, how would you describe the political groupings within the Soviet of Workers' and Soldiers' Deputies in Kazan?

GD: At first there were no groupings. One viewpoint dominated totally and unanimously.

H: Meaning the Mensheviks? Did the workers' and soldiers' deputies regard themselves as Mensheviks?

GD: No!

H: So what did it mean?

GD: There were no others! Only the Bolsheviks and they became active only much later.

H: Were [the deputies] more or less non-party types who simply supported or followed the leadership of the Soviet?

GD: Yes. The chairman of the Soviet was an officer, Lieutenant Poplavskii, who had absolutely no affiliation with political parties or organizations. But he was solidly behind me, chiefly because he regarded my every opinion as the height of wisdom.

H: Now, aside from your personal influence, did the Soviet deputies recognize the leadership of the Menshevik Social-Democratic Committee in Kazan?

GD: No.

H: It was personal leadership?

GD: Yes, and there was friction between me and the Committee, because the other members, or some of them at any rate, were annoyed that decisions were being made without them. I remember one conversation about this. I said to them, "I need to make decisions quickly. If you wish, I am ready to let the Committee make the decisions. But then you will have to attend the Soviet, rather than stay at home, and you'll have to meet more than once a week. I can't wait for your agreement. It is technically impossible for me to assemble everyone in a few minutes. So you must be here. Then I can present you with each issue as it arises."

H: Now let us return to your notion of coalition government. To be specific, there might be two elements here: one, that you couldn't cope with the situation without the bourgeoisie. But there could also be the maximalist view that you had to take power. And since this is not very orthodox, it could be defined as a coalition. To what extent did the bourgeoisie represent a significant threat of counterrevolution from the right prior to May?

GD: There's some danger of later rationalization, of course, but I would describe my position as follows. There was the so-called dual power, two sources of authority. I thought that, if there were two sources of authority, then there was no real authority. Such authority as there was was either in a state of anarchy or was on the way to becoming anarchy. Hence the thought of a coalition government, which would have an entirely concrete political character, so to speak. The Provisional Government would be transformed. Part of its members would be replaced by leading members of the Soviet. This, this was a dream, or an illusion if you will, of removing the possibility of differing political lines between the Provisional Government and the soviets. The soviets would not make any major independent political decisions; but the [country's] actual leaders – i.e., the leaders of the soviets – together with other ministers would hammer out a common [political] line.

H: But why was a coalition government needed? Why not a "homogeneous" socialist government?

GD: This was a major dilemma for me. My prognosis for the future was half right and half absolutely wrong. It took its full shape somewhat later, but was already fairly clear. What I imagined was that the Bolsheviks would seize power.

H: As early as April?

GD: Yes. I thought so as early as March. But I thought, of course, that they wouldn't be able to cope with power or to overcome all the counterrevolutionary forces.

H: Did you arrive at this when you read the leaflet?

GD: Yes, but I never imagined that Bolshevik rule could last very long. And here, of course, the pattern of the French Revolution influenced me as well. But a clearer formulation came only later on. At that time I thought that, at best, we would end up with an absolute monarchy. That was what I thought most likely. But I thought then and to the end that if there was any chance of avoiding this outcome, we should try to avert it. And this meant, above all, trying to prevent the disintegration of the country, to prop it up, and to satisfy insofar as possible at least the most pressing current needs of the population. The threat of disintegration was constantly hanging over us.

H: And this made the participation of "census" elements absolutely necessary?

GD: The unification of all forces that were not directly counterrevolutionary.

H: What did this mean?

GD: The participation of "census" elements, especially because they included people with administrative experience. It would have been very easy to get rid of Plotnikov, the Provincial Commissar in Kazan, or to remove the incumbent mayor, a very liberal man. They had the advantage of knowing their job. There were such posts and elementary things that had to be solved at every step, such as the food-supply problem. This was a major problem even before the revolution. So we needed people who knew how to obtain grain, where to buy it, how to organize transportation, and so on.

H: And this seemed more important for you than the threat of counterrevolution?

GD: Than the threat of an immediate counterrevolution.

H: Which could come only after a period of anarchy?

GD: And after a temporary triumph of the Bolsheviks.

Ninth interview

H: Let us continue our discussion of events before May 1917.

GD: In April, the Minister of War Guchkov implemented a decision to give soldiers at the front leave to return for agricultural work. I don't know how the decision was made – by Guchkov personally or by the government.[1] In any case, the appropriate order was issued by the Minister of War, and presumably he was counting on winning popularity at the front for himself and the government. But it was absolutely catastrophic from the standpoint of continuing the war. I think it hastened the collapse of the front no less, and perhaps even more, than the famous Order No. 1.[2] We were even more perplexed, because some of the more thoughtful soldier representatives in the Soviet of Workers' and Soldiers' Deputies, at any rate, pointed out that there was no way to make the soldiers on leave return to the front. And that is in fact what happened, although it might have been a hard thing to take into account. This decision also furthered the disorganization of the railways, which were in pitiful shape to begin with, because a large number of people were furloughed – not the whole army, of course, though I don't know how many. Among skeptics, at any rate, this strengthened the impression that things were hardly going well with the government.

Then there was a very interesting episode over May Day. After Guchkov had not only agreed to the removal of General Sandetskii but had even congratulated us for our resolve and decisiveness in carrying out the revolution, a new regional commander was appointed. It was done in an entirely formal manner. There were no elections. The Minister of War appointed a new person; I think that his name was General Mrozovskii, who had a fairly liberal reputation. General Mrozovskii proposed to the Soviet that a celebration with a military orchestra be organized for May 1. His idea obviously was to turn May Day into a patriotic government demonstration, although with a revolutionary tinge, of course. This proposal didn't meet with sympathy. I spoke about it in the Soviet and there was complete agreement with my position that, whereas our relationship to the present government was in no way the same as to the previous government, May Day was still a workers' holiday and a holiday of the [Socialist] International. And we could not yet reconcile ourselves to have the *Internationale* performed by a military chorus, which was still not our own, not completely ours. So that was the decision. The celebration was grandiose by local standards, with great enthusiasm and speeches.

This episode should be considered in connection with another factor, the ambiguity that permeated all the relationships of the soviets to authority. True, there was not just the Soviet of Workers' and Soldiers' Deputies; much later there was also a separate Soviet of Peasants' Deputies attached to it. The Soviet was, on the one hand, a parallel government, while on the other it remained a workers' organization. There is an issue here that for some strange reason remains completely unclear to me. I don't know why, but I never became interested in it. This is the question of the financing of both the soviets and the Social-Democratic organization. The fairly substantial amounts of money that were needed to maintain the Soviet came from the government, of course. But the delicate question of how the Menshevik organization was financed remains unclear to me.[3] I simply can't imagine that the large number of newspapers, with their considerable editorial expenses, could have been paid by membership dues. At the time I struggled to try to put both the Soviet and the Menshevik organization on their own feet, the principal motivation being that I didn't believe that an organization that couldn't sustain its own existence could be viable or independent. Nothing came of it.

But these considerations formed the basis for the peculiar and, as far as I know, unique situation that our Menshevik newspaper was part of a joint newspaper with the Soviet. I was the editor of both halves. Of course, there was another comrade who concerned himself with local affairs and news items, but the entire political section fell to me. And I was quite flattered and pleased when the Central Committee informed us that Comrade Cherevanin, who had been charged with the inspection of provincial Menshevik newspapers, had rated ours as the best in terms of quality. Incidentally, I couldn't say that our prestige rose particularly as a result, or that we were somehow considered more significant than other papers.

By this time, we were entirely swamped in work of all sorts. I have a strange sensation about it. I would say that I recall these days as a mixture of very concrete images, often very painfully real, with something completely unreal, like a dream. I think that it would take a Kafka to present it precisely. I have made attempts to reconstruct what my days were like. I was so busy that, although it took me only eight or ten minutes to get to the Soviet from my house, for weeks I had no time to get home and spend the night there. I would only dash back to change clothes and then return to the Soviet. But when I ask myself what I did and how I spent a particular day, I am unable to reconstruct a single one in all its details. I know that I had to write political articles and carry on an infinite number of discussions, as well as receive petitioners with all sorts of trivial business (though not for them, of course). But the overall sensation of time spent rather unproductively remains.

It would be interesting to determine to what extent this was particularly true of Kazan, or whether it was widespread. All the figures that are given for party members, almost 200,000 by the time of the August Conference, give an absolutely distorted picture of the number of people who were really active party members in Kazan, but I think also generally. In Kazan they were an insignificant handful. (Party life consisted chiefly of discussions.) So there was I, and there was Doctor Shergov, who worked with me strenuously for two or three months. Then he withdrew somewhat, because he was, after all, a military doctor and had to return to his medical duties. Aside from that, there were very few. They did take over a few functions; for instance, the Committee of Public Safety gradually folded of its own accord and was in effect replaced by an improvised democratic Duma, an improvised form of democratic self-government. There were a few people – two or three lawyers and a couple of others – who became Duma members and took part in its sessions and activities. There was a Socialist Revolutionary, also a lawyer, who was the Chief of Militia and very involved in this thankless task. The former policemen had been fired and new ones had been recruited on the basis of "reliability," who had to be taught the most elementary things to carry out their duties. This lawyer, who also had never had anything to do with the police, wasn't capable of managing it properly.

It was a small handful of people; an enormous amount of work fell on their shoulders, and this work made it absolutely impossible to check the Bolshevik agitation which was gradually developing. At first virtually nothing was heard or seen of the Bolsheviks. I don't think there was a single Bolshevik in the Soviet, at any rate, none spoke. As I mentioned, a Bolshevik organization was established upon Tikhomirov's arrival. They published a rather pathetic little sheet. The impression was that they were completely impotent, even if not altogether absent. Only gradually did we come to realize that the situation was otherwise. In fact, these members of the reconstituted Bolshevik organization, who had very meager qualifications in every respect, were carrying on constant, daily agitational activity at the factories. Little by little we began to become aware of it when a person arrived [at the Soviet] with a new mandate and stated that such-and-such a factory had recalled its deputy and elected this person as the new one. And later it turned out that the new deputy was a Bolshevik.

We, and I especially, also came into conflict with Bolshevik influence on the workers' movement at the time. There were many inevitable changes in labor conditons. Wage increases came through appeals to conciliation commissions, with the participation of employers' and workers' representatives and a chairman and a mediator from the Soviet, namely myself and a lawyer named Verger whom I shall speak of in another context. He was an excellent director of these conciliation commissions. He and I alternated as chairman and mediator. And the initial period went smoothly, but there was ongoing inflation. New demands arose as a result. The general pattern was that the employers agreed to substantial wage increases without much resistance, but this was in the initial period and involved chiefly factories in defense production. Wage issues would be resolved fairly simply, because the firms would simply demand more money from the government – something that made inflation more severe rather than alleviating it, because this new money circulated. The situation was more difficult, of course, with businesses that produced for the market and not for defense. Here it was harder to get the wages raised and the firms would respond by raising the prices for goods proportionately – another factor that accelerated inflation. So a vicious circle was created.

I mention this in connection with what I discovered for myself, namely the important role that the Bolsheviks had already begun to play, quite unnoticed by us. For me, the discovery came during a major strike at the Alokuzov factory. Before the war, this factory had been a major footwear producer, one of the largest in Russia, with around 3,000 workers. It was reconstructed and retooled during the war and manufactured not only footwear but also clothing for the army. I don't know the exact figures, but the number of workers might have reached 10,000. It was an enormous enterprise. And things went fairly smoothly at first. It was a business that was engaged entirely in defense production. But then the employers, the Alokuzovs, tried to contain the workers' demands. Perhaps they had in fact had some difficulties with the government over the wage increases, although I don't know this. Anyway, there was a strike either in May or in June. A meeting of the workers was arranged, and it was unbelievably wild. There were shouts when I tried to speak, and extremely malicious interruptions. I saw that nearly all of this came not from the men but from the women workers, who had previously never worked in factories and were mostly ex-prostitutes. It was a nightmare. The mobilization of large numbers of men had meant that the prostitutes were partly or completely unemployed. So they could be hired at very low wages, and supplemented them with their usual trade. This was not openly admitted, but the employers themselves understood that they had hired workers under these extremely substandard conditions, and yet the whole organization of production was based on this.

At this point – and this was a real discovery – a new and insistently repeated demand arose. And I think that it was not just in Kazan. The striking workers demanded first of all that they be shown the books! So that they could determine the employers' real profits, and how much the workers could get themselves! This was a slogan spread by the Bolsheviks, and it found a great response. I conducted some absurd negotiations with the owner, Alokuzov, who usually lived in Petrograd but had come to Kazan for the occasion. He made a fantastic offer, going as far as to say that he would raise wages eighteenfold for one category of workers. When he presented his long list, I said that it was unexpected. He said, "No, it's quite possible and very simple, because we have organized our factories on the basis of very cheap labor. In this category we have 11 absolutely unqualified women workers. If we change over to more normal wages, we can replace these 11 by two qualified workers, and so the wages for the two qualified workers will be eighteen times higher than the former one for the unqualified workers" – he didn't say "prostitutes." But the picture was entirely clear.

Never in my life – though I had to deal with some stormy mass meetings later on, particuarly in Germany – did I encounter such a savage atmosphere. At this point it became clear to me that there was a major difference between this improvised mass of workers and the workers of 1905–1906. Of course, there had been a large influx of new workers from the countryside between the revolution of 1905–1906 and the war, and then during the war itself. I gave some accounts of this in what I wrote. On the one hand there were these women workers who were infected with the general mood. On the other, there were small craftsmen who had also been mobilized as factory workers, and whose attitude was, as they shouted at one factory, "We should take everything from them. They've robbed us enough!" This was also said to me, not by one of the older workers, but by a small artisan who had been mobilized in wartime. This gave a clear picture of the spontaneous forces that erupted, and erupted savagely. These forces were not felt at first, but became more and more perceptible later, and, so far as I recall, there was literally nothing similar in 1905–1906. If before we were all bound up with the notion that Russia was a long way from being ripe for socialism, in the course of the revolution this view grew stronger rather than weaker, at least in my case and for many others. Where was that working class with which we would build socialism? This was, of course, an important part of the picture.

H: Concerning these new recruits from the countryside, can you tell me what were your feelings when these new elements appeared in Kazan?

GD: I didn't have a completely clear impression, in the sense of being able to distinguish these recent arrivals. I had a general impression that the mass of workers at that time was much less receptive to socialist propaganda in the strict sense of the term, and that they weren't as prepared as they had been in 1905 as a result of the activities of worker circles at that time, modest as they had been. It was my feeling in general that these new workers simply weren't interested in such things as socialism.

H: Now, perhaps you can answer another question: aside from the slogans about opening the books to learn how much profit the bosses were making, what were the Bolsheviks' other main slogans current during May and June?

GD: Economic slogans, higher wages, the eight-hour working day, which the Provisional Government in fact accepted. And then the pure demagoguery like "prices are rising; it's the government's fault," or "the war is continuing; it's the government's fault." There was something that happened slightly later but which belongs in this same context. We were greatly upset when we read that Skobelev (Minister of Labor in the first coalition government) had received a delegation of factory owners who demanded that certain excessive and reckless worker demands be checked. And the delegation included a former very prominent member of the Bolshevik Central Committee, Leonid Borisovich Krasin, who was a director of the German firm of Siemens and Schukert.[4] When I later went to Petrograd and was at the editorial offices of *Novaia Zhizn'*, I mentioned this. I asked what had happened to Krasin that had caused him to break with the party. I was told that, according to Krasin, he hadn't altered his convictions. In fact, he came to see us, and we asked him directly, because we were very disturbed and he said, "But I feel that if the working class behaves like sons of bitches, we Social Democrats should be the first to say so."

H: Let me try to put the question to you directly. Let us take the Bolshevik slogans of 1914, like the calls for a democratic republic, an eight-hour working day, and especially confiscation of landed gentry estates. These struck a responsive chord in Petersburg in 1913–1914. It seems to me that they did partly for the reasons you have mentioned: the people who migrated there from the countryside in 1913 and 1914 were all products of the Stolypin reforms and so on, and had these attitudes. To what extent was this a factor at this point in 1917?

GD: It was not an important factor among the city workers. Probably it was among the soldiers, who remained physically inaccessible to us, so to speak. You must bear in mind one of the wildest inanities that existed at that time. There had been the mobilization of huge numbers of people who simply couldn't be outfitted and armed properly. According to our information, there was a reserve garrison of 40,000 men in and around Kazan. It was absolutely impossible to send them to the front. There was only one occasion when soldiers were dispatched, and it fell to me to be the chief persuader. It was a staggering scene. We felt that we were obligated to act since we were the only executive organization despite the usual objection we encountered from the soldiers. "Now that the revolution had occurred, and there's freedom and the beginning of a happy life, why should we have to go off and get killed, and not enjoy this life?" It was a very hard argument to answer. We had to say, "Yes, that's true, but a German victory, capitulation to Germany will mean liquidation of the revolution, and then there'll be no happy life," and so on. At the very beginning, in April or May, this argument might have been somewhat convincing. Afterwards, particularly in view of Guchkov's action, you couldn't even think of sending people from the rear to the front. So we dropped the issue.

These 35,000 free soldiers lived in their barracks around the city, and, incidentially, made the provisioning of Kazan much more difficult, because they had to be fed. And, I think, they were generally better fed than a considerable part of the population. But as for getting to the barracks, I was able to do so once or twice, but until October, when a preliminary "October revolution" took palce in Kazan, we did not go around to the barracks and propagandize. Although I have no precise information, to judge from later developments the Bolsheviks did something there; there were a number of officers who had joined the Bolshevik party. The mass of soldiers only desired to return home to the countryside and divide up the land, and they feared lest it would be divided without them. I am still amazed that they didn't all desert, something they did immediately after the October coup. Of course, the Bolsheviks took the opportunity to mention, in speaking of the misdeeds and derelictions of the government, that land was not being given out, that landowners were not being dispossessed.

H: Now, to what extent was the social profile of the Bolshevik agitators and in particular of the Bolshevik leadership in Kazan revealed during the months between May and July? Who were the people involved in this agitation? Where did they come from?

GD: First of all, there was not a single local person who was in any way prominent. There was Tikhomirov, who had reconstituted the organization. He was in fact a native of Kazan, but he had isolated himself from local reality even before the war, and then he stayed around a relatively short time. He did his job, arranged some financial support. I don't know now. Later on I had a talk with him when he admitted receiving some amount of money. From time to time, though, a completely unknown man would appear. He was a young *intelligent* who, as I learned much later, lived quite discreetly in Kazan, but would surface sporadically. He was smart, and a surperb speaker. Then on one occasion, no one knew why, a Comrade Shenkman took the floor in the Soviet. He delivered a very well spoken, very good speech exposing the government and the "opportunism" of the Mensheviks. And then one of the most successful Bolshevik agitators was a worker named Avram Komlet who had belonged to the Bolshevik organization a long time. I had a friendly chat with him. He would travel through the province, something we couldn't do, and agitate among the peasants. This conversation occurred somewhat later, but it gives an idea of what the agitation was like. I asked, "Listen, it can't be that easy to carry on Social-Democratic agitation among the peasants." "It's easy!" "Well, how do you do it?" "It's simple – I say, 'There are Bolsheviks and Mensheviks. The Mensheviks are the ones who want to give the people less [*men'she*] while the Bolsheviks are the ones who want to give them more [*bol'she*].' And it always works! They all opt for the Bolsheviks!"

H: But isn't it true that among the peasantry in Kazan province the influence of the Socialist Revolutinaries was the greatest?

GD: In Kazan, the main influence was that of the Left Socialist Revolutinaries. And something that we simply knew nothing about and didn't suspect – they actually organized a Soviet of Peasant's Deputies. That was later on, probably in June. I'll talk about the first session of it later. Then there were Left Socialist Revolutionary speakers, like Kamkov, who came to Kazan.[5] It's a strange thing – not a single prominent Menshevik or Right Socialist Revolutionary came to visit us. Someone came from the *Edinstvo* group, and made no impression on us whatever.[6] That was all. We were limited to our own resources. In the long run, it would have been better to have fresh people. You couldn't go on talking to 90 percent of the same people on every occasion. But there was no help at all in this respect. And the people who were leaders, members of the Central Committee, remained absolutely unknown, not only to the broad strata of the population and society, but even within the party organization itself.

H: Now, to what extent did the influence of the Bolsheviks spread in the period prior to the July Days? To judge by the number of Bolshevik deputies in the Soviet, for instance?

GD: There were still very few. But it was different in July and August. In August it was already completely clear that they were winning over the soviets.

Now, about the episode concerning the German money in July.[7] In the city, Bolsheviks were still extremely weak. I remember Tikhomirov running to me and saying, "God knows what's happening! Our comrades are being beaten up in the streets! Over money! Aren't you going to stop this? You can't be in favor of these methods of political struggle?!" I said, "I am not in favor of them at all, and I am ready to take measures to stop them. Probably we'll be able to do it. But I'd like to get to the bottom of the matter." It was a very controversial question. I said, "I'm ready to make a public announcement that I don't know whether or not the Bolsheviks took German money. If they did, I condemn it, of course, but this doesn't mean that Lenin is a German agent as many people allege. If he took money, it was not in the service of the German government but for his own party. I am ready to make a public statement to that effect, and I don't doubt that it will have a great impact. But in return, you have to tell me the truth: did you or didn't you take German money?" "Yes, we did, but from Scheidemann's people, not from the German government."[8] So that from that point on I didn't know whether or not they had taken money; I had to use some rhetorical devices to skirt the issue. And I made the public announcement.

H: You have noted that, during this campaign over the Bolsheviks' German funds, the situation of the Bolsheviks in Kazan had become much more difficult. Did this affect the mass of workers?

GD: Not the workers.

H: What about the soldiers?

GD: Not them either. It affected the man in the street, merchants, shop-assistants, salesmen – such types. It becomes clear if you consider it topographically. The soldiers lived chiefly in barracks around the city. The workers were partly on the outskirts, partly in the suburbs, with only a very small number in the city itself. The beatings of the Bolsheviks occurred in the center of the city, in the daytime, when there were no workers or soldiers there. Several known Bolsheviks got beaten up. There were only a few such cases, but it created a kind of panic among Tikhomirov and other Bolsheviks; perhaps they suspected that we had organized the beatings and were resorting to such physical methods.

H: I conclude from this that there was no suppression of the Bolshevik organizations in Kazan afterward. And how long did the agitation against the Bolsheviks last among the inhabitants? A week? Two weeks?

GD: No, a few days. They soon forgot about it.

H: And then the situation was as before?

GD: Yes. It in no way impeded the rise of Bolshevism and the Bolsheviks' penetration of the soviets.

Something that started to become very evident in June, I think, was the orientation of the bourgeoisie – an alienation from us and a kind of sympathy for the Bolsheviks, a peculiar kind of sympathy. Such people openly said, "All you're doing is ruining Russia. The Bolsheviks will come to power for a few weeks or months; they won't be able to do anything and will be overthrown, and then a sensible government will be formed." I even spoke in public on this topic once. I appealed to representatives of the business community, and something was organized in a cinema, together with some demonstration. I said, "You're mistaken if you figure this way! It will be entirely different, and you won't gain from it, you'll lose. You may lose everything!" But this attitude existed and was very strong, there's no doubt about it.

H: How did it express itself concretely?

GD: At first, we could count on some sort of material assistance in case of need. My overall policy was to reduce subsidies to the minimum. I preferred, insofar as possible, to receive, you might say, voluntary donations, with some specific goal in mind. After a while it became unthinkable – there were no longer any sympathetic members of the middle class. And then, whereas before relationships were civil, even pleasant, now there was only animosity.

Tenth interview

H: We have arrived at the July Days of 1917, and that is where we will begin our discussion today.

GD: I have read with amazement in Leonard Shapiro's *History of the Communist Party* that, after the exposures of their German funds, the Bolsheviks went into a decline until the Kornilov Affair, and so on.[1] As I recall, nothing of the sort happened. And – as I will describe later, probably in the next interview – I have no reason to assume that this was true just in Kazan. It was precisely in July that I observed clear evidence of a considerable increase in the Bolsheviks' strength. The few of us who were entirely engaged in the work of the Soviet had little direct contact with the mass of workers. We had no opportunity to go to factory meetings and the like. But we were able to judge the shift in climate from several indications. First, although my impression was, as I have stated, that the level of the working class was much lower in 1905–1906, our organization and I in particular had close contact with some workers who could be called working-class intelligentsia. I'm thinking of two or three typographical workers and of one at a munitions factory – a factory not in Kazan itself, that would have been impossible, but not far off. This was a very large factory, probably with tens of thousands of workers during the war. It was through these worker-intellectuals [*rabochie intelligenty*] that we got clear information about what was going on among the lower strata of the working class. I would like to make a few remarks about these worker acquaintances who revealed to me the existence of a previously completely unknown, new type of worker.

The typographers were very sensible men who had been in the organization earlier, had attended circles, and later participated in the Labor Group of the War Industrial Committee.[2] They were very good comrades, but they didn't provide any revealing information. But Staraverov at the munitions factory did. (He is mentioned in the later Soviet literature as a progressive worker.) Staraverov was a member of the factory committee that was set up, and he was with me constantly and was very attached to me. We often talked about the situation and the mood among the workers, and he would stay until all hours and then spend the night in my office, sleeping, as I did, on a pile of newspapers instead of a bed. As a result of this acquaintance, two other members of the factory committee of the munitions factory began to come to see me, and they had Bolshevik sympathies. I remember the name of one of them, Konchenko. These were completely new types who now headed the factory committee and had actually become bosses of the plant. At a time when automobiles were extremely scarce in Kazan, in 1917, they took over the factory automobile and went around in it. They would come to see me and we would have a friendly talk, it was pleasant to chat with them. One of them was nothing special, while Konchenko was definitely clever and able. They would say, "Why do you spend all your time sitting here? Let's go for a swim, we have a car!" Or "Why not have a good time?" In fact they told me that things were very comfortable now that there were a large number of prostitutes among the workers. "It's very practical. You don't have to go hunting them." This was completely new; yet, these were pure proletarians with some status. It was also entirely obvious that they had so much money that they could spend it as they pleased!

For me such acquaintances became more interesting much later, because this type appeared in the period of Soviet power as well. They had Bolshevik sympathies, but at the same time were very friendly to me. They had a certain intellectual curiosity, and liked to come and chat with someone intelligent. At this time, their appearance was a very alarming sign, because it was entirely clear that they had become the bosses at this large munitions factory, and this had major consequences. (Later, in August, the factory was blown up, but not by the Bolsheviks as far as we knew.)

Then there were other signs. New deputies were still appearing. Their profile was initially unclear, but then things happened that made the sessions of the Soviet extremely stormy. No one made Bolshevik speeches, but our speeches began to be interrupted by cutting remarks, questions, or outcries like "And what's the government up to?" and so forth. And there would be replies in kind. The chairman of the Soviet at the time was a young officer, a very nice fellow, but he would lose control at such moments and not be able to cope with the meeting. Then I, as vice-chairman, sitting next to him, would get up. I had a booming voice and my manner could be energetic, so I could always bring the meeting to order. But all this was an enormous change from what had gone on before.

So it was clear that the character of the Soviet was changing. The change resulted from the fact that while we were sitting in the Soviet, the Bolsheviks were organizing re-elections in different factories, recalling the former delegates and sending new ones who, while they might not be formally party members, were entirely under Bolshevik influence. Thus they undermined our influence in the Soviet. In addition, two events, both very important, occurred in June. One of them is particularly interesting because it shows how complications could arise completely unforeseen by theories or rational considerations. We received an order – I don't remember if it applied to all Russia or only to some regions: "In view of the acute shortage of white (wheat) flour, the sale of white flour is to be forbidden."[3] It happened that this was at the time of a Moslem fast, which was to be followed by celebrations. And the Moslems need white flour for their ritual food. When they couldn't buy it, an insurrection flared up. Several thousand people from the Tartar and Moslem part of the city flocked to the center of town, seized the major, and threatened to kill him if they weren't given white flour. An absolutely unimaginable situation resulted. It happened that a new military commander – who later played a major role – arrived in Kazan that day. He later told me that when he arrived and saw the hordes of enraged Moslems marching to the center of town, to the Soviet and then to the Kazan Kremlin, he had the impression that everything was coming apart. But then he was struck, he said, by the influence that the Soviet still commanded. The situation seemed absolutely hopeless. At that point my close comrade, whom I already mentioned, had a brilliant idea. When the Soviet had assembled, he proposed – or virtually ordered – that all of the members of the Soviet, who wore special arm-bands, leave the premises and form a chain around the administration buildings to stop the raging crowd. And the authority of the Soviet was still so great that the appearance of a few hundred men with their Soviet arm-bands had a powerful effect. The Moslems capitulated and freed the major rather than killing him. And calm was restored within a few hours. I don't remember now what compromise was reached. I think it was some sort of rationalization: an exception from the regulation was made and the necessary amount of white flour was sold for ritual purposes. But it was an entirely unexpected occurrence that revealed new aspects of the seething passions that existed.

Now, before discussing the second event, I should mention that the situation in the Soviet was such that there were no strict rules, and essentially anyone could speak. While none of our Mensheviks or the "official" Socialist Revolutionaries ever came, one of the main leaders of the Left Socialist Revolutionaries, Kamkov, did. He delivered a speech in the Soviet, and it definitely met with a response – he was a good speaker. I answered him, although I was no longer in the habit of polemicising, since I usually made reports or gave accounts of events, and these were usually accepted unanimously or nearly unanimously as resolutions. But now I had to debate. In general his speech wasn't so frightening. Though I can't give the content exactly, it was a very revolutionary speech, very critical of the Provisional Government, but filled with the familiar Socialist Revolutionary phrases. It wasn't particularly hard to answer. I think that I handled it without particular difficulty. The situation was different when, some time later, an absolutely unknown person unexpectedly appeared – Shenkman. He was a Bolshevik speaker of a very different sort, with a businesslike style and logically developed train of thought. In this case I found myself in a very difficult position. I had a real sense that there was nothing for me to answer. He very clearly and convincingly pointed out some entirely obvious facts: how the war was affecting the overall situation, to what extent the government was unable to cope with the difficulties, and so on. What was there to object to, when I myself felt that it was essentially true? Well, there were no resolutions offered, and none were passed. But in any case, a considerable part of the Soviet was now clearly on his side. Moreover . . .

H: When was this?

GD: In July, perhaps around the 20th, after the July Days. In addition, the Soviet of Peasants' Deputies formed at about the same time. We had thought that a peasant Soviet should be convened, but there was no real peasant organization in our area. Our contacts were so slight that it came as a complete surprise when we learned of the existence of an organization that had carefully prepared the founding of this Soviet, had conducted elections, and that the organization had been formed by a Left Socialist Revolutionary leader, Kalegaev, who I think, was later a Peoples' Commissar.[4] He was intelligent, but he made the impression of someone strange and enigmatic. One fine day, everything was ready and a couple of hundred peasant deputies assembled from varous parts of Kazan province and set up the Soviet of Peasants' Deputies. It's worth describing what happened next. Although we were seeing this fellow, Kalegaev, for the first time, we learned later that he had been living secretly in the province for some time, I don't know how long, and traveling about, with funds always at his disposal. As in many other cases, it was a mystery where the money came from; we didn't have any ourselves. Of course, you can't explain it simply as Germany money, because there's no evidence that the Left Socialist Revolutionaries obtained any. But they had some opportunities for moving about and working in the countryside. Such activity involved spending some money at that time; there were no railways, so you had to travel on horseback, and then live besides. In short, Kalegaev or someone else opened the meeting, but it began with a proposal to elect so-and-so as chairman. It was said of this so-and-so that he had participated in the liberation movement for a long time, had been arrested, condemned, sentenced to penal servitude, and had returned only after the revolution. At this point an incredible scene began in the hall, with a great din and voices shouting, "The convict! [*katorzhnik*] Give us the convict! We elect the convict!" God almighty, what sort of den of savages was this? And the chairman was elected amid these shouts of "Convict!"

Kalegaev then delivered a speech, in a Socialist Revolutionary spirit, about the need to settle the land question. The speech was nothing much, but after it some peasant spoke up. The peasant had a very cunning face, venomous I would say, and began to talk in a kind of exalted, church-like tone about the war. "People perished," he said, "and so many of our valorous warriors have laid their bones on distant battlefields." What point was he trying to make? There is an expression in Russian about "laying down one's bones" [*kost'mi polozhit'*], meaning "to fall in battle." "And," the peasant continued, "bones make good fertilizer!" He moved that an expedition to the front be organized to collect the bones of dead soldiers, so as to use them for fertilizer. Well, I don't scare very easily, but I was simply horrified. It's hard for me to convey the scene. I especially remember his appearance, his dark beard, and his speaking in a kind of saccharin, pious tone about our valorous warriors. Of course, his motion was somehow suppressed.

This was the way that the Soviet of Peasants' Deputies was formed, and, quite understandably, it did not merge with the other Soviets of Workers' and Soldiers' Deputies. We weren't interested, and the Left Socialist Revolutinaries, who completely dominated the Soviet of Peasants' Deputies, didn't want it dissolved in a larger body where the workers' and soldiers' deputies would be in the majority. Although the soldiers' deputies were essentially peasants in military uniform, they were not under the undivided sway of the Left Socialist Revolutionaries. By about the end of the month it had become clear to us that the Bolsheviks' winning over the soviets was but a matter of time. And we discussed the question of what had to be done. The small circle of people who played the chief role were of one mind, that assuming that the soviets were to remain all together, they would become entirely the tool of the Bolsheviks. We wracked our brains to figure out how to get around the soviets. A point that is of some slight interest is that a Georgian, Gogua, turned up at one point.[5] I hadn't known him before . . .

H: He was a well-known Menshevik?

GD: Yes. He came not for political purposes, but in connection with certain professional business. We got to know one another and became quite close. He did not participate in our political work and didn't make speeches, but he became familiar with the situation. I mention him because I suspect that, later in Petrograd, he made reports on the situation in Kazan. And now in this already cheerless situation another issue arose in the Soviet and gradually loomed larger and larger, namely an intense anger at the All-Russian Central Executive Committee of the Soviets [*VTsIK*].[6] They said, "Well, so there was a congress of Soviets, and we elected it, and then they maintain absolutely no contact with the local Soviets. It seems they don't understand what's going on in the country. They speak on behalf of all Soviets without adequate right!" Then the announcement of the Moscow State Conference came.[7] Our Executive Committee moved that the soviets be represented in the Moscow Conference, not just by the central Soviet [i.e., *VTsIK*], but also by representatives of at least the most important local Soviets. And to deliver this resolution to the center, in a timely and energetic manner, they sent me on a mission to Moscow.

This trip was a story in itself. I arrived in Moscow and went to the Soviet. I was to speak to Chkheidze, the chairman of the All-Russian Central Executive Committee.[8] "Comrade Chkheidze is busy. Comrade Chkheidze is very busy!" Finally I said to the secretary, "Listen, our Soviet has instructed me to transmit to the *VTsIK* the demand that not only the *VTsIK* but also the most important Soviets be represented at the Moscow Conference. Deliver this message, at least, to Comrade Chkheidze." I don't remember whether it was that day or the next, but this memorable secretary – I forget his name – told me that he had communicated my message to Comrade Chkheidze, who was very interested in my proposal but was very busy at the moment with preparations for the Moscow Conference, and would willingly talk to me about my request after the conference. If I had any illusions previously about what was going on at the center, I no longer had them after this. It was really a madhouse. But during this visit I learned something startling. They had finally decided to get rid of Steklov, who had been the editor of *Izvestiia*,[9] and I found out that Comrade Gogua had suggested that I be made editor in his place. However, since I was virtually unknown and nothing came of it for other reasons, Dan became the next editor. But it meant something to me and also confirmed that, when Gogua returned to Petrograd, he had talked about both me and the situation in Kazan.

Nothing came of the Moscow Conference. Our party congress was to meet very soon afterward, but I had to return to Kazan in a hurry, because news arrived that there had been a fire at the munitions factory. By the time I got to Kazan, it was the third or fourth day of the fire – the sound was like a large artillery barrage, boom-boom-boom! It was a huge factory – one of the largest manufacturers of gunpowder. What was the cause? Of course, some people suspected the Bolsheviks had done it, but we didn't think so. For all their tactics, there was no reason to think that the Bolsheviks planned to sabotage the conduct of the war in this way. Antoher explanation, which seemed the wildest, focused on the German prisoners of the camp that was located not far from the munitions factory. The Bolsheviks, particularly, in the factory committee that had fully taken over the factory, had fraternized with their German comrades, freed them from the camp, and, we were told, these German war prisoners came around to the factory freely without being bothered. All safety measures, passes, and so on, had been eliminated. It's quite likely that some of the patriots among the prisoners – they were probably all German patriots, more or less – took the opportunity to blow up the plant. It's a very pretty genre scene of the times. The factory eventually burned down, since there wasn't anything you could do about it.

A few days later, I returned to Petrograd, this time for our party congress [the so-called August or Unification Congress]. The congress was interesting and valuable for me not so much in and of itself, but because I had the chance to meet many people from different places. It has always remained a question for me to what extent my impressions of Kazan could be generalized. Was it an exceptional case – perhaps exceptionally unfortunate – or was it typical? At that time I had the impression that the situation in Kazan was in no way unique. This became apparent not at the congress itself, but at a number of meetings that took place beforehand. Meetings were organized as the delegates arrived – 30–40 delegates at a time. The Internationalists arranged meetings with their people, the Defensists with theirs.[10] I attended the Defensists' meetings, and Tsereteli was there at least twice; I saw him up close for the first time (I had heard him earlier as a speaker).

As the local delegates spoke, I saw that their situation was generally very alarming. The picture was an unhappy one. Tsereteli listened very attentively, asked questions, and was very worried. And something came of it. At the congress, the principal speaker who framed the policy, the policy of support for particiaption in the Provisional Government, was Tsereteli, with Martov as cospeaker. Dan wasn't there at all. There was a message that Comrade Dan was unfortunately ill with a lung inflammation and couldn't be present. It was only many years later that I learned from Lydia Osipovna that the reason was entirely different – their child was dying, and both of them could think of nothing else.

So Tsereteli and Martov were there. It was a strange picture. On our side, meaning the Defensist wing of the majority, first one person would come in and sit down, and then another. The Internationalists were different, they all came to meetings together. In front were Martov, Abramovich, Martynov, Semkovskii, Astrov, and so forth. They were also dressed differently from us, since they wore the clothing they had worn in their various European emigrations. And their discipline was such that if they protested something, the whole group would start to shout excitedly all together. Tsereteli delivered a general speech. Then Martov was called upon to give a speech, while Martynov was asked for a special additional statement on foreign policy. And resolutions or theses were introduced. When I read the theses presented by Tsereteli, I had the impression that he was painting an overoptimistic picture of the general situation. I wrote a correction, which described, based on my personal experience and what I had already heard at these meetings, the critical state of the revolution and, in particular, the frictions in the soviets between the workers' and soldiers' soviets. This wasn't so true for us, but it was clear from the talk, because the soldiers' soviets were essentially peasant soviets, and the sense of urgency was much more acute among them. And I went on to say that there were many factors disrupting the unity of so-called Revolutionary Democracy. I wrote out this correction and sent it to Tsereteli, who was sitting at the table of the presidium. He looked at it and said to me, "It's a very important correction; you introduce it and substantiate it." So I offered a brief justification. It evoked a violent response from the Internationalists. Martov immediately asked to reply to it. He shouted excitedly, "It's dangerous, terribly dangerous, to talk about frictions within the revolutionary masses!" But the correction was accepted nonetheless. In my opinion, the congress was not very significant. At any rate, the memory of it was entirely overshadowed by what started on its last day – Kornilov uprising. This, you might say, completely blotted out the congress, both for myself and for others, I think. Everything was focused on the uprising. It didn't last long. In the end, there wasn't even any serious fighting, because Kornilov's troops themselves weren't about to fight. But there were several days of extreme tension. On the last day, when the Kornilov uprising had just been liquidated, a session of the Executive Committee of Soviets was held.

H: You were still in Petrograd?

GD: Yes, I remained through the session. Avksentev, the Minister of Internal Affairs, was there. He delivered an extremely energetic speech. He spoke of the death penalty for Kornilov, precisely, definitely, in colorful and vivid expressions. Then Kamenev spoke as a principled opponent to the death penalty. He said that as an opponent of the death penalty, he would oppose it even for a rebellious general. Then Tsereteli spoke – it was a strange speech. I would characterize it by the words of Doubting Thomas in the Gospel: "Lord, I believe. Help me in my lack of faith." It was delivered in very optimistic tones, but somehow you didn't believe that it fully corresponded with his feelings. At one point he uttered the phrase, "We have led democracy from victory to victory!" Nadezhda Evgenevna Grinfeld,[11] who was sitting next to me, said, "Is this possible? He sees nothing that's going on in the country! You should say something!" I answered that I had stopped arguing. "Why?" she asked. I said, "Because the time is now upon us when issues will be resolved not by words but by weapons." After this, Liber delivered a speech of startling power.[12] He was a strong speaker, and spoke very rapidly, perhaps as fast as our own Schwarz. And he said addressing the Bolsheviks, "You promised peace, bread, and freedom! Isn't that true? You will conclude a peace with Germany but you will unleash a civil war that will be more horrible than the foreign one. You talk about bread, but your policies will create an unprecedented famine in the country!" Then he went on; I'll take up the main points. "Freedom! You will set up a regime of savage terror, and put all your opponents in jail!" The effect on part of the meeting, at least, was stunning. Later, Nadezhda Evgenevna Grinfeld and I went up to Liber. She said, "Listen, Mikhail Isaakovich, do you really believe what you say?" "Absolutely! I'm convinced that I will yet have to speak through jail-bars to my little daughter when she comes to see me!" So it wasn't simply a possibility for him, he was convinced that it would happen this way. This is important, because it shows that not just people like myself, but even Liber, who was at the very top, were convinced by this time that things were heading for a Bolshevik victory. It might have been different later on, because of psychological factors – it's too hard to abandon all hope.

Then Martov spoke, and virtually no one heard him. It was a very unsuccessful speech, long and boring. Mainly he polemicized with the Menshevik majority, dreaming like Luka in Gorkii's play *The Lower Depths*, about "the land of righteousness." My impression was that his speech offered the meeting nothing except boredom. The mood was despondent. In general, I think that many Mensheviks in the majority felt that the situation was extremely perilous. It was entirely different with the Internationalists. One Internationalist, Astrov, had written an article about the Kornilov uprising that began triumphantly, "The dream of revolutionary democracy has come true. All Russia has become divided into two camps." Astrov's views changed radically afterwards. Later, he and I became quite close. When Anna Petrovna Krasnianskaia was compiling the proceedings of the congress, it happened that she simultaneously brought the notes of my speech and Astrov's at the congress. We both read them, and the transcription was very good. But Astrov asked, "Did I really say that?" "My God! Did I really say something that stupid?" In any case, at that moment there was a strangely triumphant reaction among the Internationalists, based, I think, on a total misunderstanding of the true disposition of forces. Perhaps it was one of the crucial mistakes, because it was immeasurably easier to deal with Kornilov than to deal with the Bolsheviks. For the Mensheviks, and not just for the Internationalists, the danger of counterrevolution meant that of counterrevolution from the right. In fact, Kornilov had tried, and nothing had come of it. So this main threat to the revolution was eliminated. But they didn't notice that somehow. In ways that were not completely clear, the Bolsheviks had managed to create the impression that they had dealt with Kornilov! How did they do it? I have the impression that they did in fact create this legend. They were involved, of course, but nothing would have come of the Kornilov uprising even without them.

H: I would like to return to the July Days. You observed that in Kazan it was only the man in the street who responded to the reports that the Bolsheviks were German agents, and that the workers and soldiers didn't react at all. Would you say that the reaction to the July Days in Kazan was a major factor in the strengthening of Bolshevism?

GD: Probably, but you couldn't be certain of it at the time. At any rate, there was no decisive evidence to that effect.

H: Now, another minor point. You have already noted that by June you could discern that the upper bourgeoisie in Kazan were positively disposed towards the Bolsheviks, with the secret thought that the Bolsheviks would take power and not be able to handle it, and that their regime would immediately fall apart.

GD: Yes, that it would collapse very soon.

H: Did this attitude persist?

GD: Yes, it did.

H: Now, I would like to take up the Menshevik congress in August. Since this was the first time you took part in a Menshevik party congress, this must have been your first general confrontation with the Menshevik party. What did it seem like to you?

GD: My impressions prior to the congress were much more important – all these meetings and talks, in part with old acquaintances, which unfortunately confirmed my impressions and convinced me that the Kazan experience was not unique. The most vivid moment of the congress was not Tsereteli's report, but a speech of extraordinary power given by Potresov, who painted a very pessimistic picture and warned of the illusions of the "victories of democracy" that Tsereteli had spoken of earlier. In particular, he spoke scornfully of the Socialist Revolutionaries as spiritually bankrupt, illustrating the point strikingly by describing a big "zero" in the air. His speech did make an enormous impression on everyone. But no special Potresovite trend resulted. The only point that led to differences in voting among the majority was on the restoration of the death penalty. A small minority voted against the adopted resolution, which protested against the restoration of the death penalty. I belonged to this minority, despite the fact that, both earlier and later, I had been fundamentally opposed to the death penalty. But I had a kind of mandate on this issue. When the issue was discussed in the Kazan Soviet after the death penalty had been restored, the Executive Committee of the Soviet, myself included, naturally wished to pass a protest resolution. But it met strong resistance from the soldiers' deputies, whose objection came down to the fact that, if the war continued, the death penalty was completely unavoidable. As one of the soldier speakers put it, in the current situation the soldiers would go forward to meet death only if they knew that death awaited them behind. It was an astounding argument! Still, it was a difficult decision. But the episode itself was very striking, because it was entirely unexpected that the soldiers would come up with such arguments.

Then there was a comic episode. I don't remember who else spoke about foreign policy, but Martynov demanded something like three-quarters of an hour or an hour for a supporting speech. And there was a desperate squabble over this. Finally, the majority yielded and gave him around 40 minutes or three-quarters of an hour, and he proceeded to rattle off his speech in less than 20 minutes. It ended amid general laughter.

H: Now there's another question that I'm very much interested in. How were factions formed? What was factional discipline like? Were there factional meetings where the theses of the majority were discussed?

GD: There were no theses.

H: Well, what about proposals or texts of proposed resolutions?

D: No, the texts weren't discussed. The meetings were chiefly interesting in that they involved exchanges of information about the situation and the mood of the country. It was in this spirit that the Petrograd comrades led them. The major figure was Tsereteli, who was at two meetings, and Sofia Moiseevna Zaretskaia.

H: Then it would have been more or less typical, say, for a delegate from city X to come to the debates of the congress and vote for or against major issues on his own initiative, without any preparation. Was this the case?

GD: There was voting for Tsereteli, or for Martov!

H: More or less automatically?

GD: Yes. On the majority side, at any rate, the main unifying force was Tsereteli's personality, which was then almost magical. He was so capable of winning sympathy and trust! He was so charming! I don't recall at this point which occasion it was, but I was on a trip with Doctor Sherbur, and I remember that we were at a meeting in Petrograd where Kerenskii and Tsereteli spoke. Sherbur was a physician and a specialist in psychiatry besides. Kerenskii's speech was forceful but completely hysterical – he trembled. Sherbur said to me, "You know, he's a sick man, and I could diagnose his mental problem just on the basis of this speech." Then Tsereteli spoke. When he had finished, Doctor Sherbur, who was Jewish, said "You know, that's how I imagine Jesus Christ!" Incidentally, I was told at the time that Tsereteli was ill, spitting up blood, and that "Iraklii Georgievich won't live more than six months." Apparently his doctors were convinced of it. And he went on to live for forty-odd years, I think!

H: Let me ask another question: was there a kind of "swamp" at the congress, meaning a large number of delegates who didn't know which camp they would join at the time they arrived, or who were vacillating?

GD: In my opinion, there was little or none of this. At this point, I should add something that we don't like to talk about even now, it seems. I am convinced that no small part was played by the aversion for Martov and his group – emigres who didn't understand and couldn't make sense of what was going on in Russia. This feeling was reinforced by the way they behaved at the congress which was completely uncustomary for Russian meetings – an endless number of interruptions, *zwischenrufen*, and something like attacks when ten or more people would come forward shouting something excitedly. What's more, they were decked out in strange clothes, with large hats.

H: What sort of strange clothes?

GD: It's hard to say. There was something about the style, kind of bohemian. Or take the Polish Social Democrat Lapinskii, who played an important part later on – he would shout out things in a very un-Russian accent![13] Seeing many of them for the first time, I gained the impression that the only human being among them was Abramovich. The others would wave their arms and shout. I have mentioned an episode when Martov stated, "Newspapermen who feed on bankers' handouts," and Kuchin[14] shouted from his seat, "You Paris *kafeinik!*" He used the French word *café!* So I think that if there were people who vacillated, the actions of the Internationalists made so revolting an impression that a great majority of the congress united firmly behind Tsereteli.

H: Based on your impressions of the delegates, how would you characterize the majority? What sort of people were the Mensheviks in a sociological sense?

GD: It's hard for me to distinguish my feelings at the time from what I felt later. I think that even then I had the sense that Menshevism reflected the mentality of a more advanced and more European stratum of the working class. For example, the two typographers I dealt with in Kazan, or the non-Bolshevik member of the factory committee of the munitions plant – in terms of intelligence and education,they were a head above the workers who followed the Bolsheviks. This applies to what might be called the Russian Mensheviks. The Internationalists, on the other hand, seemed to live outside of Russian reality and to continue, you might say, their emigre way of life. I personally, even earlier, had had no desire to emigrate. Then, after 1917, I had so strong an aversion to emigration, that later on, in Berlin, it was a very difficult decision not to return to Russia. And I made the decision only when I was certain, as a result of the connections I had made with the German Social Democrats while still in Soviet service working to seditious ends, that I would be able to become part of German life and have friends, and not be condemned to live a marginal existence. And, before I came to America, I essentially succeeded. But, to go back to the Internationalists, one of the decisive impressions was one of revulsion from these simply incomprehensible and alien people.

H: I get the impression, at least retrospectively, that there was a good deal of disillusionment among the Revolutionary Defensists, even in August, and doubts even among some of the leaders. I mean disillusionment with the Provisional Government and the possibility of collaborating with people like Tereshchenko and company.[15] This was particularly strong among the Georgians – not the ones who were in Petrograd, like Chkheidze and Tsereteli, but among people like Zhordania.[16] Tsereteli himself notes that he was very disillusioned. To what extent were these doubts over the policy of the coalition government – both foreign and domestic, especially about the issue of war – expressed during the congress?

GD: They weren't. For instance, take the issue of war. Well, you know that the argument was that a German victory would mean the collapse of the revolution, and that Russia would entirely cease to function. It would mean a defeat for everyone. And nearly every time I was in Petrograd, I raised the issue of the war and the prospects of ending it in discussions with members of the Central Committee – educated people. In brief, I got an answer, stated with great assurance, which was fairly mysterious but ran roughly like this: the war couldn't be ended, because even if Russia were to conclude a separate peace, the result would be that allied troops would be landed in Russia, and the war would continue on Russian territory. No details were given about it. Incidentally, as far as I know, this answer was never disseminated publicly.

H: Very well. Now, as regards the domestic situation, there was the issue you spoke of at the congress, namely the delay in land reform and in the distribution of land to the peasantry.

GD: Yes, feelings were running very high among the peasants, specifically the soldiers.

H: Did the delegates at the congress turn to Tsereteli and ask, "What is going on? Why the delay?"

GD: Yes. The explanation was that this was an impossible problem. That the commission to implement the land reform had been established, but that it couldn't be undertaken while the war continued. It was impossible to proceed with land reform because soldiers would return from the front fearing that the land would be divided without them. The usual explanation.

H: Didn't the following issue come up: wouldn't it be better for us to put together a "homogeneous" [socialist] government in some form, to take power into our own hands?

GD: No, not at all! They were afraid of that!

H: Well, to summarize, could it be said that there was a feeling among the delegates that the situation was deteriorating, but that they felt there was simply no way out?

GD: Yes.

H: Was there a sense of passivity – great pessimism?

GD: A feeling of passivity or inertia – that you had to carry on as before, to try to gain strength and to conduct policy as rationally as possible. And then, I think, it all dissipated with the Kornilov uprising. I don't think that there were many people with any sort of optimistic outlook after the Kornilov uprising.

Eleventh interview

H: Now let us continue our discussion of the Kornilov Days.

GD: The Bolsheviks were not a decisive force in rebuffing Kornilov, but after the Kornilov Days it became quite clear that the Bolsheviks, and only the Bolsheviks, had profited politically from the affair. There was a tremendous upsurge in Bolshevik influence, something explainable largely by the fact that General Kornilov was commander-in-chief and identified with the Provisional Government. Most people didn't believe, I think, that the

Provisional Government seriously opposed Kornilov. At the time I had the distinct feeling, as I expressed it, that the time for speeches and for words in general had passed, and that the issue would now be resolved by arms. This doesn't mean that everyone around me held the same opinion. But some thought about taking the offensive, about repressing the Bolsheviks. This stemmed from a conviction that a Bolshevik uprising and attempt to seize power was forthcoming. So you either had to capitulate or resist. I was one of those who felt you had to resist.

After the Kornilov Days, I returned to Kazan. As was to be expected, a radical change had occurred there. A Bolshevik majority had emerged in the Kazan Soviet. This had some rather humorous consequences. I arrived in Kazan and went to the Soviet, to the editorial offices. As I already said, our Menshevik newspaper was published there together with *Izvestiia*, the organ of the Soviet. Representatives of the new majority came to see me and said, "Well, Comrade Denike, it is like this. You understand, of course, that we're the majority now, and so it's impossible for the Menshevik paper to be published together with the Bolshevik *Izvestiia*." I said, "Of course, I quite undersand, I will immediately stop editing the *Izvestiia* of the Soviet." "But what will you do?" I replied, "I will continue to edit the Menshevik paper." "I'm afraid that doesn't suit us," one of them replied. "What do you mean?" "Well, you see, we don't really have anyone to edit *Izvestiia*. Why don't you stay on as its editor?" I said, "Listen, I would edit *Izvestiia*, but I would do so in my own way." "But couldn't you agree to something like this: publish the Menshevik paper, and edit *Izvestiia* at the same time?" I answered, "No," and the discussion ended there. So the Bolsheviks edited it themselves. I had nothing more to do with the Soviet.

At this point I had to deal with a very difficult matter, a ticklish affair for me, the preparations for the elections to the Constituent Assembly. The situation was like this. Gogua, the Georgian, who was on very good terms with us and with me in particular, gave an overly optimistic estimate of our strength, saying that our chances in the elections were very good. I think almost everyone agreed with this position. For instance, I often heard the opinion from people who were not at all Social Democrats that, if there had been a separate curia or a separate electoral district in Kazan, there would have been no doubt that I would be elected. But, as we had just learned, the electoral law was such that, except for the capital cities, the larger provincial cities were completely swamped by the countryside. For example, out of a population of more than two million in Kazan province, Kazan itself and all the cities combined didn't constitute more than ten percent of the population. And, of course, in small district towns the mood was the same as in the countryside. All this radically altered the picture.

Meanwhile our Central Committee sent a letter stating that the electoral slate should list Martov first, Gvozdev second, and so on.[1] These instructions from the Menshevik Central Committee caused a furor in the local organization. My position was to do what the organization considered self-evident, namely to put up a slate headed by me, one that would have some chance because I was well known in Kazan and the vicinity and also because I was the editor-in-chief of *Izvestiia*. There was also the special circumstance that my cousin had married into a prominent and liberal Kazan Tartar family, so I was very popular among the younger Tartars. Our Kazan organization met and discussed the candidacy issue, and the result was something I had hardly anticipated to such an extent – virtually no one had any idea of who Martov was. For some, he was the person described by Dallin – a young man with some penchant for Internationalism – while for others Martov was as he had been characterized by Tsereteli. I don't think I mentioned his famous remark, "No, Comrade Martov, the masses won't follow you to the Congress. Why should they need second-rate Bolsheviks when first-rate Bolsheviks are available?" And I became convinced that, almost without exception, the comrades in the Kazan organization regarded Martov as a second-rate Bolshevik. Why should he be entered? Then a second argument was, "But no one knows him!" I remember that there were liberals, not socialists, who said later on that there were only a small handful of Jews in the town, and that the Tartars would never vote for Jews or a slate headed by Martov. I tried to stay out of the argument, but when the attacks on Martov became very acrimonious, I took up his defense and told who Martov was and what his merits were. For most members of the organization, this was something absolutely new.

I made no proposals, but it was decided to send a letter to the Central Committee stating that a slate of this kind would lose. A very stern reply was received, over the secretary's signature. (She was Eva L'vovna Broido, whom I got to know later.)[2] She wrote that, on the basis of available information, Kazan was regarded as thoroughly reliable, that it could be counted on to elect two Mensheviks, and that it was extremely important to have Comrade Martov among the members of the Constituent Assembly. Therefore they were insisting that Martov be placed first on the list, and Gvozdev second. In short, a categorical command. All this was a sorry indication of the world of fantasy they lived in. It's hard to explain how absurd it was to assume that a slate headed by Tsederbaum-Martov would be voted in by Kazan province, where more than nine-tenths of the voters were peasants, and almost 40 percent of these were Tartars. After this, all of us lost interest in the elections to the Constituent Assembly. It was clear that it was an absolutely lost cause.

What became evident – something that neither I nor scarcely anyone else understood – was that the most perfect electoral system on paper was something unworkable in Russia, because proportional elections on the basis of slates presupposed a clear idea about parties. The situation was that the Bolsheviks and Socialist Revolutionaries had some short formulas with which they operated: "Peace, bread, and freedom," for the Bolsheviks; "All the land to the people!" for the Socialist Revolutionaries. We and the Kadets had no such short formulas. Later on, we were told that our people campaigning in the countryside met with widespread resentment, and that the peasants were saying, "We want to vote for ideas, not numbers, and not for slates numbers 1, 2, and 3, but for people that we know." Now it is recognized that it's simply impossible to deal with such a gigantic area and a population of this kind merely by direct elections. There wasn't anybody who was known to the two million or two-and-a-half million people in the province, and there were no notions whatever about parties. I imagine that the same situation in effect prevailed in other localities, and it points up the unfortunate results for the Mensheviks. From our standpoint, the elections to the Constituent Assembly were from the outset a lost cause. Of course, none of us could estimate exactly what the results would be, but you could guess pretty well that the victors would be the Bolsheviks and the SR's. What is important is that in Kazan and many other places these SR's were Left SR's.

A few weeks later, I had to return to Petrograd for the Democratic Conference.[3] It takes a particular literary talent to describe what this was like. The meetings were gigantic – I have no idea how many people there were. All sorts of organizations were cleverly gathered together; all the nationalities, represented. There were representatives of a lot of nationalities that I had never heard of, but, curiously, each of these was presented as the representative of so many million people. I (and others as well) sat and made notes – three million, five million, seven million. Finally, when it was over, they added up to 300 million. I went out into the corridor, and ran into Avksentev, who was the Minister of Internal Affairs. I asked him, "Nikolai Dmitrievich" (perhaps I called him "Comrade Avksentev"), "You're the Minister of Internal Affairs. You should know what the population of Russia is." He answered that it was his job to know. "Well, up to now I thought that there were 180 million in Russia – but it's more! More than 300 million!" I think that Chkheidze cut off the recitation. He said, "We are all interested in self-determination for the nationalities, and the sooner it is achieved the better. But I think it will be achieved sooner if we cut down on the time for speeches." And, amid more or less general laughter, this part of the session was ended.

There were some outcries at this session. There were "Cooperators",[4] who were very conservatively oriented in the terms of that time. It was here for the first time, in 1917, that I heard Trotsky speak. When he was heading for the podium, someone shouted, "Well, Comrade Trotsky, where's your permanent revolution?" He answered, "It's right here!" And he was right. But at that time I had already ceased to listen.

It was all so hopeless, so senseless that I engaged in conversations in the corridors. Mainly I talked with Konstantin Mikhailovich Ermolaev, a member of the Central Committee.[5] I had first met him, I think, in 1906; I don't remember the exact circumstances. At that time he was a Menshevik and I was a Bolshevik, but we became quite close, because we were not what was called factional people. In 1917 he traveled around Russia a great deal. My conversations with him were generally very valuable, because his impressions, garnered in various parts of Russia, were unfortunately quite similar to mine from Kazan. In these conversations that we held in the corridors of the Democratic Conference, I outlined my theory of power and the sanctions of power in a more systematic form. The two of us tried to ground this in the current situation, and to relate it to what could be expected. Our conclusion was very dismal. Specifically, the traditional power had gone, and the sanction of power created by tradition no longer existed. Of course, there could be no thought of a religious sanction for the new power – Government by the Face of God, and all that. Democratic sanction lay in agreement. But we felt it was too late, that the opportunity had passed. I and many others wondered about this point later, and whether it might have happened, but I'm not at all sure that things could have gone differently and that a government with real authority could have emerged, if instead of spending months on working out a highly sophisticated democratic electoral law, they had simply held elections a few weeks after the revolution, with some extension of the franchise, and formed a coalition. Perhaps, I don't know. But it was done this way, and I am recalling it because it was clear to me that we had absolutely no hopes at the time that the Constituent Assembly could create a regime with authority. And so our dismal conclusion was that there remained only the possibility of the consolidation of power through force. And that those who were able to employ this force would retain power.

This was our final conclusion. It reinforced my idea that we should prepare for defense in the most literal military sense of the term. Before leaving for Kazan, I went to see the Minister of War, Verkhovskii, who was regarded as very reliable and progressive.[6] The conversation was a real shock for me! I told him what the situation was, that I felt we would have to reckon with a Bolshevik attempt to seize power, and that we should organize. I suggested to him a Union for the Defense of Democracy or something of the kind. He agreed with everything, and then said, "Yes, of course, of course, it all definitely needs to be done but keep in mind that you now have a new military commander, Colonel Arkhipov – a really remarkable officer. He conducted himself so brilliantly at the front, that although he is only a colonel, he was recently placed in command of a division. Really exceptional! You stay in contact with him and bear in mind that, in view of his military experience, Colonel Arkhipov knows what the real alignment of forces is." And he ended the conversation with those words. I had the very definite impression that this loyal minister was obviously ready to give in completely to the Bolsheviks. What else could his words mean – that the military commander understood the real alignment of forces? If, for instance, he were to judge that the real alignment favored the Bolsheviks, he would give in to them. It might not have been quite this way, but still the facts indicated that there were no serious forces ready to defend the Provisional Government.

H: You returned directly to Kazan after this?

GD: Well, I remained a few more days, and was present at one meeting of the Preparliament.[7] Granny Breshko-Breshkovskaia spoke, in a pathetic sort of way.[8] I should say, though, that I simply didn't treat all this seriously any more. It was so apparent that these attempts to create popular representation artificially were utterly hopeless. None of these preparliamentary agencies or conferences had any authority, and meanwhile life – the actual alignment of forces – was taking shape along totally different lines.

H: I would like to ask a question about the period around the end of September and the first days of October. What were your impressions regarding the mood within the Menshevik party at this point? After the Kornilov Days, to what extent could you discern any shifts in outlook?

GD: Not much. But I think, that a shift toward the Internationalists began at that time.

H: What were the signs of this?

GD: I have a curious recollection about this. The Central Committee published what was called "correspondence" for the provincial press. They distributed these articles, and a major article that was published during the Kornilov Days was one by Astrov – an ardent Internationalist at that time – that began with the words "The dream of revolutionary democracy has come true. All Russia (or the whole country) has divided into two camps!" This was interpreted then as meaning a victory. The fact that this article was included in this "correspondence," was reprinted in the newspapers, indicates the shift in outlook. I didn't see other signs.

H: Aside from Ermolaev, did you talk with other members of the Central Committee at the time?

GD: During the Democratic Conference?

H: After the Kornilov Days.

GD: Well, I had conversations with Liber. Even at the end of August, during the Kornilov Days, Liber had the firm conviction that the situation was heading toward a seizure of power by the Bolsheviks.

H: You didn't speak with Dan?

GD: No, I don't know at what point he appeared. He wasn't at the Unification Congress. The delegates were told that Comrade Dan had an inflammation of the lungs.

H: His daughter had died.

GD: Yes, that's what had happened. I didn't see him at all at that time. I talked with Tsereteli a good deal during the congress, and then later on we would meet and converse. I also spoke with Sofia Moiseevna Zaretskaia.

H: What was their outlook?

GD: Tsereteli, at any rate, maintained an outward appearance of optimism. I don't know whether it was sincere; I doubt that it was. Perhaps he simply felt that he should maintain appearances. Zaretskaia's outlook was generally similar to mine.

H: I am dwelling on this because at the outset you noted that there were generally two positions after the Kornilov Days: either to resist actively or to give up.

GD: Resist or give up? I think that the attitude of the majority was neither – that is, resistance by purely verbal or purely political means. During the Kornilov Days, Martov, of course, did not speak about the need to capitulate to the Bolsheviks. He spoke still less about organizing resistance to them. But he repeated his earlier thesis about the need for liquidating the coalition government and forming a purely socialist one. This was the basis for the policy of *Vikzhel* and so forth.[9] Of the Internationalists, only Martov was on the All-Russian Central Executive Committee of the Soviets at the time. When he spoke, it was as if someone from an entirely different party was speaking, because he directed his speeches not so much against the Bolsheviks or even the bourgeoisie, but rather against Tsereteli and the others who sought out the "correct" bourgeoisie. I had the impression that the majority of the Mensheviks didn't realize what was going on – the majority in the capital cities, that is; I don't doubt that the outlook was different in the provinces. Ermolaev thought so too.

H: When you returned to Kazan, what was the mood inside the Menshevik organization?

GD: The dominant attitude was to try to organize resistance. I repeat, no one thought of taking aggressive measures. This simply didn't enter the mind, was something alien. But we expected attacks and we felt we should prepare to defend ourselves. We adopted a very noble, heroic resolution at the time: since we could not summon people – military units in particular – to an action that threatened bloodshed, and remain only in the role of speakers ourselves, a number of the more prominent comrades, myself included, were sent out among the military units and lived among them.

H: And if resistance was to be undertaken, whom would you turn to? No doubt this issue was discussed.

GD: You see, part of the workers were entirely on our side.

H: Some of the older elements?

GD: Yes, but then, you know, no one made this clear. Everyone writes that there were *junkers,* and so forth. But who were these *junkers?* A very large proportion of them were students. They were not *junkers* in the earlier sense of the term – that is, men beginning military careers. In view of the wartime necessities, the training of officers had been accelerated. The more qualified young men called up – chiefly students – were sent off immediately to *junker* schools. So they became *junkers,* not because they planned on a military career but simply as a wartime measure involving crash preparation of an officer corps. So the notion that these were children of landowners and bourgeois is completely inaccurate. They were chiefly very young men, mostly students who had been called up, with different outlooks. In terms of the alignment of forces, however, they were not reactionary elements. In general, they held approximately a Menshevik point of view.

H: What was the attitude of the Soviet of Soldiers' Deputies in Kazan at the end of September and the beginning of October?

GD: A Bolshevik majority had formed in the Soviet, but I would say that the soldiers' deputies were to the right of the workers' deputies.

H: And did they remain that way?

GD: On the whole, they did. As events showed, however, they were entirely cut off from the mass of soldiers.

H: Weren't reelections held?

GD: Yes, for them too, but Kazan soon began its own October Revolution, two weeks early! The situation was utterly preposterous! After all, what were these elections of soldiers' deputies? There were 40,000 soldiers (or, according to Bolshevik sources, 35,000) spread out over distances of dozens of versts, in dozens of barracks, and so forth. These soldiers' deputies were representatives of some particular units, more or less cohesive, and either in the city itself or close to it. The chairmen of the Soviet – the general Soviet – both the first and the second, were officers. They were officers who were popular among the soldiers. They could be said to belong to Revolutionary Democracy, perhaps with some inclination to the SR's, but generally of indeterminate views. But they stood out, and the soldiers eagerly elected them, specifically because they were officers who got along well with the soldiers – treated them like people, and showed concern for them. They enjoyed personal popularity among a certain group of soldiers. There was one fellow, Poplavskii: "Listen, Poplavskii's a good fellow! Let's elect him!" And everyone said, "A good fellow! Let's elect Poplavskii!" For personal reasons, he gave up the chairmanship, and someone else was elected, Galnov, a short fellow without any particular military bearing, pleasant and modest – a charming person. So they were elected on the basis of personal qualities.

H: Were the Soviet of Workers' Deputies and Soviet of Soldiers' Deputies originally organized as separate soviets?

GD: Yes, but they soon merged and had a common chairman.

H: When was that?

GD: In Kazan, almost from the outset. It was different in different places. For some reason that is not clear to me now, in Kazan the elections to the Soldier's Soviet took place very quickly. A workers' deputy was never chairman of the general Soviet; it was an officer from the outset. The Peasant's Soviet, on the other hand, was something separate.

H: And you say that the Bolsheviks gained a majority after the Kornilov Days?

GD: Yes.

H: Did you know anything about attitudes in the Soviet of Peasants' Deputies?

GD: It was entirely in the grip of the Left Socialist Revolutionaries. They had prepared the makeup of the Soviet of Peasants' Deputies in advance and obviously attached particular importance to it in Kazan province, because quite unexpectedly this fellow Kalegaev appeared. Later he became one of the People's Commissars in this Bolshevik/Left SR coalition.[10] [How did this come about?] I remember that Kamkov, also a leader of the Left SRs, came to Kazan. Without our noticing it at all, Kazan became one of the provinces on which the Left SRs concentrated. During the elections they put up relatively few candidates, but this was evidently their system.

H: You mean the slate system?

GD: Yes, and not to spread themselves thin over the provinces but to concentrate on certain points, where they could win most of the seats.

H: And in these slates they appeared simply as candidates of the PSR?

GD: Yes – on the slates they were simply Socialist Revolutionaries.

Twelfth interview

H: Let us talk about the October Revolution in Kazan.

GD: I would like to begin with a generalization which I think will help in understanding the days before October. More from hindsight than from the direct impressions of the time, I have come to the conclusion that most of the Defensists in 1917 were in no way socialist but rather staunch and ardent democrats. And the problems that arose in the last week before October were problems of the defense of democracy, which was widely believed to be threatened by a Bolshevik attack. The position was purely defensive. I can't recall anyone among us who would have thought of a counterattack, or some action aimed at hindering a Bolshevik coup, or attempt at a coup. The only question was how to defend ourselves and how to defend democracy. It's not very easy for me to distinguish what was thought and said, say, at the beginning of October, or soon after October. As it seemed after October, though, there was a fundamental view that democracy, which had been left with no one to defend it, had perished over a long period. To leave open even the possibility of democratic developments in the future, even in the face of an immediate defeat, democracy still had to be defended, so as to create a sense of values, a real and concrete sense of the value of democracy.

So when I arrived in Kazan, I imagined this to be my first task. The issue was defense; a Union for the Defense of Democracy was created, and some reliable military units were found, including the reknowned *junkers,* or cadets. The notion that no one was on the side of the Provisional Government except for reactionary monarchist parties is simply completely untrue. As I have stated, the *junkers* were an entirely different lot. Generally the middle stratum of the *raznochinets* intelligensia, one might say. Aside from these *junkers,* there were some other units, and we Mensheviks distributed ourselves in such a way that one of us was constantly with each such military unit. For instance, I stayed with an armored-car unit. There were no tanks in Russia at that time, but there were armored cars, two of them in this case, and a fairly large detachment – 20 or 25 men. These were not *junkers* but highly skilled industrial workers, because the job required not only drivers but also mechanics, who were constantly being summoned for all sorts of needed repairs. In short, they came from the upper stratum of the proletariat.

But these preparatory measures hadn't gotten very far when an utterly amazing thing occurred. All of a sudden, little slips of paper were distributed all around the city: "Whoever wants to make peace, come on such-and-such a date" (October 10 or 11, I don't remember) "to Adskoe Field." Adskoe Field was a large empty space on the very edge of town, between the town and the insane asylum. Where these slips had come from, and who had produced them, was a total mystery. But an enormous crowd gathered, and some really believed that peace would be concluded there!

In particular, there were a large number of soldiers, from the garrison closest to the city. The meeting was a stormy affair, and the leader who emerged was a young officer whose last name, if I remember rightly, was Pavlov. We were taken completely by surprise. Still, there were some people we knew and some connections we had, so it was possible to get in touch with the barracks and find out. It turned out that this fellow Pavlov had formerly been in Petrograd in a machine-gun company. This machine-gun company had gained the reputation – probably justifiably – of a Bolshevik outfit and had been disbanded and dispersed. This officer Pavlov – I think he was a lieutenant – had been sent to Kazan. Because of some offense, he had been placed under arrest – confined to quarters or officers' arrest. Under some pretense, against his word of honor, he was let go for a short time. But he didn't return, and instead went around to the barracks outside the city, and, with amazing speed and ease, he stirred them up. He joined up with Gratsis, a Latvian who was completely unkown in Kazan at that time, having come there from some privincial town. Gratsis was later a Bolshevik, but at the time nothing was known of him. And they incited the garrison near the city to revolt, and then went around to various barracks and stirred up agitation with the demands that peace be concluded and power be handed over to them. This was not a Bolshevik undertaking. The Bolsheviks were completely perplexed. Of course, they had information from Petrograd. The issue of an immediate insurrection wasn't raised at the time, as you know. Everything was timed to coincide with the Congress of Soviets.

Although I wasn't in the Soviet or an editor, I was still an influential figure. Two or three people from the Bolshevik committee, who were entirely unknown to me, came to me with the demand that Pavlov and Gratsis be arrested, because they were convinced that they were provocateurs and that the Bolshevik organization had absolutely nothing to do with them. They were ready to help in every way possible to halt the soldiers' revolt. The question that we then confronted was what to do.

H: Approximately when did this happen?

GD: It probably began on October 10 or 11. The Bolsheviks must have come about two days later, say October 12 or 13. I remembered it as two weeks before the October Revolution. The commander of the troops felt that an open and aggressive soldiers' revolt couldn't be tolerated and decided to send an expedition of loyal units to restore order. The expedition had to move up a long, wide street. Very soon after the line of troops began to move, there was an unexpected encounter. It could be easily discerned that four pieces of artillery had been positioned at the other end of the street. They began to fire on the oncoming troops. There would be four shots in succession, then a pause, then four more. In short, it was clear that there were four pieces, and they would fire and then reload. Something that struck me (and it was only later that I learned the reason) was the complete panic of these military men! Even Colonel Arkhipov, the commander, and the other officers were in complete confusion. At this point I displayed my tactical talents. I said, "Listen, it's quite clear that they fire four times and then reload. There's a two-or three-minute pause after each four shots. Since we have two armored cars, they should be placed on a side street away from the bombardment, and as soon as the pause comes they should come out fast with machine-gun fire, then take cover again." This was done, to great effect. No one was killed, but, as we later learned, the people manning the artillery actually fled from the machine-gun fire. As a result, the troops could move up and take the weapons. But the panic was so complete that the troops simply didn't have the resolve to do it. This didn't happen at the very start of the revolt, but some five or six days afterward, and then things were peaceful for a few days. Neither side did anything. There were efforts both on our part and on the part of the government to capture Pavlov and Gratsis, who were riding around everywhere, but it was completely obvious that they had won the sympathy of the soldiers. The soldiers hid them, and they couldn't be found anywhere.

At this point something happened that I can't account for, and there was no way to explain it later. On the eve of the coup in Petrograd, the city was bombarded. But this was no longer a matter of four field-pieces – it was a real artillery bombardment, clearly by a large number of weapons. The rebels had used the pause to prepare an organized artillery attack against the city. I'm only guessing, since it was a day before the coup in Petrograd – it began at night – but I think that the Kazan Bolsheviks had learned that an overthrow was imminent in Petrograd, made contact with the rebels, and thus started the October Revolution in Kazan. This guess of mine is confirmed by the fact that, during the bombardment, the same Bolsheviks who had demanded the arrest of Gratsis and Pavlov 10 or 12 days before now appeared before the commander of the troops with a proposal for truce negotiations. I told Colonel Arkhipov, or tried to tell him, that it was preposterous, that it was doubtless a trap, and that they were waiting for something and trying to gain time, the more so since the bombardment was continuing. But it was impossible to talk to him, that combat officer! It was only later that the psychology changed. Although only a colonel, he was in command of a division because of his military achievements. He would only rage around the room like an animal and shout, "Russian troops are bombarding a Russian city! I can't stand it! I can't stand it!" It was all very dramatic, and he went to negotiate.

At this point my guesswork was confirmed exactly. I am almost certain that the Bolsheviks already had precise information, because the truce negotiations were not yet over when the news came by telegraph from Petrograd that power had passed into the hands of the Soviets. The revolution had been carried out in Petrograd, and at this point the commander and the defense forces gave in.

That was how the October Revolution took place in Kazan. I can't say to what extent it was typical, but it is quite significant, I think, that there were already the makings for an explosion among the mass of soldiers, even without direct Bolshevik initiative.

In this case, it burst by chance, because of some piece of foul play or something of the sort – an officer who thought primarily of saving himself from unpleasant consequences and so readily stirred up tens of thousands of men, even though they were essentially peasant soldiers, of course. At that point I was in the quarters of the armored-car division, talking to the men, and we decided that I should leave, because if the Bolsheviks came my presence could hurt everyone. As for them, they had fulfilled their obligations and now they were surrendering. And indeed, the Bolshevik commissar – not a friend of mine, but a fairly good acquaintance, and one of the very few former Mensheviks in Kazan – came to the barracks, now as the Bolshevik commissar. His name was Broido, although you won't find it in bibliographical dictionaries; the name has a sinister ring to it, because his wife became one of the most notorious members of the Cheka later on.

I sat down and had a quite talk with him. I wondered: "What if they lock me up?" I had to reckon with the fact that they might kill me on the spot. I would either have to kill myself or go off at random and hide somewhere. Then one of these brave armored-car fellows, who had guessed what was up, said to me, "People like you should live, you'd better go." I left, taking a revolver so that, if I was threatened with death or beating, I would do away with myself. I made my way along the streets completely without incident. Since I was very popular among the Tartars they hid me in the Tartar section of town, a place that people from the Russian section knew nothing about. They wouldn't know where to look, and they were even afraid to venture in. So I stayed there some six or seven days. They dressed me as a peasant, and I let my beard grow. Then I left on the train and saw what was happening.

The October Revolution was on. For the huge mass of soldiers who were mobilized and in the rear, it was a signal to return home, and this only a few days after the event. There wasn't a chance of buying tickets for the train. Trains ran only once a day. They were so crowded that it was hard to even stand. People were jammed up against one another. The Bolsheviks were already looking for me; my picture had been printed in the Bolshevike press, and someone on the train who had a newspaper said, "You know this fellow Denike, they're looking for him – you look like him!" I looked at him and said, "I guess so! What an unfortunate resemblance!" So I stopped for a while to cover my tracks, and then went on to Moscow, arriving in the last days of the fighting in Moscow. Of course, it wasn't very pleasant when I got off the train and heard artillery bursts, and fighting in the streets. I found my way to some acquaintances, spent a few days resting up, and then went on to Petrograd, where I already had an invitation to be on the editorial board of the Menshevik newspaper.[1] We worked there every day. There was Dan, Martov, then Gorev, Boris Isakovich Goldman, Astrov, and myself.[2]

H: Regarding the revolution in Kazan, when it became known that a coup had occurred in Petrograd, was that the end?

GD: Yes, it was.

H: No further resistance could be imagined?

GD: No.

H: Why?

GD: Could we have resisted with our bare hands? There was a large armed force against us. Resistance would have been possible only with an armed force available. The other armed force headed by Arkhipov, who was hysterical and was probably following the instructions of the Minister of War, had capitulated. And then I should add that, as I went about the city before fleeing, I had the impression that literally the entire population had turned out onto the streets. It was my impression – seen from a car and superficial, of course – that the crowds were exultant. That was what struck me, although it was all very fleeting. I didn't catch any upset or unhappy faces. They were exultant! At last, some sort of resolution! The time of indecision that had been such a strain on everyone was now over! That's my view of the situation. But I repeat that my observations were superficial.

H: Now, before this point, you mentioned something about the Union for the Defense of Democracy and the Constituent Assembly.

GD: Yes, the Constituent Assembly that no one believed in.

H: Besides these *junker* elements that you mentioned who else was involved in it?

GD: There were these armored-car soldiers. Then there were one or two companies that were quartered in the city itself. They were outside of the mass influence of the soldiers who surrounded the city on all sides.

H: How did these armored-car troops differ from the mass of soldiers?

GD: In roughly the same way as in the west, and then in the next war, the tank soldiers differed from the infantry. They were crack soldiers, chosen on the basis of technical qualifications. Workers with such qualifications were not generally called up. When they were, it was only in the numbers needed for special technical positions.

H: Were they from Kazan?

GD: No, from various places. They had been in the war for two years. I can't recall now why they were sent to the rear.

H: And there was no support among the workers of Kazan?

GD: No. But later, among the crowds in the streets, there was a mass of workers, after the news got out . . .

H: You mean in support of the Bolsheviks?

GD: Yes. Many of them hadn't before, but now they were rejoicing.

H: And what was the mood among the city intelligentsia?

GD: I didn't see any of them; I had to disappear.

H: Yes, I understand. But what about at the time that the Union was formed, meaning before the news of the coup in Petrograd? Were they frightened?

GD: The intelligentsia was generally sympathetic to us but didn't take a particularly active part. The bourgeoisie was not sympathetic, because they believed that the Bolsheviks would soon collapse.

H: How was the support of the city intelligentsia expressed?

GD: Well, chiefly in the same way it was during the entire period of the revolution. People would come up to you, meet you in a club somewhere and have a meal, express their sympathy, and that was it! It was amazing

how few active people there were. Even in *Sotsialisticheskii Vestnik* I pro-
pounded the thesis that it is inaccurate to say that it was a coup of the
minority.[3] Of course, the Bolsheviks had only a minority of the entire population, but they had a substantial majority of the active population.

H: Now, after you arrived in Moscow during the last days of the revolution there and had rested up, did you meet with the Mensheviks there?

GD: In Moscow? No, I didn't.

H: Did you have any impression of the general mood there?

GD: No, there was nothing I could observe. First of all, when I arrived
I was completely exhausted, as a result of several nights without sleep, and
I needed to rest up. I went to my old friend, the artist Konchelovskii, who
was generally very glad to see me, and I stayed with him. I spent one night
there but the next day I already noticed that he was nervous and afraid that
they would come looking for me, and that it would be unpleasant for him.
He kept out of politics. So I moved in with another acquaintance, Kliuchni-
kov, from Kazan. He later had some part to play in events. He was a
Smenovekhovets[4] and a violinist, and he played in Italy, in Genoa. He
played with Chicherin because Chicherin was a good pianist.[5] I spent two
or three days there, and we played music, since I also played the piano and
his wife was a very good concert pianist. It was a kind of idyll against the
background of what was going on.

H: You arrived in Petrograd around the beginning of November?

GD: Yes, around the eighth or the ninth.

H: Could you describe for me your first talks with the Mensheviks
there? Whom did you talk to? What was the outlook? How did they react to
the situation? What was to be done?

GD: My impression was a curious one. There was none of the agitation
and excitement that would have been expected. The task was to put
together a newspaper.

H: So you initially established contact with them.

GD: They had summoned me to Petrograd, from Kazan, before the
coup. I had stayed on in Kazan simply because I didn't want to leave. But
they had already asked me to be on the editorial board of *Rabochaia Gazeta*.
I think that it was Gogua's suggestion, otherwise I can't explain it.

H: So as soon as you arrived in Petrograd you got right down to work?

GD: Yes. It was a very pleasant atmosphere, but there were those
among us who were really worked up!

H: But hadn't *Rabochaia Gazeta* been in operation for almost a year?

GD: Yes, but it had essentially been a [Revolutionary] Defensist paper,
but by this time it included some Internationalists, namely, Martov and
Astrov. Gorev's views were indeterminate, and then there was me. Martov
would write his article, and Dan would write the lead article. There would
be little short articles, five or six a day, and they would be divided among
us. Dan sometimes made a game of it – he was phenomenal in this respect.
He would say, "Well, gentlemen, tell me how many lines my lead article
should have." We would say 180 or 210. Dan would go off, write it in a
hurry, and have it typeset. When the galleys were brought, they would

always have exactly the number of lines we had requested. He was very proud of this. The only person who was really nervous – and more than nervous, he was tormented – was Astrov.

H: Tell me, before you started working, you probably needed to get oriented. Weren't there any preliminary talks regarding the new situation?

GD: There was no orientation whatever, simply reactions to events. For example, there was the issue that the Kadets were deprived of the right to participate in the Constituent Assembly. There was a protest on the grounds of general democratic principles. And, in addition, there was the opportunity to write on one's own initiative, before the party congress and before the change in the makeup of the Central Committee.[6] All this went very smoothly, these were topics to which the responses were self-evident. Arbitrary or capricious actions were criticized. When I began to work regularly, the *Vikzhel* affair was already behind us and no longer being dealt with.

Dan was very kind. He sometimes organized discussions. For instance, he would say, "Now here's a topic that would make a good funny short article! Everybody write, let's have a contest! We'll chose the best one!" It was completely idyllic, you would say, and then there was something that was in strange contradiction with the passionate debates of the party congress, namely, a kind of passivity on the part of Dan and Martov.

H: Had you already noted the shift in Dan?[7]

GD: Yes, of course, but above all because of his obvious complete solidarity with Martov. It was clear evidence of a shift. But I can't recall that he once discussed principles within the editorial staff.

H: Even regarding expectations for the future?

GD: No. I think that, because the congress was forthcoming, it was a period of temporizing. For instance, I wrote an article entitled "Ends and Means," not for *Rabochaia Gazeta* but rather for the party correspondence that was distributed to various newspapers. Then I wrote an article, "On the Peasantry," for *Rabochaia Gazeta*, discussing what the Bolsheviks faced in the struggle with the peasantry. Even at the time I felt that they could not be completely victorious in this struggle.

H: What were your own attitudes during November, before the Congress?

GD: The peace negotiations were paramount. As far as I can recall, my own attitude, which was generally shared (as the discussions at the party congress subsequently showed), was a negative one. That it was not only a wrong way but a criminal way to conclude peace. We expected that these negotiations with the Germans would lead to capitulation; Lenin himself called it an "obscene" peace. The talks I had were not in the editorial offices but rather with Ermolaev (whom I saw often and whom I was living with at one point) and with Dubois,[8] who was very close to Ermolaev and whom I got to know at that time. Then Bogdanov somehow attached himself to the three of us.[9]

How idyllic relationships were can be seen from the following. Once the majority in the Central Committee had changed, Dan said to me, "Iurii Petrovich, of course, you understand you can't stay on the editorial board."

I said, "Of course, I understand," and I left. At that time, however, the Central Committee organized a number of commissions that were to prepare our project for a constitution for the Constituent Assembly – I don't think that this is mentioned anywhere in the literature. One of the commissions dealt with the structure of the government and, in particular, the problem of federation with the various nationalities. This important commission included Tsereteli, Abramovich, Semkovskii, and myself.[10] So you couldn't say that it was a one-sided group.[11] Probably there was a fifth member, but I think that we only had two meetings, and the conversations were among the four of us. The chief issue was how far the right of self-determination should go; as far as secession, or not?

H: This was after the congress?

GD: Yes.

H: And, as regards the coup itself, you remained completely convinced that the Bolsheviks couldn't stay in power very long?

GD: I didn't expect a sudden change. Of course, I completely misjudged it, but I recall that the question of how long would they hold out was constantly discussed.

H: What was the dominant outlook that month?

GD: Well, it wasn't quite the same as during the first few days, of course, when we thought that everything would collapse, and so forth. I seem to remember that I said it would be two or three years. Someone mentioned, "Can you imagine? Plekhanov has gone completely crazy! He says that it'll be ten years! How absurd!" It seemed completely improbable. The old man had gone out of his mind! Incidentally, in 1917, despite the drivel that Deich writes in his memoirs, Plekhanov was totally disregarded and scorned.

H: What was Martov's opinion?

GD: I didn't hear Martov's opinion.

H: What about Dan?

GD: They didn't express them, either then or later. It was as if they had withdrawn into themselves. I don't know for sure, but probably there were discussions at the meetings of the Central Committee.

H: Did you meet with Potresov at this time, prior to the congress?

GD: No. I heard him at the August Congress, and at the December Congress as well. But I didn't yet know him personally. I found him very attractive, and yet at the same time very alien. I was never a Potresovite, so to speak.

H: Did Gorev have an opinion on this issue?

GD: That dumb windbag? He was the least interesting person in the group.

H: What about Astrov?

GD: Astrov was in the process of getting rid of his Internationalism. A sharp swing to the right.

H: Perhaps you could tell me how the paper operated?

GD: It was located in a very suitable, fairly large apartment. The editorial office consisted of one large room, where the three of us usually worked: Gorev, Astrov, and myself. Perhaps from time to time there might have been someone else there. Then there were two more rooms, one for Martov and one for Dan. Dan would arrive with a prepared layout for the paper. He always saw the paper as it should be. He was a remarkable editor, and he had an ability to work democratically. He would come out and say, "Comrades, I have the following topics." He would distribute them to us, and then go off and write the lead article. Martov never talked to anyone, except Dan, of course – after all, they lived in the same apartment. But in the editorial office he never talked to anyone. Not a word. He would sit in his office, write his article, hand it over to us, and then leave. He would come out only in rare instances, and then only to say hello. I can't recall a single conversation with Martov. And yet he was probably in a total panic, something that wasn't temperamentally true of Dan. Dan could wait so calmly for what would come next; what would come of the congress and so on. You recall Martov's letter to Axelrod cited by Dallin, which was written soon after the October Revolution – the end of November, I think.[12] Generally it points to a period in which doubts were rife: Could we take a position against the proletariat? And so forth.

H: Did the editorial staff discuss the political line to be followed?

GD: No. I remember only one later conversation with Martov and Dan, which stunned me. It was after the *Sobraniia upol'nomochennykh* [Assemblies of Representatives] were organized.[13] We didn't have enough speakers then, and there was to be a huge meeting at the Semianin Works (the railway shops). It was certain to be a very large meeting. We wanted to have a "star" for the meeting – I had already been to the Semianin Works several times, and everyone in our little group had already appeared there, and we wanted someone who had not spoken there. We asked Martov and Dan. Martov simply refused, saying that he couldn't do it. It didn't surprise me, because he was no speaker for a large meeting. But Dan said, "I'm afraid not, Iurii Petrovich – you see, Lydia Osipovna has managed to get some flour, so she's going to be making bliny today. We'll have a little vodka and then play some cards."

H: Do you think that this reflects the fact that Dan was ideologically indifferent to the *Sobraniia upol'nomochennykh?*

GD: Of course, they were very reserved about them. In the first place, they were pessimistic about it, and then I recall . . .

H: Their orientation was toward renewal of the soviets?

GD: Yes. And they didn't want to come out strongly against them, except for Abramovich. But I remember that Abramovich exaggerates his optimism, because when he says that he made speeches and so on during this period, the Central Committee was in Moscow at the time, and Abramovich spoke just once – at this same large meeting. After Martov and Dan refused, Abramovich agreed to speak. It was the only time.

H: But was there a time when they were opposed to the *sobraniia upol'nomochennykh?*

GD: No, they didn't oppose them. The secretary [of the Central Committee], Eva L'vovna Broido, with whom I was on very good terms by then, was evidently sympathetic and offered some assistance. She would tell us that a meeting was planned at such-and-such a factory. Initially my dealings with her were purely formal, and then at one point she said, "Listen, Iurii Petrovich, I didn't know but I've been told that you're a first-rate speaker." After this she would invite me to speak at such-and-such a factory.

H: To return to the newspaper as it operated in November, it's very hard for me to understand one thing. Say Dan would write a lead article. In many respects, there must have been differences among you. Didn't you discuss his articles?

GD: He would only ask how many lines were needed. You see, every one of us knew, of course, that it was a temporary arrangement. And since it was a temporary arrangement, we needed at least to . . .

H: What do you mean by "temporary arrangement"?

GD: It meant that, depending on the results of the Congress, the make-up of the editorial board would change. Dan had stayed on from old times, and Gorev too, I think, and I myself had been asked to join before October. There was a tacit agreement to stay within the limits of what was generally agreed on by everyone. Violence, arbitrary acts, restriction of freedom of the press, and so forth, were all topics on which there was and could be no disagreement.

H: I understand. But, of course, you knew that there were very substantial differences among you.

GD: Of course.

H: But it was better not to discuss them?

GD: The more so in that, after the failure of *Vikzhel*, the line favoring the formation of a government of all socialist parties, from the NS's [People's Socialists] to the Bolsheviks had collapsed. This, after all, had been the most important difference between us.

Thirteenth interview

H: Let us take up the December Congress of the Menshevik party.

GD: It was as a result of the congress that Dan and his followers went over more or less fervently to Martov's viewpoint. Though at the congress Dan stressed that he was critical of Martov's conceptions. But it was clear that a new majority was forming, as in fact happened. As far as I could see, it wasn't this issue that raised much interest at the congress, precisely because it was assumed that results had been decided in advance. Most of the principal debates were not concerned with problems of current and future politics, on which no one had clear views, at least about the methods of struggle. Rather the debates were about who had been right and who had been wrong before October, who was more to be blamed for what had happened, and for the Bolsheviks' victory and so forth.

I think that it is crucial to take account of what was actually going on in life, in Petrograd, at this time, because that is what gives the correct perspective on the movements that arose among the workers. What was Petrograd like in December? Cold and hungry and in an uproar. It was not at all surprising that a new regime, that had broken so radically with the past, could not set up a whole administration in a few weeks, the more so since it was hindered by a boycott of civil servants. I remember the winter streets, which would go for days or even weeks without being cleared of snow, so that all traffic except for pedestrians ceased. You could travel with difficulty by car, but by then cars were the symbols of those in power. There was a joke that ran, "Those aren't Mensheviks in the cars, they're Bolsheviks. A new revolution must have happened!" There was one exception, although I don't know whether it was widespread. On one occasion I managed to get to the editorial offices of *Novaia Zhizn'* with great difficulty, through the snow covering the streets.[1] It was very deep. Not everyone could get through. Then Bazarov showed up. "Well, how did you make it?" "I came on skis!" So the situation was such that you could travel about the city on skis, and in some places there was no other way of getting around.

As for food, there would be no bread for days at a time. I remember odd situations when finding bread was absolutely out of the question, and virtually nothing was available – neither bread nor vegetables. But the stores still had some more expensive things like cakes, or chunk chocolate. That's the lowest grade of chocolate, which is sold unwrapped, simply in pieces. I remember meals like soup with cake and chocolate. Anyway, I drew no political conclusions from this. But you have to imagine the mood of the masses, including the workers – in particular, those who believed in the Bolsheviks naively, without enough experience, and trusted in promises, expecting that the new regime would put an end to the disorder, that things would get better right away, just like that. And now more than a month had passed, and things hadn't gotten better, but rather much worse. I know that this is an unpleasant conclusion for those who particularly cherish the idea of the awakening of class consciousness, but I think that these circumstances – the increasing deprivation and disorder – probably played the major part in the great shift in mood and the emergence of strong and definite oppositional feelings, which we made use of at the time. At the same time, there were large numbers of robberies. There was a decree that lawbreakers were to be shot on sight, which was published by the Menshevik newspaper.

I forgot to mention this, but it's a well-known fact that the entire right bloc refused to become part of the Menshevik Central Committee.[2] Ermolaev, Dubois and myself among others had remained "unemployed" by the party, one might say. As soon as the congress was over I was told, "You understand, you can't be on the editorial board of a party paper like this one any longer," something that was entirely normal and natural for me. Of course, this created some financial difficulties. This is quite a mystery: even now I don't understand how the parties subsisted and how individuals supported themselves. I never did know what the exact sources of income were. I know that neither membership dues nor newspaper sales could sustain the party apparatus, but how was it done? I never knew whether there were people who managed these things. Others also knew nothing about it, and probably didn't want to. There were some donations. The Socialist Revolutionaries had American money, Kerenskii told me. Anyway, whatever it was, the arrangements were such that money wasn't a particular problem. The main concern was how to go on existing without foodstuffs. At the time, those of us who were "unemployed" in terms of party or organizational responsibilities were intensely involved in speaking at meetings. At the time it was chiefly Ermolaev, Dubois, and myself, and then at some point Bogdanov. Usually we would go in pairs. Without exception, we were completely successful. Consistently, right up until the existence of the *Sobraniia upol'nomochennykh*, our meetings would always end in a verbal rout of the Bolsheviks and the acceptance of our resolution. But Dubois, who was burdened with a family – a wife and two children – was a very impulsive person, and he sometimes frightened us. I remember that on one occasion there were the three of us, Ermolaev, Dubois, and myself. And when Dubois took the floor . . .

H: At a meeting?

GD: I don't remember; it was at some factory . . . I think that it was probably at the end of December. I remember that he quite literally frightened us; he began to speak in defense of looting. "As for myself, if I can't find bread for my two children, I'll go and steal it." Now, if a well-educated man and a lawyer, and of Swiss origin besides, was in such a frame of mind, you can imagine what the attitude was on the part of many workers, both Bolsheviks and non-Bolsheviks. I think that this was definitely a key element in the oppositional attitude; the rapid disillusionment with the Bolsheviks, even before the dissolution of the Constituent Assembly.

H: What line did you take at your meetings?

GD: In the first place, defense of democracy, in favor of the formation of a government that would truly represent broad strata of the country. The Bolshevik Soviet government always appeared as a government of a small handful who had seized power. And then, the circumstances – the deterioration of the situation after the seizure of power – had changed their attitude toward the war. The Bolshevik thesis, which was quite correct and had been enormously successful, was that the hunger and distintegration were all consequences of the war, and that a coalition government was not capable of dealing with the war. "We'll end the war and everything will be better!" Of course, peace wasn't concluded when the Bolsheviks came in, but in effect the war had ceased. We all knew that. Moreover, the issue wasn't so acute because the workers who still remained in Petrograd and hadn't gone to the front knew that they wouldn't have to go. For the soldiers who were in Petrograd, the issue of the dispatch of garrison troops to the front was of considerable importance, but in the last analysis there, too, they knew perfectly well that they would stay where they were.

At the front and elsewhere, where the soldier issue was also a peasant issue, the situation was entirely different. But in Petrograd, there was the fact that the war had virtually ceased, and things hadn't gotten better! They had gotten worse. And the Germans were advancing. There would be an "obscene peace" – this phrase was heard – Lenin's own! At this point, we began to speak of a popular opposition. We took our inspiration from Danton's words about a "great national convulsion," and we believed in it.

It must be borne in mind that most people, both Mensheviks and Bolsheviks, were literally hypnotized by the French Revolution. Not only was it constantly referred to, but people believed that the Russian revolution was taking the same forms. To digress for a moment, I remember that Iugov later wrote an article (this was in New York) in which he began by citing Axelrod who could not understand how people such as Lenin and Trotsky, who had studied the French Revolution in such detail, had learned nothing from it and made the same mistakes from the start.[3] I said to Iugov at the time that Pavel Borisovich [Axelrod] didn't understand precisely that what the Bolsheviks had learned from it was that the Jacobins had perished because they hadn't been able to organize their power, and had been left hanging at the decisive moment. The Bolsheviks had learned this lesson and had begun by organizing their power. But this shows how strong the hypnosis of the French Revolution (quite erroneously understood) was for someone like Pavel Borisovich. And then there were those constant, insufferably boring discussions about Thermidor.

H: Now, within the framework of these vague ideas and expectations, what was the importance of the Constituent Assembly?

GD: The results of the elections were already known.[4] At this point it became clear that the Bolsheviks would not have a majority; if they did, it would only be with the Left Socialist Revolutionaries. I think that we didn't precisely know what kind of Socialist Revolutionaries had won. It was clear that some provinces were already in the Left Socialist Revolutionary orbit. In other provinces it was different; it was very hard to judge. One thing that was entirely clear was that none of us would be at the Constituent Assembly, except the Georgians. Essentially, if we were to play any part, it would only be as a result of the personal authority of certain individuals, like Tsereteli, as was in fact the case. Although he represented only a handful of people, he delivered the major address at the Constituent Assembly. At any rate, I don't recall that the Constituent Assembly could have aroused much hope. There would have been more hope in connection with its dissolution.

H: Was it expected?

GD: Yes. I think that it was Liber who regarded it as inevitable, because a popular response was anticipated. But there was also the thought that the Bolsheviks would act cautiously toward a Constituent Assembly elected by a nationwide vote. At that time, we didn't understand as yet to what extent, as a result of this senseless electoral system, the Constituent Assembly had failed to make an impression on the people. There are countless stories about the Constituent Assembly. But what took place at the Assembly was not the major event of that day.[5] The major event was a demonstration. It amazes me how little is said about this. It is because the accounts were written by people who sat in the Assembly and didn't see the demonstration. It was a large demonstration, so large it was very difficult to count how many people were there. At any rate, there were tens of thousands. I've seen many demonstrations in my day, including some that were much bigger, particularly in Berlin – running to many hundreds of thousands. But I never saw a demonstration like this one. It was a demonstration that couldn't have been dispersed by gunfire – tens of thousands of people, with a large number of workers. Someone demanded from the outset that they disperse. This had no effect. Then there was a few minutes of shooting. People fell killed and wounded, but the entire demonstration kept on without faltering, singing as it went. Mainly they sang the Varshavianka. Probably they sang it because of its first words: "Hostile whirlwinds howl above us." The words suited the situation. The volleys were from the Lettish troops, as later became known, but they didn't disperse the demonstration, but sharpened the hostility. The demonstration was dispersed by a bayonet attack. It was something I never saw before or since! It simply couldn't be endured. I didn't exactly flee, but when a soldier would come at me with a bayonet, I would take a couple of steps sideways and then go over onto the sidewalk.

H: How was the demonstration organized?

GD: It was organized chiefly through propaganda. But for me that was of no importance. The demonstration had shown it had a definite political idea. It was a demonstration in defense of the Constituent Assembly. And it showed that there was a number of people – the number was exaggerated, but was still considerable – who were prepared to do anything, to risk their lives. It seemed to me that the earlier opposition movement had shifted from what one might call the stomach phase to the political phase. I think that the decisive impetus for the organization of an Assembly of Representatives [*Sobranie upol'nomochennykh*] was the killing of some workers. This was a colossal exposé of a regime that called itself a "workers' regime."

We went on, not knowing what was occurring in the Constituent Assembly. Later, I went to the headquarters of the Menshevik Central Committee. Tsereteli came there. So did Bramson, a People's Socialist, who was the secretary of the commission that had worked out the electoral laws.[6] They had been in a hurry, but since they were trying to work out the world's most sophisticated electoral law, they delayed and delayed. I remember a pathetic scene: Bramson entered and said hello to Tsereteli. Tsereteli said to him, "It's you who have destroyed the Constituent Assembly!" This was a serious idea! A thought that was frequently dwelled on later was that if, much earlier, with simply some improvement in the existing law, a popular government had been elected, the situation might have been entirely different. This was obviously Tsereteli's thought when he said to Bramson, "It's you who have destroyed the Constituent Assembly!"

It was at this point that the real storm began. I was with Ermolaev, probably, at a huge meeting at the Semianin factory. The Semianin factory comprised the railway shops for the Petrograd-Moscow railway line, a very large factory. They were involved in all sorts of production and maintenance operations. Two workers from the factory had been killed in the demonstration. The Bolsheviks knew that the factory was seething, and they sent to the meeting a member of the Fourth Duma, Muranov, who I think actually worked at the factory.[7] It has to be seen to be believed. They wouldn't let him speak, shouting the nastiest and most ferocious things at him – "murderers," "sons of bitches," and so forth. It was an unbelievable scene. No mater how he tried to explain things or tried to get something through the noise, he didn't succeed. The meeting was filled with an absolutely savage hatred. And I also remember another meeting at the same factory, when Ermolaev said to me, "You know, I'm absolutely terrified about what will happen when the Soviet regime is toppled. The bloodshed, the brutality, the hatred!"

A few days, perhaps a week, after the disbanding of the Constituent Assembly, Boris Osipovich Bogdanov and I were on our way to the Putilov factory. It was a long trip, and what we talked about was that we both had a sense of being at a dead end. Day after day we would speak at meetings and argue with the Bolsheviks, and invariably we would be the victors; sometimes the Bolsheviks would simply decide not to speak, but now what? Some kind of form had to be found, some kind of workers' organization needed to be created. This was the general theme of the conversation. We arrived at the huge meeting at the Putilov factory. There was a Bolshevik speaker, a good one; I think his name was Glebov. I delivered a long speech, which clearly made a great impression. The main theme, of course, was the dissolution of the Constituent Assembly, that the so-called "workers' regime" was shooting workers, and that it was supposed to be a democracy. Suddenly a group of people came hurrying in and approached the chairman, who said, "Comrades, I must interrupt our discussion for a few minutes, because Comrade Evdokimov, our representative in the Executive Committee, has just arrived, and he has an important announcement to make." Comrade Evdokimov appeared, seeming to be dreadfully agitated, and said, "Comrades, the Executive Committee of the Soviets received information today that a counterrevolutionary plot with the aim of overthrowing the Soviet government has been discovered. The plot is led by the Empress Maria Fedorovna and the Menshevik leader Tsereteli." In a loud but calm voice, I said to the entire meeting, "It's all a blatant lie!" There was a second of silence. People were at a loss; they didn't know how to reply. Bogdanov took the floor, delivering a forceful speech exposing such vile tactics, which ran something like this: "This is what they're doing in the Central Executive Committee of the Soviets. What we need is a free organization." Then, in a completely improvised fashion, he said, "I propose that this meeting choose two or three representatives" – I don't remember how many – "and send them there, so that they will report back to us." This was the beginning of the Assembly of Representatives.

H: Where were they sent?

GD: I think that they were given the address of the Menshevik Defensist Club that had been formed.[8] There is yet another episode, which, incidentally, I published in *Novyi Zhurnal* after Tsereteli's death.[9] It is connected with the Defensist Club. I don't know whether the preposterous notion that Tsereteli was plotting with the Empress Maria Fedorovna was a factor or not, but in any case there was concern about his safety, because a violent, hate-filled propaganda campaign was being waged against him. Tsereteli was forced to live in complete secrecy, and I was entrusted with the task of communicating between him and the outside world. Meanwhile, Shingarev and Kokoshkin were murdered by sailors.[10] A few days later, when I happened to be in the Defensist Club, I was given a message, I think from Gogua: "Go to Tsereteli and tell him that Lenin said to Enukidze,[11] 'I can't accept the thought that drunken sailors might kill Tsereteli in the same way they killed Shingarev and Kokoshkin. You're in touch with him: tell Tsereteli on my behalf that at this point we're not yet capable of restraining drunken sailors from doing what I mentioned. It's my personal request to him that he leave for Georgia, and he'll be given the opportunity to get there safely.'" I passed this on to Tsereteli, and he departed for Georgia. I think that this characteristic of Lenin was something very important. Nicolaevsky said that when Lenin first met with Tsereteli in the summer of 1917, they kissed each other, although they were enemies by then. If you compare this with Lenin's relationship to Martov, it's a major correction to the traditional image of Lenin. In any case, I'll vouch entirely for the fact that I passed Lenin's personal request on to Tsereteli.

H: What was Tsereteli's response?

GD: He heard me out and didn't say anything in particular, but he left soon afterward. That was arranged without my participation. As I imagine it, although this is partly reconstructed, it evidently happened like this: Lenin told Enukidze, who of course couldn't deal with it directly, but he probably knew that I was in touch with Tsereteli. He probably told Gogua, who was a member of the Central Committee who had been elected at the December Congress, and he told me.

H: Let us get back to the representatives' movement. As you observed it, this movement originated at the Putilov factory, at a meeting where Bogdanov delivered a speech.

GD: The Assembly of Representatives was conceived of from the outset as an ongoing institution. To put it simply, the Assembly of Representatives was to become parallel to the Soviet of Workers' Deputies. This accounts for the fact that something like five weeks elapsed between the first initiative and the official opening of the Assembly of Representatives. The difficulty lay in holding elections in such a way that, when the assembly actually met, it would be representative. It's not hard to understand that simply to declare that there would be elections on such-and-such a day would be pointless. There were no funds to put out such a declaration anyway. Therefore the elections were conducted so that each time, at each factory, preliminary meetings were organized and the question of holding elections was decided. It would seem like an utterly utopian idea, but there's the very curious fact that the regime didn't interfere with these Assemblies of Representatives for some months. The very fact (and it was sensed quite clearly at the time) that it was possible to conduct such elections and to create an Assembly of Representatives indicated that at this point the Bolsheviks had lost their influence among the workers to a considerable extent, if not entirely. After all, these were not simply elections in which the workers could vote for Mensheviks and Socialist Revolutionaries.

If the Bolsheviks had felt strong enough, they would also have participated; no one could have prevented them. And yet this didn't happen. Of course, although we didn't know at the time and never will, it's possible that the Bolsheviks were involved marginally, in some odd way or another; they might have wanted to have observers there. But, in any case, this had no effect on the sessions of the Assembly of Representatives. This provides the key to the understanding of the situation. The direct impetus for the movement, which caused a kind of upsurge among the workers, was simply a matter of accident. But on the basis of my impressions and recollections of the time, it was not so much the disbanding of the Constituent Assembly, but rather the disruption of the demonstration and in particular the killing of workers.

Then there was another factor, namely, the peace negotiations and how the general features of the German demands came to be known. This definitely caused a strong reaction.

H: Among the workers?

GD: Among the workers and in general. The official position, as Dallin cites it, was the creation of a national volunteer militia.[12] Again drawing on my recollections, this idea met with very strong responses. I vaguely remember my own speeches discussing the French Revolution, quoting Danton, "de l'audace, encore de l'audace," and so forth. And the response was considerable. It would seem like a paradox – people were definitely not happy about it. But what a peace! It was a peace without any conception of what it would mean. The impression was created – it is cited fairly extensively by Dallin – that even the most educated leaders felt that it was a "partition for the enslavement of Russia." Moreover, there was the related notion that, however poorly equipped for combat the disintegrating Russian army was, still, the Germans had to keep troops in the East, occupy territory, and so forth. If this assistance terminated, the general feeling was, I think, that it would mean the victory of Germany on both fronts, and if she were victorious in the West, no hope would remain for Russia. Later on, I know, there was some retreat from this position, and the idea was held to be entirely erroneous. America was ignored because the first American troops appeared on the Western front only some months later, in fairly modest numbers, and while there was material assistance, we knew nothing about American troops in Europe – indeed, as was later confirmed, there weren't any. Thus for some time there was indeed a mood on the verge of despair. I think that it was primarily in Petrograd, which was at the time under the threat that if negotiations were to break down, the Germans would advance and take the city. At any rate, my view was to resist in any way possible.

This was the atmosphere and the situation when the elections took place. The resulting composition of the assembly [of representatives] had the Mensheviks in the majority, with a number of Socialist Revolutionaries and nonaffiliated people.

This was a Menshevik specialty, and the fact that there were free workers' elections, independent worker activity, and a worker organization was something of value in itself. The question of what to do next, of what this was for, and where it might lead was somehow of secondary importance. So a parallel Soviet was set up. It wasn't stated that way, but that was clearly the idea. Therefore it is only out of confusion that it is placed in the same category with isolated demonstrations. From the outset, it was a collaborative effort, and operated continuously as an organization for a month. But this period that was felt to be very important and in general very militant didn't last very long.

An interesting thing happened in March: the government decided to move from Petrograd to Moscow. This is something that needs to be examined, which has completely vanished from history. It was announced that the government had decided to move to Moscow, and that the move would occur on such-and-such a date. The announcement prompted an extremely violent reaction, in particular at the Semianin factory. This factory housed the railway shops for the line which the members of the government were to travel from Petrograd to Moscow. And the workers said that they wouldn't let them go. What happened? The government moved to Moscow two or three days before the date announced in the papers. I have never seen this mentioned in the literature, but for me there's no doubt about it. I remember very well the sensation of something completely unexpected. It shows that the government reckoned with the possibility of acts of sabotage and the like, and essentially resorted to fairly primitive deception. One might have wondered, "Why did they announce it in advance?" No one thought of that at the time. Now, with hindsight, it is easier to suspect what was going on than it was at the time. I remember the impression that it made on the Assembly of Representatives. I would say that the assembly then felt that its activity was pointless. Up to that point, right up until the transfer of the government to Moscow, there was an enemy, one might say. Even if it couldn't be seen literally, it could be seen in essence: there had been an object and now this object had vanished. What remained was only Petrograd and its immediate needs. From that point on, I feel, there was a shift in the nature of the Assembly of Representatives. Dallin cites Baturskii's article to the effect that the Assembly of Representatives concerned itself chiefly with ongoing, chronic, or fairly narrow problems. That's true only for the period after the transfer of the government. Prior to that, there were discussions about the needs of Petrograd, but also debates on matters of principle. Our common friend Solomon Meerovich Schwarz, with his grandiose temperament, delivered a speech that ended with the words, "Comrades, I won't say, 'Back to capitalism' – no! Our slogan is, 'Forward, to capitalism!'"

H: I recall that when I put this question to you, you intended to describe these meetings, these meeting of workers' representatives before the government left for Moscow. Could you simply recall the scene and what the atmosphere was?

GD: Well, you see, I don't remember that. I recall that there was a fairly large meeting, I imagine there were more than a hundred people present. Almost all of the largest factories were represented, and more besides.

Aside from us, who stood apart, so to speak, the meeting was very much a workers' meeting in composition, without any fictitious mandates or fictitious representatives. I clearly recall the orderly, polite, calm impression made . . . the smart business-like man who ran the meeting so well . . .

H: And the question of what was to be done, was it raised?

GD: No.

H: Well, say, was it discussed among you in the Defensist Club? Now that you had this organization, what was to be done with it?

GD: There was the vague notion that it was a parallel soviet, in competition with the Soviet, and the results would be that the Assembly of Representatives would assume the authority that the Soviet had possessed in an earlier period. So there was this idea of opposition . . . that the Soviet had become bureaucratic and an instrument of the government, in contrast to this democratically elected, parallel soviet that was completely independent of any regime. Perhaps it was a vague, far-ranging hope that, as anti-Bolshevik attitudes developed among the workers, the Assembly of Representatives would develop as a self-constituted authority. But I don't think so. I had the impression, as I mentioned, that it was pointless. Subjectively, from my point of view, this expressed itself in the fact that, by April, I had the feeling that it was a dead issue. And since Kuchin, who was initially involved in organizing the Assembly of Representatives and then transferred to Moscow to the Committee of the Central Region, was urging me to come to Moscow (also on the premise that there was nothing to do in Petrograd), in April I agreed to move to Moscow, where I was appointed to the Bureau of the Regional Committee and, together with Kuchin, as an editor of *Novaia Zaria*.[13]

NOTES

Chapter 1. Lydia Dan

First interview

1 Vladimir Osipovich Tsederbaum [pseud. Levitskii], the youngest of Lidia Dan's brothers (born in 1883). Following an early political start in the student movement (in 1898–99), he joined the Menshevik faction of RSDRP (1903), contributed to several of its publications, and from 1907 to 1914 was one of its leading "Liquidators" (*see* Dan, Twelfth Interview, note 2). During the First World War and the revolution he followed Potresov's "Defensist" line (*see* Dan, Second Interview, note 22), and after October 1917 he belonged to the right-wing minority of the Menshevik Party. He was arrested several times by the Soviet authorities, spent many years in prison, and was finally shot in 1941. *See also* Dan, Second Interview, note 19.

2 The familiar form of address in Russian.

3 The respectful form of address in Russian.

4 Sergei Osipovich Tsederbaum [pseud. Ezhov], Lidia Dan's brother. a year younger than she (born in 1879). His political activity, like Lidia's, began in the Social-Democratic groups of St. Petersburg in the second half of the 1890's. Worked with *Iskra* and later in Menshevikk organizations as a *praktik*: disseminating illegal literature, organizing workers' circles and trade unions, and contributing to various Menshevik publications. In the period of "Liquidationism" he participated in both legal and illegal activities and served (1911–1916) as a member of the Central Initiative Group *(Tsentral'naia initsiativnaia gruppa)*, the Menshevik leading body inside Russia. During the 1917 revolution he belonged to the centrist Revolutionary-Defensist faction and was a member of the Menshevik central committee. After October 1917 he was active in the left-wing majority of the party and in the cooperative movement. He was arrested in 1921, spent the rest of his life in exile and prison, and was finally shot in 1941.

5 Martov [pseudonym of Iulii Osipovich Tsederbaum, 1873–1923] was Lidia Dan's older brother. He became a founder and a leader of the Menshevik Party. His life and activities are described in great detail in the following interviews and in several annotations.

6 Evgenii Arkad'evich Anan'in (1888–?) joined the Menshevik Petersburg organization in 1905 and became a contributor to Menshevik "Liquidationist" publications until his emigration in 1913. During the First World War he supported Menshevik-Internationalism, but in 1917 he remained abroad and in later years pursued an academic and literary career.

7 Nadezhda Osipovna Tsederbaum, Lidia Dan's older sister (1875–1923). *See also* Dan, Second Interview, notes 11 and 28.

8 Aleksandr Ivanovich Herzen (1812–1870), a self-exiled Russian publicist, the first theorist of Russian socialism, and founder of the influential Russian oppositional journal *Kolokol* [The Bell], published in London and Geneva in 1857–1867.

9 On December 16, 1883 Nikolai Starodvorskii and German Lopatin executed police-colonel Sudeikin, Chief of the Third Section (the secret police) in the name of the People's Will. Martov learned the details of their trial from a friend of his father, the lawyer K., who praised their brave conduct in court. Lopatin and Starodvorskii became heroes for Martov. In his memoirs Martov recounts a disillusioning encounter with his "hero" 21 years later: Martov was asked to serve as an arbitrator between Starodvorskii and Vladimir Burtsev, the emigré historian of Russian revolutionary movements. Drawing on the testimony of Lopatin, Burtsev alleged that, while in Shlissel'burg prison, Starodvorskii had addressed a letter of repentance and denunciation to the authorities. At the time, Martov was relieved to find that the evidence was inconclusive, and he cleared Starodvorskii's name. However, in 1917, Secret Police archives revealed that Starodvorskii had indeed been a paid agent of the Police (Iu. Martov, *Zapiski sotsialdemokrata*, Berlin-Petersburg-Moscow, 1922, pp. 36–37).

10 Alexander II won his image as "liberator" through the emancipation of the serfs (1861) and the other Great Reforms. His assassination by the People's Will, which was followed by a period of reaction and repression, became the subject of heated arguments.

11 The party of the People's Will [*Narodnaia volia*] was founded in 1879 and continued to exist until 1884. A party of socialist-populist ideology, it was noted primarily for its centralist organization, headed by an Executive Committee, and its acts of political terror, which culminated in the assassination of Alexander II.

12 Jewish religious primary school, where children were taught Bible and prayers.

13 Martov's unfinished memoirs, covering the period 1890–1900 (Iu. Martov, *Zapiski sotsialdemokrata*, Berlin-Petersburg-Moscow, 1922).

14 The traditional ceremony and meal of Passover's eve.

15 In 1881, in the aftermath of the assassination of Alexander II, Russia was swept by a wave of antisemitism and pogroms.

16 The *Bund* [General Jewish Workers' Union in Lithuania, Poland, and Russia] was founded only in October 1897, but Social-Democratic organizations of Yiddish-speaking Jewish workers had existed in Vilno and other towns in the Jewish Pale of Settlement since the early 1890s.

17 Boris Viktorovich Savinkov (1874–1925) was one of the most colorful figures in the Russian revolutionary movement. From 1903 he was a member of the legendary Combat Organization of the Party of Socialist Revolutionaries and participated in the assassinations of Plehve and other high-ranking tsarist officials. In 1906 he was sentenced to death, but escaped, left the PSR, and turned against its practice of political terror. From 1911 he lived in France, wrote novels (under the pseudonym V. Ropshin), and in 1914 volunteered for the French army. In 1917 he returned to Russia, served as Kerenskii's military aide, and was involved in General Kornilov's revolt. After the Bolshevik takeover, he participated in several anti-Soviet organizations, often as an underground agent, and was finally arrested by the Soviet authorities in 1924. His death sentence had been commuted but he committed suicide. His brother, Aleksandr Viktorovich Savinkov, committed suicide at a very young age, while in Siberian exile. Lidia Dan recounts some details of his death and their relationship in the Tenth Interview.

18 A card game for three players; very popular in Russia.

19 Vera Ivanovna Zasulish (1849–1919) was active in revolutionary populist groups from the late 1860s. In 1878 she shot and wounded General F. F. Trepov, the governor of Petersburg; her trial and acquittal became a *cause celebre*. Between 1878 and 1905 she lived in emigration, and in 1883 was among the founders of the first organization of Russian Social Democrats, the Group For the Emancipation of Labor. Lidia Dan became personally acquainted with her in 1901–1902 in the work of the *Iskra* editorial board, of which Zasulich was a member.

20 Vera Nikolaevna Figner (1852–1942) was active in the 1870s in populist groups working in the countryside and later in the party of Land and Freedom [*Zemlia i volia*]. After its collapse, she joined the People's Will, of which she was the acting

leader from 1881 until her arrest in 1883. Sentenced to death, and later to life imprisonment, she spent 22 years in the infamous Shlissel'burg prison.

21 Lidia Dan refers here to the attempt on the life of Alexander III which was exposed by the police before it could take place. The conspirators, among them Aleksander Ulianov (Lenin's brother), were executed on May 8, 1887.

22 Gleb Uspenskii (1840–1902), a popular author of stories about life in provincial towns and in the village, won fame for his truthful portrayal of the harsh realities of peasant life. Nikolai Nikolaevich Zlatovratskii (1845–1911) wrote stories about peasants and was noted for his authentic, if somewhat idealized, description of village life and activities. Both writers were leading representatives of the school of *narodnik* [populist] writers who were responsible for the profusion in the 1870s and 1880s of literary works concerned with realistic and detailed presentation of the countryside.

23 In 1894 the death of Alexander III and the accession to the throne of Nicholas II, who was rumored to be more sympathetic to liberal views, raised hope for a change in government policy. A number of zemstva (district and provincial organs of self-government) used their addresses to the throne to demand the "establishment of legality" and a greater participation of the zemstva in local affairs. The tsar in his answer condemned the "senseless dreams of participation by zemstvo representatives in the affairs of internal administration," and made clear his intention, "to preserve the foundation of Absolutism as strongly and as undeviatingly as did my lamented late father."

24 L. H. refers here to the 1873–74 movement of young educated men and women who went to live in the village, to help and enlighten the peasants. The movement came to a quick end as a result of both police action and the mistrust of the peasantry.

25 Bazarov was the hero of Turgenev's novel *Fathers and Sons*, published in 1862. Bazarov was described by his creator as a "nihilist," and for the Russian reading public he epitomized the generation of the 1860s, the radical "sons" of the generation of the 1840s. Dmitrii Ivanovich Pisarev (1840–68), writer and publicist, was considered the chief spokesman of the "nihilists," although he preferred to call himself a "thinking realist."

26 "The Precipice" [*Obryv*], published in 1869, described the 1860s conflict between "fathers"and "sons." In the novel, Mark Volokhov is the nihilist "son." The novel was often interpreted in Russian society as an attack on the generation of "sons."

27 Sergei Mikhailovich Kravchinskii [pseud. Stepniak, 1852–1895], a leading Populist in the 1870s and an advocate of political terror. In 1878, in Mikhailov Square in St. Petersburg, he stabbed and killed General N. V. Mezentsov, Chief of the Gendarmes and Head of the Third Section.

28 The term "nihilism" appeared in Russia first in an 1858 philosophical book where it was used as a synonym for skepticism. It was employed in Turgenev's novel *Fathers and Sons* to describe Bazarov's philosophy. The term gained widespread use in polemics against some of the more extreme figures of the 1860s.

29 Petr Frantsevich Lesgaft (1839–1909), a professor in the Faculty of Sciences at the Imperial University of St. Petersburg, was renowned for his studies in anthropology and anatomy and popular among the students for his "radicalism."

30 Nikolai Konstantinovich Mikhailovskii (1842–1904), a social theorist, literary critic, and publicist, exerted great influence on the generation of the 1870s and remained important in Russian public and intellectual life throughout the 1880s and 1890s. He developed the concept of the "repentant nobleman" to account for the liberation movement of the 1840s–1860s.

31 Fedor Mikhailovich Reshetnikov (1841–1871), author of novels and stories about the lives of peasants and miners in the Urals and the poor of the large cities.

32 Mikhail Evgrafovich Saltykov-Shchedrin (1826–1889), a satirist, published regularly in the journal *Notes of the Fatherland*. During the 1860s and early 1870s his satire often focused on the struggle between the supporters of the Great Reforms and their enemies.

33 Aleksandr Nikolaevich Ostrovskii's numerous plays on the life of the Russian merchant class were standard fare on the Russian stage in the second half of the nineteenth century. In reviewing Ostrovskii's early plays in 1859 Dobroliubov coined the expression "Dark Kingdom" as emblematic of the merchant world portrayed therein.

34 N. Avgustovskii became Martov's closest friend in 1889, when they attended the seventh grade of *First Gimnazium*. He came from a liberal family (his uncle was the popular liberal writer N. V. Shelgunov) and, like Martov, belonged to the "democratic" circle in their class. S. E. Golovin, in contrast, had been the leader of the "conservative-nationalist" circle in the class, but changed his allegiance during a summer vacation in Switzerland, where he fell under the influence of revolutionary-minded students and of the illegal literature which they supplied to him. Back in school, he joined the "democratic" circle and became a close friend of Martov. Through his acquaintances in Geneva, Golovin managed to establish contacts with some students in Petersburg who supplied him with liberal and revolutionary literature (including Marx's *Communist Manifesto*) which he and his circle read and discussed.

35 The book by Kravchinskii is most probably *Underground Russia*, originally written in Italian and later translated into Russian (1893). The book is a collection of lively sketches of the heroes of the revolutionary movement of the 1870s and their exploits.

36 The concept of a "debt to the people" was developed by the socialist philosopher Petr Lavrov in his *Historical Letters* published in 1870. Addressed to "critically thinking individuals," the *Letters* (specifically the Fifth and Sixth Letters, on "The Cost of Progress" and "The Action of Individuals") reminded them that they owed a debt to the masses whose toil had provided the material means for their education, and that they had a moral obligation to repay that debt through "the greatest possible bestowal on the masses of material comforts, intellectual and moral development, and the introduction of scientific understanding and justice to social institutions." This idea was an important inducement for the movement "To the People" and for the populism of the 1870s; the idea was later adopted and elaborated upon by Mikhailovskii.

Second interview

1 In a number of his works (among them "The Realists" and "Pushkin and Belinskii") Pisarev attacked any form of art which had no utilitarian or redeeming social value. In particular, he identified Pushkin with the "superfluous character" Eugene Onegin (from the novel in verse of the same name) and referred to him as the "drowsy figure of a lounge lizard."

2 This "utopian novel" of questionable literary merit was published in 1863 and marked the beginning of socially utilitarian literature in Russia. Its bold, confident, scientifically minded characters, "the men and women of the new age," served as models for radical Russian youth for the rest of the century.

3 Nikolai Aleksandrovich Dobroliubov (1836–1861) was a literary critic and publicist for the influential journal *Sovremennik* [The Contemporary], edited by Chernyshevskii. His articles "What is Oblomovshchina" and "Dark Kingdom" typify the realist-materialist approach to literary criticism and became standard reading for Russian radical youth throughout the second half of the nineteenth century.

4 Timofei Nikolaevich Granovskii (1813–1855), a popular and respected professor of history at Moscow University, was a leading figure in the circle of "Westerners" during the 1840s.

5 Dmitrii Ivanovich Mendeleev (1834–1907), a famous chemist responsible for the table of chemical elements named after him. From 1863 to 1890 a professor at the Imperial University in Petersburg.

6 Grigorii Isaakovich Bogrov (1825–1885) was born of an Orthodox Jewish family in Poltava, became assimilated and Russified in his early adulthood, but turned against Jewish assimilation during the last years of his life. His autobiographical novel, "Notes of a Jew" [*Zapiski evreia*], was published in *Otechestvennye zapiski* [Notes of the Fatherland] in 1871–73; in it he described the world of Orthodox Jews as he saw it – isolated from the rest of Russian society and ruled by ancient dogmas.

7 Visarion Grigor'evich Belinskii (1811–1848), one of the most famous of Russia's "progressive" literary critics of the nineteenth century and one of the first to propagate in Russia a new type of "realist" literary criticism which focused on the social and philosophical ideas contained in the literary works. Through his contribution to several important journals, such as *Otechestvennye zapiski* and *Sovremennik*, and through successive editions of his collected works, Belinskii continued to influence both readers and writers throughout the nineteenth century.

8 Dmitrii Ivanovich Ilovaiskii (1832–1920), historian and author of many works on early Russian history as well as standard texts for secondary schools. His concentration on the history of the tsars and the nobility and his close adherence to the official line of the Ministry of Education ensured the continued use of his text books in schools. Among professional historians, however, his work was not respected.

9 The older brother, Konstantin Sergeevich Shekhter [pseud. K. Grinevich], was a medical student and not directly involved in underground work, but he was arrested on December 16, 1898 (in connection with the *Rabochee znamia* arrests) because Sergei Osipovich had hidden illegal material in his apartment. In 1917 he was a member of the Bureau of the Menshevik Organizational Committee and was active in the Petrograd Soviet. The younger brother, Evgenii, was with Vladimir Osipovich in the same "circle" in the *gimnazium* and remained his best friend for many years.

10 During World War I Menshevik opinion was divided in regard to the nature of the war and the best way to end it. The basic division was between (1) the "Defensists," who called upon the workers to help defend their motherland against the attack by "German militarism," and (2) the "Internationalists," who viewed the war as a struggle between the capitalist powers and called for an international socialist effort to end the war and bring about a socialist revolution. During 1917, Defensist and Internationalist factions continued to exist within the Menshevik Party but the majority of the Mensheviks belonged to a third faction, the centrist Revolutionary-Defensist faction, which was formed in March 1917. *See also* Denike, Tenth Interview, note 10.

11 Nadezhda Osipovna married Sergei Nikolaevich Kranikhfel'd, one of Martov's close friends in the *gimnazium* and the university.

12 The brothers Nikolai and Vasilii Dmitr'evich Sokolov were the sons of the Court priest and confessor to Nicholas II. Of the nine children of the family, only Nikolai and Vasilii became involved in oppositionist activities. (During the early days of the 1917 revolution, Nikolai, a known attorney, was one of the leaders of the Petrograd Soviet.) Martov met Vasilii during the demonstration at Shelgunov's funeral; when he entered Petersburg University in the fall of 1891, Vasilii was already a second-year student, acquainted with clandestine student groups. He offered his apartment as a meeting place for Martov's own circle, introduced Martov to his older brother, Nikolai (whose circle of older students included Struve, Stranden, and Potresov), and brought Martov into contact with other, more established circles of Marxist and Populist students.

13 Ivan Dominikovich Stavskii was of peasant origin from the Ukraine. He was sent by his father's master to the *gimnazium* where he became involved in a reading circle organized by one of his teachers. According to Martov, these early experiences made Stavskii more mature and self-reliant than any of his other friends. Stavskii joined Martov's student circle in the fall of 1891 and in the summer of

1892 they both became Marxists. In late 1892 he was among the six students who founded the Petersburg Group for the Emancipation of Labor, but he abandoned all illegal activity after his arrest and short imprisonment.

14 Sergei A. Gofman was a third-year student in the Faculty of Mathematics when Martov was introduced to him by Stavskii in the fall of 1891. He was interested mainly in developing a philosophical world-view and was the driving force in Martov's circle until Martov became involved in propaganda activity. Their friendship was restored after Martov's arrest and release, and in the fall of 1892 Gofman used his father's position as a railroad employee to smuggle to Petersburg a package of illegal literature which Potresov had collected in Geneva; Martov, Gofman, and three other students (Ia. Stavrovskii, V. M. Treniukhin, M. V. Vasil'evna) became enamoured of the ideas of Plekhanov, Axelrod, and their Geneva Group for the Emancipation of Labor (see Dan, Fourth Interview, note 23) and decided to name their own circle the "Petersburg Group for the Emancipation of Labor." When Martov was sent to Vilno, Gofman continued to participate in the circle's propaganda among the workers of Petersburg and kept Martov informed of their work. He also participated in the fall of 1895 in the establishment of the Union of Struggle for the Emancipation of Labor (see Dan, Third Interview, note 18), but his political work ended with his arrest in June 1896.

15 The severe famine in the "black earth" regions of east and southeast Russia and the cholera epidemic that followed were major events in the political life of Russia: a unique opportunity for energetic public activity was presented to the zemstva and the hastily formed welfare committees in which the Populist intelligentsia played a leading role. But for much of the younger generation of the intelligentsia the famine appeared as further evidence that the future of Russia lay not with the helpless peasantry but with the development of capitalism, the industrial working class, and Marxism.

16 Martov was arrested in February 1892 after his friend Rizenkampf had "broken down" during an interrogation and had told the police of their common illegal activities. In May 1892 Martov was released on bail pending his sentencing and in November 1892 he was sentenced to five months solitary imprisonment which he served from December 17, 1892 to May 17, 1893.

17 Maria Konstantinovna Tsebrikova, a writer dedicated to "democratic" enlightened ideas, published in 1889 in London "A Letter to Emperor Alexander III," sharply criticizing tsarist policies. The letter was circulated among opposition groups and caused Tsebrikova's exile to Vologda province.

18 L. H. speaks here of a document published by George Kennan in Century Magazine [New York, November 1887] under the title "The Last Appeal of the Russian Liberals," which Martov and his friends planned to mimeograph, together with Tsebrikova's letter, for dissemination. Originally entitled "In the First Days of the Ministry of M. T. Loris-Melikov," it was a memorandum written by S. Muromtsev and signed by 25 prominent Moscow professors, lawyers and other professional men. The memorandum, which was submitted to Loris-Melikov in 1880, called for political reforms providing a limited form of national representation and legal guarantees of civil rights.

19 The first serious differences of opinion appeared in the years 1907–14 when Vladimir Osipovich [Levitskii], who lived in Moscow and in Pskov, became one of the most outspoken proponents of "Liquidationism." Martov, Lidia, and Fedor Dan were in emigration during most of these years and never embraced Liquidationism as completely as Levitskii did. Their differences deepened during World War I, when Martov became the chief spokesman for the Menshevik-Internationalists while Levitskii cooperated with other Defensists in publishing the collection Samozashchita [Self-Defense]. In 1917, Martov was the leader of the Internationalist wing of Menshevism whereas Levitskii belonged to the Defensists. After October 1917 Dan and Ezhov, who had taken a centrist Revolutionary-Defensist position all through 1917, joined the Menshevik-Internationalists headed by Mar-

tov; but Levitskii continued his complete opposition to the Bolshevik rule and became associated with the anti-Soviet League for the Regeneration of the Motherland and Freedom [*Soiuz vozrozhdeniia rodiny i svobody*] which was being condemned by the Menshevik Central Committee.

20 Shlissel'burg prison was notorious for its severe regimen and famous inmates. Its location on Lake Ladoga provided an ideal place of imprisonment for important prisoners: isolated, yet not too remote from Petersburg. In the 1880s a new section consisting of 50 solitary cells was constructed inside the walls of the fortress and in 1884 all of the *Narodovol'tsy* arrested in the wake of the 1881 assassination were transferred to that section; many died or lost their minds there. From 1884 Shlissel'burg also became the site of important executions.

21 N. Riazanov [pseudonym of David Borisovich Gol'denbakh], *see* Dan, Fifth Interview, note 18.

22 Aleksandr Nikolaevich Potresov (1869–1934) was an exception among the Mensheviks in that he came from a gentry family with some social standing. In the early 1890s, while attending university in St. Petersburg, he joined Marxist student circles and was later associated with the "legal Marxists," but in 1895 was among the founders of the underground Petersburg Union of Struggle. He was arrested in 1896, exiled to Viatka, and in 1900 left Russia for Munich where, together with Martov and Lenin, he participated in the founding and editing of *Iskra*. After the split in the RSDRP, he collaborated with Martov and Axelrod in the Menshevik wing, but following the collapse of the 1905 revolution, chose to remain in Russia, was the editor of all the Menshevik publications there, and became the champion of unqualified "Liquidationism." Disagreements with Martov deepened during World War I and the 1917 revolution when Potresov led the Defensist wing of Menshevism. After the Bolshevik takeover headed a small group of extreme right-wing Mensheviks and from 1927 to 1934 edited their journal in emigration, *Den'*.

23 Pet'r Berngardovich Struve (1870–1944) came from a family of important civil servants. He became a Marxist during his first year in the university (1890) and by the mid-1890s had attained a widespread reputation among Petersburg's Marxist youth through his writings for legal-Marxist publications and his appearances in the Free Economic Society (*see* Dan, Third Interview, note 1). By the beginning of the new century he had broken with revolutionary Marxism and joined the "Revisionist"wing of Russian Marxism, later the newly formed liberal movement, and eventually the Constitutional Democratic [Kadet] Party.

24 Aleksandra Mikhailovna Kalmykova (1849–1926), the widow of Senator Kalmykov, had a long record of public activity in education. She became acquainted with Struve through her son and during the 1890s rendered him (as well as Potresov) great help; Struve lived at her home and often at her expense. He introduced her to Marxism and Russian Marxists and even after his break with Social Democracy Kalmykova continued to contribute to *Iskra*.

25 Lidia Dan refers here to the period from April 1901 to April 1902 when the editorial board of *Iskra* resided in Munich. In fact, only four members of the board lived in Munich: Martov, Lenin, Vera Zasulich, and Potresov; Plekhanov and Axelrod continued to live in Switzerland. Lidia Dan spent a few months in Munich working for *Iskra* in late 1901 and early 1902.

26 The Sunday and evening schools were devoted to the basic education of adult workers. In most cases they operated under the auspices of philanthropic factory owners; the teachers were drawn from among the young intelligentsia. The schools enjoyed a short period of popularity and even government support from 1859 to 1862; after a long period of decline they regained their prestige in the late 1880s and 1890s. Several of the women who participated in the original Petersburg Union of Struggle were veterans of a Petersburg Sunday school, where they had become familiar with factory workers.

27 Beyond the *Nevskaia Zastava* [Neva Gate] extended a district of many big factories and workers' dwellings.

28 The Social Democratic League of Youth [*Soiuz molodezhi*] was founded in May 1920 as an affiliate of the Menshevik Party. Made up of young *intelligenty* and skilled workers, mainly printers, it attempted to mobilize opposition to the Soviet government and the *Komsomol*. The league continued its activity through 1923 despite frequent arrests. Andrei S. Kranikhfel'd, Nadezhda Osipovna's son, was the secretary of the Central Organizational Bureau of the League, of which Boris Sapir was also a member.

29 In May 1893 Martov was released from prison with the stipulation that he be exiled for two years from Petersburg and other university cities. On the advice of his friends in the movement he decided to spend those two years in Vilno, which was reputed to have an active Social-Democratic movement. He served his term in Vilno from June 1893 to May 1895 and continued to live there until October 1895, at which time he returned to Petersburg.

30 Lidia Dan refers here to the doctrine developed in the 1880s and 1890s by the founders of Russian Marxism (Plekhanov, Axelrod, and the Geneva Group for the Emancipation of Labor), according to which the Russian Revolution would consist of two distinct stages: the first stage, that of "bourgeois revolution," would establish the bourgeoisie as the ruling class while benefiting the workers with economic improvements, political and civic equality, and the freedom to organize. In the second stage, that of the "socialist revolution," the proletariat would come to power. But this stage was expected to begin only after an undetermined period of bourgeois rule, during which the working class would have developed its class consciousness, its organization, and its methods of class struggle.

31 Until the period under discussion (the early 1890s) the Russian "constitutionalists" were mostly gentry liberals who were willing to go further than other groups within gentry liberalism in calling for the establishment of a qualified constitutional order. During the 1880s and 1890s the constitutional idea took root among the intelligentsia and by the turn of the century the heretofore weak group of constitutionalists became the main stream of Russian liberalism.

32 The work referred to is *O zadachakh sotsialistov v bor'be s golodom v Rossii* [On the Tasks of the Socialists in the Struggle with Famine in Russia], published in Switzerland in 1892.

33 The term, coined in the 1880s, was used by Russian socialists, particularly Marxists, to describe condescendingly the nonrevolutionary and nonpolitical activities of gentry liberals and professional-intelligentsia employees of the zemstva in furthering education and social welfare among the peasantry during the period following the Great Reforms of the 1860s.

34 The "Bestuzhev Courses" were founded in 1878 by a circle of progressive academics headed by Professor A. N. Beketov for the purposes of offering opportunities for higher education to women. The tsarist Ministry of Education approved the courses and named Professor K. N. Bestuzhev-Riumin as their official head. Graduates of the courses were licensed to teach in secondary schools for girls.

35 Lidia Dan refers to Struve's work "Critical Remarks on the Question of Russia's Economic Development" (*Kriticheskie zametki k voprosu ob ekonomicheskom razvitii Rossii*, Petersburg, 1894). The sentence ending the book reads: "No, let us admit our lack of culture and enroll in the school of capitalism!" Struve himself explained this controversial sentence in an article written in 1895 and republished in 1902 (P. B. Struve, *Na raznye temy* [*1893–1901 g.g.*] *Sbornik statei*, Petersburg, 1902, pp. 1–59).

36 The journal of the German Social–Democratic Party.

37 Published in 1885, "Our Differences" [*Nashi raznoglasiia*] became a cornerstone of Russian Marxist thought. The book attacked Populist beliefs and asserted that capitalism was becoming the dominant economic form in Russia and, more importantly, that it was a "progressive" historical development.

38 Members of the Party of Socialist Revolutionaries (PSR). The PSR (founded in 1901), like the Populists of the last quarter of the 19th century, championed the

interests of the Russian peasantry. The debates between the Marxists and the Populists dominated the intellectual and revolutionary life of the 1890s.

39 A member of the Constitutional-Democratic [Kadet] Party, founded in August 1905, which drew its main support from the liberal intelligentsia and the professional classes.

Third interview

1 Founded by Catherine II to disseminate knowledge on rural economy, the Free Economic Society evolved in the second half of the 19th century into a forum for open discussions of the most diverse national questions. During the five-year period following the election of Count P. A. Geiden as president of the Society in March 1895, and until the Society was closed down by the authorities in 1900, the regulations restricting attendance to members and their guests were lax and the meetings attracted many university students. Most popular of all were the meetings on political economy during which Struve and Tugan-Baranovskii (using Marxist arguments) debated the Populists.

2 Mikhail Ivanovich Tugan-Baranovskii (1865–1919) taught economics at Petersburg University and led the attack on Populism, in the 1890s, at the meetings of the Free Economic Society and in the "legal" Marxist press. His most noted contribution to the Marxist-Populist debate, *The Russian Factory in the Past and the Present* [*Russkaia fabrika v proshlom i v nastoiashchem*], appeared in 1898. In the following years Tugan-Baranovskii joined Struve and others in the "revisionist" wing of Russian Marxism and in 1906 they became members of the new Constitutional-Democratic [Kadet] Party.

3 B. Gorev, *Iz partiinogo proshlogo. Vospominaniia, 1895–1905*, Leningrad, 1924, p. 6. Gorev [pseudonym of Boris Isaakovich Gol'dman] began his Social-Democratic activity in 1895 with the Petrograd Union of Struggle (*see* Dan, Fourth Interview, note 34). From then until 1917 he experienced alternate periods of exile in Siberia and of Social-Democratic work in Russia and abroad. Until 1905 he sympathized with the Bolsheviks but thereafter became an avowed Menshevik, participating in all Party congresses, central bodies, and publications. Within Menshevism he always occupied a centrist position; joined the Revolutionary-Defensist faction in 1917 and, after October, the left-wing majority of the party. In 1920 he left the Menshevik Party and turned to writing for Bolshevik publications.

4 Plekhanov's speech was delivered before a small crowd of students and several workers assembled in front of the Kazan Cathedral in St. Petersburg on December 6, 1876. This demonstration was intended as a protest against the imprisonment of hundreds of students and radicals who went "To the People" in the summers of 1874 and 1875. After the demonstration Plekhanov escaped abroad to avoid arrest.

5 Beltov, *K voprosu o razvitii monisticheskogo vzgliada na istorii* [*On the Question of the Monistic View of History*], Petersburg, 1895. The book was written by Plekhanov, who used the name Beltov as a pseudonym so that his book would be approved for publication by the censor. The book was part of a series of "legal-Marxist" publications founded by Potresov.

6 Nadezhda Konstantinovna Krupskaia and Zinaida Pavlovna Nevzorova both taught reading and arithmetic at a Sunday and evening school for adult workers in the working-class district beyond the Neva Gate in Petersburg. They were among the original founders of the Union of Struggle for the Emancipation of Labor and participated in its agitational work until their arrest in summer 1896. In 1898, while in exile in Siberia, Krupskaia became Lenin's wife.

7 The reference is to a group of Populists which had been organized in St. Petersburg in 1891 under the name *Gruppa narodovol'tsev* [The Group of Followers of the People's Will] and had conducted progaganda among a small circle of workers. In 1894 most of the *Narodovol'tsy* were arrested and, as Lidia Dan reports,

their secret press was often used by the Social Democrats until it was seized by the authorities in 1896.

8 The play "The Weavers," written in 1892 by the German playwright Gerhart Hauptmann and staged in Berlin in September 1894, became standard reading for all European socialists. The story revolves around the famine of 1844 and the bloody insurrection among the Silesian weavers; its heroes are not individuals but rather the mass movement. According to Martov, the Group of *Narodovol'tsy* in Petersburg printed "The Weavers" in the summer or fall of 1895. He does not mention any involvement on the part of the Social Democrats in this venture, although such cooperation existed, according to him, during the initial period of the Petersburg Union of Struggle in late 1895–early 1896 (*Zapiski sotsialdemokrata*, pp. 255, 273–4, 303).

9 V. M. Treniukhin was drawn into Martov's close circle in the fall of 1892 and participated in the Petersburg Group for the Emancipation of Labor. He and Gofman were the only ones left of Martov's old friends in St. Petersburg at the time of Martov's return from Vilno. They participated in the founding of the Petersburg Union of Struggle for the Emancipation of Labor.

10 *Russkoe bogatstvo* [Russian Wealth] was a "thick journal" established by a group of liberal-populist writers and publicists in 1880. By the mid-1890s, under the editorship of Mikhailovskii and Korolenko, it became one of the most widely read monthlies in Russia as well as a center for the "Legal Populist" opponents of Marxism. In the late 1890s and early 1900s its contributors included future leaders of the liberal-populist *Trudovaia gruppa* (Annenskii, Peshekhonov, and Miakotin) and of the Party of Socialist Revolutionaries (Chernov).

11 Two tabloids, published in St. Petersburg (1908–1917) and Moscow (1909–1918), respectively.

12 The "yellow ticket" served, in place of the usual internal passport, as the residence permit for women who declared prostitution as their profession. These "legal" prostitutes were allowed to work in public "Houses of Tolerance" where they were subject to inspection by the police medical committees which were established in all large cities in the 1840s.

13 The event known in the history of the Russian labor movement as the "Obukhov Defense" marked the first attempt by striking workers in St. Petersburg to defend themselves against police and army units. It occurred in 1901, during a period of deteriorating labor conditions and after several months of agitation by the Petersburg Union of Struggle and the Petersburg Committee of RSDRP. A May Day strike of 1,200 workers from the Obukhov Foundries led to their firing and a second strike, which was begun by the remaining Obukhov workers and joined by workers from two neighboring factories. Together, they fought off the police and the army by barricading themselves inside one of the buildings; they were forced to surrender only late in the night of May 7th.

14 D. Kol'tsov, *Mashina*, Geneva, 1896 (published by the Union of Russian Social Democrats Abroad).

15 Ivan Vasil'evich Babushkin (1873–1906) worked at the Semianovskii machine-building factory in St. Petersburg. From 1891 he attended evening and Sunday schools for workers and in 1893 joined a workers' circle led by Lenin and dedicated to the study of Marxism. In 1894–5 he became one of the few workers involved in the agitation activities of the Petersburg Union of Struggle. He continued these activities in exile (in Ekaterinoslav, 1896–1900) and upon his release became an *Iskra* agent. In 1905–6 was active in the RSDRP Committee and the Soviet of Soldiers' and Cossacks' Deputies in Chita where he was shot by a punitive expedition on January 31, 1906. *See also Vospominaniia I. V. Babushkina, 1893–1900*, Leningrad, 1925.

16 For the Russian Social Democrats of the 1890s, "propaganda" meant the slow process of educating workers in small study circles with the goal of inculcating in them a general political understanding and class consciousness. Martov, like others, was involved in propaganda work before his exile to Vilno, where the

experience of the Jewish labor movement led in 1894 to the development of a new strategy for Social Democracy. In his memoirs, Martov explained the new strategy of "agitation" as follows: "It was expected that agitation would bring the proletariat into conflict with its employers over the day-to-day economic needs of the workers . . . but we were convinced that through this very struggle the masses would be prepared for the assimilation of wider social and political strivings . . ." (*Zapiski sotsialdemokrata*, p. 255). The new strategy was explained to Social-Democratic circles in Russia through the pamphlet *Ob agitatsii* [On Agitation], written by a Vilno Social Democrat, Arkadii Kremer, and edited by Martov. The practice of agitation in St. Petersburg is described by Lidia Dan below.

17 Illarion Vasil'evich Chernyshev (1871–?) was a student who led a Social-Democratic circle in the Technological Institute in St. Petersburg in 1894–95. It was known as the circle of the "Youngsters" and it responded enthusiastically to the program of *Ob agitatsii*. In the fall of 1895 Chernyshev and his circle joined the founders of the Petersburg Union of Struggle. Most of them were arrested in early 1896. After a period of exile Chernyshev participated in *Iuzhnyi rabochii* (1900–1), *Iskra* (1902), and *Rabochee delo* (1902). In later years he withdrew from political activity altogether and published several studies on the agrarian economy.

18 The Petersburg Union of Struggle for Emancipation of Labor [*Soiuz bor'by za osvobozhdenie truda*] was founded in the fall of 1895 by the two Social-Democratic groups active in Petersburg: the "Youngsters" [*Molodye*] and the "Oldsters" [*Stariki*]. Martov and the *Molodye* were enthusiastic supporters of the new strategy of "agitation" while most of the *Stariki* (Lenin was one of their leaders) looked on it with some reservations. At its inception, the Union numbered 17 members, all *intelligenty*, and could also rely on a "periphery" of student supporters. The Union's agitational activities were conducted in three separate districts, each of which was led by a "Group of Propagandists." The Union's central guidance came from an "Inter-District Bureau" (also called the "Central Group" or "Committee") of five members which included Martov and Lenin. The "Central Workers' Group" (composed of veterans of the workers' study circles) was subordinated to the Central Group. The Union lost all of its original members after a series of arrests in December 1895, January 1896, and June 1896, and by 1897 a new generation of leaders had emerged. *See also* Dan, Third Interview, note 21.

19 The Putilov Metallurgical and Machine-building Works employed thousands of workers who played an active role throughout the history of the Russian labor movement.

20 Fedor Il'ich Gurvich [pseud Dan, 1891–1947], Lidia Dan's second husband. In 1895–96 he was active in the Petersburg Union of Struggle for the Emancipation of Labor and from 1901 wrote for *Iskra*. Following the 1903 split in Russian Social Democracy he became (after some hesitation) a committed Menshevik, a close collaborator of Martov, and a contributor to all Menshevik publications. After the 1913 amnesty he returned to Russia to head Menshevik activities. During World War I he collaborated with the group of "Siberian Zimmerwaldists" and following the February Revolution joined them in leading the centrist Menshevik faction of Revolutionary Defensists which dominated the Soviets. After the Bolshevik takeover of October 1917 Dan shifted his allegiance to the Leftist-Internationalist Menshevik faction headed by Martov and, following Martov's death in 1923, became the leader of this faction in emigration.

21 Stepan Ivanovich Radchenko participated in Social Democratic circles in Petersburg from the early 1890s and took part in the establishment of the Union of Struggle in 1895 as one of the leaders of the *Stariki*. His reputation as "a master of conspiracy" earned him a special standing within the Union: he and his wife remained outside the daily work of agitation and were entrusted with the technical aspects of the organization. Radchenko was the only member of the original Union who succeeded repeatedly in avoiding arrest and, from 1897, used the

organizational power concentrated in his hands to circumvent the "antiintelligentsia," "economist" tendencies of the new generation of the Union's leadership and its newspaper, *Rabochaia mysl'*. *See also* Dan, Third Interview, note 22.

22 The conflict between "Economists" and "Politicals" reached its peak from 1897 to 1900. In essence, the "Economists" called for the workers' economic struggle and the strike movement to be freed from the constraints of the intelligentsia-dominated revolutionary organizations with their emphasis on the political struggle against autocracy. The "Politicals," however, did not accept their opponent's argument that through a process of economic struggle the workers would grow "spontaneously" to political consciousness. Thus, the "Politicals" continued to claim the leadership of the labor movement for the politically oriented organizations of the Social-Democratic intelligentsia. In St. Petersburg, the "Politicals" found their support among the veterans of the original Union of Struggle (all of whom, with the exception of Radchenko, were then in exile) and the new groups around *Rabochee znamia* [Dan, Fourth Interview, note 4], while the "Economists" came mostly from the younger generation of the Union and were associated with *Rabochaia mysl'*. In emigration, the old Group for the Emancipation of Labor advocated the "political" line, while the younger Union of Social Democrats Abroad supported the "Economist" challenge. *See also* Dan, Fourth Interview, note 23 and Fifth Interview, note 11.

23 *Rabochaia mysl'* [The Workers' Thought] was published from late 1897 by the new generation of intelligentsia leaders of the Petersburg Union of Struggle, together with workers' affiliates of the Union. The journal championed a spontaneous, economic-oriented, workers' organization.

24 August (or Karl) Kok was born in an Estonian community in the Caucasus. He was trained as a mechanic and (beginning in 1891) took part in workers' circles in Tiflis. In 1896 he traveled to Germany and became strongly influenced by German Social Democracy and especially by the ideas of Edward Bernstein. From 1897 to 1899 he played a pivotal role in both the technical and ideological aspects of the journal *Rabochaia mysl'*, transforming it into a "workers' journal" with a strong antiintelligentsia bias.

25 Kozhevnikova's first husband, A. G. Rizenkampf, was a friend of Martov during their first year at the university, and together they joined E. P. Radin's circle. When all the members of the circle were arrested, in February 1892, Rizenkampf was the only one who informed on his friends. In order to escape the social stigma of "traitor" he went to Dorpat (in 1893) together with his newly married bride Vera Vasil'evna Kozhevnikova; there, she met Fedor Dan and left Rizenkampf, who then returned to St. Petersburg and committed suicide. (The Rizenkampf affair is described in detail by Martov in *Zapiski sotsialdemokrata*, pp. 121-28). Kozhevnikova's marriage also ended a few years later, in Berlin, and she returned to Russia where she became a Bolshevik.

26 *See* Dan, Third Interview, note 18.

27 Following the Petersburg textile strikes of summer 1896 and a smaller strike in January 1897, Count Witte, the Minister of Finance, pushed through the law of June 2, 1897 which reduced the legal working day to $11\frac{1}{2}$ hours. However, the law proved almost meaningless owing to legal loopholes and ineffective management.

28 *See* Dan, Third Interview, note 18.

29 The Factory Inspectorate was created as a consequence of the labor legislation of 1882 and 1884. The nine District Inspectorates reported directly to the Ministry of Finance regarding the enforcement of laws for the protection of labor (mainly child labor), and later also on the reasons for workers' unrest.

30 The Skorokhod Shoe Factory (established in 1882) was one of the largest in Russia.

31 *Novoe vremia* [New Times] was a St. Petersburg daily founded in 1856; under the editorship of A. S. Suvorin (1873) it became an advocate for the most conservative nationalist tendencies. In addition to its staunch support of the tsarist govern-

ment it was also notorious for the virulence of its antisemitic and xenophobic diatribes.

Fourth interview

1 From the late 1890s to 1902, orthodox Marxists, especially the supporters of *Iskra*, used the term *kustarnichestvo* to characterize the fragmented and "Economism-minded" labor movement of Russia; in contrast, they advocated the creation of a centralized, intelligentsia-led party to guarantee Social-Democracy's adherence to the goal of political revolution. *See also* Dan, Third Interview, note 22 and Allan K. Wildman, "Lenin's Battle with *Kustarnichestvo:* the *Iskra* Organization in Russia," *Slavic Review*, XXIII (September 1964), pp. 479–503.

2 The Group of Twenty grew out of the *Kassa* [the mutual aid organization of radical students] at the University of St. Petersburg. Its members were dedicated to the struggle for political freedom and they included N. I. Iordanskii, I. I. Lodyzhenskii, S. N. Saltykov, P. E. Shchegolev, and M. V. Kistiakovskaia (with the exception of Shchegolev, all Marxists). During the fall of 1899 the group conducted an intense agitation campaign among Petersburg workers in cooperation with *Rabochee znamia*, but in the spring of 1900 it shifted all of its energies to the students' political struggle. The arrests that followed in the summer of 1900 decimated the group.

3 The group *Sotsialist* [Socialist] was founded in the spring of 1900 by radical students from the Imperial University, the Technological Institute, and the Forestry Institute in St. Petersburg. Its members (among them P. M. Rutenberg, the brothers A. V. and B. V. Savinkov, Sofiia M. Zaretskaia, and Lidia Dan herself) had been affiliated with the Petersburg Union of Struggle but disagreed with its new "economist" leanings. During the fall of 1900 the group conducted agitation among Petersburg workers; it was closely tied to *Rabochee znamia* and to the Vilno based Social-Democratic Workers' Library (led by Eva L. and M. I. Broido) which published the group's leaflets.

4 The first *Rabochee znamia* [Workers' Banner] group was founded by students from the Petersburg Technological Institute who had grown dissatisfied with the cautiousness of the veterans of the Petersburg Union of Struggle and with the antiintelligentsia, "economist" line of its younger generation. With the help of M. V. Lur'e and his Belostok "Group of Revolutionary Workers," they printed one issue of their newspaper which called for a militant political struggle. After the arrest of the founders, their place was taken by a group from inside the Petersburg Union of Struggle, including S. V. Antropov, M. B. Smirnov, V. P. Nogin, O. A. Zvezdochetova, Lidia Dan, and her brother S. O. Ezhov, all of whom were later arrested as a consequence of the strike at the Maxwell and Paul Textile Factories in December 1898. *R.z.* continued to exist and cooperated with several groups of radical students until more arrests were made in March 1901 and the remaining members of *R.z.* joined the new organization of *Iskra*.

5 *Iskra* [The Spark] was established by Lenin, Martov, and Potresov in cooperation with the leaders of the Geneva Group for the Emancipation of Labor (Plekhanov, Axelrod, and Vera Zasulich). It was published abroad – in Munich, London and Geneva – where it remained beyond the reach of the tsarist police and whence a network of agents smuggled it into Russia. *Iskra* became the first recognized all-Russian newspaper of the Social Democrats and played a major role in the early years of the RSDRP. From December 1900 to August 1903, 45 issues of *Iskra* were edited by the six original editors; following the Second Congress and the split in RSDRP [*see* Dan, Fifth Interview, note 5 and Eighth Interview, note 15] the journal was controlled first by Lenin and Plekhanov (issues 46–51) and later by the Mensheviks (issues 52–112); it ceased publication in October 1905 when its editors returned to Russia.

6 The adjective *Russkii (Russkaia)* means simply "of Russia," or "Russian." The term *Rossiiskii (Rossiiskaia)* means "nationwide" or "empirewide," and in this sense connotes the imperialist nature of the Russian state.

7 Moisei Vladimirovich Lur'e was a typesetter of impoverished Jewish origin; proletarian in appearance and manner he was self-educated and became Russified through his contacts with Social Democratic circles. In the "Revolutionary Workers' Groups," which he established in several towns in the Western provinces in 1897, he advocated political, revolutionary action and he used his authority over the Jewish workers and his own mastery of the technique of conspiracy to operate his illegal press for a comparatively long time. After the discovery of the press in 1898 he escaped to London and organized the smuggling of various leaflets, including *Rabochee znamia*, into Russia. In 1905 Lur'e joined the Anarchists.

8 Smirnov, Antropov, and Zvezdochetova were active in the Petersburg Union of Struggle; together with Lidia Dan and her brother Sergei Ezhov they established (in 1898) an autonomous group within the Union and later joined *Rabochee znamia*. Sergei V. Antropov was the central figure in this group; a former Tolstoyan, vegetarian, and ascetic, he was distinguished by his intensive moralism. In December 1898, when the whole group was arrested, Antropov was given the heaviest sentence but escaped to London, continued to plan for a unification of Russian Social Democracy around a single political program, and eventually joined *Iskra* to become one of its first agents in Russia. Ol'ga Apolonovna Zvezdochetova was a highly idealistic and talented Sunday School teacher and propagandist, motivated more by a human and personal interest in her worker-pupils than by political impulse; she continued her propaganda and pedagogical work during her various exiles. Mikhail B. Smirnov was the "theoretician" of the group, writing and debating in the Free Economic Society against the Populists and "Revisionist" Marxists. Both Smirnov and Antropov later became Bolsheviks.

9 Aleksandr and Boris Viktorovich Savinkov and Petr Moiseevich Rutenberg were members of the *Sotsialist* group to which Lidia Dan also belonged. Rutenberg became a Socialist Revolutionary in the early 1900s and was connected with the Combat Organization of the PSR. Through his work as an engineer in the Putilov Ironworks he became involved in Father Gapon's Assembly, and in 1905 served as the link between Gapon and the SRs in St. Petersburg and Geneva. But in April 1906, he organized the execution of Gapon, who had tried to draw him into a conspiracy with the police, after which he left the PSR. Following the Bolshevik takeover, he emigrated to Palestine, where he built the first hydroelectric plant. *See also* Dan, First Interview, note 17 about the Savinkovs.

10 Mikhail Ivanovich Iordanskii (1876–1928) and Ivan Ivanovich Lodyzhenskii (1872–1957) were active in students' political circles in Petersburg, and in 1899 founded the Marxist Group of Twenty. Lodyzhenskii was supported by his landowning family and remained a kind of perpetual student; he was entrusted by Lidia Dan and other Social Democrats with organizing meetings and disseminating leaflets. In later years both Iordanskii and Lodyzhenskii joined the Menshevik wing of Russian Social Democracy. Iordanskii wrote for the Menshevik press and was elected to the party's Central Committee and to the Executive Committee of the Petersburg Soviet (in 1905). He was the editor of the important literary-political journal *Sovremennyi mir* [The Contemporary World] from 1906 and used his connections in literary circles to advance Menshevik publishing initiatives. During the war he supported the Defensist ideas of Plekhanov and served as a Military Commissar of the Provisional Government (in 1917), but in 1921 left the Menshevik party and joined the Bolsheviks. Lodyzhenskii participated in the work of various Menshevik organizations in Russia. After the Bolshevik seizure of power he sympathized with the Menshevik Right, served a term in a Soviet prison, and in 1921 left Russia.

11 The strikes which took place in December 1898 followed several months of vigorous agitation among the workers of these factories by members of the *Rabochee znamia* group and the Petersburg Union of Struggle.

12 According to Lidia Dan's brother, Levitskii, V. V. Tatarinov was a member of the Political Red Cross (a "legal" organization which helped political prisoners). He was contacted by Lidia's husband (G. Kantsel') who was a physician and not directly involved in underground activity. Tatarinov mimeographed *Rabochee znamia* leaflets on the Red Cross's machine and was arrested on December 16, 1898, together with other members of *R.z.* (V. Levitskii, *Za chetvert veka. Revoliutsionnye vospominaniia*, Vol. I, Part I, Moscow-Leningrad, 1926, p. 107).

13 Iulia G. Toporkova was a central figure in the Political Red Cross.

14 The Union of Liberation [*Soiuz osvobozhdeniia*] was founded in July 1903 by representatives from three different groups: gentry and intelligentsia activists from the zemstva and a group of young intelligentsia socialists who had earlier formed the "Revisionist" wing of Russian Marxism. This new, united liberal movement borrowed its name from the constitutionalist journal *Osvobozhdenie* [Liberation] which began publication in June 1902 in Stuttgart, Germany, under Struve. The Union sought to stir public opinion, especially among the zemstvo men, in the direction of democratic-constitutional reforms. To that purpose, its local branches began organizing numerous public "banquets" and professional unions in the fall of 1904, demanding a constitution and democratic elections. The Union fell apart in the fall of 1905 when the majority of its members joined the new Kadet Party.

15 Together with Plekhanov and Vera Zasulich, Pavel' Borisovich Axelrod (1850–1928) was one of the founders of the Geneva Group for the Emancipation of Labor and of Russian Social Democracy. One of his most important contributions to Russian Social-Democratic thought was the doctrine of the "hegemony of the proletariat," formulated for the first time in his pamphlet *Istoricheskoe polozhenie i vzaimnoe otnoshenie liberal'noi i sotsialisticheskoi demokratii v Rossii* [The Historical Situation and the Interrelation of Liberal Democracy and Socialist Democracy in Russia], published in Geneva in 1898. Against the "Economist" trend in the Russian labor movement, Axelrod argued that the Social Democrats should devote greater efforts to the "all-national" struggle for political democracy and, specifically, should encourage the participation of the historically weak Russian bourgeoisie in the organized struggle against absolutism. In this way, Social Democracy would gain "hegemony" ("leadership" in Axelrod's words) over all of the social groups opposed to autocracy and could ensure the implementation of the genuine democratic system. After the revolution of 1905, the concept of "hegemony" was given up by many Mensheviks, most notably Martov and Potresov. As Lidia Dan suggests, Lenin favored "utilization" rather than "support and alliance" as the means for securing a position of leadership for Social Democracy in the struggle against absolutism. *See also* Lidia Dan's discussion of this issue in the context of the 1905 revolution in the Ninth Interview.

16 Viktor Pavlovich Nogin (1878–1924) was a master dyer at the Paul Textile Factory in St. Petersburg; was educated in workers' Sunday Schools and in Social-Democratic circles and served as the main link between *Rabochee znamia* and the textile workers during the period of agitation in the fall of 1898. He was arrested with the rest of *R.z.*'s members in December 1898 and exiled to Poltava for three years along with Sergei Tsederbaum; there, the two friends continued their agitational activities and, on Martov's return from exile in early 1900, were initiated by him into the project for *Iskra*. Nogin served as an agent for *Iskra* throughout its existence and after the split in its ranks opted for Bolshevism though he continued to support efforts at reunification. When the Bolsheviks came to power in 1917, he was one of the leaders of the party's moderate wing.

17 The *praktiki* were those Mensheviks who conducted "practical" work in various kinds of workers' organizations allowed to operate "openly" between 1907 and 1914 – trade unions, cooperatives, and insurance associations.

18 A law from 1791 barred the Jews in the Western and Southwestern provinces of Russia (formerly part of the Commonwealth of Poland-Lithuania) from leaving their "Pale of Settlement" and traveling through Russia proper. In the course of

the 19th century the law was alternately relaxed (under Alexander II) and made harsher (under Nicholas I and Alexander III). During the period described here, only Jews who held university degrees or were registered with the first merchant guild were allowed to reside in the capital cities of Russia.

19 Vasilii and Nikolai Vodovozov were the sons of a famous Petersburg pedagogue. Nikolai (1870–1896) was among the first Marxists in St. Petersburg in the early 1890s; by the time of his premature death he had published articles in support of Marxism in a number of leading journals. The older brother, Vasilii (1864–1933), was an economist and journalist who lived in Kiev and was active in liberal-populist circles. He was among the founders of the Union of Liberation in 1903, joined the left wing of the Kadet Party in 1906, but opted for the Party of People's Socialists [*Partiia Narodnykh Sotsialistov*] when it was established in 1907.

20 Sergei Nikolaevich Bulgakov (1871–1944) was an economist, publicist, the author of several works defending Marxism against the Populists, and one of the luminaries of "Legal" and "Revisionist" Marxism in the late 1890s. But in the early 1900s he came to reject the "objective laws of history" and to view social progress not as empirical law but as an ideal. This development was reflected in a collection of essays published in 1904, "From Marxism to Idealism" [*Ot Marxizma k idealizmu*]. In later years Bulgakov turned to mysticism and Christianity.

21 N. Cherevanin [pseudonym of Fedor Andreevich Lipkin, 1869–1938] by that time had already been through several years of Social-Democratic propaganda work (in Kharkov). Beginning in 1903 he assumed a leading role in Menshevik activities, publishing and participating in congresses and central Menshevik bodies. He championed "Liquidationism" before World War I and Defensism during the war and the revolution – when he worked as an economist, first in the Union of Cities, and, in 1917, in the Economic Department of the Petrograd Soviet. After the Bolshevik takeover he joined the left-wing majority of the Menshevik Party; was arrested in the 1920s and died in prison.

22 Lidia Dan refers here to the body of ideas developed between 1897 and 1899 by the German Social-Democratic leader Eduard Bernstein and known as "Bernsteinism" or "Revisionism." Bernstein rejected many of the tenets of orthodox Marxism, in particular the notions that contemporary capitalist society was faced with an inevitable crash and that socialism was attainable only through revolution. His ideas were adopted by the Russian "Revisionists," one of whom was Tugan-Baranovskii.

23 The Group for the Emancipation of Labor [*Gruppa osvobozhdeniia truda*] was the first organization of Russian Social Democracy, founded in Switzerland in 1883 by five Russian Marxists. Its leaders – Plekhanov, Axelrod, and Vera Zasulich – exerted great influence on the young Social-Democratic movement in Russia during the 1890s. When Lenin, Potresov, and Martov planned to publish a central organ of Russian Social Democracy it was only natural that they seek the cooperation of the Group's triumvirate.

24 Boris Moiseevich Sapir (born in 1902), a Menshevik since 1919, was one of the leaders of the Social-Democratic Youth League during 1920–23. In emigration (from 1926) he collaborated with the Menshevik leaders including Lidia Dan and her husband. During the period of these interviews he lived in New York and participated in the work of the Inter-University Project on the History of the Menshevik Movement.

25 "The Southern Worker," a Social-Democratic journal published in Ekaterinoslav from January 1900 to April 1903. Owing to its militant political line, its regional rather than local orientation, and its popularity, *Iuzhnyi rabochii* became *Iskra*'s natural rival; generally it preserved its autonomy, though some of its members did cooperate with *Iskra*'s agents in Russia.

26 Lidia Dan refers here to the debate begun in 1894 as a result of Struve's polemics against Russian Populism in his *Critical Remarks*. The debate continued throughout the remainder of the 1890s in the meetings of the Free Economic Society and on the pages of Populist and Marxist publications.

27 Nikolai F. Annenskii (1843–1912) had been exiled for revolutionary activity (1880–85) and spent the years thereafter working in the statistical departments of several provincial zemstva. In the second half of the 1890s he headed the statistics section of the Petersburg municipality and became one of the editors of *Russkoe bogatstvo*. From 1901 he was again directly involved in political activity, contributing to *Osvobozhdenie*, participating in the establishment of the Union of Liberation, in the organization of the *Trudovaia gruppa* in the State Duma (1906), and in the founding of the Party of the People's Socialists.

28 The term "Legal Marxism" had two different meanings. Originally, it referred to the "legal" publication, through the initiative of Potresov and Struve, of a number of Marxist works which due to their seemingly theoretical, non-political nature were approved by the Russian censor. Published between 1894 and 1899, these works by Plekhanov, Lenin and Struve, among others, were the main vehicle for the Marxist attack on Populism. By 1900–1901, the term had acquired its second meaning; in these years "Legal Marxism" was used by the "orthodox" wing of Russian Marxism to disparage "Revisionism" and its spokesmen (e.g Struve, Tugan-Baranovskii, and Bulgakov).

29 The Literacy Committee was founded as a branch of the Free Economic Society in 1861 (the parallel Moscow Committee was founded by the Imperial Moscow Society of Agriculture) and concerned itself with organizing adult education, the reviewing and preparation of text books, and the publication of Russian writers in "cheap editions." In the 1880s the Petersburg Committee became very popular with the lower ranks of the intelligentsia who were dedicated to "small deeds," and during the famine of 1891–92 it served as a center for liberal activists to conduct relief work. Both the Petersburg and Moscow Committees were closed down by the government in 1895 but shortly afterwards were replaced by "Societies for Literacy" which functioned essentially along the same lines as the former committees.

30 Aleksei B. Peshekhonov (1867–1933) was a typical representative of the new, liberal-populist trend; he served as a statistician in the Poltava zemstvo until he was exiled for political activity; in the 1890s, while in exile, he began writing for *Russkoe bogatstvo* and in the early 1900s was a contributor to both the new liberal journal *Osvobozhdenie* and the Socialist-Revolutionary organ *Revoliutsionnaia Rossiia* [Revolutionary Russia]; between 1903 and 1905 was a member of the newly formed Union of Liberation, but in 1906 became one of the leaders of the new Party of People's Socialists.

31 Viktor Mikhailovich Chernov (1873–1952) began his revolutionary activity in the early 1890s with the populist party of *Narodnoe pravo* [The People's Right]; during his three-years' detention in Tambovsk province he wrote for *Russkoe bogatstvo*. In 1901 he became a member of the Agrarian Socialist League abroad and later the editor of *Revoliutsionnaia Rossiia*. In 1902 he was among the founders of the Party of Socialist Revolutionaries and thereafter its most distinguished leader. In 1917 he headed the majority-faction of the PSR, the largest faction in the soviets, and for a few months served as the Minister of Agriculture in the Provisional Government. After having fought against the Bolsheviks in the civil war he left Russia.

32. Venedikt Aleksandrovich Miakotin (1867–1937) was a historian, publicist, and a regular contributor to *Russkoe bogatstvo* from the late 1890s to 1915. His political career was typical of the "young generation" grouped around this journal: political activity among both "liberals" and Populists, participation in the Union of Unions in 1905, and finally, the founding of the Party of the People's Socialists in 1906.

33 Literally, "elders"; however, this word is also a generic term for any elected leaders or spokesmen who act as representatives for a definite group of people (a peasant community, the workers of a particular factory, the student body of a university).

34 B. Gorev, *op. cit.*, Chapter I (*see* Dan, Third Interview, note 3). In fact, the difficulties which Gorev encountered in establishing contact with underground workers' circles were characteristic of the years before 1895. The introduction of agitational tactics by the Union of Struggle in the fall of that year allowed student
activists like Gorev a "peripheral" role in the organization, usually mimeographing leaflets or raising contributions from sympathizers. (Gorev claimed to have
introduced the term "periphery" – borrowed from Professor Lesgaft's lectures
on anatomy – into revolutionary usage.) Gorev was eventually coopted into the
"Central Group" of the Union in the fall of 1896, after repeated arrests had eliminated its original leaders.

35 The First Congress met in Minsk on March 1, 1898; it announced the formation
of the Social-Democratic Labor Party of Russia [*Rossiiskaia sotsial-demokraticheskaia rabochaia partiia* or *RSDRP*] and elected a Central Committee. The
Petersburg Union of Struggle, which had been weakened by arrests and inroads
from Economism, did not play a role in convening the Congress but was represented by Radchenko. Other groups represented were the Bund, the Kiev, Moscow, and Ekaterinoslav Unions of Struggle, and the editorial board of a new
Social-Democratic newspaper published illegally in Kiev, *Rabochaia gazeta* [The
Workers' Gazette]. The new all-Russian party was destroyed a few weeks later
when the entire membership of the Central Committee was arrested.

36 Gorev wrote in his memoirs: "Indeed, the effect of Beltov's book was downright
magical. . . . People turned Marxists literally overnight." *Op. cit.*, p. 10 (*see* Dan,
Third Interview, note 3).

37 *Nachalo* [The Beginning] was published in Petersburg during the first half of
1899 and was closed down by tsarist authorities in June of that year. It was edited
by Struve, Tugan-Baranovskii, and other "Legal Marxists," but its contributors
also included Lenin, Plekhanov, and Zasulich. In addition, Struve attempted to
create in *Nachalo* a literary section of distinct style and quality. After early negotiations with Chekhov and the Symbolists came to nothing, the section was
entrusted to Gorkii and featured also some of the rising Modernist writers.

Fifth interview

1 Iosif Solomonovich Bliumenfel'd [German: Blumenfeld, 1865–?] was born of
Rumanian parents and reared in Russia; he was expelled from the country in
1884 for his activity in the People's Will. While abroad, he was attracted to the
Geneva Group for the Emancipation of Labor and managed its printing shop. He
performed the same role for the Union of Russian Social Democrats Abroad
(where he supported Plekhanov in his conflicts with the "youngsters") and for
Iskra (1901–05), *Golos sotsialdemokrata* (1908–11), and *Izvestiia Petrogradskogo
sovieta* (1917).

2 J. H. W. Dietz, based in Stuttgart, was the principal publisher of the German
Social-Democratic Party; he employed Russian typesetters and brought out both
Iskra and *Zaria*.

3 Upon arriving in Munich in early 1901, Lidia Dan found the following members
of the *Iskra* board there: Vera Zasulich, who had been in emigration for two decades (except for the year 1900 which she spent in St. Petersburg under an
assumed name); Potresov and Lenin, who had arrived in Germany in April and
July 1900, respectively; and finally, Martov and Krupskaia (Lenin's wife), who
had only arrived there a few months earlier.

4 Inna [Dimka] G. Smidovich-Leman had been the secretary of *Iskra* before Krupskaia's arrival and continued to help in its work afterwards.

5 In the *Iskra* editorial board the name "young ones" was reserved for the Peters-
burg trio of Lenin, Martov, and Potresov. The "oldsters" were the veterans of the
Geneva Group for the Emancipation of Labor: Plekhanov, Axelrod, and Vera
Zasulich.

6 Only three issues of *Zaria* [The Dawn] ever appeared: the first in April 1901, the second (which incorporated nos. 2 and 3) in December of that year, and the third (no. 4) in August 1902; all were published in Stuttgart.

7 The Second Congress of RSDRP took place in Brussels and London from July 30 to August 23, 1903. In the course of the congress Lenin proposed a smaller editorial board for *Iskra* (and one in which his view would command a stable majority) to consist of Plekhanov, Martov, and himself and excluding Axelrod, Zasulich, and Potresov. Lenin's proposed editorial board was approved by the congress but Martov refused to participate in it.

8 The letters were written in April and June 1902 (*Leninskii sbornik*, vol. 4, ed. L. B. Kamenev, Moscow-Leningrad, 1925, pp. 96–7, 104–5, 118, 122, 127–8, 129, 131).

9 Axelrod's involvement in the making of kefir (a kind of fermented milk) is described in Abraham Ascher, *Pavel Axelrod and the Development of Menshevism*, Cambridge, Mass., 1972, pp. 82–8.

10 Herman Greulich, a Swiss socialist leader.

11 The Union of Russian Social-Democrats Abroad [*Soiuz russkikh sotsialdemokratov za granitse*] was formed in 1895 to assist the Group for the Emancipation of Labor in publishing more popular Social-Democratic material for the instruction of the rapidly expanding labor movement inside Russia. The group reserved the right to determine the membership of the Union, which was to be drawn from among the younger generation of emigres (most of them veterans of the Social-Democratic movement of the 1890s in Russia). By 1898, however, these "youngsters," led by the "Economists" Kuskova and Prokopovich, had gained control of the Union, and in April 1900, the Group's leaders withdrew from the Union. Lidia Dan is mistaken here in assuming that at the time of his visit to Yalta (in the spring of 1900) Martov was unaware of the differences between the Group and the Union. In fact, prior to his arrival in Yalta, Martov had been informed by Lenin and Potresov of their meeting with two representatives from the Union in which the reasons for the split between the Union and the Group were discussed. (*See* Iu. Martov, "Pskov," *Leninskii sbornik*, ed. L. Kamenev, vol. 4, Moscow, 1924, pp. 51–60).

12 *Sovremennoe obozrenie* [Contemporary Review] was planned as a supplement to *Zaria* with Struve as its sole editor. During the negotiations (held in Munich from December 1900 to February 1901) it was agreed that in return for publishing *S.o.* Struve would help *Iskra* and *Zaria* in raising contributions among his liberal friends in Russia; but these plans were abandoned when Struve was arrested on his return to Russia and detained in Tver for a year. Soon afterwards, the *Iskra* leaders changed their minds about cooperation and the Russian liberals acquired their own organ, *Osvobozhdenie* (edited by Struve).

13 In March 1900, Martov, Lenin, and Potresov met in Pskov to discuss plans for a new Social-Democratic organization; these discussions led to their cooperation in *Iskra*. During their stay in Pskov, Lenin and Martov also met with Struve and Tugan-Baranovskii to negotiate collaboration between the "orthodox" and the "revisionist" wings of Russian Marxism.

14 D. E. Zhukovskii was a wealthy landowner and a zemstvo leader who was later to become one of the founders of the Union of Liberation. In early 1900 he was rumored to have offered Struve (a personal friend) a large sum of money for the publication of an oppositional journal abroad. Zhukovskii had in fact contributed 1,000 rubles to *Iskra* through his childhood friend, Potresov (who also received 2,000 rubles from Kalmykova). But he is reported to have given a far greater sum, 30,000 rubles, to Struve for the publication of the liberal-constitutional journal *Osvobozhdenie*.

15 *Osvobozhdenie* [Liberation] was a liberal-constitutional journal published abroad from July 1902 to October 1905. It was founded by a group of liberal intelligentsia and zemstvo activists, headed by Struve, and became the organ of the Union of Liberation (in 1903).

16 The *Bor'ba* [Struggle] group was formed in Paris in the summer of 1900 and made its position public in the fall of 1901. Although its leaders were in agreement with the political goals of *Iskra*, they criticized its refusal to admit its rival, the Union of Russian Social Democrats Abroad, into the new, united organization of Russian Social Democracy. At the Second Congress *Bor'ba*, which had no contacts inside Russia, was denied representation and the delegates voted to end its existence. (In an unpublished part of her interview Lidia Dan stresses that much of the dislike of *Iskra*'s editors toward *Bor'ba* was caused by the arrogance and vanity of its members.)

17 E. Smirnov [pseudonym of Emmanuil L'vovich Gurevich, 1865–?] had been living in emigration since 1888 and was close to the French socialists; before joining *Bor'ba* he was consecutively affiliated with the *Narodovoltsy*, the Russian "legal" Marxist journals, and the Union of Russian SDs Abroad. He returned to Russia in 1905, joined the Mensheviks, and was active in various Menshevik and radical-democrat newspapers as well as the SD faction of the State Duma. During World War I he supported the Menshevik-Defensists; but left the Menshevik party in August 1917 and joined the editorial board of the Right-SR newspaper, *Vlast' naroda* [People's Power]. He remained in Russia after the Bolshevik takeover and later worked in the Marx-Engels Institute.

18 N. Riazanov [pseudonym of David Borisovich Gol'denbakh, 1870–1938], the most outstanding of the three leaders of *Bor'ba*, had been active in Social Democratic circles since the early 1890s. Following the Second Congress, he remained outside the new SD factions but joined the Mensheviks in 1906, was active in the trade unions, and during World War I cooperated with the Menshevik-Internationalists in emigration. He returned to Russia in 1917 to become part of the trade-union leadership; at first he remained a Menshevik but went over to the Bolsheviks in August. Despite his frequent opposition to Lenin he held several high positions and headed the Marx-Engels Institute until 1931 when he was one of the accused in the "Menshevik trial"; died in prison.

19 Iu. Steklov [pseudonym of Iurii Mikhailovich Nakhamkes, 1873–1941] had been in the Social-Democratic movement since 1893, a member of the Union of Russian Social-Democrats Abroad, and a defender of the veterans' position against the Union's Economist "youngsters." When *Bor'ba* ceased to exist, he remained outside the new Social-Democratic factions, although he contributed to several Bolshevik publications in 1905 and thereafter. He became the editor of *Izvestiia* (the official organ of the Petrograd and All-Russian Soviet) in 1917 but remained an "independent" Social-Democrat Internationalist until the eve of the October takeover, when he joined the Bolshevik Party and continued to serve as the editor-in-chief of *Izvestiia* during the 1920s.

20 Nevzorov was then the pseudonym of Iu. M. Steklov. His article was sent to both *Zaria* and *Iskra* in response to Lenin's article "With What to Begin?" [*S chego nachat'?*], published in *Iskra*, no. 4, as the editorial board's tactical guideline. Although Nevzorov's article was sharply criticized by all six members of the *Iskra* board, three of them (Axelrod, Martov, and Potresov) favored its publication while the other three (Plekhanov, Lenin, and Zasulich) opposed it, and the article never appeared (*Perepiska G. V. Plekhanova i P. B. Akselroda*, Moscow, 1925, part II, pp. 155–7; *Pis'ma P. B. Akselroda i Iu. O. Martova*, Berlin, 1924, pp. 41–4, 53–7).

21 Elsewhere in these interviews Lidia Dan said: "The complications with Potresov came about because, while in exile in Viatka province [in the late 1890s], he had made a rather unsuccessful marriage with Ekaterina Nikolaevna . . . She was a doctor's assistant, also a Social Democrat and an activist in the Petersburg Union of Struggle. She was very primitive and completely unsuitable for Aleksandr Nikolaevich. He was an extremely versatile man, a man of European culture in the broadest sense, and extremely knowledgeable about European literature."

22 The *otrezki* were the segments of land which the peasants had cultivated under *obrok* (quitrent) before 1861 but which were cut off from their allotments and

given to the gentry landowners under the terms of the Edict of Emancipation. During the discussions described here, it was agreed that the agrarian program of the Social Democrats should include the return of the *otrezki* to the peasants; it was calculated to satisy the peasants' most urgent demand, yet stopped short of the "socialization" of land which the SRs championed. Already then Lenin was leaning toward full nationalization of the land, and in 1906 he made it the center of his agrarian program.

23 The "theory of stages" (or the "process theory," as the Economists themselves called it) was advanced by the moderate Economists grouped around *Rabochee delo* (*see* Dan, Sixth Interview, note 7). Drawing on the assumptions advanced in the pamphlet *Ob agitatsii*, they asserted that before proceeding to political agitation the Social Democrats should pass through two phases of economic agitation: first, against individual employers, and later, against the capitalist class as a whole.

24 Plekhanov's "project" was to serve as the draft of the program around which the *Iskraists* had hoped to unite Russian Social Democracy. The ten-page document, over which Plekhanov labored for the last six months of 1901, turned out to be an exegesis of the process of history and was deemed by the other *Iskra* editors as too vague. Lenin also thought that Plekhanov was mistaken in his evaluation of the respective roles of the proletariat, the liberal bourgeoisie, and the peasantry in the expected revolution.

Sixth interview

1 Iu. O. Martov, *Bor'ba s osadnym polozheniem v Rossiiskoi sotsial demokraticheskoi rabochei partii* [The Struggle Against the State of Siege in the Russian Social-Democratic Labor Party], Geneva, 1904. The pamphlet was written in the aftermath of the Second Congress of RSDRP and the split in Russian Social Democracy, at a time when the Mensheviks and the Bolsheviks began to offer their respective explanations for the split.

2 Grigorii Alekseevich Aleksinskii (1879–1967) was one of the most colorful figures in the history of Russian Social Democracy. He began his political activity in the student movement in Moscow, in 1899, and was one of the leaders of the student disturbances of 1901–02. He joined the Bolsheviks in 1905 and became the leader of the Bolshevik faction in the Second Duma, where he took an extreme "boycottist" position against any participation in liberal-parliamentary politics. In 1909 he joined the *Vpered* group of extremist Bolsheviks, but the beginning of World War I marked a complete turnabout in his political orientation: he took a strong Defensist position, cooperated with like-minded Social Democrats and Social Revolutionaries in the Paris journal *Prizyv*, and upon his return to Russia in 1917 he joined Plekhanov's group *Edinstvo*. After his emigration, in 1918, he formed ties with Russian monarchist circles.

3 Inessa Armand (1897–1920) was a French-born woman who grew up in Russia and joined the Moscow Bolshevik organization in 1904. Following her arrest and exile, she escaped abroad (1908) where she joined the Bolshevik center and became very close to Lenin; their collaboration (and rumored affair) continued through the war and the revolution.

4 Lenin's older brother, Aleksandr, was hanged in 1887 for his role in an attempted assassination of Alexander III.

5 "What is to be Done?" [*Chto delat'?*] was published in Stuttgart in 1902; in it Lenin laid down the plans for a centrally organized, all-Russian Social-Democratic party which he considered necessary if the Russian labor movement were to develop into an effective political force. These plans and expectations for the control of the "spontaneous" working class by "conscious" SD revolutionaries called forth some of the strongest opposition from Lenin's opponents at the Second Congress.

6 Lev Grigor'evich Deich (1855–1941) cooperated with Zasulich, Plekhanov, and Axelrod in founding the original Group for the Emancipation of Labor in 1883. He had been a wanted man since his earlier involvement with *Zemlia i volia* and was arrested while on a visit to Germany to arrange for the transfer of illegal literature into Russia. He spent the next 16 years in Siberia and returned to Social-Democratic activity only in 1901; remained a close follower of Plekhanov, joined the Mensheviks in 1903, and during the war and the revolution belonged to the "defensist" group *Edinstvo* together with Plekhanov and Zasulich. After the Bolshevik takeover he ceased all political activity and remained in Russia.

7 *Rabochee delo* [The Workers' Cause] was the journal of the Union of Russian Social Democrats Abroad published sporadically in Geneva from April 1899 to February 1902; it was the major organ of the moderate Economists and thus the archrival of *Iskra*. The *R.d.* group was dissolved by a resolution of the Second Congress.

8 Ekaterina Dmitr'evna Kuskova (1869–1958) and her husband Sergei Nikolaevich Prokopovich (1871–1955) were among the "youngsters" of the Union of Russian Social Democrats Abroad from 1897 to 1899. Their position from the start had been close to Economism, and in 1899 they incorporated elements of Revisionism and gave it extreme expression in the controversial brochure *Credo;* this brochure, based on a talk given by Kuskova, called on the Social Democratic intelligentsia to encourage the proletariat to a purely economic struggle and to involve itself in liberal political activities. Because of strong opposition to their views from the Group for the Emancipation of Labor they left the Union in 1899, returned to Russia, and were among the founders of the Union of Liberation and the Union of Unions (in 1905). In the years between the two revolutions they remained outside the political parties, were active in the "political Masonry" [*see* Dan, Eleventh Interview, note 13] and among the Moscow radical intelligentsia. In 1917 they associated with the right wing of the Mensheviks (Prokopovich represented the party in the Provisional Government as a Minister of Trade and Industry and later of Food Supplies). In 1921 they were arrested and banished from the Soviet Union.

9 On May 1, 1900, thousands of workers participated in a spontaneous, open street demonstration in Kharkov. This was the first of a series of significant demonstrations which would take place in various industrial cities during the next few years.

10 The meeting in Geneva, in June 1901, was attended by the two main protagonists of Russian Social Democracy abroad – the Union of Russian Social Democrats Abroad and *Iskra* – and by an intermediary group, *Bor'ba*. In fact, the meeting resulted in a provisional agreement which approved in principle the reconstruction of the Union on a more highly "political" and centralized basis. However, by the time the official "unification" meeting convened (in Zurich, in October), both sides had abandoned any pretense of compromise, and the meeting came to an end when the *Iskra* people read a statement denouncing the Economism of *Rabochee delo*, then left the hall.

11 Lev Mikhailovich Khinchuk (1868–1944) first began his revolutionary activity in 1889 for which he served a term in prison. In 1902 he was a central figure in the Moscow SD organization but was arrested in May of that year with all of the other activists in the organization (including Lidia Dan). After the 1903 split of the RSDRP he joined the Mensheviks and during the following years worked in the party's central organizations; was elected the chairman of the Moscow Soviet in 1905 and again in 1917, when he was also a member of the Menshevik Central Committee (representing the Revolutionary-Defensist faction). In 1920 he announced his resignation from the Menshevik Party, joined the Communist Party, and held a number of important economic and diplomatic positions in the Soviet Government.

12 Semen Lazarevich Vainshtein (1879–1923) became involved in Social–Democratic activity in 1899–1900 while attending university in Kharkov; in 1902 he

worked in the Moscow SD organization and was arrested in May together with its other members. In 1905 he was active in the Petersburg Soviet and wrote for the Menshevik newspaper *Nachalo*. After another term in prison he went to live illegally in Baku and participated in the leadership of the Union of Mechanical Workers; he was rearrested and spent the next seven years in Siberia. During World War I he joined the group of SD-Internationalists known as the Siberian Zimmerwaldists; together with the other members of this group he returned to Petrograd in 1917, participated in the Menshevik Revolutionary-Defensist faction, and was a member of the Bureau of the All-Russian Executive Committee of the Soviets. After the Bolshevik takeover he joined the minority right wing of Menshevism, spent time in Soviet prisons, and in 1923 was forced into emigration.

13 After a term of exile in Turukhansk for earlier Social-Democratic activities, Glafira I. Okulova became an *Iskra* agent in 1901, was arrested again in 1902, and was exiled to Olekminsk, where she became a convinced Bolshevik in the following year. She married a leading Bolshevik, Teodorovich [*see* Dan, Eighth Interview, note 17].

14 S. V. Zubatov, the chief of Moscow security police, headed an experiment in "police socialism" in 1900–1903; under the auspices of the Ministry of the Interior police agents he helped to organize the workers for cultural and economic activities hoping to divert their attention from politics. These government-sponsored trade unions were disbanded in 1903, when the authorities discovered that they could no longer control the very labor movement which they had helped to initiate.

Seventh interview

1 A system of universal internal passports had existed in Russia since the reign of Peter I. During the eighteenth and through most of the nineteenth century, this system also served as a register for taxation purposes but after 1897 passports were utilized solely as a means of controlling the movement of the populace. Passports were required of all people traveling or residing in places other than their stated place of residence; of Jews who found themselves anywhere outside the Pale of Settlement; and of every person in the capitals and other places defined by the law as being under "special protection." All travelers were under the obligation to register with the local police if intending to stay overnight.

2 Ortodox [pseudonym of Liubov Isaakovna Aksel'rod, 1870–1949] was at that time a contributor to *Iskra* and *Zaria*. She had been active in the revolutionary movement in the 1880s and later went into emigration where she became a close follower of Plekhanov in the early 1890s. She continued to follow his line in the coming years, leaned toward the Bolshevik wing in 1903 yet joined the Mensheviks a short time later, and was against "Liquidationism" in the prewar period. During World War I and the revolution she was in Plekhanov's Defensist *Edinstvo* group, but after the Bolshevik takeover ceased her party activity and held various positions in Soviet academic institutions.

3 Lidia Dan speaks here of the older brother, Boris Savinkov, who would soon join the Socialist Revolutionaries (*see* Dan, First Interview, note 17).

4 Anatolii Vasil'evich Lunacharskii (1875–1933) began conducting SD propaganda among Kiev railroad workers at the age of 17 and after a stay abroad with his sick brother Platon, during which they formed ties with the Group for the Emancipation of Labor, participated (in 1899) in the founding of the Moscow SD Committee together with Lenin's sister and Platon's wife. Arrested shortly afterward, he was exiled to Vologda, where he and Bogdanov were the center of a lively circle of Marxist thinkers. In 1903 he returned from exile, joined the Bolsheviks, and the editorial board of the Bolshevik journals in Geneva (1903–5) and Petersburg (1905–6). After 1907 he went into emigration and was associated with Bog-

danov in the Bolshevik splinter group *Vpered*. During World War I he worked with SD-Internationalists of all factions in the Paris journal *Nashe slovo* and in 1917, in Petrograd, joined the interfactional group of *Mezhraiontsy* [Interboroughists]. In late July that group joined the Bolsheviks and after October Lunacharskii became the Commissar of Education.

5 Aleksandr' Aleksandrovich Malinovskii [pseud. Bogdanov, 1873–1928] was then serving a 3-year term of exile in Vologda for his SD activity in Tula and Moscow. He had already published works in philosophy and economics and was developing, together with Lunacharskii and other SD exiles, the ideas of Empirio-criticism. After the split in RSDRP he became a Bolshevik, was close to Lenin, and held various important positions in the Bolshevik organization. From 1908 he developed deep disagreements with Lenin, joined with several other Bolsheviks in the extremist *Vpered* group, and was expelled from the party. He lived in Russia through World War I and the Revolution, maintained a staunch internationalist position, but remained outside any of the SD factions. After the October takeover he dedicated himself to scientific work and to developing "workers' culture."

6 Strumilin (pseudonym of Stanislav Gustavskii Strumillo-Petrashkevich, 1877–1974] had participated in the work of the Petersburg Union for Struggle in the late 1890s. In 1905, he returned from exile, joined the Petersburg Menshevik organization and remained a Menshevik until October 1917 after which he joined the Bolsheviks and worked as an economist in various important government and academic positions.

7 Pavel' Eliseevich Shchegolev (1877–1931) was also one of the student activists Lidia Dan came to know in *Rabochee znamia;* was one of the leading members of the Group of Twenty. After his arrest and exile, he turned his attention from political activity to the study of the history of the Russian revolutionary movement: from 1907–17 edited the historical journal *Byloe;* in 1917 he participated in the Provisional Government's Investigation Commission and edited the 7 volumes of its proceedings.

8 Elena Osipovna Stentsel recalled in an interview how Savinkov would appear before the political meetings of Russian students in Berlin (circa 1901–1902) and would argue that it was absolutely necessary to be more "revolutionary" than the Social Democrats . . . (Interview with E. O. Stentsel, June 29, 1960, p. 31, Archive of the Project on the History of Menshevism, Columbia University). In later years Stentsel became a Menshevik and worked in the Printers' Union and in the cooperative movement unitl October 1917, after which she went into emigration.

9 *Revoliutsionnaia Rossiia* [Revolutionary Russia] was published in Russia by the Union of Socialist Revolutionaries (also known as the "Northern Union") beginning in 1900. In early 1902, following the merger of the "Northern" and "Southern" unions into the united Party of Socialist Revolutionaries (PSR), the newspaper was transferred abroad where it was published until 1905 as the organ of the new party.

10 Mikhail Egorovich Bogatyrev was a worker at the Votinskii Factory in the province of Viatka and, after 1900, a member of a circle of Social-Democratic workers in Sormovo. Was arrested in 1902 for his role in organizing a May Day demonstration of Sormovo workers. It is not clear whether or not he is the Moscow worker to whom Lidia Dan refers.

11 Mikhail Alekseevich Bagaev (1873–1949), a metal worker, was drawn to Marxist circles in Ivanovo-Voznesensk in 1892–3. He lived in various cities in the 1890s, always working with local Social-Democratic groups. In 1900–1902, he worked in Nizhnii Novgorod and Vladimir for both the "Northern Union of Russian Social Democrats" and *Iskra*, was eventually arrested, and in the Taganka prison he made the acquaintance of Lidia Dan. In 1905 he returned from exile in Eastern Siberia and joined the Bolshevik organization. He was arrested again in 1908 and while in Siberian exile abandoned all revolutionary activity until 1917, when he was the chairman of the Soviet in Tomsk province. He joined the Communist

Party in 1924. (*See also* Lidia Dan's recollections of her conversations with Bagaev in the Eighth Interview; M. Bagaev, *Za Desiat'let*, Ivanovo, 1930.)

12 The idea of "people's houses," borrowed from western Europe, became popular among the more progressive zemstva and dumas in the early 1900s. The "houses" were designed as centers for educational and charitable work among the lower classes. The Petersburg People's House, financed and patronized by the liberal-minded Countess S. V. Panina, was opened in 1903 and offered a variety of services and activities: a free library, a dining hall and tea house, legal aid, evening classes for elementary education and for crafts, lectures, poetry readings, theatrical shows, and the like.

13 "People's universities" were organized in Moscow and St. Petersburg in 1906 and spread quickly to many provincial towns until 1909, when most of them were closed down by the government. The "universities" were modeled after similar institutions in Western Europe and the United States and offered workers a variety of evening courses, organized and taught by local attorneys, doctors, engineers, and high school or university teachers.

14 It is not clear to which "pamphlets" Lidia Dan alludes; at that time Vladimir Galaktionovich Korolenko (1853–1921) was a writer, journalist, editor, and public man enjoying a national reputation on the strength of three volumes of short stories and several important journalistic pieces based on his public work (the most famous of which were his relief work during the famine of 1892 and his gaining the acquittal of eight Udmurt peasants from the province of Viatka who had been falsely accused of human sacrifice); by 1902 he had become coeditor (with Mikhailovskii) of *Russkoe bogatstvo* and was preparing to participate in the defense of peasants who had been involved in agrarian disturbances in Poltava and Kharkov provinces; in the following year he would write articles condemning the pogroms against the Jews of Kishinev and Gomel.

15 Vladimir Ivanovich Charnolutskii (1866–1941) and Gavril A. Fal'bork (1864–1942) led the opposition-minded delegates of the Third Congress of Activists in the Field of Technical Education which took place in St. Petersburg in January 1904; Fal'bork also participated in the founding congress of the Union of Liberation meeting in St. Petersburg at the same time. Both men were arrested in January 1904, but were again in St. Petersburg in late 1904 and played an important role in the Union of Unions. In later years both were active in the Union of Teachers and, after 1917, in Soviet educational institutions.

16 *Vestnik Evropy* [The Europe Courier] was published monthly in St. Petersburg from 1866 to 1917 and was in the general tradition of the "thick journals," combining literary pieces with articles on historical, political, cultural, and popular-scientific topics. Voicing a moderate liberal view in the spirit of the "Great Reforms" of the 1860s, it limited its criticism of the tsarist regime to specific issues of justice, education, local government, etc., and at the same time argued against both the Populist and the Marxist revolutionary movements. After the turn of the century served mainly as an organ of the moderate liberals and the academic intelligentsia.

17 Perhaps Lidia Dan has in mind Lev Naumovich Kleinbort, the SD commentator who later contributed regularly to the journal *Sovremennyi mir* [Contemporary World] on the life of the workers and published a volume on workers' culture (*Rabochii klass i kultura*, vol. I: *kak skladyvalas' rabochaia intelligentsiia*, Moscow, 1925).

18 *Russkaia mysl'* [Russian Thought] was published in Moscow from 1880 and was one of the most widely read monthlies in Russia. Although at its inception it had voiced enlightened-Slavophile sentiments, from 1885 onward it took a more "progressive," broad-minded attitude, and published articles by both the "Legal Populists" and the "Legal Marxists."

19 *Russkie vedomosti* [Russian News] was a Moscow daily which began publication in 1863. It was known for its high level of journalism (though chided by radicals for its restraint in criticizing the tsarist government) and was widely read among

the Moscow "professors" and other intelligentsia as well as the provincial intelligentsia throughout Russia.
20 *See* Dan, Third Interview, note 31.
21 *Russkoe slovo* [The Russian Word], a Moscow daily, started publication in 1895 but gained popularity only around the turn of the century when a new owner made it into a modern newspaper, more concerned with "news" than with promoting a political line.
22 *Tovarishch* [Comrade] was a daily which appeared from March 1906 to December 1907; its political line was close to the left-wing Kadets though there were a few Mensheviks among its contributors. *Den'* [Day], also a daily, appeared from 1912 to 1917; unitl May 1917 its list of contributors included a variety of moderate socialists and liberals; thereafter, under the editorship of Potresov, it became the organ of the Menshevik-Defensists.

Eighth interview

1 In the Russian (Cyrillic) alphabet V is the third letter, E is the seventh.
2 Part of Lidia Dan's letter was quoted by Martov in his letter of June 21, 1902 to Lenin which was published in *Leninskii sbornik*, vol. 4, pp. 124–6.
3 Mariia [Mania] V. Vil'bushevich [later Shokhat] was arrested with many other Minsk Bundists at the beginning of 1900. During their interrogation by Zubatov she and several others were persuaded to establish a legal workers' organization which would be committed to a purely economic struggle and which would have police protection. Their efforts brought about the founding (in July 1901) of the Minsk "Jewish Independent Workers' Party" which momentarily attracted a large following and led a number of successful strikes. However, the collapse of Zubatov's plans in other cities and the Kishinev pogrom brought about the disintegration of the party in July 1903. Vil'bushevich's disillusion with both legal and illegal labor organizations in Russia turned her to Zionism and she eventually emigrated to Palestine, where she was among the founders of an underground self-defense organization.
4 P. O. Lissagaray, *Histoire de la Commune de 1871*, Brussels, 1876.
5 A. Tun [Thun], *Istoriia revoliutsionnykh dvizhenii v Rossii*, Geneva, 1903.
6 N. P. Bogolepov, formerly a Professor of Law and Rector of Moscow University, became the Minister of Education in 1898 and immediately instituted severe measures to stem student political activity, most notably the conscription of student demonstrators into the army. He was shot on February 14, 1901 by P. V. Karpovich (a student who had been expelled from Moscow University) and died on March 2, after which most of his measures were revoked.
7 These two works by Plekhanov were published abroad in 1883 and 1885 respectively and became the cornerstone of Russian Social-Democratic thought. In these early pieces Plekhanov argued that Russia, like Europe, had to pass through a stage of capitalist development, and he outlined the political struggle which the Social Democrats would have to undertake during this period.
8 Count V. A. Kugushev, a landowner, was drawn into Social-Democratic affairs by the manager of his estate, Aleksandr Dmitrievich Tsuriupa (a Social Democrat and later a Bolshevik). Although his involvement was mostly limited to financial aid, he was arrested in 1902, spent several months in prison (where Lidia Dan became acquainted with him), and was exiled without trial to Olonetsk province. After escaping and living abroad he returned to Russia in the fall of 1905 and resumed his agricultural enterprises. Through the mediation of Lidia Dan he contributed great sums to the Menshevik publications *Iskra* and *Nachalo* (1905).
9 The prison administration was removed from the Ministry of the Interior and placed under the Ministry of Justice in 1895.
10 The Aleksandrovsk Central Prison was situated near Irkutsk; next to the Central Prison was the "transit" prison where exiles were lodged while awaiting transfer

to various Eastern Siberian locations. Prisoners arriving from European Russia would get off the Tran-Siberian train at Usol'e, a village situated across the River Enisei from Irkutsk, and would walk or travel by wagon or sleigh to Aleksandrovsk.

11 Lidia Dan's brother and his wife, Konkordiia Ivanovna Zakharova, were smuggled out of the Aleksandrovsk Central Prison in two laundry baskets. Their celebrated escape was described by Ezhov in "Twenty Hours In a Basket" [*Dvatset' chasov v korzine*], published in *Sovremenik*, 1913, no. 12, and reprinted in Zakharova's and Ezhov's memoirs *(Iz epokhi "Iskry," 1900–1905gg.*, Moscow, 1924).

12 The Second Congress of RSDRP adopted a resolution which labelled the SRs as "nothing more than a bourgeois-democratic faction to which the general attitude of Social Democracy cannot be any different than toward the liberal representatives of the bourgeoisie as a whole" and emphasized the need to draw a clear distinction between the SRs and the SDs (an assertion that was most likely prompted by the appearance of combined SR-SD committees in several Russian cities). The draft resolution prepared by Axelrod recognized the possibility of cooperation between the two parties in isolated instances, but the congress approved the proviso introduced by Plekhanov that any such cooperation should be subject to the authority of the Central Committee.

13 The *Bund* [General Jewish Workers' Union in Lithuania, Poland, and Russia] broke with the RSDRP during the Second Congress after the majority of the delegates to the congress had voted against the Bund's demand for autonomy and for the right to exclusive representation of the Jewish workers in the RSDRP.

14 On July 15, 1904 the Minister of Interior, Viacheslav Plehve, was assassinated in St. Petersburg by the SR E. Sazonov. Plehve's name had been connected with the brutal repression of the peasant disturbances in Kharkov and Poltava provinces (1902) and in Georgia (1903); he had also been involved with experiments in police-sponsored trade unions and was accused of attempting to divert the growing national protest movement by waging war against Japan. His assassination and replacement by the more moderate Prince Sviatopolk-Mirskii signaled the beginning of a surge in oppositional activities which culminated in the revolution of 1905.

15 L. H. refers here to the split between Mensheviks and Bolsheviks which occurred during the Second Congress of RSDRP in the summer of 1903. While the leaders abroad engaged in polemical exchanges which progressively broadened the area of disagreement between the two factions, many Social Democrats in Russia remained unaware of the split or unclear about its cause.

16 Olekminsk was a small village in Eastern Siberia to which Lidia Dan was sent in July 1904 to serve the sentence of her exile.

17 *See* Dan, Sixth Interview, note 13 for details about Glafira Okulova. Ivan Adolfovish Teodorovich (1875–1940) had been a member of the Moscow Union of Struggle from 1895 and a member of the Moscow Committee and an agent of *Iskra* in 1901–2. He became a Bolshevik already in 1903, during a term of exile in Olekminsk, and after his escape from exile in the summer of 1905 worked in Bolshevik organizations in Petersburg (1905–7) and the Urals (1908). Another arrest put an end to his revolutionary career in 1908, but in 1917 he was back in Petrograd as a Bolshevik member of the City Duma, and after the October takeover served as the Commissar of Food Supplies and other important positions in the Soviet government.

18 Mikhail Solomonovich Uritskii (1873–1918), the son of a poor Jewish family in the Western provinces, began organizing Social-Democratic student circles during his *gimnazium* years in the early 1890s and continued to do so while attending university in Kiev (from which he graduated in 1897). Became a Menshevik in 1903, during a term of exile in Iakutsk province, and remained active in the Menshevik underground even after 1905, until repeated arrests (and escapes) forced him to leave Russia. During World War I joined the SD-Internationalists in emigration and, in 1917, became a member of the Bolshevik Party and its Central

Committee. Thereafter, and until his assassination in August 1918, adopted a militant position, taking an active part in the preparations for the October seizure of power and in the dispersal of the Constituent Assembly, and serving as Chairman of the Petrograd *Cheka* (secret police).

19 F. P. Shipulinskii (1876–1942) was active in Social-Democratic organizations in Ekaterinoslav and other southern cities beginning in 1898, but according to one Soviet source, he joined the Mensheviks only in 1905 (*Tretii s'ezd RSDRP*, Moscow, 1959, pp. 350, 749–50). Left the Menshevik party in 1920, joined the Communist Party in 1932, and was ousted from it in 1936.

20 Konstantin Andreevich Popov (1876–1949) began his Social-Democratic activity in 1899, in the Petersburg Group for Self-Emancipation of Workers. He underwent many changes of position: at first inclined toward Economism, he became a supporter of *Iskra* in 1901; after the 1903 split declared himself a Menshevik, but joined the Bolsheviks three years later; left the Bolshevik Party in 1917 and joined the SD-Internationalists, only to rejoin the Communist Party in 1922. Until that year Popov's activity (both before and after 1917) had been centered in Omsk; after 1922, he occupied a variety of high political and academic positions in Moscow.

21 Boris Solomonovich Tseitlin [pseud. Baturskii, 1879–1920], Avram Moiseevich Ginzburg [pseud. Naumov, 1878–?], and his wife Anna Rozenfel'd were all born of wealthy Jewish families in Vitebsk, became active in the Bund in 1897, and founded the journal *Iuzhnyi rabochii* in Ekaterinoslav in 1900. They were arrested and exiled in 1902 and returned to political activity as Mensheviks in 1905. Tseitlin and Ginzburg were both "Liquidators" before World War I and Defensists during the war. Tseitlin-Baturskii served as a member of the Menshevik Organizational Committee and the editor of the journal *Strakhovanie rabochikh* [Workers' Insurance] in the years before 1917 and sat on the Menshevik Central Committee and on the editoral board of *Rabochaia gazeta* during the Revolution, but after October 1917 joined the minority of right-wing Mensheviks. Ginzburg terminated all illegal activity after his arrest in 1910 and wrote for the newspaper *Kievskaia mysl';* was Deputy Mayor of Kiev and Deputy Minister of Labor in 1917; ceased political activity after the October takeover and worked in several Soviet economic institutions in Moscow until his arrest in 1930; was sentenced in 1931, together with other defendants in the "Menshevik Trial," to ten years in exile.

22 V. K. Kurnatovskii (1868–1912) was by then a venerable veteran of the revolutionary movement: he had participated in Populist circles (in 1886), joined the Geneva Group for the Emancipation of Labor (1893), conducted SD work in Russia and Georgia (since 1897), and was serving a second term of exile in Eastern Siberia. In 1905 he was sentenced to hard labor for life for his role in organizing the Chita Soviet but escaped abroad in 1906 and died there.

Ninth interview

1 The Combat Organization was born in 1902 together with the Party of Social Revolutionaries and was headed by Evno Fishelevich Azef, a member of the Central Committee of the PSR; although financed by the party, the organization was ostensibly independent in choosing its targets and planning its attacks. The central organization and its local "brigades" were responsible for nearly 200 attacks (almost all of them successful) on tsarist officials; among them such important figures as the Ministers of Interior Plehve and Sipiagin and Grand Duke Sergei Aleksandrovich. The organization disintegrated in 1908 when it was revealed that Azef had been a double-agent working for the police. *See also* note on Plehve, Dan, Eighth Interview, 14.

2 Iurii Larin [pseudonym of Mikhail Aleksandrovich Lur'e, 1882–1932] was then in exile for his participation in the Crimean SD organization. He escaped from

exile in 1904 and began a long period of work in various Menshevik organizations; he never entirely joined the "Liquidationist" trend and, in 1911, was among the founders of the semiclandestine Initiative Group. During the revolutionary revival of 1912–14 he drew closer to Trotsky and his "centrist" position between the Mensheviks and the Bolsheviks, adopting Internationalism during World War I. He returned to Russia after February 1917 and tried to bring about a break between the Internationalist wing of Menshevism and the party's Revolutionary-Defensist majority, but in August joined the Bolshevik Party. After October he worked in Soviet economic institutions.

3 Lidia Dan speaks here of Aleksandr Savinkov, with whom she had an affair of the heart.

4 The *Skoptsy* [Castrated] were one of several sectarian religious groups which originated with the great schism in the Russian Orthodox Church in the second half of the seventeenth century. The *Skoptsy*, who practiced castration in order to foil temptation, appeared in the second half of the eighteenth century in several provinces around Moscow, and by the late nineteenth century they numbered many merchants in their ranks. They were organized into communities called "ships," each guided by a "helmsman" through whom the Spirit "spoke" during special ritualistic vigils. All of the schismatic and sectarian groups were subjected to some persecution by the tsarist state, especially those, like the *Skoptsy*, who were declared to be "pernicious."

5 The word is of Mongol derivation and means "runaway"; it was used in Eastern Siberia for the local peasantry of Russian origin.

6 No information regarding Bobinskii could be found. Mark Samoilovich Khinoi (1885–1968) had had only a formal elementary education and training as a typesetter. He had been operating illegal SD printing shops in various towns in the western provinces of Russia from 1901 until his arrest in 1903. After his return from exile in 1905, he joined the Mensheviks and worked in the Ekaterinoslav Soviet. During the next three years he was arrested several times, but he always escaped, and continuing to live illegally in St. Petersburg until finally, in 1908, he emigrated to France. In 1913, he settled in the United States, where he became a contributor to the Russian and Yiddish socialist press, including the Menshevik journal *Sotsialisticheskii vestnik*.

7 The Erfurt Program, drafted by Karl Kautsky, was adopted by the German Social-Democratic Party in 1891 and served as its platform until the collapse of Imperial Germany. The first part of the program outlined the Marxist view of social development and presented the socialist ideal of a complete transformation of society. The second part detailed the goals which the SDs should attempt to realize within the framework of capitalist society; these aims reflected the immediate political and economic interests of the workers.

8 *Pravo* [The Law] was established in 1898 by a group of Petersburg liberals; it began as a weekly on jurisprudence but in the fall of 1904 became a general political newspaper of pronounced liberal-constitutionalist tendencies. Its publisher, Professor V. M. Gessen, and most of its editors were among the founders and leaders of the Kadet Party.

9 *Nasha zhizn'* [Our Life], a general political daily, appeared in St. Petersburg from November 1904 to July 1906; it was close to the left wing of the Kadets and edited by V. V. Vodovozov.

10 The "broad movement" of January 1905 designates three simultaneous developments: the strike that had begun on January 2 at the Putilov Ironworks in St. Petersburg and which, by January 7, had engulfed most of the capital's factories; the week of frenzied activity in the branches of Gapon's "Assembly of Russian Factory and Mill Workers" that culminated on Sunday, January 9, in the workers' attempt to petition the tsar and the subsequent massacre of scores of unarmed men, women, and children; and finally, the general wave of strikes and demonstrations, which spread from Petersburg to Moscow and to other cities in the aftermath of that "Bloody Sunday."

11 Father Georgii Apolonovich Gapon (1870–1906) founded the Petersburg "Assembly of Russian Factory and Mill Workers" in February 1904 as a loyal organization, acting under police protection, for the cultural betterment of the workers. However, in the fall of 1904, the general social restiveness and the Assembly's unique status as a legal workers' organization helped turn its eleven branches into lively centers of working-class activity and involved the Assembly in the workers' struggle for economic improvement. In January 1905, Gapon supported the Putilov strike, initiated the general Petersburg strike and the political demands it promoted, was responsible for the idea of a petition to the tsar, and led the workers' fateful procession to the Winter Palace on January 9. The Social-Democratic organizations in St. Petersburg became aware of the Assembly's growing significance only on the eve of the Putilov strike. The Bolsheviks continued to condemn Gapon, while the Mensheviks were divided: their Petersburg Group criticized the Assembly, but Menshevik agitators in some of the city's districts followed the workers into the Assembly's halls. In fact, on the eve of "Bloody Sunday," the local Menshevik leader Somov [pseudonym of I. A. Peskin] tried to dissuade Gapon from the planned procession, but several other Mensheviks favored it and participated in it.

12 In the aftermath of "Bloody Sunday" the government decided to convene a commission of government officials and elected representatives of the capital's workers and employers to "determine the causes of workers' discontent." Senator N. V. Shidlovskii was chosen to head the Commission, and on February 7 he published the rules for the election of workers' representatives: On February 13, each factory was to elect its electors, and on February 18, 9 groups of electors were to choose their representatives to the Commission. Both the Mensheviks and the Bolsheviks vacillated between their opposition to this limited, government-initiated body and their desire to exploit the opportunity for agitation and organizational work. Because of the rapid turn of events there were no directives from the leaders in emigration and the local SD agitators (especially the Mensheviks among them) responded to the clear desire of the workers in the factory to go through the first stage of the elections. Later, however, the SDs induced the workers-electors to eschew participation in the second stage of the elections unless guaranteed the freedom to discuss their needs openly. On February 18, when a resolution in this spirit was denied by the government, the electors refused to continue with the elections and called for a general strike.

13 Virgilii Leont'evich Shantser [pseud. Marat, 1867–1911], a lawyer, had indeed been working for *Iskra* since 1900 (in Moscow). Following two years of Siberian exile (1902–1904), joined the Bolshevik organization in Moscow and was among the organizers of the insurrection in December 1905. Additional arrests and escapes led to a period of emigration (1907–1910) during which he joined other extremist Bolsheviks in the *Vpered* group.

14 In the Eleventh Interview Lidia Dan discusses in detail these "maximalist attitudes" which were prevalent also among some of the Mensheviks who wrote for the daily *Nachalo* in November and December of 1905.

15 According to the census of 1897, illiteracy was less universal than indicated by Lidia Dan – 79 percent for the country as a whole, 55 percent for urban population.

16 See above, Eighth Interview, note 8.

17 Martynov [pseudonym of Aleksandr Samuilovich Pikker, 1865–1935] began his revolutionary activity in the early 1880s in the People's Will but was in exile and military service from 1886 to 1899. After his release he worked at first in organizations connected with *Iuzhnyi rabochii*, then emigrated (1900), joined the Union of Russian Social Democrats Abroad, and in articles written for *Rabochee delo* attacked *Iskra* from an Economist point of view. However, after the split among *Iskra*'s editors, Martynov joined the Menshevik faction and remained one of its leading figures until 1918, contributing to all party publications and serving on all its central bodies. In 1905, he took an extremist-maximalist position in the

Menshevik newspaper *Nachalo*, and during World War I and the Revolution he was in the Internationalist wing of the party. After a period of political inactivity (1918–1922) he joined the Communist Party and became active in the Comintern.

Tenth interview

1 The *Iskra* editorial board elected by the Second Congress (which included Lenin, Plekhanov and Martov) never operated at full complement because of Martov's refusal to join it [*see* Dan, Fifth Interview, note 7]. In October 1903 Plekhanov, too, began to demand the cooptation of the three ousted editors and in reaction to this demand Lenin resigned his post as a co-editor. From that time and until it ceased publication in October 1905, *Iskra* was a Menshevik organ.

2 The "Third" Congress took place in London from April 12 to April 27, 1905. It was convoked by the Bolshevik-dominated Central Committee of RSDRP but was boycotted by the Mensheviks who, in turn, assembled some of their own supporters from Russia in Geneva during April and May 1905 and called that meeting the "First All-Russian Conference of Party Workers." These two assemblies were dedicated to the discussion of the tactical and organizational questions raised before the two factions by the events of early 1905.

3 Vikentii Anitsetovich Gutovskii [pseud. Evgenii Maevskii, 1875–1919] began his Social-Democratic activity in 1899 in the Petersburg Group for Self-Emancipation of Workers but was soon arrested and deported to his hometown of Tobol'sk, where he became active in the Siberian Committee which later elected him as a delegate to the "Third" Congress. Following his "defection" and participation in the Mensheviks' Geneva Conference, became one of the principal Menshevik activists in St. Petersburg, a member of the party's central bodies, and a contributor to several Menshevik publications. He was a "Liquidator" and a Defensist, worked in the Labor Group of the Central War-Industrial Committee during World War I, and belonged to the Menshevik Defensists in 1917 and 1918. In 1919, he became the editor of a Menshevik newspaper in Siberia and was shot by Kolchak's forces.

4 For an extensive discussion of this question see the Sixth Interview.

5 Lidia Dan probably refers to Martov's introduction to his brochure, "The Struggle Against the State of Siege in the Party" (dated February 1904), in which he explained his failure to argue against Lenin's organizational statutes on the eve of the Second Congress and ascribed this failure to his concern that *Iskra* appear united before the congress. He had intended, he wrote, to criticize specific points in Lenin's presentation at the congress.

6 S. I. Gusev [pseudonym of Iakov Davidovich Drabkin, 1874–1933], a former member of the Petersburg Union of Struggle and an SD organizer in Rostov-on-Don, was among Lenin's most loyal supporters during the Second Congress. He was later accused by the Mensheviks of having circulated a list, allegedly compiled by Martov and his supporters, containing Martov's "nominees" for the Central Committee (Aleksandrova, Levin, Rozanov, Trotsky, and Krokhmal, all considered "soft liners"). After the congress, he toured many cities in Southern Russia in an effort to enlist support for the Bolshevik position and in the coming years continued to support Lenin's position completely. Before 1917 and in the early years of Soviet rule he worked in various provincial organizations; after 1923 he occupied several important positions in the Communist Party.

7 Iu. Martov, *Ob odnom "nedostoianom" postupke (otvet' Leninu, Liadovu i Ko.)* [Regarding One "Mean" Action. A reply to Lenin, Liadov and Co.], Geneva, May 1904.

8 Ekaterina Mikhailovna Aleksandrova (1864–1943), a veteran of Populist and Social-Democratic groups in St. Petersburg and an *Iskra* member since 1902, was a member of the Organizational Committee for the Second Congress and was present at the congress itself where she favored the "Menshevik" position. After

the congress, she worked in the central Menshevik organizations, but following the 1905 revolution she ceased all political activity except for a brief return in 1912 as a supporter of Trotsky's *Pravda* group.

9 Andrei Ivanovich Zheliabov was one of the central figures in the People's Will and participated in several of its terroristic acts, including the assassination of Alexander II. He stood trial for this act and was executed on April 3, 1881.

10 Martin Nikolaevich Liadov [pseudonym of Mandel'shtam, 1872–1947] had begun his Social-Democratic activity in Moscow in 1892 and had spent five years in exile before fleeing abroad, where he aided Lenin in his struggle against the "Menshevik" editors of *Iskra* during the Second Congress and afterwards. In 1909, he joined the extremist group *Vpered*, but returned to Russia in 1911 and worked in legal workers organizations in Baku, where, in 1917, he was active in the Soviet as a "non-factional Social Democrat." He moved to Moscow in 1920, joined the Communist Party, and occupied several high positions in the field of education until 1932.

11 Nikolai Ernestovich Bauman (1873–1905) participated in several SD organizations: the Petersburg Union of Struggle (1896–7); the Union of Russian SDs Abroad (1899–1900); *Iskra* (he was its agent to the Moscow Committee in 1902–3). Represented the Moscow Committee at the Second Congress, where he joined the Bolshevik faction which then sent him to work in the Northern Bureau of CC. He was arrested three times, escaped twice, and was finally freed (on October 10, 1905) by the governor of Moscow province in response to the demands of demonstrators. He was killed during a demonstration, and his funeral (on October 20) turned into a huge political demonstration.

12 The "expropriations," i.e., the armed robberies carried out by SR and Bolshevik "Combat Brigades" for the purpose of financing their revolutionary activities, began during the period of disorder in 1905 and peaked in 1906 and 1907. They were condemned and prohibited by the Fourth and Fifth Congresses of RSDRP, were never acknowledged by the Bolsheviks, and caused sharp disagreement between the Bolsheviks and the Mensheviks and even among the Bolshevik leadership itself. The "expropriations" ended after the Bolsheviks were implicated in the famous robbery of the State Bank in Tiflis in June 1907.

13 *Samoupravlenie, samostoiatel'nost', samodeiatel'nost'* [lit. self-government, autonomy, self-activity] were terms used by the Mensheviks to express the need for the "active involvement" of workers in public affairs, especially in "their" party [i.e., RSDRP], as a means of ensuring the proletarian character of the party, and as a "school for the development of class consciousness in the proletariat." These concepts were developed by the Menshevik editors of *Iskra* following their 1903 split with Lenin and provided the doctrinal foundations for the work of the *praktiki* in 1907–14. *See* in particular P. B. Akselrod, "Ob'edinenie Rossiiskoi sotsialdemokratii i eia zadachi" and "K voprosu ob istochnike i znachenii nashikh organizatsionnykh raznoglasii," *Iskra*, nos. 55, 57, 68 (December 15, 1903; January 15 and June 25, 1904).

14 Pavel' Nikolaevich Miliukov (1859–1943), a prominent historian and a professor at Moscow University, belonged to the younger intelligentsia generation of Russian liberalism. Was among the founders of the constitutionalist journal *Osvobozhdenie* in 1901 and the Union of Liberation in 1903. Established the Kadet Party in 1905 and was its most widely recognized leader throughout its existence, representing it in the Third and Fourth Dumas and in the first cabinet of the Provisional Government in 1917.

15 Ivan Ivanovich Petrunkevich (1843–1928), a landowner from Chernigov province, became in the late 1870s a proponent of constitutionalism, first in the Chernigov zemstvo, and after his banishment from that province, in the Tver zemstvo. During the 1880s and 1890s he was the most outspoken of gentry liberals. He was among the founders of the Union of Liberation and the Kadet Party.

16 In late October 1904, the Second Congress of the Union of Liberation met in St. Petersburg and decided that under the spirit of "public confidence" declared by

the new Minister of Interior, Sviatopolk-Mirskii, the time was ripe to press for constitutional demands through the forthcoming Third Zemstvo Congress (scheduled to convene in St. Petersburg from November 6 to 9), through the district and provincial zemstvo assemblies which were scheduled to follow the congress, and finally, through a series of "banquets," which the Union's members were to organize in all major cities, beginning on November 20, 1904, the fortieth anniversary of Alexander II's judicial reforms. These meetings of zemstvo men and members of the professions called for constitutional reforms often with specific mention of a constitution and a constituent assembly. In two "Letters to the Party Organizations" in Russia (published as leaflets in November and December 1904) the Menshevik editors of *Iskra* called upon their followers to organize workers' demonstrations around the banquets for the purpose of lending their support to the political demands of the zemstva and the professional unions while at the same time impressing on them the more extensive political and social demands of the workers. However, Menshevik agitators in Russia often sought to use these demonstrations to show the workers the chasm that separated them from the zemstva.

17 Aleksei Ivanovich Kabtsan (1883–1924) had been active in the Odessa SD organization before he went to Geneva in 1905 and began working in the *Iskra* secretariat. He returned to Russia in the fall of 1905 and worked in the Samara Printers' Union. During World War I he supported Defensism and headed the Labor Group of the Samara War-Industrial Committee until his arrest in late 1916. During the 1917 Revolution he served as the Chairman of the Samara Soviet, Chairman of the Samara City Duma, and editor of the Samara SD organ *(Vechernaia zaria)*. After October he joined the right-wing minority of the Menshevik Party and supported the anti-Bolshevik regional governments of Samara and Ufa.

18 The Mutiny on the flagship of the Russian Black Sea Fleet began on June 15 off the shores of Odessa. Following an incident involving tainted meat rations, the sailors killed or imprisoned all their officers, but they failed in their attempts to turn the ship's guns on the government forces on shore. All but one of the other ships in the Fleet declined to join the mutiny and the Potemkin fled to Constanza, Rumania, where her crew sunk the ship and sought refuge on land. Despite its futile end the Potemkin mutiny aroused great hopes among the revolutionaries for similar insurrections in the army and the navy.

19 In July 1899, Plekhanov delivered a brief speech to the founding congress of the Second Socialist International; he concluded the speech with the prophecy: "The revolutionary movement in Russia can triumph only as a revolutionary movement of workers" (G. V. Plekhanov, *Sochineniia*, vol. IV, Moscow-Petrograd, 1923, p. 54).

20 Grigorii Iakovlevich Aronson (1887–1968) was drawn into Social-Democratic activity in 1902 while still a *gimnazium* student. Beginning in 1903 he was an active propagandist, first for the Bolsheviks, and from 1907 for the Bund. Aronson settled in Vitebsk only in 1913; had spent most of his earlier years in Gomel' and Minsk which, like Vitebsk, were situated in the Jewish Pale of Settlement; their large population of impoverished Jews provided the Bund with its strongest following. In Vitebsk, Aronson was the secretary of the workers' "Sick Fund," and in February 1917 was elected Chairman of the local Soviet and Council of Trade Unions. After October, he joined the right wing of the Menshevik Party but also continued his activity in the Bund and in various workers' organizations. He was expelled from the country in 1922, following two terms in Soviet prisons, and became a member of the Delegation Abroad of RSDRP [Mensheviks] (in which he represented the right wing) as well as a prolific contributor to the Yiddish and Russian press in New York.

21 After the fall of the tsarist regime, in February 1917, the Mensheviks emerged as the leaders of the Workers' and Soldiers' Soviets which sprang up in Petrograd and all over Russia. The soviets enjoyed the full support of the urban lower

classes, acted as their organs of self-government, and had to be reckoned with in every way. However, the Mensheviks were opposed to the soviets' taking power since they believed that this course would result in the isolation and consequent defeat of the working class. At the same time they also refused to participate in a coalition government with the "bourgeois" parties for fear of raising undue hopes among the workers. Only in May, when they came to believe that their participation alone could save the Provisional Government, did the Mensheviks decide to join a coalition cabinet. As a result, their freedom of political action was seriously curtailed, and when they failed to achieve peace and economic reforms, their leadership became compromised in the eyes of the workers.

Eleventh interview

1 Victor Adler (1852–1918) was the founder and leader of the Austrian Social-Democratic party.
2 In 1917, Kshesinskii Palace (formerly the residence of the tsar's mistress, the ballerina M. F. Kshesinskaia) served as the headquarters of the Bolshevik Party. In periods of upheavals, such as the July Days, workers and soldiers sympathetic to the Bolshevik slogans would gather in the Palace's courtyard to listen to speeches by Lenin and others.
3 The events immediately preceding and following the October Manifesto marked the high point of the 1905 revolution. These events began on October 8 with a strike by the Union of Railroad Employees and Workers. By October 15 a general strike, called by the Union of Unions [*see* note 12 below] had completely paralyzed the lines of communication throughout the country. To satisfy the strikers' demands and in order that peace may be restored in the country, the Tsar issued on October 17 an Imperial Manifesto which promised "to grant the people the immutable foundations of civil liberty, based upon genuine inviolability of the person and the freedoms of conscience, speech, assembly, and association; to admit immediately to participation in the State Duma ... [the elective body granted by the Tsar on August 6] those classes of the population who are at present entirely deprived of electoral rights . . .; to establish it as an immutable right that no law shall take effect without the approval of the State Duma." The Manifesto was widely interpreted as a charter of general political liberties and its publication marked the beginning of the "days of freedom": newspapers of every political opinion were openly published in defiance of the obligatory preliminary censorship (which was temporarily waived on November 24); various political and social organizations appeared and began to exercise the freedom of assembly even before it had been put into the law in March 1906; and the socialist parties, though still subject to arrest and harrassment, began working in the open. The limited amnesty of October 22 also encouraged many Social Democrats to return from their European emigration. At the center of the SD's activity in late October and November was the Petersburg Soviet (Council) of Workers' Deputies, which had been created on October 13 to direct the general strike in Petersburg, but which soon became the self-governing body of the city's workers. The SDs exercised strong influence over the Soviet though the workers' deputies refused to be bound by an official acceptance of the SD program. The SD leadership itself had initially favored concentration of all forces on the political struggle against tsarism, but became increasingly drawn into supporting the workers' economic struggle against their employers and, consequently, found itself fighting on two fronts: on October 29, the Soviet called for a strike in support of the workers' demand for an 8-hour working day but had to call it off on November 6; on November 1, it asked also for a general political strike to protest the expected court-martial of the Kronstadt mutineers and the imposition of martial law in Poland; this strike, too, remained confined chiefly to Petersburg and to its working class and demonstrated the Soviet's weakness; finally, on November 23, the

Soviet called also for a "financial boycott" against the government. On November 26, the government counterattacked with the arrest of the Soviet's titular head, G. S. Khrustalev-Nosar. There was no dramatic reaction on the part of the Soviet, and on December 2, while the Soviet was meeting in the hall of the Free Economic Society, the building was surrounded by troops and 190 deputies (including all of their principal leaders) were arrested. On December 7, a nationwide general strike was called to protest the arrests, but by this time the workers were exhausted and many of the professionals and employees who had struck in October for the liberal-constitutionalist goals of the Union of Unions did not join this time; the strike ended without any concessions from the government. In the wake of the "December strike" there occurred an armed uprising in Moscow which was led by the Moscow Social Democrats and the Moscow Soviet. The uprising began on December 10 and was only crushed on December 17 after loyal troops (among them the Semenovskii Guard Regiment) had been brought into the city. During these events and following them, the authorities, often aided by employers, moved on to curtail the newly-gained freedoms: they arrested members of soviets, searched and disarmed workers, and closed down radical newspapers, thus bringing the "Days of Freedom" to an end.

4 *Nachalo* [The Beginning] was published legally in Petersburg from November 13 to December 2, 1905 (16 issues appeared altogether) and was the principal organ of the Mensheviks. The editorial board included Dan, Iordanskii, Martov, Martynov, Potresov, Parvus, and Trotsky (see A. M. Bourguina, *Russian Social Democracy. The Menshevik Movement. A Bibliography*, Stanford, California, 1968, p. 330).

5 Alexander Parvus [pseudonym of Israil Lazarovich Gelfand, 1869–1924], a Russian Jew who had settled in Germany, won distinction among German Social Democrats in the 1890s for his writing on economics and Marxist thought and for his polemics against the reformist trend. He wrote for *Iskra* both before and after the 1903 split, returning in October 1905 to Russia where he and Trotsky gained control of the Petersburg radical-liberal daily *Russkaia gazeta* and transformed it into a popular newspaper with a strongly radical line. After his arrest in 1906 and a term of Siberian exile, he returned to Germany and combined journalistic and propaganda work with somewhat suspect business dealings. (During World War I he used the profits from his black-marketeering to publish the socialist-patriotic journal *Die Glocke*.)

6 The theory of "permanent revolution," as it was developed by Trotsky and Parvus in November 1905, postulated that the workers' role in the Russian revolution would grow in dominance until the proletariat would have to assume power and, once in power, to implement a socialist program. Trotsky wrote that "a revolutionary continuity would thus be established between the minimal and the maximal programs of Social Democracy," i.e., between the program for the "bourgeois revolution" and that for the "socialist revolution" ("Sotsial-demokratiia i revoliutsiia," *Nachalo*, November 25, 1905). The theory's success relied on the strength of the proletariat, the support of the peasantry, and the establishment of socialism throughout Europe.

7 In an unpublished section of this interview Lidia Dan mentioned that she had known Saltykov since her student days. "He was a student and a prominent student activist in Petersburg. In addition, he was a good practical worker; later he was involved in publishing and managed rather well. After that, he was in the Second Duma and was even condemned to penal servitude. I think that he was a very decent person politically and had a great desire for acting in the forefront. I imagine that he would have been just as active in any other progressive party besides the Social Democrats. Or perhaps not. It was primarily his student past that attached him to Social Democracy – he had grown up in it."

8 Boris Sapir, "Predtechi i zarozhdenie menshevizma" [The Precursors and origin of Menshevism], an unpublished study written for the Inter-University Project on the History of the Menshevik Movement, Columbia University.

9 The Fourth Congress of RSDRP took place in Stockholm, in April and May 1906, with both Mensheviks and Bolsheviks in attendance; it was intended to define the lessons of 1905 and to formulate the party's plans for the next revolutionary outbreak. *See also* Dan, Twelfth Interview, note 4.

10 In the early part of his autobiography, Martov recounts his childhood memories of the 1881 pogrom in Odessa (pp. 18–19). He adds that years later, in 1905, he was "deeply shaken" by the sight and the stories of Jewish refugees from all over Russia whom he met at the Vilno railroad station.

11 Axelrod's idea was expounded for the first time in a pamphlet entitled "The People's Duma and the Workers' Congress" [*Narodnaia duma i rabochii s'ezd*] published in the fall of 1905. He hoped to make use of the new opportunities for a mass working-class movement and called on the Social Democrats to launch an agitational campaign for the election of workers' deputies to an all-Russian congress; he expected that the election campaign and the discussions at the congress itself when it met, would involve broad segments of the working class in political activity. The idea of a workers' congress gained prominence among Mensheviks in 1906 but was rejected by the Fifth Congress of RSDRP in 1907; it was revived again in 1916 by the leaders of the Labor Groups in the War-Industrial Committees, who were among the founders of the Petrograd Soviet in February 1917.

12 The Union of Unions was founded in May 1905 by representatives of 14 all-Russian unions (of lawyers, teachers, and other liberal professions). Its program was dictated by the Union of Liberation and consisted of political demands, the most important of which was the demand for the "four-tail" election formula (universal, equal, and direct suffrage and secret balloting). Under the chairmanship of Miliukov it united oppositional groups ranging from zemstvo activists to railroad workers, but its unity collapsed in the heated atmosphere of the summer of 1905 and especially so after the acceptance by Miliukov of the first Manifesto on the elections to the State Duma (August 6). The majority of the Union (claiming 100,000 members in the autumn) continued to press for the "four-tail" formula, primarily through a planned general strike which finally took place in October 1905. In the aftermath of that strike and the October Manifesto, the Union began losing its influence and its remaining leaders broke into two groups: the Prokopovich-Kuskova "economist" group and a populist group that later founded the Party of People's Socialists (NSs).

13 Lidia Dan's statement on the role of the Masons in the Union of Liberation should be qualified. All memoirists and historians who have written on this subject agree that Russian Masonry revived only after 1905 (it had been completely banned by Alexander I). There is evidence that three of the 20 founders of the Union of Liberation became Masons; but only after the Union had disintegrated. Of the three, only two (Kuskova and Prokopovich) belonged to the Russian "political Masonry," which according to Kuskova's letters to Lidia Dan (published in G. Aronson, *Rossiia nakanune revoliutsii*, New York, 1962, pp. 138–140) was conceived as a replacement for the Union of Liberation and its coalitionary strategy.

14 Nikolai Vladislavovich Volskii [pseud. Valentinov, 1879–1964], *Encounters with Lenin*, London and New York, 1968 (translation of the Russian *Vstrechi s Leninym*, New York, 1953).

15 *Severnyi golos* [The Northern Voice] began its publication after the Menshevik organ in St. Petersburg *(Nachalo)* and its Bolshevik counterpart *(Novaia zhizn')* were closed down by the tsarist authorities. Four issues appeared (the fourth under the name *Nash golos*) from December 6 to 18, 1905.

16 B. M. Knuniants [pseud. Radin, 1878–1911] began his revolutionary activity in 1897 in the Petersburg Union of Struggle and later worked in various SD organizations in Baku. As the Baku Committee's delegate to the Second Congress he supported Lenin's position, and after the split in the party participated in the Bolshevik Petersburg organization (in 1905 he served also in the Executive Committee of the Petersburg Soviet). In 1908 he escaped from exile and returned to

Baku, drew close to the Menshevik "Liquidators," and contributed to their journal *Nasha zaria.*

Twelfth interview

1 The elections to the First Duma took place in March and April 1906, and as Lydia Dan explains, they were boycotted by the Bolsheviks who chose to concentrate their efforts on the organization of an expected armed insurrection. But the Mensheviks did not campaign actively either, with the important exception of Georgia, where the elections were held at a later date and where the Mensheviks won all of the Duma seats.

2 The term "Liquidationism" was coined by Lenin in 1909 and applied by his followers to the Mensheviks whom they accused of advocating the "liquidation" of the Social Democratic party as a revolutionary organization. This accusation grew out of the Menshevik call for an open labor party and open, self-managed workers' organizations in the aftermath of the revolution of 1905–7. Some Mensheviks added to that vision a rejection of the old conspiratorial, sectarian organizations of the intelligentsia (which had in any case disintegrated in the period of reaction from 1907–11) and an overly optimistic view of Russia's chances for an "organic," nonrevolutionary transformation into democracy.

3 Petr Pavlovich Maslov (1867–1946), an economist of Social-Democratic leanings who later became a Menshevik (1903), a "Liquidator" (1907–1914), and a Defensist (1914–1917), always remained detached from underground work, participating instead in Legal Marxist publications at the turn of the century and, later, acting as the publisher of the Menshevik-sponsored series on the history of the 1905 revolution (*Obshchestvennoe dvizhenie v Rossii v nachale xx veka* [The Social Movement in Russia at the Beginning of the 20th Century], Petersburg, 1909–12). Both his scholarly work and his contributions to the party's program were in the area of agriculture and included the Menshevik plan for the "municipalization" of land. A member of Plekhanov's extreme Defensist group in 1917, he left all political activity after the Bolshevik victory and continued his scholarly work to become, in 1929, a member of the Academy of Science of USSR.

4 At the Fourth Congress of the RSDRP which took place in Stockholm in April and May 1906, the party was formally reunited under one Central Committee. The Mensheviks, who had the majority at the "Unification" Congress, succeeded in having most of their program adopted. *See also* Dan, Eleventh Interview, note 9.

5 The Menshevik Party was never officially granted legality by the tsarist government, but its electoral activities were silently tolerated during the election campaigns for the Duma.

6 In his pamphlet *Regarding One "Unworthy" Action* Martov emphasized the "ethical principle which ought to guide a socialist in his relations with the party and his comrades" (*Ob odnom "nedostoianom" postupke,* p. 10). See also Dan, Tenth Interview, pp. 180–1 for the circumstances surrounding the writing of this pamphlet.

7 Martov wrote: "Today, the 'toleration' of forgers; tomorrow – free access to the Degaevs" (*Ob odnom "nedostoianom" postupke,* p. 1). Sergei Degaev was one of the leaders of the "Combat Organization" of the People's Will who had agreed to serve as a police informer in 1882 and was responsible for the arrest of Vera Figner and many other members of the organization in 1883.

8 Roman Vatslavovich Malinovskii (1878–1918), a metalworker and a member of the Bolshevik CC, was elected to the Fourth Duma and chaired its Bolshevik faction until his sudden resignation in May 1914. Documents captured after the revolution of February 1917 substantiated the suspicions which several Mensheviks and Bolsheviks had had about Malinovskii – it turned out that he had been a police agent all along, had been elected to the Duma with the help of the police, and had later resigned only because of his dismissal from its service. He was tried and executed in 1918.

Chapter 2. Boris Nikolaevsky

First interview

1 The ceremony of ordination of priests into the Orthodox Church.
2 According to a law of 1889, Land Captains [*zemskie nachal'niki*] were appointed by the government as superintendents of the local peasantry and were given administrative and judicial powers in the village; were usually chosen from the local gentry.
3 Konstantin Dmitrievich Ushinskii (1824–70), writer and reformer in the field of education.
4 The conference, which took place in Vienna in August 1912, was convoked by the Mensheviks and Trotsky's *Pravda* group in an effort to unite all of the anti-Leninist factions in the RSDRP (the Leninists had met earlier in 1912 in Prague). The "August Bloc" which was formed at the conference had already shown signs of disunity in 1913 and collapsed completely with the onset of World War I.
5 Aleksei Rykov (1881–1938) had worked in various cities for *Iskra* and the underground Bolshevik organization and had been a member of the Bolshevik Central Committee. After the February revolution returned from emigration and was one of the leaders of the Moscow Bolshevik organization. In spite of some disagreement with Lenin headed the Supreme Council on the People's Economy, and later, the Council of People's Commissars. Was demoted in 1930 because of his opposition to Stalin, arrested in 1937, and executed in 1938.
6 The "Red Guards" – the detachments of armed workers organized between February and July 1917 and with increasing speed after the Kornilov Affair in August 1917 – were moved to the front after October; they fought the advancing German army and later formed the backbone of the new Red Army.
7 The attack on Kronstadt in March 1921 ended the revolt of this Baltic sea port against the Soviet government. Formerly, Kronstadt had supplied the military force for the Bolshevik seizure of power in October 1917.
8 Acronym for *Sovet narodnogo khoziaistva* [Council of the People's Economy]; B.N. had in mind the Supreme Council of the People's Economy [VSNKh], which Rykov headed during 1918–21.
9 Aleksandr Vasilevich Kruglov (1853–1915); Pavel' Vladimirovich Zasodimskii (1843–1912). *See also* Dan, First Interview, note 22 for a definition of the "*narodnik* writers.*"
10 Groups of extreme right-wing elements who saw themselves as self-appointed defenders of the Russian state and church; involved in the early 1900s with anti-Jewish pogroms. After the October Manifesto of 1905 they became part of the organized Right and increased their activity, attacking not only Jews but also students, liberals, and all those suspected of "revolutionary" sympathies.
11 A journal of general readership dedicated to popular history, nature, and travel.

Second interview

1 The two-century-old fortress of St. Petersburg (construction began in 1703) where opponents of the tsars were imprisoned; most of the famous revolutionaries of the nineteenth century found their way there.
2 The Decembrists were the organizers of an abortive uprising against Nicholas I on December 14, 1825, upon his accession to the throne. They came mainly from the ranks of the liberal-minded officers of the Guards and had been influenced by the ideas of the Enlightenment and the French Revolution; their plans for Russia included various constitutional and agrarian reforms but their loosely organized "secret societies" were easily crushed, their leaders executed, and nearly 100 were exiled to Siberia. Nonetheless, their lofty ideals, heroism, and suffering were

celebrated in literature and art and they came to serve as models for the revolutionary intelligentsia later in the century.

3 B. N. uses here the term "realist" to designate a student from the Realschule.

4 Mikhail Aleksandrovich Vedeniapin (b. 1879) had become involved in the students' protest in 1901 and had joined the SRs during a stay abroad. He led the Samara SRs in 1905, for which activity he was sentenced in 1906 to several years of hard labor. As a member of the SR Central Committee in 1917 adopted a staunchly Defensist position and after the October seizure of power fought against the Bolsheviks in the Samara area. Later he renounced the SR struggle against Soviet power, volunteered to fight with the Red Army in Poland, and during the Trial of the SRs in 1922 his 10-years hard-labor sentence was commuted. During the 1920s he wrote for the journal of the Society of Political Prisoners, *Katorga i ssylka. See also* the Sixth Interview with Nikolaevskii.

5 Thomas Mayne Reid (1818–1883) and Gustave Aimard [pseudonym of Olivier Gloux, 1818–1883] were British and French novelists, respectively, who wrote stories of the American frontier and the Mexican wars; both were widely read at the turn of the century in Russia.

6 Vsevolod Vladimirovich Krestovskii (1840–1895) wrote poetry in the "democratic-realistic" style of the 1860s but later, in the 1870s, turned to novels and wrote in the genre of the "reactionary novelists," satirizing the young generation and new radical ideas; the usual story of that genre pitted an aristocratic hero against Nihilism and Jewish or Polish intrigue.

7 General Petr Semenovich Vannovskii (1822–1904) was appointed Minister of Education in March 1901 in an effort to end unrest in the institutions of higher education (two years earlier he had quelled student demonstrations by ordering the troops to shoot into the crowd). Resigned after one year, when his draconian "Provisional Rules" caused only greater unrest; his only durable "reform" put an end to the teaching of Greek in Russian *gimnazia.*

8 Evgenii Nikolaevich Chirikov (1864–1932) wrote numerous stories about the life of the intelligentsia in provincial towns. In the 1890s and early 1900s these stories were published in the "thick" journals of both Populist and Marxist tendencies. Emigrated after October 1917.

9 *Samarskii vestnik* [Samara Herald], a local provincial daily, was taken over in 1896 by a group of SDs headed by P. P. Maslov. Struve and Tugan-Baranovskii were also among the contributors.

10 Upon rereading these interviews B. N. added the following information: "Vasilii Petrovich Artsybushev was a disciple of Zaichnevskii's, of *Nabat* [a Geneva journal established in 1875 by the radical Populist P. N. Tkachev who urged the Russian intelligentsia to raise the Russian countryside in rebellion—ed.]. He was descended from a noble family of military men, had graduated from the Orlov Military Academy, and became one of the first *Nabatovtsy* of the 1870s. He was arrested, exiled, and wandered around Siberia for some twenty years. When he settled in Samara, he had already become a Social Democrat and was associated with Krzhizhanovskii, the chief figure in the Eastern Bureau of the Central Committee, previously the Eastern Bureau of *Iskra.* Martov's sister, Nadezhda Osipovna, had also been in Samara but I didn't know these people personally though I was told a great deal about them since I was very interested and was a good listener." G. M. Krzhizhanovskii (1872–1959) had been a member of the Petersburg Union of Struggle in the 1890s, was close to Lenin during their exile in Siberia, and became one of *Iskra*'s principal agents, carrying on communications through the Samara zemstvo board where he was employed as an engineer. Was active in the Bolshevik Party throughout its history and after 1920 held a series of high-ranking positions in Soviet institutions concerned with the economy and energy.

11 The pamphlet, published in Geneva in 1903 by the League of Russian SDs Abroad, reproduced Plekhanov's lecture, on "The People and the Intelligentsia in the Poetry of N. A. Nekrasov," delivered at a memorial meeting held in Geneva on

January 10, 1903, in commemoration of the twenty-fifth anniversary of Nekrasov's death (*Sochineniia*, 2nd ed., 1925, vol. 10, pp. 373–392).

12 Herzen, the father of Russian socialism and the most important revolutionary writer of the 1840s and 1850s, was the illegitimate son of an aristocratic Russian nobleman, I. A. Iakovlev, and his German mistress.

13 The term *raznochintsy* (literally, "various ranks") designated people who had left the social estate of their birth (i.e., gentry, townspeople, peasantry, and clergy) but had not formally entered another legal class; in the second half of the nineteenth century was often used to describe the professional intelligentsia.

14 Pavel' Ivanovich Preobrazhenskii (1874–1944).

15 In February–March 1901, and again in the same months in 1902, large student strikes and demonstrations took place in the universities of Petersburg, Moscow, Kiev, Kharkov, and Kazan. Most of these began as protests against Vannovskii's "Provisional Rules" but ended up presenting general political demands.

16 For more details on Bekenskii see the Third Interview with Nikolaevskii, p. 241.

17 Kliment Arkad'evich Timiriazev (1843–1920), a prominent Russian botanist at the Petrov-Razumovsk Academy in Moscow and later at Moscow University, wrote many articles and books that popularized the evolutionary theories of Darwin; his book *Life of the Plants* (1878) was published in numerous editions in Russian and other languages.

18 The *Reading Library* [*Biblioteka dlia chteniia*], a popular journal of the 1830s (published 1834–1865), featured articles on nature, folklore, scientific topics, as well as works by major Russian writers.

19 Nikolai Maksimovich Minskii (1855–1937) was one of the forerunners of the school of literary Symbolism in Russia in the late 1880s and 1890s, although today he is not regarded as having been a major contributor to that school of writing.

20 Nikolai Gerasimovich Pomialovskii (1835–1863) was one of the notable "*raznochintsy* writers"; his most famous work, *Seminary Sketches* (1862–3), was based on first-hand knowledge of the brutality of scholastic life in Orthodox seminaries and provided a good example of literature's concern to depict with grim realism every aspect of Russian life.

21 Leonid Nikolaevich Andreev (1871–1919) and Stepan Gavrilovich Skitalets [pseudonym of Petrov, 1869–1941] contributed to *Znanie* [Knowledge], which was under the editorship of Gorkii; the journal promoted literature of a strong social concern. Forty issues appeared between 1903 and 1913.

Third interview

1 *Zhizn'* [Life], a literary-political journal published in Petrograd from 1897–1901 (and thereafter in London and Geneva), was controlled by the "Legal Marxists." Among its contributors were Tugan-Baranovskii, Struve, and more rarely Lenin, as well as many leading writers (Gorkii, Chekhov, Skitalets, Chirikov, Bunin, and others).

2 *See* Dan, Seventh Interview, note 5.

3 Martov's pamphlet "The Workers' Cause in Russia" [*Rabochee delo v Rossii*] was published twice (anonymously in 1899 and under his name in 1903) by groups close to *Iskra*. The pamphlet "Red Banner in Russia" [*Krasnoe znamia v Rossii*] was published by *Iskra* in December 1900 with an introduction by Axelrod.

4 Veniamin Pavlovich Bulatov (b. 1879), a metalworker from Sormovo, had been involved in Social Democratic circles since 1899; after repeated arrests was placed under police surveillance in Samara (in 1902) but was rearrested in 1903, again for Social Democratic activity, and exiled to Eastern Siberia.

5 *Narodnichestvo*, or Populism, found its most active manifestation in the movement "To The People" in the 1870s (*see* Dan, First Interview, note 24); its failure led to disagreement in the ranks of the revolutionary intelligentsia over the tactics to be followed in the political struggle against the tsarist regime, with one

wing (the People's Will) turning to political terrorism; it was members of that party (the *Narodovoltsy*) who eventually assassinated Alexander II in 1881.

6 Aleksandr Ivanovich Levitov (1835–1877) spent most of his life wandering all over Russia and wrote stories on the life of homeless tramps and pilgrims and on the miseries and ignorance of the peasantry.

7 *See* Nikolaevskii, Second Interview, note 10.

8 The anti-Jewish pogrom in Kishinev in Bessarabia stirred public opinion in Russia and abroad not only because of the degree of its violence but also because it was condoned, if not actually encouraged, by the government itself; it began on Easter Day (April 6) 1903, and lasted for two whole days before the authorities intervened to stop the riots; hundreds of Jews were killed or injured, and their homes and businesses were ransacked. The April 1903 strike at the state-owned armor factory in the town of Zlatoust in the Urals was also the scene of unusual violence; units commanded by the Governor of Ufa Province, N. N. Bogdanovich, fired into a crowd of workers, killing 65 and wounding 250; it resulted in widespread workers' protests and the assassination of Bogdanovich.

9 *See* Nikolaevskii, Second Interview, note 7.

10 Fedor Gardenin was an agronomist with the Ufa zemstvo. At least three of his children are reported to have been very active in Social Democratic, and later Bolshevik organizations: Maria (born 1880) was arrested in 1901 while attending the Women Courses in Petersburg; returned to Ufa and worked for the zemstvo; eventually became involved first with SR and then SD circles. Boris (born 1881) was a member of the Ufa Committee of Social Democrats until his expulsion in the fall of 1903; was later convicted of some involvement with the assassination of Bogdanovich. Sergei (born 1883) worked in 1902–3 for the Ufa zemstvo, became involved in SD circles, and was a local agent for *Iskra*. All three worked later in Bolshevik organizations and after 1917 in Soviet institutions.

11 Vasilii Viktorovich Leonovich (1875–1932) contributed to many Populist publications of the 1890s, often under the pseudonym Angarskii or Viktorov.

12 Roman Emil'evich Tsimmerman [pseud. Gvozdev, 1866–1900] published articles in Legal-Marxist and Liberal-Populist journals at the turn of the century and was the chief editor of *Samarskii vestnik*. His views on the peasant economy were laid down in his work *Kulachestvo-rostovshchichestvo; ego obshchestvenno-ekonomicheskoe znachenie* [Kulachestvo and Usury; Its Social-Economic Significance], published in 1898.

13 The executive boards [*upravy*] of the zemstva were elected by the district and provincial zemstvo assemblies to carry on the business of local government; their chairmen had to be approved by the provincial governor and the Interior Minister, respectively, but their members were often drawn from the liberal-minded professionals who headed the zemstva's departments of statistics, health, education, etc.

14 *Novoe slovo* [New Word] was acquired by Struve and a group of Social Democrats in the winter of 1896–97 and was published in Petrograd until it was closed down by the government in December 1897. *See* Dan, Fourth Interview, note 37 on *Nachalo*.

15 Martov's article, *Narodnichestvo, prezhde i teper'* [Populism, Before and Now] was published in *Novoe slovo*, November–December 1897, under the pseud. A. Egorov. Potresov's article, signed by him and published in *Nachalo*, no. 1/2, 1899, was entitled *O nasledstve i naslednikakh* [On Heritage and Heirs].

16 B. N. refers here to Lenin who wrote at that time for *Nachalo* under the pseudonym V. Il'in.

17 Elsewhere in these interviews B. N. relates that the younger brother, Ibniamin, had also begun his political career as a Social Democrat but later became active in Muslim political groups which he represented in the Third Duma. Ibragim remained loyal to Social Democracy.

18 B. N. probably has in mind the 12 issues of *Narodnaia volia*, published underground by the Party of the People's Will between 1879 and 1885, or the 7 issues of *Listok narodnoi voli* published by the same party between 1880–1886.

19 *Za sto let, 1880–1896*, compiled by Vladimir L'vovich Burtsev, and published by the Russian Free Press Fund in London in 1897 (with the English subtitle "A Century of Political Life in Russia, 1800–1896"), reproduced important proclamations and other documents related to the revolutionary movement; the second half of the book was a chronological record of events which noted the dates of arrests, trials, the establishing and the closing down of journals, and the appearance of important publications.

20 Mikhail Petrovich Dragomanov (1841–1895), a Ukrainian historian, ethnographer, and publicist; settled abroad in 1876 and published works advocating Ukrainian cultural and political autonomy, and calling for support of the zemstvo liberals in Russia. His memoir, *Zhit'e i slovo* [Life and Word], appeared in 1894.

21 Nikolai Ivanovich Novikov (1744–1818), writer, editor and dean of Russia's literary life during the reign of Catherine the Great; sought to create Russian national culture and promoted the education of the lower classes. Was imprisoned by Catherine in 1792 and even after his release by her successor, Paul I (in 1796), was not allowed to reopen his schools and publishing houses.

22 A Tun (Thun), *Istoriia revoliutsionnykh dvizhenii v Rossi* [A History of Revolutionary Movement in Russia], Geneva, 1903.

23 Aleksandr Pavlovich Serebrovskii (1884–1938), the son of a *Narodovolets* exile from Ufa, joined the revolutionary movement in his early youth and became a Bolshevik in 1903. During a period of emigration (1908–1911) studied engineering and, from 1920 on, held prominent positions in the oil and gold industries of the Soviet Union. B. N. adds: "He was a liberal whom the Mensheviks [in the Soviet Union] huddled around, and he was executed."

24 B. N. refers here to the militant political strategies, the close contacts between the Social Democratic intelligentsia and the workers, and the regional (rather than local) orientation – all of which were associated with the journal *Iuzhnyi rabochii* [Southern Worker].

25 During his short career in the Russian revolutionary movement Sergei Genadievich Nechaev (1847–1882) made his name synonymous with political terror and a strict revolutionary organization, but eventually discredited his very methods by murdering in 1869 one of his own followers in the Secret Society. Was arrested for the murder and ended his days in a tsarist prison completely repudiated by the revolutionary movement.

26 *Otechestvennye zapiski* [Notes of the Fatherland], published in Petersburg from 1839–1884, enjoyed two periods of immense popularity and influence over the revolutionary-democratic intelligentsia: in the first decade of its existence, when it was in the hands of the "westernizers," under the strong influence of Belinskii, and published works by Herzen, Nekrasov, Turgenev, and Lermontov; and again, from 1868–1884, when it was edited by Nekrasov (and after his death by Mikhailovskii) and published works by Ostrovskii, Uspenskii, and Pisarev among others. Though close in view to the Populists, the editors allowed for a broad range of opinions in the journal.

27 *Domostroi* [Household Manual], a mid-sixteenth century book of rules on the proper performance of religious duties, the upbringing of children, and general everyday living; it reflected the conservative mores of townsmen and merchants in Muscovite Russia.

Fourth interview

1 *Delo* [The Cause], a literary-political monthly of great influence among the "democratic" intelligentsia, was published in Petersburg from 1866 to 1888. Among its contributors were Pisarev, Lavrov, Shelgunov, Reshetnikov, and Uspenskii.

2 Valentin Ivanovich Khaustov (b. 1885), a metal-turner of peasant origins, was elected to the Fourth Duma by the General Assembly of Electors in the province of Ufa. He belonged to the Duma's SD faction and after its split to the Menshevik faction.

3 Grigorii Andreevich Gershuni (1870–1908) was one of the founders of the Party of Socialist Revolutionaries and the first head of its legendary Combat Organization. He was arrested in 1903 and sentenced to death (later commuted to life imprisonment) for his role in organizing daring acts of political terror.

4 Lenin's book, a scholarly study entitled "The Development of Capitalism in Russia" [*Razvitie kapitalizma v Rossii*] was published in Petersburg in 1899.

5 The reference is most probably to the series of articles entitled "Types of Capitalist and Agrarian Evolution" [*Tipy kapitalisticheskoi i agrarnoi evoliutsii*], published in 1900 in the Populist journal *Russkoe bogatstvo* (issues nos. 4–8 and 10). Another article by Chernov, entitled "Toward the Question of Capitalist and Agrarian Evolution" [*K voprosu o kapitalisticheskoi i agrarnoi evoliutsii*] was published in the eleventh issue of the same journal.

6 A. Kovrov [pseudonym of Grigorii Aleksandrovich Grossman, b. 1863] wrote for both Marxist and Populist journals at the turn of the century. Later, he was close to the Mensheviks and left Russia after 1917.

7 Evgenii Andreevich Solov'ev [pseud. Andreevich, 1863–1905], critic and publicist, wrote for a number of journals around the turn of the century. Though not a Marxist, he was critical of the Populists and published (in 1899) a series of nine articles on the intelligentsia of the 1870s in the Legal-Marxist journal *Zhizn'*.

8 In the summer of 1902, peasant disturbances broke out all over southern Russia but with particular ferocity in the provinces of Kharkov and Poltava in the Ukraine and along the Volga.

9 The reference is to the article published in January 1899 in the Legal-Marxist journal *Zhizn'* (no. 1, part 2) under the title "The Alleged Contradictions of the Labor Theory of Value" [*Mnimyia protivorechiia trudovoi teorii stoimosti*].

10 E. A. Solov'ev, *D. I. Pisarev: ego zhizn' i literaturnaia deiatel'nost'* [D. I. Pisarev: His Life and Literary Activity], St. Petersburg, 1899.

11 A novel, published in Moscow in 1908. *See also* Dan, Seventh Interview, note 5.

12 Two Petersburg newspapers of liberal tendencies which began publication on the eve of 1905. *Nasha zhizn'* [Our Life] was published daily from November 6, 1904 to July 11, 1906 and was close to the left wing of the new Kadet Party. *Syn otechestva* [Son of the Fatherland], also a daily, was published from December 18, 1904 to December 2, 1905; was controlled at first by the editors of *Russkoe bogatstvo*, but in November 1905 became the organ of the SRs.

13 Aleksei Aleksandrovich Lopukhin (1864–1928) was the Director of Police from 1902–1905; in early January 1905, in a report submitted to the Council of Ministers, argued that the Police could not cope with the revolutionary movement. After his dismissal supplied secret information to various revolutionaries and sympathizers: the text of his 1905 report was published for example by the Bolsheviks in Geneva; he gave materials documenting the government's involvement in pogroms in 1906 to the lawyer representing the arrested members of the Petersburg Soviet; finally, he also provided Burtsev with information regarding the double-agent Azef. He was sentenced to exile in 1909 for all of these activities; was later pardoned and lived abroad. B. N. added that Lopukhin's widow had told him of a conversation between her husband and Count Witte at which she heard the latter say "that Nicholas would destroy Russia, that his policies would lead to utter ruin, and that he had to be removed."

Fifth interview

1 Sofia L'vovna Perovskaia (1853–1881) participated in several Populist circles of the 1870's and in the movement "To the People" (in the province of Samara). In

1878 he joined the revolutionary party *Zemlia i volia* [Land and Freedom], became one of its leaders and underground operators and, together with A. I. Zheliabov, participated in the assassination of Alexander II in March, 1881 (for which they were both executed).

2 Aleksandr Konstantinovich Solov'ev (1846–1879), a Populist, became a member of *Zemlia i volia* in 1876 and worked among the peasants of the Volga region in 1877–78; he tried to assassinate Alexander II on his own initiative on April 12, 1879, but failed and was executed.

3 Iosif Fedorovich Dubrovinskii (1877–1913), who headed the Samara SD Committee at that time, had been active in Populist circles (1893–95) and SD workers' organizations in Moscow and Kaluga (1896–97), and had served time in Siberia where he formed ties with the *Iskra* circle. After the split in the RSDRP he considered himself a Bolshevik but favored a "reconciliation" with the Mensheviks. In 1913 he was arrested and sentenced to a term in Siberia, but committed suicide in order to avoid slow death from tuberculosis.

4 Konkordiia Nikolaevna Samoilova (1876–1921) became a Social Democrat while attending the Women Courses in Petersburg in the late 1890s. She joined the *Iskra* organization in 1903 and began working in several local Bolshevik organizations in 1905, including Baku and Lugansk where she married another Bolshevik, A. A. Samoilov. In 1912 she became the secretary of the Bolshevik newspaper *Pravda* and an organizer of women workers; she continued as organizer after 1917. She died during the cholera epidemic in the Volga region.

5 Nikolai Vasilevich Shelgunov (1824–1891), a professor at the Petersburg Institute of Forestry, became close to Mikhailovskii and Chernyshevskii and wrote undergound leaflets for the revolutionary circles of the 1860s. He was arrested in 1863 and spent many years in prisons and exile, during which he wrote for the "democratic" journals of the time. His funeral in 1891 was the occasion for a mass political demonstration.

6 Elsewhere in this interview, B. N. reports that Konovalov became a telegraph operator for the railroads in the town of Nikolaev in Saratov province and an aspiring writer; that he spent time in solitary confinement which destroyed him psychologically; that he eventually turned an informer for the Secret Police but tried to break off and finally, in 1911, committed suicide. *See also* the discussion of this case by Iu. P. Denike in his Second Interview, p. 313; Fifth Interview, p. 358; and Seventh Interview, p. 388.

7 *See* Dan, Tenth Interview, note 16.

8 *See* Dan, Tenth Interview, note 2.

9 Petr I. Voevodin (1884–1964) worked for the Bolshevik party and later for the Soviet government in various provincial towns.

10 Boris Pavlovich Pozern (1882–1939) worked in the Bolshevik organizations of several provincial towns; he served in the Red Army during the Civil War and afterward did party and government work. During his term as Secretary of the Leningrad District Committee of the Communist Party (1931–34) he became close to S. M. Kirov (1886–1934), another old Bolshevik and Civil War veteran who was the Secretary of the Party's Leningrad Provincial Committee at that time; Kirov's assassination on December 1, 1934, is thought to have been ordered by Stalin and to have opened the period of the Great Terror which culminated in the years 1936–38 (when Ezhov was the Commissar for Internal Affairs). Pozern's date of death is given by various Soviet sources as having been 1938, 1939, or 1940.

11 At that time Russia was at war with Japan and had already suffered a momentous defeat with the fall of the fortress of Port Arthur to the Japanese on December 19, 1904.

12 *See* Dan, Ninth Interview, note 10.

13 Aleksandr Aleksandrovich Korostelev (1887–1937) joined the Bolsheviks in 1905 but continued to work as a metal-turner in Samara and Orenburg. Headed the Orenburg Soviet in 1917 and served in the Red Army during the Civil War as a political commissar. Later worked in the trade unions and in Soviet economic

institutions, becoming eventually a member of the Central Committee and the Presidium of Soviets.

14 The "Party," the "organization," and the "committee" to which B. N. refers in these pages are the RSDRP (Russian Social Democratic Labor Party) and its local committees.

15 Aleksandr Nikolaevich Naumov (1868–1950), *Iz utselevshikh vospominanii, 1868–1950*, 2 vols., NY, 1954–55.

16 Nikolai Dmitrievich Avksent'ev (1878–1943) was one of the leaders of the Party of Socialist Revolutionaries and headed its "Right" wing throughout the Party's history. During the revolution of 1917 he served as Chairman of the All-Russian Soviet of Peasants' Deputies, as the Minister of Internal Affairs in the Second Coalition, and as the Chairman of the Preparliament. He was a member of the anti-Bolshevik "Ufa Government" during the Civil War and later emigrated to Paris where he headed the Russian Lodge of Free Masons.

17 The term *obyvateli* was often used synonymously with the actual legal terms *meshchane* or *meshchanstvo* to define the lower groups of the city population – petty tradesmen, artisans, and so forth. However, in the parlance of the Russian intelligentsia *obyvatel'*, *obyvatel'shchina*, and *meshchanstvo* referred specifically to the spiritual attributes that set the petty-bourgeoisie apart from the intelligentsia – a concern for material comfort and respectability coupled with a lack of spiritual enlightenment, individuality, or social activism. *See* Ivanov-Razumnik's study, "The History of Russian Social Thought" [*Istoriia Russkoi obshchestvennoi mysli. Individualizm i meshchanstvo v Russkoi literature i zhizni xix v.*, St. Petersburg, 1911].

18 Grigorii I. Prigornyi [pseudonym of Kramol'nikov, b. 1880] began his revolutionary activities in the Siberian Union of RSDRP in 1898 and after 1903 worked in Bolshevik organizations in Russia; however, joined the Mensheviks in 1906 and gravitated to the "Liquidators." Was a "Right wing" Menshevik in 1917 (when, according to B. N., he wrote "the best work against Lenin") and left the Party altogether after the Extraordinary Congress of 1917; joined the Communist Party in 1919 and worked in the Marx-Engels Institute until 1941.

19 In a later interview, on February 9, 1961, B. N. asked to be allowed to correct this statement: "The Black Hundred campaign had already started, as I told you, in the summer, but the von Galin affair only after the events of October. Only then, did the governor legalize, more correctly recognize, the public committee. . . ." About the events of October 1905, *see* Dan, Eleventh Interview, note 3.

20 *Proletarii*, an underground Bolshevik daily established by the "Third Congress," was published in Geneva from May 14 to November 12, 1905 (only 26 issues ever appeared).

21 The *Iskra* plan was worked out in November 1904 by the Mensheviks; it envisioned the organization of working class demonstrations before each zemstvo "banquet" in order to convince the zemstva of the need for broader political demands; according to Axelrod the goal was "to indicate the proletariat's readiness to support the bourgeois opposition in its struggle for freedom and to demand, at the same time, of this opposition support for its strivings." In his criticism of that plan Lenin presented his own alternative: rather than try to push forward the reluctant liberals, the Social Democrats should organize the working class for a decisive blow against absolutism, an effort which would result in a fully democratic revolution and a shortening of the future struggle for socialism.

22 *See* Dan, Eleventh Interview, note 3.

Sixth interview

1 A section of the local SD organization which concentrated on propaganda and recruitment among the soldiery.

2 The First State Duma convened on April 27, 1906.

3 See Dan, Tenth Interview, note 12 about the controversy concerning the "expro-priations" and "partisan actions."

4 B. N. added the following about the Kadantsev family: "The three Kadantsev brothers took over the group after me. They were from a military family. They had a sister named Inna, an active worker and Social Democrat. The oldest of the Kadantsev brothers, Erazm, was an officer who had served in the Russo-Jap-anese War. He did not return until after my departure, so I never saw or got to know him. I knew Ivan, who was in my class at the *gimnazium* but in a different section. Then there was his younger brother Mikhail, who was a Cadet in the Orenburg Cadet Corps. When the *druzhina* began to expand its activities in 1906, Erazm was the chief of staff. The real organizer, Ivan, was the contact for all the liaison operations. Erazm is still living; he received the Order of Lenin in 1955. He wrote a brief memoir that is far from truthful. Ivan died in 1917 after catch-ing a bad cold. He had revived the whole *druzhina*, but in carrying out some train-ing maneuvers, he caught cold lying on the ground, became seriously ill, and died." *See* also pp. 252-53, where B. N. speaks of the Kadomtsev [sic!] family.

5 The Second State Duma opened on February 20, 1907. I. G. Tsereteli, son of a famous literary family in Georgia and the leader of the Georgian Duma delega-tion (all Mensheviks), was chosen by the Menshevik-dominated CC to head the SD faction in the Second Duma and implement the policy of cooperation with other opposition parties. He became noted for his oratorical skill, forthrightness, and charisma.

6 Few biographical details are available about Pavel Nikolaevich Kolokolnikov, who was a typical Menshevik-*praktik* and a staunch opponent of Bolshevism. A "Liquidator" and a war-time "Defensist," he was active in "open" trade unions and workers' consumer cooperatives. During 1917 he belonged to the Revolution-ary Defensist faction, and from May of that year he served in the Provisional Government as Deputy Minister of Labor in charge of trade unions and labor mediation. After the October seizure of power he left the CC to protest its negotiations with the Bolsheviks, refusing to return even when these were broken.

7 The Central Committee elected at the Fourth Congress of RSDRP (April 1906) was dominated by the Mensheviks; the one elected at the Fifth Congress, by the Bolsheviks.

8 See Dan, Third Interview, note 3.

9 B. N. may be referring to either of two conferences that took place in Tammer-fors, Finland: The exclusively Bolshevik conference of December 11–17, 1905; or the Second Conference of RSDRP (also known as the First All-Russian) which met in November 16–20, 1906.

10 Deputies to the Second State Duma were elected in January and February 1907.

11 The Fifth Congress of RSDRP met in London, April 30–May 19, 1907. Although the Bolsheviks commanded a majority in the congress, a Menshevik resolution condemning "partisan actions and expropriations" was adopted against the objections of Lenin and other staunch Bolsheviks.

12 About Axelrod's idea of a "workers' congress," *see* Dan, Eleventh Interview, note 11.

13 *Soznatel'naia Rossiia* [Conscious Russia], a "legal" SR journal under Chernov's editorship, was published in St. Petersburg in the fall of 1906.

14 The differences mentioned by L. H. concerned both the revolutionary value of trade unions and their proper relations with the SD party. Whereas the Men-sheviks welcomed the opportunities created by tsarist concessions for legal or semi-legal working-class activity, the Bolsheviks regarded the non-party, class organizations that appeared during 1905 with suspicion because of their poten-tial to divert the workers' attention from the task of a popular uprising. Thus, in May 1905, the Menshevik Geneva Conference decided to support "a permanent liaison between the Party organizations and the trade unions" and to provide

"constant assistance" to them, whereas the Bolshevik "Third" Congress resolved "to exploit . . . the unions . . . in order to ensure Social Democracy a predominant influence over them."

15 *See* Dan, Eleventh Interview, note 9 and Twelfth Interview, note 4.

16 *See* Dan, Fifth Interview, note 22; Denike, Second Interview, note 7 and Third Interview, note 13.

17 Both Bolsheviks and Mensheviks advocated participation in the election campaign for the Second Duma, but debate continued over the practice of joint candidate-lists with other parties. Many local party organizations departed from the resolution of the Second RSDRP Conference (November 1906), which allowed such lists only in cases where these would prevent the election of a Black Hundreds' (i.e., reactionary) candidate; prohibited these lists altogether in the workers' curia; and gave preference to electoral agreements with Populist parties over the Kadets.

18 Marxist literary-political journals published during the second half of the 1890's; *see* Dan, Fourth Interview, note 37 and Nikolaevskii, Third Interview, notes 1 and 14.

19 *Otkliki sovremennosti* [Contemporary Responses], a "legal" publication put out by a group of Mensheviks in Petersburg, appeared in five volumes in March–June 1906.

20 Paul Louis (b. 1872), a French historian of socialist leaning, wrote several works on socialism; perhaps B. N. has in mind his "Socialism in the Contemporary State," which was published in Russian in 1906 (*Sotsializm v sovremennom gosudarstve*, St. Petersburg).

21 Friedrich Zorge (1828–1906), a German Socialist, follower of Marx and Secretary of the First Socialist International (1872–74), emigrated to the USA in 1852 and was active in American socialist labor organizations. His book, *The Labor Movement in the United States*, was published in Russian in 1907.

22 B. N. may have in mind one of several articles by Potresov: "An Urgent Task" [*Neotlozhnaia zadacha*], in which he argued the value of "open" organizations for Russian Social Democracy (vol. 2); or his later article, "About the kadets" [*O kadetakh*] (vol. 5); or perhaps "The Duma – An Organizing Center" [*Duma - Organizuiushchii tsenter*], printed in the Menshevik workers' daily *Kur'er* (no. 3), in May 1905.

23 Kautsky's work appeared in Russian in 1907, titled *Dvizhuiushchie sily i perspektivy russkoi revoliutsii* (1907).

24 The article, "K. Kautsky and the Russian Revolution," was published in vol. 2 (1907) of the Menshevik Petersburg publication *Otkliki* [Responses].

25 *See* Dan, Eleventh Interview, note 5.

26 B. N. might be referring to Trotsky's introduction to a volume of his essays entitled "Our Revolution" [*Nasha revoliutsiia*, Petersburg, 1906]; written in prison in 1906, the introduction, entitled "The Balance and the Prospects – The Moving Forces of the Revolution" [*Itogi i perspektivy-Dvizhushchie sily revoliutsii*], gave the fullest exposition of the idea of "permanent revolution," developed during 1905.

27 *See* Dan, Eleventh Interview, note 6.

28 Lenin's "Two Tactics of Social Democracy in the Democratic Revolution," written in Geneva in June and July 1905, compared the Menshevik tactic of prompting the liberals to lead the revolution toward the creation of a "bourgeois democratic republic," to his own, more radical tactic of raising a popular insurrection, under Marxist leadership, with the aim of creating a "democratic dictatorship of the proletariat and the peasantry."

29 *See* Dan, Tenth Interview, note 2.

30 *See* Dan, Tenth Interview, note 3.

31 *Vpered* [Forward], a Bolshevik daily, was published in Petersburg from May 26 to June 14, 1906.

Chapter 3. George Denike

First interview

1 According to the Gregorian calendar used in the West the Bolshevik seizure of power occurred on November 7, 1917, whereas according to the Julian calendar, then in use in Russia, it took place on October 25.

2 The reference here is specifically to the judiciary reforms of November 20, 1864, which were, in principle at least, committed to the notions of the equality of all before the law, the independence of the judiciary, and the right to representation by qualified members of the bar.

3 According to the Table of Ranks instituted by Peter the Great in 1722, all offices in both the military and the civilian branches of state service were arranged in an hierarchical order of 14 ranks. Each state official began his career at the fourteenth rank and rose gradually up the ladder; the attainment of the eighth rank brought with it an automatic title of nobility.

4 Aleksandr Fedorovich Kerenskii (1881–1970), a lawyer of Populist leanings, was elected to the Fourth Duma and headed its moderate faction of *Trudoviki*. As the best-known socialist deputy of the Duma he played a key role in establishing the Provisional Government (in March 1917) and in securing the support of the Petrograd Soviet for that government and became successively the Minister of Justice (March–April), the Minister of War (May–September), and Premier (July–October) in that government. He emigrated in 1918.

5 Joseph Hoffman (1876–1957), a Polish-born, world-renowned pianist.

6 Ernst Mach (1838–1916), Austrian physicist, psychologist, and philosopher; his writings inspired the "school of empirio-criticism" in Russia and caused sharp controversies among the Social Democrats (*see* Denike, Third Interview, note 14). The writings referred to by Denike were published in Russian under the following titles: *Mekhanika. Istoriko-kriticheskii ocherk ee razvitiia*, St. Petersburg, 1909; *Analiz oshchushchenii i otnoshenie fizicheskogo k psikhicheskomu*, 2nd ed., Moscow, 1908.

7 R. Abramovich [pseudonym of Rafail Abramovich Rein, 1880–1963] was a leading member of the Bund and the Menshevik organization in Russia for many years. He emigrated in 1912, and during First World War supported the Center-Zimmerwald position. In 1917 he returned to Russia and belonged to the Internationalist factions of both the Menshevik Party and the Bund. In November 1917 he participated in the negotiations for the establishment of a "homogeneous socialist government," and in early 1918 represented the Menshevik opposition inside the Soviet and in the Assemblies of Representatives. He left Russia with Martov in 1920, and from 1921 until his death was one of the editors of *Sotsialisticheskii vestnik*, living in Berlin, Paris, and New York.

8 Anatolii Eduardovich Dubois (1882–1959), a Petersburg lawyer, joined the Mensheviks in 1906 after a short period as a Bolshevik. He supported "Liquidationism" and was active in legal trade unions and the legal labor press. During First World War he belonged to the Defensist wing of Menshevism, and at the beginning of the Revolution was sent by the Petrograd Soviet as its Commissar to the Northern Front. In 1917, from May until October, he served as Deputy Minister of Labor in the Provisional Government. After the Bolshevik seizure of power, he belonged to the right-wing minority of the party, fought against the Bolsheviks, and was arrested and expelled from the Soviet Union in 1923. He continued activity in the Menshevik Party abroad and became a member of its left wing in 1940.

9 *See* Dan, Tenth Interview, note 16.

10 Vladimir Viktorovich Adoratskii (1878–1945) had joined the Social Democratic movement in 1900 during his studies at the University of Kazan and had been the Secretary of the Kazan Bolshevik Committee since 1904. He spent the years after 1905 in prison, exile, and emigration. After the revolution of 1917 he became the head of the Central Archives and, later, of the Marx-Engels Institute.

11 Francois-Alphonse Aulard (1849–1928), leading historian of the French revolution, was known for meticulous scholarship and a "democratic" political orientation.

12 *Pravda* [The Truth], a Social-Democratic monthly published in Moscow from January 1904 to February 1906, dedicated considerable space during its first year of publication to the presentation of Mach's ideas on philosophy, aesthetics, and ethics.

Second interview

1 S. A. Lozovskii [pseudonym of Drizdo, 1878–1952] grew up in a poor Jewish family in the Pale of Settlement; with financial help from his brother, he began studying in his twenties and successfully passed the *gimnazium* equivalency examinations. He joined SD (Social Democrat) circles in 1901 and became a member of the Bolshevik organization in Kazan in 1905. He was arrested in 1908, escaped, and settled in Paris where he became active in French trade unions, in the Bolshevik organization, and, during the First World War, in Internationalist publications. After his return to Russia in June 1917, he occupied a series of high positions in the trade union movement.

2 V. A. Desnitskii [pseudonym of Stroev, 1878–1958] joined the SD (Social Democrat) movement in 1897 and its Bolshevik faction in 1903. He left the Bolsheviks in 1909 to join the *Vpered* group, and became a writer for the SD-Internationalist journal *Novaia zhizn'* in 1917. After the civil war, he began working in the Soviet education system.

3 Denike probably has in mind an article by Axelrod published in *Iskra* (no. 68, June 25, 1904) under the title "K voprosu ob istochnikov i znachenii nashikh organizatsionnykh raznoglasii" [Toward the Question of the Origins and the Significance of Our Organizational Differences].

4 Solomon Meerovich Schwarz [pseudonym of Monoszon, b. 1883], like Denike, had been a Bolshevik from 1903 to 1907, first in his hometown of Vilno and, beginning in 1905, in Petersburg. He studied law abroad between 1907 and 1915, but during a year-long stay in Russia in 1913 he worked in the Menshevik-led trade unions and wrote extensively on the question of social security for workers. During the war he took a Defensist position and was the secretary of the Labor Group of the Moscow War-Industrial Committee. He headed the Department of Social Security in the Ministry of Labor of the Provisional Government in 1917. After the Bolshevik seizure of power, he was among the organizers of a strike of all state employees against the new government, but at the end of 1919, joined the left-wing majority of the Menshevik Party and enlisted in the Red Army. He was arrested and expelled from the Soviet Union in 1921 and continued his activity in the Menshevik Party in Berlin and New York.

5 *See* Dan, Eleventh Interview, note 3.

6 Vladimir Matveevich Gessen should not be confused with his better-known cousin, Iosif V. Gessen, also a jurist, who was one of the leaders of the Kadet Party and the editor of its newspaper *Rech'*.

7 The agrarian program of the PSR – officially endorsed only at the party's First Congress in 1906 – called for the "socialization" of lands, i.e., for the expropriation of all privately owned land without compensation and for an egalitarian distribution of the land funds among "all those who work the land with their own toil" to be carried out by local and regional elected bodies.

8 Nikolai Gurevich Poletaev (b. 1872), a skilled metal worker was elected to the Third Duma from the Workers' Curia of Petersburg province.

9 *See* Dan, Fifth Interview, note 22.

10 On permanent revolution *see* Dan, Eleventh Interview, note 6.

11 Ianovskii was the pseudonym used by Trotsky in 1905. Georgii S. Nosar' [pseudonym of Khrustalev, 1877–1918] had been a member of the Union of Lib-

eration and an attorney for the Union of Printers. He joined the Menshevik organization in Petersburg in 1905 and in October was elected the first chairman of the Petersburg Soviet. He was arrested on November 26 and was sent into exile, from which he escaped abroad. He returned to Russia in 1917 as an extreme Defensist and during the Civil War was arrested and shot by the Bolsheviks.

12 Mikhail Vladimirovich Bernatskii served in the Provisional Government, first as the head of the new Department of Labor in the Ministry of Trade and Industry, and in September–October as the Minister of Finance. During the Civil War he was a member of Denikin's government, and later of Wrangel's; he emigrated after their defeat.

13 *Novaia zhizn'* [New Life] was the first Bolshevik newspaper published legally inside Russia. Twenty-eight issues appeared in Petersburg between October 25 and December 3, 1905.

14 Sofiia Moiseevna Zaretskaia had been an active member of the Menshevik faction since 1903; in the Moscow organization (1905), as the Secretary of the SD faction of the Second Duma (1907), and as workers' organizer in Moscow and Saratov. She supported "Liquidationism" and Defensism. She was a member of the Central Committee of the Menshevik Party and of the Executive Committee of the Soviets in 1917 but belonged to the right-wing minority of the party after October 1917; she remained in the Soviet Union and was active in the Menshevik Moscow organization in the 1920s.

15 Peter Anan'evich Krasikov [pseudonym of Pavlovich, 1870–1939], a veteran of 15 years in the revolutionary movement and one of Lenin's chief operatives from 1900; he was the Bolshevik representative to the Executive Committee of the Petersburg Soviet in 1905. He left political activity after his arrests (December 1905; 1906) and practiced law in Petersburg. He became a Bolshevik delegate to the Petrograd and the All-Russian Executive Committees of the Soviets in 1917 and after the Bolshevik seizure of power held several high-level positions in the Soviet judicial system.

Third interview

1 The reference here is to the collective volume *Ocherki realisticheskogo mirovozreniia* (Petersburg, 1904) in which the Empiriocriticists fully articulated their views. The leading Social Democrats Lunacharskii, Bazarov, A. Bogdanov, and P. Maslov were among the volume's contributors.

2 Vladimir Aleksandrovich Bazarov [pseudonym of Rudnev, 1874–1937] had by then established himself as a philosopher and an economist, had had a decade of SD activity behind him, and was a contributor to all the Bolshevik publications of 1905–7. In the period after 1907 he remained outside the various groupings of Russian SD, but wrote for Menshevik journal *Nasha zaria*. He joined the journal *Letopis'* with several other unaffiliated SD-Internationalists in 1915, established the daily *Novaia zhizn'* in 1917, and played an important role in the Petrograd Soviet and the Soviet's Economic Section. He cooperated with the Menshevik Internationalists in 1918–19, but later worked in the Communist Academy and Gosplan until his arrest in 1930 in connection with the "Menshevik Trial." He died in prison.

3 The People's Socialist Party [*Narodnaia Sotsialisticheskaia Partiia*] was founded in 1906 by Miakotin and other members of the Populist wing of the Union of Unions who insisted on the exploitation of all legal possibilities and, thus, did not join the Party of Socialist Revolutionaries which was dedicated to a boycott of the Duma elections.

4 Aleksandra Kollontai (1872–1952) joined SD circles in the 1890s and was close to the Mensheviks until World War I. Joined the Bolsheviks in emigration in 1915 and worked in their Military Organization in Petrograd in 1917. Was a leader of

the "Women's Section" and the "Workers' Opposition" in the early years of Soviet rule but after 1923 worked exclusively in the Soviet diplomatic service.

5 I. P. Goldenberg (1873–1922) had joined SD circles in 1892 and the Bolshevik faction in 1903. Was one of the leading Bolsheviks inside Russia, a delegate to several congresses, and a member of the Central Committee. Left the Bolsheviks during World War I to support Plekhanov's extreme Defensism, but after the Bolshevik victory in the Civil War joined the Communist Party.

6 The First Duma was dissolved by the tsarist government on July 9, 1906 after only a ten week existence. Two hundred deputies of the Duma from the Kadet Party and the Group of Trudoviki responded by crossing the Finnish border to Vyborg, where they signed a call "To the People From the People's Representatives" on July 10. The "Vyborg Manifesto" urged the Russian populace to "passive resistance" of the government by refusing to pay taxes not approved by the Duma and by not handing over military recruits. In contrast to the expectations of the socialist parties, the dissolution of the Duma did not cause the revival of widespread unrest in the cities and the countryside.

7 Vladimir Savel'evich Voitinskii (1885–1960) had been a Bolshevik agitator in Petersburg in 1905–7 before his arrest and exile to Siberia. See Denike, Eighth Interview, note 9 on his later association with the Mensheviks.

8 Denike probably refers to the revolt which took place in the Baltic port of Sveaborg in the second half of July 1906. Having learned of the revolt on July 19, the Bolshevik Petersburg Committee called for a sympathy strike and began preparing for a general uprising. However, the revolt in the fleet was quickly crushed and only a small number of workers in Moscow and Petersburg responded to the Bolshevik directions.

9 The *Trudoviki* were members of the *Trudovaia gruppa* [Toilers' Group] which was organized as a parliamentary faction from among the peasants' deputies to the First Duma. Led by SR *intelligenty* (whose own party had boycotted the duma elections), the *Trudoviki* gained great popularity among the peasant voters. In spite of their decision in the summer of 1906 not to form a party, they were returned to the Second Duma with an even greater number of seats.

10 A united Central Committee was established by the "Unification" Congress which met in Stockholm in April and May 1906.

11 Konstantin Mikhailovich Ermolaev (1884–1919) had been involved in "practical" party work since 1904. After 1910 became one of the most outspoken "Liquidators" and one of the three Mensheviks who refused to serve with the Bolsheviks in one Central Committee. Belonged to the group of "Siberian Zimmerwaldists" during World War I and to the leadership of the Revolutionary Defensist bloc in 1917. Joined the right-wing minority of the Menshevik party after October and supported armed opposition to the Bolsheviks.

12 Soon after the First Duma opened on April 27, 1906, most of the workers' deputies joined the Georgian deputies (all of whom were Social Democrats) in one Social Democratic faction.

13 The reference here is to the agrarian program of the Mensheviks which called for a takeover of all lands by local (rural and municipal) institutions. The Menshevik program had been adopted by the party at the "Unification" Congress in Stockholm, where Lenin's proposal for an outright nationalization of all lands had been defeated.

14 The Empiriocriticists (who included A. Bogdanov, Bazarov, Luncacharskii, P. S. Iushkevich, and other Social Democrats who had been influenced by the Austrian philosopher, A. Mach) published their ideas in two major collections: *Ocherki realisticheskogo mirovozreniia* [Essays on a Realistic Worldview], Petersburg, 1904, and *Ocherki po filosofii marksizma* [Essays on Marxist Philosophy], Petersburg, 1908. They were severely criticized by Lenin in his treatise *Materializm i empiriokrititsizm* (1909) which caused a split in the Bolshevik Party.

15 See V. I. Lenin, *Polnoe sobranie sochinenii*, 5th ed., Moscow, 1964, vol. 47, pp. 103–6.

16 The freedom of political activity which had reasserted itself so dramatically during the Days of Freedom in October-November 1905 and which had been given at least a limited legal grounding in the "Provisional Rules" enacted in late 1905 and early 1906, was increasingly encroached upon by the government in the following years; most notable in this regard were the dissolutions of the First and Second Dumas (in July 1906 and June 1907, respectively) and the enactment of the "Emergency Rules of Summary Justice" in August, 1906.

17 On Axelrod's idea of a Workers Congress *see* Dan, Eleventh Interview, note 11.

Fourth interview

1 Klimentii Efremovich Voroshilov (1881–1969), a metalworker, joined the Bolshevik organization in Lugansk in 1903 and was its delegate to the Fourth and Fifth Party Congresses and the First all-Russian Conference of Metalworkers in 1906–07. He spent the years after 1907 in underground work and in prison; he returned to Lugansk in 1917 as chairman of the local soviet, the city duma, and the Bolshevik organization. He began a military career during the Civil War which eventually led him to become a distinguished Soviet commander during World War II; after the war he was a top political figure.

2 The election to the State Duma was conducted in two stages: first, the curiae of landowners, urban proprietors, peasants, and workers selected their electors (the last two curiae in a two- and even three-stage process); and second, the electors from all the curiae of each province met and elected the province's deputies to the Duma.

3 Grigorii Evgenevich Belousov (1876–1916), a glass worker and union organizer in the Donbas region in 1905, was elected to the Second Duma from the workers' curia of Ekaterinoslav province; he was arrested with the faction in June 1907 and imprisoned until 1911. He was transferred to Siberia, escaped abroad, and during First World War wrote for ultra-Defensist publications in Paris and New York.

4 A Menshevik leader. *See* Dan, Sixth Interview, note 11.

5 *See* Nikolaevskii, Fifth Interview, note 4.

6 The Fifth Party Congress took place in April and May 1907.

7 Agents of the *Okhranka*, the tzarist secret police.

Fifth interview

1 V. M. Molotov (b. 1890), Arosev, and V. A. Tikhomirov were all students in the Kazan *Realschule*, where they disseminated Bolshevik propaganda from 1907 until their arrest in 1909. All three worked for the Bolshevik party in the following years, though Molotov was especially active. He emerged as one of Stalin's lieutenants in the 1930's, serving principally as the Chairman of the Council of Ministers and as Foreign Minister. Tikhomirov, the son of a rich merchant, placed his financial means at the service of the party until his death during the Civil War. According to information supplied by Denike elsewhere, Arosev worked for the Soviet government arranging cultural exchanges and living in Molotov's apartment in the Kremlin until his arrest and eventual execution during the purges.

2 The "Lena Massacre" which occurred on April 4, 1912 and marked the beginning of a two-year wave of labor unrest. The massacre followed a bitter strike by some 6,000 goldminers. About 2,500 of them assembled on April 4 to demand the release of their imprisoned strike committee; when calls to the strikers to disband were not heeded, government troops were ordered to shoot directly at the men, killing 270 and wounding some 250 others.

3 According to the "Provisional Rules" of November 24, 1905, preliminary censorship of periodicals was abolished; instead, issues containing matters allegedly in

contravention of the law could be seized and the 'responsible editor' of the journal placed under arrest. To ensure editorial continuity in such cases, it was customary for a person other than the actual editor to sign the licensing forms.

4 Fedor Avgustovich Stepun (1884–1965) belonged to the school of Russian Christian Existentialists in emigration. Wrote in Russian and German on questions of religious philosophy and Russian literature. His memoir, entitled *Byvshoe i nesbyvsheesia* [What Was and What Was Not] was published in New York in 1956.

5 *Vekhi* [Landmarks], subtitled a "A Collection of Essays on the Russian Intelligentsia," was published in Moscow, in 1909, by a group of writers and thinkers which included Struve, N. A. Berdiaev, S. N. Bulgakov, M. O. Gershenzon, A. S. Izgoev, V. A. Kistiakovskii, and S. L. Frank. In the aftermath of the revolution of 1905–7, these authors, who had been formerly associated with the radical intelligentsia, turned against its materialist, atheist, and radical traditions, in a sense, against their own upbringing, and called for a recognition of the primacy of the spiritual life of the individual over the outward forms of social and political life.

6 Denike refers here to Ivan Vasil'evich Godnev (b. 1856), a member of the Octobrist Party and a deputy from Kazan Province to the Third and Fourth Dumas. He served in the Provisional Government as State Controller from March to July, 1917.

Sixth interview

1 Konstantin Sergeevich Stanislavskii [pseudonym of Alekseev, 1863–1938], an actor and director, had already become famous for his innovative approach to theater and acting, which he implemented in the Moscow Art Theater.

2 The "Association of Wanderers" [*Peredvizhniki*], established in 1870 under the impact of the aesthetic ideas of the 1860's, brought together artists who sought their subject matter among the simple people of Russia, depicting them in a "critical-realistic" and expressive genre; among them were such famous Russian painters as Repin and Levitan. The "World of Art" [*Mir iskusstva*] was a journal around which gathered a group of young artists and art lovers headed by A. N. Benois and the editor-impressario S. P. Diagilev; its members were close to the West European Modernists, and between 1900–14 sought to promote an interest in native and foreign art and to reestablish the purely aesthetic view of art. From 1910 to 1924, the "World of Art" group was responsible for a revival of the Russian theater and for the exportation of Russian arts to Western Europe.

3 The main goal and effect of the "Stolypin reforms" (beginning with an imperial decree of November 9, 1906 and including Duma legislation from June 14, 1910, and May 29, 1911) was to turn individual members of the peasant commune into independent farmers who would own land privately.

4 Aleksandr Aleksandrovich Kizevetter (1866–1933), a historian of eighteenth and nineteenth century Russian political and institutional history, taught at Moscow University from 1898 until his resignation in 1911 (*see* note no. 11 to this interview) and at the University of Prague after being forced into emigration in 1922.

5 The brothers Aksakov, Ivan Sergeevich (1826–1886) and Konstantin Sergeevich (1817–1860), were among the chief public exponents of Slavophilism, which extolled the virtues of the "true" traditional Russian ways (the communal spirit of the people and the Orthodox Church, the paternal authority of the tsar) as superior to those of the "decadent" West.

6 Michael [Mikhail Mikhailovich] Karpovich (1888–1959) studied Medieval and Byzantine history of the Sorbonne (1907–1908) and Russian history at Moscow University (1908–14). His academic career was interrupted by the First World War (during which he served in the Ministry of War, helping to coordinate military industrial production) and the Revolution (when he was a confidential aide to the Provisional Government's ambassador to Washington). He taught history and Russian literature at Harvard University from 1927 to 1957.

7 Robert Iur'evich Vipper (1859–1954) taught at Moscow University from 1894 until 1924 and, again, after 1941. The book to which Denike refers, *Ivan Groznyi*, was published privately in Moscow in 1922 and reprinted several times by Soviet publishing houses in the 1940s.

8 Struve's article was entitled "The Question of the Growth of Productive Forces in the theory of Social Development" and was published in the collection *Sbornik statei posviashchennykh Vasiliu Osipovichu Kliuchevskomu*, Moscow, 1909.

9 Dmitri Moiseevich Petrushevskii (1863–1942) belonged to the "social-economic" school of Russian historians of the European Middle Ages. Wrote on the origins and nature of feudalism in Western Europe and on the particular features feudalism assumed in England. His first work, published in two volumes in 1894–1901, was a study of the 1381 peasant revolt led by Wat Tyler *(Vosstanie Uota Tailera)*. After 1917 continued to teach in Soviet universities.

10 Pavel' Gavrilovich Vinogradov (1854–1925) had taught at Moscow University since 1884 until he left for Oxford, England in 1903; returned to Moscow in 1908 only to resign again in 1911 (*see* following note). Wrote several important works on the social and legal history of medieval England; returned to Oxford in 1918.

11 In February, 1911, a large number of faculty of Moscow University resigned in protest over actions taken by the Minister of Education, L. A. Kasso, against striking students as well as against the autonomy which the universities had been granted in 1905.

Seventh interview

1 *See* Denike, Sixth Interview, note 3.

2 P. A. Stolypin, President of the Council of Ministers and Russia's principal policy-maker since 1906, was shot on September 1, 1911 by a revolutionary who was a double agent for the police.

3 "Our Dawn," a monthly published in Petersburg from 1910 to 1914. Edited by Potresov and featuring articles by all of the Menshevik leaders, *Nasha zaria* was the most important journal in the development of Menshevik thought between the Revolution of 1905 and World War I.

4 During the years from 1907 to 1914, the Mensheviks published several collections of their own writings on the origins, character, and consequence of the 1905 revolution. The most important of these efforts was the 4-volume study *Obshchestvennoe dvizhenie v Rossii v nachale XX veka* [The Social Movement in Russia At the Beginning of the 20th Century], published in Petersburg in 1909–1912.

5 The First Balkan War, waged by Montenegro, Greece, Serbia, and Bulgaria against Turkey, began on October 8, 1912 and ended in April 1913, in a victory for the Balkan allies. A Second Balkan War followed in the summer of 1913 in which the Balkan countries fought among themselves (Bulgaria against an alliance of Serbia, Rumania, and Greece), thus enabling Turkey to recover some of its earlier losses.

6 Nikolai Sevastianovich Derzhavin (1877–1953), a philologist from Petersburg University who wrote several scholarly books on Bulgarian culture and history. In 1914 he published a more political brochure on the Bulgarian-Serbian conflict over Macedonia: *Bulgarsko-serbskie vzaimootnosheniia i Makedonskii vopros*, Petersburg, 1914.

7 Denike's information regarding Lenin's letters to Gorkii could not be verified.

8 The collection, including also Russian and Oriental Art, was assembled by the Moscow merchant Petr Ivanovich Shchukin and confiscated by the state after the October Revolution; it is now housed at the Pushkin Museum in Moscow.

9 *Pravda* [Truth], a Bolshevik daily for workers, was published in Petersburg from April 1912 to July 1914; under various different names during the last years. *See* also Denike's article *"Kupecheskaia semia Tikhomirov"* [The Tikhomirov Merchant Family], *Novyi zhurnal*, no. 68 (1962), pp. 280–87.

10 In accordance with the desire for unity among their electors, the six Bolshevik and seven Menshevik deputies to the Fourth Duma formed a united SD faction. But in October 1913, Roman Malinovskii, a double agent of the secret police as well as one of Lenin's closest associates, convinced the other Bolshevik deputies to form a separate faction. *See also* Dan, Twelfth Interview, note 8.

11 Mendel Beilis, a Jewish laborer from Kiev, was accused of the ritual murder of a Russian boy whose body was discovered in March 1911 in a cave outside Kiev. His trial became a cause celebre because of its antisemitic implications and ended in acquittal in October 1913.

12 *See* Dan, Twelfth Interview, note 8.

13 *See* Nikolaevskii, Fifth Interview, note 6.

14 The Defensists were those Mensheviks (and other socialists) who advocated socialist and workers' support of the war effort against Germany. Most Menshevik-Defensists followed A. N. Potresov's view of the war as a struggle between West European democracy and German militarism.

15 During the Duma's debate of the government's request for special wartime credits, on July 26, 1914 (August 8 in the Gregorian calendar), the Social Democratic deputies (both Mensheviks and Bolsheviks) declared their denunciation of the war and the tsarist government and walked out, refusing to vote for the war credits. Their behavior was in sharp contrast to that of the German Social Democrats who had voted together with the whole Reichstag (on August 4) in favor of granting war credits to their government.

Eighth interview

1 The third volume of V. S. Voitinskii's Russian memoirs, describing the events of 1917, was never published. The manuscript, entitled *"Gody pobed i porazhenii, 1917-yi god"* [Years of Victories and Defeats; The Year of 1917], is deposited in the Nicolaevsky Collection at the Hoover Institution on War, Revolution, and Peace, Stanford, California. The telegram to which Denike refers was sent to railroad stations all over Russia by Aleksandr Aleksandrovich Bublikov, a Duma deputy of the Octobrist Party, in his capacity as the Commissar of Transportation in the Provisional Committee which the Duma had established on February 27 in order to bring about the formation of a new government.

2 Bublikov's telegram, which was in the form of an appeal to the railroad workers to carry out their duties, was sent on February 28 and thus preceded the formation of the Provisional Government on March 2; it merely announced that "the Committee of the State Duma has undertaken" to form a new government.

3 The term "dual power" [*dvoevlastie*], as used in 1917, described the political arrangement which emerged after the February overthrow of the tsarist government and which continued until the creation of a coalition government in early May. The "duality" of power resulted from the fact that the soviets, which enjoyed the unquestioned loyalty of the workers and many of the soldiers, refused to participate in the government together with the representatives of the upper classes, and furthermore, conditioned their support of the Provisional Government upon its implementation of a specific program of policies and reforms. As Denike explains below, such suspicion and division of power did not exist in many provincial towns like Kazan.

4 During 1917 a variety of soviets [councils] existed in towns, districts, and fronts all over Russia. In some places, Petrograd for instance, workers and soldiers were united in one soviet; in others, like Moscow, there were two separate soviets, one of workers, another of soldiers; in rural districts the soviets usually included only peasants; and in areas close to the front lines – only soldiers.

5 *See* Denike, First Interview, note 4.

6 The controversy inside *Pravda* was between its original editor, Molotov, and three prominent Bolsheviks (Kamenev, Stalin, and M. K. Muranov) who returned from

Siberia in mid-March and seized control of the paper. Under Molotov and the Bureau of the Bolshevik Central Committee, *Pravda* had espoused a staunch Internationalism and a categorical opposition to the Provisional Government. But on March 14 its line suddenly moderated and its editorials began advocating continued military defense against Germany and at least a limited support for the Provisional Government.

7 In all likelihood, the pamphlet to which Denike refers originated in the most radical of the three Bolshevik organizations which existed at that time in Petrograd, i.e., the Committee of the Vyborg District. The "Petersburg Group" to which he refers included in fact the three members of the Bureau of the Bolshevik Central Committee – A. N. Shliapnikov, Molotov, and P. A. Zalutskii – whose immediate aim was not a Soviet government but a "provisional revolutionary government" controlled by socialists. Even more moderate was the Bolshevik Petersburg Committee, established on March 5th; it shared the Bureau's staunch Internationalism but accepted the formula of conditional support for the Provisional Government adopted by the Soviet.

8 In the months following the February Revolution there surfaced a desire on the part of many local Menshevik and Bolshevik organizations to reunite in one party. "United" party organizations existed in many provincial towns; during the First All-Russian Conference of Soviets (March 29–April 3) preparations were even begun for an all-Russian "unification" congress. However, when Lenin returned to Russia on April 4, it became clear that there was no real hope for such unity.

9 Voitinskii's early association with the Bolsheviks is described in Denike, Third Interview, note 7. During the First World War, while in exile in Irkutsk, he became close to Tsereteli and participated in his circle of "Siberian Zimmerwaldists," which espoused moderate Internationalism. Was one of the most effective propagandists for Tsereteli's Revolutionary Defensist policies in 1917, first in Petrograd, where he was the chief editor of *Izvestiia* and a popular speaker, and after August as the Soviet's Commissar to the Twelfth Army stationed around Riga. After the Bolshevik takeover in October, he worked for the independent government of Georgia until its collapse in 1921. Went into emigration, first in Germany, and later in 1935, in the USA, where he worked as an economist and statistician for various government organizations and continued to publish extensively.

10 Iraklii Georgievich Tsereteli (1881–1959), a Menshevik from Georgia, first became famous as the chairman of the Social Democratic faction of the Second Duma. Was arrested in 1907, spent six years in prison and lived in Siberia, near Irkutsk, from 1914 to 1917; there he became the leader of a circle of moderate Internationalists (mostly Mensheviks but including also SRs and former Bolsheviks) called the "Siberian Zimmerwaldists." Returned with his supporters to Petrograd in March 1917 and gained the support of the majority of the Petrograd Soviet and the Menshevik Party for his program of "Revolutionary Defensism"; i.e., a program which prescribed an energetic pursuit of international agreement to end the war and an equally energetic defense against Germany so long as the war continued. Tsereteli's program also called for greater cooperation between the Soviet and the Provisional Government, and when a coalition government was established in May 1917, he became the leading representative of the Soviet in the cabinet. After the Bolshevik takeover in October and the dissolution of the Constituent Assembly in January 1918, he escaped to Georgia and served the newly independent Georgian Republic in diplomatic missions. Later lived in Paris and in New York (from 1948), where he largely withdrew from political activity.

11 *Rabochaia gazeta* [The Workers' Gazette], published daily in Petrograd from March 7 to November 17 (and thereafter under different names), was the official newspaper of the Menshevik Organizational Committee. Between May and October its political line was almost exclusively that of Revolutionary Defensism.

12 In fact, the reference here is to a number of SD-Internationalists who played a leading role in the early days of the Petrograd Soviet and in the establishment of "dual power"; they were not affiliated with either the Menshevik or the Bolshevik organizations, though N. N. Sukhanov and Iu. M. Steklov joined the Internationalist faction of the Menshevik Party in the late summer of 1917. These people worked for the Soviet government in the 1920s (Sukhanov and Bazarov as economists, Steklov as the editor-in-chief of *Izvestiia*) but only Steklov joined the Communist Party and escaped prosecution in the "Menshevik Trial" of 1930.

13 The conflict referred to concerned Miliukov's diplomatic Note of April 18 (*see* note 16 below). The resignation of the leader of the Kadet Party, P. N. Miliukov, from the Provisional Government came after the cabinet had agreed to accept the foreign policy demands of the Soviet in order to facilitate socialist participation in a new, coalitionary cabinet.

14 The Mensheviks held their first All-Russian Conference in Petrograd from May 7 to 13. At that time, the majority of the party adopted the political strategy of Revolutionary Defensism and approved the party's participation in the coalition government that had been established on May 5.

15 The term "Revolutionary Democracy" was used in 1917 as a collective name for all the elements that coalesced around the soviets: the workers, the soldiers, the organized peasants, and the socialist parties.

16 During the second half of March and in early April there were repeated clashes between the leaders of the Soviet and the Minister of Foreign Affairs, Miliukov. While Miliukov was trying to secure Russia's right to annex the Dardanelles, which had been promised to her by her Allies, the Soviet vowed (in its "Appeal to the Peoples of the World," on March 14) to "resist the policy of conquest" and committed itself (in the resolution of the First All-Russian Conference of Soviets on March 30) to "peace without annexations or indemnities." The most serious of the clashes occurred when it became known that in his Note to the Allies on April 18, Miliukov had restated Russia's claim for annexations and indemnities under the phrase "guarantees and sanctions." The uproar caused among the supporters of the Soviet, and the mass demonstrations staged by them on April 20 and 21, forced the cabinet to reject Miliukov's policy and presaged the collapse of the first Provisional Government.

17 The United States declared war on Germany on April 6, 1917 and on Austro-Hungary on December 7, 1917.

Ninth interview

1 It is not clear whether the order was in fact given by Guchkov himself, but in any case, the Provisional Government decided in late April to allow all soldiers over forty to return temporarily to their villages for field work for four weeks and to discharge all those over forty-three. Supplementary instructions stipulated that dismissals for field work should not exceed 15 percent of any given unit (the soldiers' committees were assigned the role of determining precedence), and in June the government recalled the over-forties to take part in the summer offensive. All this worsened the problem of discipline in the army and caused havoc on the country's railroads.

2 Order No. 1, which was issued by the Petrograd Soviet to the garrison of the Petrograd District on March 1, sanctioned the demands of the soldiers for full civic and political rights, mandated the election of soldiers' committees to conduct the nonmilitary aspects of their lives, and made the soldiers' obedience to the military authorities conditional on the latter's compliance with the provisions of the Order. Similar "orders" were issued later to the army at the front and were blamed by many for the breakdown of military discipline.

3 As Denike indicates, some, though not all, of the Soviet's budget came from the Provisional Government; no information is available on the finances of the Menshevik Party.

4 Before leaving political activity Krasin (1870–1926) had been an organizer and technical man for *Iskra* and, beginning in 1903, for the Bolsheviks. He had worked in Baku, participated in the Petersburg Soviet of 1905, and had been a delegate to all party congresses. Stopped all political activity in 1909 and worked as an engineer and manager until after October 1917 but returned to the party in 1918 to play an important role in foreign trade negotiations and in attracting other engineers to participate in the Soviet economy.

5 B. D. Kamkov [pseudonym Kats, 1885–1938], a statistician by profession, emerged as a leader of the left wing of the PSR in 1917. Like other SRs, he supported the Bolshevik government after October, but opposed the Treaty of Brest-Litovsk in March, and was among the organizers of the Left SR revolt in July 1918. He was sentenced to prison but later worked as a statistician in Soviet institutions.

6 *Edinstvo* [Unity], a daily, was published in Petrograd from March 19, 1917 to January 1918 by a group of SD-Defensists led by Plekhanov. That group, which assumed the newspaper's name and subscribed to its leader's ultra-defensist views, remained outside the Menshevik Party and was even denied representation in the Executive Committee of the Soviet.

7 On July 4, at the height of two days of mass demonstrations by soldiers and workers under the Bolshevik slogan of "All Power to the Soviets," the Minister of Justice of the Provisional Government released documents to the press alleging that Lenin had been a paid agent of the German government for many years. These allegations brought a temporary but sharp decline in the popularity of the Bolsheviks and are still debated by historians.

8 Philipp Scheidemann was one of the more conservative leaders of the German Social Democrats. During the First World War supported *burgfrieden*, i.e., a policy of social peace and full support of the war effort by the socialists.

Tenth interview

1 The reference is to the attempt made in the last week of August by the Chief of Staff, General Kornilov, to replace Kerenskii's coalition government with a dictatorial Council under his own leadership and to crush the power of the Soviet and the soldiers' committees. Units loyal to Kornilov were ordered to advance from the front to Petrograd and only their agreement to turn back a few days later prevented a bloody confrontation with the supporters of the Petrograd Soviet. Bolshevik workers and leaders figured prominently in the Soviet's plan for the defense of Petrograd, and thus, while the Kornilov affair exposed the counter-revolutionary intentions of right wing circles and the complicity of many moderates, it is also believed to have improved the political fortunes of the Bolsheviks.

2 The War-Industrial Committees were established in 1915 by the national organizations of the Russian industrialists in order to mobilize and coordinate war-related economic activity. In July 1915 workers were invited to send their representatives to the Committees, a move which was opposed by the Bolsheviks and the Menshevik-Internationalists abroad but welcomed by many Mensheviks inside Russia. Most of the workers participating in the Labor Groups of the War-Industrial Committees were veterans of the Menshevik-led trade unions.

3 Denike's assertion that the Provisional Government prohibited the sale of wheat flour could not be ascertained. What is known is that the Provisional Government enacted a law "On the Transfer of Grain to the State" on March 25, 1917; that its Ministry of Agriculture established rationing of all grains in most of Russia on

April 29; and that on July 17 its newly created Ministry of Food ordered that no grains be processed into flour without the Ministry's authorization.

4 A. L. Kalegaev, a railroad employee from Kazan province, was a peasant organizer in that province during 1917 and emerged as an important leader of the Left SRs in the fall of that year. Was selected by his party to serve as the Commissar of Agriculture in the first Soviet government formed by Bolsheviks and Left SRs in November 1917, but resigned in March 1918 when his party withdrew from the government over the issue of the Treaty of Brest-Litovsk.

5 No details could be found about K. G. Gogua [pseudonym Davydov] except that he had been an important member of the Georgian Menshevik organization since at least 1906 when he represented the Tiflis Committee at the Stockholm Congress.

6 The All-Russian Central Executive Committee of Soviets [*VTsIK*] was elected at the First All-Russian Congress of Soviets which took place in Petrograd in June. The 300-member body included 100 representatives of provincial soviets, who did not participate in the daily work of the Executive Committee but who were called to an "extra-ordinary session" in Petrograd in the aftermath of the July Crisis.

7 The decree of the Provisional Government calling for a State Conference was published on July 13 and the conference itself met in Moscow from August 12 to 15. With 2,500 delegates from every organization and party in Russia, the conference had been expected to mobilize support for the Provisional Government; instead, it served as a stage for right-wing attacks on the coalition, was boycotted by the Bolsheviks, and caused a one-day general strike in Moscow, thus underscoring the polarization of the country and the isolation of the Provisional Government.

8 Nikolai Semenovich Chkheidze (1864–1926), a Menshevik from Georgia, had been the Chairman of the Social Democratic faction in the last two Dumas and was elected Chairman of the Petrograd Soviet on the day that body was formed in February 1917. Served as the Chairman of that body until September and of the All-Russian Central Executive Committee until October, pursuing in both bodies the policies of Revolutionary Defensism. Remained staunch opponent of the Bolsheviks after October, escaped to Georgia and became the Chairman of its Constituent Assembly. Was a member of the Georgian government-in-exile from 1921 until his death by suicide in 1926.

9 In fact, Steklov had resigned from the editorial board of *Izvestiia* in May, when he had come under attack from other members of the board (particularly Voitinskii) for expressing his differences with the Revolutionary Defensist leadership of the Soviet, and because a change in the composition of the board had left him in the minority (*see Petrogradskii sovet rabochikh i soldatskikh deputatov. Protokoly zasedanii Ispolnitel'nogo Komiteta i biuro I.K.*, Moscow-Leningrad, 1925, pp. 138, 233).

10 By the time of the August "Unification" Congress of the Menshevik Party, the divisions that existed within the party in 1917 had become clearly drawn. Three factions were represented at the Congress: the Revolutionary Defensist faction, which commanded the loyalty of two thirds of the delegates and followed Tsereteli's policies (*see* Denike, Eighth Interview, note 10); the small Defensist faction, led by Potresov, whose support of the coalition government and of Russia's war against Germany was far less qualified than that of the Revolutionary Defensists; and the Internationalist faction (with about 30% of the delegates to the August Congress) which was opposed to socialist participation in a coalition government and demanded greater pressure on the Provisional Government for an immediate armistice. The Menshevik-Internationalists were led by Martov and his colleagues (Martynov, Abramovich, Lapinskii, Semkovskii, and Astrov) all of whom returned from emigration only in May 1917.

11 Nadezhda Evgenevna Grinfeld (1887–1918) had joined the Bund in Kishinev in 1903 and except for short periods in prison and emigration was continuously

active in Menshevik organizations in Odessa, Kiev, and Petersburg. Was a popular speaker at mass meetings in Petrograd and Kronstadt during 1917.

12 Mikhail Isaakovich Gol'dman [pseudonym Liber, 1880–1937] was one of the leaders of the Bund and a veteran of the Menshevik Party since its inception in the Second Congress (1903); had represented the Bund in the Central Committee elected by the Fifth Congress (1907) and in the Bureau of the "August Bloc" (1912). During those years he was a "Liquidator" and became a Defensist in 1914. He served on the Executive Committee of the Petrograd Soviet and the All-Russian Executive Committee in 1917 and was one of the leaders of the Revolutionary Defensist bloc in the soviets. During the Civil War and until his arrest in 1923 was a leading figure in the right-wing minority in the Menshevik Party.

13 Pavel' Lapinskii [pseud. of Levinson], the leader of the left wing of the Polish Socialist Party *(PPS-Levitsa)*, became a close associate and friend of Martov in emigration during the years of First World War. Returned with him to Russia in May 1917 and was prominent among the Menshevik-Internationalists. Worked in the Soviet Commissariat of Foreign Affairs and in the Comintern after October 1917, but remained close to Martov until the latter's death in 1923. Was executed during the Great Purge.

14 Georgii Dmitrievich Kuchin was a lawyer and a Menshevik (since 1912) but serving as an artillery officer on active duty at that time; he belonged to the Defensist wing of the Menshevik Party during World War I and became the Chairman of the Soldier's Committee of the 12th Army in 1917, and later, of the Northern Front. He represented these bodies in the All-Russian Executive Committee of Soviets, in the Menshevik Central Committee, and at various congresses. He belonged to the right-wing minority of the Menshevik Party after the Bolshevik seizure of power and was active in the Assemblies of Representatives and other anti-Bolshevik workers' organizations. Even after fighting in the Soviet-Polish War, he continued underground Menshevik work until his final arrest in the late 1920s.

15 Mikhail Ivanovich Tereshchenko (1886–1956), a sugar magnate from the Ukraine and the former head of the Kiev War-Industrial Committee, served in all the cabinets of the Provisional Government, first as Minister of Finance, and from May to October as the Minister of Foreign Affairs. Like the Left Kadet N. V. Nekrasov and the Progressists A. I. Konovalov and I. N. Efremov, belonged to the group identified by the Mensheviks as the "progressive bourgeoisie." This group was responsible for the Provisional Government's invitation to the Soviet to join a coalition government.

16 Noi Nikolaevich Zhordania (1870–1953) was among the founders of Georgian Social Democracy in the 1890's. Represented the Georgian Mensheviks in all the party congresses and in the First Duma, but continued to live in Georgia. Was Chairman of the Tiflis Soviet in 1917; supported Revolutionary Defensism but was opposed to the Soviet's participation in the coalition. Headed the independent government of Georgia in 1918–21 and after its defeat was the main figure in the Georgian government-in-exile.

Eleventh interview

1 Kuzma Antonovich Gvozdev (1883–?), born of a peasant family and apprenticed to a railroad shop at the age of 13, began attending SR-influenced workers' circles in the early 1900s; was arrested several times and exiled to Siberia. Returned in 1909 and worked at the Putilov Works in Petrograd, where he became chairman of the Menshevik-led Union of Metalworkers and headed the Labor Group of the Central War-Industrial Committee during the First World War. During 1917 he was a member of the Executive Committee of Soviets, deputy Minister of Labor (from May), and Minister of Labor (from September). Soon after the Bolshevik

seizure of power, he left political activity and worked in workers' cooperatives, and later, in the 1920s, in the Supreme Economic Council of the Soviet Union.

2 Eva L'vovna Broido (b. 1876) had joined the Social Democratic movement in 1900; from 1905 onward she and her husband, Mark Isaakovich Broido, were active in the trade union movement, first in Baku, and later in Petersburg. In later years she was elected to responsible positions in the Menshevik Party: Secretary of the Menshevik Organizational Committee (1912); a member of the Menshevik Central Committee (August 1917); Secretary of the CC (December 1917). During these years she was also active in the party's semi-legal "Initiative Group" (1912–1914) and the group of Menshevik-Internationalists that was assembled in Minusinsk, Eastern Siberia, during World War I. She left Russia in 1921 to become a member of the Menshevik Delegation Abroad, but was sent to the Soviet Union in 1927 for underground work. She was arrested in 1928 and kept in prison until her death some time in the 1930s.

3 In the aftermath of the Kornilov Affair the All-Russian Executive Committee of Soviets called for the representatives of "democratic Russia" to decide what government should rule the country until the Constituent Assembly. Between September 14 and 20, more than a thousand delegates from soviets, soldiers' committees, trade unions, consumer cooperatives, and elected local governments met in Petrograd but failed to reach agreement on either of two proposed solutions: that which called for a continued coalition between the soviets and the "bourgeois" organizations; and that calling for "homogeneous government" made up exclusively of the democratic organizations. Instead, the Conference elected a 367-member Council of Democratic Organizations to choose a new government and to oversee it until the Constituent Assembly convened.

4 Members of consumer cooperatives.

5 *See* Denike, Third Interview, note 11.

6 Aleksandr Ivanovich Verkhovskii (1886–1938), a Major-General in the tsarist army, had cooperated with the forces of the February Revolution from the outset and had been elected Deputy Chairman of the Sevastopol' Soviet. Began serving as Minister of War in Kerenskii's government in August but resigned in October in an effort to force an end to the war. Attempted to organize military forces in support of a "homogeneous" socialist government after the Bolshevik takeover but later joined the Red Army (1919) and served in prominent positions until his execution in the Great Purge.

7 Popular name for the Council of Democratic Organizations which was elected by the Democratic Conference on September 20. On September 23 this body adjourned to await its formal opening by the Provisional Government, thus allowing Kerenskii to establish a new coalition cabinet and to supplement the Preparliament (now officially named the Council of the Republic) with 150 representatives of "bourgeois" organizations. The Preparliament (minus the Bolshevik delegates who left in protest) was in session from October 7 until its dispersal by the Military Revolutionary Committee on October 25, but accomplished nothing.

8 Ekaterina Konstantinova Breshko-Breshkovskaia (1844–1934) participated in the Populist movement of the 1870s and was among the organizers of the SR Party at the beginning of the twentieth century. She spent more than twenty years in prison and was widely known as the "grandmother of the revolution." She belonged to the Defensist wing of the PSR in 1917 and emigrated after the civil war.

9 In the immediate aftermath of the October seizure of power by the Bolsheviks, *Vikzhel* [the All-Russian Executive Committee of the Railroad Union] tried to negotiate the establishment of a "homogeneous" socialist government including all the socialist parties and factions, from the People's Socialists on the Right to the Bolsheviks on the Left.

10 In November 1917, the Bolsheviks and the Left SRs established a new government (called the Council of People's Commissars). This coalition collapsed in March 1918, when the Left SRs withdrew from the government in protest over

the German-Soviet peace treaty of Brest-Litovsk. For additional information on Kalegaev *see* Denike, Tenth Interview, note 4.

Twelfth interview

1 *Rabochaia gazeta* remained the official Menshevik newspaper after the October seizure of power, but it had to change names often in order to evade Bolshevik repression. Other names used during this period were *Luch'* [Ray of Light] and *Novyi luch'* [New Ray of Light].

2 Gorev was the pseudonym of B. I. Gol'dman, *see also* Dan, Third Interview, note 3 and Fourth Interview, note 34.

3 *Sotsialisticheskii vestnik* [The Socialist Herald], published from 1921 to 1965 in Berlin, Paris, and New York, was the central organ of the Menshevik Party in emigration.

4 The movement *Smenovekhovstvo* took its name from a collection of essays published in Prague, in the summer of 1921, by a group of Russian emigrés of Kadet and Octobrist leanings under the title *Smena vekh* [A Change of Landmarks]. This and other collections and journals published in emigration in the early 1920s viewed the New Economic Policy launched by the Soviet government as the beginning of Russia's passage back to capitalism and pluralism, and they encouraged the Russian professional intelligentsia to collaborate with the Soviet government in order to reinforce the new trends brought about by the NEP.

5 Georgii Vasil'evich Chicherin (1872–1936), born of noble origin; left Russia in 1904 after several years with the Ministry of Foreign Affairs. In emigration grew close, first to the Mensheviks, and later, during the First World War, to the Internationalists. Returned to Russia in 1918 and headed Soviet foreign affairs until 1930.

6 The Menshevik Party held an Extraordinary Congress in Petrograd from November 28 to December 6, 1917. Even before the congress convened the Revolutionary-Defensist majority of the Menshevik Central Committee had split over the question of negotiations with the Bolsheviks for the formation of a "homogeneous" socialist government; four Revolutionary Defensists (Dan, Cherevanin, Gorev, and G. M. Erlikh) had joined the Internationalists, thus giving them a majority in the Central Committee. When a new Central Committee was elected by the Extraordinary Congress, it included only supporters of the new Internationalist majority.

7 Between March and October 1917 Dan was the most influential supporter of Tsereteli and his Revolutionary Defensism in the Menshevik Party. But in the aftermath of the Bolshevik seizure of power his position grew closer to that of the Internationalists until, at the Party Congress in December, he emerged as Martov's principal collaborator in the party's new Internationalist majority.

8 Anatolii Eduardovich Diubua (1882–1959), a Petersburg attorney, had been a Bolshevik in 1905 but joined the Mensheviks in 1906 and participated in their organizational and journalistic work in the legal trade unions, supporting "Liquidationism" and Defensism. He served as Commissar of the Petrograd Soviet to the Northern Front and as deputy Minister of Labor in the Provisional Government in 1917, and after October belonged to the right-wing minority of the party, participating in the anti-Bolshevik uprisings of 1918. He was arrested, exiled to Siberia (1922–23), and eventually expelled from the Soviet Union. In emigration he belonged first to the right wing of the party and, after 1941, to its left wing.

9 Boris Osipovich Bogdanov (1884–1956), a Menshevik since 1905, had been a Defensist from the beginning of First World War and had served as the Secretary of the Labor Group of the Central War-Industrial Committee. He was among the organizers of the Petrograd Soviet and its Labor Section in 1917 and a member of the Menshevik Central Committee. After the Bolshevik seizure of power he left the Central Committee in protest over its negotiations with the Bolsheviks and

joined the right-wing minority of the party. He was arrested in the early 1920's and spent the next 30 years in camps and prisons.

10 S. Iu. Semkovskii [pseudonym of Bronshtein, 1882–?] lived in emigration between 1907 and 1917 and was close both to the Mensheviks and to Trotsky's *Pravda* group; was among the organizers of the 1912 Vienna Conference and the August Bloc (*see* Nicolaevsky, First Interview, note 4). During the First World War and the revolution belonged to Martov's group of Menshevik Internationalists, but joined the extreme-left minority of the Menshevik Party in 1918; left the party altogether in 1920. Thereafter worked in various Soviet academic institutions.

11 Two of the Committee's members (Abramovich and Semkovskii) belonged to the Internationalist faction of the party, while Tsereteli and Denike had been associated with the Revolutionary Defensist majority which became the minority faction in November.

12 The letter is cited in L. H. Haimson, ed., *The Mensheviks*. Chicago: University of Chicago Press, 1974, pp. 102–3.

13 An Assembly of Representatives from Petrograd factories was organized in March 1918 with the encouragement and the help of a group of Menshevik Defensists. On March 27 the Assembly already counted 170 representatives elected in more than 50 factories, including the largest factories of the capital; similar assemblies were organized in Moscow and in many provincial towns. An All-Russian Conference of Factory Representatives was convened in Moscow on July 20, 1918; however, the arrest of all of the delegates on July 21 put an end to the movement.

Thirteenth interview

1 *Novaia zhizn'* [New Life], a daily published in Petrograd from April 18, 1917 to July 1918, was established by Gorkii and a group of SD-Internationalists who had sought to bridge the Menshevik-Bolshevik division among Internationalists (*see also* Denike, Eight Interview, note 12). However, after Martov's return to Russia some of the *NZh* editors became closely associated with the Internationalist faction of the Menshevik Party, and during the summer and fall of 1917 it was the only mass publication to which Martov and other Menshevik-Internationalists contributed.

2 On November 1, a group of eleven Defensists and Revolutionary Defensists (M. I. Liber, B. S. Baturskii, L. I. Gol'dman, F. A., Iudin, K. A. Gvozdev, A. N. Smirnov, P. A. Garvi, K. M. Ermolaev, S. M. Zaretskaia, P. Kolokol'nikov, and B. N. Krokhmal') resigned from the Menshevik Central Committee in protest over the Committee's decision to participate in the attempt to organize a government of all the socialist parties, including the Bolsheviks. Except for Kolokol'nikov, all of the members of this "Right bloc" returned to the Central Committee on November 10, when it appeared that the negotiations with the Bolsheviks had broken off but were excluded from the new Committee elected on December 7, 1917.

3 Aron Abramovich Iugov (1886–1954), a self-taught economist, was an active member of the Menshevik organization in Rostov-on-Don and was elected to the Menshevik Central Committee in December 1917. He left the Soviet Union in 1922 and became the Secretary of the Menshevik Delegation Abroad; he wrote on economic affairs for its journal, *Sotsialisticheskii vestnik*, and was Dan's closest associate until 1939 when he began collaborating with the Communist Party.

4 The elections to the Constituent Assembly took place in early November 1917; the results became known gradually in late November and early December. Of the 37.5 million votes cast nearly 16 million went to the SRs who, together with the Ukrainian SRs, captured 380 seats out of a total of 703; the Bolsheviks received close to 10 million votes while the Mensheviks could claim no more than 1,364,826 votes, 570,000 of which came from the Trans-Caucasus region (mostly from Georgia).

5 The Constituent Assembly met for only one day, January 5, 1918, before it was dissolved by the Soviet Government.

6 Leontii Moiseevich Bramson (1869–1944), a lawyer and a noted Jewish activist, began his political activity in the Union of Liberation and was a member of the secretariat of the Union of Unions in 1905. He was among the organizers of the *Trudovaia gruppa* in the First Duma but later joined the Party of People's Socialists. He belonged to the Defensist wing of the Executive Committee of the Petrograd Soviet in 1917 and later emigrated.

7 Matvei Konstantinovich Muranov (1873–1959) was born of a peasant family; beginning in 1907 was active in the Union of Railroad Workers in Kharkov. He was elected to the Fourth Duma in 1912 as the Bolshevik candidate in the workers' curia of Kharkov. He was arrested with the Bolshevik faction in late 1914 and exiled to Siberia until 1917, when he returned to Petrograd to become one of the editors of *Pravda*. After October he worked in party and government institutions until his retirement in 1939.

8 Elsewhere in this interview Denike said: "It is now difficult for me to recall at what point it happened, but a kind of 'defensist club' took shape. It wasn't a distinct organization, but rather a place that the Defensists rented and at which they would gather. . . ." Apparently this "club" had been organized in November or December, after the Defensists had left the Central Committee, but Denike became aware of its existence only in March 1918.

9 The incident is mentioned briefly in Denike's necrologue for Tsereteli, *"Pamiati ushedshikh. I. G. Tsereteli,"* Novyi zhurnal, no. 57 (1959), pp. 284–85.

10 Fedor Fedorovich Kokoshkin and Andrei Ivanovich Shingarev had been among the leaders of the Russian liberal movement since the days of the Union of Liberation; they were prominent Kadets and members of the Provisional Government. They were murdered by angry sailors on January 7, 1918, while in Bolshevik prison.

11 Avel' Safronovich Enukidze (1877–1937), like Tsereteli and Gogua, was a native Georgian and a veteran of the Georgian SD movement which he had joined in 1896. He joined the Bolsheviks in 1903 and until 1917 worked as a union organizer in Baku and Petersburg. He was for many years the Secretary of the Central Executive Committee of the Soviets. He was shot during Stalin's Great Purge.

12 In this and other references to Dallin's writing, Denike most probably had in mind a manuscript on "The Menshevik Party Under Soviet Rule," which David Dallin was preparing at the time for the Inter-University Project on Menshevik History. Large parts of this manuscript were published in L. H. Haimson, ed., *The Mensheviks from the Revolution of 1917 to the Second World War*, Chicago, 1974. David Iul'evich Dalin [pseudonym of Levin, 1889–1962] had become active in Menshevik organizations during his *gimnazium* years (in Rogachev) and continued while attending university in Petersburg (1907–10), Berlin, and Heidelberg (where he received a Doctorate of Philosophy and Politics in 1913). During World War I adhered to the internationalism of the Zimmerwald Left and after his return to Russia (May 1917) became one of the principal spokesmen for Menshevik Internationalism, representing his faction in the party's Central Committee. Remained a staunch Internationalist even after October and participated in the work of the Bolshevik-dominated trade unions, the Moscow Soviet, and the Councils on National Economy. Was arrested in 1921 and allowed to leave for Berlin, where he joined the Delegation Abroad and collaborated with Dan and Martov. By 1934, earlier doubts about the future of socialism in the Soviet Union and the evidence of Stalin's brutal methods caused his break with the Delegation and advocacy of unrelenting struggle against the Soviet regime. But in 1939 he created (with Nikolaevskii and Abramovich) a new "centrist" majority in the Menshevik Party and remained an active participant in its work even after his move to New York in 1940. In the United States engaged in scholarly work (pub-

lished 11 monographs and many articles, some in *The New Leader*) which established him as a major scholar in the field of Soviet studies.
13 *Novaia zaria* [New Dawn] was published by the Committee of the Central Region
of the RSDRP which the Defensists dominated. Four issues were published, two
of them double (3-4 and 5-6), between April 22 and June 10, 1918.